FIDUCIARY OBLIGATIONS IN BUSINESS

The scholarship on fiduciary duties in business organizations is often pulled in two directions. While most observers would agree that business organizations are one of the key contexts for the application of the fiduciary obligation, corporate law theorists have often expressed disdain for the role of fiduciary duties, with the result that fiduciary law and theory have been out of step with the business world. This volume aims to rectify this situation by bringing together a range of scholars to analyze fiduciary relationships and the fiduciary obligation in the business context. Contributing authors examine fiduciary obligations in fields ranging from entity structure to bankruptcy to investment regulation. The volume demonstrates that fiduciary law can inform pressing corporate governance debates, including discussions over stakeholder models of the corporation that move beyond shareholder interests.

Arthur B. Laby is Professor of Law at Rutgers Law School and Co-Director of the Rutgers Center for Corporate Law and Governance.

Jacob Hale Russell is Associate Professor of Law at Rutgers Law School.

T0381681

Fiduciary Obligations in Business

Edited by

ARTHUR B. LABY

Rutgers Law School

JACOB HALE RUSSELL

Rutgers Law School

CAMBRIDGE
UNIVERSITY PRESS

CAMBRIDGE
UNIVERSITY PRESS

Shaftesbury Road, Cambridge CB2 8EA, United Kingdom

One Liberty Plaza, 20th Floor, New York, NY 10006, USA

477 Williamstown Road, Port Melbourne, VIC 3207, Australia

314–321, 3rd Floor, Plot 3, Splendor Forum, Jasola District Centre, New Delhi – 110025, India

103 Penang Road, #05–06/07, Visioncrest Commercial, Singapore 238467

Cambridge University Press is part of Cambridge University Press & Assessment, a department of the University of Cambridge.

We share the University's mission to contribute to society through the pursuit of education, learning and research at the highest international levels of excellence.

www.cambridge.org
Information on this title: www.cambridge.org/9781009387095

DOI: 10.1017/9781108755849

First published 2021
First paperback edition 2023

A catalogue record for this publication is available from the British Library

Library of Congress Cataloging-in-Publication data
NAMES: Laby, Arthur B., editor. | Russell, Jacob Hale, editor.
TITLE: Fiduciary obligations in business / edited by Arthur B. Laby, Rutgers University School of Law; Jacob Hale Russell, Rutgers University School of Law.
DESCRIPTION: Cambridge, United Kingdom ; New York, NY : Cambridge University Press, 2021. | "The chapters in this book were the subject of a two-day workshop held at Rutgers Law School in Camden, N.J. in October 2019" – ECIP asknowledgements." | Includes bibliographical references and index.
IDENTIFIERS: LCCN 2021009977 (print) | LCCN 2021009978 (ebook) | ISBN 9781108485128 (hardback) | ISBN 9781108755849 (ebook)
SUBJECTS: LCSH: Corporate governance – Law and legislation – United States – Congresses. | Trusts and trustees – United States – Congresses.
CLASSIFICATION: LCC KF1422.A75 F53 2021 (print) | LCC KF1422.A75 (ebook) | DDC 346.73/0664–dc23
LC record available at https://lccn.loc.gov/2021009977
LC ebook record available at https://lccn.loc.gov/2021009978

ISBN   978-1-108-48512-8   Hardback
ISBN   978-1-009-38709-5   Paperback

For Rachel, Sonia & Ethan, with love – A.B.L.
For Elizabeth & August, my principals – J.H.R.

Contents

Contributors

CO-EDITORS

Arthur B. Laby is Professor of Law at Rutgers Law School and Co-Director of the Rutgers Center for Corporate Law and Governance.

Jacob Hale Russell is Associate Professor of Law at Rutgers Law School.

AUTHORS

Quinn Curtis is Professor of Law at the University of Virginia School of Law.

Deborah A. DeMott is the David F. Cavers Professor at Duke University School of Law.

Jared A. Ellias is the Bion M. Gregory Chair in Business Law and Professor of Law at the University of California, Hastings College of the Law.

Jennifer G. Hill is Bob Baxt AO Chair in Corporate and Commercial Law, Monash University Faculty of Law.

Christine Hurt is George Sutherland Chair and Professor of Law at J. Reuben Clark Law School, Brigham Young University.

Howell E. Jackson is James S. Reid, Jr., Professor of Law at Harvard University.

Edward J. Janger is David M. Barse Professor of Law, and Associate Dean of Faculty Research and Scholarship, at Brooklyn Law School.

Lyman Johnson is Professor of Law at the University of St. Thomas (Minneapolis), and the Robert O. Bentley Professor of Law, Emeritus, at Washington and Lee University.

Christoph Kumpan is Dr. Harald Hack Foundation Professor of Private Law, Corporate Law and Capital Markets Law at Bucerius Law School, Hamburg, Germany.

Amir N. Licht is Professor of Law at the Harry Radzyner Law School, Interdisciplinary Center Herzliya.

Paul B. Miller is Professor and Associate Dean for International and Graduate Programs, and Director of the Notre Dame Program on Private Law, Notre Dame Law School.

Dana M. Muir is Robert L. Dixon Collegiate Professor of Business and Arthur F. Thurnau Professor of Business Law at Stephen M. Ross School of Business, University of Michigan.

Steven L. Schwarcz is the Stanley A. Star Distinguished Professor of Law & Business, and Founding Director of the Global Financial Markets Center, at Duke University.

Robert J. Stark is a partner and Restructuring Practice Group Leader at Brown Rudnick LLP.

Masayuki Tamaruya is Professor of Law at the University of Tokyo.

Julian Velasco is an Associate Professor of Law at Notre Dame Law School.

Kelli Alces Williams is the Matthews & Hawkins Professor of Property at the Florida State University College of Law.

Editors' Acknowledgments

We are thankful to all the colleagues, friends, and family who helped make this project successful. Our greatest debt, of course, is to our contributors. The chapters in this book were the subject of a two-day workshop held at Rutgers Law School in Camden, N.J. in October 2019. In addition to our authors, we are grateful to Richard R. W. Brooks, Asaf Raz, and Andrew Tuch, who attended the workshop and offered many helpful comments. Tremendous thanks are due to Carol Shaner, who coordinated the workshop and, as she always does, made us appear more organized than we are.

In preparing the volume, we were greatly aided by three student research assistants, Lauren Bonanno, Ryan Duffy, and Zhao Li, and by Nancy Talley and Genevieve Tung in the law school library.

Many thanks to Matt Gallaway and his excellent team at Cambridge University Press, and to the four anonymous reviewers who offered comments on the project. We thank Arc Indexing for preparing the index.

We are grateful for the enthusiastic support of the Rutgers Center for Corporate Law and Governance, and in particular for the Center's outstanding Advisory Board and Alumni Steering Committee. We thank our colleague, Doug Eakeley, the Center's Co-Director, for his unflagging support of this project and others, and our law school's Co-Deans, Kimberly Mutcherson and David Lopez, for their steady leadership and encouragement. We benefited from sound advice on the project offered by John Oberdiek and Dennis Patterson.

Arthur thanks Tamar Frankel, and remembers B. Sharon Byrd, who spurred interest and inquiry on these issues. Jacob thanks Michael Klausner and Travis Laster, who have greatly shaped his perspective on these subjects.

Introduction

The Decline and Rise of Fiduciary Obligations in Business

Jacob Hale Russell & Arthur B. Laby[*]

I THE CONTRACTARIAN WAVE IN FIDUCIARY LAW AND SCHOLARSHIP

Recent years have seen a surge of scholarly interest in the fiduciary relationship. The collapse of Enron in 2001 and WorldCom and 2002 led to an explosion of scholarship on corporate law,[1] including scrutiny of the role fiduciary duties might play to enhance governance. The Sarbanes-Oxley Act of 2002 appeared to adopt some underlying logic from fiduciary law, particularly in its emphasis on the personal responsibility of senior corporate officers to certify their firms' financial statements. The 2008 financial crisis further trained the focus of scholars, regulators, lawyers, and courts on the failures of intermediaries, gatekeepers, and others who arguably breached their duties. New fiduciary rules have been proposed and implemented to govern investment intermediaries.

In addition—or perhaps in response—to these developments, a number of excellent books and articles have appeared on the doctrinal, philosophical, and historical aspects of fiduciary law.[2] Legal scholars have applied fiduciary theory to a growing number of actors, including voters,[3] government officials,[4] judges,[5] politicians,[6] parents,[7] and even friends.[8] They have drawn links between previously disparate doctrinal domains—from trust law to corporate law to family law to public law—through the lens of fiduciary theory.

In many ways, the law of business organizations would seem to be the obvious focal point for such work. Some of the most well-known statements of a fiduciary's obligation appear in the

[*] We are grateful to Vice Chancellor J. Travis Laster for helpful comments on a portion of this Introduction.
[1] The trajectory of corporate governance scholarship is chronicled by Mariana Pargendler, *The Corporate Governance Obsession*, 42 J. CORP. L. 360, 361–3 (2016); *see also* Ronald J. Gilson, *From Corporate Law to Corporate Governance*, in OXFORD HANDBOOK OF CORPORATE LAW AND GOVERNANCE (Jeffrey N. Gordon & Wolf Georg Ringe eds., 2018) (tracing the history of how agency theory led to "a search for the organizational Holy Grail, a technique that bridges the separation of ownership and control").

[2] Representative examples include: RESEARCH HANDBOOK ON FIDUCIARY LAW (D. Gordon Smith & Andrew S. Gold eds., 2018); CONTRACT, STATUS, AND FIDUCIARY LAW (Paul B. Miller & Andrew S. Gold eds., 2016); PHILOSOPHICAL FOUNDATIONS OF FIDUCIARY LAW (Andrew S. Gold & Paul B. Miller eds., 2014); THE OXFORD HANDBOOK OF FIDUCIARY LAW (Evan J. Criddle, Paul B. Miller, & Robert H. Sitkoff eds., 2019).

[3] Edward B. Foley, *Voters as Fiduciaries*, 2015 U. CHI. LEGAL F. 153, 158, 181–82 (2015).

[4] Max Schanzenbach & Nadav Shoked, *Reclaiming Fiduciary Law for the City*, 70 STAN. L. REV. 565 (2018); *see generally* FIDUCIARY GOVERNMENT (Evan J. Criddle et al. eds., 2018).

[5] Ethan J. Leib et al., *A Fiduciary Theory of Judging*, 101 CALIF. L. REV. 699 (2013).

[6] D. Theodore Rave, *Politicians as Fiduciaries*, 126 HARV. L. REV. 671, 706–11 (2013).

[7] Lionel Smith, *Parenthood is a Fiduciary Relationship*, 70 U. TORONTO L. J. 395 (2020).

[8] Ethan J. Leib, *Friends as Fiduciaries*, 86 WASH. U. L. REV. 665, 707–14 (2009).

context of business organizations. Judge Cardozo's widely quoted elucidation of the fiduciary standard appeared in a 1928 case about partners (coadventurers, to be precise) in a real estate investment scheme.[9] The duty of care and the prudent person rule, broadly applicable to fiduciary management of property, derived from the trust case of *Harvard College* v. *Amory*, a hundred years before *Meinhard*.[10] Fiduciary duties in the trust context can be traced even further to England's law over 500 years ago.[11]

Fiduciary obligations pervade business law: from the duties owed by directors, officers, and controlling shareholders;[12] to duties regulating a host of intermediaries critical to business dealings,[13] and debates over the role of fiduciary duties in alternative entities. Sometimes these duties develop organically in the common law. Other times they develop through statutory interpretation. For example, a rich body of fiduciary case law has developed under the federal securities laws,[14] and another under the Employee Retirement Income Security Act (ERISA).[15] Courts apply these precedents in turn to other areas, much like *Meinhard* is often applied to contexts outside of partnership.[16]

But the business law scholarship on fiduciary duties has a Janus-faced character. Despite the close doctrinal relationship, the expressed attitude of much corporate law scholarship reflects several decades of disdain for the role of fiduciary duties. The wave of corporate law and economics scholarship that began in the 1980s could be openly scornful of fiduciary theory. This sentiment of Frank Easterbrook and Daniel Fischel is representative: "Fiduciary duties are not special duties; they have no moral footing; they are the same sort of obligations, derived and enforced in the same way, as other contractual undertakings."[17]

The apparent marginalization of fiduciary duties in business law scholarship tracks, in part, developments in the substantive law. Since the mid-1980s, legislative and judicial developments in Delaware and other states have gradually lessened both the applicability and enforceability of fiduciary duties. For instance, following the famous 1985 decision in *Smith* v. *Van Gorkom*, Delaware amended its corporate statute to allow companies to eliminate personal financial liability for a director's breach of the duty of care.[18] Such provisions are now widespread in corporate charters. In 2000, Delaware amended its statute to permit corporations to limit the fiduciary duty of loyalty by waiving certain corporate opportunity claims.[19] All told, the likelihood of financial liability for a director stemming from a fiduciary breach is very low.[20]

In addition, the rise of alternative entities like limited liability companies, which now far outpace the formation of corporations, has brought with it nearly unlimited freedom to contract around fiduciary duties. A principal rule of construction in the Delaware alternative entity acts is "to give the maximum effect to the principle of freedom of contract," and fiduciary duties can be "expanded or restricted or eliminated" in operating agreements.[21]

---

9   Meinhard v. Salmon, 164 N.E. 545 (1928).

10   26 Mass. 446 (1830).

11   *See* David J. Seipp, *Trust and Fiduciary Duty in the Early Common Law*, 91 B.U.L. Rev. 1011 (2011).

12   *See* Lyman Johnson, *The Three Fiduciaries of Delaware Corporate Law*, ch. 3 (this volume).

13   *See* Steven L. Schwarcz, *Examining Trustee Indenture Duties*, ch. 5 (this volume).

14   *See* Howell E. Jackson, *New Challenges for Fiduciary Protections for Investors in Mutual Funds*, ch. 7 (this volume).

15   *See* Arthur B. Laby, *Trust, Discretion, and ERISA Fiduciary Status*, ch. 4 (this volume).

16   Knowles v. State ex rel. Lindeen, 222 P.3d 595, 598 (Mont. 2009) (state securities law); Bessemer Trust Co. v. Branin, 949 N.E.2d 462, 469 (N.Y. Ct. App. 2011) (restrictions on soliciting customers of a former employer).

17   Frank H. Easterbrook & Daniel R. Fischel, *Contract and Fiduciary Duty*, 36 J. L. & Econ. 425, 427 (1993).

18   488 A.2d 858 (Del. 1985); Del. Gen. Corp. L. § 102(b)(7).

19   Del. Gen. Corp. L. § 122(17).

20   Bernard S. Black et al., *Outside Director Liability*, 58 Stan. L. Rev. 1055 (2006).

21   6 Del. Code § 18–1101(b) and (c) (LLCs); 6 Del. Code § 17–1101(c) and (d) (LPs).

Beyond doctrinal developments, the erosion of fiduciary duties over the past three decades was also born of theoretical conviction. Early contractarians like Easterbrook and Fischel made two moves, one descriptive, and the other normative. Descriptively, since a corporation was simply a "nexus of contracts" among various constituents, fiduciary duty was conceptualized as a contract term between a principal (usually a shareholder) and its agent (usually a manager).[22] Normatively, contractarians tended to frame those duties as part of a freely chosen arm's-length bargain, which ought to be waivable, rather than a non-abrogable court-imposed duty stemming from the relationship between the parties or the firm's origins in trust.

When corporate charters and LLC agreements began narrowing fiduciary duties, this seemed further proof to contractarians of the inefficiency of mandatory fiduciary rules. To the extent fiduciary duties still existed in business ventures, at least as a default, their purpose was merely to remedy standard problems identified by information economics. Fiduciary duties might reduce the cost of contracting and fill gaps in contracts that, without implied fiduciary duties, would insufficiently constrain agency costs.

Easterbrook and Fischel famously emphasized this point. For them, fiduciary law was always subsidiary to contract. Corporate law existed to aid, not displace, actual bargains.[23] In 1993, they dismissed critics of the contractual view of fiduciary duties—scholars who felt that fiduciary duties carried moral significance, or even as a doctrinal matter that they occasionally required standards of conduct higher than would-have-been-bargained-for-terms—for having no theory whatsoever.[24] Easterbrook and Fischel could find nothing distinctive about fiduciary law. Simple maximization of the contractual bargain could always explain results across a wide range of topic areas, even in cases like *Meinhard* replete with moralizing language.[25]

Other law and economics scholars adopted and extended this line of argument. Many considered fiduciary duties so ancillary that they simply ignored them: as Easterbrook and Fischel noted in 1993, of the law and economics textbooks in print, only Richard Posner's so much as mentioned fiduciary duties in the index.[26] Others explicitly argued for further flexibility in these duties—that is, more enabling legislation that would allow parties to contract around them. Both Larry Ribstein and then-Delaware Chief Justice Myron Steele argued that fiduciary law should not even be the default stance for alternative entities—critiquing, as Steele contemptuously termed it, "the commonly accepted puritanical default fiduciary duty norm."[27]

Still, subsequent years have seen the erosion of various elements of what we term the "proto-contractarian" position. By proto-contractarian, we refer to the early views of authors like Easterbrook and Fischel, who made strong assumptions about the optimality of corporate governance on the belief that natural selection processes would inevitably lead to efficient results in firms' contracting decisions.[28] Although their work has had an enormous influence on business law scholarship, relatively few scholars or courts today hew exactly to the strongest

---

[22] Michael C. Jensen & William H. Meckling, *Theory of the Firm: Managerial Behavior, Agency Costs, and Ownership Structure*, 3 J. FIN. ECON. 305 (1976).

[23] FRANK EASTERBROOK & DANIEL FISCHEL, THE ECONOMIC STRUCTURE OF CORPORATE LAW 34 (1991).

[24] Easterbrook & Fischel, *supra* note 17, at 434.

[25] *Id.* at 440.

[26] *Id.* at 427 at n.4 (noting that "there is surprisingly little commentary from other scholars on the economics of fiduciary duty").

[27] Larry Ribstein, *Are Partners Fiduciaries?* 2005 U. ILL. L. REV. 210; Myron Steele, *Freedom of Contract and Default Contractual Duties in Delaware Limited Partnerships and Limited Liability Companies*, 46 AM. BUS. L. J. 221 (2009).

[28] It is debatable whether those strong assumptions were more the result of their "proto" nature (i.e., these were early sketches of models, rough by necessity, that were later fleshed out) or because those authors held a normative agenda (i.e., more of an orthodoxy). The "second generation" of economic analysis of corporate law was both empirically and theoretically critical of the "first generation," which we term the proto-contractarians. *See* Robert Daines and

descriptive and normative claims made by the early contributors. Rather, those claims have evolved within the law and economics tradition, resulting in more nuance and have been subject to heavy criticism from outside that tradition.

Likewise, doctrine has not given as much ground as hoped for by the strongest advocates for freedom of contract. For instance, the Delaware LLC statute was amended in 2013 to make it clear that fiduciary duties were the default for alternative entities in Delaware.[29] Though not technically part of fiduciary law, Delaware courts have also used equitable powers, as well as the contractual principle of the implied covenant of good faith and fair dealing, to provide for fiduciary-like remedies even when otherwise limited.[30] And the drafters of the Uniform Limited Liability Company Act explicitly rejected the strongly contractarian idea that fiduciary duties are "merely a set of default rules" in favor of a balance between freedom of contract and protection of vulnerable parties.[31] Meanwhile, duties that are sometimes seen as relatively marginal because they are so hard to enforce—such as *Caremark* claims for breach of the duty of oversight—have arguably been revitalized by Delaware decisions in 2019.[32]

These developments render the time ripe for a new collection of essays on the role of fiduciary duties in business, possibly the first such volume since the seminal *Principals and Agents: The Structure of Business* in 1985.[33] The authors in our collection come from a range of perspectives. Some argue for more limited approaches to fiduciary duties in particular contexts; others for more expansive ones. Nonetheless, all chapters point to important gaps in the current scholarship about fiduciary duties in business, which we hope this volume goes some way to addressing.

In the next section of this introduction, we explain some of the ways in which the proto-contractarian position on fiduciary duties has eroded, categorizing its demise into three key areas, and situating our contributors' works within that framework. We then provide a roadmap for the book and outline our contributors' arguments.

II THREE CHALLENGES TO PROTO-CONTRACTARIANISM

This section outlines the erosion in the proto-contractarian characterization of fiduciary duties. Although our authors did not develop their chapters within this framework, we situate aspects of

---

Michael Klausner, *Economic Analysis of Corporate Law, in* THE NEW PALGRAVE DICTIONARY OF ECONOMICS (Palgrave Macmillan 2008).

[29] The change to Sec. 18-1104 of the Delaware LLC Act, which added an explicit reference to the background rules of fiduciary duties, was adopted to eliminate confusion created by a Delaware Supreme Court decision, Gatz Properties LLC v. Auriga Capital Corp., 59 A.3d 1206 (Del. 2012). A series of Chancery rulings had consistently expressed the view that LLCs carried default fiduciary duties. In *Gatz*, the Delaware Supreme Court—whose Chief Justice, Steele, had expressed distaste for default duties, *see supra* note 27—affirmed one such Chancery ruling while expressly limiting its fiduciary discussion to dictum. *See also* Feeley v. NHAOCG, 62 A.3d 649 (Del. Ch. 2012) (finding default fiduciary duties in LLCs in the wake of *Gatz* and discussing the history of Chancery rulings on the topic).

[30] In re Carlisle Etcetera LLC, 114 A.3d 592 (Del. Ch. 2015) (extensive discussion of the role of equity, and the history of equitable jurisdiction, as a backstop).

[31] Drafters' Comments to § 105(d)(3), UNIFORM LIMITED LIABILITY COMPANY ACT (last amended 2013).

[32] These are discussed in Jennifer G. Hill, *Corporations, Directors' Duties and the Public/Private Divide*, ch. 15 (this volume).

[33] PRINCIPALS AND AGENTS: THE STRUCTURE OF BUSINESS (John W. Pratt & Richard J. Zeckhauser eds., 1985). Featuring contributions from as many economists as law professors, *Principals and Agents* made the argument that the principal-agent relationship was the "recurrent pattern" of business that could "explain a great deal about how business is organized," based on the central principle of "enabl[ing] principals to exert an appropriate influence on the actions of agents." In a chapter focused on the legal contours of fiduciary duties, Robert Clark outlined key attributes of the fiduciary relationship. His contribution, like his later work, pushed back on what he called the "extreme contractualist viewpoint" of Jensen and Meckling, which he felt did not capture the complexity of the agency relationships within a corporation.

their contributions within our taxonomy. In doing so, we shall sketch a rough account of three paths—which we call "market realist," "stakeholder/pluralist," and "fiduciary traditionalist"— that scholarship on fiduciary duties in business has followed since the proto-contractarian wave of the 1980s. Each of these poses a potential challenge to the view that fiduciary law is a mere contractual gap-filler between shareholders and managers, or that full freedom of contract is always warranted.

The first two paths accept many of the premises of contractarianism, but with modifications. What we term the "market realist" approach is often the most contractarian: it does not necessarily reject the premise of the contract metaphor, but it comes with more caveats and deeper empirical texture. The second position, "stakeholder/pluralism," can still be viewed as contractarian, but it widens the focus well beyond the narrow, stylized shareholder-manager contract. Although both of these positions can be quite critical of the early contractarians, they do not necessarily challenge the basic paradigm. The broad consequences of the contract paradigm, including how it refocused the key questions of corporate governance, are a primary concern of Jennifer Hill and Jacob Russell's contributions to this volume.

The third "fiduciary traditionalist" position comes closest to a full rejection of contractarian ideas and the presentation of a separable theory. Scholars termed fiduciary traditionalists, many of whom are part of a broader growth in scholarship on fiduciary duties outlined at the start of this introduction, rarely approach these questions from a law and economics or contractual framework. They are more likely to draw on earlier bodies of doctrine, including equity, agency law, and trust law, and on philosophical and moral justifications for the imposition of fiduciary duties.

As readers will note, although our focus is on fiduciary duties, these three paths track larger debates in corporate law theory. Market realism is part of the broader turn in law and economics scholarship to a more realistic, empirical portrayal of corporate governance. Stakeholderism, as the name suggests, invokes one of the most hotly contested topics in business law: the basic purpose and nature of the corporation. As noted earlier, fiduciary theorists have contributed in many ways to our understanding of the robust role fiduciary law plays across a range of business domains, from firm governance to investor protection.

We shall now briefly describe each of these three pathways. We make no pretense that this is an exhaustive literature review. Beyond sketching this taxonomy, our goal is to note some of the ways in which we believe the chapters in this volume connect to and extend these themes.

A *The Market Realist Path*

The market realist critique is part of a broader scholarly intervention that stemmed from the first wave of contractarianism. These scholars are often sympathetic to the contractarian position, and like the proto-contractarians, they draw primarily on economic approaches in analyzing business. Nonetheless, they typically reject the most stylized proto-contractarian claims. Early scholars assumed that evolutionary processes led to optimal results. Michael Jensen and William Meckling's article *Theory of the Firm*, which is one of the most cited social-science writings, is most often used today to support the proposition that the separation of ownership and control in the corporation leads to agency problems. Fewer recall their optimistic conclusion that the survival and dominance of the corporate form suggest that the corporation is well-suited to reducing agency costs.[34]

The challenges to the early assumption that individual firm design will be optimal proceed along both theoretical and empirical grounds.[35] One theoretical argument noted that economic forces, including network effects, could lead to the adoption of boilerplate whose specific terms may be suboptimal for individual firms.[36] Other scholars advanced empirical arguments buttressing the theoretical critiques. The earliest such work typically studied the corporate charter, which contractarians assumed were a major site of contracting behavior. Empiricists noted a high degree of uniformity in charters, both in the choice of jurisdiction (Delaware) and in content—which suggested that the real world saw little of the contractual bargaining assumed by proto-contractarians.[37]

Few people now dispute the relevance of a more textured approach to analyzing the firm. Such texture is characteristic today both in quantitative empirical work and in more theoretical and doctrinal descriptions. Kelli Alces Williams's contribution to this volume is an example. In rejecting the fiduciary regime as an inapt description of the publicly traded corporation, Williams draws attention to the practical reality of large firm governance—a group of diversified shareholders with different risk tolerances, making it nearly impossible to identify a singular set of goals for managers to pursue. This method tracks market realism, in that it draws on a mismatch between the nitty-gritty reality of public corporations, compared to the high-level stylized assumptions of those (both contractarians and noncontractarians) who use the fiduciary paradigm to describe the manager-shareholder relationship.

In a different context, ERISA law, Dana Muir makes a similar move, noting the difficulty of characterizing principals and agents along simplistic lines. Although it is more common to characterize only employees and plan participants as retirement plan "beneficiaries," Muir notes that employers are also beneficiaries; otherwise, they would not voluntarily create such plans. The concerns of Williams and Muir echo Robert Clark's 1985 warning that the "nexus of contracts" stylization runs the risk of obscuring the multitude of complex relationships that make a typical firm interesting and worthy of study.[38]

The proto-contractarians typically believed that fiduciary duties should be fully waivable. Nowhere was their goal achieved more than in the explosion of alternative entities, which has led some commentators to express alarm at practitioners' rush to limit or waive fiduciary duties.[39]

---

[34] Jensen & Meckling, *supra* note 22 (concluding that "whatever its shortcomings, the corporation has thus far survived the market test against potential alternatives").

[35] For a more extensive synthesis of this literature, *see* Daines & Klausner, *supra* note 28.

[36] The scholars who advanced this point noted two additional explanations—agency costs between law firms and their clients, and behavioral biases—that could also result in convergence on standard terms, without any guarantee that the "substantive content of a term maximizes firm value." Marcel Kahan & Michael Klausner, *Path Dependence in Corporate Contracting: Increasing Returns, Herd Behavior and Cognitive Biases*, 74 WASH. U. L. Q. 347, 348–49 (1996).

[37] *See, e.g.*, Robert Daines, *The Incorporation Choices of IPO Firms*, 77 N.Y.U. L. REV. 1559 (2002).

[38] Clark, *supra* note 33.

[39] For instance, two Delaware jurists argued strongly that contractual freedom was a "siren song," of questionable merit on theoretical grounds and demonstrably problematic in practice, given the many LLC cases with poorly written waivers. Leo Strine & J. Travis Laster, *The Siren Song of Unlimited Contractual Freedom*, in ELGAR HANDBOOK ON ALTERNATIVE ENTITIES (Mark J. Lowenstein & Robert W. Hillman eds., 2004); *see also* Brent Horton, *Modifying Fiduciary Duties in Delaware: Observing Ten Years of Decisional Law*, 40 DEL. J. CORP. L. 921 (2016) (studying real-world examples of such modifications and noting the problems that commonly arise). In one decision illustrating issues that arise when courts interpret fiduciary modifications, then-Chancellor Strine memorably described a "linguistically challenging" clause purporting to modify fiduciary duties as "prepared by a member of a cold-

Still, most today accept that there is a role for at least some flexibility, for instance, in the context of appropriately drafted limitations on the corporate opportunity doctrine, part of the fiduciary duty of loyalty. The key questions on freedom of contract today are not usually binary choices, but rather a debate on where to draw the line.

The line-drawing problem is illustrated well in what Christine Hurt's chapter calls "extra large partnerships," such as publicly traded partnerships. This organizational form questions many of the premises that long distinguished small, closely held partnerships from large corporations and the laws that govern them. Unlike publicly traded corporations, publicly traded partnerships can limit fiduciary duties. Hurt notes the possibility that doing so may be less a policy decision and more simply the result of the drafters of the relevant uniform acts not anticipating the growth of partnerships to the extra large size.

Other market realists have challenged the standard proto-contractarian claim that evolutionary forces will lead to optimal outcomes both in contract decisions and governing law, including the right level of fiduciary protection.[40] Historical analysis can provide a corrective to this oversimplification, as evidenced by three historical chapters in this volume—Jared Ellias and Robert Stark on fiduciary duties near insolvency, Masayuki Tamaruya on the turn to fiduciary duties in Japanese nonprofit law, and Jacob Russell on the recasting of fiduciary obligations in American nonprofits. In each chapter, the authors draw attention to how fiduciary duties have evolved alongside a changing mix of other bodies of doctrine, including trust law. Fiduciary duties are rarely about optimizing one single element, and the level of duties has waxed and waned. For instance, Ellias and Stark note that judges have swung back and forth between arguing that contract sufficiently protects creditors and fearing that it does not. This history suggests the pendulum has not likely made its last swing. Path dependence, not just a teleological trend toward efficiency, plays an important role in all three historical chapters.

Even if rules did evolve to be optimal, sophisticated parties might still evade them through regulatory arbitrage. To the extent a large partnership chooses its organizational form primarily for fiduciary flexibility, and to the extent the drafters of the uniform partnership laws did not expect that, Hurt's chapter may provide one example. Howell Jackson's chapter provides another example in the mutual fund context. As he notes, the U.S. system for governing mutual funds is an elaborate investor protection regime based on fiduciary duties, and the U.S. Securities and Exchange Commission has repeatedly rejected a more contractual model used in Europe and elsewhere. Yet, certain investment vehicles with parallel policy implications are not always covered by the regime.

B *The Stakeholders/Pluralism Path*

A second line of critique has focused on the narrow shareholder-manager relationship generally emphasized by proto-contractarians. In fact, a range of players inhabit the corporation, and fiduciary duties may thus govern a multiplicity of principal-agent relationships in complex, interactive ways. The stakeholder critique has generally accepted the focus on managers and

blooded species, rather than a breathing, feeling member of our species trying to capture in words an actual human state of mind." Gelfman v. Weeden Investors, 859 A.2d 89, 112 (Del. Ch. 2004).

[40] Within corporate law, Easterbrook and Fischel, *supra* note 23, are probably the best known proponents of this view. Henry Hansmann's approach is also representative of this assumption, as he uses variations in firm structure—like nonprofits, employee-owned firms, and customer-owned cooperatives—to infer underlying contracting problems faced by each of these venture types. HENRY HANSMANN, THE OWNERSHIP OF ENTERPRISE (2000). This is a standard move in law and economics scholarship generally, although, over time, the field has adopted more refined approaches for understanding when the law might evolve toward efficiency. ROBERT COOTER AND THOMAS ULEN, LAW AND ECONOMICS 419–53 (6th ed. 2016).

directors as agents but has argued that understanding the principal to be "shareholders" is too narrow, both descriptively and normatively. The team production model advanced by Lynn Stout and Margaret Blair in 2003 provides a well-known focal point for this critique and directly assails the economic theory adopted by proto-contractarians.[41] Of course, today, fights over stakeholder and shareholder theory represent a central tension in corporate law—one that has spilled into major newspapers and political campaigns—a history that both Amir Licht and Jennifer Hill summarize in their chapters for this volume.

Beyond debates over how best to characterize the primary principle in corporate law, others—who we call pluralists—have widened the lens of the agency focus in other ways. The earliest proto-contractarians tended to focus especially on the manager-shareholder relationship. That focus meant relatively less attention was paid to the many other fiduciary or fiduciary-like relationships in the corporate galaxy, whether debt governance, controlling shareholders, or fiduciary relationship in other bodies of law like ERISA and investment management, often imposed on aspects of firm behavior.

For instance, in his chapter for this volume, Lyman Johnson suggests that even the characterization of Delaware as having a singular corporate "fiduciary law" is problematic. There are three distinct sets of fiduciary obligation regimes within the corporation with distinct beneficiaries, agents, and underlying paradigms. Kelli Alces Williams's intervention also falls squarely under this umbrella, given her argument that in public corporations, one cannot realistically describe a singular shareholder constituency to whom the board is beholden.

The stakeholder/pluralist critique notes that corporate law, and its fiduciary duty regime, is often called upon to solve broader social problems—thus taking the domain of fiduciary duties beyond the identifiable parties to the proto-contractarians' "nexus of contracts." Hill's chapter reminds us of the long shadow that corporate governance casts, particularly in the wake of financial scandals from Enron in 2000 onward, and that limiting harm to society may be a key purpose of fiduciary law. Similarly, Tamaruya's chapter explains how fiduciary principles were ported into Japanese nonprofit law with the goal of protecting societal interests. In a different domain—the fiduciary duties that govern various forms of retirement savings and investing—Quinn Curtis emphasizes a saver's overall retirement lifecycle planning process. In invoking this as the regulator's primary goal, Curtis's chapter implies that calibrating fiduciary regimes must consider goals far beyond the narrow domain of gap-filling individual contracts.

Two chapters advance suggestions about the practical implementation of more robust stakeholder consideration—in Amir Licht's case, a mechanism for adjudicating issues that arise when boards owe duties to multiple constituents, in Julian Velasco's case the implementation of benefit corporation statutes. Licht's proposed mechanism is rooted more in historical trust law doctrine, where the duty of impartiality that he proposes emerged, rather than in contract law. Likewise, although Velasco endorses shareholder primacy, his analysis extends beyond the proto-contractarians' conventional focus on shareholder profits.

Still, other chapters remind us of the many other ways fiduciary law may affect firm governance. Several analyze creditor relationships, drawing attention to the fact that the proto-contractarians may have given short shrift to tensions between creditors and shareholders.[42] Two

---

[41]   Margaret M. Blair & Lynn A. Stout, *A Team Production Theory of Corporate Law*, 85 Va. L. Rev. 248, 249, 254–5 (1999).

[42]   There are, to be sure, exceptions among the proto-contractarians; for instance, much of Michael Jensen's work was focused on the interaction between debt and equity. Michael Jensen, *Agency Costs of Free Cash Flow, Corporate Finance, and Takeovers*, 76 Am. Econ. Rev. 323 (1986). Nonetheless, the proto-contractarian position today is often characterized as emphasizing the shareholder-manager relationship to the exclusion of all else. *See* Hill, *supra* note 32.

contributions, Ted Janger's and Ellias and Stark's, examine the moment where that tension comes into the sharpest relief: the zone of insolvency. Both analyze the ways in which fiduciary law has, can, and should solve tensions between shareholder and creditor needs in that complex moment. Steven Schwarcz's chapter, which analyzes the fiduciary paradigm in the context of indenture trustees, comes to a contract-focused conclusion—that no duties should be imposed beyond the contract. However, this framing explicitly challenges the proto-contractarian focus on shareholders, especially given the vast size of debt relative to equity.

Other chapters examine areas beyond creditor law where fiduciary law impacts governance, such as Tamaruya and Russell's not-for-profit chapters. Both Arthur Laby and Dana Muir focus on ERISA, a legal regime that affects nearly every business and draws heavily on fiduciary principles. Consistent with the pluralist critique, both draw attention to the complexity of identifying a precise principal and agent. For Muir, a key issue is that players in the ERISA context may wear multiple hats, as in her comment that employers are in an important sense, beneficiaries to the plans they create. For Laby, the key challenge revolves around identifying a fiduciary and, as discussed in the next sub-section, arguing for the role that fiduciary theory can play in drawing those lines.

C *The Fiduciary Traditionalist Path*

A third challenge to the proto-contractarians stems from the surge of scholarly interest in fiduciary duties over the past ten to fifteen years. Scholars have identified and debated what unifies fiduciary obligations across disciplines, giving rise to new insights about when heightened duties are warranted. Their method and approach are often at odds with proto-contractarians and draw on a wider range of doctrine—especially trust law and equity—more than contract law. Often these scholars do not engage the contractarians directly.[43] Instead, they present a different approach to thinking about fiduciary law. Intellectually, many contributors in this field come less from a law and economics background, and are more likely to draw on philosophy. The explosion of this scholarship in recent years is quite notable.[44] This work has created a scholarly community that transcends narrow doctrinal fields, one which hardly existed at the time of the proto-contractarians.

Laby's approach to ERISA is characteristic, in that he explicitly argues for how the interpretation of the statutory regime has failed to but can and should draw on first principles of fiduciary law. For instance, understanding the fiduciary nature of advice giving, which has been a topic of discussion within fiduciary theory, may help courts answer practical questions about how to identify fiduciaries under ERISA's thorny regime. Other authors in the volume emphasize the trust or agency law origins of particular fiduciary duties, which brings the non-contractual aspects into sharp relief. Muir, for instance, emphasizes the trust and fiduciary origins of ERISA in explaining why courts distinguish certain investment decisions as "inherent fiduciary functions" rather than discretionary choices under the settlor doctrine.

---

[43] There are prominent examples of fiduciary theorists directly tackling the question of whether fiduciary law is best seen as a contract, an argument raised not just by Easterbrook and Fischel but also subsequently by some trust law scholars, most notably John Langbein. *See, e.g.,* John Langbein, *The Contractarian Basis of the Law of Trusts,* 105 YALE L. J. 625 (1995); Charlie Webb, *The Philosophy of Fiduciary Law,* in OXFORD HANDBOOK OF FIDUCIARY LAW, *supra* note 1, at 689–95; Deborah A. DeMott, *Beyond Metaphor: An Analysis of Fiduciary Obligation,* 1988 Duke L. J. 879; Daniel Markovits, *Sharing Ex Ante and Sharing* Ex Post: *The Non-Contractual Basis of Fiduciary Relations,* in PHILOSOPHICAL FOUNDATIONS OF FIDUCIARY LAW 209 (Andrew S. Gold & Paul B. Miller eds., 2014).

[44] *See supra* note 1.

Deborah DeMott, long one of the staunchest critics of the overuse of the "contract metaphor,"[45] continues to unearth distinctive aspects of the fiduciary relationship in her contribution. These aspects are at odds with standard contract doctrine, and thus cannot easily be reconciled with the conception of fiduciary obligations as a mere species of contract. Paul Miller's emphasis on equity as the source of fiduciary constraints draws attention to other limits of the contract-based perspective on fiduciary law. By its nature, equity is designed to address conduct that is otherwise lawful, but that is inequitable and unfair. Christoph Kumpan likewise draws attention to the complex role of fairness, a consideration the proto-contractarians would likely put to the side. In assessments about director independence, Kumpan provides a comparative analysis of how courts could consider subtle ties, for instance, emotional ones: this analysis appears to be rooted in equity and fairness rather than contract.

Finally, several contributors who focus on the societal values that fiduciary law may serve, including Hill, Curtis, and Tamaruya, also indirectly challenge the idea that fiduciary duties are a mere species of contract.

III ROADMAP OF THE VOLUME

We could have taken several different approaches to organize the chapters in this volume. We chose to arrange the book along broad thematic lines that transcend specific subfields of business law. As more fully described in this section, there are four sets of challenges or aims discussed by these authors: (i) identifying fiduciaries and their duties, (ii) describing gaps in, and alternatives to, fiduciary regimes, (iii) assessing historical or comparative perspectives, and (iv) evaluating fiduciary law from the perspective of stakeholders and society. This section provides a roadmap to the chapters, with a brief précis of each.

We are mindful that we have not organized the volume along traditional doctrinal lines, although the collection certainly covers a wide array of fields. For example, readers interested in debt and bankruptcy should review the contributions by Steven Schwarcz, Ted Janger, and Jared Ellias and Robert Stark. Those interested in funds, advisors, and other aspects of investment management should focus on the chapters by Howell Jackson, Quinn Curtis, Dana Muir, and Arthur Laby. Jacob Russell, Masayuki Tamaruya, and Julian Velasco cover nonprofit organizations and benefit corporations. Corporate fiduciary duties are addressed by Lyman Johnson, Paul Miller, Kelli Alces Williams, Christoph Kumpan, Jennifer Hill, and Amir Licht. Partnership is the subject of Christine Hurt's chapter, and agency the subject of Deborah DeMott's. In our view, however, organizing the book along purely doctrinal lines would mask the depth of the contributions and insights they provide about fiduciary governance and fiduciary theory.

A *Identifying Fiduciaries and Their Duties*

The first set of challenges or aims the authors address is the difficulty of identifying fiduciaries and the duties they owe to principals. The first chapter, by Deborah DeMott, takes up this project not by considering whether a given party should be deemed a fiduciary, but rather by exploring situations when fiduciary duties do not run coterminously with the relationship itself. She assesses when agents and principals may owe duties to one another either before an agency relationship has formed or after it has ended, and the justification for imposing such duties. The

---

[45]   DeMott, *supra* note 43.

chapter reviews aspects of the formation and termination of agency relationships, which, unlike relationships grounded in property interests or bilateral contract, require no formality to create. DeMott uses the metaphor of a dimmer switch, as opposed to an on/off switch, to describe the application of agency doctrine and the beginning and end of an agent's fiduciary duties.

DeMott then examines the periods before and after a relationship's formal existence. She discusses grounds on which duties may be owed by an agent to a prospective principal, such as an investment firm employee who might defraud an investor before a relationship has formed. In that case, the employee's association with the firm allows her to identify prospects to defraud and lends plausibility to the agent's conduct. DeMott also observes duties owed following termination, such as an agent's duty not to use or disclose a former principal's confidential information. She concludes by discussing the implications of the chapter for theoretical accounts of fiduciary law.

In the second chapter, Christine Hurt moves from agency to partnership. She observes that partnerships were once small-scale "livelihood" businesses, but are now often huge enterprises, organized as investment vehicles with limited liability, delegated management, and a public float. Hurt examines both limited liability partnerships (LLPs) and publicly traded partnerships (PTPs), often known as master limited partnerships (MLPs). She claims that while these partnerships resemble corporations in many respects, investors lack the protections normally afforded to corporate shareholders—especially because MLPs can waive fiduciary duties. Fundamentally, Hurt questions whether and when a person should be considered a partner in these organizations, which has important implications for fiduciary duties. Furthermore, whether an LLP partner should really be considered an employee raises thorny issues regarding the application of other bodies of law, such as employment discrimination law, securities regulation, and bankruptcy protection.

Hurt contrasts business organizations characterized by separation of ownership and control, such as a corporation, a limited partnership, and an LLC (in most cases), with business organizations where partners are both owners and managers, such as a general partnership. She situates an LLP as a hybrid, where partners, in theory, retain both ownership and control, although control may be illusory due to the presence of a powerful management committee that operates much like a corporate board. Also, while limited partnerships and LLCs often can eliminate fiduciary duties by agreement, MLPs are sold to strangers. Thus, just as corporate law provides for unwaivable fiduciary duties to shareholders, perhaps the same should be true for MLPs. Hurt concludes that these very questions demonstrate that partnerships have outgrown partnership law.

After this tour through agency and partnership, Lyman Johnson turns to corporate law. His aim is not to identify fiduciaries in corporate law, who are well known, but rather to identify differences in the character of the fiduciary duties these actors owe. Johnson begins by noting that corporate law recognizes three fiduciaries, officers, directors, and controlling shareholders. He then explains that these fiduciaries are distinct with respect to the beneficiary of their fiduciary duties, the reasons for imposing the duties, and the demands of loyalty and care. Thus, Johnson makes an important contribution by demonstrating that corporate law fiduciary duties are not monolithic and by casting doubt on claims of unitary coherence in the fiduciary duties of corporate law and corporate governance. Furthermore, sometimes the scope of one's fiduciary duty is unclear even within a given category. For example, Johnson points out that under Delaware's corporate law, there is a lack of consensus regarding whether officers' fiduciary duty (as opposed to directors') is one of ordinary care or gross negligence.

The chapter also comments on the distinction between the standard of conduct and standard of review in fiduciary law, which was the subject of a well-known 1993 article by Melvin Eisenberg. Johnson argues that Eisenberg did not write about an existing distinction between the two; rather, Eisenberg launched the distinction through the publication of the article. Johnson demonstrates that the standard of conduct and standard of review tend to converge, not diverge, with respect to both loyalty and care. In Johnson's view, this renders Eisenberg's famous distinction unhelpful.

Arthur Laby examines the complex question of who is considered a fiduciary under ERISA. Identifying ERISA fiduciaries has been the subject of countless lawsuits and extensive deliberation at the U.S. Department of Labor, which implements and enforces ERISA. Laby addresses the topic by widening the lens and comparing the ERISA statutory regime with the common law, an apt comparison because ERISA is based, at least in part, on common law fiduciary duties.

Laby draws three parallels between ERISA and the common law with respect to identifying fiduciaries with the first being the structure of fiduciary categories. Laby sees the standard common law distinction between categorical and ad hoc fiduciaries as present under ERISA, albeit with different labels attached. The second is the approach under both the common law and ERISA to determining fiduciary status. Laby highlights and critiques the attention paid to discretionary authority as the acid test for identifying a fiduciary, a development that he observes in both the common law and in ERISA jurisprudence. The third parallel, linked to the second, is the challenge to determining fiduciary status presented by advice giving. Laby explains that common law courts are not consistent in their treatment of advisors as fiduciaries. Similarly, under ERISA, regulators and courts struggle to determine when advice, in the absence of discretionary authority, should give rise to fiduciary status. Laby concludes that trust can serve as a foundation for an advisor's fiduciary status both in the common law and under ERISA.

Steven Schwarcz looks beyond the standard pantheon of corporate fiduciaries, such as officers and directors, to the world of indenture governance and indenture trustees in the multitrillion dollar bond market. Indenture trustees are financial institutions that administer the complex contracts between bond issuers and investors. Schwarcz explains that indenture trustee duties can be divided into two time periods, pre-default and post-default. In other work, Schwarcz has analyzed post-default decision-making. In this chapter, he turns his attention to pre-default indenture governance. The question of what duties are owed pre-default has become more important as activist investors have made increasing demands on indenture trustees to take actions prior to default and sued trustees for the failure to take such actions.

Schwarcz provides an illuminating history, explaining that, since the early twentieth century, the prevailing view is that trustees have no fiduciary duties pre-default. He then develops a normative argument that an indenture trustee's duties should be limited to those specified contractually in the indenture. Moreover, he claims, a trustee can refuse to take action that would create a conflict among investors, provided that the refusal is not a violation of the indenture. The chapter then applies the rule to a number of scenarios that arise in suits against trustees, including taking enforcement actions, investigating red flags, monitoring servicers, and monitoring for events of default.

B Gaps and Alternatives in Fiduciary Regimes

The second set of chapters focuses on gaps in and alternatives to fiduciary law. As some of these papers remind us, even within highly regulated fiduciary regimes, conduct which one might expect to be addressed often slips between the cracks. In other instances, the authors compare the imposition of fiduciary duties with alternative schemes for promoting fairness.

Quinn Curtis observes a series of gaps in the regulation of financial advice given to retail investors. Using a fictitious investor, Curtis looks broadly at financial advice given over an investor's lifecycle to demonstrate the difficulty of aligning incentives. A narrow focus on sales commissions paid to financial advisors detracts from risks created by other types of compensation, by the overall cost of advice, and by the fact that no compensation structure will truly align the interests of advisors and clients. Curtis defends the claim that "every compensation model gives rise to conflicts of interest," and the chapter provides a rich account of conflicts that might affect an investor's decisions.

The chapter reviews common compensation schemes and identifies the resulting misalignment of incentives. For example, while commission-based compensation is often identified with the risk of "churning" a customer's account, fee-based compensation based on assets under management can result in "reverse churning"—the tendency to ignore an account because the advisor will be paid regardless of the effort expended. Curtis then applies his framework to two alternative approaches, the Department of Labor's (now vacated) fiduciary rule and the Securities and Exchange Commission's Regulation Best Interest for broker-dealers, to evaluate how they fare with regard to his expanded notion of conflicts of interest. Curtis argues that the two approaches both suffer from adopting a narrow view of how conflicts distort incentives. Both approaches seek to identify and resolve discrete conflicts, as opposed to looking more holistically at an investor and considering how to improve the overall outcome across that investor's lifecycle.

Howell Jackson is similarly focused on investor protection and describes the elaborate system of mutual fund regulation in the United States, heavily based around fiduciary duties and reinforced by other regulatory mechanisms. This fiduciary regime comprises the double helix of duties owed by both a fund's independent directors and a fund's investment advisor. These duties are buttressed by regulations around portfolio restrictions, shareholder approvals, mandatory disclosures, and rights of redemption. In Jackson's view, however, the detailed regime has led to regulatory arbitrage whereby certain industry participants create alternative vehicles that escape many, and sometimes all, fiduciary protections designed for fund investors. These alternative vehicles may reduce costs and satisfy client demands, but they raise questions for policy makers.

As examples of regulatory arbitrage, Jackson examines various distribution practices that allow funds to bypass the well-developed system of fiduciary protections. He highlights the use of omnibus accounts whereby a brokerage firm, acting as a sub-transfer agent, is arguably paid for distribution efforts, thereby avoiding certain regulatory safeguards. Another example is the distribution of funds through individual accounts, whereby brokers and advisors allocate retail investor assets into various funds. When the allocation is the same across many investors, the result looks like a fund-of-funds, generating similar, if not identical, returns for a large number of retail investors, but without traditional mutual fund regulation. Jackson challenges regulators and academics to consider whether there should be more uniformity in investor protection across these disparate vehicles.

In her contribution, Dana Muir addresses regulatory arbitrage in a different context, employee benefit plans governed by ERISA. Although employee benefit plans give rise to a number of fiduciary relationships, Muir focuses on the relationship between employers, who sponsor the plans, and employees, who participate in them. Muir recounts two important developments in employee benefits starting in the 1980s. First, the structure of retirement plans shifted from defined benefit (DB) to defined contribution (DC) plans. DC plans, however, operate outside of many of ERISA's traditional requirements. Many rules intended for DB plans are inapplicable to DC plans, and the lower regulatory burden contributed to DC plans' rise, suggesting arbitrage akin to the development discussed by Jackson. The second development is that health care and disability insurance plans rose in importance. However, operating a health care plan differs from operating a retirement plan, and ERISA regulates health care plans relatively lightly.

Muir then points out that employer treatment by ERISA varies depending on whether it is acting as a sponsor establishing the plan, or as a plan fiduciary. Two implementing rules address the potential tension between these roles. First, under the settlor doctrine, plan sponsors do not act as plan fiduciaries when establishing, amending, or terminating plans — leaving a potential gap in the regulation of ERISA plans. Second, according to the standard of review for claims denials, as long as a plan adopts discretionary grants of authority, the standard is the deferential arbitrary and capricious standard. Muir contends that a deferential standard of review might result in increased costs that either are randomly distributed or, if a decision maker acts opportunistically, result in inappropriate denials.

Ted Janger focuses on financial distress and financially troubled firms. In particular, Janger compares the role of fiduciary duties, on the one hand, and the role of "clawback" (addressing preferential and fraudulent transfers), on the other, in regulating the behavior of officers, directors, and investors when a firm is in the vicinity of insolvency. Janger contrasts the U.S. and U.K. approaches. In the United Kingdom, officers and directors of a firm in the vicinity of insolvency owe creditors a relatively strong fiduciary duty, but that is no longer the case in Delaware. By contrast, the United States takes a strict approach to clawback, while the United Kingdom requires culpability before clawback will occur. Janger concludes that both the U.S. and the U.K. approaches have gaps. They both fail to see that duty and clawback serve complementary functions when a firm is in the vicinity of insolvency, namely the equitable treatment of creditors. Thus, a more balanced approach would be preferable. In that regard, Janger advocates for a regime of "equitable duty" whereby fiduciary principles (duty) and avoidance (equity) work together so that similarly situated claimants are treated correspondingly, and no constituency will be made worse off.

Paul Miller maintains a focus on equity but turns his attention to intra-shareholder tensions that sometimes arise in the corporate governance context. Miller argues that equity has moved between two strategies to achieve fairness among shareholders. The first is ex ante imposition of fiduciary duties on controlling shareholders to better align shareholder interests; the second is ex post equitable intervention on the grounds of oppression, facilitating shareholder exit or addressing the misalignment of shareholder interests prospectively. Just as Janger contrasts two alternatives, duty and clawback in the United States and the United Kingdom, Miller contrasts two alternatives across jurisdictions, claiming that American equity prefers a fiduciary approach whereas Commonwealth jurisdictions prefer the oppression doctrine.

Miller begins by identifying problems of group decision-making in a corporate structure, in particular the corporate tyranny that can result from majoritarian rule. He then contrasts the two approaches: American equity protects minority shareholders ex ante by deeming controlling shareholders to be fiduciaries, whereas Commonwealth equity operates ex post to enable judicial review of conduct on the basis of oppression. Next, Miller builds a case against the fiduciary approach, arguing, among other things that it is inconsistent with accepted fiduciary theory and disrespects shareholders' formal equality. By contrast, the oppression remedy has advantages based on the philosophy of corrective intervention as opposed to supplementing first-order law. Toward the end of the chapter, Miller describes ways in which the oppression remedy is substantively equitable. This might surprise some readers as oppression is a modern innovation and lacks foundation in the historical equity of the chancery courts.

C Historical and Comparative Perspectives

The next set of papers employs historical and comparative perspectives when examining fiduciary duties in a variety of business contexts. These perspectives are essential to the study of fiduciary law and fiduciary theory. Historical perspectives inform how and why a legal regime is organized today. This is particularly true in fiduciary law where many of the key concepts are rooted in centuries-old doctrines, such as the law of trusts, yet have also been stretched and modified as they came into contact with novel entity forms and contemporary business practices. Similarly, comparative perspectives help one gain a deeper understanding of one's own legal system and find ways to enhance or perfect one's own legal regime.

Jared Ellias and Robert Stark's contribution traces the evolution of Delaware corporate law as courts decide how to treat creditors of insolvent firms. As Ted Janger discusses in his contribution, and as Ellias and Stark make clear, Delaware corporate law today provides little protection to creditors of troubled firms. But that was not always the case, and the pendulum may well swing back toward more protection for creditors of troubled companies.

The chapter chronicles these shifts over time. The nineteenth century saw the rise of the trust fund doctrine, whereby creditors of insolvent firms sought protection in a manner, sometimes resembling modern fiduciary law. Under the doctrine, a director's duty shifts from protecting shareholder interests to preserving creditors' value, just as a trustee is meant to preserve a trust's value for beneficiaries. The trust fund doctrine, however, began to fall from favor around the turn of the twentieth century and was largely eradicated by the mid-twentieth century. The pendulum, however, swung again. In the 1990s, Delaware courts began to find that management owed a fiduciary duty to creditors in the case of insolvency. However, this development reversed around the time of the 2008 financial crisis, particularly in Delaware, and Delaware courts no longer recognize a direct claim against directors for breach of fiduciary duty by creditors of an insolvent firm, or one in the zone of insolvency. Those creditors are left to look to other areas of the law for protection, such as bankruptcy, contract, or fraudulent conveyance law, unless and until the pendulum swings again.

Fundamental to aspects of the corporate director's fiduciary duty of loyalty is the director's independence—the ability to make decisions free from extraneous influences. Christoph Kumpan employs a comparative approach and examines director independence in Germany and the United States, paying particular attention to Delaware. Although the two systems might appear very different, particularly in light of Germany's two-tier board structure, Kumpan claims that the structures tend to converge in some respects.

The chapter contrasts how independence is determined in each jurisdiction. In Delaware, independence is determined on a case-by-case basis depending on factors and concepts developed mainly through case law, such as the presence or absence of economic ties, personal ties, and coinvestments. A case-by-case approach, Kumpan argues, preserves flexibility but undermines legal certainty as courts can arrive at unpredictable conclusions. By contrast, Germany follows a more standardized rules-based approach, which promotes certainty but lacks the flexibility needed for individual cases. Kumpan claims that although the concept of independence is similar in both jurisdictions, the implementation differs significantly. In Germany, decisions with regard to independence are made ex ante, and by insiders, as independence decisions are left to the board itself. In Delaware, decisions are made ex post by outsiders—the courts. In Germany, however, the supervisory board (the higher tier of the two-tier structure) must communicate its decision to the public. In that regard, the potential market reaction will play a role ex post as well. Finally, Kumpan offers suggestions about how Delaware's approach might be improved to ensure more legal certainty for directors and shareholders alike.

The next two chapters turn to nonprofit organizations, employing both comparative and historical perspectives. Jacob Russell's chapter is an intellectual history of the transformation in charitable law toward a contract-based approach. Before the 1980s, charitable law was grounded in property and trust law, and focused on ideas of the "public" contained in concepts like "public trust" or "public ownership." Nonprofit boards had broad autonomy, and fiduciary duties were meant to address fraud and self-dealing. Beginning in the 1980s, however, the contract paradigm entered discussions of charitable law, moving the law from its trust origins closer to the law of business organizations.

In the second section of the chapter, Russell shows that contractarianism has more influence over the non-profit sector than is widely known. He uses a series of examples to demonstrate how the contract paradigm has left its mark on non-profit fiduciary duties. The first of these is donor rights: organizations are increasingly held responsible to donors, who have increased ability to sue the organization. The second is the role of attorneys general in enforcing bargains with donors, as opposed to vindicating the public interest. The third is the rise of references to the "duty of obedience," referring to a duty to the contract with one's non-profit donors. Russell concludes by offering a warning against viewing the law of a previous era in the light of a later prevailing paradigm—the new paradigm may not be wrong, but it should not be used as a tool to recast history.

Masayuki Tamaruya examines Japanese nonprofit law from both a historical perspective, dating back to the nineteenth century, and a comparative perspective, as many aspects of Japan's law borrow from Germany's. The chapter chronicles the law's evolution, including an important shift in nonprofit governance since the 1990s, and assesses its achievements. Tamaruya demonstrates extensive changes in the law over the last quarter century, including the introduction of 2006 legislation to replace the 110-year old Civil Code provisions regulating nonprofits.

The chapter provides a historical overview of Japanese nonprofit law from the late nineteenth century to the late twentieth century, beginning with the 1896 Civil Code, based in part on the German Civil Code, and running through the 1980s. The law was a product of both indigenous nonprofit tradition and influences from civil law and common law jurisdictions. During this time, nonprofit oversight was delegated to governmental departments, leaving little role for internal fiduciary governance. However, as the role of government in regulation increased, so did the incidence of mismanagement, corruption, and scandal, paving the way to reform.

The 2006 legislation represented a comprehensive overhaul of Japanese public interest corporation law. The law provided for a major shift from external governance, relying on government mandates, to internal governance, relying strictly on fiduciary principles and transparency. Although the legislation is no longer new, there is not yet sufficient data regarding how the new approach will work in practice. Tamaruya concludes that reform efforts will likely continue. In 2020, for example, new public interest trust legislation was proposed.

D Stakeholders and Society

The last set of chapters look beyond fiduciary relationships and evaluate fiduciary law from the perspective of stakeholders and society. Although chapters in other sections of this volume address various stakeholders, these papers focus more explicitly on stakeholders and society.

Jennifer Hill's contribution begins with the premise that the public corporation is an ambiguous entity. Conceptions of the corporation have long vacillated between a private "nexus of contracts" approach and a public approach, where greater attention is paid to stakeholder interests and social responsibility. The tension between these approaches has implications for director and officer duties. Recent scandals in the United States and Australia highlight how corporate law attempts to address multiple concerns, such as financial performance and negative externalities, which at times may require trade offs.

Hill begins with an overview of corporations from the perspective of the public-private divide. U.S. corporations have strong public roots. During the nineteenth century, however, the idea of the corporation as a public body melted away, and a private contractual conception emerged. The chapter then discusses implications of the public-private tension for directors' fiduciary duties, tracing this tension to the 1932 Berle-Dodd debate over the nature of directors' duties. The chapter then considers developments in corporate culture against a backdrop of recent banking scandals in the United States and Australia. In light of these scandals, Hill points to a focus by key players on stakeholders and society, as well as a renewed focus on corporate culture. Finally, the chapter explores, from a comparative view, the magnitude of directors' liability for flawed cultures that result in negative externalities. The United States represents the smallest likelihood of liability. The United Kingdom might be somewhat higher, but the lack of litigation likely negates a higher standard. These two jurisdictions can be contrasted with Australia, where the risk of liability may be greater due to public enforcement of directors' duties.

Amir Licht similarly takes up the private-public divide in the role of the corporation, which he terms the monistic-pluralistic divide. Licht points out that the debate over the pluralist position, which would balance the interests of multiple stakeholders, has been largely over *whether* to adopt the approach and not over *how* to implement it. Licht, therefore, advances a proposal, drawn from trust law, for a mechanism to implement a pluralist approach, namely that directors should exercise their discretion impartially. The greatest advantage of the proposal, Licht says, is its workability.

Like Hill, Licht engages the longstanding debate over the role of the corporation. Licht surveys several jurisdictions, including the United States, United Kingdom, Canada, Israel, and India. Most jurisdictions express a need to consider stakeholders' interests but provide little guidance on how to do so. Licht also revisits the Berle-Dodd debate and notes that the arguments on each side tend to come from different sources. The pluralist approach draws on ethics, politics, and psychology, while the monistic approach draws more on economics.

Licht then advocates for his duty of impartiality. This duty already regulates conflicts between trustees and trust beneficiaries and can be applied to address the interests of stakeholder constituencies. When directors and other corporate fiduciaries make business judgments in a company's best interest, Licht maintains, they should be required to treat the corporation's stakeholders impartially. Licht explains that stakeholder impartiality could be useful in legal systems that both endorse a pluralist approach and favor a monistic approach.

Picking up on themes in the previous two chapters regarding the shareholder-stakeholder debate, Julian Velasco turns to benefit corporations. Velasco questions the commonly held belief that benefit corporations were created to overcome a bias toward shareholder primacy. Instead, Velasco argues that benefit corporations are consistent with the shareholder primacy norm, but not the wealth maximization norm. He carefully distinguishes between these two concepts. The former states that the corporation must operate in shareholders' interests; the latter insists that it must operate with shareholder wealth creation as the goal. In that regard, shareholder wealth maximization, which assumes that shareholders are primarily interested in wealth creation, can be viewed as one instantiation of shareholder primacy. But that assumption, Velasco argues, may not always hold. Shareholders may seek a legal form that allows them to join with likeminded investors and commit to a purpose other than wealth creation. A benefit corporation is the result, but it is no less shareholder-centric than a conventional business corporation.

Thus, Velasco argues that both the benefit corporation and the traditional business corporation should be understood in the light of shareholder primacy. However, shareholders of a benefit corporation have signaled their interest in pursuing other socially desirable goals. Velasco rejects the claim that the benefit corporation was created for the purpose of benefiting stakeholders and society. It is better understood in terms of shareholder altruism—empowering shareholders who are inclined to be altruistic—as opposed to stakeholder rights.

Kelli Alces Williams closes the volume with a sobering view of corporate fiduciary duties and the real role of corporate officers and directors in society. Williams claims that the modern public corporation is far different from the corporation envisioned by early drafters of state corporate laws. According to Williams, operating a modern public corporation today is not a fiduciary enterprise, and she provides three reasons why officers and directors should not be described as fiduciaries. First, corporate managers cannot pursue the best interest of multiple beneficiaries, whose goals are not monolithic. Second, managers are expected to pursue their own interests, including incentive compensation, when the application of the fiduciary obligation would require renouncing self-interest. Third, well-diversified shareholders are not vulnerable to managers' decisions. Thus, in most cases, officers and directors do not act on behalf of a well-defined beneficiary, and they are not selfless in defining the corporate interest or pursuing it.

The impoverished state of corporate fiduciary duties has many sources, Williams claims, including the decline of the business judgment rule, the decline of the duty of care, the complexity of large scale enterprises, market demands, and political culture. In any case, whatever principle guides corporate managers, it is not fiduciary in nature. Furthermore, continuing to identify corporate governance relationships as fiduciary is detrimental because it gives investors a false sense of security—they wrongly take solace in the integrity that fiduciary duties inspire. Williams advises that acknowledging the truth will allow investors to better protect themselves and hold managers accountable through other means.

IV CONCLUSION

All told, this collection brings together nineteen distinct and thoughtful voices on the role of fiduciary law and fiduciary duties in business. Whether readers approach this volume as a practitioner, scholar, jurist, policy maker, or businessperson, we expect they will find a range of insights across a broad set of subfields. As is clear from the roadmap, and will be clearer from the chapters, the contributors' perspectives differ widely.

Yet each chapter is united by a common thread: identifying and filling gaps in the understanding of fiduciary obligations in business. This story is not yet finished. As this introduction suggests, the contractarian revolution's impact on corporate law and scholarship is still reverberating. It has resulted in significant change, but it has also prompted pushback and reconsideration. We hope this volume provides both a synthesis of the current state of fiduciary law in business and a thoughtful forecast on critical debates that lie ahead.

PART I

Identifying Fiduciaries and Their Duties

Fiduciary Duties on the Temporal Edges of Agency Relationships

Deborah A. DeMott[*]

I INTRODUCTION

The common law of agency imposes duties that principal and agent owe to each other, including an agent's fiduciary duties to the principal. Although not mirror images, these duties usually run parallel in duration because most of the time, a principal's duties, like an agent's, are coterminous with the relationship. This chapter explores situations in which temporal lines of demarcation do less work. The absence of a fully formed relationship of agency does not mean that the parties owe each other no duties of any sort. For example, consider an employee of an investment firm who may defraud investors who are not yet clients of the firm. Although the employee acts without actual or implied authority and in transactions not conducted through the firm, the employee may have identified prospects to defraud through his connection to the firm. This chapter analyzes situations like these. Likewise, a relationship's end does not obviate continuing obligations stemming from the now-concluded relationship. The character and content of duties on the peripheral edges of relationships vary, as do the justifications for imposing duties and whether they are derived from doctrines apart from agency law. Additionally, the resolution of issues at the temporal edges of agency relationships may yield to bright-line determinations or require fact-specific and nuanced inquiries. The ubiquity of agency relationships—spanning otherwise-disparate contexts, including organizational settings—makes these issues matter.[1]

Among fiduciary relationships, agency is distinctive because both principal and agent hold ongoing power to terminate the relationship at will, albeit in breach of contract. The distinctive structure of agency—empowering both parties to act unilaterally to end their relationship, often preceded by a unilateral process of reflection and planning—assures the presence of issues about duties on the periphery of termination. This dimension of agency's distinctive structure has implications for broader accounts of fiduciary obligation, especially those grounded in cognitive dimensions of an actor's loyalty. Agency doctrine generally permits an employee or other agent

---

[*] Portions of this chapter expand on points made more briefly in Deborah A. DeMott, *Fiduciary Principles in Agency Law, in* THE OXFORD HANDBOOK OF FIDUCIARY LAW (Evan J. Criddle, Paul B. Miller & Robert H. Sitkoff eds., 2018). An earlier version benefitted from discussions at the 2019 Fiduciary Law workshop and the editorial conference for this volume, the Tokyo University Law Faculty Private Law Forum and the Trust Future Forum, Kansai, and the Altara Kaufman 2018 Conference on Global Perspectives on Fiduciary Law at IDC Herzliya; and the comments of Howell Jackson, the editors of this volume, and other colleagues.

[1] *See* Great Minds v. FedEx Office & Print Servs., Inc., 886 F.3d 91, 95 (2d Cir. 2018) 2018) (noting "mundane ubiquity" of agency relationships; licensor's counsel failed to address agency relationships linking licensees with non-employee copying service when terms of license, which permitted reproduction and distribution for non-commercial purposes by licensee, did not prohibit delegation whether to licensee's employees or non-employee agents).

to plan to compete with the principal following termination; but empowered to end the relationship at any time, an agent's commitment to it may always appear contingent, at least as seen in retrospect by a now-former principal. Of course, a principal who appreciates agency's implications may attempt to structure the relationship's terms to protect its interests. Additionally, agency doctrine, applicable to ongoing relationships between parties whose perspectives and preferences may shift over time, accommodates interim bargaining to adjust a relationship's terms going forward, each party always empowered to exit. This is not the structure that underlies what is often assumed to be the prototype for a fiduciary relationship, a donative trust.

The chapter opens by sketching aspects of the formation and termination of common-law agency relationships. Requiring no formality to create, agency relationships are also relatively fragile, in contrast with legal relationships grounded in property interests, donative trusts, limited-liability entities, or bilateral contract. Next, the chapter identifies and examines the distinct bases on which agents might owe duties to prospective principals, including the possibility of a distinct status or category, "agent-in-waiting," with the consequence that fiduciary duties would apply to all actors within the category. The chapter then examines the duties owed by principals and agents following the termination of an agency relationship as well as the more contestable stage that precedes termination. Implications for more general or theoretical accounts of fiduciary law conclude this section.

II THE FORMATION AND TERMINATION OF AGENCY RELATIONSHIPS

Agency relationships are distinctive among fiduciary relationships, including those, like agency, for which fiduciary character is ascribed by status or legal convention.[2] Outside these settled categories, courts impose fiduciary duties in particular relationships in response to specific circumstances, specifically the potential for opportunism and abuse when one party invites and a vulnerable party reposes trust.[3] As Daniel Kelly observes, these cases usually fall "along the borderline ... between an arms-length transaction, in which each party may act according to its own self-interest, and a fiduciary relationship, in which the law requires a party to act in the sole or best interests of another."[4] A signal trait of agency law is the relative ease and informality with which two parties may create an agency relationship and, later on, exit from it. The common law defines agency as "the fiduciary relationship that arises when one person (a 'principal') manifests assent to another person (an 'agent') that the agent shall act on the principal's behalf and subject to the principal's control, and the agent manifests assent or otherwise consents so to act."[5] Creating a common-law agency relationship does not require compliance with specified formalities, such as executing a written instrument, nor does it require any filing with the state comparable to the requisites to form a corporation or other type of limited-liability business entity. In this respect, an agency relationship resembles a general partnership formed when parties agree to co-own a business for profit and requires no compliance with specified formalities. The parties' intention to formalize their relationship later on, structuring it through a to-be-formed limited-liability entity, does not preclude the existence of a general partnership.[6]

---

[2] On status-based fiduciary relationships, see Andrew S. Gold & Paul B. Miller, *Introduction, in* Philosophical Foundations of Fiduciary Law 1, 2–3 (Andrew S. Gold & Paul B. Miller eds., 2014).

[3] *See* Daniel B. Kelly, *Fiduciary Principles in Fact-Based Fiduciary Relationships, in* Oxford Handbook of Fiduciary Law 12 (Evan J. Criddle, Paul B. Miller & Robert H. Sitkoff eds., 2019).

[4] *Id.* at 4.

[5] Restatement (Third) of Agency § 1.01 (Am. Law Inst. 2006).

[6] For implications, see Christine Hurt, *Startup Partnerships*, 69 B. C. L. Rev. —(forthcoming 2020).

Agency law also enables principal and agent, as between themselves, to define the scope of their relationship, including specifying domains in which the agent may act free of fiduciary duties to the principal.[7] More generally, the law recognizes that another type of legal relationship—such as a debtor-creditor relationship—may co-exist with agency and confer rights on the agent to act in ways contrary to the principal's interests, as would a securities broker who liquidates an over-margined account notwithstanding the client's objections.[8] The law also recognizes relationships that are not agency relations as defined by the common law but nonetheless resemble agency's most basic consequence: one actor's conduct affects the legal position of another, but the agent-like actor has an economic interest distinct from the relationship, which privileges actions taken solely to benefit that actor. In such relationships—for example, those created by a power given as security—contractual provisions can control when and how the relationship may be terminated.[9] Corporate law acknowledges and defines roles for an important category of agents, corporate officers.

Although agency is consensual, an enforceable contract between principal and agent need not accompany or underlie its creation; many agency relationships are formed gratuitously.[10] Thus, a relationship of common-law agency may link an agent to a principal prior to any enforceable contract. As a consequence, agency relationships can arise with fluidity and lack the harder-edged moment of formation or initiation integral to conventional accounts of contract formation.[11] Some agents—corporate officers, for example—may commence acting in a de facto capacity, in advance of compliance with formal requisites, including those imposed by a firm's governance documents.[12] Many contemporary statutes enable agency-like relationships typified by precisely-drawn triggers that initiate the relationship and the duties that follow, such as durable powers of attorney.[13]

Simple to form, agency relationships are also terminable at will by either principal or agent, albeit in breach of any contract between them. A principal has the power to terminate the agent's actual authority to act on the principal's behalf by making a manifestation of revocation to the agent. Likewise, an agent has power, through a manifestation to the principal, to terminate their relationship by renouncing authority.[14] More vividly, "you're fired" and "I quit" operate as performative utterances to end an agency relationship, even when a contract between the parties provides otherwise.[15]

---

[7]   For these possibilities, see Deborah A. DeMott, *Defining Agency and Its Scope (II), in* COMPARATIVE CONTRACT LAW 396 (Larry A. DiMatteo & Martin Hogg eds., 2016).

[8]   For more on the defined scope of agency relationships, see *id.* at 403.

[9]   RESTATEMENT (THIRD) OF AGENCY § 3.12 (AM. LAW INST. 2006). Conventional examples are powers, given as security, to protect a legal or equitable title held by the power's holder, as well as powers to exercise voting rights associated with securities or membership interests.

[10] *Id.* § 1.01 cmt. d.

[11] For a critique of hinging contractual obligations on "a specific hypothetical moment of contract formation," see Shawn J. Bayern, *The Nature and Timing of Contract Formation, in* COMPARATIVE CONTRACT LAW 77, 88 (Larry A. DiMatteo & Martin Hogg eds., 2016).

[12] *See In re* the Walt Disney Co. Derivative Litig., 906 A.2d 27, 48 (Del. 2006) (defining "*de facto* officer" as "one who actually assumes possession of an office under the claim and color of an election or appointment and who is actually discharging the duties of that office, but for some legal reason lacks *de jure* legal title to that office.").

[13] *See* Estate of Alford v. Shelton, 89 N.E.3d 391 (Ill. 2017) (applying ILL. COMP. STAT. 45/2–10.3(a) (West 2010); child designated as successor agent in parents' durable powers of attorney owed no fiduciary duties prior to the exit of original agent).

[14] RESTATEMENT (THIRD) OF AGENCY. § 3.10 (AM. LAW INST. 2006). If the "agent" instead holds a power given as security, it may be made irrevocable, typically by a term in the written instrument creating or evidencing the power. *Id.* § 3.12.

[15] Unless, as discussed above, the "agent" holds a power expressly made irrevocable that is supported by a distinct economic interest.

Why are common-law agency relationships so relatively fragile? And why does agency law privilege one party's present preferences over both parties' inconsistent earlier preferences to bind themselves to an ongoing relational commitment? The underlying premise of agency is consent, in particular, the principal's consent on an ongoing basis to legally effectual representation by the agent. By revoking an agent's actual authority, the principal retrieves or calls back an extension of its own legal personality.[16] Renouncing and thereby terminating an agency relationship also frees the agent from most constraints imposed by the relationship, including the agent's duty to comply with the principal's lawful instructions and the agent's fiduciary duty of loyalty to the principal. Possessing a unilateral power to terminate should lower a prospective agent's anticipated costs of undertaking to act on behalf of any particular principal, including an employer. Although the agent may be obliged to forego attractive opportunities during the relationship, opportunities of the same type may rightfully become available once the agent exits the relationship.[17]

Agency doctrine overall mixes immutable characteristics—including the agent's fiduciary duties to the principal and the unilateral powers held by principal and agent to terminate the relationship—with those subject to agreement between agent and principal, including agreements defining the scope of the agency relationship to privilege conduct by the agent that would otherwise breach the agent's duties to the principal, as discussed above. Thus, subject to limits grounded in public policy concerns, an agent may agree not to compete with the principal following termination.[18] An agreement may also contain provisions that price out the cost to the agent of early termination by the principal, as in many executive employment agreements. In other relationships, contract provisions—typically drafted by the agent—may impose fees on the principal if the principal terminates the relationship within a set period. Termination or exit fees charged by asset managers ("investment advisers" in the United States), although fairly common, can be problematic.[19] Assets under management in a client's account belong to the client as principal, not the manager, who holds the assets as an agent who is the client's fiduciary. Often clients exit a management relationship when they are unhappy with the manager, which implies that an exit fee can operate as a penalty geared to retain clients and function inconsistently with the adviser/manager's fiduciary duty to place the clients' interests before its own as their agent.

Just as a prospective agent may owe duties to the principal prior to the formation of an agency relationship or a contract encapsulating the parties' agreement, terminating an agency relationship does not end all duties the parties owe each other. Some linger post-termination, echoing the operation of an agent's "lingering authority" to bind the principal, that is, the appearance of authority that may survive following the termination of actual authority.[20] Additionally, when an agent contemplates terminating the relationship—perhaps in the prospect of competing with the principal—the agent's commitment to the principal and orientation toward its interests may no longer be as whole-hearted as loyalty requires as assessed in retrospect by the now-former

---

[16] For this rationale, see Francis Reynolds, *When Is an Agent's Authority Irrevocable?, in* MAKING COMMERCIAL LAW: ESSAYS IN HONOUR OF ROY GOODE 259, 259 (Ross Cranston ed., 1997). On the implications of understanding an agent as an extension of the principal's legal personality—and not as a substitute for the principal—see Deborah A. DeMott, *The Fiduciary Character of Agency and the Interpretation of Instructions, in* PHILOSOPHICAL FOUNDATIONS OF FIDUCIARY LAW 321, 322 (Andrew S. Gold & Paul B. Miller eds., 2014) (hereinafter DeMott, *Fiduciary Character*).

[17] RESTATEMENT (THIRD) OF AGENCY § 3.10 cmt. b (AM. LAW INST. 2006).

[18] *Id.* § 8.04 cmt. b.

[19] Jason Zweig, *The Intelligent Investor: Should You Have to Pay A Fee to Fire an Adviser?*, WALL ST. J. (July 26, 2014).

[20] RESTATEMENT (THIRD) OF AGENCY § 3.11 cmt. c (AM. LAW INST. 2006). "Lingering authority" requires that the third party's belief that the agent acts with authority be reasonable. *Id.*

principal. Even when the agent's conduct does not contravene duties of loyalty, investing effort and ingenuity to prepare for new adventures can sap the agent's diligence on behalf of the (present) principal.[21]

Long-established doctrine permits an agent to take otherwise lawful steps to prepare to compete once an agency relationship is terminated,[22] and to do so without disclosure to the principal.[23] When preparations to compete overlap with continued service, ambiguity can cloud inquiries into the agent's conduct and motives. For example, consider an agent/employee whose duties require visible interactions with major customers of the principal/employer's business. When the agent is especially responsive and effective in customer-facing interactions, was the agent motivated to solidify a relationship that will follow her to a competitor? Or simply to do good work on behalf of the principal?[24] As elaborated below, permissible (and secret) preparations to compete imply that an agent's duty of loyalty to the principal, or at least its scope or intensity, may diminish when the agent contemplates ending the relationship. Of course, if an agent abandons her plan and decides to stay, the duty of loyalty should resume its earlier dimensions.

The prospect of fiduciary duties that precede the formation of an agency relationship, like the duties that linger following termination and may dim if not lessen preceding termination, complicates schematic accounts of fiduciary relationships that position parties at arm's length prior to and following a relationship. A visual or mechanical metaphor may help conceptualize these peripheral duties: the purchaser of a switch to control an electric light has a choice between an on-off toggle function or a dimmer control through a rheostat that enables a user to vary the light's degrees of brightness. Agency doctrine operates at times more like a dimmer switch than an on-off toggle, in particular in the inception and expiration of fiduciary duties. This lack of precise demarcation increases the need for fact-specific inquiries to resolve disputed situations, a consequence not unique to agency law.[25] Bright-line determinations are not absent from cases applying agency law, just not universal.

III AGENTS' DUTIES PRECEDING AGENCY RELATIONSHIPS

Prospective principals and agents owe duties to each other derived from other bodies of law, including tort law. In one line of cases, an employee of a brokerage firm defrauds investors who are not—or at least not yet—clients of the firm, acting without either actual or apparent authority to bind the firm and through transactions that explicitly are not conducted through the firm. But the employee's association with the firm enabled the employee to identify prospects to defraud, while a known association with the firm lent plausibility to the employee's conduct. In the brokerage context, it is well established that an agency relationship begins only when a client

---

[21] An agent's duties of performance require that the agent "act with the care, competence, and diligence normally exercised by agents in similar circumstances," subject to any agreement with the principal. *Id.* § 8.08.

[22] *Id.* § 8.04; *accord*, Restatement of Employment Law § 8.04 cmt. c. (Am. Law Inst. 2015).

[23] An agent's duties include "a duty to use reasonable effort to provide the principal with facts that the agent knows ... when the facts are material to the agent's duties to the principal . . . ." Restatement (Third) of Agency § 8.11 (Am. Law Inst. 2006). This general duty does not encompass the fact that the agent plans to compete with the principal. *Id.* § 8.04 cmt. c. Nor does the agent's fiduciary duty of loyalty require disclosure. *Id.*

[24] *Id.* § 8.04 cmt. c. Overall, if an agent who plans to exit does not explicitly solicit the principal's customers or employees to join the competing enterprise, the fact that customers or employees follow the agent does not establish disloyalty on the agent's part; excellent work performance itself is not an indicium of disloyalty. Mercer Mgmt. Consulting, Inc. v. Wilde, 920 F. Supp. 219, 234 (D.D.C. 1996).

[25] For an example, see Adam J. Hirsch, *Inheritance on the Fringes of Marriage*, 2018 Univ. Ill. L. Rev. 235, 276 (observing that "[t]he simple truth is that persons enter and leave our lives at times distinct from crowning acts").

places an order, and the broker agrees to execute it.[26] However, if the firm acted negligently in hiring its employee—perhaps one with a prior history of client complaints or regulatory infractions—or in supervising or retaining the employee, the firm could be subject to liability on a tort theory. In accepting this theory, a recent case analogized the premise for the brokerage firm's liability to the liability of a burglar alarm company that hires, as a door-to-door salesman, a felon known to be violent who kidnaps a prospective alarm-system customer.[27] An employee's fraud also subjects the employee to liability to the prospective customer. The brokerage firm's liability is direct, not vicarious; the employee acted without actual or apparent authority on behalf of the firm but the firm itself, if negligent, is subject to liability.[28]

Apart from law of general applicability, prospective agents are subject to duties to prospective principals in particular domains. Relationships between lawyers and prospective clients are instructive, given that lawyers are treated as their clients' agents for many purposes.[29] Only to a client does a lawyer owe the full complement of duties that reflect the fiduciary character of a lawyer-client relationship.[30] However, it would be mistaken to assume that a lawyer owes a prospective client no legal duties other than those derived from tort law. Lawyers owe prospective clients a duty not to use or disclose confidential information learned through consultation with the prospective client, subject to exceptions not germane to this chapter. In possession of a prospective client's confidential information, a lawyer is subject to constraints in representing clients whose interests are materially adverse to prospective clients.[31] Likewise, a lawyer owes duties to a prospective client concerning property in the lawyer's custody.[32] To the extent the lawyer furnishes legal services, the lawyer owes the prospective client a duty of reasonable care.[33] Contracts in which clients or prospective clients express advance consent to conflicts—with the lawyer's own interests or representation of other clients—that may later emerge in the relationship are effective only when the client is fully informed, and the lawyer reasonably believes no client's interest will be adversely affected.[34]

The same suite of duties applies even when no lawyer-client relationship eventuates. And why? The sharing of confidential information is a frequent linchpin in seeking legal services, situating prospective clients much like clients. The vulnerability that follows for clients, once confidential information has been shared, seems essential to a relationship with a lawyer, even when the relationship is tentative or prospective, or the client is sophisticated. And when a lawyer

---

[26]   Le Marchant v. Moore, 44 N.E. 770 (N.Y. 1896); *In re* Enron Corp. Sec. Derivative & "ERISA" Litig., 238 F. Supp. 3d 799, 843 (S.D. Tex. 2017).

[27]   Owens v. Stifel Nicholaus & Co., 650 Fed. App'x 764 (11th Cir. 2016) (discussing salience of Underberg v. S. Alarm, Inc., 643 S.E.2d 374, 375 (Ga. App. Ct. 2007)).

[28]   RESTATEMENT (THIRD) OF AGENCY § 7.03 (AM. LAW INST. 2006) (distinguishing between direct and vicarious liability).

[29]   *See* Deborah A. DeMott, *The Lawyer as Agent*, 67 FORDHAM L. REV. 301 (1998).

[30]   RESTATEMENT (THIRD) OF THE LAW GOVERNING LAWYERS § 16 (3) and cmt. b (AM. LAW INST. 2000) (stating that "[a] lawyer is a fiduciary . . . .").

[31]   *Id.* § 15(1)(a) & (2).

[32]   *Id.* § 15(1)(b).

[33]   *Id.* § 15(1)(c).

[34]   MODEL RULES OF PROF'L CONDUCT r. 1.7(b) (AM. BAR ASS'N 1983). On the efficacy of general open-ended waivers, compare Galdene Labs., L.P. v. Activis Mid Atl. LLC, 927 F. Supp. 2d 390 (N.D. Tex. 2013) (denying a motion to disqualify counsel subject to unrelated conflict pertaining to the current client; client gave informed consent to open-ended general waiver that would ordinarily be ineffective but acted through general counsel who frequently retained outside counsel, including large law firms) with Celgene Corp. v. KV Pharma. Co., No. 07-4819SDW, 2008 WL 2937415, at *8 (D.N.J. July 29, 2008) (granting motion to disqualify when the retention agreement included comparable waiver language; agreement did not manifest informed consent because it did not specify types of conflicts, such as the concurrent representation of generic pharmaceutical companies in patent cases). *Galdene* and *Celgene* both shift the burden—ordinarily borne by the party moving to disqualify counsel—to the law firm resisting disqualification.

gives advice or otherwise furnishes legal services to a prospective client, the recipient is likely to rely, perhaps by failing to form a lawyer-client relationship either with the advice-giver or another lawyer.

As their clients' agents, lawyers are distinctive. They are officers of the court and members of a largely self-regulated profession and agents whose representative role comes packaged with other significant functions, most importantly furnishing advice to clients on a confidential basis. Their distinct duties—including those owed to prospective clients regardless of whether a lawyer-client relationship is formed—stem from the lawyer's status as a lawyer. Revisited in this light, brokers—the agents with which this section began—are disanalogous in significant ways. Any duty a broker owes a customer concerning investment advice is distinct from the agency duties the broker owes in executing an order from the customer to buy or sell.[35] In contrast, the structure of a lawyer-client relationship, including one in formation, situates the client or prospective client in a position that entails sharing confidential information with the vulnerabilities that follow. Nonetheless, might a broker ever have duties as a sort of "agent-in-waiting" before receiving an order for execution?

IV THE STATUS OF "AGENT-IN-WAITING"?

The imposition of duties (whether or not deemed fiduciary in character) that anticipate the formation of an agency relationship could be conceptualized in several ways, each with its distinct rationale. First, pre-agency duties may be grounded in the application of other bodies of law. These include tort law, which furnishes the basis for brokerage firm liability to prospective clients in the "bad broker" cases discussed above. Second, pre-agency fiduciary duty may be grounded in a fact-specific, case-by-case determination of whether a particular relationship was characterized by trust invited by one party and justifiably reposed by the other. Lawyers' duties to prospective clients, discussed above, operate categorically but the underlying justifications resemble those for the imposition of fact-specific fiduciary duties. Third, pre-agency fiduciary duties could follow from treating a relationship as an instance of a category in which all relationships are fiduciary ones, perhaps termed "agency-in-waiting."[36] Grounding pre-agency duties in a distinct state that anticipates the formation of an agency relationship calls into question whether the duties arise when no agency relationship ensues. Perhaps only a limited suite of duties follows; recall that a lawyer owes duties to a prospective client but not the broader-reaching fiduciary duties owed to a client. Statutes and regulatory provisions may also be relevant to shape or dominate analysis and resolution. The sections that follow explore pre-agency duties for two significant groups: de facto and de jure corporate officers, and brokers.

A *Corporate Officers, De Facto and De Jure*

An actor who assumes to act as an agent in a formally defined category when requisite formalities have not been met—typified by a de facto corporate officer—owes fiduciary duties in the de facto phase, which may or may not precede a de jure phase. This is because the actor in question has assumed to act as an agent, in de facto officer cases with some appearance of rightful occupancy of the office, such as acquiescence by the corporation's board of directors. Thus, the status of the de facto officer is not an instance of acting as a poseur—purporting to be an agent when that is not

---

[35] *In re Enron*, 238 F. Supp. 3d at 843.
[36] Thanks to Richard Brooks for urging me to develop the implications.

true at the time of holding out—or a fiduciary *de son tort*—unilaterally taking on a fiduciary status (or its appearance) without a regular appointment to it.[37] By definition, de facto officers do not act unilaterally in assuming a particular office. The consequences for the corporation are closely linked to apparent authority because it is requisite that a de facto officer, in exercising the functions of an office, reasonably appears to hold the office.[38] To exercise the functions of an office in interactions with third parties as a corporation's representative is to act as the corporation's agent. Like a formal appointment or election to an office, whether an agent exercises an office's functions is readily determinable.

Returning to the potential status of "agent-in-waiting," consider the position of an individual whose announced appointment as a corporate officer will become effective at a future time, who, in the meantime, prepares to undertake the office's responsibilities. In *In re the Walt Disney Co. Derivative Litigation*, the court held that the corporation's new president did not owe fiduciary duties before assuming office, including duties concerning the terms of his employment agreement.[39] Not having purported to assume the duties of the presidency before his announced start date, the officer-in-waiting was not a de facto officer; his activities to prepare himself for the office did not amount to exercising its functions.[40] Additionally, the facts fell short of the bases on which courts impose fact-specific fiduciary duties. More generally, whether an actor has entered the realm of corporate officeholders and their fiduciary duties—even as a de facto officer—is relatively amenable to a bright-line or toggle-switch determination.[41]

B Brokers

In contrast with corporate officeholders, the facts of the leading brokerage case, *Martin v. Heinold Commodities, Inc.*,[42] illustrate situations in which multiple bases for pre-agency fiduciary duties may be present. In *Martin*, the Illinois Supreme Court held that a commodities broker had a duty to explain the nature of its opaque fee and commission structures to prospective clients. The court stressed that "where the very creation of the agency relationship involves a special trust and confidence on the part of the principal in the subsequent fair dealing of the agent, the prospective agent may be under a fiduciary duty to disclose the terms of his employment as an agent."[43] It is not clear whether the imposition of the duty of disclosure applies at a categorical level and thus becomes applicable when the parties intend to create a relationship of a particular type, or whether the duty applies (and the prospective agent's

---

[37] On poseurs, see Deborah A. DeMott, *The Poseur as Agent, in* AGENCY LAW IN COMMERCIAL PRACTICE 35–54 (Danny Busch et al. eds., 2016). On fiduciaries *de son tort*, see Andrew S. Gold, *The State as a Wrongful Fiduciary, in* FIDUCIARY GOVERNMENT 183, 190–93 (Evan J. Criddle et al. eds. 2018).

[38] *See* Lowder v. All Star Mills, Inc., 330 S.E.2d 649, 655 (N.C. Ct. App. 1985) (individual found to have acted as an officer signed corporations' income tax returns as corporate president and assistant treasurer, had input into corporations' formation and operation, and took over their management). On de facto officers in general, see RESTATEMENT (THIRD) OF AGENCY § 3.03 cmt. e (AM. LAW INST. 2006).

[39] 906 A.2d 27, 48–49 (Del. 2006). I testified as an expert witness on other issues in this litigation.

[40] *Id.* at 41 n. 14. Both determinations were made on the basis of a summary judgment record. *See In re* the Walt Disney Co. Derivative Litig., No. CIV.A. 15452, 2004 WL 2050138 (Del. Ch. Sept. 10, 2004).

[41] Along these lines, the trial court observed, "[a] bright line rule whereby officers and directors become fiduciaries only when they are officially installed, and receive the formal investiture of authority that accompanies such office or directorship, is a more reasonable and desirable rule" than imposing fiduciary duties at an earlier point, which could prove indeterminate in practice. *Id.* at * 4. Likewise, a corporation's directors and controlling shareholder are not as such agents of the corporation. *See* Lyman Johnson, *The Three Fiduciaries of Delaware Corporate Law—and Eisenberg's Error*, ch. 3 (this volume).

[42] 643 N.E.2d 734 (Ill. 1995).

[43] *Id.* at 740.

failure to make the requisite clarifying disclosure breaches the duty) only following a case-specific inquiry into the qualities of the relationship between a particular broker and its prospective principal. If the latter, a sophisticated or experienced investor could confront a higher barrier in establishing that the broker owed a duty, assuming that such an investor, acting skeptically and at arm's length, would inquire about fee and commission structures. Regardless of an investor's degree of sophistication, the broker possesses an informational advantage, here concerning the terms and operation of its fee and commission structure; a sophisticated investor might be expected to realize this fact, ask questions, and consider going elsewhere for brokerage services if unsatisfied by the broker's answers.

Like securities brokers, commodities brokers are agents who operate in a context shaped by regulation, which does not explicitly or comprehensively resolve all questions that may arise. General agency law could be salient to a practice of some brokers, anticipatory front-running. Regulation requires that commodities brokerage firms adopt internal prohibitions against front-running by individual brokers, that is, practices that prioritize trades in proprietary accounts or accounts in which a broker has an interest, ahead of executable customer orders in the same commodity. By front-running a customer's order an agent competes with the principal (the customer), contravening the agent's fiduciary duty of loyalty unless the customer consents.[44] Front-running can also injure the principal when a broker's front-running transaction is large enough to move the market price. If the broker profits through the front-running strategy, the broker also nets more from the transaction than the commission agreed by the customer. In any event, by accepting or undertaking to execute an order to buy or sell on behalf of a customer, the broker has consented to and formed an agency relationship with the customer and thus owes fiduciary duties to the customer as its principal.

In contrast, anticipatory front-running could be prompted by a prospective customer's request for a quote from a commodities broker, not an executable order. Informational asymmetries are present in the relationship because the broker can access real-time information about the relevant market that the customer lacks, including information about order flow. Commodities regulation itself imposes no explicit prohibition on "trading ahead" of prospective customer orders, as opposed to orders that are "executable." However, commodities regulation in the United States now includes a prohibition on insider trading—narrower than the counterpart applicable to insider trading in securities—that proscribes the use of misappropriated information in breach of a pre-existing duty.[45] The reasoning in *Martin* could ground liability in a pre-existing duty, either because the circumstances surrounding a particular request for a quote led the customer to repose trust and confidence in the broker, or because circumstances or structures generally in commodities markets necessitate that prospective customers repose trust and confidence in brokers.

To be sure, anticipatory front-running is riskier for a broker than conventional forms of front-running because if the request for a quote is not followed by an order, the broker may hold an illiquid position. This reduces the likelihood that the broker will profit through front-running as well as the likelihood of injury, here to a prospective customer who may never place an order to

---

[44] Restatement (Third) of Agency § 8.05(2) cmt. c (Am. Law Inst. 2006).

[45] Commodity Exchange Act §§ 4b(a), (c) (2015); 7 U.S.C. §§ 6b, (c) (West 2020). The Dodd-Frank Act amended the language of section 6 (c) in 2010 to grant the Commodity Futures Trading Commission (CFTC) authority to prohibit the use of manipulative or deceptive devices or contrivances in contravention of CFTC regulations. The amendment imposes no affirmative disclosure obligations except where necessary to prevent or correct a misleading statement. The CFTC brought and settled its first insider trading proceedings in 2015 and 2016, both against traders who front-ran their employers' proprietary trading plans. *In re* Motazedi, CFTC No. 16–02, (Dec. 2015) and *In re* Ruggles, CFTC No. 16–34, (Sept. 29, 2016).

be executed. If so, grounding "agent-in-waiting" liability in the prospective principal's vulner-ability to injury does not seem compelling in this scenario, nor does a commodities broker as such, unlike a lawyer, occupy a status that engenders fiduciary obligations to prospective clients. In contrast, consider the vulnerabilities created by agreeing to co-own a business—which creates a general partnership, as discussed above—and the likelihood that the partners will share ideas well before they create a formal (and limited-liability) business firm. Sharing at "the dawn of the relationship," in Christine Hurt's terminology, is both crucial to future viability and a source of vulnerability for the partners, who risk betrayal by each other. Within this "danger zone," the law categorically assigns the relationship among business co-owners to a general partnership and its imposition of fiduciary duties.[46]

C *Implications of Ubiquity of Agency Relationships*

As one court recently noted, agency relationships are characterized by "mundane ubiquity,"[47] given their presence in a range of recurrent situations. Although agency relationships are governed by general doctrines—including those defining an agent's fiduciary duties—it is unsurprising that at their temporal edges, the duties imposed on agents-in-waiting are not uniform. Creating a lawyer-client relationship in itself likely creates vulnerabilities for the prospective client, given the need to share confidential information with the lawyer to form the relationship coupled with the likelihood that the prospective client will rely on any advice given by the lawyer. Thus, as a categorical matter, lawyers owe duties to prospective clients, including constraints in the representation of other clients with materially adverse interests. In contrast, brokers are not categorically subject to fiduciary (or fiduciary-like) duties to prospective customers; and it is not evident why imposing such duties would be warranted when a prospective customer never places an order. As *Martin* illustrates, a court may be persuaded that the specifics of a broker's relationship to a customer warrant the imposition of fiduciary duties (in that case, a duty of disclosure), based either on the nature of the relationship and the vulnerability it creates for the client or on informational advantages possessed by the broker and used to disadvantage the client. Separately, for some recurrent situations, articulating a bright-line rule is preferable to case-by-case inquiry into factual specifics. Thus, lawyers owe duties to prospective clients as a categorical matter; corporate officers-in-waiting are not subject to fiduciary duties unless or until they purport to perform the functions of the office. Up to then, the potential for abuse and opportunism by all officers-in-waiting is not compelling enough to offset the benefits of a clear line of demarcation.[48]

v DUTIES ON THE PERIPHERY OF TERMINATION

Terminating an agency relationship does not end all duties that the agent and principal owe to each other, most obviously duties imposed by an enforceable contract between them. Additionally, both principal and agent hold unilateral power to terminate the relationship. The fact that either or both contemplate ending the relationship does not eliminate their duties, although the agent's continuing duty of loyalty to the principal co-exists—if awkwardly—with

---

[46]   Hurt, *supra* note 6, at (ms.) 55. Likewise, the absence of a written agreement for M&A advisory services does not necessarily bar the conclusion that a bank that furnishes advice and other services owes a fiduciary duty to the party engaging it. I thank Andrew Tuch for this point.

[47]   *Great Minds*, 886 F.3d at 95.

[48]   For comparable reasoning as applied to determinations of fact-based fiduciary status, see Kelly, *supra* note 3, at 11–12.

any undisclosed plan to depart and preparations toward that end. Consider first ongoing duties that survive termination; then duties owed when either agent or principal, or both, contemplate exit.

A Duties Following Termination

Distinct from duties imposed by contract, an agent's duty not to use or disclose the now-former principal's confidential information for the agent's own purposes or those of a third party survives termination of the agency relationship,[49] as does the agent's duty not to retain or use the principal's property without the principal's consent.[50] It is irrelevant whether the agent has memorized the information or retained a physical record.[51] The ongoing fiduciary duty of confidentiality owed by former agents is not absolute because otherwise privileged information may be revealed to protect the agent's superior interest or that of a third party.[52] A former agent's revelation about the principal to a third party may breach the agent's fiduciary duty to the former principal even when neither the former agent nor the third party breaches another distinct legal prohibition, in particular, those applicable to tipping and trading in securities on the basis of inside information. In *Dirks v. S.E.C.*, in which a former corporate officer and other employees told an investment analyst that the corporation was rife with fraud, the revelation may or may not have breached fiduciary duties owed by the former officer and his colleagues, but neither they nor the analyst—who traded on the information—engaged in a "fraud or deceit" on the corporation's shareholders.[53] Under the Court's construction of federal securities law, a corporate insider breaches the fiduciary duty owed to shareholders through tipping only when the prospect of gain to the insider makes the tip improper; the tippee's use of the information cannot constitute a "fraud or deceit" unless the tip itself breaches the insider's duty.[54] On its facts—unusual for an insider-trading case—the tippers in *Dirks* did not reveal information to obtain a monetary or personal benefit; thus the tippee was not an after-the-fact participant in an insider's breach.[55]

Following the termination of an agency relationship, the now-former agent owes the principal a duty to cease acting as an agent or purporting to do so,[56] even when the principal breaches a contract by terminating the agent's authority. Agents who do not follow what could be termed the principal's countermanding or final instruction act wrongfully toward the principal by persisting. But within agency's taxonomy of duties, the agent's refusal to comply—for example, by remaining in possession of property the agent manages on the principal's behalf—breaches not a fiduciary duty but a duty of performance.[57] This distinction carries implications for remedies against the now-former agent who, of course, is no longer an agent subject to the full suite of an agent's duties. In particular, an agent's breach of a duty of loyalty is a basis on which the principal may seek forfeiture of commissions or other compensation paid or payable to the agent during the period of disloyalty, for which the duration may be disputed.[58] The agent's

---

[49]   RESTATEMENT (THIRD) OF AGENCY § 8.05(2) & cmt. c (AM. LAW INST. 2006).
[50]   *Id.* § 8.05(1).
[51]   *Id.* cmt. c; *accord*, RESTATEMENT (THIRD) OF UNFAIR COMPETITION § 39 (AM. LAW INST. 1995).
[52]   RESTATEMENT (THIRD) OF AGENCY § 8.05 cmt. c (AM. LAW INST. 2006) (noting that agent does not breach duty through revelation to law-enforcement authorities that principal is committing or is about to commit a crime).
[53]   463 U.S. 646, 660 (1983). Thanks to Sung Hui Kim for highlighting this case.
[54]   *Id.* at 664.
[55]   *Id.* at 666.
[56]   RESTATEMENT (THIRD) OF AGENCY § 8.09 cmt. b (AM. LAW INST. 2006).
[57]   DeMott, *Fiduciary Character of Agency*, *supra* note 16, at 334; Strategis Asset Valuation & Mgmt., Inc. v. Pacific Mut. Life Ins. Co., 805 F. Supp. 1544 (D. Colo. 1992).
[58]   RESTATEMENT (THIRD) OF AGENCY § 8.01 cmt. (d)(2) (AM. LAW INST. 2006).

persistence, characterized as disobedience to an instruction from the principal, would not be disloyal conduct that forfeits the agent's right to compensation for prior service.[59] Likely more significant to most former principals, a now-former agent lacks apparent authority to bind the principal to a third party who knows or has good reason to know that the agency relationship has ended.[60]

Post-termination, a principal's duties to a former agent—beyond those created by contract—are fewer in number, just as they are throughout the relationship. This seeming imbalance reflects a basic consequence of agency itself: the relationship situates the agent (and only the agent) in a representative position to take action with legal consequences for the principal, and often in proximity to the principal's property.[61] Nonetheless, a principal may engage in conduct that, although not conventionally tortious, will foreseeably inflict loss on a now-former agent. In *Shen v. Leo A. Daly Co.*, the principal terminated the agent it had engaged as its general manager for Taiwan, which requires that the principal officially designate a "responsible person" to conduct business and affix that agent's signature-equivalent to tax returns.[62] Following the termination, the principal did not remove its designation of its now-former agent as its responsible person despite warnings from the agent that the failure might subject the agent to adverse legal consequences in the event of tax disputes between Taiwan and the principal. Following a final adverse tax determination, the principal refused to pay the amount claimed, prompting Taiwanese authorities to notify the former agent that he was forbidden to leave the country pending resolution of the country's tax dispute with the principal. The court held that the principal was subject to liability for loss suffered by its former agent, including the attorneys' fees he incurred. Rejecting the former agent's argument that the principal's conduct constituted false imprisonment,[63] the court held that the principal breached the duty of good faith and fair dealing it owed its former agent, which, in the court's analysis, was tortious.

Necessarily co-existing with the principal's ongoing power to terminate the relationship,[64] the scope of the duty of good faith and fair dealing is crimped as a consequence. Whether the duty is embraced and how it is formulated varies across jurisdictions. Framing the inquiry within contract law, a relatively recent Australian case declined to imply a duty of mutual trust and confidence that would be breached when an employer undercut a soon-to-be-former employee's ability to utilize helpful mechanisms created by the employer. In *Commonwealth Bank v. Barker*, the bank decided to make the employee's position redundant and terminate his employment in about four weeks. The bank also hoped that the employee could be redeployed within its organization.[65] His manager sent the employee an email urging him to work with a career-support officer, who also emailed the employee, using the employee's bank email address. However, the employee's access to his bank email account was terminated at the time of the redundancy notice; he alleged that, as a consequence, he did not become aware of a position description that may have fitted him. The court rejected the implication of a term of mutual trust and confidence, instead characterizing employment as a domain dominated by

---

59 *Strategis*, 805 F. Supp. at 1551–52.
60 Sullivan v. Pugh, 814 S.E.2d 117, 120–121 (N.C. Ct. App. 2018) (purported transferee of legal and equitable interests in claims or proceeds stemming from fire damage to transferor's property had good reason to know transferor's former president lacked authority to bind it).
61 RESTATEMENT (THIRD) OF AGENCY ch. 8, Topic 2, intro. note (AM. LAW INST. 2006).
62 222 F.3d 472 (8th Cir. 2000) (applying Nebraska law).
63 The court found that "the country of Taiwan is clearly too great an area within which to be falsely imprisoned." *Id.* at 478.
64 RESTATEMENT (THIRD) OF AGENCY § 8.15 cmt. b (AM. LAW INST. 2006).
65 [2014] HCA 32. Thanks to Matthew Conaglen for alerting me to this case.

legislation. The court explicitly declined to follow authority from the United Kingdom, which held that former (and innocent) employees of a scandal-ridden bank stated legally viable claims in the bank's winding-up proceeding. The U.K. court held that the bank owed its employees an implied duty of trust and confidence that would be breached by mismanagement that leaves employees unemployable elsewhere due to the stigma created by their former employer.[66]

B *Preparing for Termination*

Agents or principals who plan to end an agency relationship do not owe each other a duty to disclose that fact, potentially giving each the advantage of an informational asymmetry in continued dealings with the other. Although (subject to exceptions not relevant here) an agent owes the principal a duty to disclose facts that are material to the agent's duties to the principal,[67] the duty does not require an advance warning that the agent will renounce authority. Additionally, if the parties negotiate over the terms of their relationship—to continue it with modifications or terminate on mutually-agreed terms[68]—the principal and the agent likely negotiate to further their own interests as each then understands them.

This reality requires some tempering of the content or scope of the agent's overarching duty of loyalty to the principal, which is "to act loyally for the principal's benefit in all matters connected with the agency relationship."[69] By participating in the negotiations, the principal has not consented to the agent's self-interested stance because the principal does not know all material facts, which include the agent's undisclosed objectives and negotiating strategy.[70] More plausibly, the agent's conduct in renegotiating the relationship's terms falls outside its scope, as would the agent's knowledge of the fact that the agent plans to renounce authority and thereby end the relationship. To be sure, the agent's actions in negotiating are "connected with" the agency relationship in a causal or factual sense because the relationship still exists. However, the agent's actions are insufficiently within its scope to justify requiring that the agent renegotiate solely for the principal's benefit. The principal, knowing the identity of the party with whom it is negotiating, would not reasonably expect the agent to bargain toward achieving the principal's benefit, as opposed to the agent's own objectives. And just as the principal holds unilateral power to terminate the relationship, so does the agent. Accordingly, a principal may try to structure incentives to keep key agents on board and motivate them, especially once they become aware that the relationship will end.[71]

Likewise, an agent may make preparations to compete with the principal once the agency relationship ends. Agency law defines "preparations" to exclude conduct—albeit preparatory to competition—too proximately situated to the principal's business operations and assets, including soliciting existing customers or employees of the principal to follow the agent.[72] Such

---

[66] Malik v. Bank of Credit & Commerce Int'l S.A., [1998] A.C. 20 (H.L.). *See* Restatement (Third) of Agency § 8.15, reporter's notes (Am. Law Inst. 2006) (citing *Malik*).

[67] Restatement (Third) of Agency § 8.11 (Am. Law Inst. 2006).

[68] *Id.* § 3.09.

[69] *Id.* § 8.01.

[70] C&E Servs., Inc. v. Ashland, 601 F. Supp. 2d 262, 270 (D.D.C. 2009).

[71] *See, e.g.,* Act II Jewelry, LLC v. Wooten, 301 F. Supp. 3d 905 (N.D. Ill. 2018) (incentive bonus agreement with key manager adopted following the firm's announcement of the business division's wind-down for which manager responsible). In *Act II*, after learning the plan, the manager incorporated a competing business prior to her termination date. The court found a genuine issue of material fact on whether the manager owed the LLC a fiduciary duty, stressing that under general agency law employees of Delaware LLCs owe fiduciary duties to their employers. *Id.* at 916–17.

[72] Restatement (Third) of Agency § 8.04 cmts. b & c (Am. Law Inst. 2006).

conduct is analogous to an agent's extraction of the principal's property or confidential informa-tion for subsequent competitive use, which would breach the agent's fiduciary duties.[73] Beyond instances of active solicitation, an agent—especially one positioned within a principal's organ-ization—may be better situated to design a competitive plan than are potential third-party competitors, who may lack established ties to the principal's suppliers or customers, as well as ties to the principal's personnel. Agents may also be able to time their departures to inflict maximum competitive damage on the principal. In extreme cases—such as calculated en masse departures at a sensitive time for the principal—courts may determine that the agents' conduct went beyond mere "planning" to compete to the commencement of a competitive business while still engaged by the principal.[74]

The general rule permitting preparations to compete does not formally differentiate among types of employee-agents, whose roles range from providing non-managerial services to broad responsibilities as an entity's executive officers. It is hard to generalize from reported cases across jurisdictions. For example, one court categorically treated preparations to compete by corporate officers as breaches of fiduciary duty.[75] Some courts impose a heightened duty on officers, in particular, a duty not to act in ways that impede the firm's ability to continue in business.[76] Officers who agree with each other to compete post-termination may thereby breach their fiduciary duties, especially when their agreement is colored by extreme or egregious conduct.[77] A fair generalization about many cases is that "actions of corporate executives are likely to receive particular scrutiny."[78] Sometimes subtle interactions between motive and conduct can situate post-termination disputes over pre-departure preparations beyond bright-line determinations, into the realm of fact-intensive inquiry.

As this chapter illustrates, agents are heterogenous in the specifics of the duties they owe, including those connected to termination. Recall the discussion above of a lawyer's duties in dealing with a prospective client. Although a lawyer may terminate the representation of a client, the lawyer owes the client a duty to take steps to the extent reasonably practicable to protect the client's interests, including giving notice to the client of the termination or impending termination.[79] In contrast, agency law does not impose a general duty on either principals or agents to act in a harm-minimizing fashion, as opposed to the more minimal duties surveyed in this chapter; the court's justification for imposing liability on the principal in *Shen* is ingenious and unusual. And exiting from an agency relationship frees the agent to compete with the principal and take other actions adverse to the principal's interests. In contrast, lawyers owe duties to former clients that constrain their rights to undertake the representation of parties with materially adverse interests in the same or a related matter.[80] General agency law—the realm of corporate officers and brokers—defines duties and the conduct that breaches them in terms that accommodate a broader range of actors and activities than would be tolerable in the realm of lawyers' roles and duties.

---

[73] *Id.* § 8.05.
[74] RESTATEMENT (THIRD) OF AGENCY § 8.04 cmt. c (AM. LAW INST. 2006).
[75] Steelvest, Inc. v. Scansteel Serv. Ctr., 807 S.W.2d 476 (Ky. 1991).
[76] Veco Corp v. Babcock, 611 N.E.2d 1054, 1059 (Ill. App. Ct. 1993).
[77] RESTATEMENT (THIRD) OF AGENCY § 8.04 cmt. c (AM. LAW INST. 2006).
[78] RESTATEMENT OF EMPLOYMENT LAW § 8.04 reporter's notes to cmt. d.
[79] RESTATEMENT (THIRD) OF THE LAW GOVERNING LAWYERS § 8.04 cmt. c (AM. LAW INST. 2000). *See* Maples v. Thomas, 565 U.S. 266 (2012) (lawyers for death-row inmate breached duties to client and terminated agency relationship by accepting employment that prevented ongoing service to client, without giving notice to the client or court; unrepresented, client not bound by failure to file timely appeal).
[80] RESTATEMENT (THIRD) OF THE LAW GOVERNING LAWYERS § 132 (AM. LAW INST. 2000).

VI THEORETICAL IMPLICATIONS

These dimensions of agency doctrine have implications for scholarly accounts of fiduciary law more generally. When the assumed prototype for the general category of actors subject to fiduciary duties is a trustee, and the prototypical fiduciary institution is a trust,[81] agents and agency relationships can appear to be discordant, non-conforming, or marginal instances. It is essential to an agency relationship that the principal have the right or power of control over the agent—and thus the power to furnish binding instructions on an interim basis—while the extent of a principal's control and how it is exercised can vary widely. An actor who is not subject to control of any sort exercised by a principal is not an agent, with the consequence that the parties' relationship is not one of common-law agency.[82] However, the irreducible requisite of control for agency relationships means they lack an essential property of fiduciary relationships specified by leading theories: possession by an actor of discretionary powers, or the exercise of discretionary power over a critical resource of the beneficiary.[83] To be sure, an agent has the power to disregard the principal's instructions, but agency law does not entitle an agent to treat the bounds of actual authority, including the principal's interim instructions, as mere suggestions or precatory expressions that are not binding.

As this chapter demonstrates, fiduciary duties within agency doctrine reflect signal characteristics of agency relationships not present in relationships governed by trust-law doctrine. A trustee's duties are tied to the trustee's exercise or non-exercise of powers as a trustee[84] and decisions about whether and how to exercise those powers,[85] which circumscribes their scope and duration, unlike the more fluid duties owed by agents, including former and prospective ones. The scope of a trustee's duty of loyalty focuses on the administration of the trust,[86] in contrast to the broader or less specified range of an agent's duty. Additionally, agency doctrine applies to ongoing relationships between two parties whose perspectives and preferences may shift over time. Thus it accommodates relationships in which parties may bargain with each other on an interim basis to adjust the terms of their relationship going forward, each always holding a unilateral power to exit. Relatedly, agency doctrine also accommodates the possibility that agents, while still employed, may take measures to prepare to compete with the principal. This is not the structure that underlies a prototypical donative trust created by a manifestation of a settlor as a fiduciary relationship through which the trustee holds title to property and is subject to duties to deal with the property for the benefit of others.[87]

The duties that prospective agents may owe to principals also cast new light on a long-established dimension of contract law, which "accords parties the freedom to negotiate without risk of precontractual liability."[88] The duty of fair dealing that's generally imposed on parties to

---

[81] *See, e.g.*, D. Gordon Smith, *Firms and Fiduciaries, in* CONTRACT, STATUS, AND FIDUCIARY LAW 293, 308 (Paul B. Miller & Andrew S. Gold eds., 2016) (characterizing the trust as "the quintessential fiduciary relationship").

[82] Hollingsworth v. Perry, 570 U.S. 693, 713 (2013).

[83] Julian Velasco, *Delimiting Fiduciary Status, in* RESEARCH HANDBOOK ON FIDUCIARY LAW (D. Gordon Smith & Andrew S. Gold eds., 2018); Alice Woolley, *The Lawyer as Fiduciary: Defining Private Law Duties in Public Law Relations,* 65 U. TORONTO L. J. 285, 309–315 (2015). For accounts that specify essential properties, see Paul B. Miller, *The Idea of Status in Fiduciary Law, in* CONTRACT, STATUS, AND FIDUCIARY LAW 25, 48 (Andrew S. Gold & Paul B. Miller eds., 2016); D. Gordon Smith, *The Critical Resource Theory of Fiduciary Duty,* 55 VAND. L. REV. 1399 (2002).

[84] RESTATEMENT (THIRD) OF TRUSTS § 70 (AM. LAW INST. 2007).

[85] *Id.* § 86.

[86] *Id.* § 78.

[87] RESTATEMENT (THIRD) OF TRUSTS § 2 (AM. LAW INST. 2003) (defining a trust as the "fiduciary relationship with respect to property, arising from a manifestation of intention to create that relationship and subjecting the person who holds title to the property to duties to deal with it for the benefit of charity or for one or more persons, at least one of whom is not the sole trustee").

[88] E. Allan Farnsworth, CONTRACTS 189 (4th ed. 2004).

an existing contract does not reach precontractual negotiations.[89] Despite cases and secondary authority recognizing a theory of liability grounded in one party's reasonable reliance engendered by negotiations toward a contract that is never concluded, only rarely do litigants in the United States seek relief on this basis. Parties engaged in negotiations toward a contract may be unaware that justifiable reliance can support liability; or perhaps, as Allan Farnworth suggests, parties are generally content with "the common law's aleatory view of negotiations," which might also reflect broader social disinterest in the outcome of negotiations.[90] Against this contract-law backdrop, the prospect that agents may owe duties beyond those imposed by tort law to prospective principals, or be subject to affirmative duties of disclosure in dealings with prospective principals, can appear discordant.[91]

However, both the *Martin* brokerage precedent and the duties that lawyers owe to prospective clients—instances discussed at length above—could be distinguished from negotiations toward a paradigmatic bilateral contract. First, consider the structures that particular relationships necessitate. Dealings undertaken in anticipation of an agency relationship often (and maybe even prototypically) involve informational asymmetries that reflect more than disparities in expertise. In *Martin*, as in the hypothetical instance of anticipatory front-running, the broker had access to material information legally unavailable to its prospective principal. Agents—like lawyers—whose functions require knowledge of their clients' or principals' confidential information typically deal with a party, a prospective client, who is made vulnerable by sharing information necessary to proceed toward an agency relationship. Separately, consider the nature of the prospective agent's activity. The scope of pre-agency duties could place them outside "negotiations" as a category of activity; the disclosure of fee and commission structures that *Martin* may require could precede negotiations, a distinct phase of activity. Additionally, by front-running on the basis of a client's order or request for a quote, a broker is not negotiating with a client or prospective client, just exploiting an informational advantage. Finally, and much more broadly, negotiations toward an agency relationship could be treated as a basis for the imposition of fiduciary duties full stop (or categorically), but such breadth is inconsistent with much decisional law as well as with more tailored rationales that ground pre-agency duties in structures that entail vulnerability or induce reliance.

Duties owed at the temporal edges of agency relationships also have implications for general accounts of fiduciary duties, even apart from those premised on assuming a trust to be the prototype of a fiduciary relationship. Some accounts of the fiduciary duty of loyalty emphasize a cognitive dimension, that is, a focus on how the fiduciary deliberates and the connection between such deliberation and the fiduciary's actions. In recent scholarship, Stephen Galoob and Ethan Leib demonstrate that a fiduciary's cognition can bear on whether the fiduciary has satisfied duties of loyalty imposed by the law,[92] building on their earlier work identifying loyalty, deliberation, conscientiousness, and robustness as the cognitive dimensions of loyalty.[93] A cognitive account of fiduciary loyalty provides a different framework for resolving issues when an agent prepares to compete with the principal before the agency relationship has come to an end, or even engages in a calculated assessment of whether to quit. For Galoob and Leib, the fiduciary duty of loyalty requires robust commitment; preparing to compete could betray the principal, or attempt betrayal, as a consequence of the agent's abandoned or weakened

[89]   *Id.*
[90]   *Id.* at 198–99.
[91]   I owe this insight to Norio Higuchi.
[92]   Stephen R. Galoob & Ethan J. Leib, *Fiduciary Loyalty, Inside and Out*, 92 S. Cal. L. Rev. 69 (2018).
[93]   Ethan J. Leib & Stephen R. Galoob, *Fiduciary Political Theory: A Critique*, 125 Yale L. J. 1820 (2016).

commitment to the principal.[94] To the extent that agency law tolerates preparations to compete, and pre-preparation strategizing over exit, there is a limit to the fit between cognitivist accounts and the law.

Additionally, to encompass duties on the peripheries of agency relationships within a cognitivist account would require deepening the cognitivist account. If an agent plans (or hopes) to exit from the relationship and does not disclose that fact to the principal, is the non-disclosure an instance of disloyalty that makes forfeiture of compensation due to the agent an available remedy to the principal? Alternatively, the structure of agency itself—a fiduciary relationship that empowers both parties to act unilaterally to end the relationship—may mean that conduct will often reflect a mix of motivations and that the retrospective lens of litigation will often require factually intensive scrutiny.

VII CONCLUSION

Agency relationships, so quotidian, can elude theoretical frameworks premised on other types of legal relationships. The reasons why prospective agents might owe fiduciary duties to principals, and the status of those duties when an agent plans to terminate an agency relationship, have broader implications for accounts of fiduciary obligation within business firms.

---

[94] Galoob & Leib, *supra* note 92, at 101. The authors acknowledge that agency law "suggests ... some room for permissible preparation. . . ." *Id.* n.111.

2

Extra Large Partnerships

Christine Hurt

I INTRODUCTION

The beginning of the twentieth century was the dawn of partnership law. The Uniform Partnership Act (UPA) was promulgated in 1914, and the Uniform Limited Partnership Act (ULPA) quickly followed in 1916. The United States Constitution was amended in 1913 to add the Sixteenth Amendment, which allows the federal government to institute an income tax, and the first income tax regime created a lasting and important division between partnerships, which are taxed once at the partner level, and corporations, which are taxed once at the entity level and once at the shareholder level. At the time, partnerships were generally small, with two or three partners, and most were livelihood businesses.[1] Accordingly, the new tax code treated these enterprises taxing the partner-owners like joint sole proprietors with business income. The UPA treated general partnerships similarly, with the partners owing fiduciary duties to one another and being liable for the obligations and debts of the partnership. Limited partnerships were governed differently, but under the same theories of responsibility: those with discretion over limited partnership assets and the right to manage limited partnership affairs had fiduciary duties to the entity and remained personally liable.

Now at the beginning of the third decade of the twenty-first century, the partnership landscape is very different. General partnerships may be quite large, and though some professional partnerships may be livelihood enterprises with full-time partner-managers, they do not have to be. Large general partnerships may have limited liability through the limited liability partnership form, and large limited partnerships will have achieved full limited liability and may have completely eliminated all fiduciary duties previously owed by managers. Large limited partnerships may be more likely to be investment vehicles for passive limited partners than livelihood businesses. The largest of these limited partnerships may be publicly traded with freely transferable shares. In effect, twenty-first-century partnerships have become more corporate-like than the twentieth century (and twenty-first century) corporations.

This chapter will analyze two of the most extreme examples of partnerships that have outgrown partnership law: limited liability partnerships (LLPs) and publicly traded partnerships (PTPs), known in the investment community as master limited partnerships (MLPs). Both reflect the tension between traditional partnership law and legislatively-granted limited liability and contractual flexibility. Just as corporation statutes apply awkwardly to small, closely held

---

[1] In this chapter, the term "livelihood business" refers to small businesses that provide compensation for the owners' regular work relied upon by the owners for income, whether that income is paid as salary, dividend, or distribution.

corporations, partnership and limited partnership acts apply even more awkwardly to extra large partnerships.

General partnership law naturally limits the size of those partnerships due to the fact that all partners are liable for the misconduct of all partners, whether the partners know one another or not. In addition, partners in a general partnership have the ability to comanage, which helps partners monitor and supervise one another to mitigate personal liability. This means that partners are not employees and that partnership interests are not securities under federal law. However, the ability of general partnerships to elect to be LLPs changes some basic assumptions about general partnerships. With a liability shield, LLPs can be very large, with partners in the hundreds or possibly thousands. Management will necessarily have to be delegated, with many partners looking much more like possibly employees or even passive investors. Applying securities law, bankruptcy law, and even employment law to these general, but limited, partnerships has become quite complex.

Likewise, some large, complex enterprises may have outgrown even the limited partnership form. Though the form contemplates passive investors delegating management to a general partner, MLPs use the form to do something even more corporation-like than the corporation-like limited partnership structure originally imagined 100 years ago. Investors in MLPs, however, do not have the protections of corporate shareholders, which makes the investment in MLPs a very different type of investment. Because MLPs can waive fiduciary duties, investors in these vehicles end up in a structure that is not like a limited partnership or a corporation at all, but a financial contract completely different from equity ownership in any of these entities.

II LIMITED LIABILITY PARTNERSHIPS

A *Background*

The LLP, though its name may suggest otherwise, is a general partnership, not a limited partnership (LP). As such, it is governed by general partnership law. In contrast to corporations, the owners of a general partnership have unlimited personal liability, fiduciary duties to the partnership and other partners, the right to comanage the business, and vicarious liability for the actions of the other partners. Though these hallmarks of a general partnership seem fairly harsh compared with a corporate structure, partnerships were created for active owners with the right and discretion to employ the assets of the enterprise, who arguably should have constraints on their own opportunism. Fiduciary duties provide a backstop to guard against such opportunism.

Moreover, a partnership is a voluntary business relationship. Forcing partners to be liable for one another's wrongdoings creates incentives for partners to choose partners wisely and monitor one another's actions. Partners are better positioned to minimize losses and damages than third-party plaintiffs, particularly tort plaintiffs.[2]

The LLP, however, replaces one important characteristic with a corporate one: limited liability. Emerging in the early 1990s, the LLP was created for a particular type of general partnership, the professional firm.[3] Professionals such as attorneys and accountants were restricted in many states from forming corporations, specifically because of the fear that

---

[2] *See* Leonard Bierman & Rafael Gely, *So, You Want to Be a Partner at Sidley & Austin?*, 40 Hous. L. Rev. 969, 984 (2003) ("Partners, particularly in smaller partnerships, have the ability to easily monitor each other's behavior."); Henry Hansmann, *Ownership of the Firm*, 4 J. L. Econ. & Org. 267 (1988) ("Workers in nearly all industries are in a very good position, in comparison with other classes of patrons, to monitor the management of the firm.").

[3] *See generally* Christine Hurt, *The Limited Liability Partnership in Bankruptcy*, 89 Am. Bankr. L. J. 567 (2015).

professionals, who owed fiduciary duties to their clients, could insulate themselves both from those duties and liability for breach of those duties.

However, as professional firms grew larger in the global economy, the theory that a partner on the U.S. East Coast could monitor a partner in Hong Kong did not seem to fit, and general personal liability for all partners for the acts of near strangers seemed unfair,[4] particularly when far-flung partners did not necessarily choose incoming partners.[5] A partner voluntarily joined or withdrew from a partnership, but did not necessarily have the opportunity to negotiate a partnership agreement, participate in management, or choose and monitor other partners.[6]

Initially, the LLP statutes granted partners immunity from the tort liability of their partners, so long as they did not supervise the tortfeasor or otherwise participate. Partners would not have an obligation to indemnify the partnership or an individual partner for those claims, whether by contribution or otherwise. To prevent prospective plaintiffs from being under-compensated, some states required professional LLPs to maintain insurance coverage or other proof of financial responsibility.[7] However, second-generation statutes quickly expanded the "tort shield" to a "full shield," covering contract obligations of the partnership as well.[8] Though original arguments for a tort shield do not logically extend to limited contractual liability, persuasive industry participants prevailed legislatively. Because professional service firms, such as law firms, hold little in the way of partnership capital,[9] they greatly benefit from a full shield provision.[10]

Of course, leaving no individual liable for obligations is the feature, not the bug, of all limited liability entities, and limited liability has become ubiquitous among business entities. Absent a separate agreement, no individual shareholder or manager is liable for the debts of a corporation, and no individual manager or member in a limited liability company is liable for the debts of the LLC, and no limited partner, even if they participate in management, is liable for the debts of an LP. Even the general partner in an LP may insulate itself from liability,

---

4   *See* William H. Clark, Jr., *Rationalizing Entity Laws*, 58 Bus. Law. 1005 (2003) (describing how accounting firms, stunned by the malpractice-induced bankruptcy of Laventhol & Horwath, lobbied for the LLP statutes as an interim measure until LLC statutes were passed).

5   For example, Section 4.2 of the Dewey & LeBoeuf LLP Partnership Agreement stated that the partners generally had the right to vote on the admission of a new partner, but that the Executive Committee could determine that a majority vote of a subset of partners could suffice, and that subset might be merely the Executive Committee. *See* Dewey & Leboeuf LLP, Partnership Agreement (Oct. 1, 2007) (amended April 2, 2010) (on file with author).

6   *See* Robert W. Hillman, *Organizational Choices of Professional Service Firms: An Empirical Study*, 58 Bus. Lawyer 1387, 1389 (2003) (noting that as professional service firms grow to "hundreds or even thousands of partners" that no true bargaining occurs between the partners and that the partnership agreement is a "take it or leave it" document).

7   *See, e.g.*, Mass. Gen. Laws ch. 108A, § 45(8)(a) (2020); *but see* Tex. Bus. Orgs. Code Ann. § 152.804 (2011) (repealed in 2011).

8   *See* Clark, *supra* note 4, at 1009 (stating that the first "full shield" statute was passed by Minnesota in 1994, with New York passing the second in the same year). Currently, all state statutes would be described as "full shield," though some states use language from the Revised Uniform Partnership Act (RUPA) § 306(c) referring to "debt, obligation, or other liability," while others refer to obligations "arising in tort, contract, or otherwise." *See* Christine Hurt & D. Gordon Smith, Bromberg & Ribstein on LLPs, Revised Uniform Partnership Act, and the Uniform Limited Partnership Act T.3.1 (2d ed. 2018).

9   *See* Henry Hansmann, *When Does Worker Ownership Work? ESOPs, Law Firms, Codetermination, and Economic Democracy*, 99 Yale L. J. 1749, 1772 (reasoning that workers in worker-owned firms put their capital and labor at risk in the same enterprise and therefore may want to limit contributed capital).

10 *See* Susan Saab Fortney, *Law as a Profession: Examining the Role of Accountability*, 40 Fordham Urb. L. J. 177 (2012) (lamenting that in the rush to expand LLP statutes to further limit attorney liability, there was little criticism or voiced concerns over diminishing accountability of the legal profession).

either by forming a limited liability entity as the general partner or, in some states, by creating a "limited liability limited partnership" (LLLP).[11]

What makes LLPs different from these other hybrid entities is that it is still a general partnership for governance purposes, with all the characteristics of general partnership that come with that designation. In practice, the LLP may operate like a closely held corporation or member-managed LLC, and of course, those owners combine management control and personal liability.[12] What seems to separate the LLP from the closely held corporation, which comprises shareholders with no right to comanage, and a member-managed LLC, which comprises members with a right to comanage, is that some LLPs can be extra large.[13]

B *Separation of Ownership and Control*

The theory of the firm focuses on the separation of ownership from control—situations in which "owners," those who contribute capital while taking the risk of both profit and loss, delegate "control" to non-owner agents. This separation creates agency costs, resulting from agents controlling in ways that deviate from the owners' directions and ultimate objectives.[14] Because continued monitoring and supervision of agents are costly and at some point, ineffective, fiduciary duties provide a backstop against agent opportunism and serious neglect.

The quintessential entity for explaining agency costs is the corporation, in which owner-shareholders delegate management power to the board of directors.[15] Fiduciary duties ensure that the board will not abandon the interests of the owners. This same dynamic is present in LPs (limited partners delegate management control to the general partner) and in manager-managed LLCs (members delegate management control to the manager), and those managers generally owe the owners fiduciary duties, except in those states, like Delaware, that allow for the elimination of those duties.

In a general partnership, partners are both owners and managers in a worker-owned firm.[16] With each addition of an additional partner, ownership and control are dispersed, but each partner retains the right to comanage. Though agency costs are still present, monitoring theoretically should limit those losses.[17]

---

[11] Unif. Ltd. P'ship Act §§ 201(a)(4), 404(c) (Unif. Law Comm'n 2001); Del. Code Ann. tit. 6, § 17–214(c) (2020). Prior to the LLLP statutes' passage, parties could create a similar effect by having the general partner or general partners of an LP be a limited liability entity, such as a corporation.

[12] *See* Susan E. Woodward, *Limited Liability in the Theory of the Firm*, 141 J. Inst. & Theoretical Econ. 601 (1985) ("In particular, the most important feature of limited liability is that it accommodates transferable shares."). However, for closely held corporations and general partnerships, free transferability is rarely desired, leaving risk-aversion as the explanation for limited liability in these firms. *See id.*

[13] Whether a member of an LLC has the right to comanage depends on whether it is member- or manager-managed, and subject to the operating agreement. Whether most large LLCs are manager-managed is an empirical question and not researched here.

[14] *See* Michael C. Jensen & William H. Meckling, *Theory of the Firm: Managerial Behavior, Agency Costs, and Ownership Structure*, 3 J. Fin. Econ. 305 (1976) ("In most agency relationships the principal and the agent will incur positive monitoring and bonding costs (non-pecuniary as well as pecuniary), and in addition, there will be some divergence between the agent's decisions and those decisions which would maximize the welfare of the principal.").

[15] *See* Paul Rose, *Common Agency and the Public Corporation*, 63 Vand. L. Rev. 1353, 1361 (2010)("Under a classic theory of the firm, agency costs in a corporate context increase as ownership is separated from control. As the manager's ownership of shares in the firm decreases as a percentage of the total, the manager will bear a diminishing fraction of the costs of any nonpecuniary benefits he takes out in maximizing his own utility.").

[16] *See* Hansmann, *supra* note 2 (describing worker-owned firms as stereotypically service firms in which the workers have homogeneity of interests, such as law and accounting firms).

[17] Hillman, *supra* note 6, at 1389 ("Partnership law, for example, assumes a model partnership that is relatively small and populated by partners with roughly equal status within the partnership.").

Extra large LLPs are both corporation and partnership. Theoretically, the partners each retain ownership and control, dedicating their full-time attention to the operations of the LLP. However, this control may be more theoretical than real. Many large law firm LLPs are managed by a committee, which may or may not be appointed by all partners. These committees function similarly to a corporate board of directors comprising entirely inside directors. These committee members are owners, and the investment of financial and human capital may create conflicts. Historically, general partnership law has limited this temptation by creating personal liability. An LLP, however, has eliminated that limitation on opportunism.[18]

Though the stereotypical large LLP is a professional firm, in many states, any business activity may be organized as an LLP. Professional firms have reputational constraints on adding new partner-investors to their firms; each partner brings a professional reputation for good or ill that inures to the firm. However, nonprofessional LLPs may not have the same constraint and may intentionally recruit partner-investors that are strangers to them merely for their investment and not for their participation or reputation. Though personal liability and the right to comanage would make this undesirable for a general partnership, the LLP shield has created a mechanism whereby managers can recruit pseudo-passive (or not so pseudo-) "partners." Examples of these firms, and how they skirt securities laws, are described below.

C *Are Extra Large LLPs Really Partnerships for Employment Purposes?*

One of the traditional characteristics of partnership law is the right to comanage. From this right flows the necessity for fiduciary duties and justification for personal liability. Partner-managers do not admit partners without their consent, and they are able to monitor the other partners as well. The LLP grants all partners limited liability except for liability for their own torts, and this limited liability allows LLPs to grow quite large, with partners who do not fear joining their fortunes with strangers. Partners in LLPs share fortunes, but not disasters. This reality allows partners to agree to cede their management rights in large LLPs to designated managers or management committees because the need to monitor is greatly decreased.

The result then is a partnership with partners who do not manage. Though management rights may not seem like a necessary characteristic of a partner, in a livelihood business, that partner may seem more like an employee than a partner.

Though one can easily imagine scenarios in which partners are discriminated against by their fellow partners on account of their race, gender, or even age, federal laws (and their state counterparts) prohibiting such discrimination will apply only to employees, as distinguished from employers, partners, and owners.[19] Though questions on decisions to elevate employees to partner status may be covered by such status,[20] once individuals become partners, the question of whether discrimination law applies is murkier.[21] As partnerships grow in size and complexity, the question of whether a participant is a partner-employer or employee is not as clear as one might think.[22]

[18] *But see* Douglas R. Richmond, *Law Firm Partners as Their Brothers' Keepers*, 96 KY. L. J. 231, 251 (2007) (arguing that firms transitioning to LLPs were also devoting significant resources to risk management, rebutting a theory that those firms were looking to be more aggressive).

[19] Title VII of the Civil Rights Act of 1964, 42 U.S.C. § 2000e (2018) (prohibiting discrimination on the basis of race, color, religion, sex, or national origin); Age Discrimination in Employment Act, 29 U.S.C. § 630(f) (2018).

[20] Hishon v. King & Spalding, 467 U.S. 69 (1984).

[21] *See* Hopkins v. Price Waterhouse, 920 F.2d 967 (D.C. Cir. 1990) (declining to consider whether Title VII protects employees after they become partners).

[22] *See* Joel Bannister, *In Search of a Title: When Should Partners Be Considered "Employees" for Purposes of Federal Employment Antidiscrimination Statutes?*, 53 U. KAN. L. REV. 257 (2004).

In the prototypical early general partnership under the UPA or RUPA with few partners, all of whom have equal management rights, invested capital, and personal liability, discrimination is not unthinkable but might be disincentivized. Although the majority of partners may be irrationally averse to one partner based on race, gender, or age, poor treatment of the partner would lead to that partner having the right to dissociate and dissolve the firm. However, modern LLPs under later versions of RUPA can avoid this consequence in detailed partnership agreements. Whereas early general partnerships were characterized by partners choosing their partners, and therefore less likely to discriminate against them later, and by partners having the right to withdraw and dissolve the partnership, large modern partnerships admit partners under much different circumstances.

Courts wrangling with the question of whether a partner in a partnership may ever be considered an employee for federal law purposes agree the mere internal classification does not answer the question.[23] Courts must make a case-by-case determination, and recent courts use a multi-factor test from a case involving a professional corporation of shareholder-physicians.[24] Earlier cases predating LLP statutes attempted to distinguish between modern "general partners," and mere employees focused on liability for loss, profit sharing, and selectivity of admission.[25] Even when general partners retained personal liability, the absence of other partner characteristics such as voting rights, management authority, and share of profits created an employment relationship subject to federal discrimination laws.[26] A partnership agreement may on its face grant partners typical partner rights and obligations, but if a partner could not exercise those rights in an extremely large general partnership and was treated more like an employee on a day-to-day basis, employee discrimination laws would apply.[27] However, if partners retained some control and partner-like rights and obligations, particularly unlimited liability, "a few indicia of employee status did not destroy plaintiff's status as a partner."[28]

One of the most prominent pre-LLP cases involving a large general partnership and its partners over this issue is *Equal Employment Opportunity Commission* v. *Sidley Austin Brown & Wood.*[29] In 1999, the law firm Sidley Austin demoted 32 of its 500 partners, spurring litigation brought by the E.E.O.C. on behalf of the partners under the Age Discrimination in Employment Act. In a decision regarding a discovery dispute, Judge Richard Posner held, in a majority opinion that there was enough question whether the demoted partners were

---

[23] Equal Emp't Opportunity Comm'n v. Sidley Austin Brown & Wood, 315 F.3d 696, 709 (7th Cir. 2002) ("[A]n employer may not evade obligations under federal law by plastering the *name* "partner" on someone whose legal and economic characteristics are those of an employee.") (Easterbrook, J., concurring); *see also* Clackamas Gastroenterology Assocs. v. Wells, 538 U.S. 440, 450 (2003) ("The mere fact that a person has a particular title— such as partner, director, or vice president— should not necessarily be used to determine whether he or she is an employee or a proprietor.").

[24] *Clackamas Gastroenterology Assocs.*, 538 U.S. at 450 (2003) (listing from the EEOC Compliance Manual six factors relevant to the inquiry: whether the organization can hire or fire the individual or set the rules and regulations of the individual's work, and to what extent the individual is supervised and reports to someone higher in the organization, to what extent the individual may influence the organization, intent of the parties, and sharing in the profits, losses, and liabilities of the organization).

[25] Wheeler v. Hurdman, 825 F.2d 257 (10th Cir. 1987), *cert. denied*, 484 U.S. 986 (1987); *but see* Ehrlich v. Howe, 848 F. Supp. 482 (S.D.N.Y. 1994) (general partner not employee where jointly and severally liable for partnership debts, shared profits and losses, had significant voting interest, participated in hiring decisions, and could be terminated only by unanimous vote). Federal courts addressing the partner classification issue use the test set out in *Clackamas Gastroenterology Associates v. Wells*, 538 U.S. 440 (2003).

[26] Simpson v. Ernst & Young, 100 F.3d 436 (6th Cir. 1996).

[27] Strother v. S. Cal. Permanente Med. Grp., 79 F.3d 859 (9th Cir. 1996).

[28] Rhoads v. Jones Fin. Co., 957 F.Supp. 1102, 1110 (E.D. Mo. 1997).

[29] 315 F.3d 696 (7th Cir. 2002); *see also Simpson*, 100 F.3d at 444 (upholding jury finding that dismissed partners were "employees" and discriminated against in violation of the ADEA).

"employers" under federal law when the firm was controlled by a self-perpetuating executive committee, with nonmember partners having little power. The E.E.O.C. continued its discovery, filed a lawsuit against the law firm in 2005,[30] and settled in 2007 in favor of the demoted partners.[31]

Interestingly, Judge Easterbrook, who concurred with Judge Posner in the discovery dispute, seemed ready to concede that the partners were indeed partners because they had unlimited liability, substantial capital accounts, and profit sharing. However, twenty years later, large law firms like Sidley Austin (and including Sidley Austin) are LLPs or a similar limited liability entity. Presumably, a large LLP or an LP may have many partners who may be partners under state law, but not partner-employers under federal law,[32] and some high-profile cases are currently in litigation.[33] Over twenty years ago, Judge Martha Craig Daughtrey opined in her concurrence in *Simpson* v. *Ernst & Young*, to "encourage the legislative branch of our federal government" that

> [I]n a world-wide organization like Ernst & Young that employs almost 2200 "partners," however, the nominal co-owners of the company are, by necessity, so far removed from the seat of actual power as to be subject to the reach of the invidious acts that employment discrimination statutes seek to remedy. Only by statutory modifications redefining the class of individuals to be protected from such mistreatment can we ensure that hiring, promotion, and firing decisions are undertaken with proper regard for the law of the land.[34]

Relatedly, and perhaps even more importantly, the trend in law firm partnerships to classify attorneys as "non-equity partners" creates considerable doubt whether these types of partners are partners under state law or federal law.[35]

D *Are Extra Large LLPs Really Partnerships for Securities Law Purposes?*

Generally, one thinks of partners in a general partnership as working partners, active managers devoting their full-time attention to a joint enterprise. Unlike limited partners in an LP, these

---

30 United States Equal Emp't Opportunity Comm'n v. Sidley Austin Brown & Wood LLP, 406 F. Supp.2d 991 (N.D. Ill. 2005).

31 Press Release, U.S. Equal Employment Opportunity Commission, $27.5 Million Consent Decree Resolves EEOC Age Bias Suit Against Sidley Austin (Oct. 5, 2007) (on file with author) (resulting in a median payment of almost $900,000 to the plaintiffs).

32 *See* Panepucci v. Honigman Miller Schwartz and Cohn, LLP, 408 F.Supp.2d 374 (E. D. Mich. 2005) (denying motion to dismiss as more facts were needed to determine whether "percentage partner" was indeed a partner-employer and not an employee); Baskett v. Autonomous Research LLP, No. 17-CV-9237 (VSB), 2018 WL 4757962 (S. D.N.Y. Sept. 28, 2018); *but see* Von Kaenel v. Armstrong Teasdale, LLP, 943 F.3d 1139 (8th Cir. 2019) (holding that equity partner was a bona fide partner and not employee under the ADEA); Simons v. Harrison Waldrop & Uhereck, L.L.P., No. CIV.A. V-05-71, 2006 WL 1698273 (S. D. Tex., June 14, 2006) (reasoning that in 2005, "the only cases which have considered equity partners as "employees" under common law principles dealt with large partnerships where control is concentrated in a small number of managing partners").

33 Campbell v. Chadbourne & Parke LLP, No. 16-CV-6832, 2017 WL 2589389 (S.D.N.Y. June 14, 2017), *cert. denied*, 138 S.Ct. 684 (2018) (denying summary judgment because facts were required to determine whether partners at a large law firm were in fact employer-partners for purposes of Title VII of the Civil Rights Act of 1964); Ramos v. Superior Court, 28 Cal.App.5th 1042 (Cal. Ct. App. 2018), *cert. denied*, 140 S.Ct. 108 (2019) (reversing the decision that partner's claims against Winston & Strawn, LLP must be arbitrated and allowing the claim to be litigated because California law disfavoring arbitration agreements applied to her as an "employee," and even though she was a partner signatory to the partnership agreement with the arbitration clause).

34 Simpson v. Ernst & Young, 100 F.3d 436, 445–46 (6th Cir. 1996).

35 *See, e.g.*, Davis v. Loftus, 778 N.E.2d 1144 (Ill. App. Ct. 2002) (holding that "income partners" that received a fixed salary plus bonus, with no profit or loss sharing, were not partners under state law and therefore not personally liable for malpractice claim).

partners are not passive investors; they are on-site monitoring and supervising their venture and are experts in that venture. "Investors" in a general partnership are active owners and comanagers, not purchasers of a financial product. However, the LLP shield's existence makes these assumptions not necessarily true. With no personal liability, LLPs could have passive investor-partners with little downside from being unable to expertly monitor and manage the venture. As state LLP statutes have moved away from the requirement that LLPs be limited to certain professions, partners in an LLP could be virtual strangers and completely passive. An LLP with a restrictive LP agreement could be a mere investment vehicle, like an LP. Furthermore, because general partnership interests have been presumed not to be securities under federal law,[36] promoters may attempt to turn a typical LP investment vehicle into a general partnership with an LLP shield and escape securities registration requirements.

The federal securities laws apply to transactions involving a "security," which includes, in addition to specific types of instruments, any investment contract.[37] The leading Supreme Court case, *Securities and Exchange Commission* v. *W. J. Howey Co.*, defined "investment contract" to mean "a contract, transaction or scheme whereby a person invests his money in a common enterprise and is led to expect profits solely from the efforts of the promoter or a third party."[38] The *Howey* test attempts to distinguish between consumer and investment purchases and also between active management participants and passive investors. General partners have usually invested money in a common enterprise with an expectation of profit; however, their profits usually result from their own efforts and those of their partners. Additionally, the securities laws are designed to cure informational asymmetry through mandatory disclosure, and general partners can demand and obtain information from their own general partnership.

Moreover, partners may usually exit the partnership and have their capital contributions returned, unlike participants in other types of business entities. This safeguard may protect partners easily in ways that the securities laws could only after litigation. However, if a purchaser of a general partnership interest in an LLP finds themselves defrauded as to the nature and profitability of the investment, then federal securities law may also protect the investor-partner.

Earlier cases understood that some partnership interests would be more passive than others, and so created a special "subtest" to the *Howey* test to determine whether partnership interests satisfy the last prong of the *Howey* test: "solely from the efforts of others." This additional test, the *Williamson* test, comes from *Williamson* v. *Tucker*.[39] This test looks not only at the partnership agreement as it is written, but also as to how it operates:

> A general partnership or joint venture interest can be designated a security if the investor can establish, for example, that (1) an agreement among the parties leaves so little power in the hands of the partner or venturer that the arrangement in fact distributes power as would a limited partnership; or (2) the partner or venturer is so inexperienced and unknowledgeable in business affairs that he is incapable of intelligently exercising his partnership or venture powers; or (3) the partner or venturer is so dependent on some unique entrepreneurial or managerial ability of the promoter or manager that he cannot replace the manager of the enterprise or otherwise exercise meaningful partnership or venture powers....[40]

---

[36] *See* Blaine F. Burgess, *Securities Prosecution: Unconventional Securities and the Inherently Defective Common Enterprise Rules*, 41 N. KY. L. REV. 159 (2014); Joshua Eihausen, *SEC v. Shields: For Investors, A Bad Presumption Yields Bad Results*, 92 DENV. U. L. REV. 539 (2015).

[37] *See* 15 U.S.C. §§ 77b, 78c (2018).

[38] Sec. & Exch. Comm'n v. W. J. Howey Co., 328 U.S. 293, 298–99 (1946).

[39] 645 F.2d 404 (5th Cir. 1981).

[40] *Williamson*, 645 F.2d at 423, 424.

More than a decade before the first LLP statute was passed, *Williamson* anticipated that the larger the general partnership, the more "security-like" the partnership interest would become, and "comanagement" will become more like shareholder voting than management.[41]. In addition, the court understood that the mere labels of "limited partnership" and "general partnership" were not particularly useful in determining whether certain types of partnership interests were active ownership.

One of the first federal cases to specifically encounter a passive investment in LLP clothing was *Securities and Exchange Commission v. Merchant Capital, LLC.*[42] The Eleventh Circuit found that though the investors had formal powers under the agreement, including the power to remove the general partner by unanimous vote, they lacked the effective ability to exercise these powers. Despite the investors' general business experience, it was significant that they had no independent experience in the debt-purchase business; the general partner could be removed only for cause by unanimous vote; the partners were geographically dispersed and had no preexisting relationships; the general partner controlled information and did not give the investors enough data to make an informed decision as to how much the partnership's debt pool was worth, and the voting process favored the general partner because unvoted ballots counted for management. Other cases involving general partnerships have held likewise, looking at the underlying facts through the lens of the *Williamson* test.[43]

Some state statutes explicitly characterize interests in LLPs as investment contracts;[44] other statutes apply only to LLPs in which some members are passive.[45] One industry that is wrestling with this issue is the oil and gas industry, which regularly uses the joint venture or general partnership form.[46] These cases are currently in litigation, but one can imagine different rules for an industry of repeat partner-investors with some experience in the same types of joint ventures.[47] However, the sophistication and expertise of the investor in an oil and gas venture should arguably not change the determination of whether the investment is a security but instead

---

[41]   *See id.* at 424.

[42]   483 F.3d 747 (11th Cir. 2007). Courts currently differ on whether in the LLP context, the *Williamson* test creates a presumption that general partnership interests are not securities or whether it is "simply a guide." *See id.* at 755; *see also* Rome v. HEI Resources, Inc., 411 P.3d 851 (Colo. App. 2014) (rejecting the "strong presumption" that general partnerships interests are not securities under state law in favor of "economic realities" test).

[43]   *See* Sec. & Exch. Comm'n v. Lowery, 633 F.Supp.2d 466, 480 (W. D. Mich. 2009) (reasoning that given LLP partners' limited liability, and therefore their reduced incentive to be active in the business, the partnership presumption against security "is not appropriate when the investment is in a limited liability partnership."). *See also* United States v. Wetherald, 636 F.3d 1315 (11th Cir. 2011) (upholding jury determination in a criminal case that LLP units were securities where management involvement by nonexperts was minimal).

[44]   *See* Conn. Gen. Stat. § 36b-3(19) (2020) ("'Security' includes … (B) as an 'investment contract,' an interest in a limited liability company or limited liability partnership….").

[45]   *See* Iowa Code § 502.102(28)(e) (2020) (defining as a security an interest in an LLP, "provided 'security' does not include an interest in a limited liability company or a limited liability partnership if the person claiming that such an interest is not a security proves that all of the members … are actively engaged in the management of the … limited liability partnership").

[46]   Sec. & Exch. Comm'n v. Sethi, 910 F.3d 198 (5th Cir. 2018); Sec. & Exch. Comm'n v. Shields, 744 F.3d 633 (10th Cir. 2014) (holding that the SEC had successfully rebutted the presumption that the joint ventures were not securities and raised a fact question); Sec. & Exch. Comm'n v. Mieka Energy Corp., 259 F.Supp.3d 556 (E.D. Tex. 2017) (holding that interests were securities where partners did not know each other's identity and had no experience in the oil and gas industry).

[47]   Sec. & Exch. Comm'n v. Arcturus, 171 F.Supp.3d 512 (N.D. Tex. 2016) (granting summary judgment for SEC on the question of whether joint ventures were securities), *rev'd and remanded*, 928 F.3d 400 (5th Cir. 2019) (vacating earlier opinion that held that all three prongs of *Williamson* test had disputed facts and holding that the second prong had disputed facts but the other two were undisputed in defendants' favor).

could qualify the investment offering as a private placement exception to the registration of the "security."[48]

Assuming LLP interests are securities under federal law, offerings of the securities must be registered under the Securities Act of 1933 unless the sales are entitled to exemptions, such as those for limited offerings,[49] private offerings,[50] or for intrastate transactions.[51] Whether or not LLP interests are exempt from registration, if they are securities, they are subject to the anti-fraud provisions.[52] To date, neither private plaintiffs nor the S.E.C. has attempted to apply federal securities laws to LLP interests in livelihood partnerships in which all partners devote their daily attentions, whether as partners with substantial management authority or not. However, one can imagine a large LLP partner who makes a capital contribution only to find negative consequences on the other side of the partnership buy-in wondering whether the securities laws hold a remedy.

E Are Extra Large LLPs Really Partnerships for Bankruptcy Purposes?

As a corporation approaches insolvency, boards of directors, particularly in closely held corporations, may have an incentive to favor certain potential claimants over others. To favor owners, boards would distribute assets of the corporation as dividends in respect to stock. State law prohibits such dividends if the corporation is insolvent when the dividends are made. Additionally, individual directors who voted for the prohibited dividend are personally liable.

When approaching insolvency, partners in a general partnership might not favor distributions over payment of firm obligations. Because each partner is liable for the obligations of the partnership, distributing the assets of the partnership may defer creditor satisfaction, but the partners will eventually have to contribute to partnership obligations.[53] When the partnership is an LLP, however, partners will have the same desire to preserve firm cash for the benefit of owners, not creditors, as owner-managers in a closely held corporation. However, state laws do not restrict partnership distributions as strictly as corporate dividends.[54] Most notably, distributions to partners "constituting reasonable compensation for present or past services" are not considered prohibited distributions.[55] In a general partnership, partners receive distributions in lieu of salaries for devoting their full-time attention to the partnership, which they are required to do under partnership law.[56] Though near-in-time distributions will be subject to fraudulent

---

[48] See Megan Conner, *The Death of the Joint Venture Exemption in Oil and Gas Securities Regulation*, 3 ONE J: OIL & GAS, NAT'L RES., & ENERGY J. 1309 (2018).

[49] See Regulation D, Securities Act Rules 501–08, 17 C.F.R. §§ 230.501–230.508 (2020).

[50] Securities Act of 1933, § 4(2), 15 U.S.C. § 77d(2) (2018).

[51] See Securities Act Rule 147, 17 C.F.R. § 230.147 (2020); Securities Act Rule 147A, 17 C.F.R. § 230.147A (2020).

[52] See Securities Act of 1933 Act §§ 12(2) and 17(a), 15 U.S.C. §§ 77l(2), 77q(a) (2018); Securities Exchange Act of 1934 Act § 10(b), 15 U.S.C. § 78j(b) (2018), Securities Exchange Act Rule 10b-5, 17 C.F.R. § 5 (2020).

[53] Unless each partner is equally wealthy and subject to a lawsuit, individual partners will have differing preferences over keeping assets in the partnership or distributing all available cash and subjecting themselves to individual suit.

[54] The 2013 amendments to the RUPA provide for a clawback of distributions in certain cases in insolvency. See REVISED UNIF. P'SHIP ACT §§ 406 (amended 2013) (restricting distributions if the LLP is insolvent before or after the distribution), 407 (imposing liability on a partner that knowingly consents to a wrongful distribution); see also OHIO REV. CODE ANN. §1776.84(A) (West 2020) (restricting distributions made if "after giving effect to the distribution, all liabilities of the limited liability partnership exceed the fair value of the assets of the limited liability partnership").

[55] The RUPA definition of "distribution" does not include "amounts constituting reasonable compensation for present or past service or payments made in the ordinary course of business under a bona fide retirement plan or other bona fide benefits program." See REVISED UNIF. P'SHIP ACT § 102(4)(B) (amended 2013).

[56] Under UPA and RUPA, partners are not owed compensation for services to the general partnership. See UNIF. P'SHIP ACT §18(f) (UNIF. LAW COMM'N 1918) ("No partner is entitled to remuneration for acting in the partnership business,

transfer restrictions, distinguishing between "compensation" for work performed and a return on capital is inexact at best.[57]

Perhaps because under general partnership law, an insolvent partnership would not be considered "insolvent" unless all of its general partners were insolvent, the Bankruptcy Code does not seem to anticipate the bankruptcy of general partnerships.[58] LLPs are not mentioned in the Bankruptcy Code, and "partnership" is undefined. Because the definition of "corporation" includes a "partnership association" if it is "organized under a law that makes only the capital subscribed responsible for the debts of such association,"[59] LLPs have been treated as corporations in bankruptcy.[60]

III PUBLICLY TRADED PARTNERSHIPS

The limited liability of passive investment in the LP form has always enabled LPs to have more total partners than general partnerships. Limited liability for limited partners is the norm, and unlike a general partnership, limited partners do not have a default right to comanage the firm. LPs can then grow larger than a traditional general partnership, with passive investors recruited to provide mere capital, not reputation, management expertise, or business connections. The three limitations on the size of an LP (by the number of partners) are transferability of shares, retaining flow-through taxation, and federal securities laws. For the past several decades, the main driver of sizable LPs were sophisticated market participants creating entities for investment vehicles. These highly specialized LPs benefitted from the state of Delaware allowing LPs (and LLCs) to eliminate fiduciary duties. Because these entities are generally formed between known participants, then parties could bargain and price fiduciary duties and create contractual covenants that might better suit their arrangements.

The original partnership forms, even the LP form, are not well-suited to extra large enterprises or publicly held entities. Theoretically, the personal liability of the general partner in an LP would limit the size of the enterprise. Even if the general partner were a corporation, 100 per cent liability for the enterprise in return for a lesser ownership interest might not be ideal. General partners would also be liable for breaches of fiduciary duties to limited partners, and public ownership attracts litigation. However, the PTP takes advantage of the ability to eliminate fiduciary duties in Delaware (and some other jurisdictions) to elevate the LP to a publicly traded firm that is even more corporate-like than a corporation.

---

except that a surviving partner is entitled to reasonable compensation for his services in winding up the partnership affairs."); REVISED UNIF. P'SHIP ACT § 401(h) (amended 2013) ("A partner is not entitled to remuneration for services performed for the partnership, except for reasonable compensation for services rendered in winding up the business of the partnership.").

57 Putting aside the difficulty in distinguishing whether a partnership distribution is compensation for services rendered or a return on capital, states following the UPA may decide the matter differently than states following the RUPA. *See* In re Dewey & LeBoeuf LLP, 518 B.R. 766, 789–90 (Bankr. S.D.N.Y. 2014) (holding that partners are not entitled to a "reasonably equivalent value" defense allowing them to argue that distributions were compensation for services and not a return on capital accounts because the New York UPA follows a "no compensation" rule).

58 The Bankruptcy Reform Act of 1994 accepted only one proposal of the ABA Business Law Section's Ad Hoc Committee on Partnerships in Bankruptcy, was an amendment to Bankruptcy Code §723(a) so that a partnership debtor trustee would have recourse against a general partner only "to the extent that under applicable nonbankruptcy law such general partner is liable for such deficiency." *See* 11 U.S.C. § 723(a) (2018).

59 11 U.S.C. § 101(9)(A)(ii) (2018).

60 In re Rambo Imaging, L.L.P., No. 07–11190-FRM, 2008 WL 2778846 (Bankr. W. D. Tex. July 15, 2008); In re Promedicus Health Grp., LLP, 416 B.R. 389 (Bankr. W.D.N.Y. 2009).

A *Freely Transferable Shares*

One of the hallmarks of all partnerships is that interests of general partners in a general partnership and all partners in an LP may not be transferred to those outside the partnership without the consent of the remaining partners. If a partner attempted to transfer her shares to a third party, then that transferee received the "transferable interest" only, generally the right to distributions. Transferees did not have the right to comanage or even vote as a limited partner, even though limited partners do not have the default ability to bind the partnership or comanage beyond limited voting powers. By designing LPs with nontransferable shares, the uniform acts ensured that LPs formed under a similar act would honor the partnership maxim that participants "pick their partners" and be treated as a partnership under federal tax law.[61]

Two developments changed the landscape for transferring LP interests: one change in Delaware law and one change in federal taxation law. In 1985, just prior to the 1985 amendments to the 1976 Act, Delaware adopted revisions to its own Delaware Revised Uniform Limited Partnership Act (DRULPA). These 1985 Delaware amendments "clarified the prior law, codified practices that had developed in the LP area, and increased flexibility in the structuring of LPs."[62] These amendments, among other things, allowed partnerships to have different classes of limited partners with various rights[63] and also allowed for the certification of LP interests,[64] for ease of transfer. In other words, LPs could be more corporation-like, with liquid partnership interests with different financial and governance rights. The impetus for many of these changes was the evolution of the LP structure for use with large numbers of limited partners.[65]

Additional amendments by the Delaware legislature in 1988 targeted the growing number of publicly traded master limited partnerships (MLPs), allowing for easy transfer of LP certificates without the use of depositary receipts.[66] For example, LP interests could be traded without the incoming partner executing the partnership agreement by following a different procedure provided for by the LP agreement.[67]

However, the regulatory abandonment of the *Kintner* factors ratified and enabled the ability of hybrid partnerships to become whatever the creators wanted. The appearance of LLPs[68] and LLCs[69]

---

[61] Until 1996, partnerships that wanted to avoid corporate taxation could have no more than two of four corporate characteristics (free transferability of shares, perpetual life, centralized management, and limited liability). *See* the United States v. Kintner, 216 F.2d 418 (9th Cir. 1954). These *Kintner* factors were codified as Treasury Regulations. *See* Treas. Reg. §§ 301.7701–2; 24 (1959). Because LP owners were most interested in limited liability and centralized management, most LPs retained restrictions on transferability of shares and continuity of life.

[62] Craig B. Smith, *Limited Partnerships—Expanded Opportunities Under Delaware's 1988 Revised Uniform Limited Partnership Act*, 15 DEL. J. CORP. L. 43 (1990).

[63] DEL. REVISED UNIF. LTD. P'SHIP ACT § 17–302(a) (1985).

[64] DEL. REVISED UNIF. LTD. P'SHIP ACT § 17–702(b) (1985).

[65] Joseph J. Basile, Jr., *The 1985 Delaware Revised Uniform Limited Partnership Act*, 41 BUS. LAW. 571 (1986).

[66] DEL. REVISED UNIF. LTD. P'SHIP ACT § 17–101(10) (1988).

[67] DEL. REVISED UNIF. LTD. P'SHIP ACT § 17–101(12) (1988) ("A partner of a limited partnership or an assignee of a partnership interest is bound by the partnership agreement whether or not the partner or assignee executes the partnership agreement.").

[68] The first LLP statute was adopted in 1991 in Texas, and by 1994, thirteen states including Delaware had also adopted LLP statutes, with almost as many adopting LLP in the first half of 1995, including California. *See* HURT & SMITH, *supra* note 8, at 9–11.

[69] The first LLC statute was adopted in 1977 by Wyoming, which was blessed by the IRS as creating a "partnership" in 1998. By 1997, forty-seven additional states had passed similar statutes. *See* William W. Bratton & Joseph A. McCahery, *An Inquiry into the Efficiency of the Limited Liability Company: Of Theory of the Firm and Regulatory Competition*, 54 WASH. & LEE L. REV. 629 (1997).

in the early 1990s created more tax classification problems.[70] Rather than continue to classify entities and state statutory frameworks piecemeal,[71] the IRS adopted regulations in 1996 that allowed entities with two or more owners not incorporated under a corporate statute to choose whether to be taxed as "partnerships" under Subchapter K or corporations.[72] In other words, any entity that was not a corporation would automatically receive tax partnership status, regardless of whether the entity created by statute and agreement looked more like, or exactly like, a corporation. Tax rules enabled changes to partnership law. The differences between LPs, LLCs and corporations would become very formalistic and quite thin.

B *Partnership Taxation*

Though "check-the-box" regulation made it easier for most noncorporate entities to qualify for partnership tax treatment, a different tax provision, dating from 1985, continued to resist partnership taxation in one area: publicly traded entities.

However, the 1986 tax reforms, aimed in part at the abuses of the LP form, introduced new Section 7704, which requires MLPs to be taxed as corporations unless ninety per cent or more of the partnership's gross income consists of "qualifying income." Though "qualifying income" is generally passive income, it also includes one category of operating income, which is income associated with "any mineral or natural resource."[73] Because of these restrictions, most post-1987 PTPs are in the oil and gas industry, real estate, and finance.[74] Creative structuring allows certain companies to meet the ninety per cent test and retain partnership taxation, even though ownership interests are publicly traded.[75]

---

[70] The first wave of LLC statutes can be described as either "bulletproof" statutes designed to create tax partnerships and "flexible" statutes that created uncertainty for tax classification. *See* Karen C. Burke, *The Uncertain Future of Limited Liability Companies*, 12 Am. J. Tax Pol'y 13, 40 (1995).

[71] *See, e.g.*, Rev. Rul. 95–2 (listing state versions of RULPA that satisfied the classification test in Treas. Reg. 301.7701–2 and superseding similar Revenue Rulings in 1994); Rev. Rul. 93–93 (issuing guidance that an Arizona LLC may be classified as a corporation or a partnership depending on the structure adopted in the operating agreement); Rev. Rul. 88–76 (1988) (classifying an LLC organized under the Wyoming statute as a partnership).

[72] Treas. Reg. § 301.7701–1 et seq.; Victor E. Fleischer, *"If It Looks Like a Duck": Corporate Resemblance and Check-the-Box Elective Tax Classification*, 96 Colum. L. Rev. 518 (1996).

[73] I.R.C. § 7704(d)(1) (1986). "Qualifying income" includes

(A) interest,
(B) dividends,
(C) real property rents,
(D) gain from the sale or other disposition of real property (including property described in section 1221(1),
(E) income and gains derived from the exploration, development, mining or production, processing, refining, transportation (including pipelines transporting gas, oil, or products thereof), or the marketing of any mineral or natural resource (including fertilizer, geothermal energy, and timber),
(F) any gain from the sale or disposition of a capital asset (or property described in section 1231(b) held for the production of income described in any of the foregoing subparagraphs of this paragraph, and
(G) in the case of a partnership described in the second sentence of subsection (c)(3), income and gains from commodities (not described in section 1221(1) or futures, forwards, and options with respect to commodities.

[74] Energy Infrastructure Council, Publicly Traded Partnerships Trading on U.S. Exchanges (Sept. 10, 2020), https://eic.energy/uploads/mlpsonexchanges_09102020.pdf [hereinafter MLP Data] (72 oil & gas, 4 real estate, 8 investment firms, and 3 "other").

[75] *See* Victor Fleischer, *Taxing Blackstone*, 61 Tax L. Rev. 89 (2008) (describing how The Blackstone Group, a private equity investment firm organized as a limited partnership that profited from a combination of nonqualifying fees and qualifying investment income was able to restructure so as to retain partnership taxation and be publicly traded).

Until 2018, the number of publicly traded entities had been on the rise.[76] In 2016, for example, 140 exchange-traded entities were classified as partnerships for tax purposes. Of those, 123 were LPs, and 10 were LLCs.[77] Notably, 111 of the exchange-traded entities were in the oil, gas, coal, marine, and natural resources industries. Four were real estate firms, and fourteen were financial firms.[78] In addition to the 140 individual firms, there were eleven MLP indexes. The number of new PTPs entering the market reflects changes both in taxation and in the price of oil: Prior to 1996, it was normal for two MLPs to have an initial public offering.[79] Following the "check-the-box" regulations, the number of public offerings of MLPs began to climb, reaching eighteen a year by 2006,[80] roughly following a pattern in crude oil prices.[81] Following a dip during the financial crisis, offerings rose again in 2011 (13); 2012 (15); 2013 (20); and 2014 (18). Mirroring problems in the oil and gas industry,[82] MLP initial offerings were low in 2015 (8), 2016 (2), and 2017 (5). However, various factors resulted in a much lower number of MLPs by July 2018.[83] By September 2020, there were 73.[84]

C *Fiduciary Duties*

Eliminating fiduciary duties is not required to become an MLP, but it definitely reduces the possibility of costly litigation and increases future structuring and business options for the managers. Corporations cannot eliminate all fiduciary duties under state statutes, even though Delaware corporations may choose to limit liability for the duty of care and even waive the corporation's rights to corporate opportunities. Even in Delaware, most of the duty of loyalty, including the duty surrounding conflicted transactions, is unwaivable. However, LPs (and LLCs) organized in Delaware and some other jurisdictions, may choose to eliminate all fiduciary duties that would otherwise be owed by the general partner (or LLC manager) to the entity and the owners.

Hybrid entities, such as LPs and LLCs, can be conceptualized as bundles of contractual rights, and the Delaware courts have prioritized recognizing and enforcing the terms in the

---

[76] *See* Mohsen Manesh, *Contractual Freedom Under Delaware Alternative Entity Law: Evidence from Publicly Traded LPs and LLCs*, 37 J. CORP. L. 555 (2012) [hereinafter *Contractual Freedom*] (noting that PTPs are an "increasingly significant part of the business world").

[77] Interestingly, the publicly held LLCs differ from the standard MLP model, with some of them mirroring corporations, with a board of directors that stands for election and has director-type fiduciary duties. *See* John Goodgame, *New Developments in Master Limited Partnership Governance*, 68 BUS. LAW. 81, 87–91 (2012).

[78] In the mid-1990s, several private equity firms went public, including Apollo Global Management LLC, KKR & Co. LP, Fortress Investment Group, and The Blackstone Group LP. The Carlyle Group, L.P. went public in 2012.

[79] *See History of MLP IPOs*, ALERIAN, https://www.alerian.com/education/resources/figures-and-tables.

[80] *See id.*

[81] At the same time, oil prices climbed gradually during the first decade of the 2000s, reaching over $60 per barrel by the beginning of January 2005 to a high of over $150 per barrel in 2008. *See Crude Oil Price History Chart*, MACROTRENDS, https://www.macrotrends.net/1369/crude-oil-price-history-chart.

[82] Oil prices fell from a modern high of over $100 per barrel in July 2014 to temporarily below $30 per barrel in June 2016. *See id.*

[83] 2017 saw a wave of consolidations and mergers in the MLP industry, with the MLP merging with the related general partner. The 2017 tax reforms and changes in energy regulation may have also contributed to the decline. *See* Stuart Carter & Shawn Amini, *FERC Issues Final Rule on Pipeline Tax Policy*, OPPENHEIMERFUNDS.COM (July 19, 2018), https://www.oppenheimerfunds.com/advisors/article/ferc-issues-final-rule-on-pipeline-tax-policy. By July 2018, there were 114 PTPs (9 LLCs and the rest LPs), with 94 in the oil and gas industry, four in real estate, and twelve in finance. By July 2019, the number was 99 PTPs (4 LLCs and the rest LPs). *See* MLP DATA, *supra* note 74.

[84] MLP DATA, *supra* note 83.

governing documents of those entities based on theories of private negotiation.[85] Recently, Delaware courts have attempted to give full force and effect to LP agreements that have eliminated all fiduciary duties, giving relief only under the terms of the agreement and the implied duty of good faith and fair dealing.[86] The courts will only resort to analyzing whether an action violates the duty of good faith if the LP agreement's contractual provisions have "gaps," which can create uncertainty about the general partner's ability to take certain actions.

MLPs, however, sell units to strangers, who are bound by an agreement that they certainly have not negotiated, and probably have not read. Corporate law anticipates passive, unconnected shareholders and gives them both unwaivable fiduciary duties and statutory protections, such as the right to regular meetings. Limited partners do not have the same statutory protections, perhaps because drafters of RUPA did not anticipate extra large partnerships.

D *Jurisdiction*

One of the starkest examples of traditional concepts of partnership creating absurd results has to be federal diversity jurisdiction. To bring a lawsuit against a partnership, limited or general, in federal court, any litigant must allege either a federal question or diversity of citizenship between or among the "parties."[87] Diversity must be complete: No plaintiff may have the same citizenship as any defendant. In cases against an individual and a corporation, the two parties are diverse if the individual is domiciled in a state that is different from the corporation's state of incorporation. However, if the corporation is instead an unincorporated entity (partnerships, LP, or LLC), then each partner or member of the entity must be domiciled or incorporated in a state different from the individual,[88] even for MLPs with thousands of unitholders that change daily. Though LPs could be seen as separate entities for diversity jurisdiction purpose, the U.S. Supreme Court has held that they are not.[89] Therefore, a corporation with one shareholder will have the citizenship of its state of incorporation, but an MLP with hundreds of thousands of unitholders will have the citizenship of each of its unitholders.[90] Realistically, limited partners in an MLP have no ability to bring a nonfederal cause of action, such as breach of fiduciary duty or breach of contract, in federal court.[91] In addition, large LPs may find

---

[85] *But see* William W. Clayton, *The Private Equity Negotiation Myth*, 37 YALE J. ON REG. 67 (2020) (debunking the myth that sophisticated limited partners would negotiate for fuller fiduciary duty protections in the governing documents for all limited partners when they prefer to negotiate for individual "side letter" protections).

[86] *See, e.g.*, Bandera Master Fund LP v. Boardwalk Pipeline P'ners, LP, No. 2018–0372-JTL, 2019 WL 4927053 (Del. Ch. Oct. 17, 2019) (dismissing fiduciary duty claims in complaint but retaining some of the breaches of contract claims). Recently, the Delaware Supreme Court reinstated actions by limited partners in the MLP context under the implied contractual duty of good faith and fair dealing. *See* Dieckman v. Regency GP LP, 155 A.3d 358 (Del. 2017); Brinckerhoff v. Enbridge Energy Co., Inc., 159 A.3d 242 (Del. 2017).

[87] 28 U.S.C. § 1332 (2018).

[88] Chapman v. Barney, 129 U.S. 677, 682 (1889).

[89] Carden v. Arkoma Assocs., 494 U.S. 185 (1990) (recognizing that the result "can validly be characterized as technical, precedent-bound, and unresponsive to policy considerations raised by the changing realities of business organization"). Though the dissent argued that the limited partnership's citizenship should be determined by its general partners, the 5–4 decision in *Carden* was reaffirmed fourteen years later by the Court in Grupo Dataflux v. Atlas Glob. Grp., L.P., 541 U.S. 567 (2004).

[90] Grynberg v. Kinder Morgan Energy Partners, L.P., 805 F.3d 901 (10th Cir. 2015).

[91] Pathfinder Transp., LLC v. Pinnacle Propane, LLC, 259 F.Supp.3d 949 (W.D. Ark. 2017); Markwest Liberty Midstream & Res., L.L.C. v. Bilfinger Westcon, Inc., No. 5:16-CV-118, 2016 WL 6553591 (N.D.W. Va. Nov. 4,

that they cannot access federal courts to press nonfederal claims because of the same rule.[92]

This lack of access to federal courts due to an outdated conception of partnerships almost certainly continues for political reasons.[93] By requiring complete diversity of all owners in an unincorporated entity, courts reduce the number of federal lawsuits. In remanding these cases back to state court, federal courts repeat to litigants that the cases are clear,[94] and only Congress has the power to change these absurd results.[95] However, Congress does not seem eager to do so.

IV THE FUTURE OF EXTRA LARGE PARTNERSHIPS

Partnerships have outgrown partnership law. In 1913, when the federal tax code first enshrined a tax distinction between partnerships and corporations, partnerships were very different from corporations. Corporations suffered double taxation as the price for limited liability to third parties for all owners and the negative externalities that might occur from having a large enterprise with passive, non-monitoring owners and limited liability. However, modern enterprises may look nothing like the stereotypes of the form they have chosen.

The tax code perpetuates the myth that corporations and partnerships are always different. Subchapter C taxes corporations on income and gain earned at the corporate level then taxes certain distributions and liquidations again to shareholders. Subchapter K does not tax partnerships on income and gain earned at the partnership level but taxes the individual partners on their allocations of gain and loss regardless of distributions. Confounding this problem, the Tax Cuts and Jobs Act of 2017, results in virtually identical tax rates for many types of businesses, operating under two different, complex regimes.[96] Instead of retaining an artificial categorization between corporations and unincorporated entities, which are much closer in governance and operation than in 1913 or even 1995, the tax code could treat all business entities the same for tax purposes.

This new "Subchapter B" would replace Subchapter C and Subchapter K of the Internal Revenue Code and create one master tax regime for business entities. Legislators could target small businesses for tax "nudges" or tax relief by having a separate regime for small business by assets, profits, revenues, or the number of owners. In the alternative, legislators could create a separate regime for livelihood businesses, following the *Howey* test for securities. In other

---

2016) (denying argument that "unitholders" were not "limited partners" under the limited partnership agreement); Trafigura AG v. Enter. Prods. Operating LLC, 995 F.Supp.2d 641 (S.D. Tex. 2014).

[92] *See* CNX Gas Co., LLC v. Lloyd's of London, 410 F.Supp.3d 746, (W.D. Pa. 2019) (remanding to state court cause of action brought by large LLC, which had not determined the citizenship of 1800 members, against its insurer).

[93] *See* Charles J. Cooper & Howard C. Nielson, Jr., *Complete Diversity and the Closing of the Federal Courts*, 37 Harv. J. L. & Pub. Pol'y 295 (2014).

[94] Huntcole, LLC. v. 4-Way Elec. Svcs. LLC, No. 4:17-cv-65-DMB-JMV, 2017 WL 6375978 (N.D. Miss. Dec. 13, 2017) (rejecting "the suggestion that this Court should disregard the long recognized vehicle of the limited partnership, such as those at issue in this case, and instead treat these limited partnerships as if they were of questionable stature as artificial entities . . . is not even colorable.").

[95] Grynberg v. Kinder Morgan Energy Partners, L.P., 805 F.3d 901 (10th Cir. 2015) (acknowledging that such a rule precludes diversity jurisdiction over publicly traded partnerships, but that Congress would need to address that issue, not the courts); Cabrera v. Aboytes-Munis, No. H-14-2725, 2015 WL 5093230, at *3 (S.D. Tex. Aug. 7, 2015) ("absent any action from Congress, an MLP should be treated as an unincorporated entity").

[96] The Bush Tax Cuts of 2001 cut the effect of double taxation in half by drastically reducing the rate at which dividends and capital gains are taxed. The Tax Cuts and Jobs Act finished this work by drastically reducing the corporate tax rate. *See* Christine Hurt, *Partnership Lost*, 53 U. Rich. L. Rev. 491 (2019).

words, entities that issue no "securities" or "investment contracts" would have lighter taxation than entities with passive owners holding securities. Distinguishing between entities based on size, externalities, or passive ownership makes more sense in the twenty-first century than distinguishing based on illusory entity categories.

Furthermore, laws as unrelated as employment law and securities law start from a presumption that partnerships resemble 1913 general partnerships, not modern partnerships. This stereotype needs to be eliminated or reworked as the exceptions may swallow the presumptions.

3

The Three Fiduciaries of Delaware Corporate Law—and Eisenberg's Error

Lyman Johnson

I INTRODUCTION

The duties of care and loyalty are central to the discourse of corporate law. Although sanctions for a duty of care breach by directors are unlikely, due to widespread adoption of exculpation provisions, directors of public companies nonetheless generally give ex ante attention to proceeding in a careful manner, the essence of care. And a robust duty of care for officers—the law on which is surprisingly undeveloped in Delaware—might revive the prospect of remedies for a care breach by senior executives, who cannot be exculpated. The more demanding duty of loyalty, however, undoubtedly remains the chief focal point of fiduciary analysis and litigation under Delaware law.

In imposing duties of loyalty and care, Delaware corporate law is similar to other fields of law where fiduciary obligations play a key role—agency, partnership, trusts and estates, guardianships, conservatorships, and attorney-client relationships. But corporate law also is strikingly, and uniquely, different from those other areas. Within corporation law, not one, not two, but three distinct actors owe fiduciary duties—executive officers, directors, and controlling shareholders. Moreover, the object or beneficiary of those actors' duties is not the same. For example, directors owe unremitting duties to both the corporation and all of its shareholders, but controlling shareholders only occasionally owe duties and, when they do, they do not likewise owe reciprocal duties to directors, but only to minority shareholders. Similarly, officers owe duties to the corporation, but it is not clear that they owe duties directly to shareholders.

The reasons for these three actors owing fiduciary duties also differ. Officers owe duties because they are agents of the corporation,[1] but they are not agents of the shareholders. Directors are not agents of the corporation or shareholders,[2] and, after decades of fretful and inconclusive theorizing, owe duties to both of them in a sui generis capacity.[3] Controlling shareholders (sometimes) owe duties for pragmatic policy reasons largely centering on their control.

Finally, the nature, scope, and demands of care and loyalty can differ markedly for the three actors. To cite one example, the controlling shareholder duty of care seems to arise only in the

---

[1] Amalgamated Bank v. Yahoo, Inc., 132 A.3d 752, 780 (Del. Ch. 2016).
[2] Arnold v. Soc'y for Sav. Bancorp, Inc., 678 A.2d 533, 539–40 (Del. 1996).
[3] Lyman Johnson & David Millon, *Recalling Why Corporate Officers Are Fiduciaries*, 46 WM. & MARY L. REV. 1597, 1605 n. 25 (2005).

highly unusual "looting" context and has a limited reach, whereas director and officer duties of care apply more pervasively, even though they differ from one another.

Thus, in corporate law—unlike other areas where fiduciary duties arise—there does not appear to be *a* singular duty of care and loyalty, but multiple variations of those duties owed by multiple actors. The beneficiary of the duties, the reasons for imposing the duties, and the nature and demands of the duties can differ for the three actors. This oft-overlooked doctrinal point is the chapter's first contribution, and it cautions restraint in over-claiming how much totalizing theoretical coherence can be brought to the fiduciary area, at least in corporate law where the governance structure is more complex and the duties more nuanced.

The second contribution is to identify when and why, given the straightforward fiduciary duty analysis seen in other areas of the law, Delaware's judiciary instead introduced a prolix standard of conduct-standard of review construct into its corporate fiduciary analysis. The source, it turns out, is an influential but mistaken distinction first hailed by Professor Melvin Eisenberg in 1993.[4] Professor Eisenberg posited that Delaware corporate law could be explained in terms of that distinction. Fiduciary duties (sometimes called standards of conduct) are acknowledged by Delaware courts, but, analytically, they receive little emphasis in corporate law and often are overshadowed by the ever-evolving judicial formulation of separate, more deferential standards of review to which courts give greater attention. Fiduciary duties (standards of conduct), moreover, apply to the conduct of corporate governance actors and are fairly simple while standards of review pertain to the behavior of judges in assessing that conduct and can be complex.[5] Here too, according to Eisenberg, corporate law appears to part ways with other areas of law where the standards align.[6]

Professor Eisenberg's account was historically and descriptively inaccurate. At the time he wrote—1993—Delaware courts had only infrequently used the terms "standard of conduct" and "standard of review." Only *after* Eisenberg's article did Delaware courts use those terms with any frequency. Professor Eisenberg thus did not describe a pre-existing state of positive law; instead, he provided theoretical support for a subsequent, unhelpful change in positive law.

The two sets of standards, moreover, often converge and are identical, both for directors and for shareholders, thus raising a question of whether the distinction is uniformly accurate in corporate law and whether unenforceable conduct standards can be considered "law" at all where they do diverge. For officers, mistakenly likened to directors by Professor Eisenberg, the two standards appear to be one and the same, in any event. In the corporate governance context, then, the disparate fiduciary duties of the three actors and the modern focus of the judicial lawmaking enterprise on standards of review, rather than fiduciary duties, combine to form what might better be described as Delaware's law of *fiduciaries* than Delaware's fiduciary *law*.

Section II of this chapter identifies salient differences in the Delaware judiciary's treatment of fiduciary duties for officers, controlling shareholders, and directors. Sub-section A begins with officers, even though the judiciary's expounding of fiduciary law for officers is still strikingly undeveloped. Officers are agents, and the fiduciary analysis is, or should be, straightforward and, so far, it remains uncomplicated by the use of a separate standard of review, such as the business

---

[4] Melvin A. Eisenberg, *The Divergence of Standards of Conduct and Standards of Review in Corporate Law*, 62 Fordham L. Rev. 437 (1993).

[5] *See, e.g., In re* Trados Inc. Stockholder Litigation, 73 A.3d 17, 45 (Del. Ch. 2013).

[6] This was a key jumping-off point for Professor Eisenberg in distinguishing judicial review practices in corporate law from those in other fields of law. As explained in section III, however, Delaware courts rarely used the "standard of conduct" construct prior to Professor Eisenberg's article, and the Supreme Court has only infrequently used it since the article.

judgment rule. The fiduciary analysis of officers, as long as it continues unencumbered by the default business judgment rule review standard, is a model of simplicity and serves to refute the divergence theory. Sub-section B examines the limited contexts in which controlling shareholders owe duties, including a landmark 2014 decision where Delaware restored corporate law's duty of loyalty to a more traditional fiduciary duty analysis while also needlessly employing a business judgment standard of review to do so. Sub-section C addresses director duties and judicial lawmaking practices concerning them. Director cases are by far the most numerous and complex, and the area where various standards of review are used most widely, if unnecessarily. Section III assesses the inaccuracy and disutility of the supposed standard of conduct-standard of review distinction in light of significant convergence. Fiduciary analysis in Delaware corporate law, as elsewhere, can and should be much more straightforward.

II THE THREE FIDUCIARIES

A *Officers*

Delaware law says very little about the governance responsibilities or fiduciary duties of the most influential actors in corporate affairs—i.e., executive officers. From a business success or failure standpoint, corporate well-being is predominantly *officer*-centric, even though, from a legal and corporate governance standpoint, *director* primacy prevails.[7] Yet, Delaware's law of officer duties is sparse. The undeveloped state of the law, moreover, has endured for the many decades Delaware has dominated corporate law.

Delaware's corporate statute contains few provisions pertaining to officers. Those that do exist deal with electing and removing officers, preventing voidability of conflict of interest transactions, and indemnification.[8] Unlike many other states, Delaware has no statutory standards of conduct, nor does Delaware permit exculpation of officers—thus making officers far more vulnerable to personal liability for care breaches than directors—and it does not expressly allow officers to rely on designated persons.

Very little case law exists on officer duties. Only in 2009 did the Delaware Supreme Court in *Gantler v. Stephens* finally hold that officer fiduciary duties of care and loyalty "are the same as those of directors . . . ."[9] Before then, corporate law tended to lump directors and officers together as discharging general "management" or "manager" responsibilities, even though they occupy starkly different roles in public companies. A decade after the *Gantler* ruling, it is not at all clear that the duties are "the same" because very little has been clarified about officer duties, and many issues remain utterly unresolved. Notably, the *Gantler* court did not use the business judgment rule in analyzing the claims against corporate officers. Rather, the court's review of officer conduct was straightforward, seemingly bypassing the rule as a separate standard of review in ruling that the plaintiffs "state a claim that they [the defendants] breached their fiduciary duties as officers."[10] Unlike the case with directors, where, historically, the business judgment rule preceded a clear articulation of the duty of care and the standard of conduct (care) thus became

---

[7] *See, e.g.*, Gorman v. Salamone, No. 10183-VCN, 2015 WL 4719681, at *15 (Del. Ch. July 31, 2015) (describing "bedrock statutory principle of director primacy").

[8] DEL. CODE ANN. tit. 8, §§ 142–45 (2015). The statutory provision authorizing a corporation to waive in advance specified corporate opportunities also applies to officers, along with directors and stockholders, subject to fiduciary duty analysis. DEL. CODE ANN. tit. 8, § 122 (17) (2015).

[9] Gantler v. Stephens, 965 A.2d 695, 708–09 (Del. 2009).

[10] *Id.* at 709.

embedded in the standard of review (the business judgment rule),[11] with respect to officers, the duty of care emerged first, and the business judgment rule construct has yet, if ever, to appear.

The Delaware Chancery Court continually notes that the applicability of the business judgment rule to officers is unsettled,[12] and a recent federal court decision bluntly stated there is no Delaware case law supporting such an application.[13] Scholarly opinion on the subject remains divided,[14] but the policy case for applying the rule to officers is far weaker than for directors and, in any event, the rule is unnecessary. A stringent or deferential standard of conduct for officers on policy grounds can be achieved simply by calibrating the duty of care standard at ordinary or gross negligence, as desired. There is, moreover, no substance to the duty of care in a decision-making context—it is a process-oriented duty only[15]—and thus the business judgment rule's substantive element is unnecessary for establishing that point.[16]

Although the business judgment rule has not been applied to officers, Delaware law clearly recognizes that corporate officers, unlike directors, are agents of the company.[17] Consequently, officers owe fiduciary duties to the company and must act solely for its benefit and subject to its directives and control,[18] as administered through the board of directors. Several intriguing implications would seem to follow from such a fiduciary position, but Delaware law has not addressed these issues.

First, Delaware has not settled whether the appropriate standard of care for an officer is the traditional, demanding agency law standard of ordinary care/negligence or the more deferential director-like standard of gross negligence.[19] Given director dependence on officers for providing full, timely, and accurate business information, and the director's statutory right to rely on officers, one would expect a stricter standard of care for officers than the lax gross negligence standard applied to directors.[20] Directors, and the shareholders they represent, also need to know that because directors delegate significant responsibilities to senior officers, those officers are acting only as authorized and are careful, not reckless, in their numerous dealings on behalf of the corporation. Second, Delaware has not fully articulated the nature and contours of officer monitoring and oversight duties; the scope of an officer's duty of disclosure to superior officers, directors, or shareholders; whether or the extent to which, officers may, like directors,[21] consider noninvestor stakeholders in carrying out their

---

[11] Henry Ridgely Horsey, *The Duty of Care Component of the Delaware Business Judgment Rule*, 19 Del. J. Corp. L. 971, 985, 995 (1994). History, not logic, thus made the business judgment rule, not fiduciary duties, preeminent in Delaware's judicial lawmaking.

[12] *See, e.g.*, Chen v. Howard-Anderson, 87 A.3d 648, 666 n.2 (Del. Ch. 2014).

[13] Palmer v. Reali, 211 F. Supp. 3d 655, 666 n.8 (D. Del. 2016).

[14] *Compare* Lyman Johnson, *Corporate Officers and the Business Judgment Rule*, 60 Bus. Law. 439 (2005), *with* Lawrence A. Hamermesh & A. Gilchrist Sparks III, *Corporate Officers and the Business Judgment Rule: A Reply to Professor Johnson*, 60 Bus. Law. 865 (2005).

[15] Brehm v. Eisner, 746 A.2d 244, 264 (Del. 2000).

[16] Of course, if the business judgment rule is narrowly and properly understood only to preclude judicial review of the merits of business decisions—and not, wrongly, as an overarching analytical construct—then use of the rule would be unobjectionable, but still unneeded. *See* Lyman Johnson, *The Modest Business Judgment Rule*, 55 Bus. Law. 625 (2000) (describing proper, limited nonreview function of the rule).

[17] *See supra* notes 1–2. For an explanation of how persons who are not de jure agents can, under certain circumstances, take on agent-like duties, *see* Deborah A. DeMott, *Fiduciary Duties on the Temporal Edges of Agency Relationships*, ch. 1 (this volume).

[18] Restatement (Second) Agency § 387 (Am. Law Inst. 1958); Restatement (Third) Agency § 8.01 (Am. Law Inst. 2006) (duty to act for the principal's benefit).

[19] *Amalgamated Bank*, 132 A.3d at 780 n.24.

[20] Deborah DeMott, *Corporate Officers as Agents*, 74 Wash. & Lee L. Rev. 847 (2017).

[21] *Compare* Unocal Corp. v. Mesa Petroleum Co., 493 A.2d 946, 955–56 (Del. 1985) (directors may consider non-shareholder interests) *with* Revlon, Inc. v. MacAndrews & Forbes Holdings Inc., 506 A.2d 173, 181 (Del. 1985) (directors must exclusively consider shareholder interests in corporate break-up context).

responsibilities; the scope of an officer's right to rely on others; and whether officers, who are not subject to direct control by shareholders and are not agents of them, owe duties to shareholders that can properly be pursued via direct rather than derivative litigation.

Importantly, if Delaware takes its characterization of officers as agents seriously, the fiduciary duty analysis can, as *Gantler* suggests, remain straightforward and uncomplicated by any need for a separate judicial standard of review such as the business judgment rule. After all, under agency law, no such separate standard of review obtains. Instead, a court examines a fiduciary duty claim for wrongdoing by focusing on only two elements: "that a fiduciary duty existed" and "that a defendant breached that duty."[22]

For various reasons, Delaware has not spoken to these basic and important issues about officer fiduciary duties,[23] although it repeatedly has done so for directors. The point here is that, to date, Delaware does not treat officers the same as directors. One cannot say that officers owe the same duties as directors, that courts will review their conduct similarly, or that the consequences of a fiduciary duty breach are identical. Delaware's fiduciary law of officers is not, today, the fiduciary law of directors.

B Controlling Shareholders

Like officers, controlling shareholders owe fiduciary duties, but, unlike officers, they do so only occasionally. Duties are not owed for the same reason, moreover, nor do they appear to be owed to the same persons. The nature and demands of the duties also differ.

Controlling shareholders, unlike officers, are not agents of the company (or of other shareholders) and they do not owe duties for that reason. Nor do they owe duties because they govern the business and affairs of the corporation as do directors. Rather, controlling shareholder duties, when they arise, are predicated on their ability to control who sits on the board of directors and on their power to remove those directors for not complying with the controller's wishes with respect to a particular matter.[24] Similarly, minority shareholders voting on a transaction involving a controller might perceive that an adverse vote would lead to retribution by the controller. The perception of possible retaliation or coercion leads to policy concerns that control might be used to extract corporate value for the disproportionate benefit of the controller, rather than for all shareholders.[25] Thus, although shareholders as a group generally are *owed* fiduciary duties, in certain settings controlling shareholders also *owe* duties.

A controller's duty of care as a shareholder appears to be quite limited. It likely arises only where the controller, without conducting an adequate investigation, sells control of a corporation to a person under such circumstances as would alert a reasonable seller that the buyer may loot the company.[26] Such a duty is owed to the company and its minority

---

[22] *See, e.g.,* Beard Research, Inc. v. Kates, ASDI, Inc., 8 A.3d 573, 601 (Del. Ch. 2010). Interestingly, in July 2019, Vice-Chancellor Laster cited *Beard's* two elements in analyzing a fiduciary duty claim against a defendant who was the CEO and a director. Clark v. Davenport, No. CV 2017–0839-JTL, 2019 WL 3230928, at *8 (Del. Ch. 2019). Prior to that decision, Vice-Chancellor Laster frequently employed the standard of conduct-standard of review construct. *See infra* notes 65–68.

[23] *See* Lyman Johnson, *Dominance by Inaction: Delaware's Long Silence on Corporate Officers, in* Can Delaware Be Dethroned? Evaluating Delaware's Dominance of Corporate Law (S. Bainbridge ed., 2017).

[24] *See* Ann M. Lipton, *After Corwin: Down the Controlling Shareholder Rabbit Hole,* 72 Vand. L. Rev. 1977 (2019).

[25] *Id.*

[26] Harris v. Carter, 582 A.2d 222 (Del. Ch. 1990). Occasionally, courts make broad statements about the breadth of duties owed by controlling shareholders in unusual circumstances. *See, e.g.,* Cinerama, Inc. v. Technicolor, Inc., No. 8358, 1991 Del. Ch. LEXIS 105, at *63 (a controlling shareholder who exercises "power by directing the actions of the corporation, assumes the duties of care and loyalty of a director of the corporation."). Unlike many other states,

shareholders, and, one court explicitly assumed, is breached only by grossly negligent conduct.[27] No divergent standard of review was used in analyzing such shareholder conduct. Plainly, the duty of care is not the same for controlling shareholders as it is for officers, being narrower in scope and likely more lax in its required standard, thus dispelling the notion that there is a single duty of care in corporate law.

As to the duty of loyalty, again only controlling shareholders owe such a duty, not all shareholders, and such a duty is owed only in certain settings, not pervasively. Delaware law recently has spent considerable time explaining how non-majority shareholders may be considered controlling shareholders.[28] This is an especially important determination after *Kahn v. M&F Worldwide Corporation ("MFW")*[29] — discussed below — where the Delaware Supreme Court charted a much narrower path to a business judgment rule standard of review for controllers than noncontrollers.[30]

Even controllers, however, are unconstrained by duties in much of their capacity as shareholders. They can vote for whomever they wish as directors, even for themselves or their relatives and affiliates, without breaching any duty. They can sell their stock when and on such terms and to such third persons as they wish — subject to the looter exception noted — without owing a duty to provide minority shareholders an equal opportunity to sell.

Controlling shareholders also can engage in conflict of interest transactions free of loyalty claims, provided that such transactions do not involve self-dealing or result in them obtaining a material benefit not received by shareholders generally.[31] Even here, such self-dealing and unique benefit transactions do not automatically constitute a breach of the duty of loyalty. Rather, under Delaware's entire fairness standard of judicial review — its most exacting — if a controller can prove ex post that a challenged transaction was entirely fair to the corporation, no breach of loyalty or invalidity will be found. In many non-corporate law fields, self-dealing transactions lacking the ex ante consent of beneficiaries are void, whereas in corporate law they are not, although they are subject to an ex post company option to try to invalidate them and/or to seek damages, an effort that fails if the fiduciary proves fairness. Here, Delaware corporate law appears to depart from, and is more permissive than, other areas of law where more absolutist prohibitory fiduciary principles apply.[32]

Delaware does not recognize special duties for majority shareholders toward minority shareholders in close corporations. Nixon v. Blackwell, 626 A.2d 1366 (Del. 1993). Like other states, however, Delaware in an appropriate context may grant corporate dissolution or other relief to a minority shareholder. *See* Paul B. Miller, *Equity, Majoritarian Governance, and the Oppression Remedy*, ch. 9 (this volume).

[27] Harris, 582 A.2d at 235–36.

[28] *See, e.g.*, In re Tesla Motors S'holder Litig., No. CV 12711-VCS, 2018 WL 1560293 (Del. Ch. 2018).

[29] Kahn v. M&F Worldwide Corp., 88 A.3d 635 (Del. 2014).

[30] In brief, under *MFW* where controllers are involved and engage in self-dealing, *both* independent director approval and uncoerced, disinterested shareholder approval are required to obtain business judgment rule review. Where no controlling shareholder is involved, approval of a transaction by a majority of fully informed, uncoerced, disinterested shareholders *alone* leads to business judgment rule review, even if, absent such approval, a stricter standard of review would apply. Corwin v. KKR Fin. Holdings, LLC, 125 A.3d 304 (Del. 2015). In the latter setting, considerable focus understandably is now placed on the quality of the disclosures made to shareholders, *see, e.g.*, Morrison v. Berry, 191 A.3d 268 (Del. 2018), because if disclosures are inadequate, *Corwin* does not apply and a possibly stricter standard of review may be triggered. Note here the legal wrangling over standards of review, not fiduciary duties.

[31] *See, e.g.*, Pers. Touch Holding Corp. v. Glaubach, No. CV 11199-CB, 2019 WL 937180, at *19 (Del. Ch. Feb. 25, 2019).

[32] Amir Licht, *Farewell to Fairness: Towards Retiring Delaware's Entire Fairness Review* (European Corporate Governance Institute Working Paper No. 439, Feb. 2019), https://papers.ssrn.com/sol3/papers.cfm?abstract_id=3331097. Professor Licht traces how entire fairness developed in corporate law and how it deviates from general fiduciary principles as seen in the strict "no further inquiry" principle applicable to conflict of

In fact, even though controllers play a limited role in corporate governance and, unlike officers and directors, make no business decisions on behalf of a corporation, their self-dealing behavior can now be reviewed under the "business judgment" standard of judicial review. After flirting with a business judgment rule standard early in the 1970s,[33] in the 1980s and 1990s, the Delaware Supreme Court retreated and imposed the demanding entire fairness standard of review,[34] from which there appeared to be no transactional escape route for a controller except to adopt a tender offer/freezeout deal structure. That changed in 2014 in *MFW*. There, the Supreme Court held that to obtain a deferential business judgment rule standard of review, controllers must, at the outset and prior to substantive deal negotiations,[35] condition the transaction on the approval of (i) a special committee of independent directors who comply with their duty of care and who are empowered to freely select their own advisors and definitively say "no" to a deal; and (ii) a majority of informed, uncoerced, disinterested shareholders.

The court's endorsement of a business judgment rule standard of review for a controlling shareholder transaction added nothing because the policy goal of offering a transactional path around the entire fairness standard could have been achieved without overlaying the business judgment rule standard. Moreover, the business judgment rule was designed for reviewing business decisions made by directors, and its several policy underpinnings are aimed at them, not shareholders. In addition, its use for controlling shareholders reveals once again how Delaware's standards of review occupy much of the judiciary's lawmaking in the corporate context and can obscure a more forthright focus on fiduciary duties.

In a manner similar to the approach taken for officers in *Gantler*, the Supreme Court in *MFW* could have considered the issue before it as a straightforward matter of fiduciary duty. The business judgment rule—designed for directors, rooted in their plenary governance role, and central there only because it emerged in Delaware before a clear duty of care—could have, and should have, been bypassed. To speak of "business judgment" in the controlling shareholder context is incoherent because such a shareholder makes no "business" judgment on behalf of the corporation in the same statutory way directors do. To be sure, in a third-party merger, shareholder approval is necessary to effectuate the merger, but shareholders in that setting—controlling or otherwise—owe no fiduciary duties to the corporation or other shareholders, provided they receive no unique material

---

interest dealings. He argues as well that the entire fairness standard of review amounts to a license for controllers and insiders to appropriate value from vulnerable shareholders. In economic terms, the ex post standard of review serves to set a price range for such appropriation but still permits it. Andrew Tuch argues, however, that advance consent and fairness are both "exceptions" to a strict duty of loyalty. Andrew Tuch, *Reassessing Self-Dealing: Between No-Conflict and Fairness*, 88 FORDHAM L. REV. 939. Yet, assuming a self-dealing transaction is properly authorized—whether or not by a neutral actor—it is legally valid in a fairness regime like corporate law, subject to ex post fairness review if challenged, but in an advance consent of beneficiary regime like trust law, the transaction would not seem to be valid in the first place.

    Section 144 of the Delaware General Corporation Law operates similarly, but not identically, to Delaware's common law of fiduciary duties. Satisfying section 144 only means that a challenged director or officer transaction—it has no bearing on shareholder dealings—is not void or voidable solely because of a conflict of interest if its requirements are satisfied. *See* Benihana of Tokyo, Inc. v. Benihana, Inc. Int., 891 A.2d 150, 185 (Del. Ch. 2005), *aff'd* 906 A.2d 114 (Del. 2006). The different but related question of whether an interested transaction might give rise to a breach of fiduciary duty claim is for the common law to decide, under somewhat different requirements. *In re* Cox Commc'ns S'holder Litig., 879 A.2d 604, 614–15 (Del. Ch. 2005).

[33] *See, e.g.*, Getty Oil Co. v. Skelly Oil Co., 267 A.2d 883, 887 (Del. 1970).

[34] Weinberger v. UOP, Inc., 457 A.2d 701, 711 (Del. 1983); Kahn v. Lynch Comm. Sys., Inc., 638 A.2d 1110 (Del. 1994), *aff'd* 669 A.2d 79 (Del. 1995).

[35] The key date is the beginning of substantive financial negotiations. Olenik v. Lodzinski, 208 A.3d 704, 716–18 (Del. 2019).

benefit. Instead, they can and do vote based on whether, as investors, they self-interestedly believe a proposed merger is financially beneficial to them. When minority shareholders similarly are empowered under a majority-of-the minority provision in a controlling shareholder self-dealing merger of the type in *MFW*, they too lack fiduciary duties, can vote based on self-interest, and are not required to advance the company's best interests or those of any other person. And when the ostensibly controlling shareholder in that setting votes on the merger, it does not "self-deal"[36] or "control" the outcome, given the agreed-to dual approval mechanisms, and thus it likely and properly votes in accordance with its own financial interests as an investor.

The issue of advancing the best interests of the corporation in this sanitized setting is a matter of concern only for directors and officers. Moreover, there simply is no reason to import the business judgment rule's feeble element of "rational business purpose" into reviewing the conduct of a shareholder who does not act on behalf of the company. The Supreme Court did so, however, because it apparently saw one standard of review — the business judgment rule construct — as the only alternative to another standard of review, entire fairness. The court was ensnared in the realm of second-order, judicially created standards of review rather than proceeding directly on the first-order fiduciary duty issue.

In the *MFW* setting, after all, the underlying concern is whether the controlling shareholder fulfills its duty of loyalty as it seeks to gain for itself complete ownership of the stock (or other advantage) to the exclusion of the minority shareholders. Triggered by the desire of the controller to gain something from, or to the detriment of, the minority, a traditional fiduciary duty of loyalty approach would require the controller to refrain from such a transaction unless it received prior consent.[37] Delaware, however, like other jurisdictions, long ago departed from that strict ex ante duty of loyalty requirement in its corporate law jurisprudence. In its place, Delaware adopted an entire fairness test under which ex ante self-restraint is not required, and fiduciary self-dealing is permitted (without prior consent) if, ex post, the fiduciary can prove to a court's satisfaction that a transaction, if challenged, is substantively fair.

The *MFW* court in part restored Delaware's corporate law duty of loyalty to the traditional duty of loyalty by providing for (dual) prior approvals. It did not, however, return the default standard of review to a prohibition of (and voidability of) unconsented-to self-dealing, but instead preserved entire fairness. Scholars differ as to whether entire fairness should be maintained as a default standard, scrapped, or worked around as in *MFW*.[38] Whichever way the court went on that issue, however, it should have stopped there. Nothing was added by then placing the business judgment rule on top of the requirement that a controller must obtain two sets of director and shareholder consents. If, as the *MFW* court mandated, the controller conditions the proposal from the outset on the dual approval mechanisms, then ex ante the controller *fulfills* its duty of loyalty, subject only to ex post allegations of fiduciary wrongdoing by the independent committee of directors or tainted approval by the minority shareholders. Beyond addressing those possible challenges, there appears to be nothing left for a court to review — under any standard. The duty of loyalty, unaided by a separate standard of review, can directly achieve the same desired policy outcome.

---

[36]   Vice-Chancellor Laster aptly made this point before the MFW decision. *In re* CNX Gas Corp. S'holders Litig., 4 A.3d 397, 412 (Del. Ch. 2010).

[37]   Licht, *supra* note 32.

[38]   Professor Licht advocates dropping the substantive aspect of entire fairness but acknowledges that scholars differ sharply on that point. *Id.* at 54. *See, e.g.,* James Cox et al., *Understanding the (Ir)Relevance of Shareholder Votes in M&A Deals*, 69 Duke L. J. 503 (2019). *See also* Tuch, *supra* note 32.

C Directors

Directors owe two fiduciary duties under Delaware law, the duty of care and the duty of loyalty.[39] These duties are straightforward and are not frequently modified.[40] Most lawmaking on corporate law by Delaware judges over the last thirty years centers on standards of review, which do change with some regularity. This sub-section will briefly describe key features of director duties to contrast them with the duties of officers and controlling shareholders. Section III will then critically examine the inter-relationship between standards of judicial review and so-called standards of director conduct (fiduciary duties).

1 The Duties

Early Delaware decisions refused to countenance breaches of trust (loyalty) by corporate directors,[41] and by the 1920's directors were described as "fiduciaries." In Justice Randy Holland's recounting, the imposition of duties was an equitable response to the power conferred on directors as a matter of statutory power.[42] To power and control as underpinnings of loyalty, information advantages vis-à-vis investors also explain director duties. Unlike officers, directors are not agents of the corporation, and thus do not owe duties as a matter of agency principles. Rather, they humanly act for the inanimate corporate principal.

In essence, loyalty "mandates that the best interest of the corporation and its shareholders take [] precedence over any interest possessed by a director ... not shared by the stockholders generally."[43] The classic example that implicates the duty of loyalty is when a director appears on both sides of a transaction or receives a material personal benefit not shared by all shareholders. But loyalty also prohibits wrongly appropriating corporate opportunities, using confidential information for personal advantage, and competing with the corporation. Since *Stone*, it also encompasses director conduct not taken in good faith, a breach of which requires intentional dereliction or conscious disregard of duties.

Unlike loyalty, the duty of care is a relative newcomer to Delaware corporate law, apparently first appearing in the early 1960s,[44] after the business judgment rule.[45] Although sometimes phrased as "that amount of care which ordinarily careful and prudent men would use in similar circumstance,"[46] deficiencies in director conduct are actionable only if directors are grossly negligent. This is true both in the decision-making context and the oversight context.[47] Grossly negligent conduct is described as reckless conduct,[48] a high bar, and somewhat difficult to

---

[39] Stone v. Ritter, 911 A.2d 362, 370 (Del. 2006).

[40] In *Stone*, the Supreme Court did clarify that good faith is a component of loyalty, not a separate fiduciary duty. *Id.*

[41] Randy J. Holland, *Delaware Directors' Fiduciary Duties: The Focus on Loyalty*, 11 U. PA. J. BUS. L. 675, 680 (2009) (tracing case law development).

[42] *Id.* at 678. Control over another's property also is stated more generally as a basis for imposing fiduciary duties. Sokol Holdings, Inc. v. Dorsey & Whitney, LLP, No. CIV.A. 3874-VCS, 2009 WL 2501542, at *3 (Del. Ch. 2009).

[43] Cede & Co. v. Technicolor, Inc., 634 A.2d 345, 361 (Del. 1993).

[44] The history is described in Horsey, *supra* note 11, and Johnson, *The Modest Business Judgment Rule, supra* note 16.

[45] Although the phrase "business judgment rule" first appeared only in 1959, the phrase "business judgment" was used by Delaware courts many decades before. Johnson, *The Modest Business Judgment Rule, supra* note 16, at 639.

[46] Graham v. Allis-Chalmers Mfg. Co., 188 A.2d 125, 130 (Del. 1963). *Graham* often is cited as the first decision explicitly addressing care, but three years earlier, the Court of Chancery at least observed that directors had "carefully weighed and evaluated" various factors in their decision. Kors v. Carey, 158 A.2d 136, 141 (Del. Ch. 1960).

[47] *In re* Walt Disney Deriv. Litig., 907 A.2d 693, 748 n.418, 749–50 (Del. Ch. 2005), *aff'd*, 906 A.2d 27 (Del. 2006), Chancellor Chandler noted how an earlier possibility that a negligence standard of care might apply in the oversight context had been "eclipsed" by subsequent decisions. *Id.*

[48] *See, e.g.*, McPadden v. Sidhu, 964 A.2d 1262, 1274 (Del. Ch. 2008).

distinguish from good faith's demanding "intentional" standard, designed to be an even higher bar. Moreover, there is no substance to the duty of care, at least in the decision-making context.[49]

Unlike the slender duty of care owed by controlling shareholders, directors, like officers, owe such a duty pervasively, both in and out of the decision-making context. Directors owe duties for different reasons, however, and are held to a loose standard of gross negligence, whereas the standard for officers in Delaware is unclear. As agents, officers typically would owe an ordinary level of care. Directors, unlike officers, can be exculpated from liability for a duty of care breach.

As to loyalty, there are some overlaps and some differences for the three actors. All are proscribed from unconsented-to self-dealing absent proving fairness ex post. Unlike controlling shareholders, directors have *Revlon* and *Unocal* duties,[50] and are forbidden from directly competing with the corporation. The limitation on directors competing appears narrower than it would be for officers who are full-time employees, however. Finally, as addressed below, the beneficiary of director duties may be different, and that subject unquestionably has been the most widely debated and controversial issue in corporate law over the last century.

2 The Beneficiary

Disagreement over the beneficiary of director duties arises at both the doctrinal and normative levels and is longstanding. There is no parallel debate about the rightful object of the officer and controlling shareholder duties. The subject, moreover, is vast and addressed here only to highlight yet another difference in the discourse about director duties as compared to the other two corporate actors.

Under positive law, directors owe fiduciary duties to the corporation and all of its shareholders.[51] Some commentators take "corporation" and "shareholders" to be equivalent in such phrasing,[52] but that seems to be a faulty reading. First, although occasionally duties are described as benefitting shareholders, frequently both "corporation" and "shareholders" are included in the description of director duties and such recurrent expressions appear purposeful. Second, a corporation is a distinctive legal person, with its own discrete commercial purposes, and is economically, socially, politically, and juridically separate from its shareholders. This is evident not only in the feature of limited shareholder liability for corporate obligations, but also in Delaware's distinction between derivative litigation and direct litigation. The latter seeks to vindicate shareholder claims while the former pertains to corporate claims. The difference centers on who suffered the wrong and who will obtain the recovery,[53] and in making that determination distinct corporate personality matters immensely. Finally, Delaware courts emphasize a duty owed to shareholders alone when they wish to, as in a *Revlon* sale of control setting, where directors must focus solely on shareholder financial welfare, and when directors wrongly interfere with shareholder voting rights.[54] In short, directors owe duties both to the

---

[49] *See supra* note 15.

[50] *See* Revlon, Inc. v. MacAndrews & Forbes Holdings, Inc., 506 A.2d 173 (Del. 1986) (directors must maximize the share price in a corporate break-up or sale of corporate control setting); Unocal Corp. v. Mesa Petroleum Co., 493 A.2d 946 (Del. 1985) (establishing an intermediate reasonableness standard of review of corporate defensive measures).

[51] *See, e.g.*, Aronson v. Lewis, 473 A.2d 805, 811 (Del. 1984).

[52] *See* Julian Velasco, *Fiduciary Principles in Corporate Law, in* THE OXFORD HANDBOOK OF FIDUCIARY LAW 8 (Evan J. Criddle, Paul B. Miller & Robert H. Sitkoff eds., 2018). *But see* Model Business Corporation Act § 8.30, official cmt. at 8–193 ("corporation" refers to the business enterprise and also to the shareholder body).

[53] Tooley v. Donaldson, Lufkin & Jenrette, Inc., 845 A.2d 1031 (Del. 2004).

[54] *Revlon*, 506 A.2d at 181 (sale of control); Blasius Indus., Inc. v. Atlas Corp., 564 A.2d 651, 659 (Del. Ch. 1988) (distinguishing corporate interest from shareholder voting rights).

corporate enterprise and to the shareholders, unlike officers, who as agents of the company (but not shareholders), may owe duties only to the company.[55]

To the extent that duties do run to shareholders, the debate also exists as to whether directors must maximize shareholder wealth or, rather, must act to "benefit" shareholders but not "maximize" for them, at least outside the limited *Revlon* sale of control context. Doctrinally, and notwithstanding the scholarly writing of former Chief Justice Leo Strine,[56] the "benefit" position more closely reflects judicial holdings.[57]

At the normative level, the debate over the proper object of director duties has been, and remains, the most contentious subject in modern corporate law.[58] Scholars remain divided. Many advocate a strict shareholder wealth maximization focus,[59] while others support a "team production" model[60] or various forms of a multi-constituency stakeholderism.[61] Some scholars advocate that directors should advance the interests of the enterprise itself or its avowed business mission,[62] not solely shareholder interests which can diverge from those of the company. Profits certainly result from a healthy, purpose-driven company, but maximizing them is not necessarily the sole, avowed aim of many companies. The point here, however, as with the doctrinal points, is that such a fierce, recurrent debate about fiduciary duties concerns only director duties. At least in legal literature, scant debate addresses the descriptive and normative focus of controlling shareholder or officer duties. This too reveals how corporate law discourse treats these three actors differently concerning fiduciary duties.

III DUTIES AND STANDARDS IN DELAWARE

With respect to fiduciary duties, then, Delaware corporate law appears to be unique in at least two ways. First, unlike other settings where fiduciary duties arise, three different actors owe duties. Each actor owes *a* duty of care and *a* duty of loyalty, but not exactly the *same* duties of care and loyalty. Instead, as observed by Professor Mark Hall in another setting, "general principles of fiduciary obligation give rise to various sets of rules in many settings . . . which share only broad,

---

[55] Of course, directors delegate responsibilities to officers. But those are operational matters pertaining to the business enterprise, not the directors' own functions as representatives of shareholders, which include monitoring corporate officers.

[56] Leo E. Strine, Jr., *Our Continuing Struggle with the Idea that For-Profit Corporations Seek Profit*, 47 Wake Forest L. Rev. 135 (2012).

[57] *See, e.g.*, N. Am. Cath. Educ. Programming Found., Inc. v. Gheewalla, 930 A.2d 92, 103 (Del. 2007) ("benefit" stockholders); Paramount Commc'n, Inc. v. Time, Inc., 571 A.2d 1140, 1150 (Del. 1989). Vice-Chancellor Laster seeks to reconcile the two positions in part by describing the director duty as promoting or maximizing the value of the corporation for the benefit of shareholders. *In re Trados*, 73 A.3d at 36–37.

[58] Strine, *supra* note 56, at 147 n.34, 147–48 n.35 (collecting commentary). In August 2019, the influential Business Roundtable, an association of chief executive officers of leading American companies, altered its Statement on the Purpose of a Corporation to move away from earlier statements that corporations exist principally to serve shareholders. The new Statement emphasizes a commitment to create value for all stakeholders, whose long-term interests are said to be inseparable. For shareholders, the companies state that they will be "generating long-term value." *Statement on the Purpose of a Corporation*, Business Roundtable, http://opportunity.businessroundtable.org/our commitment/.

[59] *See, e.g.*, Stephen Bainbridge, *Director Primacy: The Means and Ends of Corporate Governance*, 97 Nw. U. L. Rev. 547 (2003) (advancing director primacy as the means to the goal of shareholder wealth).

[60] Margaret Blair & Lynn Stout, *A Team Production Theory of Corporate Law*, 85 Va. L. Rev. 248 (1999).

[61] Andrew Keay, The Corporate Objective 173–230 (2011) (describing and critiquing multi-stakeholderism).

[62] *Id.* at ch. 4 (corporation as an entity has its own distinctive objective); Lyman Johnson, *Relating Fiduciary Duties to Corporate Personhood and Corporate Purpose*, in Research Handbook on Fiduciary Law (D. Gordon Smith & Andrew S. Gold eds., 2017) (articulated corporate goals are the proper director focus).

familial resemblance."[63] The reasons for the duties, the beneficiaries, the scope, the demands, and the consequences of breach all can differ for the three fiduciaries of corporate law.

Second, in Delaware most notably, courts evaluating alleged fiduciary misconduct in the corporate setting do not routinely determine simply whether a duty existed and whether it was breached. Instead, courts purportedly use a different set of more prolix analytical constructs— called standards of review—to examine alleged wrongdoing. These standards of review are said to diverge from and are not the same as the underlying fiduciary duties. Much of Delaware's corporate "law," in fact, concerns standards of review, not fiduciary duties, particularly for directors. This ostensible divergence is claimed to be unique to corporate law, setting it apart not only from other areas of fiduciary law but other areas of law more generally.

It turns out, however, that Delaware courts only infrequently used the standard of conduct-standard of review rubric before the early 1990s, when Professor Melvin Eisenberg first wrote about the supposed phenomenon.[64] Only *after* Eisenberg wrote, however, was there an upsurge in deploying those terms, and unhelpfully so. Professor Eisenberg did not describe an existing state of law; rather, he prescribed and launched legal change.

This purported deviation of judicial review standards from a more direct analysis of fiduciary conduct in Delaware corporate lawmaking will briefly be revisited from several angles. These include its current use in corporate lawmaking and its modern emergence; certain anomalies in Delaware's dualism; whether, and to what extent, divergence currently exists; and what really is the corporate "law" of fiduciaries in Delaware, in light of judicial review standards. The focus will be on directors because section II A and B explained how the construct is not used for officers and only recently was redeployed for controlling shareholders.

A *Judicial Use of the Standard of Conduct/Standard of Review Construct*

Recent opinions by Vice-Chancellor Laster succinctly contrast the two sets of standards. He explains how the "standard of conduct describes what directors are expected to do and is defined by the content of the duties of loyalty and care. The standard of review is the test the court uses when evaluating whether directors have met the standard of conduct."[65] In a subsequent opinion, he noted that Delaware has three tiers of review for evaluating director decision-making: the business judgment rule, enhanced scrutiny, and entire fairness.[66] He explained that the standard of review is "more forgiving of directors and more onerous for stockholder plaintiffs than the standard of conduct."[67] Applying the enhanced scrutiny standard of review to director conduct, Vice-Chancellor Laster nonetheless granted the director defendants summary judgment, even though they had acted unreasonably because plaintiffs offered no evidence that the directors had acted in bad faith.[68] Here we see that failing to comply with the more forgiving standard of review does not necessarily result in liability. The standard of review, therefore, although more lax than the standard of conduct, is not also a standard of director liability.[69]

The divergence of standards theory was first advanced by Professor Melvin Eisenberg in 1993.[70] Some Delaware judges subsequently seized on it in academic writings and judicial

---

[63]   Mark A. Hall, *Law, Medicine, and Trust*, 55 STAN. L. REV. 468, 490–91 (2002).
[64]   Eisenberg, *supra* note 4.
[65]   *In re* Trados Inc. S'holder Litig. (*Trados II*), 73 A.3d 17, 35–36 (Del. Ch. 2013).
[66]   Chen v. Howard-Anderson, 87 A.3d 648, 666 (Del. Ch. 2014).
[67]   *Id.* at 667.
[68]   *Id.*
[69]   An evident anomaly here will be addressed below.
[70]   Eisenberg, *supra* note 4.

opinions.[71] As David Kershaw notes, however, "there is no support at all for this distinction in *any* jurisdiction prior to very recent Delaware case law."[72] A words and phrases survey reveals that the Supreme Court made only seven references to "standard of conduct" in corporate fiduciary decisions before Professor Eisenberg's article, one in each of 1939, 1975, and 1985, and two in 1981 and 1991. In only three cases—one involving a charitable corporation—were both of the phrases "standard of conduct" and "standard of review" used by the Supreme Court before Eisenberg wrote.[73] After the article, the Supreme Court did not use the phrase "standard of conduct" for the next seven years. Since 1998, in many years the phrase has not been used at all, and in no year does it appear more than once.[74] Remarkably, only one Supreme Court case since Eisenberg wrote contains both the "standard of conduct" and "standard of review" phrases.[75]

The Supreme Court used the phrase "standard of review" by itself only eleven times in corporate fiduciary cases before Eisenberg's article, once in each of 1979, 1991, and 1992, twice in 1985, and three times in 1989 and 1990. Since 1993, that phrase has not been used in seven of the ensuing years, used once in eight years, used twice in seven years, three times in three years and four times in two years. The Chancery Court uses both phrases far more than the Supreme Court, but uses "standard of conduct" far less often than "standard of review," with use of the latter rising considerably since 2010.

This quite modern construct, in essence, serves to rationalize a potential disjunction between the demands of fiduciary duties and the more deferential judicial review of director compliance with those duties. It may not, however, play as central a role in the Supreme Court as is commonly thought, and it played a very limited role when Eisenberg wrote. Possibly, Professor Eisenberg did not so much describe an existent legal phenomenon but instead sought to launch one.

B *Anomalies*

The *Chen* decision, where the director defendants failed to comply with a standard of review more forgiving than the standard of conduct, but nonetheless were not liable, reveals an anomaly in the divergence approach. If plaintiffs had successfully offered evidence of, and ultimately proven, director bad faith, the director defendants would have been liable. But if directors had acted in bad faith, either by consciously disregarding their responsibilities or by acting in subjective bad faith, then "they breach their duty of loyalty by failing to discharge that fiduciary obligation in good faith."[76] A divergent, more deferential standard of review might filter out a liability claim earlier—although it did not do so in *Chen*—but the journey through such

---

[71] *See, e.g.*, William Allen, Jack Jacobs, Leo Strine, *Realigning the Standard of Review of Director Due Care with Delaware Public Policy: A Critique of Van Gorkom and Its Progeny as a Standard of Review Problem*, 96 Nw. U. L. Rev. 449 (2002). At the time of their writing, William Allen had retired as Chancellor of the Court of Chancery, and Jack Jacobs and Leo Strine were serving as Vice-Chancellors. Later, Jacobs and Strine became justices on the Delaware Supreme Court.

[72] David Kershaw, The Foundations of Anglo-American Corporate Fiduciary Law 185 (2018) (emphasis in original).

[73] Kahn v. Sullivan, 594 A.2d 48 (Del. 1991); Oberly v. Kirby, 592 A.2d 445 (Del. 1991); Smith v. Van Gorkom, 488 A.2d 858 (Del. 1985), *overruled in part* by Gantler v. Stephens, 965 A.2d 695 (Del. 2009).

[74] A table summarizing the Supreme Court's and Court of Chancery's use of the two phrases from 1939 through 2018 is available from the author.

[75] Gatz Properties, LLC v. Auriga Capital Corp., 59 A.3d 1206 (Del. 2012).

[76] Stone v. Ritter, 911 A.2d 362, 370 (Del. 2006). The Supreme Court recently forthrightly held that a *Caremark* claim was stated against directors for a bad faith breach of loyalty in an oversight context because the directors utterly failed to attempt to assure that a reasonable information and reporting system existed. Marchand v. Barnhill, 212 A.3d 805 (Del. 2019). This conclusion was reached in the straightforward manner proposed here.

a review standard is unnecessary given the absence of a breach of the underlying duty in either instance. The duty of loyalty (standard of conduct) here *is* the standard of liability, at least for money damages. One can argue whether intentional wrongdoing is too demanding a standard of loyalty (and liability), but that debate is not advanced by using a different standard of review.

Another anomaly emerging from the divergence construct involves the interaction between the duty of care and the business judgment rule. In *Cede & Co.* v. *Technicolor, Inc.*, the Supreme Court held that if a plaintiff overcomes the business judgment rule standard of review by establishing a breach of the duty of care, then the standard of review switches to an entire fairness standard, with the directors having the burden of proof.[77] No authority cited by the court supports that unprecedented ruling.[78] Overcoming one standard of review by proving a breach of a particular duty (care) thus leads only to invoking a second, stricter standard of review designed exclusively for a different duty (loyalty). Directors who believe ex ante that the pertinent standard for decision-making is to be careful, thus learn, ex post, that the standard has become a standard of fairness. The standard should not change retroactively.

Breaching a fiduciary duty by itself should create director liability, subject only to the issues of causation, damages, and exculpation. Again, the court in *Cede* was enamored by standards of review rather than directly focusing on fiduciary duties. And because a duty of care breach by directors simultaneously overcomes the deference of the business judgment rule review standard, the two standards align, not diverge.

C *Divergence or Convergence?*

The business judgment rule standard of review is the default standard of review and is "a presumption that in making a business decision the directors acted on an informed basis, in good faith, and in the honest belief that the action taken was in the best interests of the company."[79] To rebut the presumption, a plaintiff must provide evidence that directors "breached their duty of loyalty or care."[80] The duty of care, recall, is process-oriented only,[81] essentially demanding an informed decision-making process and due deliberation, and gross negligence is the standard by which the discharge of care is measured.[82] As a result, if a director complies with the fiduciary duty of care (standard of conduct) — setting loyalty aside — the business judgment rule standard of review obtains. If, however, a director breaches the duty of care (standard of conduct), the business judgment rule standard of review does not apply. The standard of review for the duty of care thus requires that the standard of conduct be fulfilled. The former is not more forgiving, it is equivalent in its demands, pointing toward convergence of the two, not divergence.[83]

As to loyalty, there appears to be no bifurcated standard of conduct-standard of review rubric for directors with respect to wrongfully usurping a corporate opportunity,[84]

---

[77] Cede & Co. v. Technicolor, Inc., 634 A.2d 345 (Del. 1994).
[78] Lyman Johnson, *Rethinking Judicial Review of Director Care*, 24 Del. J. Corp. L. 787, 799 (1999).
[79] Aronson v. Lewis, 473 A.2d 805, 812 (Del. 1984).
[80] RCS Creditor Trust v. Schorsch, No. CV 2017–0178-SG, 2017 WL 5904716, at *9 (Del. Ch. Nov. 30, 2017).
[81] *Brehm*, 746 A.2d at 264. As noted earlier, *supra* notes 15–16 and text, given this fact, substance should not be an element of the rule, not even the frail "rational purpose" aspect that often is mistakenly included. The quality of a business decision, as opposed to the quality of the decision-making process, should be off-limits under any judicial approach to reviewing the duty of care.
[82] Smith v. Van Gorkom, 488 A.2d 858, 873 (Del. 1985).
[83] *See* Johnson, *supra* note 16, at 651. Professor Kershaw also makes this point, Kershaw, *supra* note 72, at 108–09, 220–22, as does Licht, *supra* note 32, at 11–12.
[84] Broz v. Cellular Info. Sys., Inc., 673 A.2d 148 (Del. 1996) (multi-factor test as a guideline on corporate opportunity).

appropriating confidential information,[85] or directly competing with the corporation.[86] With respect to self-dealing, the default standard of review for a transaction not pre-approved by neutral directors or shareholders is entire fairness. Professor Eisenberg, however, stated that the standard of conduct also was fairness, thus himself aligning the two.[87] Even if the director standard of conduct is better described as "loyalty," not "fairness," where informed, independent directors or uncoerced, informed, disinterested shareholders approve a - transaction,[88] the duty of loyalty *is* fulfilled, even under traditional fiduciary principles.[89] Thus, the divergence of standards for directors seems narrowly to be that the default standard of review for self-dealing transactions lacking neutral pre-approval is entire fairness rather than the outright prohibition of such dealings seen in other fiduciary settings.

With respect to *Unocal* and *Revlon* claims, the ostensible standard of review is a demand for reasonable director conduct, but the monetary liability standard is, absent self-dealing, intentional wrongdoing, as *Chen* points out.[90] Or, if disinterested, uncoerced shareholders approve a transaction, *Corwin's* business judgment rule standard applies. The reality then, outside the injunction context, is that the *Unocal/Revlon* standard of conduct applicable to directors is to be careful and not engage in intentional wrongdoing. Factoring in injunctions as a possible remedy, the standard of conduct in the *Unocal/Revlon* setting is to be careful and behave reasonably. The standard of conduct thus converges with the remedial standard,[91] with no need for an intermediate standard of review.

D *Fiduciary "Law" for Directors*

Professor Eisenberg insisted that Delaware's standards of conduct are "law," as does Professor Julian Velasco, more recently.[92] Certainly, in states where the Model Business Corporation Act has been adopted, the standard of conduct set forth in Section 8.30 of that Act is "law" in the sense that it was adopted by legislative bodies. Its status in relation to the weaker standard of liability (Section 8.31) also contained in the Act remains unclear and problematic, however. Delaware has no statutory standard of conduct and director standards are not "law" simply because judges pronounce them; judges pronounce nonbinding dicta as well.

The conduct/review dichotomy fails the congruence feature argued by Lon Fuller to be one of eight necessary characteristics for a rule to be a "legal" rule and thus recognizable as law.[93] Congruence, for Fuller, demands that a rule as announced must be the rule as applied. It fails as well under an imperative theory of law described by Joseph Raz as an obligation backed by a sanction because, supposedly, as seen in *Chen*, violating a standard of conduct may not result in a sanction.[94] Even expressive theories of law, according to which laws embody and convey

---

[85] *See, e.g., Oberly*, 592 A.2d at 463 (it is an act of disloyalty for a fiduciary to profit from confidential corporate information).

[86] *See, e.g.,* Thorpe v. CERBCO, Inc., 676 A.2d 436, 442 (Del. 1996).

[87] Eisenberg, *supra* note 4, at 451, 464.

[88] *Corwin*, 125 A.3d 304.

[89] *Licht, supra* note 32, at 11.

[90] *See supra* notes 66–68 and accompanying text.

[91] Of course, the usual factors associated with injunctive relief will still apply, such as the likelihood of success on the merits and so on.

[92] Eisenberg, *supra* note 4, at 464 (conduct standards are "legal rules"); Julian Velasco, *The Role of Aspiration in Corporate Fiduciary Duties*, 54 Wm. & Mary L. Rev. 519 (2012).

[93] Lon Fuller, The Morality of Law 39, 81, 208–09 (rev. ed. 1969).

[94] Joseph Raz, The Concept of A Legal System: An Introduction to the Theory of a Legal System 126 (2d ed. 1980).

community norms,[95] would seem to demand that a potential sanction accompany the expression of norms, not that shared norms alone constitute law.

Analogies to constitutional review standards such as "rational basis" or "strict scrutiny" review in Equal Protection claims likewise are inapt.[96] In the former, the legislative standard for enacting economic regulation is that a law be "rationally related" to a legitimate government interest, the same as the judicial standard of review. In the latter, legislatures must narrowly tailor a law to advance a "compelling government interest," the same factors examined by courts. The legislators' lawmaking standard of conduct and the reviewing court's standard of review thus focus on the same factors.

The laudable aim for articulating demanding standards of conduct in corporate law, of course, is not just remedial. It seeks as well to have directors internalize the norms of care and loyalty. Other factors besides law also influence director conduct ex ante, however. Particularly in Delaware, judicial "sermonizing,"[97] the custom of providing lengthy and instructive dicta, evolving best practices promulgated by various professional groups and transmitted by lawyers, recent federal initiatives,[98] and community norms generally, all combine to produce more desirable governance norms. One hopes as well that loyalty remains a strong social norm — though doubt exists[99] — but the fact that various factors besides standards of conduct may improve director behavior ex ante does not give them the force of law.

Perhaps it does not matter whether standards of conduct constitute "law" under one or more jurisprudential theories to the extent they might diverge from standards of review. That alone may not be grounds to abandon them. It would, after all, be fairly disquieting to assert that there are no legal duties of loyalty and care for Delaware directors. The better move is the opposite — i.e., to employ fiduciary duties more explicitly, emphatically, and frequently. Delaware courts should acknowledge that there is less divergence than Eisenberg suggested, and where possible, downplay standards of review in favor of directly assessing whether directors fulfilled or breached a particular duty.[100] This will impart a renewed generative force to fiduciary duties in Delaware and, possibly, revive a slackened commitment to enforcing them.

IV CONCLUSION

Corporations have a more complex governance structure than other legal arrangements where fiduciary duties obtain. Three different actors — officers, directors, controlling shareholders — play disparate roles. Not surprisingly, then, the various aspects of the fiduciary duties owed by these diverse actors also differ. Discourse about fiduciary duties in Delaware corporate law should be more actor-specific, not general as in other areas.

[95] *See, e.g.,* Matthew D. Adler, *Expressive Theories of Law: A Skeptical Overview,* 148 U. Pa. L. Rev. 1363 (2000) (providing a description of expressive theories).

[96] *See, e.g.,* FCC v. Beach Commc'ns, 508 U.S. 307, 315 (1993) (rational basis); Loving v. Virginia, 388 U.S. 1 (1967) (strict scrutiny).

[97] Edward Rock, *Saints and Sinners: How Does Delaware Corporate Law Work?,* 44 UCLA L. Rev. 1009 (1997).

[98] The Sarbanes-Oxley Act of 2002 and the Dodd-Frank Wall Street Reform and Consumer Protection Act of 2010 are the outstanding examples. Each of these federal acts addresses, among other matters, officer and director-related governance matters.

[99] Lyman Johnson, *After Enron: Remembering Loyalty Discourse in Corporate Law,* 28 Del. J. Corp. L. 27 (2003) (citing indications of loyalty's decline as a shared business and cultural value). Professor Eisenberg argued more generally that common law doctrine must have "substantial support in the community." Melvin Eisenberg, The Nature of the Common Law 14, 29 (1988). If loyalty is waning as a cultural norm, that does not bode well for the duty of loyalty, if congruence between norms and law is important for legitimacy.

[100] Vice-Chancellor Laster very recently did just that. *Supra* note 22.

Relatedly, the particular duties owed by a challenged actor's behavior should receive greater judicial attention and standards of review should be downplayed in fiduciary analysis. Divergence between standards of conduct and standards of review is less common than appreciated and, generally, divergence is unnecessary. Restoring fiduciary duties to prominence will simplify judicial analysis and, one hopes, reinvigorate the much-needed qualities of care and loyalty.

4

Trust, Discretion, and ERISA Fiduciary Status

*Arthur B. Laby**

I INTRODUCTION

Debates over fiduciary status under the Employee Retirement Income Security Act of 1974 (ERISA) gained national attention in 2010 when the U.S. Department of Labor (DOL) attempted to expand the definition of an ERISA investment advisor fiduciary. The DOL proposed a significant new rule but withdrew it in the face of industry backlash.[1] It reproposed the rule in 2015 and adopted it in 2016 notwithstanding significant opposition from the business community.[2] The DOL's triumph, however, was short-lived. The U.S. Chamber of Commerce challenged the rule in the courts and won a resounding victory when a U.S. Court of Appeals vacated the rule in its entirety.[3] Controversy over the definition of an ERISA fiduciary is not limited to investment advisors. ERISA's definition of "fiduciary" raises questions regarding whether and when a large number of professionals and service providers, such as banks, brokers, advisors, insurance companies, trustees, and attorneys, are considered ERISA fiduciaries.

Although developments under ERISA are linked closely to the statute, ERISA law is also strongly connected to the broader fiduciary landscape. ERISA fiduciary law is based on the common law of trusts.[4] In *Firestone Tire & Rubber Co. v. Bruch*, the Supreme Court observed that "ERISA abounds with the language and terminology of trust law."[5] Therefore, it is not surprising that there are many parallels between ERISA law and the common law of fiduciary obligation with respect to determining fiduciary status. Yet commentators regularly fail to

---

* For helpful comments I thank Dana Muir, Robert Plaze, Jacob Russell, Natalya Shnitser, Peter Wiedenbeck, and participants at the Rutgers Law School Workshop on Fiduciary Duties in Business, the Ninth Annual Employee Benefits and Social Insurance Conference, and the Cambridge University International Fiduciary Law Workshop.

[1] *See* Definition of the Term "Fiduciary," 75 Fed. Reg. 65,263 (proposed Oct. 22, 2010) (to be codified at 29 C.F.R. pt. 2510) (withdrawn Apr. 20, 2015); *see also* JOHN H. LANGBEIN ET AL., PENSION AND EMPLOYEE BENEFIT LAW 475–76 (6th ed. 2015).

[2] *See* Definition of the Term "Fiduciary," 80 Fed. Reg. 21,927 (proposed Apr. 20, 2015) (to be codified at 29 C.F.R. pts. 2509, 25010) (proposal); Definition of the Term "Fiduciary"; Conflict of Interest Rule—Retirement Investment Advice, 81 Fed. Reg. 20,946 (Apr. 8, 2016) (adoption), vacated by Chamber of Commerce v. Dep't of Labor, 885 F.3d 360 (5th Cir. 2018). For a discussion, see Quinn Curtis, *Conflicts of Interest in Investment Advice: An Expanded View*, ch. 6 (this volume).

[3] *Chamber of Commerce*, 885 F.3d 360.

[4] *See, e.g.,* Central States, Southeast & Southwest Areas Pension Fund v. Central Transp., Inc., 472 U.S. 559, 570 (1985) ("[R]ather than explicitly enumerating *all* of the powers and duties of [ERISA] trustees and other fiduciaries, Congress invoked the common law of trusts to define the general scope of their authority and responsibility."); *see also* Dana M. Muir, *Fiduciary Relationships in Employee Benefit Plans*, ch. 10 (this volume).

[5] Firestone Tire & Rubber Co. v. Bruch, 489 U.S. 101, 110 (1988).

explore these parallels in any detail, and courts fail to recognize their implications—a gap filled by this chapter. My goal is to elucidate these comparisons and consider ways in which identifying them might lead to sounder decisions concerning who is considered a fiduciary. Given that ERISA is based on common law fiduciary duties, courts adjudicating ERISA fiduciary-related claims should pay close attention to common law fiduciary developments.

This chapter will explore three parallels between the common law and ERISA in determining fiduciary status. The first is the structure of fiduciary categories. In the common law, fiduciaries divide between categorical, status-based, or de jure fiduciaries, on the one hand, and ad hoc, fact-based, or de facto fiduciaries on the other. Categorical fiduciaries are treated as fiduciaries as a matter of law based on their professional or social status. They include trustees, partners in a general partnership, lawyers, company directors, and others. Ad hoc fiduciaries are considered fiduciaries on an ad hoc basis depending on the facts and circumstances surrounding their relationship with a principal. They include banks, accountants, advisors, clergy, family members, and many more.

The split between categorical and ad hoc fiduciaries exists within ERISA as well, although ERISA has its own vernacular. ERISA, for example, employs the term "named" fiduciary, analogous to a categorical fiduciary. And it uses the term "functional" fiduciary, analogous to an ad hoc fiduciary of the common law. Named fiduciaries (and certain other fiduciaries) are individuals or firms, which are always considered fiduciaries to an ERISA plan. By contrast, functional fiduciaries are individuals or firms which, depending on the relevant facts and circumstances, may be considered fiduciaries with respect to a plan. As in the broader fiduciary landscape, a professional—such as a lawyer, accountant, or trustee—who is considered an ERISA functional fiduciary for one plan might not be considered a fiduciary with respect to another. Furthermore, the key legal and policy debates in fiduciary law and fiduciary theory today concern who is considered an ad hoc fiduciary in the common law and a functional fiduciary under ERISA. The law regarding common law categorical fiduciaries and ERISA's named fiduciaries is fairly well-settled.

The second parallel focuses on the approach to determining fiduciary status. When determining whether a person is a common law fiduciary, some courts and commentators look to whether one person has discretionary authority over the assets or affairs of another. A focus on discretion has gained currency among many fiduciary scholars, who claim that discretion is an essential ingredient of a fiduciary relationship. Contrary to the discretionary authority thesis, however, other activities, such as providing advice, should and do result in a common law fiduciary relationship. The common law's emphasis on discretion parallels developments in ERISA. When determining ERISA fiduciary status, many courts focus primarily, if not exclusively, on whether a person has discretion over aspects of a plan or plan assets. Although discretion is an important component of ERISA's definition, it is only one consideration and ignores other aspects of the definition, such as whether a person provides investment advice. However, in the ERISA context, as we shall see, the DOL has limited the circumstances when one is considered an investment advisor fiduciary.[6]

A third parallel, closely related to the second, is the challenge under both the common law and ERISA presented by giving advice. Common law courts are inconsistent when considering whether advisors are fiduciaries. Under ERISA, the treatment of advisors is similarly unclear. Although the statute refers to investment advice, in 1975, the DOL instituted a five-part test for determining when a person provides such advice. Under the five-part test, the person must

---

[6] *See* 29 C.F.R. § 2510.3–21(c) (2016).

provide advice, on a *regular basis*, under a *mutual agreement*, where the advice is the *primary basis* for investment decisions, and the advice is *individualized* based on the particular needs of the plan.[7] Thus, the challenge in common law and under ERISA is to clarify whether and when advisors, and investment advisors, in particular, are and should be considered fiduciaries to their clients.

Fiduciary status is of paramount practical importance in the common law and under ERISA. In the common law, fiduciary status subjects the fiduciary to a heightened risk of liability and additional forms of punishment. Under ERISA, fiduciary status leads to an enhanced standard of conduct and a wide set of duties and obligations.

The chapter will proceed in five sections. Following this introduction, the next three sections will discuss each of the parallels mentioned above. Section V is a short conclusion.

II FIDUCIARY CATEGORIES

It is well-recognized in the common law that certain individuals and firms are categorical or status-based fiduciaries. Categorical fiduciaries are treated as fiduciaries as a matter of law by virtue of their status.[8] Other fiduciaries are ad hoc or fact-based fiduciaries. The latter group does not fit into a recognized category of fiduciaries. Instead, they are deemed to be fiduciaries on an ad hoc basis by virtue of the facts and circumstances surrounding their relationship with a principal. What is perhaps less well known is that ERISA mirrors this structure to a considerable degree. ERISA employs a system of named and functional fiduciaries analogous to the categorical and ad hoc fiduciaries of the common law. This section outlines the common law distinction between categorical and ad hoc fiduciaries and compares it to the ERISA regime.

A *Common Law Categorical and Ad Hoc Fiduciaries*

Categorical fiduciaries include those professionals and other persons who the courts always, or nearly always, treat as fiduciaries as a matter of law. They include trustees, guardians, partners in a general partnership, corporate directors, lawyers, and others.[9] Once an individual becomes a trustee, for instance, the person's status as a fiduciary is well accepted and seldom questioned. A trustee is a fiduciary based on her status as a trustee. The same is true for lawyers, guardians, partners, and so on.

The existence of categorical fiduciaries has advantages and disadvantages. One advantage is to provide legal certainty to both fiduciaries and principals in organizing their affairs. A second advantage is to provide broad fiduciary protections to principals in all relationships with these nominal fiduciaries. However, there are also drawbacks to this approach. First, rigid categories may promote the view that every objectionable act taken by a categorical fiduciary is a fiduciary breach when that is not the case.[10] Second, the approach can be overbroad. In some cases, a person may find herself to be a categorical fiduciary, but the actual relationship contains few or none of the features characteristic of most fiduciary relationships. In weighing the pros and cons, courts presumably have determined that the cases that would result in injustice are a reasonable

---

[7] *See id.* In July 2020, the DOL formally reinstated the five-part test, challenged in the litigation mentioned above. *See* Conflict of Interest Rule—Retirement Investment Advice: Notice of Court Vacatur, 85 Fed. Reg. 40,589 (July 7, 2020).

[8] Andrew S. Gold & Paul B. Miller, *Introduction, in* Philosophical Foundations of Fiduciary Law 2 (Andrew S. Gold & Paul B. Miller eds., 2014).

[9] *See id.* at 3.

[10] *See* Robert Flannigan, *The Boundaries of Fiduciary Accountability*, 83 Can. B. Rev. 35, 50 (2004).

tradeoff for the certainty that some relationships will always be considered fiduciary and the attendant protections provided.[11]

Fiduciaries other than categorical fiduciaries are ad hoc or fact-based fiduciaries. As the term "ad hoc" implies, these individuals or firms are considered fiduciaries on an ad hoc basis depending on the facts and circumstances of their relationship with a principal. Ad hoc fiduciaries are too numerous to list, but they include banks, accountants, advisors, clergy, family members, and many more. A bank, for example, although not normally considered a fiduciary to a customer, may be deemed a fiduciary if the bank gives advice or otherwise develops a relationship with a customer that is worthy of special protection.[12]

Courts determine whether someone is an ad hoc fiduciary by identifying attributes of the relationship apart from a category into which one of the parties might fall. Commonly cited attributes include trust and confidence, discretion, undue influence, vulnerability, dependence, inequality, and access.[13] Notwithstanding the large number of individuals and firms that have been deemed fiduciaries, courts tend to be reluctant to expand the number of ad hoc fiduciaries due to concerns over the expansion of liability.[14]

The difference between categorical and ad hoc fiduciaries is well accepted in fiduciary law. Perhaps less familiar is that ERISA's statutory and interpretive structure bears similarities to the common law regime, although the labels are not the same. I next describe ERISA's structure for determining fiduciary status and compare it to the common law.

B ERISA's Categorical and Ad Hoc Fiduciaries

ERISA's approach to fiduciary status parallels that of the common law. Although ERISA defines the term fiduciary in terms of particular functions, the statute also requires the existence of certain categorical fiduciaries, including "named" fiduciaries, who are always considered plan fiduciaries. This section outlines the difference between ERISA's categorical and ad hoc fiduciaries.

Before beginning a discussion of ERISA fiduciaries, let us briefly review an example of a common ERISA plan, to make the discussion that follows more concrete. Although there are many possible variations, consider a typical defined contribution plan governed by ERISA.[15] In this example, an employer, known as the "plan sponsor," establishes a plan to attract and retain quality employees. The employees, and perhaps former employees, who participate, and who are entitled to plan benefits, are the "plan participants." The plan will often have one or more trustees, often affiliated with the employer, such as corporate officers or directors. A trustee, however, can also be an unaffiliated third party, such as a bank. The trustee might then determine which investments will be offered to the participants, and monitor those investments, or the trustee might engage an investment manager to do that. The investment manager will often include its in-house investment products, such as mutual funds, in the menu of available options, as well as funds offered by other companies. The trustee might select a plan administrator; if no administrator is selected, under ERISA, the plan sponsor will be the administrator. The trustee might also select a plan recordkeeper, which keeps track of the plan participants, the

[11] *See* Robert Flannigan, *The Fiduciary Obligation*, 9 OXFORD J. LEGAL STUD. 285, 301 n.91 (1989).

[12] *See, e.g.,* Buxcel v. First Fidelity Bank, 601 N.W.2d 593 (S.D. 1999) (concluding that bank acting in an advisory capacity to loan customer was considered a fiduciary).

[13] *See* Paul B. Miller, *Justifying Fiduciary Duties*, 58 McGILL L. J. 969, 1010–11 (2013); Flannigan, *supra* note 11, at 302.

[14] *See* Paul B. Miller, *A Theory of Fiduciary Liability*, 56 McGILL L. J. 235, 241 (2011).

[15] *See* Muir, *supra* note 4 (explaining the difference between defined contribution and defined benefit plans).

investments they own, and the flow of funds in and out. In some cases, the trustee might perform the functions of the administrator or recordkeeper. In a defined contribution plan, the plan participants decide how to allocate their individual contributions among investment options.

Armed with this illustration of an ERISA plan, we can return to the difference between ERISA's categorical and ad hoc fiduciaries. For ease of explanation, I shall begin with a discussion of functional fiduciaries, analogous to ad hoc fiduciaries, and then move to a discussion of named fiduciaries and other categorical ERISA fiduciaries.

1 Functional Fiduciaries Under ERISA

ERISA contains a single definition of the term "fiduciary" in section 3(21)(A). The definition is functional in nature. Any individual or firm is considered a fiduciary if the person or firm meets the functional test. Generally, a person or firm is considered a fiduciary with respect to a plan "to the extent" that the person or entity:

- Exercises discretionary authority or discretionary control regarding plan management, or exercises any authority or control regarding the management or disposition of plan assets
- Provides investment advice for compensation with regard to plan assets, or has authority or responsibility to do so, or
- Has discretionary authority or discretionary responsibility with regard to plan administration.[16]

ERISA's functional fiduciaries are analogous to the common law's ad hoc fiduciaries. One must examine a person's activities—the relevant facts and circumstances—to determine whether the activities fall within the statutory functions.[17] Moreover, the DOL has clarified that professionals, such as lawyers, accountants, actuaries, and consultants, some of whom are otherwise considered fiduciaries, will not be deemed plan fiduciaries while performing their usual professional roles. However, if their activities fall within the functions set forth in ERISA section 3(21)(A), then those professionals would be considered fiduciaries to a plan.[18] As discussed below, like in the common law, the scope of responsibilities of a functional fiduciary is role-specific; becoming a functional fiduciary does not expose one to fiduciary liability with respect to all plan operations. Finally, like in common law, the definition of an ERISA fiduciary,

---

[16]   The section reads as follows:

> Except as otherwise provided in subparagraph (B), a person is a fiduciary with respect to a plan to the extent (i) he exercises any discretionary authority or discretionary control respecting management of such plan or exercises any authority or control respecting management or disposition of its assets, (ii) he renders investment advice for a fee or other compensation, direct or indirect, with respect to any moneys or other property of such plan, or has any authority or responsibility to do so, or (iii) he has any discretionary authority or discretionary responsibility in the administration of such plan. Such term includes any person designated under section 405 (c)(1)(B).

> Although this provision establishes the test for "functional" fiduciaries, possession of discretionary authority or discretionary control (under the third prong) is not exactly a function. This prong can be contrasted with the other two, which entail exercising authority or control or providing investment advice, which can both be better characterized as functions. Possession of discretionary authority or control is more akin to an attribute. In the ERISA context, however, this third prong is included as a "function."

[17]   See Peter J. Wiedenbeck, *Untrustworthy: ERISA's Eroded Fiduciary Law*, 59 Wm. & Mary L. Rev. 1007, 1015 (2018) ("Hence actions and authority, rather than formal conveyancing and consent, establish who owes duties to plan participants.").

[18]   See Questions and answers relating to fiduciary responsibility, 29 C.F.R. § 2509.75–5 (2020).

as a functional definition, means that the group of persons included in the definition is always expanding.[19]

One might object to the analogy from ERISA to the common law on the basis that courts deciding ERISA functional fiduciary cases look to a person's function whereas courts deciding common law ad hoc fiduciary cases look to the nature of the relationship between the parties. Courts deciding common law ad hoc fiduciary cases, in other words, must determine whether the relationship itself is characterized by trust, dependence, dominance, vulnerability, and so on. But an inquiry into a relationship, according to the objection, is different from an examination of a person's function.

The reply to the objection can be found in ERISA and cases interpreting ERISA. Under the statutory language, the functional inquiry often depends on whether a defendant exercised discretionary authority or control or possessed discretionary authority or responsibility. To make that determination, courts often must look into the nature of the relationship itself. For example, courts have examined whether the relationship between a service provider and a plan was characterized by influence[20] or control,[21] which would argue in favor of fiduciary status, or, in contrast, whether it was characterized by independence,[22] which would militate against it. Thus, for practical purposes, the functional inquiry often reduces to an examination into the nature of the relationship. The analogy, therefore, between ad hoc fiduciaries of the common law and functional fiduciaries under ERISA is apt.

2 Categorical Fiduciaries Under ERISA

In the ERISA context, so-called "named" fiduciaries are analogous to categorical fiduciaries encountered in the common law. They are considered fiduciaries with respect to an ERISA plan (although not all of their activities will necessarily be fiduciary activities). Moreover, for an ERISA named fiduciary, the functional analysis described above is unnecessary—a named fiduciary is a categorical fiduciary.

ERISA's named fiduciaries are a product of the statute, but not the definitional section discussed above. ERISA provides that every employee benefit plan must be established and maintained through a written instrument. The written instrument must provide for one or more "named fiduciaries." In some cases, the named fiduciary is the employer itself. In other cases, it can be the company's board of directors, an administrative committee, or another service provider.[23] In any case, the named fiduciaries must be given authority to control and manage both plan operation and administration.[24] Thus, ERISA contains a requirement for a written plan and for the naming of at least one fiduciary, or for a process to identify at least one named fiduciary. Moreover, the named fiduciary, or fiduciaries, will be vested with the authority to control and manage the operation and administration of the plan. ERISA also defines the term "named fiduciary" as "a fiduciary who is named in the plan instrument, or who, pursuant to

---

[19]   *See* Mertens v. Hewitt Assoc., 508 U.S. 248, 262 (1993) ("ERISA, however, defines 'fiduciary' not in terms of formal trusteeship, but in *functional* terms of control and authority ... thus expanding the universe of persons subject to fiduciary duties ....").

[20]   Pappas v. Buck Consultants, Inc., 923 F.2d 531, 538 (7th Cir. 1991).

[21]   Yeseta v. Baima, 837 F.2d 380, 385 (9th Cir. 1988).

[22]   Painters of Phila. Dist. Council No. 21 Welfare Fund v. Price Waterhouse, 879 F.2d 1146, 1150 (3d Cir. 1989).

[23]   Dep't of Labor, Employee Benefits Security Administration, Meeting Your Fiduciary Responsibilities 2 (Sept. 2017).

[24]   Employee Retirement Income Security Act (ERISA), 29 U.S.C. § 1102(a)(1) (2018). Although the plan must provide for at least one named fiduciary, the named fiduciary must not necessarily be named in the plan itself. The statute provides for other mechanisms to identify the named fiduciaries. *See* ERISA, 29 U.S.C. § 1102(a)(2) (2018).

a procedure specified in the plan, is identified as a fiduciary ... ."[25] The statutory language is clear, and the existence of ERISA's named fiduciaries is well accepted.[26]

An advantage to requiring at least one named fiduciary, like the common law identification of categorical fiduciaries, is legal certainty. Plan participants and beneficiaries will know who is in charge of the plan by reviewing the governing documents, and the appointments and delegations made under those documents.[27]

In addition to ERISA's named fiduciaries, the statute provides that an "investment manager" will be a fiduciary as long as certain conditions are met. The investment manager must have "the power to manage, acquire, or dispose" of plan assets, meet specific registration or qualification requirements, and have acknowledged in writing that it is a plan fiduciary.[28] Note that an "investment manager," a defined term under ERISA, is not the same as an investment advisor fiduciary, which is part of the functional definition discussed above. Moreover, the appointment of an investment manager insulates the plan trustee—a categorical fiduciary—from liability for most investment decisions.[29] An "investment manager" necessarily has discretion or control over plan assets, but an investment advisor fiduciary does not—a theme I return to below.

Finally, besides the designation of named fiduciaries and investment managers, ERISA provides a catch-all for other categorical fiduciaries based on the nature of their role. The DOL has stated that certain offices or positions, such as plan administrators and plan trustees, "by their very nature" qualify as fiduciaries.[30] To serve in those roles, the DOL explained that one would *necessarily* act as a functional fiduciary.[31] The DOL's determination is akin to common law courts holding that if one is acting as a trustee, partner, lawyer, and so on, then one is automatically a fiduciary because undertaking those roles raises certain risks that merit fiduciary protection.

To summarize, there are four categorical fiduciaries under ERISA: (i) named fiduciaries under section 402(a)(1); (ii) investment managers, as long as they meet certain statutory requirements; (iii) administrators, because they invariably function as fiduciaries; and (iv) trustees, because they have authority and discretion over plan assets unless otherwise provided. In addition to these categorical fiduciaries, anyone can be a functional fiduciary depending on the facts and circumstances.

3 Controversies in Fiduciary Jurisprudence

Before discussing how courts determine fiduciary status, it is worth noting that the key debates regarding fiduciary status typically are over ad hoc fiduciaries in the common law and

[25] ERISA, 29 U.S.C. § 1102(a)(2) (2018). The identification must be made by the employer with respect to a plan, by the employee organization with respect to a plan, or by both acting jointly.

[26] McCaffree Fin. Corp. v. Principal Life Ins. Co., 811 F.3d 998 (8th Cir. 2016); Nelsen v. Principal Glob. Inv'r Trust Co., 362 F.Supp.3d 627, 635 (S.D. Iowa 2019).

[27] *See* Paul J. Schneider & Brian M. Pinhero, ERISA: A Comprehensive Guide § 6.08[A] (4th ed. 2018); *Panel 4: ERISA and the Fiduciary*, 6 Drexel L. Rev. 359, 363 (2014) (comments of Russell Mueller).

[28] ERISA, 29 U.S.C. § 1002(38)(A) (2018).

[29] *See* ERISA, 29 U.S.C. §§ 1103(a)(2), 1105(d)(1) (2018).

[30] The situation is different for a so-called "directed trustee," who is subject to the direction of a named fiduciary (who is not a trustee). A directed trustee's duties are circumscribed compared to a discretionary trustee. *See* Employee Benefits Security Administration, Field Assistance Bulletin No. 2004-3; *see also* Susan Peters Schaefer & Joseph Kolbe Urwitz, *The Directed Trustee in the Post-*Dudenhoeffer *World*, BNA, Benefits Practitioners' Strategy Guide, Employee Benefits Litigation, Dec. 15, 2014.

[31] DOL-EBSA, Questions and answers relating to fiduciary responsibility under the Employee Retirement Income Security Act of 1974, Interp. Bull. 75-8, 40 Fed. Reg. 47,491 (Oct. 9, 1975), redesignated 41 Fed. Reg. 1,906 (Jan. 13, 1976), reprinted in 29 C.F.R. § 2509.75-8, at D-3. The term "administrator" is defined in section 3(16), and section 3(14) refers to administrators as fiduciaries. Trustees are governed by section 403 and deemed to have authority and discretion to manage and control plan assets unless otherwise provided.

functional fiduciaries in ERISA. The established list of common law categorical fiduciaries is well accepted and tends to engender little debate. If an established category of fiduciary actors were often challenged, the category would lose its place in the pantheon of categorical fiduciaries and instead be subject to determinations on a case-by-case basis. In some ways, the whole point of establishing categorical fiduciaries is to eliminate questions over their status.[32]

By contrast, a glance at the analogical reasoning employed in ad hoc fiduciary disputes reveals why these cases can be so vexing. The law applicable to ad hoc fiduciaries is based in some respects on the law of categorical fiduciaries.[33] Courts often analyze whether someone is an ad hoc fiduciary against a backdrop of categorical fiduciaries.[34] If similar concerns that arise in a categorical fiduciary relationship are present under a new set of facts, then those concerns will serve as reasons to find an ad hoc fiduciary relationship. This reasoning, however, is not based on any agreed set of criteria.[35] And courts are not always clear or consistent when explaining which relationships should be considered ad hoc fiduciary relationships.[36]

The same is true under ERISA—the real controversies are over functional fiduciaries, not named fiduciaries. Like in the common law, naming someone an ERISA plan fiduciary makes that person a fiduciary without inquiry into her function. However, if someone is not named as a fiduciary, one must still perform a functional analysis to determine if that person is a fiduciary. The definition of a functional fiduciary is complex, and many of the terms are subject to interpretation. A quick review of statutory terms, such as "authority" and "discretionary authority," "control" and "discretionary control," "management," "investment advice," "administration," and so on, reveals the difficulties surrounding whether someone will be deemed a functional fiduciary.

Moreover, two other considerations bedevil courts deciding whether someone is a functional fiduciary. First, one must properly apply the phrase "to the extent" in the definition. The definition states that "a person is a fiduciary with respect to a plan *to the extent*" he undertakes the functions in the definition.[37] This limitation is essential to the operation of ERISA's fiduciary principles. A person is only considered a fiduciary insofar that the person undertakes the particular functions described in the definition.[38] Second, one must consider the extent to which parties can define their roles by private agreement. In common law, businesspersons generally cannot completely contract around fiduciary duties.[39] Similarly, agreement in an ERISA plan document that a person will perform a "purely ministerial function" will not avoid fiduciary responsibility if the characterization is incorrect.[40] In both contexts, however, debates

---

[32] *See* Flannigan, *supra* note 11, at 289 n.45.

[33] *See* Mathew Harding, *Fiduciary Law and Social Norms, in* THE OXFORD HANDBOOK OF FIDUCIARY LAW 798 (Evan J. Criddle, Paul B. Miller & Robert H. Sitkoff eds., 2019).

[34] *See* Deborah A. DeMott, *Relationships of Trust and Confidence in the Workplace*, 100 CORNELL L. REV. 1255, 1265 (2015).

[35] *See* Miller, *supra* note 13, at 1010.

[36] *See* Evan J. Criddle, *Liberty in Loyalty: A Republican Theory of Fiduciary Law*, 95 TEX. L. REV. 993, 1034 (2017).

[37] ERISA, 29 U.S.C. § 1002(21)(A) (2018) (emphasis added).

[38] McCaffree Fin. Corp. v. Principal Life Ins. Co., 811 F.3d 998, 1002 (8th Cir. 2016).

[39] *See* Mark J. Loewenstein, *Fiduciary Duties and Unincorporated Business Entities: In Defense of the "Manifestly Unreasonable" Standard*, 41 TULSA L. REV. 411, 422 (2006) ("[T]hese and other cases demonstrate the continuing importance of fiduciary duties and suggest that courts will view waivers skeptically, at best."); *but see* Moshen Manesh, *Contractual Freedom Under Delaware Alternative Entity Law: Evidence from Publicly Traded LPs and LLCs*, 37 J. CORP. L. 555, 557 (2012)("Since August 1, 2004, limited partnerships ... and limited liability companies ... organized under Delaware law have been permitted to contractually modify, limit, and even eliminate the fiduciary duties of their managers arising under common law.").

[40] IT Corp. v. Gen. Am. Life Ins. Co., 107 F.3d 1415, 1419 (9th Cir. 1997).

flourish over the extent to which the parties can limit their fiduciary duties by private contract. These two considerations add to the difficulties in determining functional fiduciary status under ERISA.

The analogy between the common law and ERISA regarding the approach to fiduciary status is clear. The common law recognizes categorical fiduciaries. If one does not fall into a relevant category, the person may still be considered a fiduciary on an ad hoc basis. ERISA similarly provides for categorical fiduciaries. If one is not a categorical fiduciary, the person may still be considered an ERISA functional fiduciary depending on the person's function. And not surprisingly, the important debates today are over ad hoc and functional fiduciaries.

III DISCRETIONARY AUTHORITY

Now that we have established the parallel structure of fiduciary categories, this section looks more closely at determining the substantive approach to fiduciary status in the common law and under ERISA. When assessing the common law of fiduciaries, courts and commentators have increasingly focused on discretion as a necessary condition for a fiduciary relationship to arise.[41] This development also appears in the ERISA context. Many courts seem to view discretionary authority as the passkey to defining who can be an ERISA fiduciary. Discretionary authority is, of course, one important aspect of ERISA's definition. But some courts and commentators appear to view discretion as necessary, while the language of the statute is otherwise. This section discusses these developments and argues that an emphasis on discretion is incomplete. I begin with a discussion of discretion in the common law and proceed to related developments under ERISA's definition.

A *The Discretionary Authority Approach in the Common Law*

The discretionary authority approach to determining fiduciary status in the common law has gained currency among courts and commentators.[42] Under this approach, discretionary authority is often viewed as a necessary feature for a fiduciary relationship. In some respects, this is a logical claim. After all, the paradigmatic fiduciary is a trustee, who typically has broad discretionary authority. According to the *Restatement of Trusts*, a trustee has all of the power over the trust property that an individual has with respect to individually owned property.[43] Other fiduciaries similarly have discretion and control over a person or property. Consider guardians who are charged with making key decisions about the health, property, and affairs of their wards, who are often incapable of taking care of themselves.[44] In these paradigmatic cases, individuals who have power and control over others are charged with strict duties of loyalty and care because of the lurking danger of abuse and the risk of shirking.

Consistent with these paradigmatic cases, legal scholars have developed arguments to support the claim that discretion is a necessary feature of a fiduciary relationship. In 1975, Ernest Weinrib argued that two elements form the core of the fiduciary concept, namely the ability to exercise discretion and the discretion must be capable of affecting the principal's

---

[41] *See* Arthur B. Laby, *Advisors as Fiduciaries*, 72 FLA. L. REV. 953, 977–996 (2020); *see also* Kelli Alces Williams, *Self-Interested Fiduciaries and Invulnerable Beneficiaries: When Fiduciary Duties Don't Fit*, ch. 18 (this volume).

[42] For a more detailed discussion and critique of the discretionary authority view, *see id.*

[43] RESTATEMENT (THIRD) OF TRUSTS § 85 (AM. LAW INST. 2019).

[44] *See, e.g.*, Muse v. Treadaway, 561 S.E.2d 481, 482 (Ga. Ct. App. 2002); Nelson v. Nelson, 878 P.2d 335, 339-40 (N.M. Ct. App. 1994).

legal position.[45] In the 1980s, Tamar Frankel argued that one of two "central features" of fiduciary relationships is obtaining power to make changes that would affect the principal.[46] Deborah DeMott has explained that the only general assertion about the fiduciary obligation that can be sustained is that it serves as a device to control one's discretion.[47] More recently, Paul Miller has developed his fiduciary powers approach, arguing that, in a fiduciary relationship, one party (the fiduciary) exercises discretionary power over the significant practical interests of another.[48] According to Miller, possession of discretionary power over the practical interests of a principal is the "essential characteristic" of all fiduciary relationships.[49] In *Fiduciaries of Humanity*, Evan Criddle and Evan Fox-Decent make a related claim in the public law context.[50]

The discretionary authority approach has apparently convinced certain courts as well; some cases state explicitly that discretion is a necessary feature of a fiduciary relationship. In a leading insider trading case from the Second Circuit, *United States* v. *Chestman*, the court wrote, "A fiduciary relationship involves discretionary authority and dependency: One person depends on another—the fiduciary—to serve his interests."[51] Delaware Chancery has written, "The hallmark of a fiduciary relationship is that one person has the power to exercise control over the property of another as if it were her own."[52]

Although the discretionary authority approach is appealing, it is incomplete. The presence of discretionary authority might explain some common law fiduciary relationships—both categorical and ad hoc—but the approach is belied by many examples of fiduciary relationships that lack discretionary authority, particularly relationships between advisors and clients.[53] As a purely descriptive matter, there are many examples of fiduciary advisors in various contexts who do not possess discretionary authority. Clients may follow their advisors' advice most of the time, or perhaps all of the time, but the advisors lack the power to act on the client's behalf.

Furthermore, one might even view discretion in precisely the opposite way as those who promote a discretionary authority approach. Instead of viewing fiduciaries as endowed with discretionary authority, one might view a fiduciary as helping to ensure that a principal maintains the *principal's discretion* over her own affairs. Under the law of agency, for example, the agent acts subject to the principal's control—not the other way around.[54] Alice Woolley has

---

45   Ernest J. Weinrib, *The Fiduciary Obligation*, 25 U. Toronto L.J. 1, 4 (1975) ("First, the fiduciary must have scope for the exercise of discretion, and, second, this discretion must be capable of affecting the legal position of the principal.").

46   Tamar Frankel, *Fiduciary Law*, 71 Calif. L. Rev. 795, 808–09 (1983).

47   Deborah A. DeMott, *Beyond Metaphor: An Analysis of Fiduciary Obligation*, 1988 Duke L. J. 879, 915.

48   Paul B. Miller, *The Fiduciary Relationship, in* Philosophical Foundations of Fiduciary Law 69 (Andrew S. Gold & Paul B. Miller eds., 2014).

49   *Id.* at 90.

50   Evan J. Criddle & Evan Fox-Decent, Fiduciaries of Humanity: How International Law Constitutes Authority 31 (2016).

51   947 F.2d 551, 569 (2d Cir. 1991) (en banc), *cert. denied*, 503 U.S. 1004 (1992).

52   Sokol Holdings, Inc. v. Dorsey & Whitney, LLP, No. 3874-VCS, 2009 WL 2501542 at *3 (Aug. 5, 2009).

53   *See, e.g.*, Sec. & Exch. Comm'n v. Capital Gains Research Bureau, Inc., 375 U.S. 180 (1963) (holding that publisher of investment advisory newsletter was a fiduciary); MidAmerica Fed. Savings & Loan Ass'n v. Shearson/Am. Express Inc., 886 F.2d 1249, 1251 (10th Cir. 1989) (holding that broker-dealer for a non-discretionary account was a fiduciary resulting from broker's position of strength in the relationship); Hahn v. Mirda, 54 Cal. Rptr. 3d 527 (Cal. Ct. App. 2007) (holding that physician was a fiduciary in the capacity of failing to advise patient about a misdiagnosis); Cendant Corp. Sec. Litig., 139 F.Supp.2d 585, 608 (D.N.J. 2001) (holding that auditor who also provided advice was a fiduciary); Buxcel v. First Fidelity Bank, 601 N.W.2d 593 (S.D. 1999) (holding that bank acting in an advisory capacity to loan customer was considered a fiduciary and advice was conflicted).

54   The definition of agency posits that the agent acts subject to the principal's control. *See* Restatement (Third) of Agency § 1.01 and cmt. c (Am. Law Inst. 2006) ("The person represented has a right to control the actions of the agent.").

written that the attorney-client relationship allows the *client* to exercise discretion as opposed to the lawyer exercising discretion on the client's behalf.[55] A lawyer has a legal and ethical obligation to leave decision-making to the client.[56] A previous edition of *Black's Law Dictionary* explained that the term "advise" means that the person *receiving* the advice has discretion over whether she will follow it.[57] Although the discretionary authority approach is incomplete, it is widely held, and it finds strong support in the ERISA context, discussed in the next section.

B *Discretionary Authority Under ERISA*

Developments under ERISA are consistent with the discretionary authority approach applied in the common law. Certain ERISA courts seem to focus on discretionary authority, notwithstanding contrary language in the statute. General agreement exists that the definition of fiduciary should be broadly construed.[58] Yet, some ERISA courts and commentators appear to construe the definition narrowly to require the exercise or possession of discretionary authority.

The ERISA definition—slightly reordered here—provides multiple avenues to becoming a functional fiduciary:

- Exercise discretionary authority or discretionary control with respect to plan management[59]
- Possess discretionary authority or discretionary responsibility in the administration of a plan[60]
- Exercise any authority or control with respect to the management or disposition of plan assets[61]
- Render investment advice for a fee, with respect to the money or property of a plan[62]
- Have authority or responsibility to render investment advice for a fee, with respect to the money or property of a plan[63]

As a preliminary matter, note that ERISA does not define "discretion" and courts do not employ a consistent definition. The term, however, usually suggests decision-making power and not mere advice giving. The court in *Coldesina* v. *Simper* stated that discretion exists when a party has the "power of free decision" or "individual choice."[64] Other courts have expanded on this definition, stating that to have the power of decision or choice, "a person must know that he can decide an issue and be aware of the choices he has."[65] For a person to exercise discretion, he must "engage in conscious decision-making or knowledgeable control over assets."[66] Commentators suggest that discretion in the ERISA context essentially means having

---

[55] Alice Woolley, *The Lawyer as Fiduciary: Defining Private Law Duties in Public Law Relations*, 65 U. Toronto L. J. 285, 288 (2015).

[56] *Id.* at 312.

[57] Black's Law Dictionary 50 (5th ed. 1979).

[58] *See, e.g.*, Edmonson v. Lincoln Nat'l Life Ins. Co., 725 F.3d 406, 413 (3d Cir. 2013); LoPresti v. Terwilliger, 126 F.3d 34, 40 (2d Cir. 1997); Nelson v. Principal Glob. Inv'rs Trust Co., 362 F.Supp.3d 627, 635 (S.D. Iowa 2019).

[59] ERISA, 29 U.S.C. § 1002(21)(A)(i) (2018).

[60] ERISA, 29 U.S.C. § 1002(21)(A)(iii) (2018).

[61] ERISA, 29 U.S.C. § 1002(21)(A)(i) (2018); *see* Chao v. Day, 436 F.3d 234, 236 (D.C. Cir. 2006).

[62] ERISA, 29 U.S.C. § 1002(21)(A)(ii) (2018).

[63] ERISA, 29 U.S.C. § 1002(21)(A)(ii) (2018).

[64] 407 F.3d 1126, 1132 (10th Cir. 2005).

[65] Herman v. NationsBank Trust Co. (Georgia), N.A., 126 F.3d 1354, 1365 (11th Cir. 1997).

[66] *Id.* at 1367.

the final say over key decisions.[67] Discretion is not the same as control, although the difference between them is not clear. The *Coldesina* court said only that the distinction in the definition of fiduciary shows that Congress intended to treat control over assets differently than control over management or administration.[68] Other courts distinguish discretion or control on the one hand from mere influence over investment decisions on the other.[69]

Under ERISA, discretion and advice are separate concepts; discretion does not include advice. Only two of the five functions described in the bullet points above entail discretion— Congress included the word in some parts and omitted it in others.[70] Congress pointed to discretion as giving rise to fiduciary status, but Congress also pointed to advice as giving rise to fiduciary status. If discretion included advice giving, there would be no reason to enumerate both discretion and advice giving as separate bases for fiduciary status. However, several courts seem to impute a "discretionary" requirement into the entire definition. For example, in *Maniace v. Commerce Bank of Kansas City*, the Court of Appeals for the Eighth Circuit stated that "discretion is the benchmark for fiduciary status under ERISA." In *Maniace*, a relevant trust document limited the party's discretion and, therefore, the court reasoned, the party could not be a fiduciary.[71] Other courts repeat the claim that discretion is the benchmark for the definition.[72] In *Useden v. Acker*, the Eleventh Circuit repeated the entire definition but focused exclusively on the discretionary clause and applied the language to both a bank and law firm.[73]

In *Hecker v. Deere*, the Seventh Circuit addressed whether someone who serves as an investment advisor for a 401(k) plan is a fiduciary.[74] Under Deere's arrangement, Fidelity Trust advised Deere on what investments to include in the plans; another entity, Fidelity Research, advised the Fidelity funds offered by the plans. Deere and Fidelity Trust agreed that investment selections would be limited to Fidelity funds. The plaintiff claimed that Fidelity Trust and Fidelity Management were functional fiduciaries. In its analysis, the court stated that to find that Fidelity Trust or Fidelity Management were functional fiduciaries, one must look at whether they exercised discretionary authority or control over plan management, plan administration, or the disposition of funds.[75] There was no mention of whether the Fidelity entities would be considered functional fiduciaries by virtue of their role of providing investment advice for a fee.[76]

Other courts take a broader view—while still ignoring the advice prong—stating that *either* discretion *or* control is necessary to be considered an ERISA fiduciary. In *Herman v. Nations Bank Trust Company*, the court stated, "The plain language of the definition clearly states that

---

[67] Schneider & Pinhero, *supra* note 27, at § 6.08[D].

[68] *See Coldesina*, 407 F.3d at 1132.

[69] *See* Schloegel v. Boswell, 994 F.2d 266, 271 (5th Cir. 1993) ("Mere influence over the trustee's investment decisions, however, is not effective control over plan assets."); Pappas v. Buck Consultants, Inc., 923 F.2d 531, 535 (7th Cir. 1991) ("discretionary authority" and "discretionary control" refer to "actual decision-making power rather than to the influence that a professional may have over the decisions made by the plan trustees she advises.").

[70] *See* Chao v. Day, 436 F.3d 234, 237 (D.C. Cir. 2006) ("To the extent that the Useden court imports a "discretionary" requirement to the disposition clause, we reject its approach . . . .").

[71] 40 F.3d 264, 267 (8th Cir. 1994).

[72] *See* Nelsen v. Principal Glob. Inv'rs Trust Co., 362 F.Supp.3d 627, 635 (S.D. Iowa 2019). The *Nelsen* court later recognized that the defendants were fiduciaries because they acted as investment advisors. *Nelsen*, 362 F. Supp. 3d at 637.

[73] *See* 947 F.2d 1563, 1574-77 (11th Cir. 1991).

[74] Hecker v. Deere & Co., 556 F.3d 575, 578 (7th Cir. 2009).

[75] *Id.* at 583.

[76] Perhaps the framing of the allegation, and not the court, is to blame. The plaintiffs claimed only that Fidelity Trust "played a role" in selecting investments options. The court stated that merely playing a role or providing professional advice is not enough for fiduciary status. *Id.* at 584.

a person is not a fiduciary unless he either has discretion or exercises authority or control with respect to plan assets. If a person does not have discretion or exercise authority or control in a given situation, he does not meet the definition of a fiduciary."[77] This statement inexplicably ignores the investment advice prong of the definition, although, as discussed, the statute treats discretion and advice separately.

The DOL at times has fallen into a similar shorthand exposition of fiduciary status and focused exclusively on discretion. In a 2017 publication entitled *Meeting Your Fiduciary Responsibilities*, the DOL wrote, "The key to determining whether an individual or an entity is a fiduciary is whether they are exercising discretion or control over the plan."[78] The same bias is present among commentators. When first summarizing the definition of fiduciary, a leading casebook mentions discretion over plan administration and control over the management or disposition of assets but ignores the advice.[79] Then, after summarizing the entire definition, the authors remark that "ERISA's definition is discretion-centered."[80] In a brief mention of advice, the authors write that if a person provides investment advice for compensation, "fiduciary-level discretion is presumed."[81]

As I have tried to argue, however, there is no reason why discretion should be presumed if a person provides investment advice for compensation. The statutory language is otherwise. On several occasions, ERISA distinguishes between a person who has discretionary authority or control with respect to assets, on the one hand, and a person who provides investment advice for a fee with respect to the assets, on the other.[82] If investment advice always entailed discretion, there would be no reason for Congress to differentiate between discretionary authority and investment advice.

A brief detour into the federal securities laws demonstrates that investment advice is not always characterized by discretionary authority. The term "discretion" may not be defined in ERISA, but it is defined in the securities laws. The Securities Exchange Act of 1934 provides that a person exercises investment discretion if the person "is authorized to determine" which assets will be bought or sold for an account, or "makes decisions" as to what assets will be bought or sold for the account.[83] Not all paid investment advisors exercise discretion as defined in the securities laws. In fact, the Securities and Exchange Commission requires SEC registered investment advisors (many of whom advise ERISA plans) to disclose whether they have discretion over client accounts.[84] There is no doubt that some fiduciary advisors are shorn of discretionary authority. Thus, one should not assume that fiduciary-level discretion is presumed in the case of an ERISA investment advisor. The investment advisor portion of the ERISA definition is capacious enough to include discretionary and non-discretionary advisors. Why read this limitation into the text?

Even the dissent in the Fifth Circuit decision vacating the DOL rule, which argued for a *broad* interpretation of "investment advice fiduciary," inexplicably assumed that advice was coterminous with discretionary authority. After making this assumption, the dissent argued that the advisors covered by the DOL rule exercised discretion. But that reasoning was unnecessary,

---

[77] *See* Herman v. Nations Bank Trust Co. (Georgia), N.A., 126 F.3d 1354, 1365 (11th Cir. 1997).
[78] DEP'T OF LABOR, *supra* note 23.
[79] *See* LANGBEIN, ET. AL., *supra* note 1.
[80] *See id.* at 477.
[81] *See id.*
[82] ERISA, 29 U.S.C. §2510.3-101 (2018) (defining "plan assets"); ERISA, 29 U.S.C. § 1108(b) (2018) (providing exemptions to prohibited transactions); ERISA, 29 U.S.C. § 1108(b)(18)(D) (providing exemptions to prohibited transactions).
[83] Securities Exchange Act of 1934 § 3(a)(35); 15 U.S.C. § 78c(35) (2018).
[84] *See* Sec. & Exch. Comm'n, Form ADV, Part 1, Item 5(F), available at https://www.sec.gov/about/forms/formadv-part1a.pdf.

and not persuasive. Instead of relying on the definition of fiduciary in the statute, the dissent cited *Mertens v. Hewitt Associates*,[85] and argued that an investment advisor fiduciary exercises discretionary authority or control over plan management, administration, or assets.[86] The dissent, however, did not have to claim that the covered investment advisors exercise discretionary authority or control. The investment advice prong of the fiduciary definition is broader than that and does not reference discretion.

This section demonstrates that another strong parallel between the common law and ERISA's definition of fiduciary is the attention paid to discretion by courts and commentators. Although it is tempting to focus on discretion, given the paradigmatic fiduciary relationships, fiduciary law is richer and broader than the discretionary authority approach would suggest. A focus on discretion in the common law omits many fiduciary advisors, and the same is true in the ERISA context. In the final section of the paper, I shall examine when advice should be considered a fiduciary activity, both in the common law and under ERISA.

IV ADVICE AND FIDUCIARY STATUS

Section I demonstrated that the common law and ERISA both differentiate between categorical and ad hoc fiduciaries. Section II explained that both the common law and ERISA focus perhaps too narrowly on discretionary authority and neglect advice giving, which also can qualify one as a fiduciary. This section addresses when providing advice should generate a fiduciary relationship and, potentially, fiduciary liability. Common law courts are inconsistent regarding advice. Well-known common law cases such as *Burdett* v. *Miller* start from the proposition that investment advisors are not categorical fiduciaries.[87] However, years earlier, the U.S. Supreme Court suggested that the common law recognizes advisors as fiduciaries.[88] The treatment of advisors is similarly unclear under ERISA. Although the DOL put significant resources into a project to define an investment advice fiduciary, the Fifth Circuit, as discussed, vacated the DOL's rule. Thus, one faces a challenge in both contexts to clarify whether and when advisors and investment advisors, in particular, are and should be considered fiduciaries to their clients.[89] I begin with a discussion of advisors under the common law and then turn to ERISA.

A *Advisors as Common Law Fiduciaries*

Why are advisors considered fiduciaries under the common law in many circumstances, especially when they lack discretionary authority over their clients' assets or affairs? Why should the mere provision of advice lead to fiduciary liability? This is a complex question, which I have addressed in more detail elsewhere.[90] In this sub-section, however, I will outline my argument in brief. When certain individuals or firms provide advice, the advice is given in the context of a high level of trust, which becomes a key component of the advisory relationship. Trust is often accompanied by vulnerability and the potential for abuse through conflicts of interest, shirking,

---

[85]   508 U.S. 248 (1993).
[86]   Chamber of Commerce v. Dep't of Labor, 885 F.3d 360, 392 (5th Cir. 2018) (Stewart, C.J., dissenting).
[87]   Burdett v. Miller, 957 F.2d 1375, 1381 (7th Cir. 1992).
[88]   Sec. & Exch. Comm'n v. Capital Gains Research Bureau, Inc., 375 U.S. 180, 191-94 (1963).
[89]   For purposes of this discussion, I am omitting reference to investment advisors regulated under the Investment Advisers Act of 1940, which are always considered fiduciaries to their clients under the statute and cases interpreting the statute.
[90]   *See* Laby, *supra* note 41.

and other misbehavior, which a principal often cannot detect. The fiduciary duties of loyalty and care protect against those abuses.

Both advice and trust are complex concepts, and social scientists have explored their meanings in a variety of contexts too extensive to elucidate here. Instead, I shall briefly highlight the connection between advice and trust, which helps to inform why advisors, or many of them, are and should be considered fiduciaries.

The philosopher Edward S. Hinchman considers the act of advising a client to be an *invitation* to the client to repose trust in the advisor.[91] What makes advice different from other communications is that the advisor purports to act from a point of view that will help the client, and presumes to know as well or better than the client what is in the client's best interest.[92] An advisor invites the client to trust the advisor regarding the client's interests even if the advisor's perspective conflicts with the client's perspective.[93]

According to Hinchman's account, trust serves as the foundation of advice. The presumption inherent in advice giving is that the advisor gives the client a reason to act (regardless of whether the client actually acts) by virtue of the client's recognition that the advisor's reason for the client to act is what the advisor intends. As Hinchman writes, when you advise another, "you invite him to trust your perspective on what he should do: to treat it as a direct source of practical reasons, reasons grounded solely in your status as worthy of his trust."[94]

Understanding an advisor's role as inviting another to trust conforms with our intuitions about advice. When a career counselor advises a student about course selection, the counselor invites the student to trust her, and the student trusts (or may trust) that the counselor will advise based on the student's interests and not another criterion, such as what might be best for the school or another student. When a librarian advises a patron on a book selection, the librarian invites the patron to trust her, and the patron trusts the librarian to advise based on the reader's interests, not based on the librarian's own tastes, or her affiliation with the author. Trust is a key component of advice.

Trust, however, has a dark side. Trust and vulnerability often go hand in hand. Many definitions of trust point to the acceptance of a vulnerable situation where one person believes that another will care for the interests of the first.[95] Moreover, the greater the level of vulnerability one faces, the greater the potential for trust.[96] Trust and vulnerability can be viewed as inseparable—trust leads to vulnerability, but one's vulnerability also generates the need for trust.[97]

Once a client reposes trust in an advisor, he becomes vulnerable to various forms of abuse. Two forms of abuse ubiquitous in advisory relationships are receiving conflicted advice and receiving ill-informed or incomplete advice. Advice might be conflicted because it is motivated by an advisor's self-interest or interest in benefiting a third party. The client, however, may be

---

[91] *See* Edward S. Hinchman, *Advising as Inviting to Trust*, 35 CAN. J. PHIL. 355 (2005).

[92] *Id.* at 358.

[93] *Id.* at 359.

[94] *Id.* at 361.

[95] *See, e.g.,* Jay B. Barney & Mark H. Hansen, *Trustworthiness as a Source of Competitive Advantage*, 15 STRATEGIC MGMT. J. 175, 177 (1994); Mark A. Hall, Elizabeth Dugan, Beiyao Zheng & Aneil K. Mishra, *Trust in Physicians and Medical Institutions: What Is It, Can It Be Measured, and Does It Matter?*, 79 MILBANK Q. 613, 615–16 (2001); Mark A. Hall, *Law, Medicine, and Trust*, 55 STAN. L. REV. 463, 474 (2002); Denise M. Rousseau, Sim B. Sitkin, Ronald S. Burt & Colin Camerer, *Not So Different After All: A Cross-Discipline View of Trust*, 23 ACAD. MGT. REV. 393, 394–95 (1998).

[96] T.K. Das & Bing-Sheng Teng, *The Risk-Based View of Trust: A Conceptual Framework*, 19 J. BUS. & PSYCH. 85, 103 (2004); Hall, Dugan, Zheng & Mishra, *supra* note 95, at 615; Hall, *supra* note 95, at 474.

[97] *See* Hall, Dugan, Zheng & Mishra, *supra* note 95, at 615.

unaware of the conflict or unable or unwilling to inquire and protect himself. Or perhaps *because* the client trusts the advisor, he does not believe that any inquiry is required. Even if advice is not conflicted, the advisor might not have undertaken the proper amount of due diligence to ensure that the advice is sound. And the client is unable to monitor how much due diligence is necessary or even whether the advice is satisfactory. These vulnerabilities raise the need for legal protections.

The trust inherent in advisory relationships raises the risks directly addressed by the fiduciary duties of loyalty and care. The duty of loyalty, among other things, addresses conflicts of interest and helps ensure that an advisor acts in a client's best interest as opposed to the interest of the advisor or a third person. The duty of care helps ensure that an advisor is well-informed about the client's circumstances and undertakes the requisite diligence to serve the client's interests.

This claim is not new. The connection between trust and fiduciary duties has deep roots in case law and fiduciary scholarship. Deborah DeMott surveyed dictionary definitions of the term "fiduciary" and concluded that a fiduciary is someone who another should be able to trust to be loyal to the interests of the first.[98] Case law points to a relationship of trust as resulting in fiduciary duties.[99] Also, many courts characterize fiduciary relationships as relationships of trust and confidence.[100]

Notwithstanding the connection between trust and advice, not every act of advice giving leads or should lead to a fiduciary relationship. Indeed the guidance counselor and librarian mentioned above would likely not be subject to strict fiduciary liability. However, when certain persons or firms offer advice, a client will have a reasonable expectation that the advisor will act in a fiduciary capacity. The difficulty is determining when such reasonable expectations will arise. There is no single answer to this question. One must examine the social and economic context of the relationship and determine whether it is reasonable for a client to expect fiduciary liability to follow. These expectations are a matter of social customs and norms that develop over time as opposed to rigid criteria to be applied. As I have argued elsewhere, a key consideration is whether and how an advisor holds herself out to a client. If she holds herself out as a professional, who has developed expertise and can be trusted to apply that expertise to the client's situation, it is appropriate for a court to hold the advisor to a fiduciary standard.[101]

B ERISA Advisors

These common law principles can be applied in the ERISA context. As discussed, ERISA defines an investment advisor fiduciary as one who provides investment advice for compensation with regard to plan assets or has the authority or responsibility to do so. Not every investment advisor, however, is considered an ERISA fiduciary.

---

[98] DeMott, *supra* note 34, at 1259.

[99] *See, e.g.*, Calvin Klein Trademark Trust v. Wachner, 123 F.Supp.2d 731, 734 (S.D.N.Y. 2000) (fiduciary relationship can arise when "when one party's superior position or superior access to confidential information is so great as virtually to require the other party to repose trust and confidence in the first party."); Panato v. George, 383 N.Y.S.2d 900 (N.Y. App. Div. 1976) ("Broadly stated, a fiduciary relationship is one founded upon trust or confidence reposed by one person in the integrity and fidelity of another.").

[100] *See, e.g.*, Anderson v. ReconTrust Co., 407 P.3d 692, 697 (Mont. 2017) ("an otherwise arms-length relationship between a lender and borrower or applicant may ripen into a fiduciary relationship 'of trust and confidence,' with attendant fiduciary duties . . . .); TBF Fin'l, LLC v. Gregoire, 118 A.3d 511, 522 (Vt. 2013) ("The close relationship of trust and confidence necessary to establish a fiduciary relationship did not exist between the parties.").

[101] Arthur B. Laby, *Selling Advice and Creating Expectations: Why Brokers Should Be Fiduciaries*, 87 WASH. L. REV. 707, 767 (2012). Other relevant considerations are the advisor's primary role vis-à-vis the principal, and the advisor's compensation. *See* Laby, *supra* note 41, at 1016-18.

Limitations have been imposed both by governmental fiat and by the courts. As discussed earlier, in 1975, a year after ERISA was passed, the DOL adopted a five-part test to determine who is a fiduciary under the investment advisor provision in the definition. Under the test, an investment advisor fiduciary is someone who provides advice, on a regular basis, under a mutual agreement, where the advice serves as the primary basis for investment decisions and is individualized based on the needs of a plan.[102] (The limitations of the 1975 five-part test combined with changes in the retirement marketplace were reasons for the DOL's ill-fated 2016 rule.)

There can be little question that the five-part test has constrained courts in finding advisors that lack discretion to be fiduciaries. For example, in *Schloegel v. Boswell*, a bank established a profit-sharing plan, which purchased life insurance policies for Schloegel using funds from his profit-sharing account. Laurie Boswell was a pension consultant and insurance broker, who had advised the bank in various capacities for several decades. Boswell recommended that senior bank executives use assets from their profit-sharing accounts to purchase life insurance. He procured policies for Schloegel and received commissions on insurance premiums Schloegel paid.[103] The plan later discovered that the premiums ran afoul of federal tax regulations and canceled the policy. Schloegel and the plan sued Boswell for breach of fiduciary duty. The court determined that Boswell was not an ERISA fiduciary of the plan. After determining that Boswell did not have control over plan assets, the court turned to whether Boswell gave investment advice and the five-part test. There was no evidence in the record that Boswell gave advice "on a regular basis" or that Boswell and the plan had a mutual agreement that Boswell's advice would be the "primary basis" for the plan's investment decisions. The court concluded that the relationship fell short of what is required by the five-part test.[104]

Beyond the context of the five-part test, case law has limited the extent to which ERISA advisors are considered fiduciaries. *Hecker v. Deere*, discussed above, demonstrates that not every investment advisor for a plan will be considered a fiduciary. As mentioned, Fidelity Trust advised Deere on which investments to include in Deere's plans. Because Deere and Fidelity Trust agreed that selections would be limited to Fidelity funds, Deere and not Fidelity Trust had the "final say" on which investment options would be included.[105] Merely discussing these options with Fidelity Trust did not give Fidelity Trust discretion. Although the plaintiffs alleged that Fidelity Trust "played a role" in the selection of investment options, the court concluded that "[m]erely playing a role or furnishing professional advice is not enough to transform a company into a fiduciary."[106]

If playing a role in providing advice, or furnishing professional advice, are not enough to satisfy the definition, then what should be sufficient? To the extent an advisor "exercises *any* authority or control regarding the management or disposition of plan assets,"[107] the advisor will already be covered under the definition, and there is no need to determine whether she is an investment advisor fiduciary. The question becomes, should an investment advisor be an ERISA fiduciary when the advisor lacks authority or control over plan assets. This question is similar to the question posed under the common law: when should an advisor without discretion be considered a fiduciary?

---

[102]   *See* 29 C.F.R. § 2510.3-21 (2016).
[103]   994 F.2d 266, 268 (5th Cir. 1993).
[104]   *Id.* at 273.
[105]   556 F.3d 575, 583 (7th Cir. 2009).
[106]   *Id.* at 584.
[107]   ERISA, 29 U.S.C. § 1002(21)(A)(i) (2018) (emphasis added).

For the reasons discussed above with respect to the common law, one might look to whether an ERISA advisor is in a position of trust with respect to a plan, and the reasonable expectations of the plan sponsor and plan participants. In that regard, the *Chamber of Commerce* case, vacating the DOL rule, provides a helpful starting point when considering who should be an ERISA advisor.

The core of the *Chamber of Commerce* opinion focused on trust. Recall that the court was deciding a challenge to the DOL's expanded definition of an investment advisor fiduciary. As a lead-in to its decision, the court provided a short disquisition on fiduciary law. It began by explaining that by using the word "fiduciary," Congress intended to incorporate the well-settled meaning of the term in the common law.[108] The court explained that the intent to incorporate the common law definition was especially apt because of ERISA's common law roots. The court then explained that fiduciary status "turns on the existence of a relationship of trust and confidence between the fiduciary and client."[109] The court quoted no fewer than three venerable treatises to bolster the point that fiduciary responsibility is closely linked to trust and Congress intended to incorporate a relationship of trust and confidence into the meaning of fiduciary.[110]

The court's focus on trust as a justification for a fiduciary duty on advisors was sound. The court, however, veered off track when it applied its analysis to broker-dealers and others, and found that no such relationship of trust exists with these professionals. The court concluded that stockbrokers and insurance agents are not fiduciaries when selling products to their clients.[111] Stockbrokers and insurance agents, the court stated, are paid only for completed sales, and not based on their pitch. Although the court is correct that historically brokers engaged primarily in sales (and gave only incidental advice), while investment advisors engaged exclusively in investment counsel, that distinction belongs to a bygone era.[112] Today, a stockbroker's role is primarily advice giving; execution of a securities transaction is accomplished in milliseconds with a stroke of a key or a tap on a mobile device. The court ignored reality when it concluded that brokers do not render investment advice.[113]

Instead, like in the common law, a better approach would be to determine if a person holds herself out as an advisor and invites a relationship of trust. If yes, then a customer or client would reasonably expect the fiduciary protections discussed above and the advisor should be considered a fiduciary—even if the advisor lacks discretion or control. If a person holds herself out as a trusted advisor, the person should be considered a fiduciary under the common law and ERISA.[114]

---

[108]   Chamber of Commerce v. Dep't of Labor, 885 F.3d 360, 369-70 (5th Cir. 2018).

[109]   *Id.* at 370.

[110]   *Id.* at 370-71.

[111]   *Id.* at 372.

[112]   *See* Arthur B. Laby, *Reforming the Regulation of Broker-Dealers and Investment Advisers*, 65 Bus. Law. 395, 421-24 (2010).

[113]   *Chamber of Commerce*, 885 F.3d at 373. The court also appears to have misread the statute. The court wrote, "Only in DOL's semantically created world do salespeople and insurance brokers have 'authority' or 'responsibility' to 'render investment advice.'" *Id.* at 373. But that is not what the statute requires. The definition of fiduciary states that a person is a fiduciary if she "renders investment advice for a fee or other compensation, direct or indirect, with respect to any moneys or other property of such plan, or has any authority or responsibility to do so . . . ." Thus, as long as the broker actually renders advice, she is picked up by definition, regardless of whether she is given the formal authority to do so. As I have documented elsewhere, there can be little doubt that brokers provide advice. *See* Laby, *supra* note 101.

[114]   The same is true under Securities and Exchange Commission regulation—although not the focus of this paper. The SEC's adoption of Regulation Best Interest applies this reasoning to broker-dealers, who historically were not considered fiduciaries to their customers, and applies a best interest standard. *See* Regulation Best Interest: The Broker-Dealer Standard of Conduct, 84 Fed. Reg. 33,318, 33,434 (July 12, 2019) ("Regulation Best Interest enhances

v CONCLUSION

The courts teach that both ERISA and the common law of fiduciary obligation are based on the common law of trusts. Thus, when evaluating fiduciary status, it is no surprise to see similarities under the common law and ERISA regulation. Both have a similar structure with respect to categorical and ad hoc fiduciaries. The important debates today in both contexts are over who is an ad hoc fiduciary. Both look—perhaps too narrowly—to the feature of discretion to decide fiduciary status and sometimes ignore advice giving as a predicate to fiduciary responsibility. Both grapple with whether advice giving should lead to fiduciary liability. This chapter addresses these parallels and considers their implications. To the extent that any advisor, whether under ERISA or the common law, holds herself out as a trusted professional and engenders a reasonable expectation of fiduciary protections, courts and regulators should treat the person as a fiduciary, regardless of whether the person has discretionary authority over another's assets or affairs.

the broker-dealer standard of conduct beyond existing suitability obligations, and aligns the standard of conduct with retail customers' reasonable expectations.").

5

Examining Indenture Trustee Duties

*Steven L. Schwarcz**

I INTRODUCTION

This volume's topic—fiduciary obligations in business—often focuses on corporate governance. In contrast, this chapter examines fiduciary and other obligations that apply to indenture governance—the manner in which indenture trustees should exercise power in managing the administration of bond indentures on behalf of investors.[1] A bond indenture refers, in this context, to the contract governing the relationship between investors in, and the issuer of, corporate bonds.[2] Indentures are customarily administered by financial institutions which, in that administrative role, are called indenture trustees.[3] For simplicity, this chapter will refer to indenture trustees performing that role as "trustees," without suggesting they have, or should have, the fiduciary duties of a common law trustee.[4]

In contrast to shareholders, who are the primary beneficiaries of corporate governance, bondholders are the primary beneficiaries of indenture governance. Therefore, in a sense, indenture governance is to bondholders as corporate governance is to shareholders. Although that analogy provides a perspective, it is, of course, imperfect.

For example, because bondholders are only entitled to principal and accrued interest on their investments, indenture governance should seek to protect that value.[5] In contrast, because shareholders are residual claimants of the firm (and entitled to all surplus value),

---

   * This chapter is based largely on *Indenture Trustee Duties: The Pre-Default Puzzle*, 88. U. Cin. L. Rev. 659 (2020), part of a symposium issue based on the University of Cincinnati College of Law 30th Corporate Law Symposium, on "The Business Uses of Trust."

   [1] Indenture governance is thus different than what scholars sometimes call "debt governance," which refers to how debt may discipline corporate performance or otherwise intersect with governance.

   [2] In this chapter, the term "bonds" includes all long-term corporate debt securities.

   [3] Richard T. McDermott, Legal Aspects of Corporate Finance 144–45, 154–56 (3d ed. 2000). Indenture trustees administer indentures for virtually all issuers of bonds, both in the United States and abroad. *Cf.* Steven L. Schwarcz, *Commercial Trusts*, available at http://ssrn.com/abstract=2182267 (discussing indenture trustees for bonds issued in China).

   [4] *Cf.* Meckel v. Cont'l Res. Co., 758 F.2d 811, 816 (2d Cir. 1985) ("Unlike the ordinary trustee, who has historic common-law duties imposed beyond those in the trust agreement, an indenture trustee is more like a stakeholder whose duties and obligations are exclusively defined by the terms of the indenture agreement."); *In re* E. F. Hutton Sw. Prop. II, Ltd. v. Union Planters Nat'l Bank, 953 F.2d 963, 969 (5th Cir. 1992) ("There is no doubt . . . that if an indenture trustee owes any fiduciary duties to the beneficiary above and beyond those duties explicitly recited in the trust indenture, they are much more attenuated than those normally owed by trustees.").

   [5] *See* Steven L. Schwarcz, *Commercial Trusts as Business Organizations: Unraveling the Mystery*, 58 Bus. Law. 559, 561 (2003).

corporate governance should seek to increase shareholder value.[6] Also, measured solely by the amounts invested, indenture governance would appear to be more important than corporate governance. Worldwide, bondholders invest many times the amount invested by shareholders.[7] Realistically, though, corporate governance is considered more important for several reasons: corporations and stock markets are much more visible, and thus more tangible, to most people; and because corporate governance seeks to increase shareholder value, it involves much more judgment and discretion, and thus can be more nuanced and interesting (and more desirable of scholarly study), than indenture governance.

Indenture governance is nonetheless interesting and critically important. Historically—and as this chapter explains, also logically—indenture governance bifurcates trustee duties into two time periods: pre-default, and post-default. Post-default, meaning after a formal "Event of Default" has occurred (and while it remains continuing) under an indenture,[8] U.S. and most foreign law requires the trustee to act on behalf of the bondholders as would a prudent person in similar circumstances regarding its own affairs.[9] Many post-default decisions—such as whether to accelerate debt or liquidate collateral—require exquisite judgment calls, and ex ante no given decision may be clearly right.[10] Decision making is made more difficult by what I have called a "protection gap": when things go wrong, investors often blame parties with deep pockets, especially trustees, for failing to protect them.[11] I previously have analyzed this post-default decision making from a normative perspective.[12]

The analysis of post-default indenture governance becomes even more complex when the bondholders themselves have conflicting interests—such as conflicting priorities or conflicting sources of payment. Then, the trustee not only is subject to being second-guessed ex post for decisions that are essentially judgment calls, but also faces the difficult task of trying to understand and balance the respective obligations owed to conflicting classes—sometimes called "tranches"—of investors. The law does not clearly address bondholder conflicts. Although trust law addresses conflicts among gratuitous-trust beneficiaries by imposing a duty of impartiality on the trustee, that duty does not extend to commercial trusts.[13] I previously have also analyzed, again from a normative perspective, post-default decision making in the face of bondholder conflicts.[14]

---

[6] *See id.*

[7] *See, e.g.,* SIFMA FACT BOOK 45-46 (2018), https://www.sifma.org/wp-content/uploads/2017/08/US-Fact-Book-2018-SIFMA.pdf (showing that, in 2017, global long-term bond issuance was $21,099.7 billion versus global equity issuance of only $720.7 billion—or almost 30 times higher).

[8] Indentures customarily define an Event of Default as a default that continues after notice or a specified lapse of time, or both.

[9] *See, e.g.,* Trust Indenture Act of 1939 § 315(c), 15 U.S.C. § 77ooo(c) ("The indenture trustee shall exercise in case of default . . . the same degree of care and skill . . . as a prudent man would exercise or use under the circumstances in the conduct of his own affairs."); RESTATEMENT (THIRD) OF TRUSTS § 77(1) (AM. LAW INST. 2007) ("The trustee has a duty to administer the trust as a prudent person would, in light of the purposes, terms, and other circumstances of the trust."); Solomon Y. Deku, Alper Kara, & David Marques-Ibanez, *Trustee Reputation in Securitization: When Does It Matter?*, at 5 (2018), http://irep.ntu.ac.uk/id/eprint/33837/1/11286_Deku.pdf (stating that the post-default prudent-person standard applies in the United Kingdom). *Cf.* Corporation Act, 2001, § 283DA(c) (Austl.) (requiring a trustee to "do everything in its power to ensure that the [issuer] remedies any breach" unless the breach is immaterial).

[10] *See* Steven L. Schwarcz & Gregory M. Sergi, *Bond Defaults and the Dilemma of the Indenture Trustee*, 59 ALA. L. REV. 1037, 1040 (2008) ("Indenture trustees for defaulted bonds . . . face the conundrum that they are required to act prudently but lack clear guidance on what prudence means.").

[11] Steven L. Schwarcz, The Roberta Mitchell Lecture: *Structuring Responsibility in Securitization Transactions*, 40 CAPITAL U. L. REV. 803, 804 (2012).

[12] *See id.* at 810; *see also* Schwarcz & Sergi, *supra* note 10.

[13] Meckel v. Cont'l Res. Co., 758 F.2d 811, 816 (2d Cir. 1985) (indenture trustees, unlike ordinary trustees, are not subject to a duty of undivided loyalty).

[14] Steven L. Schwarcz, *Fiduciaries With Conflicting Obligations*, 94 MINN. L. REV. 1867 (2010).

Pre-default indenture governance, however, has even less legal guidance. However, it is critical to define a trustee's pre-default duties because activist investors, including hedge funds and so-called "vulture fund" investors that purchase defaulted bonds at deep discounts, increasingly are making pre-default demands on trustees. Activist investors are also suing trustees for losses on their bonds, alleging the trustee should have taken pre-default actions to protect the bonds. Trustees must know how to respond.

This chapter therefore examines and attempts to provide guidance for pre-default indenture governance. To that end, the next section provides a historical overview of a trustee's pre-default duties. The third section then analyzes, more normatively, a trustee's pre-default role. Thereafter, the fourth section applies that normative analysis to the types of pre-default issues that may arise in lawsuits against trustees. Finally, the concluding section examines steps that trustees could take to help guide their decision making when investors make pre-default demands.

II HISTORICAL OVERVIEW

The history of enactment in the United States of the Trust Indenture Act of 1939 (the "TIA"), which provides a statutory framework for the conduct of trustees under TIA-qualified indentures,[15] provides a valuable record of the original debate over the trustee's pre-default responsibilities. Congress enacted the TIA in order to restore investor confidence in the bond markets following the stock-market crash of 1929 and the ensuing Great Depression. Although the TIA currently requires the appointment of a trustee for bondholders in most public bond issuances over $10 million,[16] many of its fundamental principles—including those articulating the trustee's role—are followed in the model indenture provisions included in virtually all bond indentures.[17] The trustee's basic role, according to the TIA, is to help solve the collective action problem that individual bondholders may be unable to coordinate their actions with other bondholders effectively.[18]

The 1929 report of the Securities and Exchange Commission ("SEC") that led to the enactment of the TIA criticized the passive, or "ministerial," pre-default role generally taken at that time by indenture trustees.[19] The SEC recommended that a post-default "prudent man" standard should apply to trustee performance both prior to, and after, the occurrence of an Event of Default,[20] and that trustees should be required to actively monitor actions of an issuer.[21] Almost a decade later, when the TIA was enacted, however, the pre-default ministerial role had become widely accepted in market practice and was codified into the TIA.[22]

---

[15] Trust Indenture Act of 1939, ch. 411, 53 Stat. 1149 (1939) (codified as amended at 15 U.S.C. §§ 77aaa–77bbbb).
[16] 15 U.S.C. § 77ddd(a)(9).
[17] *Cf. infra* note 111(illustrating model indenture provisions).
[18] *See* 15 U.S.C. § 77bbb(a)(1) (stating that the TIA was enacted because "individual action by [investors] . . . is rendered impracticable by reason of the disproportionate expense," "concerted action by [investors] in their common interest is impeded by reason of the wide dispersion of [investors] through many states," and relevant information may not be available to all investors).
[19] Sec. & Exch. Comm'n, Report on the Study and Investigation of the Work, Activities, Personnel, and Functions of Protective and Reorganization Committees, Part VI—Trustees Under Indentures 110 (1936).
[20] Wilber G. Katz, *Trustees and Federal Trust Indenture Act*, 26 A.B.A. J. 290, 291 (1940).
[21] Stewart M. Robertson, *Debenture Holders and the Indenture Trustee: Controlling Managerial Discretion in the Solvent Enterprise*, 11 Harv. J. L. & Pub. Pol'y 461, 472–73 (1988).
[22] 15 U.S.C. § 77ooo(a)(1).

The trustee's pre-default duties have not been seriously re-examined since 1929 (when the SEC report was written), although the bond market has changed dramatically since then. Banks, pension funds, hedge funds, and other institutional investors now dominate; there are few individual retail bond market investors. Indeed, institutional investors now hold over 80 percent of corporate and foreign bonds.[23] By virtue of their sophistication and the size of their bondholding, institutional investors face less of a collective action problem than retail investors.[24] Moreover, certain institutional investors are increasingly actively engaging in high-risk strategic investing.

Whether or not due to these market changes, there are at least two views today of the trustee's pre-default role. By far the dominant view—and the view that comports with existing law and the plain language of indentures—is that trustees have no fiduciary duties to investors prior to an Event of Default.[25] Rather, their duties are ministerial and limited to the specific contractual obligations specified in the indenture.[26] Those obligations typically include administrative functions such as document custody, payment-priority ("waterfall") analytics, and payment processing.

Since the 2007–08 financial crisis (the "financial crisis"), some investors argue that trustees—especially trustees of securitized bond issues—should have some pre-default fiduciary duties. Understanding this requires an understanding of the categories of bond issues. In unsecured bond issues, which dominate bond issuance, the trustee acts for the benefit of investors whose right to payment is based on a contract claim against the issuer, little different from how an "agent bank" acts for a syndicate of unsecured lenders.[27] In secured bond issues, the trustee acts that same way and, usually, also as a collateral agent for the investors. In securitized bond issues,[28] however, the trustee acts for the benefit of investors whose right to payment is limited to collections on specified financial assets, such as mortgage loans, that have been purchased by a trust or other special purpose entity.[29]

---

[23] Financial Account of the United States: Flow of Funds, Balance Sheets, and Integrated Macroeconomic Accounts; Second Quarter 2015, table F-122 (Sept. 18, 2015), https://www.federalreserve.gov/releases/z1/20150918/z1r-1.pdf.

[24] *Cf.* Andrei Shleifer & Robert W. Vishny, *Large Shareholders and Corporate Control*, 94 J. Political Econ. 461, 462 (1986) (making that argument in the context of large shareholders).

[25] Even after its post-default duties are triggered, the trustee is not a traditional fiduciary-trustee. Schwarcz & Sergi, *supra* note 10, at sections III(A) and IV(A).

[26] *See, e.g.*, Trust Indenture Act, 15 U.S.C. § 77ooo(a)(1); Elliott Assocs. v. J. Henry Schroder Bank & Trust Co., 838 F.2d 66, 68–71 (2d Cir. 1988) (holding that a trustee's pre-default duties are limited to those duties expressly provided in the indenture).

[27] Unsecured bond issues create, at most, a hybrid form of a trust because there is, technically, no trust corpus. *See Commercial Trusts as Business Organizations*, *supra* note 5, at 569–70. *Cf.* Restatement (Third) of Trusts § 2 cmt. f (Tentative Draft No. 1, 1996) (emphasis added): "A trust involves three elements: (1) a trustee, who holds the trust property and is subject to duties to deal with it for the benefit of one or more others; (2) one or more beneficiaries, to whom and for whose benefit the trustee owes the duties with respect to the trust property; and (3) *trust property, which is held by the trustee for the beneficiaries*."

[28] The indenture in a securitized bond issue is often designated a pooling and servicing agreement, or "PSA." In the author's experience, the relevant provisions concerning the trustee of a securitized bond issue are identical whether it uses an indenture or a PSA (and this Chapter generically will refer to both as an "indenture"). Also, some securitized bond issues, even though involving a public offering, have been interpreted to be outside the scope of the TIA. *See* Ret. Bd. of Police v. Bank of New York Mellon, 775 F.3d 154 (2d Cir. 2014) (holding that certain pass-through mortgage-backed securities were exempt from the TIA under § 304(a)(2) because they were "'certificate[s] of interest or participation in two or more securities having substantially different rights and privileges,' namely, the numerous mortgage loans held by each trust"). This chapter's normative analysis of securitized bond issues is not dependent on whether such bond issues are subject to the TIA.

[29] Steven L. Schwarcz, *What is Securitization? And for What Purpose?*, 85 S. Cal. L. Rev. 1283, 1295–98 (2012).

Even prior to the financial crisis, certain credit-rating agencies had suggested that trustees of securitized bond issues may have greater duties than trustees of other categories of bond issues. Standard & Poor's ("S&P") stated, for example, that trustees of securitized bond issues consisting of mortgage-backed securities ("MBS") "act as fiduciaries that protect the interests of" investors.[30] Moody's Investors Service ("Moody's") stated that trustees in MBS transactions have an affirmative duty to investigate likely servicer defaults and be proactive participants.[31] In contrast, however, Fitch Ratings stated that such "unrealistic reliance on trustees" in MBS and other securitization transactions not only "misses the mark," but also "increases the risk to investors by potentially masking other more important considerations" such as the quality of servicer performance.[32] An FDIC manual regarding MBS trusteeships suggests that trustees of securitized bond issues have duties to ensure that the underlying loans are "properly serviced." However, that manual states that it is intended to provide general guidance subject to the provisions of governing agreements and "duties and actions are specified in the indenture and the corporate trustee/agent is limited to the provisions of the indenture."[33]

At least during the financial crisis, some practitioners also have observed expectations that trustees of securitized bond issues may have higher pre-default duties than trustees of other bond issues.[34] Whether or not inspired by these precedents, the author has seen a number of complaints in recent lawsuits alleging that pre-default, a trustee of a securitized bond issue should "police the deal" for or otherwise protect the investors.[35] To date, however, courts have not ruled that trustees have greater duties in securitized bond issues.

III ANALYZING PRE-DEFAULT DUTIES

To analyze what a trustee's pre-default duties should be, consider the possible normative frameworks for legally imposing duties in a business context. There appear to be at least two potentially overlapping frameworks: to correct market failures, discussed in sub-section A, and maximize efficiency, discussed in sub-section B. Sub-section C also considers a formalistic rationale for imposing such duties. Based on that analysis, sub-section D articulates a normative rule for determining a trustee's pre-default duties.

---

[30] Standard & Poor's Corporation, S&P's Structured Finance Criteria 100 (1988).

[31] Claire Robinson, *Moody Re-examines Trustee's Roles in ABS and MBS*, at 3–4, Moody's Rating Methodology Report (Feb. 4, 2003).

[32] Fitch Ratings, *Seller/Servicer Risk Trumps Trustee's Role in U.S. ABS Transactions* (Feb. 24, 2003).

[33] FDIC Manual, Section 6, Part C.

[34] *See, e.g.*, Christopher J. Brady, Marla Chernof Cohen, & Harold L. Kaplan, *The Role of the Trustee in Securitization Transactions, in* Securitization of Financial Assets Ch. 9, at 9-3 (Jason H. P. Kravitt ed., 2d ed. Supp. 2007) (observing that "especially in securitization and other asset-backed transactions, expectations about [both pre- and post-default] trustee responsibilities have increased").

[35] *See, e.g.*, Commerzbank AG v. Bank of New York Mellon, No. 1:15-cv-10029 (S.D.N.Y. Dec. 23, 2015), ¶ 22 (contending that prior to an Event of Default, a trustee for a securitized bond issue is "required to police the deal for investors"). *Cf.* Barry S. Fagan, *Commerzbank AG Has Sued Wells Fargo Bank For Over $100 Million Dollars in Toxic Mortgage-Backed Securities Losses* (Jan. 10, 2016), https://www.jdsupra.com/legalnews/commerzbank-ag-has-sued-wells-fargo-bank-00245/ (discussing complaints filed in the Southern District of New York in which plaintiff alleged that "Investors were dependent upon . . . Wells Fargo [Bank, as trustee,] to police the deal and to protect their contractual and other legal rights").

A *Correcting Market Failures*

The fundamental normative justification for financial regulation is to correct market failures.[36] Therefore, the primary justification for regulating the duties of a trustee pre-default should be to correct pre-default market failures.[37]

When the TIA originally was enacted in 1939, many of the bondholders for whom trustees acted were retail investors. They were unable to adequately protect themselves because of a collective action problem,[38] a type of market failure. In modern times, however, institutional investors dominate the bond markets,[39] greatly reducing the retail-investor collective action problem.[40] As a result, the role of trustees to protect bondholders by solving the collective action problem should be less urgent today than in 1939.

Even in 1939, however, trustees' pre-default duties were ministerial and limited to the specific terms of the indenture.[41] Therefore, other things being equal, trustees should not be held to higher pre-default duties today. Other things, however, may not be equal. The rise of activist investors and the advent of securitized bond issues have potentially created other market failures. The rise of activist investors has created a possible agency failure: such investors do not necessarily act for the benefit of the other investors. The advent of securitized bond issues has also created a possible information failure: some securitized bond issues are so complex that investors do not always fully understand them.[42]

Activist investors, not trustees, are responsible for the possible agency failure. Ideally, indentures should be drafted to limit the ability of investors to cause that failure. Nonetheless, so long as that failure could arise, trustees—as a matter of best practices, and to reduce risk—should not want to exacerbate the failure. To that end, a trustee might wish to consider, when requested to take action, whether that action could create or exacerbate a conflict of interest among investors. If it might, the trustee at least should have the right to refuse to take that action[43]—provided that refusal violates neither the indenture nor formal investor directions.[44]

---

[36]   Paul A. Samuelson & William D. Nordhaus, ECONOMICS 756 (15th ed. 1995).

[37]   This chapter uses the term "market failure" loosely because the economic literature defines it loosely. Economists define market failure as a "situation" in which there is an economic inefficiency. Traditionally, market failures are often associated with imperfect information (such as information asymmetries), non-competitive factors (such as a monopoly), principal-agent conflicts, or externalities.

[38]   See *supra* note 18 and accompanying text.

[39]   See *supra* note 23 and accompanying text (finding that institutional investors now hold over eighty percent of corporate and foreign bonds).

[40]   See *supra* note 24 and accompanying text (finding that, by virtue of their sophistication and the size of their bondholding, institutional investors face less of a collective action problem than retail investors). But *cf. infra* notes 75–81 and accompanying text (discussing practical issues that might impair the ability of even an institutional investor to form a coalition of investors having the requisite voting rights to direct the trustee).

[41]   See *supra* note 26 and accompanying text.

[42]   Steven L. Schwarcz, *Securitization and Post-Crisis Financial Regulation*, 102 CORNELL L. REV. ONLINE 115, 131 (2015).

[43]   A recent lawsuit questions whether trustees have the right to protect bondholders pre-default. Except as specifically addressed herein, this chapter focuses on duties and not rights per se. A few observations, nonetheless, may be relevant. Most indentures include a "Certain Rights of the Trustee" provision that allows the trustee to consult with counsel and to rely on "the written advice" or "an opinion" of counsel" as "full and complete authorization and protection for any action taken, suffered or omitted by it in good faith and in accordance with such advice or opinion." Even absent that provision, the author's experience is that the post-duties are not intended to preclude pre-default rights.

[44]   *Cf.* Harold L. Kaplan & Mark F. Hebbeln, "The Anglo-American Indenture—Covenant Enforcement and Bond Defaults—U.S. Experience and Lessons from Canada and the U.K." (ABA Business Law Section, Chicago, Ill., 2009) (observing that "the indenture trustee's role under the indenture still can be viewed as including facilitating a level playing field for all bondholders . . . [which entails] ever more difficult issues of balancing countervailing interests in doing what is right"); Lee C. Buchheit & G. Mitu Gulati, *Sovereign Bonds and the Collective Will*, 51 EMORY L. J. 1317, 1336 (2002) (arguing that the trustee is the representative of the minority voice, which may be oppressed by competing interests).

Nor should trustees have a pre-default duty to protect bondholders by trying to correct the information failure. This failure is certainly real; securitizations can be extremely complex. A study of securitization deals from 2002 to 2007 found that, on average, it takes thirty-eight pages to describe the underlying financial assets and twenty-seven pages to describe the payment-priority "waterfall."[45] Large securitizations may be especially complex, particularly if they include multiple types of underlying financial assets and multiple tranches of bonds, complicating the relationship between asset performance and payment on the issued bonds.[46] As a result, some practitioners suggest that securitized bond issues "require a level of [trustee] sophistication and specialization that is different from that of the traditional indenture trustee."[47]

There is no evidence, however, that sophisticated or specialized trustees could correct the information failure. Trustees generally have no disclosure duties, nor is there a rationale that they should have such duties. Nor do trustees have (nor should they have) a duty to recommend investments. Furthermore, even if they otherwise could help to correct the information failure, trustees for securitized bond issues are not—at least, currently—significantly more sophisticated or specialized than other trustees. Trustees receive relatively tiny fees, and the trust departments of financial institutions normally contract only to engage in relatively ministerial tasks.[48] Trustees rarely negotiate the terms of the indentures; they usually are presented with the transaction documents at the last minute and asked to sign, with little to no opportunity to make changes.[49]

In contrast, investors in securitized bond issues normally are highly sophisticated financial institutions, of which activist investors tend to be the most sophisticated.[50] In the Rule 144A-exempt transactions that characterize many securitized bond issues, the investors must be qualified institutional buyers (QIBs), the highest SEC ranking of investor sophistication and size. It is unlikely that even sophisticated and specialized trustees would better understand complex securitized bond issues than those investors.[51]

B *Maximizing Efficiency*

Another normative justification for financial regulation is maximizing efficiency. In theory, correcting market failures should make private markets work most efficiently. Sub-section A's

---

[45] Andra C. Ghent et al., *Complexity in Structured Finance* 14 (Nov. 2, 2017) (unpublished draft), https://papers.ssrn.com/sol3/papers.cfm?abstract_id=2325835.

[46] Craig Furfine, *Complexity as a Means to Distract: Evidence From the Securitization of Commercial Mortgages* 7–8 (Sept. 2012) (unpublished draft), https://www.kellogg.northwestern.edu/~/media/Files/Faculty/Research/Furfine_Complexity.ash.

[47] Brady et al., *supra* note 34, at 9-6.

[48] American Bankers Association, Corporate Trust Committee, The Trustee's Role in Asset-Backed Securities 4 (Mar. 12, 2003), https://www.aba.com/advocacy/policy-analysis/trustees-role-asset-backed-securities. *Cf.* Hunton & Williams LLP, Client Alert—Dealing With Bondholders In Troubled Times 1 (Dec. 2008), https://www.huntonak.com/images/content/1/6/v3/1601/dealing-with-bondholders-in-troubled-times.pdf ("[T]he nominal annual fee paid for standard trust services provides little incentive for an indenture trustee to [represent the bondholders].").

[49] American Bankers Association, Corporate Trust Committee, The Trustee's Role in Asset-Backed Securities 4 (Nov. 9, 2010), https://www.aba.com/aba/documents/press/RoleoftheTrusteeinAsset-BackedSecuritiesJuly2010.pdf (observing that indenture trustees usually are asked to sign transaction documents that are pre-negotiated by other parties).

[50] *Cf.* Sharon Hannes, *Super Hedge Fund*, 40 Del. J. Corp. L. 163, 193–94 (2015) (discussing how activist investors employ "expensive, time-consuming" tactics to achieve their goals).

[51] *But cf. supra* note 42, at 9 (discussing risk marginalization, which might reduce an investor's incentive individually to try to understand).

analysis of correcting market failures, therefore, should be sufficient, in principle, to maximize efficiency.

In particular, though, maximizing efficiency requires avoiding any unwarranted duplication of efforts. In bond issues, including securitized bond issues, parties have specified roles. The pre-default duties of trustees are usually limited to administrative tasks such as mailing notices or selecting bonds for redemption[52] or delivering certificates, preparing and transmitting reports, and forwarding notices.[53] As a condition to investing, investors that want the trustee to perform additional roles could demand the indenture to require that performance.[54] A trustee would then want to be compensated, however, for performing those additional roles. If those additional roles are substantive or expose the trustee to liability, that compensation might be substantial, especially compared to the relatively tiny fees that trustees are currently paid.[55] And that, in turn, would reduce the value of the trust estate. Perhaps for that reason, the author is unaware of bond indentures imposing additional roles on trustees.

Moreover, even if investors wanted parties to perform additional roles, trustees may not be the best choice of parties to perform substantive roles. As discussed, they may not be sufficiently sophisticated or specialized.[56] Officials of the federal government recently reached this same conclusion:

> A number of prominent investors have told us over the past year that a trustee fiduciary duty is . . . the only way, of accounting for all of the failures of the legacy model. Based on all of our work and irrespective of legacy terms and contracts, even if we believed in imposing a fiduciary duty, we have concluded the trustee is the wrong party for that duty going forward. The core competency of trustees is in carrying out administrative functions, not in forensic activities that require subjectivity and judgment, which is ultimately what a fiduciary must exercise.[57]

The current equilibrium of small trustee fees and (except when the trustee is formally directed by investors, as later discussed[58]) ministerial pre-default duties appears to represent a market consensus, or at least the market practice, on balancing costs and benefits. Market practice, in turn, suggests a presumption of efficiency and a pragmatic balance: post-default, investors rely on the trustee's expertise to address the default and maximize recovery on their claims—which requires taking calculated risks[59]; pre-default (absent the above-mentioned formal investor directions), investors expect the trustee only to perform the duties expressly stated in the indenture, to preserve the trust estate.[60]

---

52 *Cf. In re* Enron Corp. Securities, Derivative & "ERISA" Litigation, No. CIV. A. 03-5808, 2008 WL 744823, at *8 (S.D. Tex. Mar. 19, 2008) (explaining that until an Event of Default occurs, an indenture trustee performs certain administrative tasks such as mailing notices or selecting bonds for redemption).

53 *Cf.* CFIP Master Fund, Ltd. v. Citibank, N.A., 738 F. Supp. 2d 450, 473 (S.D.N.Y. 2010) (listing some duties that the indenture trustee had, including "delivering certificates . . . preparing and transmitting reports . . . and forwarding notices . . .").

54 *Cf.* John H. Langbein, *The Secret Life of the Trust: The Trust as an Instrument of Commerce*, 107 YALE L. J. 165, 183 (1997) ("Trust fiduciary law is default law that the parties can alter to their needs.").

55 *See supra* note 48 and accompanying text.

56 *See supra* notes 47–48 and accompanying text.

57 Press Release, Remarks by Counselor to the Secretary for Housing Finance Policy Dr. Michael Stegman Before the Structured Finance Industry Group 1st Annual Private Label Symposium (Nov. 12, 2014), https://www.treasury.gov/press-center/press-releases/Pages/jl2694.aspx.

58 *See infra* note 75 and accompanying text.

59 *Cf. Bond Default and the Dilemma of Indenture Trustee, supra* note 25, at 1068.

60 *Id.* at 1069.

C *Formalism*

The author has encountered a formalistic rationale for imposing additional pre-default duties on trustees of securitized bond issues: because securitized bond issues involve purchased financial assets, they more closely resemble a traditional trust; and trustees of a traditional trust have fiduciary duties. In a business context, however, that argument is not compelling.

In classic language, the Supreme Court has observed that saying "that a man is a fiduciary only begins the analysis; it gives direction to further inquiry. To whom is he a fiduciary? What obligation does he owe as a fiduciary?"[61] Although fiduciary law develops by drawing analogies with established prototypes, that method should not apply when cases are not analogous.[62]

The traditional fiduciary duty applicable to common law trustees serves to prevent them from taking advantage of beneficiaries.[63] However, trustees in securitized bond issues cannot take advantage of bondholders because their powers to deal with trust assets and apply collections thereof are contractually specified.[64] Any formalistic argument for imposing fiduciary pre-default duties on trustees of securitized bond issues, therefore, appears weak.

D *Articulating a Normative Rule*

The above analysis of a trustee's pre-default duties suggests the following normative rule. Pre-default, the trustee's only duties should be specified in the indenture. A trustee also should have the right to refuse to take an action that could create or exacerbate a conflict of interest among investors, provided that the refusal violates neither the indenture nor formal investor directions.

This normative rule sometimes could result in a pre-default protection gap, insofar as the indenture fails to assign any specific party to enforce pre-default remedies. For example, although some indentures require the servicer to enforce cure-or-repurchase remedies for breaches of representations and warranties regarding purchased financial assets and resolve defects in the documents evidencing or relating to those financial assets, others are silent. For indentures that are silent, the investors can protect themselves by marshaling the requisite voting rights (and providing adequate indemnification of costs) to contractually direct the trustee to enforce those remedies.[65]

Investors unable to marshal the requisite voting rights to direct the trustee would have little basis to argue that the trustee should have an implied duty to enforce those remedies. As discussed, most indentures are explicit in that the trustee's duties are ministerial and limited to the specific terms of the indenture,[66] and many further clarify that the trustee is not subject to any implied duties. These limitations on trustee pre-default duties also will be shown to be economically efficient.[67] Sophisticated investors should be responsible for the rights and obligations they contractually agree to; it is not the job of courts to create implied protections.[68]

---

[61] Sec. and Exch. Comm'n v. Chenery Corp., 318 U.S. 80, 85–86 (1943).

[62] Tamar Frankel, *Fiduciary Law*, 71 CAL. L. REV. 795, 805–07 (1983).

[63] D. Gordon Smith, *The Critical Resource Theory of Fiduciary Duty*, 55 VAND. L. REV. 1399, 1408 (2002).

[64] *See* section II. C, *infra* (examining additional duties that arise in securitized bond issues).

[65] *See infra* notes 74–75 and accompanying text.

[66] *See supra* note 26 and accompanying text.

[67] *Cf. infra* notes 93–95 and accompanying text (explaining why imposing a pre-default servicing duty on the trustee would be inefficient) and notes 96–97 and accompanying text (explaining why imposing a pre-default monitoring duty on the trustee would be inefficient).

[68] *Cf.* Metro. Life Ins. Co. v. RJR Nabisco, Inc., 716 F. Supp. 1504 (S.D.N.Y. 1989) (refusing to find an implied covenant protecting investors where the bond indenture lacked that protection).

IV APPLYING THE PROPOSED PRE-DEFAULT NORMATIVE RULE

This section applies the foregoing normative rule for determining a trustee's pre-default duties to the types of issues that may arise in lawsuits against trustees.

A *Taking Enforcement and Other Remedial Actions*

A problem can arise in a bond issue even prior to a formal Event of Default.[69] One or more investors may demand that the trustee take some enforcement or other remedial action to try to correct the problem. Compliance with that demand could be expensive; trustees normally are entitled to reimbursement of their enforcement costs from the trust estate, which would reduce the value of that estate for investors generally. Therefore, taking remedial action could create a conflict if it would disproportionately benefit only certain investors.

For example, activist investors may purchase subordinated (junior) bonds of a barely solvent issuer at pennies on the dollar. Those investors may then demand that the trustee take expensive enforcement action, with relatively little chance of success but a high upside if successful.[70] Taking that action would be unlikely to generally have a positive expected value for the investors.[71]

To illustrate this, assume that activist investors purchase all $100 of subordinated bonds of an issuer for their current trading value of $1 and other investors hold all $500 of the issuer's senior bonds, which are trading at par. The activist investors then demand that the trustee take an enforcement action likely to cost $300, which has a 90 percent chance of recovering nothing and a 10 percent chance of recovering $400. The expected value of taking that enforcement action would be calculated as follows:

> Expected value = (10% chance of enforcement action being successful) × ($400 recovery from that success − $300 cost of taking action) + (90% chance of enforcement action being unsuccessful) × ($0 recovery from that failure − $300 cost of taking action) = negative $260.

From the investors' standpoint generally, taking action would be expected to be harmful, significantly reducing recovery on the senior bonds without increasing recovery on the subordinated bonds. The activist investors nonetheless would want the trustee to take that action. Absent that action, their $100 face-amount of subordinated bonds are worth only $1, so that is the most they would lose if the action fails; whereas taking action gives them a small chance of being paid in full if it is successful, yielding a $100 recovery on their $1 investment.

Absent formal investor directions discussed in the next section, a trustee should have the right to refuse to take that action. Similarly, absent formal investor directions, a trustee should have the right to refuse to take any action not specifically required by the indenture.[72] In case of doubt, a trustee could seek—or request the investor(s) demanding the action to arrange for—formal

---

[69]   *Cf. infra* note 70 and accompanying text (discussing such problems).

[70]   Longstanding investors in those subordinated bonds might, of course, have a similar incentive. The above expected value analysis should apply regardless of who holds the subordinated bonds.

[71]   Expected value is a statistical methodology to help predict whether an action is likely to be beneficial or harmful or compare the value of alternative proposed actions. Calculating an expected value involves identifying each possible outcome and its probability of occurring, then multiplying each such outcome by its probability, and finally summing all of those values. *See, e.g.*, Steven L. Schwarcz, *Misalignment: Corporate Risk-Taking and Public Duty*, 92 NOTRE DAME L. REV. 1, 33 (2016).

[72]   A trustee especially should avoid taking action if a rough cost-benefit balancing suggests that its costs might exceed the benefits. *Cf.* section IV.D, *infra* (arguing that lacking other guidance, a trustee should be able to fall back on basic common sense, including a rough cost-benefit balancing).

investor directions. An indenture typically allows investors with at least 25–50 percent of voting rights to direct the trustee to act and indemnify the trustee[73] for the cost of taking action.[74] Investors with the requisite voting rights may seek to direct the trustee to commence a lawsuit, for example.[75] Provisions authorizing formal investor directions can increase efficiency by leveraging the expertise of sophisticated investors.

Practical issues might sometimes impair the formation of a coalition of investors having sufficient voting rights to direct the trustee to act. For example, although the trustee often controls the investor list, the indenture might restrict turning it over unless some minimum number of investors (e.g., three) request it—thus creating a potential catch-22. However, it is more typical for indentures to authorize trustees to provide information to any investor seeking to assemble an investor group for directing trustee action. The TIA provides and even indentures not governed by the TIA sometimes similarly provide,[76] that investors may communicate with other investors with respect to their rights under the indenture.[77] The fact that bonds are traded under a worldwide indirect holding system[78] creates another practical issue: the trustee might only have a list showing a securities depository or clearinghouse—such as the Depository Trust Company ("DTC," or its nominee Cede & Co.) in the United States or Euroclear in Europe— as the holder of a single "global" certificate.[79] That could require a concerned investor to examine the bonds' chain of transfers to ascertain their owners.[80]

Even if investors are unable to direct trustee actions, they may be able individually to pursue their claims in appropriate cases.[81] They also can ask regulators and enforcement agencies to address their grievances. In response to the financial crisis, for example, the U.S. Department of Justice, the U.S. SEC, and other regulators have filed numerous cases and regulatory actions against securitization parties and recovered billions of dollars.[82]

---

[73] Although indentures usually indemnify the trustee, this specific indemnification requirement appears to intend to shift risk to the investors requesting the action.

[74] *See, e.g.,* Adam Levitin, *The Paper Clause: Securitization, Foreclosure, and the Uncertainty of Mortgage Title,* 63 Duke L. J. 637, 709 (2013) (observing that a typical indenture allows holders of more than 25 percent principal amount of bonds to control trustee actions). The TIA requires indentures to authorize at least majority bondholders to direct the trustee's exercise of power. 15 U.S.C. § 77ppp(a)(1).

[75] *See, e.g.,* Complaint at 1, Bear Stearns Mortg. Fund Trust 2006-SL1 v. EMC Mortg. and JP Morgan Chase Bank (2012) (No. 7701-CL) (pleading that the trustee filed the lawsuit "acting at the direction of certain holders of Certificates issued by the Trust"); Complaint at 1, HSBC as trustee of Merrill Lynch Alt. Note Asset Trust, Ser. 2007-OAR5 v. Merrill Lynch Mortgage Lending (2016) (No. 652793/2016) (pleading that the trustee filed the lawsuit "at the direction of a certain holder of residential mortgage-back securities issued by the Trust").

[76] *Cf. supra* note 17 and accompanying text (observing that many of the TIA's fundamental principles are followed in the model indenture provisions included in virtually all bond indentures).

[77] TIA § 312(b).

[78] *Cf.* Steven L. Schwarcz, *Intermediary Risk in a Global Economy,* 50 Duke L. J. 1541, 1547–49 (2001) (describing the indirect holding system for securities).

[79] *Id.* at 1547.

[80] *See, e.g.,* Thomas G. Ward & Daniel M. Dockery, *How the Indirect Holding System Affects Investor Suits,* Law 360 (Sept. 29, 2015).

[81] *See, e.g.,* Federal Housing Finance Agency, *FHFA Announces $5.5 Billion Settlement with Royal Bank of Scotland,* (July 12, 2017), https://www.fhfa.gov/Media/PublicAffairs/Pages/FHFA-Announces-$5pt5-Billion-Settlement-with-Royal-Bank-of-Scotland.aspx (announcing settlement by FHFA as conservator of Fannie Mae and Freddie Mac of the 17th case of the 18 cases filed by FHFA against participants in the mortgage finance sector and that FHFA received a favorable verdict in the 18th case).

[82] *See, e.g.,* The Department of Justice, *Bank of America to Pay $16.65 Billion in Historic Justice Department Settlement for Financial Fraud Leading up to and During the Financial Crisis,* (Aug. 21, 2014), https://www.justice.gov/opa/pr/bank-america-pay-1665-billion-historic-justice-department-settlement-financial-fraud-leading.

B *Investigating "Red Flags" and Other Suspicious Occurrences*

Investors may become aware of so-called red flags and other suspicious occurrences in a bond issue even prior to a formal Event of Default. One or more investors may then demand that the trustee investigate the event. Compliance with that demand could be costly, and (as discussed[83]) trustees normally are entitled to reimbursement of their enforcement costs from the trust estate, which could reduce the value of that estate for investors generally. The trustee's engaging in an investigation could, therefore, create a conflict if it would disproportionately benefit only certain investors. For example, an investor in subordinated bonds who might benefit from an expensive investigation would have an incentive to direct the trustee to make that investigation if the costs of an unsuccessful investigation are disproportionately borne by investors in more senior bonds.[84]

Although the requested investigation might create or exacerbate a conflict of interest among investors, many indentures have language specifically addressing the right of investors to direct the trustee to take an action, which should include the right to make an investigation.[85] In that case, the same analysis of whether investors may direct the trustee to take a specific remedial action should apply to the question of whether investors may direct the trustee to make a specific investigation.[86]

Even absent an investor demand, investors sometimes use the trustee's failure to investigate a red flag or other suspicious occurrences as a basis for a later claim against the trustee, as a deep pocket. Although indentures typically absolve trustees from liability unless they act negligently or with willful misconduct, investors who suffer losses—even activist investors who purchase bonds at pennies on the dollar and fail to obtain payment of the full face value of those bonds[87]—sometimes argue that a trustee's failure to investigate would be negligent, if not evidence of willful misconduct. Reading an indenture as a consistent whole, however, the more specific governing text would appear to be the standard provision that the trustee "undertakes to perform ... only such duties as are specifically set forth" in the indenture and has no duty to investigate any "facts or matters" unless appropriately requested by investors to do so. An omission cannot be negligent if there is no duty to act.

C *Monitoring and Supervising Servicers (and Other Parties)*

In securitized bond issues, the bondholders are dependent on collections on the purchased financial assets.[88] Invariably, therefore, these transactions require a party, usually called a servicer (or sometimes collection agent), to service those financial assets and collect payment thereon.[89] In litigation filed following the financial crisis, which caused widespread defaults on residential mortgage loans, some investors argued that trustees in MBS transactions should have monitored or supervised the performance of the mortgage loan servicer.[90]

[83]   *See supra* notes 69–70 and accompanying text.
[84]   *Cf. supra* note 70 and accompanying text (illustrating this type of a conflict).
[85]   *See supra* notes 74–80 and accompanying text.
[86]   *Cf.* Bear Stearns Mortg. Funding Tr. 2006-SL1 v. EMC Mortg. LLC, No. CV 7701-VCL, 2015 WL 139731, at *2–3 (Del. Ch. Jan. 12, 2015) (discussing that certain investors directed the trustee to "ask[] EMC for loan origination files, servicing records, and other loan documentation for the Mortgage Loans").
[87]   *See supra* note 70 and accompanying text.
[88]   *See supra* note 29 and accompanying text.
[89]   The servicer normally is required to act in the "best interests" of the investors. Steven L. Schwarcz, *Protecting Financial Markets: Lessons from the Subprime Mortgage Meltdown*, 93 Minn. L. Rev. 373, 391 (2008).
[90]   *See, e.g.,* Ellington Credit Fund Ltd. v. Select Portfolio Serv., Inc., 837 F. Supp.2d 162, 178 (S.D.N.Y. 2011) (alleging that trustee of securitization breached its duty for insufficient supervision of servicer).

An indenture could specifically require the trustee to supervise the servicer or assure that it complies with the indenture.[91] However, more typically in the author's experience, indentures provide that the trustee has no duty to monitor or supervise the servicer. Instead, the servicer itself typically attests periodically to its compliance, and the trustee is entitled to rely on the truth and accuracy of that attestation.[92]

Without clear indenture language, should the trustee have a pre-default duty to monitor or supervise the servicer? Notwithstanding the claim that trustees have duties to ensure that mortgage loans in MBS transactions are "properly serviced,"[93] imposing a monitoring or servicing requirement would be duplicative and expensive—and thus inefficient. Servicers provide a wide array of services, including collecting principal and interest payments, communicating with borrowers, addressing borrower delinquencies and bankruptcies, working out loan modifications or other borrower difficulties, foreclosing on properties, maintaining foreclosed homes, and selling real estate-owned properties after foreclosure. They charge arm's length fees for performing these services.[94] Because most trustees are not equipped or compensated to monitor or supervise that performance, they should not have that pre-default duty.[95]

D *Monitoring for Events of Default*

Investors sometimes claim that a trustee should have a pre-default duty to monitor for the existence of an Event of Default. Likewise, some practitioners have suggested that trustees for securitized bond issues might have this duty.[96] Indentures normally provide, however, that notwithstanding the actual existence of an Event of Default, the trustee's post-default heightened duty is not triggered until a responsible officer of the trustee has "actual knowledge" or, if the indenture provides, written notice of the Event of Default.

Even absent that language in an indenture, a trustee should not have such a pre-default monitoring duty. Requiring such a duty would require the trustee to constantly investigate all events that might trigger an Event of Default. That would be expensive and time-consuming— and thus, inefficient—with investors bearing the cost.[97] It also could expose the trustee to indeterminate liability if it failed, even for reasons beyond its control, to become aware of an Event of Default. Uncertainty of the standard—one that is merely ministerial, or one requiring prudence and judgment—by which their performance would be judged would discourage financial institutions from acting as trustees or at least motivate them to charge higher fees to compensate for the risk.

---

[91] *See, e.g.*, Michael J. Canning et al., *Committee Educational Session: Real Estate Tranche Warfare: Real Estate Restructurings: Issues Raised By Complex, Multi-Tranche Financial Structures*, 120910 ABI-CLE 573 (2010).

[92] Sometimes an experienced master servicer may be appointed to supervise the servicer's performance.

[93] *See supra* note 33 and accompanying text.

[94] *See, e.g.*, Residential Capital LLC, *Annual Report (Form 10-K)*, at 9 (Feb. 27, 2009), http://www.secinfo.com/d14D5a .s16Ca.htm (reporting that Residential Capital, LLC, a mortgage loan servicer, charged approximately 15 basis points (0.15%) for servicing insured mortgage loans and 25 basis points (0.25%) for servicing uninsured mortgage loans).

[95] Also, for these same reasons, a trustee that allegedly is aware of a servicing failure should not have a pre-default duty to correct the failure absent indenture language requiring it to do so.

[96] Brady et al., *supra* note 34, at 9-6 (discussing the additional sophistication and specialization needed for such a trustee "to achieve an appropriate awareness of possible weakening financial condition of an issuer or servicer or to determine early amortization events"). *Cf. id.* at 9-16 (stating that a "diligent and competent trustee [for a securitized bond issue] will be able to recognize certain warning signals that may precipitate a trigger event in the documents").

[97] *Cf.* FEDERAL SECURITIES CODE xl (AM. LAW INST. 1980) ("It has been persuasively urged that extension of the 'prudent man' test for purposes of ascertaining the occurrence of a default . . . would be impracticable and prohibitively expensive in terms of increased trustees' fees.").

Sometimes one or more investors may notify the trustee that an Event of Default has occurred, but the notification lacks specific, actionable information clearly showing the existence of the Event of Default. What should be the duty of a trustee regarding an alleged but unproven (or disputed) Event of Default? The answer should take into account and balance practical considerations—which could include seeking or requesting that those investors obtain formal investor directions.[98] Otherwise, investors who cannot muster the requisite number to direct the trustee to make an investigation could repackage their demands by alleging that an Event of Default requires the trustee to act. If the trustee were then required to expend trust assets to investigate the Event of Default, those investors could achieve indirectly what they could not do directly.

In one case, for example, the author is aware that a "complaining investor" sent a notice to the trustee describing improper servicing by the servicer and alleging that constituted an Event of Default. The complaining investor's information was based on publicly available statements about, and regulatory investigations and proceedings pertaining to, the servicer's servicing practices, as well as rating-agency downgrades of the servicer's servicing ratings. In responding to the trustee's inquiry, the servicer said it was properly performing its servicing duties. The trustee then sent the investors a notice describing the complaining investor's arguments and the servicer's response, stating that it had not formed any view as to whether an Event of Default had occurred, and requesting direction by a requisite number of investors. Not receiving such direction, the trustee concluded that no further action was warranted in the absence of additional information. That conclusion appears reasonable under the circumstances.

E Agreeing to Settlements (And Making Other Decisions that Could Affect Investor Recovery)

Questions sometimes arise about a trustee's pre-default duty when making decisions that could affect investor recovery, such as deciding whether a trustee should settle a lawsuit or other claims against third parties or accept a debt restructuring on the bonds to avoid a default. For example, shortly after The Bank of New York Mellon, as a trustee, entered into a settlement agreement with Bank of America to settle Countrywide's repurchase liability for $8.5 billion, investors accused the trustee of having a conflict of interest, acting in bad faith, and breaching fiduciary duties in the course of administering the trusts and/or concluding the settlement.[99]

Indentures sometimes contain collective action clauses ("CACs") that allow a supermajority of investors to make these types of decisions, binding on all investors.[100] In those cases, the trustee could seek to obtain supermajority investor consent to the decision. In the United States, however, the TIA prohibits changing core payment terms of corporate bonds—their principal amount, interest rate, or maturity—without unanimous bondholder consent.[101] Therefore, relatively few indentures contain CACs.[102] This can lead to otherwise favorable debt restructurings being "held hostage" by one or more bondholders, acting as holdouts in the hope that they

[98]   *See supra* note 75 and accompanying text.

[99]   Bank of New York Mellon v. Walnut Place, LLC, No. 11-cv-5988 (S.D.N.Y. Aug. 26, 2011) (removing action entitled *In re the Bank of New York Mellon*, Index No. 651786/2011 (N.Y. Sup. Ct.)). Regulators also moved to join the suit. Memorandum and Order on Motions to Intervene Filed by Attorney Generals of Delaware and New York, at Dkt. No. 140 (Nov. 18, 2011).

[100]   W. Mark C. Weidemaier & Mitu Gulati, *A People's History of Collective Action Clauses*, 54 Va. J. Int'l L. 51, 53 (2014).

[101]   15 U.S.C. § 77ppp. *See also* Marblegate Asset Mgmt. v. Educ. Mgmt. Corp., 846 F.3d 1, 2 (2d Cir. 2017).

[102]   CACs are more commonly found in sovereign bond indentures. Buchheit & Gulati, *supra* note 44, at 1328.

will receive special premiums for consenting.[103] Resolution of that holdout behavior is beyond the scope of this chapter.[104]

F RESOLVING DOCUMENT DEFECTS

Securitized bond issues sometimes require the trustee to hold documents evidencing the underlying financial assets. For example, indentures in MBS transactions often require the trustee (or a custodian acting on the trustee's behalf) to hold certain mortgage-loan documents such as the mortgage note, the mortgage with evidence of recording, an assignment of mortgage, and the original title policy. What should be the pre-default duty of a trustee to try to obtain documents that it fails to receive or to correct documents that are defective on their face?

Because the trustee's performance costs typically would be paid from the estate, such a duty should not be triggered, if at all, unless the failure to receive a document or defect would actually harm investors.[105] That, in turn, should be judged in light of the purpose of document-delivery requirements—normally, to enable the servicer to service the loans properly and enforce those loans and mortgages against defaulting borrowers.[106] If a missing or defective document is unnecessary for such servicing and enforcement, its absence or defect would lack harmful consequences.

The party best able to assess whether or not a missing or defective document would be needed for such servicing and enforcement—and the party most often assigned that responsibility, in practice—is the servicer, who actually services and enforces the loans.[107] Trustees are not ordinarily equipped to assess those consequences. Furthermore, assessing those consequences would require the exercise of judgment and, absent an Event of Default, trustees are not, and should not be, required to exercise judgment.[108] Ideally, indentures should, therefore, require servicers to assess those consequences and provide a procedure whereby the trustee could make that inquiry of the servicer.

G DISCLOSING PROBLEMS

Investors sometimes claim that trustees should have a pre-default duty to disclose problems of which they become aware, such as documents that the trustees are required to hold being missing or defective.[109] Trustees, however, have no general disclosure duties, and there is no rationale that they should have such duties.[110] As a matter of best practices and to reduce risk,

[103] Andrew G. Haldane et al., *Optimal collective action clause thresholds* (Bank of England, Working Paper no. 249, 9, 2003).

[104] The author separately has examined this type of holdout behavior and, at least in the sovereign debt context, its resolution. *See, e.g.,* Steven L. Schwarcz, *Sovereign Debt Restructuring Options: An Analytical Comparison,* 2 HARV. BUS. L. REV. 95 (2012).

[105] *Cf. In re* Bankers Trust Co., 450 F.3d 121,127–29 (2d Cir. 2006) (even though a trustee breached its pre-default duty of inspecting certain issuer certificates and providing notice to bondholders, the court awarded bondholders only nominal damages because, even if the trustee "had been punctilious in its inspection of the certificates," that "would not have prevented the [bondholders'] losses").

[106] Patrick E. Mears & Mark R. Owens, *Representing Special Servicers in "Cleaning Up" Defaulted CMBS Loans,* PROBATE & PROPERTY 21, 23 (May/June 2011).

[107] *See supra* note 106 and accompanying text.

[108] Nothing in this chapter suggests that an Event of Default unrelated to missing documents should require a trustee to exercise judgment about the consequences, hence the materiality, of missing documents.

[109] *See supra* note 105 and accompanying text.

[110] *See* text accompanying notes 47–48, *supra.*

however, trustees may wish to disclose material problems of which they become aware. Investors then could consider whether to direct the trustee to act on those problems.

Their ability to disclose material problems turns on trustees becoming aware of such problems, which cannot always be presumed. The author's experience in numerous securitization transactions, for example, is that many of the documents evidencing the underlying financial assets are missing or defective. Without a procedure enabling the trustee to inquire about materiality with the servicer, the trustee may be unable to assess the materiality of those missing and defective documents.[111] Future indentures ideally should provide such a procedure.

v RESOLVING AMBIGUITIES

Any normative rule for determining a trustee's pre-default duties, including the rule proposed by this chapter, inevitably will face ambiguities. This section examines how a trustee could try to resolve those ambiguities.

A *Seek Legal Opinion*

A trustee could seek a legal opinion to try to resolve ambiguities. Section 8.01 of most indentures, entitled "Duties and Responsibility of the Trustee," usually allows trustees acting in good faith to "conclusively rely" on opinions that conform to the indenture's requirements.[112] Furthermore, § 8.02 of most indentures, entitled "Certain Rights of the Trustee," usually allows trustees to consult with counsel and to rely on "the written advice" or "an opinion" of counsel" as "full and complete authorization and protection for any action taken, suffered or omitted by it in good faith and in accordance with such advice or opinion."[113]

Sometimes, however, a lawyer may be unable to clearly resolve the ambiguity, perhaps because its resolution transcends legal considerations or the law itself is unclear. In those cases, the trustee may wish to seek investor instructions (discussed below in sub-section B) or even judicial guidance (discussed below in sub-section C).

B *Seek Investor Instructions*

As discussed, indentures typically authorize a requisite number of investors to instruct the trustee.[114] In appropriate cases, the trustee could seek such instructions. If it then receives instructions, the trustee should be justified in following them. Absent instructions, the trustee should be justified in not taking further steps.

C *Seek Judicial Guidance*

In more difficult or sensitive cases, a trustee could seek judicial guidance. Two basic types of judicial procedures—interpleader and declaratory judgment actions—may be appropriate.[115]

---

[111] *See supra* note 108 and accompanying text.
[112] *See, e.g.,* National Association of Bond Lawyers, Model Form of Trust Indenture, § 8.01(a)(2), https://www.nabl.org/portals/0/documents/nablformalreportsmodeldocs-nablformtrustindenture.pdf.
[113] *Id.* § 8.02(d).
[114] *See supra* notes 74–80 and accompanying text.
[115] *See generally* Robert J. Coughlin et al., *Rule 22 to Resolve a Catch-22: Defensive Maneuvers for Corporate Trustees Faced with Conflicting Claims, in* New Developments in Securitization 771, 777 (PLI Com. L. & Prac. Course Handbook Series No. 14108, 2008).

Interpleader, which is available under both federal and state law, is a procedure whereby a party with property subject to competing claims may compel the parties asserting those claims to litigate their dispute in a single proceeding.[116] Federal law provides two broadly similar types of interpleader, rule interpleader and statutory interpleader,[117] with statutory interpleader having more lenient jurisdictional requirements.[118] State law, including New York law, is similar to federal interpleader with one exception: it does not require the disputed property to be placed under the court's control (whereas federal interpleader does).[119]

A trustee could also request a declaratory judgment to have a court determine its rights, prior to taking action to expose it to liability.[120] Unlike interpleader, a declaratory judgment action requires the existence of an "actual controversy."[121] The federal declaratory judgment procedure allows the court to order a speedy hearing of the controversy.[122] That could be valuable because attempts to seek judicial guidance often can involve lengthy delays.[123] Choosing between a federal or a state declaratory judgment procedure may also be influenced by jurisdictional requirements or strategic concerns.[124]

Some states provide even more targeted statutory procedures for trustees to obtain judicial directions.[125] Because these procedures are usually designed to apply only to gratuitous trusts, it is uncertain whether they could be applied to indenture trustees[126] or used in a commercial context.[127]

D *Exercise Common Sense*

Lacking other guidance, a trustee ultimately should be able to fall back on basic common sense, including a rough cost-benefit balancing. For example, regardless of what the trustee's duty otherwise should be, the occurrence of a suspicious event should not trigger a duty to investigate occurrences and events unrelated to that event. Such an extraneous investigation could significantly reduce trust assets without commensurately benefitting the investors. Similarly, absent formal investor directions, a trustee should not generally take an action that would be expensive but unlikely to lead to a net favorable outcome—such as investigating whether a bankrupt or clearly insolvent party had breached one or more of its representations and warranties.[128] Even if the trustee could prove such a breach, a damage claim against that party may be unrecoverable.

[116] CYCLOPEDIA OF FEDERAL PROCEDURE § 22.01 (3d ed. 2005).

[117] Rule interpleader arises under Federal Rule of Civil Procedure 22; statutory interpleader arises under 28 U.S.C. § 1335 (2006).

[118] CYCLOPEDIA OF FEDERAL PROCEDURE, *supra* note 116, at § 22.05.

[119] *See* N.Y. C.P.L.R. 1006 (McKinney 2009); *see also* Coughlin et al., *supra* note 115, at 778–79 (noting this distinction between federal and New York interpleader laws).

[120] Coughlin et al., *supra* note 115, at 782–83 (quoting Banos v. Winkelstein, 78 N.Y.S.2d 832, 834 (Sup. Ct. 1948)).

[121] *See id.* at 783.

[122] FED. R. CIV. P. 57 ("The court may order a speedy hearing of an action for a declaratory judgment . . . .").

[123] *Cf.* Schwarcz, *supra* note 14, at 1901–07 (discussing how using interpleader to try to resolve fiduciary conflicts can involve lengthy litigation, and comparing that with the much speedier English judicial procedures to resolve those types of conflicts).

[124] *See* Coughlin et al., *supra* note 115, at 784–85.

[125] *See, e.g.,* N.Y. C.P.L.R. 7701 (McKinney 2009) (providing a legal mechanism for a special proceeding for express trusts).

[126] *Cf. supra* note 27 (discussing the hybrid nature of a trustee on an indenture).

[127] *See* Coughlin et al., *supra* note 115, at 779. N.Y. C.P.L.R. 7701 provides, for example, that a "special proceeding may be brought to determine a matter relating to any express trust except a voting trust, a mortgage, [or] a trust for the benefit of creditors . . . ." N.Y. C.P.L.R. 7701.

[128] Originators and sometimes sponsors of securitization transactions make representations and warranties about the quality of the financial assets being sold, for which they are liable for breach. *See supra* note 29.

VI CONCLUSIONS

This chapter has examined the duties of indenture trustees, focusing primarily on pre-default duties. Whereas outstanding scholarship focuses on post-default duties, investors increasingly are making pre-default demands on trustees in the multi-trillion-dollar bond market, requiring them to know how to respond.

The chapter shows that, pre-default, the trustee should only have the duties specifically set forth in the bond indenture. It then applies that analysis to the types of issues that typically arise in lawsuits against trustees. Finally, the chapter examines how trustees could try to resolve any ambiguities relating to those duties.

PART II

Gaps and Alternatives in Fiduciary Regimes

6

Conflicts of Interest in Investment Advice: An Expanded View

Quinn Curtis

I INTRODUCTION

A longstanding problem in the regulation of financial advice is ensuring that advisor[1] compensation does not distort recommendations to the detriment of investors. The classic case is the problem of commission-compensated brokers who may push funds with significant sales commissions rather than funds in the best interest of clients. This issue has attracted a number of interventions. Most recently, the Securities and Exchange Commission ("SEC") adopted Regulation Best Interest[2] ("Reg BI") that requires brokers to act in the best interest of their clients. Reg BI itself steps into the space vacated by the now-defunct Department of Labor fiduciary rule ("fiduciary rule"),[3] which sharply limited certain compensation models likely to distort investment recommendations in favor of high commission products. Both rules are oriented to giving investors at least some degree of protection against being advised to purchase the wrong product due to their broker's compensation structure.

The existence of conflicts of interests in investment advice that distort recommendations to retail investors is well documented, and reforms aimed at mitigating the problem have the potential to leave investors better off. But when investors plan their financial lives, their welfare depends not on a particular investment decision, but on the cumulative effect of a lifetime of investing choices. Conflicts of interest affecting investment advice can alter these choices in a number of important ways, but regulators often focus narrowly on how compensation incentives might affect the choice of a particular product at a particular time. Put simply, the regulatory attention given to the genuine problems created by sales commissions has distracted from the risks created by other types of compensation, from the overall cost of advice, and the fact that there is simply no compensation structure that perfectly aligns the interests of a financial advisor with a client.

In the next section, we consider in detail how various compensation schemes give rise to other types of conflicts of interest. Financial advice is costly to provide, and a number of compensation models are used in practice. Each of these compensation models has strengths

[1] Throughout, we will use the term "advisor" to refer to any professional providing financial advice. When we intend to indicate advisors with a fiduciary duty under the Investment Advisers Act, we will use the term "RIA."
[2] Regulation Best Interest: The Broker-Dealer Standard of Conduct, Release No. 34-86031, 84 Fed. Reg. 33,318 (July 12, 2019).
[3] Definition of the Term "Fiduciary"; Conflict of Interest Rule—Retirement Investment Advice, 81 Fed. Reg. 20,946 (Apr. 8, 2016).

and weaknesses in aligning advisor incentives with their clients' goals. The form of compensation will affect not just the *content* of advice, but its timing, price, the assets the advice pertains to, and from whom—if anyone—professional advice is received. Investment advice during the lifecycle of an investor is a complex problem of incentive alignment that will, inevitably, only be solved imperfectly.

This chapter begins by laying out, in some detail, the lifecycle investing problem that retail investors aim to solve. By taking a more comprehensive, investor-centric view of the problem of conflicted advice, it is hoped that the impact of conflicts of interest on the underlying goal—to retire on time and in comfort—can be better highlighted. It then reviews common compensation schemes and enumerates misalignments of incentives that could arise within an advice relationship. Finally, it applies this framework to the fiduciary rule and Reg BI to evaluate how these interventions fare with respect to these expanded notions of conflict of interest. The fiduciary rule and Reg BI take contrasting approaches to the problem of conflicts in investment advice, and—while the fiduciary rule has been struck down—comparing the DOL's more aggressive approach with the newly adopted Reg BI is instructive as they reflect different approaches to a long-standing regulatory problem.

This chapter will argue that, when these recent regulatory interventions are considered from a stylized investor's point of view, neither intervention is wholly satisfactory. While the fiduciary rule would have applied stringent fiduciary duties to some investment accounts, the effect on investors' overall welfare would have been ambiguous. Reg BI is more comprehensive, but its focus on disclosure tends to aggravate the complexity that retail investors hope to avoid by seeking professional advice in the first place. The effective application of fiduciary duties to protect retail investors requires taking a comprehensive view of the financial life and goals of retail investors.

II THE LIFE-CYCLE SAVINGS PROBLEM

To give some concreteness to these issues, consider an investor saving for retirement. For convenience, let us call her "Sue." Sue is 45 years old, a computer programmer by trade, and is relatively sophisticated as individual investors go—she even minored in economics twenty years ago—but Sue is a busy person and is sophisticated enough to recognize her own limits as a money manager. She would be more comfortable investing with the help of a financial professional. Sue is in the prime of her fairly lucrative career and has several hundred thousand saved in a 401(k) and another hundred thousand in an investment account. She would be an attractive client for any number of professional advisors.

Sue's ultimate goal is to retire comfortably and on schedule with minimal impact on her current lifestyle.[4] To do this, she needs an understanding of what constitutes sufficient retirement savings, how much she needs to save now given her intended timing of retirement, and guidance on how to invest the savings. With respect to the latter, she must choose an appropriate mix of assets in her retirement portfolio, rebalance those assets over time as they appreciate, and respond to deviations from anticipated returns by

---

[4] This is a simplification of a more fulsome statement of Sue's goals which would need to take account of her risk-aversion and perhaps other characteristics. Nevertheless, it is sufficient for present purposes to observe that the provision of high-quality financial advice is only a means to the end of financial welfare and not an end in itself.

potentially adjusting her savings strategy. Of course, Sue must also respond to unexpected life events that have a financial impact and perhaps even adjust her plan in response to her own changing goals about when she wants to retire and how she wants to live in retirement. All of this requires a savings plan and investment strategy subject to intermittent updating.

Given the complexity of these issues, it is no surprise that Sue would seek professional help. It is also no surprise that a substantial industry has grown up around delivering that professional assistance. The question for Sue is what type of advisor she wants to engage, and how that advisor is to be compensated. A corollary question, perhaps not much on Sue's mind but nevertheless bound up with these other choices, is the regulatory regime that will apply to the advisor in question. How Sue answers these questions will affect her savings outcomes and ultimately, whether she can achieve her retirement goals.

The "ideal" form of investment advice is, as we will see, far from clear, but Sue's goal in pursuing professional advice is the same as her overarching goal: retire on time, with sufficient savings, with minimal impact on her lifestyle in the interim. This point bears some emphasis: Sue's goal in deciding how to obtain financial advice is the same as her goal in saving in the first place. Sue's calculation in seeking out professional advice is that engaging a professional financial advisor will lead to better outcomes *net of the cost of advice* than attempting to go it alone, even though financial advisors are costly.

It is not the ambition of this paper to develop a formal mathematical model of investment advice but describing Sue's problem in a simplified framework will sharpen the analysis below. To that end, let us consider a very compact version of the problem Sue is trying to solve. First, Sue has a pool of assets that she wants to invest with an eye toward retirement and other goals—like her children's education. Since we assume, consistent with the lifecycle hypothesis,[5] that Sue will smooth her consumption, her goal is to meet those financial needs while maintaining the highest possible lifestyle both now and in retirement.

In the spirit of an economic model, but without the formalism, let us reduce Sue's lifecycle problem to three simple decision points: Right now, at Time 1, Sue has decided to plan her financial life and is considering engaging an advisor to assist her. The outcome of this planning process will be a plan for allocating assets to various investment accounts and asset mixes (and to consumption) going forward. At some point in the future, at Time 2, Sue will potentially face the need to revisit this plan. This need may or may not be obvious to Sue. For example, one of Sue's children may get into an Ivy League school, and Sue may decide to spend more than she anticipated on college as a result. Sue would be aware that this is a deviation from her plan, and she needs additional advice to revisit her goals. On the other hand, the asset mix in Sue's portfolio might grow unexpectedly, requiring rebalancing, and Sue might be unaware of this need. At Time 2, Sue could engage her advisor again, or perhaps her advisor would invest the resources necessary to become aware of the change and reach out to Sue.

Finally, at Time 3, Sue will enter the drawdown phase of her life (retirement). A fundamental question at this point is whether she has accumulated sufficient resources to retire. As at Time 2, there may also be a need to adjust her asset mix. She will also need to decide how quickly to consume her accumulated savings.

---

[5] Franco Modigliani & Richard H. Brumberg, *Utility Analysis and the Consumption Function: An Interpretation of Cross-Section Data*, in POST-KEYNESIAN ECONOMICS 388 (Kenneth K. Kurihara ed., 1955).

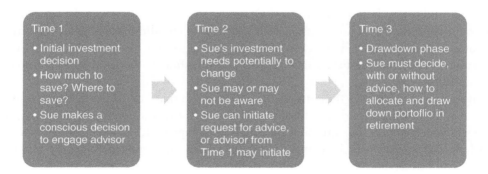

In laying out Sue's series of decisions this way, the intention is to highlight the conventional portfolio allocation choices that Sue must make alongside the broader financial choices Sue faces, like how much to save in each period. Also incorporated is the potentially ongoing need for investment advice. Sue can create a financial plan now, but what if other plans change? More importantly, what if plans do not change, but markets do, and Sue's broad portfolio deviates from her optimal allocation in ways that may not be transparent to her? Also present are strategic decisions that Sue faces, like whether to delay retirement and how to allocate assets between a Section 529 college savings plan and her 401(k) account.

III CONFLICTS OF INTEREST IN INVESTMENT ADVICE

This chapter aims to provide a richer account of potential conflicts of interest that might affect Sue's investment decisions. To that end, rather than focus on conflicts that are likely to be legally cognizable as material conflicts of interest, we focus on the broader class of principal-agent problems generally. After all, Sue's goal is not to avoid conflicts of interest but to retire on schedule and live a financially sound life in the interim. Whenever her interests differ from her advisor, material or not, disclosed or not, Sue should be concerned that her goals may be compromised. The principal-agent framework captures the various ways in which compensation models might cause deviations from her goals. To the extent that some of these deviations are not covered under Reg BI or other conflict of interest rules, this lack of coverage is perhaps food for regulatory thought rather than an indication that such potential problems should be ignored.

As with any business relationship, the interests of Sue and her financial advisor will not be perfectly aligned. There is no aspect of life in which those we hire to do a job fully internalize our interests. In some cases, these misaligned incentives may be inconsequential: if we get the product we need at a competitive price, that is often enough. Some conscientious agents might even do a better job than we would have done on our own, even if we are similarly skilled, but the fact is that agents always have incentives that differ from their principals'. Financial advice is no different. How Sue's advisor is compensated will affect the nature of the advice Sue receives. We begin by reviewing the various compensation models typically used with respect to financial advice.

A *Compensation Models for Financial Advice*

A number of different compensation models are used to pay for financial advice. A very brief overview is provided below.[6] It should be noted that combinations of the various structures are not uncommon, further complicating the analysis of incentives.

Regulations concerned with conflicted investment advice are often motivated by the perceived lower quality of *commission-compensated* financial advice. In this compensation scheme, associated with brokers, Sue would not pay for advice directly, but instead, receive advice incidental to transactions which generate trading or sales commissions for the broker. These commissions generally take the form of sales charges when the trade is made but may also be paid out on a deferred basis over a number of years.

By contrast, *fee-only* financial advice is often held to be the gold standard. Here, Sue pays a fee as a percentage of assets under the advisor's management. This is the compensation scheme associated with certain registered investment advisors (RIAs) subject to a full fiduciary duty and was the regime favored by the fiduciary rule.

The hybrid of fee and commission advice is common enough to be called out: in a *fee-based* model, Sue would pay a flat fee, but the advisor might also receive commissions related to particular transactions.

Sue might also buy financial advice for a *flat fee*. This is not uncommon when the advice takes the form of a comprehensive financial plan. Sue might sit down with a financial planner, describe her goals and current assets, and for a fee of, say, $1,000, receive a comprehensive plan with instructions on how much to deposit in each of her accounts going forward, how to maximize the value of various tax-favored accounts, which mutual funds to pick, and so on. Such plans can provide a useful roadmap for investors who do not mind implementing the advice but need some help in ensuring they are on track for their goals.

Sue could find an advisor who bills *hourly*. Here, the scope of advice could be quite flexible, from instructions on rebalancing a retirement account, to the type of full-blown plan described above. Sue might also work with an hourly advisor who also charges a retainer. In this structure, Sue is committed to paying an amount equal to, say, eight hours of the advisor's time, regardless of her needs, and hours beyond that are billed at an hourly rate.

Two other models merit mentioning, though they will not be extensively discussed here. Sue might receive advice free as an *ancillary service* to some existing financial relationship. For example, many employer-sponsored retirement plans offer call-center based financial advice at no cost to plan participants. This advice is provided as a benefit to plan participants and ultimately financed by the fees generated by managing the plan assets.

Finally, Sue might pay for investment advice indirectly in exchange for *access to her financial data*. While this is not currently a widely used model, the proliferation of very low-cost robo-advisors and financial information services like Mint or SigFig, combined with the increasing value of personal data as a commercial commodity, makes this a model worth noting, even if only as a potential future development. Financial advice provided for "free" simply as a means of gaining access to the valuable financial data of the advice recipient raises intriguing questions but is beyond the scope of this chapter.

Another compensation issue that might not be transparent to Sue is that the advisor she chooses to work with might receive compensation from his employer that distorts his incentives, even though Sue does not directly pay this compensation. For example, when funds engage in

---

[6] *See generally* John H. Robinson, *Who's the Fairest of Them All? A Comparative Analysis of Advisor Compensation Models*, 20 J. FIN. PLAN. 56 (2007).

revenue sharing, they pay brokerages a share of the income generated from asset management fees. Even though this compensation goes to the firm rather than the individual advisor, it is nevertheless a potentially important source of revenue, and the firm has an incentive to encourage the broker to sell funds that generate this type of income. This could take the form of sales targets, bonuses, vacations, and so on. What ultimately affects Sue is how her advisor, the natural person using his discretion, is compensated.

B *A Taxonomy of Agency Problems in Investment Advice*

Each of the above compensation models gives rise to distortions in how a financial advisor will advise a client. This simple point is worth emphasizing: *every compensation model gives rise to conflicts of interest.* This includes the fee-only model commonly associated with advice from RIAs held to a fiduciary duty. Below we consider a set of potential distortions of the advice an investor like Sue might receive, and how each type of compensation could exacerbate or alleviate the distortion in question.

1 Which Product to Recommend

By far the most widely discussed distortion of investment advice is when conflicts of interest motivate an advisor to recommend the wrong product from a menu of potential product offerings. The best-studied variant of this problem is the recommendation of load mutual funds to investors who would better be served by no-load mutual funds.[7] Since load mutual funds pay sales commissions to brokers who sell them, these brokers have an incentive to prefer them to no-load funds that the academic literature suggests are generally stronger performers.[8] The academic literature has concluded that these distortions harm retail investors, insofar as investors who receive commission-compensated advice are likely to end up holding investments that are worse than other options in the market. There is evidence that it is precisely because these funds are poor performers that they must resort to paying commissions to generate business.[9] While this problem is studied extensively in the mutual fund market, other financial products carry sales commissions as well, and similar dynamics are likely present in other markets where financial products are sold on commission.

But the commonly cited conflict-generating incentive to recommend high commission funds is not the only source of distortion arising from sales commissions as a compensation scheme. Commission-compensated brokers also have an incentive to recommend products that are likely to need frequent rebalancing. For example, selling a target-date fund is a particularly unattractive option for a broker as the fund is designed to be held for decades. Recommending an equivalent portfolio of the underlying funds is a more promising strategy that will generate occasional commissions as rebalancing is required. Notably, this type of distortion would not show up in the empirical tests that document the underperformance of broker-sold mutual funds, since the performance of both types of funds could be identical.

---

[7] Jason Furman & Betsey Stevenson, *The Effects of Conflict Investment Advice on Retirement Savings*, THE WHITE HOUSE: PRESIDENT BARACK OBAMA (Feb. 23, 2015), https://obamawhitehouse.archives.gov/blog/2015/02/23/effects-con flicted-investment-advice-retirement-savings.

[8] Susan E. K. Christoffersen, Richard Evans & David K. Musto, *What Do Consumers' Fund Flows Maximize? Evidence from Their Brokers' Incentives*, 68 J. FIN. 201, 205 (2012); Daniel Bergstresser, John M. R. Chalmers & Peter Tufano, *Assessing the Costs and Benefits of Brokers in the Mutual Fund Industry*, 22 REV. FIN. STUD. 4129 (2009).

[9] Christoffersen et al., *supra* note 8.

By contrast, fee-only advice is generally understood to be free of this sort of conflict. The fiduciary rule largely focused on shifting investors to the fee-only advice model. The economic case for the rule relied extensively on the benefits that would accrue to investors if the distortions of commissions in the mutual fund market were addressed.[10] Since commission-based mutual funds underperform, the DOL argued that eliminating commission-based conflicts of interest would enhance returns for investors.

While fee-only advice is less distortive of asset recommendations, it is not the case that it is entirely free of such distortions. For example, a fee-only asset manager has an incentive to recommend high-yielding investments, as—all else equal—the higher the expected return on the account, the more future assets there will be to manage.[11] This could induce a fee-only advisor to push a client to take on too much investment risk as she approaches retirement. To be sure this is a second-order effect, but it is also the case that a fee-only investment advisor's compensation is first-order neutral as to the recommended asset mix. That is, fee-only advisors do not have bad incentives when it comes to which products to recommend, but they do not have direct positive incentives either. As such, a second-order distortion might still be important.

Investment advisor risk-seeking may affect asset recommendations for another reason: Investment advisors may hope to generate new clients by delivering a particularly strong performance. This is undoubtedly a significant source of incentives for mutual fund advisors,[12] and it stands to reason that it would influence retail financial advisors as well. The incentive to generate strong returns is, to some extent, a wholesome one, but it creates a misalignment of incentives to the extent it generates motivation to take excessive risk. While the quality of asset management should be judged on a risk-adjusted basis, evidence suggests that most retail investors pay attention to unadjusted returns.[13] Thus an advisor seeking positive word of mouth, or even just satisfied clients, might shade toward too much risk-taking.

Designing compensation to eliminate asset choice distortions is not an easy task. The fiduciary rule ran into a related problem in attempting to eliminate compensation structures that would distort portfolio recommendations. In attempting to preserve the availability of commissions, while reducing their distortive effect, it was suggested that firms might simply equalize commissions among different assets on the menu. If every asset carries a 3 percent commission, then the broker's recommendation will not be distorted by a higher payment for recommending a particular product, just as a flat fee asset manager's choice is (relatively) undistorted.

Unfortunately, this reform created another problem: A 3 percent commission may be low for equities, but quite high for bonds that can be expected to have a lower rate of return. If all products pay the same commission, then the advisor does not have a commission-based reason to favor one product over another. However, the flat commission makes some products artificially less attractive to the investor net of sales charges, which simply relocates the distortionary effect without leaving the investor better off.

That a flat commission is problematic suggests that the traditional fee-based model would be problematic in a parallel way. A 1 percent annual fee for assets under management is much easier

[10] U.S. Dep't of Labor, Regulating Advice Markets: Definition of the Term "Fiduciary," Conflicts of Interest – Retirement Investment Advice, Regulatory Impact Analysis for Final Rule and Exemptions (2016) [hereinafter Regulatory Impact Analysis.]

[11] Strictly speaking, unless an advisor can diversify recommendations across accounts, the incentive would be for the advisor to make recommendations with a risk profile more attuned to the advisor's risk tolerance than the clients, but this would be most egregious in the case of clients with very low-risk tolerance, like retirees.

[12] Erik R. Sirri & Peter Tufano, *Costly Search and Mutual Fund Flows*, 53 J. Fin. 1589 (1998).

[13] Diane Del Guercio & Jonathan Reuter, *Mutual Fund Performance and the Incentive to Generate Alpha*, 69 J. Fin. 1673 (2014).

to swallow when the expected return on a portfolio of equities is 7 percent, compared with the moment when Sue is nearing retirement, and her portfolio can only be expected to earn 2–3 percent before the 1 percent cost. This is yet another reason that even a fee-only advisor might encourage too much risk-taking.

In fact, this is a fundamental problem in designing compensation. Any compensation regime that eliminates the *advisor's* incentive to favor particular options by equalizing compensation across products decreases the *client's* appetite for low-yielding investments. As a simple matter of portfolio theory, the client needs to take marginally more risk to offset the compensation. The broker's incentives will be distorted by the compensation or the client's will. It is not clear that Sue is left better off if the distortion is simply shifted to her own savings incentives.

Flat fee and hourly models do best at eliminating asset choice distortion. Because the advisor has no financial exposure to the particular mix of assets, either through commissions or subsequent performance, these compensation models are best suited to encourage a neutral decision. It is worth noting that neutral is not an ideal outcome. Corporate boards do not settle for their CEOs being neutral with respect to firm performance by eliminating self-dealing and hoping for the best. Nevertheless, performance-based compensation is quite rare in retail financial advice.

Which product to recommend to a client is obviously an important choice for an advisor with significant consequences for the client, but it is certainly not the only source of conflicts, and it is far from clear that it is even the most important one. In the balance of this section, we consider other types of distortion that tend to get less attention.

2 When to Give Advice

Most discussions of conflicts of interest in investment advice consider how compensation will affect the delivery of advice, conditional on the advice being sought. That is, we typically assume that an investor is already looking for help making a decision and ask how advisor compensation will affect the advice she receives. However, in describing Sue's lifecycle problem, it is clear that the timing of investment advice is an endogenous part of the advice relationship. That is, either Sue or the advisor can initiate the process of advice being rendered at any time. It may be the case that Sue seeks advice when she does not need it, and equally that Sue needs advice that she does not seek. How compensation affects the *timing* of advice is not an unfamiliar problem in regulating investment advice, but it is one that has been grappled with only partially.

The timing-related conflict of interest that receives the most attention is the commission-motivated practice of churning. Commission-compensated brokers have incentives to recommend high commission products over low commission products, but sales commissions generate another incentive as well: the incentive to recommend more frequent transactions. If a broker is compensated with a sales commission paid at the time of purchase, then more purchases will lead to more commissions and more income for the broker. Severe churning may lead to allegations of lack of suitability, but a commission-compensated broker will always have incentives to recommend more trading rather than less. In an age where set it and forget it financial products like target-date funds are increasingly common, commission-compensated financial advisors may face additional pressure to engage in unnecessary trading to generate commissions.

However, a fee-only investment advisor does not eliminate timing-related conflicts of interest. The fee-based compensation structure is relatively poor when it comes to motivating advisors to give attention to clients' existing accounts. If the advisor gets a fee for assets under management, then the advisor receives this fee whether or not he or she actually spends time servicing the account. The income from managing the account is not directly coupled to the advice given, and the advisor's primary motivation is to give attention to adding new accounts or to accounts that seem likely to depart. Servicing existing accounts is essentially overhead for a fee-only advisor.

As it happens, "reverse churning"—the issue of fee-only investment accounts that go without substantial attention from advisors—is a recognized problem. Stories of investment advisors letting accounts sit unattended while collecting considerable fees are not uncommon. When RIAs are egregiously inattentive, this could violate their fiduciary duties, but more modest degrees of neglect are unlikely to create problems for advisors even if they disadvantage clients. Advisors would surely respond that neglecting a client account would eventually result in the loss of that client's business, but this is not a persuasive response to the issue. *Any* failure to serve a client resulting from a misalignment of interests could potentially cause the loss of the client's business. If clients were fully attuned to how well their interests were being served and able to act effectively on that information, conflicts of interest would not be problematic in any case.

If both fee-only and commission-based compensation create conflicts of interest around timely attention to clients' accounts, might other models resolve such conflicts? Unfortunately, neither the hourly nor flat fee model seems particularly promising. While these models at least do not incentivize churning, they nevertheless create an incentive for an underworked advisor to induce a client to pay for unneeded advice. A flat fee to "update" a still serviceable plan or hourly billing for unnecessary services are risks associated with these models.

Returning to Sue's lifecycle problem, if she anticipates that the need for further financial advice might arise at some future point, is there a compensation structure, even, in theory, that might mitigate this conflict of interest? Or must Sue simply be vigilant against an irreducible agency problem as she seeks to navigate changing circumstances? Two models have some promise.

The first potential solution would be to seek a compensation structure where the time dimension creates an incentive to revisit clients who are likely to need additional advice. For example, typical class B mutual fund shares pay the sales commission out over time, and then stop after about five years. This structure of commission payout could incentivize brokers to revisit accounts once the commission is fully paid. If the timing of the commission payout is reasonably well-calibrated to the time a typical client needs attention, then this could create an alignment of incentives. Unfortunately, the need to specify the commission structure at the fund level means that this structure cannot be customized to the needs of individual investors. Nevertheless, the possibility of using bespoke compensation arrangements to address conflicts of interest illustrates that commission structures unavailable in a fee-only account might reduce conflicts around the timing of investment advice if such structures are well designed.

Another more innovative approach is the fee-only compensation model, coupled with a robo-advisor-style screen for changing circumstances. The notion here is that a robo-advisory service can evaluate client needs without increasing marginal costs to the advisor, or at least while keeping them very low relative to the cost of genuine human attention. As such, a fee-only robo-advisor would reduce the agency problem related to the timing of advice in a fee-only account by keeping the incremental cost of attention low.

3 How Much to Save in a Particular Account

The investment landscape in the United States is characterized by a growing list of specialized, tax-favored accounts. It is not uncommon for a single family like Sue's to hold investments in multiple 401(k) accounts, an IRA or two, a Health Savings Account (HSA), and one or more section 529 college savings accounts. The contributions to these accounts are restricted in purpose and therefore not fungible, and each account is likely to have different investment options. Sue's family may have assets in a non-tax-preferred brokerage account and rely on a financial advisor servicing that account for advice across all of the family's assets.

This common arrangement gives rise to yet another pernicious conflict of interest. In this case, depending as usual on the manner of compensation, the advisor may face incentives to encourage investors to save too much in the brokerage account and not enough in the other accounts or to prefer some tax-favored accounts over others.

Consider how this would play out with a typical commission-compensated broker. In that case, the broker's payment would depend on the amount of assets invested in accounts that paid a commission. Assets outside of tax-preferred accounts would fit that bill, as would assets in an IRA plan managed by the broker. On the other hand, assets in a 401(k) plan or HSA would not generate commissions for the broker. If Sue relies on the broker for recommendations regarding her overall balance of assets, the broker will have an incentive to have Sue over-save in those accounts.

Section 529 college savings plans present an even more complicated question because Sue has a choice of which college savings plan to choose, and the tax benefits depend on that choice.[14] If Sue lives in a state with an income tax, her state likely offers a tax break for using the state's plan, but if Sue goes out of state to invest in a 529 plan, she may give up that tax break. Most large brokerages have 529 plans that pay commission compensation, but unless Sue happens to be located in the same state as one of those plans (or happens to live in a state with no income tax or that gives tax breaks for out of state plans), then her broker's compensation in the form of commissions is at odds with her tax break. This is not a hypothetical scenario: The Financial Industry Regulatory Authority (FINRA) has taken action against brokerages that steered clients to out of state 529 plans to the detriment of their in-state tax breaks.[15]

Switching to a fee-only structure is unlikely to help. Fees are generally charged against assets under management, and if those assets are in employer accounts that are not part of the assets managed by the fee-only advisor, then the advisor will not receive compensation related to those accounts. As with commission compensation, a fee-based advisor has incentives to encourage assets to be directed to accounts that generate revenue. The advisor might limit advice to assets Sue chooses to have managed by the advisor, but that would greatly limit the degree to which the advice solves Sue's overall investment problem.

Charging a flat or hourly fee is the optimal solution here. When Sue seeks advice about where to direct her savings, that advice is least likely to be tainted by conflicts of interest when compensation is not tied to the choice of accounts in which assets are saved. The challenge for Sue is that such advice can be hard to find. To be sure, some advisors will deliver a financial plan for a flat or hourly fee, but Sue will find that most of those advisors also manage — either through a fee or commission structure — other investment accounts. If Sue pays an advisor a flat fee for a comprehensive financial plan, and the broker also provides fee or commission-compensated financial advice, then the flat fee for the plan does not do much to resolve the conflict of interest if the advisor can benefit by suggesting, as part of the plan, that Sue invest some of her assets through a conflict-laden channel. In practice, Sue will find it difficult to fully escape this conflict of interest.

[14] Quinn Curtis, *Costs, Conflicts, and College Savings: Evaluating Section 529 Savings Plan*, 37 YALE J. ON REG. 116 (2020).

[15] Press Release, Nat'l Ass'n Sec. Dealers, NASD Issues Investor Alert on 529 College Savings Plans (Sept. 13, 2004), http://www.finra.org/newsroom/2004/nasd-issues-investor-alert-529-college-savings-plans.

The resilience of this type of conflict is a pernicious problem because allocating assets across various savings options is surely one of the more difficult problems that modern investors face. How many of us are truly confident that we are making the right savings choices between 401(k), 529, and IRA plans? By comparison, getting a reasonably well-calibrated and diversified portfolio in any of these accounts, conditional on a sensible allocation of assets across the various accounts, may be as simple as choosing a single, low-cost target-date fund.

The problem of getting unconflicted, holistic financial advice across a variety of accounts highlights the shortcoming of our existing system of regulating financial advice, and indeed of our system of individual investing generally. Considerable regulatory effort has been put into ensuring that, within a particular account, investors get advice that is, to varying degrees, free from conflicts of interest. But when it comes to the much more challenging problem of allocating savings between or among accounts, investors are often left to their own devices or forced to seek help from advisors with conflicting incentives. The atomization of our financial lives into 401(k)s, 529s, HSAs, IRAs and so on—rarely all managed by a single firm—means choices among these accounts are often made under the guidance of an advisor with a financial interest in some, but not all, of those accounts.

4 When to Retire and How to Manage Post-Retirement Assets

If Sue inquires at Time 3 about whether she has accumulated sufficient assets to retire, the answer may depend on how she is paying for the advice. As long as Sue is working and contributing new money to an account, a commission-based advisor has an incentive not to advise her to stop. The significant, immediate commission Sue generates with each deposit is the broker's primary source of income from the account, but new deposits likely cease upon retirement. While the broker might receive trailing fees and some commissions related to rebalancing after Sue retires, Sue's value as a client declines when her career ends and the influx of new assets into the account (and the associated commissions) declines.

A fee-only advisor has an incentive to ensure that Sue's account has a balance as large as possible. This would create a more modest incentive to advise Sue to work another year or two, but the fee-only advisor's compensation continues so long as the account holds assets, and so this would be less dramatic than the commission-compensated broker. The fee-only advisor, though, would have an incentive to encourage Sue to draw down the account relatively slowly. As the account balance declines, so does the fee-only advisor's compensation.

An hourly or flat fee is robust against these problematic incentives. Since these compensation schemes do not directly link compensation to account balance[16] or new dollars invested, there is no distortion of the incentive to render sensible advice.

5 The Existence of an Advice Relationship

Suppose that Sue simply does not need professional advice but is not aware of this fact. Here, the compensation model for the advisor is basically irrelevant: the mere fact of a potential advice relationship is enough to create a conflict of interest. Only a particularly scrupulous advisor could be expected to turn away a potential client on the basis that the client would be perfectly fine going it alone. This type of conflict is hardly farfetched, and—indeed—it was recognized

---

[16] There may be an indirect link between hourly compensation and account balance, as a larger asset base might require more time to service.

implicitly in the DOL fiduciary rule, which required brokers to document why investor interests were served by rolling assets out of a 401(k) plan.

An investor could seek unneeded advice for several reasons. First, Sue might overestimate the difficulty of the investment challenge she faces. Indeed, it is questionable whether many investors with ordinary financial situations require professional advice. Over the last decade, the retirement savings landscape has transformed as a wave of 401(k) lawsuits have caused many employers to revise their plans in ways that make them simpler to use and less likely to result in costly allocation mistakes.[17] Recent years have also seen explosive growth in target-date funds, which allow investors to attain a well-calibrated, well-diversified portfolio by merely picking a prospective retirement date.[18] Investors also increasingly have access to free resources through their employers. Many large 401(k) plans now provide call-center based advice that—while based more on superficial assessments than traditional financial advising—nevertheless provides individually tailored answers to common questions.

With retirement plans providing improved options at decreasing costs and richer advice options for investors, the need for other sources of investment advice has declined. The bottom line is that, for a not insignificant number of investors like Sue, paying for advice—at least at the prices usually commanded by conventional full-service advisors—may well leave them with less money than they would have if they simply went it alone using the resources made available to them through their employers.

The reality is that, in some cases, financial advisors would serve would-be clients best by declining their business, especially those whose financial situations are well served by existing employer-based infrastructure. But the incentive to accept a client is a conflict of interest that cannot be resolved simply by tweaking the compensation regime. No matter how an advisor is paid, the mere fact that an advisor-client relationship entails payments makes accepting a client a potentially attractive option. As options for free- or low-cost advice proliferate, including employer-based options and robo-advisors, investors are unquestionably vulnerable to full-service advisors' self-interest when it comes to creating a client relationship. Our regulatory regimes have done very little to address this growing concern.

To summarize, while conflicts of interest in product recommendations get most of the attention in the regulation of investment advice, they are not the only problem that an investor seeking advice will face. Indeed, they are not even clearly the most important type of conflict. Investors who find managing their financial life a bewildering task face an equally bewildering array of options for getting professional help and mistakes in seeking help will have deleterious consequences for their investment outcomes no less severe than some investment mistakes. In the next section,. we examine how two recent regulatory interventions: the DOL fiduciary rule and Regulation Best Interest address these issues.

IV REGULATING CONFLICTS OF INTEREST

There have long been calls to unify the fiduciary standard for investment advice between brokers and RIAs under a single fiduciary standard.[19] Two recent rulemakings have directly addressed

---

[17] Stephen Miller, *Less Is More: Sponsors Simplify 401(k) Menus*, SHRM.org (June 19, 2014), https://www.shrm.org/resourcesandtools/hr-topics/benefits/pages/simpler-401k-menus.aspx.

[18] Jeff Holt, *A Brief Overview of How the Target-Date Fund Landscape Is Evolving*, MORNINGSTAR (May 9, 2019), https://www.morningstar.com/blog/2019/05/09/target-date-fund.html.

[19] *See, e.g.*, Arthur B. Laby, *Fiduciary Obligations of Broker-Dealers and Investment Advisers*, 55 VILL. L. REV. 701, 702 (2010).

conflicts of interest in investment advice: The Department of Labor fiduciary rule and the SEC's new Reg BI. While the rules take different approaches, both suffer from adopting a narrow view of how conflicts distort advice incentives. That is, both rules are the product of regulators identifying a conflict of interest and seeking to reduce its impact, rather than beginning with the question of how to improve outcomes for investors like Sue to maximize her retirement assets net of the cost (and quality) of advice. This section discusses these rules in light of the expanded account of conflicts of interest discussed above.

A *The Fiduciary Rule*

In 2016, the U.S. Department of Labor proposed a package of rules known collectively as the fiduciary rule.[20] The rules were designed to subject brokers and other professionals dealing with assets in 401(k) plans and IRAs to a fiduciary duty. The explicit economic argument for the rule was based in research demonstrating that high commission paying mutual funds were generally inferior performers, suggesting that brokers pushed these funds due to a conflict of interest related to receiving a higher commission payment (the product-recommendation conflict discussed above).[21] Before it took full effect the rule was struck down by the Fifth Circuit in a ruling the Trump administration declined to appeal.[22]

The rule's most important impact would have been on IRA accounts advised by commission-compensated brokers. The rule required that brokers advising such accounts either forgo sales commissions and other third-party compensation or enter into a contract—privately enforceable—that required them to act in the best interest of investors and take steps to mitigate conflicts of interest created by commissions.[23] The so-called best interest contract exemption would have sharply curtailed the ability of brokers to take differential commissions that might have distorted their recommendations. In doing so, it would have reduced the severity of the conflict of interest identified in the top left cell of Table 1: the distortive effect on sales commissions. This was the DOL's explicit goal in promulgating the rule. But in focusing on this particular conflict, the DOL left open the larger question whether, on net, the fiduciary rule would have left investors better off.

Return to our investor Sue, who is trying to manage her wealth over her lifecycle. What would be the effect of the fiduciary rule on her investment decisions? For starters, Sue would be more likely to receive advice on a fee-only basis. One of the chief effects of the fiduciary rule would have been to create substantial legal risks for commission-compensated advisors, at least to the extent they were helping Sue manage retirement assets, say, in an IRA. (One of the main shortcomings of the fiduciary rule was that it could not, due to the DOL's jurisdictional limits, affect non-retirement brokerage accounts.) By pushing advisors toward fee-based models, the fiduciary rule would have reduced the incentive to push low-quality products in order to receive commissions.

If Sue were to receive advice on an account subject to the fiduciary rule while it was in effect, there is little doubt that the specific recommendations she would receive would be a better fit for her needs simply because advisors would have been sharply limited in accepting compensation for recommending other products. But it does not follow that Sue would have been better off. Two

---

[20] *Supra* note 3.
[21] REGULATORY IMPACT ANALYSIS, *supra* note 10.
[22] Chamber of Commerce v. U.S. Dep't of Labor, 885 F.3d 360 (5th Cir. 2018).
[23] *See* Best Interest Contract Exemption, 29 C.F.R. § 2550 (2016).

TABLE 1 *Summary of Impact of Compensation Structure on Advice Incentives*

COMPENSATION STRUCTURE

NATURE OF ADVICE	Sales Commissions	Fee-Only Advice	Flat Fee	Hourly Fee
Choice of Product	Commissions distort recommendations.		No conflict. Advisor is neutral as to choice of product.	
Timing of Advice	Sales commissions incentivize churning.	Cost of attention incentivizes reverse churning.		Incentive to offer unnecessary advice to generate billings
Allocation to Accounts	Compensation is tied to choice of account, distorting recommendations.		No conflict. Advisor is neutral as to account choice.	
When to Retire	Sales commissions are maximized by delaying retirement to maximize new contributions.	Compensation is tied to account size, creating modest incentive to suggest delaying retirement.	No conflict. Advisor is neutral as to retirement date choice.	
Existence of Advice Relationship	Advisor has an interest in accepting a client, regardless of actual need for advice.			

other factors would need to be weighed. First, would *other* conflicts of interest have been exacerbated by the rule? Second, would the advice that Sue received come at a higher price, conflicts aside?

Taking the second issue first, it is clear that fee-based advice generally comes at a premium price to commission-compensated advice. The DOL reported that the average commission actually paid by investors was 1.58 percent,[24] but that commission is spread over the fund's holding period, say seven years, while the annual fees for fee-only asset management hover just above 1 percent.[25] While the advice Sue received under the fiduciary rule would have been of higher quality, in the sense that she would hold funds that likely performed better, Sue would likely pay more for that advice. Whether Sue would be better off with the more expensive, but superior, advice is unclear.[26] The lack of clarity on which regime would leave Sue better off at retirement reflects the shortcomings of the DOL's narrow focus. By fixating on one type of conflict of interest and relegating the cost of advice to secondary consideration, the DOL ended up with a rule whose impact on the welfare of the investors it was meant to protect was genuinely ambiguous.

The narrow focus on commissions also caused the DOL to overlook the impact of other types of conflicts. One immediate conclusion is that Sue might have been more vulnerable to reverse churning and general neglect as an investment client under the fiduciary rule. To the extent that fee-only compensation would have been the dominant model, Sue's account would generate revenue for the advisor whether or not it was serviced, at least unless Sue became so dissatisfied that she decided to take her business elsewhere.

The fiduciary rule might have also exacerbated conflicts with regard to what account Sue should target for savings. In particular, the rule applied only to certain types of accounts within the jurisdiction of the DOL. While 401(k)s and IRAs would have been subject to more stringent oversight of compensation models, ordinary investment accounts and other types of accounts like 529 Plans would not have been subject to limitations on commission compensation. The differential treatment of the account types is significant because Sue may well rely on a single financial planner for advice on allocating her savings. If that planner could receive a more attractive compensation for assets saved in accounts not subject to the fiduciary rule, there would be an obvious incentive to advise Sue to save in those accounts.

The possibility that the constraints of the fiduciary rule would induce advisors to push clients to invest in less stringently regulated accounts illustrates a pervasive issue with the regulation of financial advice: the economic case for the fiduciary rule takes the context of advice-giving as fixed, but the fiduciary rule alters that context. Advice with respect to an IRA account would indeed be higher quality under the fiduciary rule, but if a financial planner steers dollars to a broker-sold 529 account instead, then the hypothetically higher quality of the never-received IRA advice is of no benefit to Sue. By heightening liability, the fiduciary rule created disincentives to service certain types of investment accounts without considering the role that an advisor might play in advising investors in which account to save.

Intriguingly, the fiduciary rule did include one of the few examples of a regulation explicitly acknowledging this sort of problem. Among the requirements of the rule was a provision that required a broker advising a rollover from a 401(k) into an IRA to document a basis for believing

---

[24] Regulatory Impact Analysis, *supra* note 10.

[25] *See Average Financial Advisor Fees & Costs*, Advisory HQ (2020), http://www.advisoryhq.com/articles/financial-advisor-fees-wealth-managers-planners-and-fee-only-advisors.

[26] Quinn Curtis, The Fiduciary Rule Controversy and the Future of Investment Advice, 9 Harv. Bus. L. Rev. 53 (2019).

that moving the money out of the 401(k) account was in the best interest of the investor. The DOL was sensitive to the possibility that brokers might steer assets into accounts that will generate fees for them, but the DOL seems to have overlooked the bigger picture that advisors have significant scope to suggest that assets be invested in accounts that would not have been covered by the fiduciary rule at all.

Finally, the DOL assumed that, with the fiduciary rule in effect, Sue would find advice readily available. The fiduciary rule heightened potential liability for financial advice, a risk for which advisors would be likely to demand compensation and may have constrained access to advice. There is evidence that some advisors reduced the scope of their services, and some 401(k) plans that had provided call-center based advice ceased doing so. While these reductions in services are not conflicts of interest per se, they nevertheless might have materially impacted Sue's success as an investor.

The fiduciary rule might well have represented progress for retail investors: that is a close empirical question. What is clear, though, is that the rule was not the product of comprehensive consideration of how to improve outcomes for investors like Sue, but rather was an intervention focused on mitigating a particular type of conflict. That the distortionary effects of sales commissions are well documented does not mean that other types of distortions can be safely ignored, and certainly does not mean that the impact of increased costs can be disregarded. The DOL would have been well served to take Sue's lifecycle problem as a starting point and build a regulatory impact analysis aimed at supporting her savings goals.

B *Regulation Best Interest*

The most recent attempt to address conflicts of interest in investment advice is the SEC's Reg BI[27] and Form CRS.[28] Reg BI[29] addresses many of the same concerns as the fiduciary rule and can be understood as the SECs replacement for the now-defunct DOL effort. Reg BI is both broader in application and more modest in impact than the fiduciary rule. On the one hand, while the fiduciary rule covered only specific types of retirement-related accounts, Reg BI covers all advice given to retail investing clients by brokers, whether the advice applies to retirement assets or not. On the other hand, Reg BI has a much lighter regulatory touch than did the fiduciary rule: It does far less to limit the use of sales commission compensation, it permits the disclosure of conflicts as a curative mechanism and steers clear of a private right of action. Notably, the dissenting commissioners cited the relatively weak protection it would offer investors in declining to support it.[30]

---

[27] Regulation Best Interest, *supra* note 2.
[28] Form CRS Relationship Summary; Amendments to Form ADV, 84 Fed. Reg. 33,492 (July 12, 2019).
[29] I will somewhat casually refer to Reg BI to cover both the Regulation Best Interest and Form CRS rulemakings when discussing their general impact.
[30] Steven Lofchie, Maurine R. Bartlett & Conor Almquist, *SEC Adopts Regulation Best Interest*, Nat. L. Rev. (June 6, 2019). *See also* Public Statement, Robert J. Jackson Jr., Commissioner, SEC, Statement on "Proposed Rulemakings Relating to Investment Adviser / Broker Dealer (IABD) Standards of Conduct" (April 18, 2018), https://www.sec.gov/news/public-statement/proposed-rulemaking-retail-investor-relationships-investment-professionals; Public Statement, Kara M. Stein, Commissioner, SEC, Statement on "Proposals Relating to Regulation Best Interest, Form CRS, Restrictions on the Use of Certain Names or Titles, and Commission Interpretation Regarding the Standard of Conduct for Investment Advisers" (April 18, 2018), https://www.sec.gov/news/public-statement/stein-statement-open-meeting-041818.

Substantively, the regulation requires that brokers act in the "best interest"[31] of retail customers, a standard meant to be more demanding than the suitability requirement that generally applies to broker advice. The rule provides that it is satisfied if a broker complies with four requirements:[32]

- The broker must provide a disclosure document that describes the nature of the broker relationship, associated fees, and any "material facts relating to conflicts of interest."
- The broker must exercise reasonable care and diligence in making the recommendation and have a reasonable basis to believe that the broker is not placing his interests ahead of the client, considering the entire investment profile of the client.
- The broker must maintain and enforce written policies designed to "at a minimum disclose . . . or eliminate, all conflicts of interest."
- The broker must otherwise adopt policies to ensure compliance with Reg BI.

Reg BI seems initially promising in addressing a broader set of conflicts than simply distortions of what product to recommend. The definition of "conflict of interest" in Reg BI is circularly given as "an interest that might incline a broker ... to make a recommendation that is not disinterested."[33] While unhelpful as a definition, this at least has the advantage of not ruling out any particular conflict of interest. As such, it is tempting to be optimistic that Reg BI could more effectively sweep in subtle conflicts of interest than did the fiduciary rule, which was squarely aimed at conflicts anticipated by the regulators. If brokers are left to think broadly about what might cause their interests to deviate from those of their client, then perhaps some of the other types of conflicts outlined above will be addressed to some extent.

Interestingly, Reg BI is drafted in a way that is ambivalent regarding the scope of conflicts of interest it is likely to cover. On the one hand, Reg BI seems to internalize the fixation on conflicts that create incentives to recommend particular products, perhaps at the expense of other types of conflicts. The key phrase in Reg BI is that the requirement applies "when making a recommendation."[34] That is, Reg BI establishes requirements for making a recommendation, conditional on a recommendation being made. The question of the timing of advice as outlined above, for example, would not be covered. In regulating recommendations, Reg BI essentially treats the process by which the retail client and the broker decide to give and receive advice as exogenous to the regulatory environment, just as the fiduciary rule did.

On the other hand, some aspects of Reg BI seem likely to play some role in addressing other aspects of incentive misalignment. For example, the requirement that the broker believes that the recommended transaction is in the best interest of clients in light of their "investment profile"[35] would arguably discourage brokers from advising an investment in a particular account managed by the broker if it would be in the client's interest to save in a different account. Contrast this provision with the fiduciary rule's approach of essentially requiring commission-receiving firms to adopt level commissions across different products, which would fully eliminate problematic differential commissions

---

[31]   17 C.F.R. § 240.15l-1(a)(1) (2020).
[32]   17 C.F.R. § 240.15l-1(a)(2) (2020).
[33]   17 C.F.R. § 240.15l-l(b)(3) (2020).
[34]   17 C.F.R. § 240.15l-1(a)(1) (2020).
[35]   17 C.F.R. § 240.15l-1(a)(2)(ii)(A) (2020).

while doing nothing to discourage advising assets into the commission-based account in the first place.

While Reg BI evinces some awareness of these other types of conflicts, where it fails investors like Sue, is in the degree it relies on disclosure to address conflicts that might have deleterious effects. While SEC Chair Clayton noted that firms would not be able to comply with Reg BI "solely" through disclosure, firms are nevertheless not explicitly required to eliminate any particular compensation practices, even if they create conflicts. The language of the conflict-of-interest provision is "at a minimum disclose ... or eliminate,"[36] with the phrase "at a minimum disclose" arguably rendering the "or eliminate" superfluous.

Under the new rules, if Sue turns to a broker for advice, she will now receive a two-page form, written in plain English, describing her broker's compensation, as well as any conflicts of interest that compensation might create, at least insofar as those conflicts are regarded as material to the recommendations that the broker may make. The form will tell her whether she can expect additional monitoring of her account from the broker. This latter requirement, in particular, seems directed at addressing the timing of potential future advice and the client's needs to monitor her own investments.

But it is not clear that this additional information leaves Sue better off from the perspective of the problem she set out to solve. Just as the DOL did, the SEC has set out, in its new rules, to target conflicts of interest, with only a secondary emphasis on the broader goals of investors like Sue. Sue's fundamental problem, the one that motivated her to seek advice in the first place, is navigating the complex decisions around allocating assets to save for retirement. Sue believes (perhaps incorrectly) that professional advice will help her achieve a better outcome net of the cost of that advice. With Reg BI and Form CRS, Sue gets additional information about conflicts of interest that might contaminate the advice she receives, but this just means that Sue now faces the not-obviously-less-complex problem of navigating the decision of how to pay for advice about allocating assets for retirement. The problem with disclosing conflicts of interest to retail investors and asking them to act effectively on that information is that it may not reduce the burden of complexity associated with attempting to meet their retirement goals. Put simply, does Reg BI leave an investor like Sue any closer to her goal of retiring comfortably, or does it merely replace one complex decision with another? Just as with the fiduciary rule, the answer is ambiguous.

v CONCLUSION

The fiduciary rule and Reg BI have different weak points. The fiduciary rule understood potential conflicts too narrowly, even as it mandated substantive changes to address those conflicts. Under the fiduciary rule, Sue might have received better advice at a higher cost, raising the question of whether the tradeoff would actually improve her retirement outcome. Reg BI takes a broader view of potential conflicts but relies too heavily on disclosure, merely replacing Sue's problem of managing her money with the challenge of navigating the market for advice. At root, the insufficiency of both rules arises from their failure to address the *real* problem that Sue faces. Sue's challenge is not that she might receive conflicted advice; it is that saving for retirement is challenging. Reducing conflicts of interest that distort the mix of recommended financial products might make saving easier, but if it exacerbates other conflicts of interest, raises Sue's costs, or limits her access

---

[36] 17 C.F.R. § 240.15l-1(a)(2)(iii)(A) (2020).

to advice, then whether she is better off is an empirical question. Similarly, more fulsome disclosures about conflicts might make it easier for Sue to identify incentive problems, but it is far from clear that disclosure actually makes it easier for her to meet her retirement goals.

Future regulations should be designed from Sue's perspective. What changes to our system of financial advice will leave Sue better off? While addressing conflicts of interest might be one avenue of reform, Sue might be served as well or better by reforms that increase access to free advice or simply reduce the complexity of the lifecycle savings problem. For Sue, any reform that increases the chance of successful retirement is a positive one.

7

A System of Fiduciary Protections for Mutual Funds

Howell E. Jackson[*]

I INTRODUCTION

Fiduciary duties are most familiar in the context of the responsibilities owed by a single legal entity (for example, a trustee) to another (such as a beneficiary). But fiduciary duties also exist within more elaborate regulatory structures, creating what I describe in this chapter as a system of fiduciary protections: that is, an interconnected network of legal requirements centered on a limited number of specific fiduciary duties reinforced by disclosure requirements, portfolio restrictions, and investor approval mechanisms. These fiduciary systems are often overseen by an active cohort of government supervisors and supplemented in certain domains with private litigation operating under unique liability rules. As outlined in section II of this chapter, the mutual fund industry in the United States operates under just such a system of fiduciary protections. Over time, as explained in section III, this system has evolved through a series of supervisory adjustments and accommodations, but the essence of a legal regime grounded on fiduciary protections remains robust and extensive. In part as a result of the intensity and cost of this system's operation, I argue in section IV, industry participants have adjusted their product offerings to create alternative vehicles for offering investors collective investment opportunities that escape the full application of fiduciary protections designed for mutual funds, sometimes escaping that regime entirely. This exercise of regulatory arbitrage likely reduces costs and satisfies client demands, but also raises a number of challenging questions for policymakers, some of which I sketch out in section V. Beyond outlining the structure of the system of fiduciary protections that governs mutual funds in the United States, the goal of this chapter is to encourage government officials and legal scholars to consider whether aspects of that system of protections — most likely disclosure obligations related to performance and fees — should be extended to the increasingly large number of financial products that are functionally

[*] In preparing this chapter, I benefitted from suggestions of participants at the Harvard Law School Corporate Group Luncheon, as well as helpful comments from Paul Cellupica, Deborah DeMott, Joseph Franco, Clifford Kirsch, Arthur Laby, Patricia McCoy, Eric Roiter, Jacob Russell, and Susan Wyderko. This chapter builds on a taxonomy of fiduciary duties in financial regulation previously introduced in Howell E. Jackson & Talia B. Gillis, *Fiduciary Law in Financial Regulation, in* OXFORD HANDBOOK OF FIDUCIARY LAW (Evan J. Criddle, Paul B. Miller & Robert H. Sitkoff eds., 2019). A number of pending SEC proposals in mid-2020 implicate issues discussed in this chapter, some but not all of which are addressed in the text and footnotes. As it relates to the subject matter of this chapter, I would note that I am an independent trustee of CREF and affiliated TIAA-CREF Mutual Funds. The views expressed in this chapter, however, do not reflect the opinion of that organization. Additional information on my outside activities is available at https://helios.law.harvard.edu/Public/Faculty/ConflictOfInterestReport.aspx?id=10423.

similar to mutual funds but structured to fall, in part or entirely, outside of the system of fiduciary protections described in this chapter.

II TRADITIONAL MUTUAL FUND REGULATION AS THE APOTHEOSIS OF FIDUCIARY DUTIES

The system of supervisory oversight established under the Investment Company Act of 1940 ("1940 Act") and the Investment Advisers Act of 1940 ("Advisers Act"), along with supporting obligations arising under other federal securities laws as well as the requirements of self-regulatory organizations represents what is likely the world's most elaborate system of fiduciary protections for investors. Throughout this chapter, I refer to this collection of legal obligations as mutual fund regulation. The regime consists of an intricate set of portfolio restrictions, open-ended standards of conduct, disclosure requirements, share-holder consent or approval mechanisms, liability regimes, and strict price regulation for exit and entry. The structure is administered by phalanxes of lawyers and compliance officers as well as several different government agencies backed up by a well-staffed financial press and an aggressive network of plaintiff attorneys. Without question, the regime is costly and intrusive, but also safeguards much of the financial wealth of working- and middle-class America.[1]

In this section, I sketch out the key components of mutual fund regulation, concluding with a short defense of my characterization of the entire regime as embracing a comprehensive system of enhanced fiduciary protections. These descriptions are necessarily summary, but hopefully sufficient to give a flavor of the scope of the regime and the internal logic connecting its components.

A *Mandatory Independent Board Members*

A central and distinctive feature of U.S. mutual fund regulation is the requirement that each fund is overseen by a board of directors, of whom a substantial number must be independent of the fund's investment advisor.[2] These directors, typically supported by separate counsel for independent directors, serve as fiduciaries for mutual fund investors, with numerous statutory and regulatory obligations to safeguard those investors' interests. Among other things, mutual fund boards must make annual determinations about the appropriateness of management fees paid to fund advisors, sign off on major corporate actions, and oversee a host of operational details. Several decades ago, when the European Union adopted an alternative approach to policing collective investment vehicles that lacked analogous board oversight, SEC staff briefly considered and promptly rejected a proposal to permit exceptions from board oversight in U.S. mutual funds. The reasoning was that the European Union's more "contractual ... structure is fundamentally incompatible with the regulatory

---

[1] *See* INVESTMENT COMPANY INSTITUTE, INVESTMENT COMPANY FACT BOOK 2019, at 23, 28 (2019) (hereinafter "ICI 2019 FACT BOOK") (reporting net assets of regulated mutual funds in the United States to be $21.1 trillion as of year-end 2018, representing 21% of U.S. household wealth).

[2] The statutory requirement is for 40 percent of the directors to be independent, but SEC exemptive relief (discussed below) effectively raises that requirement to a supermajority, and many funds have an even greater number of independent directors. For a discussion of these requirements, *see* MICHAEL S. BARR, HOWELL E. JACKSON & MARGARET E. TAHYAR, FINANCIAL REGULATION: LAW AND POLICY 1060–65 (2d ed. 2018) (hereinafter "BARR-JACKSON-TAHYAR"). For an excellent overview of mutual fund governance requirements, *see* Eric D. Roiter, *Disentangling Mutual Fund Governance from Corporate Governance*, 6 HARV. BUS. L. REV. 1 (2016).

philosophy of the [1940] Act, which relies on boards of directors to monitor investment company operations and resolve conflicts of interests."[3]

B *Fiduciary Obligations of Investment Advisors*

The second front of fiduciary protections for mutual fund investors comes from the federal courts' interpretation of the Advisers Act as imposing a fiduciary duty on investment advisors to their clients, including their mutual fund clients.[4] This obligation extends to all actions taken by an advisor with respect to a mutual fund, such as the provision of ancillary services and the best execution of portfolio trades. These Advisers Act obligations are supplemented for investment advisors to mutual funds in section 36(b) of the 1940 Act, which imposes a specific and novel form of fiduciary duty for advisors of investment companies concerning compensation. This duty is enforceable by a fund shareholder on behalf of the fund and has been the subject of considerable litigation, as well as academic commentary, and was formalized into the Second Circuit's *Gartenberg* test, substantially endorsed by the Supreme Court several years ago.[5] Critically, a mutual fund's board of directors plays a central role in policing an advisor's obligations under section 36(b), largely accomplished through annual contract renewals required under section 15(c) of the 1940 Act.[6] The board also has more general obligations to review all outside services to mutual funds to check for potential conflicts of interest.[7] In addition, under Rule 12b-1, a mutual fund board must satisfy specific regulatory obligations before a fund advisor can make use of fund assets to finance the costs of distribution.[8] In short, mutual fund regulation doubles up on fiduciary duties with the belt of the advisor's obligations being shored up by the suspenders of oversight from a fund's board.[9]

---

[3] *See* U.S. Sec. & Exch. Comm'n, Division of Investment Management, Protecting Investors: A Half Century of Investment Company Regulation 254 (May 1992).

[4] *See* Investment Advisers Act of 1940 § 206, 15 U.S.C. § 80b-6 (2018). *See also* Investment Company Act of 1940 § 36(a), 15 U.S.C. § 80a-36(a) (2018) (authorizing SEC civil actions against, among others, investment advisors to mutual funds for fiduciary breaches). For a recent overview of Investment Advisor duties, see Commission Interpretation Regarding Standard of Conduct for Investment Advisers, 84 Fed. Reg. 33,669, 33,669 (July 12, 2019) ("The Advisers Act establishes a federal fiduciary duty for investment advisers."). *But see* Public Statement, Robert J. Jackson Jr., Commissioner, U.S. Sec. & Exch. Comm'n, Statement on Final Rules Governing Investment Advice (June 5, 2019), https://www.sec.gov/news/public-statement/statement-jackson-060519-iabd (criticizing aspects of the Commission's interpretation).

[5] *See* Investment Company Act of 1940 § 36(b), 15 U.S.C. § 80a-36(b) (2018), *interpreted in* Jones v. Harris Assoc. L.P., 559 U.S. 335 (2010) (adopting the standard articulated in Gartenberg v. Merrill Lynch Asset Mgmt., Inc., 694 F.2d 923 (2d Cir. 1982)). For an overview of the *Jones* litigation and additional background on the *Gartenberg* standard, *see* Barr-Jackson-Tahyar, *supra* note 1, at 1053–60.

[6] Investment Company Act of 1940 § 15(c), 15 U.S.C. § 80a-15(c) (2018). The thoroughness of these annual contract review measures, particularly with respect to independent trustees, is an important factor in claims brought under section 36(b).

[7] *See* U.S. Sec. & Exch. Comm'n Division of Investment Management, IM Guidance Update No. 2016–01, at 3–4, 13 (Jan. 2016), https://www.sec.gov/investment/im-guidance-2016-01.pdf.

[8] Investment Company Act of 1940 Rule 12b-1, 17 C.F.R. § 1 (2020).

[9] Of course, the fiduciary obligations of investment advisors are necessarily compromised by the inherent conflicts between advisor interests and those of mutual fund shareholders, justifying the additional fiduciary obligations at the mutual fund level. For a helpful exploration of fiduciary duties in this context, see Arthur B. Laby, *The Fiduciary Structure of Investment Management Regulation*, in Research Handbook on the Regulation of Mutual Funds 79 (William A. Birdthistle & John D. Morley eds., 2018).

C *Extensive Portfolio Restrictions*

Mutual fund regulation also imposes a number of stringent portfolio restrictions, supplemented in critical respects by the requirements of the Internal Revenue Code. Diversification requirements, liquidity rules (recently enhanced), and severe limitations on leverage and complex capital structures, all impose substantial restrictions on the operations of mutual funds.[10] Also, section 17 of the 1940 Act establishes strict limitations on transactions between mutual funds and affiliate parties, restrictions designed to eliminate the kinds of tunneling and sweetheart deals that plagued investment companies in the 1920s and 1930s.[11] These restrictions substantially constrain the scope of mutual fund operations, but are susceptible to—and, as I will shortly discuss, have been markedly ameliorated through—SEC exemptive relief.[12]

D *Mandatory Shareholder Approvals*

Notwithstanding the presence of statutorily imposed fiduciary duties on both fund boards and investment advisors, mutual fund regulation also delegates a number of specific responsibilities to fund shareholders. For one thing, a majority of fund directors must, at any time, be elected by shareholders, and the ability of the current board to fill vacancies is contingent upon shareholder election of two-thirds of the board.[13] Shareholder approval is also required for changes in fundamental investment policies,[14] the ratification of new advisory contracts when the advisor experiences a change in control,[15] and major corporate events, including many fund mergers.[16] In addition, shareholders must sign off on increases in advisory fees[17] and certain other charges, such as the adoption of 12b-1 fees.[18] As all of these events are typically preceded by approval of a fund's board of directors, these shareholder approvals afford a potential (albeit rarely exercised) opportunity for fund investors to override board decisions on important matters.

[10] For an overview of these restrictions and their logic, *see* BARR-JACKSON-TAHYAR, *supra* note 1, 1023–24, 1065–72.

[11] Investment Company Act of 1940 § 17, 15 U.S.C. § 80a–17 (2018). *See also* BARR-JACKSON-TAHYAR, *supra* note 1, at 1019–21; Investment Company Act of 1940 § 17(d), 15 U.S.C. § 80a–17(d) (2018) (restrictions on joint transactions between funds and affiliates).

[12] For contrasting views on the relationship between portfolio shaping rules and fiduciary duties *compare* Mercer Bullard, *The Fiduciary Study: A Triumph of Substance over Form?*, 30 REV. BANKING & FIN. L. 171, 175 (2010) (arguing that formal rules of conduct displace fiduciary duties), *with* Laby, *supra* note 9(contending that rules of conduct do not, at least in U.S. practice, fully displace fiduciary duties).

[13] Investment Company Act of 1940 § 16(a), 15 U.S.C. § 80a–16(a) (2018). Notwithstanding these election requirements, annual election of board members is not customary for mutual funds as these vehicles are typically organized under state laws that do not require regular elections. *See also infra* section III.C (discussing other corporate governance accommodations).

[14] Investment Company Act of 1940 § 13(a), 15 U.S.C. § 80a–13(a) (2018).

[15] Investment Company Act of 1940 § 15(a), 15 U.S.C. § 80a–15(a) (2018).

[16] *See* MUTUAL FUND DIRECTORS FORUM, PRACTICAL GUIDANCE FOR FUND DIRECTORS ON MUTUAL FUND MERGERS (2019). *See also* Investment Company Act of 1940 Rule 17a-8, 17 C.F.R. § 270.17a-8 (2019) (exempting certain affiliate fund mergers from shareholder approval requirements).

[17] This requirement derives from the specification in section 15(a) of the Investment Company Act that shareholder-approved advisory contracts for mutual funds must "precisely describe[] all compensation to be paid thereunder." Investment Company Act of 1940 § 15(a), 15 U.S.C. § 80a–15(a) (2018). *Cf.* INVESCO, SEC No-Action Letter, 1997 WL 434442 (Aug. 5, 1997) (providing no-action relief for sub-advisory contracts where advisor fees are reallocated from investment advisor to sub-advisor, causing no net increase in expenses charged to shareholders).

[18] Investment Company Act of 1940 Rule 12b-1, 17 C.F.R. § 1 (2020). *See* U.S. SEC. & EXCH. COMM'N DIVISION OF INVESTMENT MANAGEMENT, REPORT ON MUTUAL FUND FEES AND EXPENSES (Dec. 2000) ("Pursuant to rule 12b-1 under the Investment Company Act, a fund may adopt a 12b-1 plan to provide for the payment of distribution expenses. Because of the possible conflicts of interest involved in a fund's payment of distribution expenses, the Commission requires funds to follow procedures similar to those required by the Investment Company Act for the approval of an investment advisory contract.").

E *Elaborate Disclosures Regime*

Federal laws establish an elaborate system of disclosure obligations for mutual funds to assist mutual fund investors (as well as third party service providers, such as Morningstar and Broadridge) in monitoring mutual fund operations. Building off the Securities Act of 1933 and the Securities Exchange Act of 1934, mutual fund regulation requires a comprehensive system of the prospectus, registration statement, annual report, and proxy statements for mutual funds.[19] These disclosure forms bear only passing resemblance to the disclosures required of ordinary corporate issuers and include a host of disclosure provisions targeted at specific features of mutual fund regulation. For example, the disclosure items regarding mutual fund board approval of advisory fees track the *Gartenberg* test closely for compliance with section 36(b).[20] In addition, the disclosure rules for mutual funds—as well as the associated FINRA rules governing mutual fund advertising—have detailed requirements designed to ensure standardized reporting of past investment performance and mutual fund fees.[21]

Moreover, and of particular relevance to later discussions, the regulatory regime has elaborate rules for factoring in the underlying fees for a mutual fund organized as a "fund-of-funds," that is, a mutual fund that invests in other mutual funds.[22] These rules are designed to ensure that when an investor considers purchasing the top level of a fund-of-funds, the fee information includes all of the costs of operating the underlying funds.[23] Target-date funds—typically picked as default investments for retirement savings plans—are often organized as funds-of-funds, and so the rules for funds-of-funds are of particular importance in today's markets, especially for retirement savings.[24]

F *NAV Requirements for Entry and Exit with Board Oversight*

A final, but arguably critical, safeguard for mutual fund investors is the right to enter or exit mutual funds on at least a daily basis at a regulated price designed to equal the net asset value of fund assets ("NAV").[25] NAV pricing is itself overseen by fund boards on a number of dimensions most notably with respect to the fair valuation of securities when a market price is not readily

---

[19] Investment Company Act of 1940 § 8, 15 U.S.C. § 80a–8 (2018). For an overview of SEC reporting requirements, *see* U.S. Sec. & Exch. Comm'n, Investment Company Registration and Regulation Package (Dec. 21, 2004), https://www.sec.gov/investment/fast-answers/divisionsinvestmentinvcoreg121504htm.html.

[20] For the SEC release adopting these requirements, see Disclosure Regarding Approval of Investment Advisory Contracts by Directors of Investment Companies, Securities Act Release No. 8433, Exchange Act Release No. 49,909, Investment Company Act Release No. 26,486, 69 Fed. Reg. 39,798 (June 30, 2004).

[21] For an overview of FINRA review procedures for mutual fund advertising and other matters, see FINRA, Mutual Funds Rules & Guidance, https://www.finra.org/rules-guidance/key-topics/mutual-funds. For an overview of performance investment in mutual fund reports, see U.S. Sec. & Exch. Comm'n, Office of Investor Education and Advocacy, How to Read a Mutual Fund Shareholder Report, https://www.sec.gov/files/ib_readmfreport.pdf. Mutual funds are also required to make disclosures on portfolio holdings periodically.

[22] The SEC recently issued a proposal to consolidate its past exemptive relief and rulemaking with respect to fund of funds. *See* Fund of Funds Arrangements, 84 Fed. Reg. 1286 (proposed Feb. 1, 2019) (hereinafter SEC Fund of Funds Proposal) (adopted in final form 85 Fed. Reg. 73,924 (Nov. 19, 2020)).

[23] *See* Fund of Fund Investments, Securities Act Release No. 8713, Investment Company Act Release No. 27,399, 71 Fed. Reg. 36,640, 36,640 (June 27, 2006) ("The[se] amendments improve the transparency of the expenses of funds of funds by requiring that the expenses of the acquired funds be aggregated and shown as an additional expense in the fee table of the fund of funds.").

[24] *See* ICI 2019 Fact Book, *supra* note 1, at ch. 8.

[25] Investment Company Act of 1940 § 22(c), 15 U.S.C. § 80a–22(c) (2018); Investment Company Act of 1940 Rule 22c-1 (a), 17 C.F.R. § 270.22c-1(a) (2020).

available,[26] and offers essential protection for investors who become dissatisfied by fund performance.[27] Among other things, NAV pricing grants fund investors a daily out option for fund shares at regulated prices, in effect, a continuously operating right of appraisal. NAV pricing also protects current shareholders from dilution by ensuring that new shareholders pay an adequate price for their investments.

G A Comprehensive System of Fiduciary Protections

Let me now attempt to defend my characterization of this elaborate system of mutual fund regulation as a regime of enhanced fiduciary protections. Quite clearly, there are fiduciary protections at the core of this regulatory requirement, embracing both boards and investment advisors. But one might object, the other components of mutual fund regulation — like disclosure requirements imposed under more general federal securities laws or the portfolio restrictions imposed under the 1940 Act — are simply other kinds of protections that happen to apply to mutual funds in addition to fiduciary obligations of boards and advisors.

While I do not deny that many of these other regulatory requirements could be conceptualized as fully separate, many are closely related to fiduciary duties and thus are, in my view, better denominated as part of that system. A prime example discussed previously, are disclosure rules that directly pick up fiduciary obligations, such as those imposed under the *Gartenberg* test. However, even more general disclosure requirements for mutual funds have a fiduciary valence if one takes into account the mandatory election requirements for fund directors and the number of major issues for which shareholder approval is required. In traditional fiduciary law, fiduciaries must disclose to their beneficiaries a good deal of information about certain matters and some conduct is permissible only if ratified by the beneficiary with informed consent. The shareholder approval requirements of mutual fund regulation perform exactly the same function, with the disclosure rules (emanating from both federal securities laws and FINRA advertising requirements) creating a highly formalized analog to the less well-defined disclosure and consent duties of traditional trustees, providing a critical component to this fiduciary system. Indeed, the heightened formality of mutual fund regulation makes this apparatus a system of fiduciary protections and not just a straightforward application of fiduciary law.

While portfolio restrictions might not commonly be characterized as fiduciary obligations, these restrictions substantially constrain the operations of mutual funds — establishing a set of non-waivable obligations — that restrict the activities of investment advisors and the monitoring responsibilities of fund boards. As I explored with Talia Gillis in an earlier piece, one of the complexities of applying traditional fiduciary duties in a regulated context is determining when those duties actually proscribe certain conduct.[28] The portfolio restrictions of mutual fund regulation solve that problem by defining the boundaries of permissible fund activities; there are certain things that investment advisors cannot do with respect to the management of 1940 Act

---

[26] Investment Company Act of 1940 § 2(a)(41), 15 U.S.C. § 80a–2(a)(41) (2018) (mandating, when market quotations not readily available, "fair value as determined in good faith by the board of directors"); Investment Company Act of 1940 Rule 2a-4, 17 C.F.R. § 270.2a-4 (2020). The SEC's new liquidity rule, requiring that 85% of funds be marketable without a significant change in value within seven days, is intended to further safeguard NAV protections. *See* Investment Company Act of 1940 Rule 22e-4, 17 C.F.R. § 270.22e-4 (2020).

[27] For an overview of the importance of NAV determinations, see Good Faith Determinations of Fair Value, 85 Fed. Reg. 28,734, 28,735 (proposed May 13, 2020) (hereinafter SEC Proposal on Fair Valuation) (adopted in final form 86 Fed. Reg. 748 (Jan. 6, 2021)). *See also* John Morley & Quinn Curtis, *Taking Exit Rights Seriously: Why Governance and Fee Litigation Don't Work in Mutual Funds*, 120 YALE L.J. 84 (2010) (emphasizing the centrality of NAV exit rights for investors in mutual funds); Roiter, *supra* note 2 (stressing importance of exit to mutual fund governance).

[28] *See* Jackson & Gillis, *supra* star (*) note.

funds, even with board approval and informed shareholder consent. For example, NAV pricing adds another mandatory term enhancing beneficiary authority for self-help in the face of poor fiduciary performance. The nexus between these portfolio restrictions and fiduciary obligations is nicely illustrated by the SEC's practice in a host of exemptive actions to condition the relaxation of many portfolio restrictions on fiduciary oversight of the terms of relaxation in the hands of fund trustees. In these cases, portfolio restrictions and fiduciary duties are tightly interwoven. But even when the SEC has not conditioned regulatory accommodations on board oversight, there is a general obligation on fund boards to ensure that funds and advisor have in place "written policies and procedures reasonably designed to prevent violation of the Federal Securities Laws."[29] Through this obligation to review and approve compliance policies and protections, the fiduciary duties of fund trustees extend into all aspects of fund operations.

While it is certainly possible and perhaps more familiar to conceptualize the components of mutual fund regulation as a discrete collection of distinct regulatory strategies, and other scholars have done so with considerable cogency,[30] it is also defensible—and for me more useful—to conceptualize them together as an enhanced system of fiduciary protections.

III SUPERVISORY ACCOMMODATIONS OVER TIME

The overarching fiduciary structure of mutual fund regulation can be, I think, more clearly seen in the ways in which the SEC and, in some instances, Congress have adjusted regulatory requirements for mutual funds over time. I argue that the supervisory accommodations ameliorate excessively rigid and costly requirements of those outlined above, but simultaneously maintain basic investor protections of the regime. In this section, I review some of the most prominent examples of these accommodations, highlighting the extent to which the adjustments relax statutory requirements while preserving the underlying logic of fiduciary protections. I also flag several instances in which the SEC has been reluctant to acquiesce to industry efforts to obtain more aggressive cutbacks that might, in fact, undermine the overall regime. At several points, ongoing debates are flagged that reflect the continuing dynamic of adjusting fiduciary duties in this area of the law. By and large, these accommodations leave the basic structure of mutual fund regulation in place, but smooth out some of its rougher (and costlier) edges while safeguarding investor interests.

A *Exemptive Relief from Statutory Restrictions*

The best and more prominent example of supervisory accommodations comes in the elaborate system of exemptive relief that the SEC has adopted over the years with respect to mutual fund regulation. One of the distinctive features of the original 1940 Act was the delegation of expansive powers to the SEC to adopt exemptive relief, and the Commission has exercised that authority with considerable frequency.[31] Indeed, the modern mutual fund complex could not exist were it not for these accommodations. In many cases, these exemptive rules permit a practice—such as

---

[29] *See* Investment Company Act of 1940 Rule 38a-1, 17 C.F.R. § 270.38a-1 (2020).

[30] *See* Laby, *supra* note 9.

[31] For an overview of the scope of board governance aspects of the SEC's exemptive relief, see Investment Company Governance, Investment Company Act Release No. 26,520, 69 Fed. Reg. 46,378 (Aug. 2, 2004), *vacated in* Chamber of Commerce v. U.S. Sec. & Exch. Comm'n, 412 F.3d 133 (D.C. Cir. 2005). *See also* Investment Company Act of 1940 Rule 0–1(a)(7), 17 C.F.R. § 270.0–1(a)(7) (2020) (defining fund governance standards). These standards are often (and accurately) characterized as efforts on the part of the Commission to improve corporate governance of mutual funds, but the point made here is to emphasize the extent to which exemptive relief applying these governance standards

cross-trading between affiliated mutual funds—that is formally prohibited under the 1940 Act, but is now authorized under exemptive relief, typically with an elaborate set of substantive guardrails and the requirement of some degree of enhanced fiduciary oversight by the fund board of directors. For example, many instances of exemptive relief require a higher percentage of independent directors than the 40 percent imposed under the 1940 Act itself. Rule 12b-1, mentioned earlier, which allows advisors to use mutual fund assets to finance distribution costs, utilizes this approach. Exemptive relief of this sort relaxes prophylactic requirements, but within the confines of a system of fiduciary protections, as oversight is typically delegated to the fund board, which serves as an overarching fiduciary.

Within the mutual fund industry, there is now considerable discussion whether the accumulation of exemptive relief orders, with the many obligations they impose on mutual fund directors, might impose excessive burdens on fund directors, requiring them to engage in "check-the-box" exercises that provide little value to investors and distract from more important work. Dalia Blass, current director of the Division of Investment Management, has focused particularly on this issue[32] and started to push through several reforms designed to diminish the routine work assigned to fund directors and allow them to focus more on larger policy questions. For example, boards are now allowed to rely more heavily on compliance personnel to review cross-trades and play a less active role in this aspect of fund operations.[33] In effect, these additional accommodations demote these activities from the fiduciary obligations of fund boards into the regime of compliance, which boards must still oversee but not themselves manage. Accommodations of this sort soften but do not eliminate, the overarching fiduciary framework.

B *Statutory Adjustments for Soft Dollar Practices*

Sometimes it is Congress that provides accommodations. A good case in point is the relief provided by soft dollars under section 28(e) of the Securities Exchange Act of 1934. Back in the waning days of the NYSE's fixed commission era, the securities industry developed various techniques for giving rebates on commissions paid by institutional clients with large orders. There followed a series of lawsuits alleging that mutual fund advisors and mutual fund boards violated their fiduciary duties (among other legal obligations) by not passing these rebates on to mutual fund shareholders. In 1975, Congress passed legislation ending the fixed commission era, but also adopted section 28(e) specifying that it would not be a violation of fiduciary duty (under federal or state law) for investment advisors of mutual funds (as well as other clients) to use trading commissions to finance the purchase of research and certain other services.[34] The amendment thus narrowed the fiduciary obligations of mutual fund advisors

---

substitutes more stringent fiduciary oversight for relaxed mandatory rules. The development of exchange traded funds (ETFs) is itself a product of exemptive orders. *See* Barr-Jackson-Tahyar, *supra* note 2, ch.10.2.

[32] *See* Dalia Blass, Director, Division of Investment Management, U.S. Sec. & Exch. Comm'n, Keynote Address: ICI Securities Law Developments Conference (Dec. 7, 2017). *See also* Letter from Amy Lancellotta, Managing Director, Independent Directors Council, to Dalia Blass, Director, Division of Investment Management, U.S. Sec. & Exch. Comm'n (Oct. 16, 2017) (on file with U.S. Sec. & Exch. Comm'n) (encouraging "modernization" of fund director responsibilities).

[33] *See* Lori L. Schneider, Fatima S. Sulaiman & Christopher Bellacicco, *SEC Staff No-Action Letter Eases Board's Burden in Reviewing Affiliated Transactions*, K&L Gates (Nov. 1, 2018), https://www.klgates.com/SEC-Staff-No-Action-Letter-Eases-Boards-Burden-in-Reviewing-Affiliated-Transactions-11-01-2018. The Commission's recent proposal regarding the board's role in Fair Valuation procedures is similarly in this vein. *See* SEC Proposal on Fair Valuation, *supra* note 27.

[34] *See* Securities Exchange Act of 1934 § 28(e), 15 U.S.C. § 78bb(e) (2018). The history outlined in this paragraph is recounted in Barr-Jackson-Tahyar, *supra* note 2, ch. 10.2.

(among others) on the view that the safe harbor would promote the production of research with positive externalities for capital markets. This tailored narrowing of fiduciary protections has been in the news in recent years as the E.U.'s MiFID II banned the practice of bundled commissions and questions have been raised as to whether the United States should follow suit.[35] For current purposes, however, section 28(e) represents a prominent adjustment of fiduciary duties, creating an exemption within a larger regime of fiduciary responsibilities.[36]

C *Accommodations with Respect to Corporate Governance*

Another example of accommodations is the election procedures required for board directors. Practically speaking—and as noted above—the 1940 Act requires that a majority of fund directors be elected by fund shareholders. But SEC interpretations have diminished the actual control that fund shareholders have over the election of directors for their own funds. To begin with, fund elections are typically organized around a "series" of funds.[37] That is, the electorate for fund elections are not the shareholders invested in a single investment company (as defined under the 1940 Act), but a series of investment companies, typically organized as a business trust with a large number of investment mandates and separate portfolios. For matters that affect only one portfolio—like changes in investment policies—fund shareholders vote on their own, but when an issue put to shareholders is of common concern, like the election of directors, the votes of all shareholders in the series are aggregated.[38] That structure substantially diminishes the control over shareholder elections should problems arise with the management of a specific investment company, such as poor investment performance. Of course, the operation of modern fund complexes, with a single (or only a couple) of boards for potentially hundreds and hundreds of funds located in multiple series, makes the removal of individual directors for a particular investment company, or even series of investment companies, a practical impossibility. Still, at least nominally, fund directors are subject to shareholder election, so a semblance of shareholder supremacy in this domain remains.[39]

D *Adjustment to Definition of Fundamental Investment Policies and Use of Sub-Advisors*

Another illustration of marginal accommodations to a full-throated approach to policing fiduciary duties in the context of mutual fund regulation over the years relates to the 1940 Act's requirement that any changes in fundamental investment policies be subject to shareholder

---

[35] *See* Howell E. Jackson & Jeffery Y. Zhang, "*Nobody Is Proud of Soft Dollars*": *The Impact of MiFID II on U.S. Financial Markets* (Jan. 24, 2021) (forthcoming J. Fin. Reg.).

[36] When investment advisors engage in activities that fall outside the scope of section 28(e), the fiduciary duties articulated in pre-1975 case law presumably still apply.

[37] *See* K&L Gates, Organizing a Mutual Fund 5–6 (2013), http://www.klgates.com/files/Upload/DC_IM_03-Organizing_Mutual_Fund.pdf. For an excellent recent overview of the evolution of series funds, *see* Joseph A. Franco, *Commoditized Governance: The Curious Case of Investment Company Shared Series Trusts*, 44 J. Corp. L. 233 (2018).

[38] *Id.*

[39] *See* Alan R. Palmiter, *Mutual Fund Board: A Failed Experiment in Regulatory Outsourcing*, 1 Brook. J. Corp. Fin. & Com. L. 165, 171 (2006) ("When the election of directors does occur, the process is 'largely ritualistic.'"). Responding to the challenges in gaining quorum in matters put to shareholders of mutual funds and the costs of proxy solicitation more generally, the Investment Company Institute recently recommended the SEC further adjust the procedural requirements for mutual fund shareholder approvals in all contexts. *See* Letter from Paul Schott, President, Inv. Case Inst., to Vanessa Countryman, Secretary, U.S. Sec. & Exch. Comm'n (Jun. 11, 2019) (on file with U.S. Sec. & Exch. Comm'n) (hereinafter "ICI Proxy Letter") (recommending, among other things, a lowering of quorum requirements accompanied by offsetting safeguards on shareholder approval rates (75%) and board support (unanimity)).

approval.[40] Over the years, SEC staff has made modest adjustments to the definition of "fundamental investment policies," and common law of fund practice has grown around which investment policy changes can be implemented without shareholder approval.[41] Industry groups have recently lobbied for further relaxation of these shareholder approval requirements.[42] Similarly, the 1940 Act itself contemplates that delegation of investment authority to a new sub-advisor would require shareholder approval. However, SEC orders have provided exemptive relief for so-called "Managers of Managers" which allows for the creation and amendment of advisory arrangements without shareholder approval.[43]

E Two Counter Examples: Full Elimination of Fund Boards and Reluctance to Eliminate Board Oversight on Fair Valuation

Finally, it bears emphasizing a few areas in which the SEC staff has been slow to accept proposals to weaken fiduciary protections for mutual fund investors. The first, already recounted, are proposals to eliminate board directors. While, in practice, shareholder control over the election of fund directors is limited, the Commission has been unwilling to eliminate that role. Indeed, as mentioned earlier, the Commission tends to rely so heavily on fund directors to police conflicts of interest that the SEC staff is now focused on slimming down those obligations to reduce the boardroom's burdens and free up mutual fund directors for more important issues.[44]

A second area where the SEC has been slow to relax board obligations has been the role of directors in valuing securities when market quotations are not readily available. Such valuations are necessary when a security is distressed or ceases to trade for some other reason. With respect to foreign securities, fair valuation may be needed if superseding events occur after the home market closes, but before the NYSE closes. Under section 2(a)(41) of the 1940 Act, in such circumstances, "fair value [is to be] determined in good faith by the board of directors."[45] In practice, fair valuation is nowadays accomplished, to a considerable degree, through matrix pricing models and other fair valuation services that rely on various kinds of algorithmic practices. How directors are supposed to engage in the required "good faith" determinations, and how much those determinations can and should be delegated to expert service providers overseen by management personnel and compliance officers, has been hotly contested among mutual fund practitioners in recent years. The Commission staff has been subject to considerable criticism for not reconciling arguably inconsistent pronouncements on the subject.[46]

For current purposes, however, the important point is that the SEC staff has been reluctant to allow for a complete delegation of this board function in the face of substantial external pressure, and recently put forward a proposal that acknowledges the reality that the day-to-day

---

[40] *See* Investment Company Act of 1940 § 13(a), 15 U.S.C. § 80a–13(a) (2018), which cross-references Investment Company Act of 1940 § 8(b)(3), 15 U.S.C. § 80a–8(b)(3) (2018). *See also* Stradley Ronon Stevens & Young, LLP, SEC No-Action Letter (Jun. 24, 2019), https://www.sec.gov/investment/stradley-062419 (accommodations from shareholder approval requirements triggered by changes in composition of stock indices that otherwise would make funds non-diversified).

[41] *See, e.g.,* SEC Investment Company Act of 1940 Rule 35d-1, 17 C.F.R. § 270.35d-1 (2020).

[42] *See* ICI Proxy Letter, *supra* note 39, at 7–9.

[43] For a discussion of these provisions along with a recommendation that they be codified for general use, see ICI Proxy Letter, *supra* note 39, at 9.

[44] *See supra* notes 31–33.

[45] 15 U.S.C. § 80a–2(a)(41) (2018).

[46] *See, e.g.,* Letter from Robert E. Buckholz, Chairman, Fed. Reg. of Sec. Comm., ABA Bus. L. Section, to Dalia Blass, Director, and Paul G. Cellupica, Director and Chief of Counsel, Div. of Inv. Mgmt., U.S. Sec. & Exch. Comm'n (July 22, 2019) (on file with U.S. Sec. & Exch. Comm'n).

responsibility of implementing a system of fair valuation necessarily falls to management but retains considerable oversight responsibilities at the board level.[47] To the extent that accurate fair valuations are critical to creating daily NAVs and that accurate NAVs are critical to safeguarding mutual fund shareholders' ability to exit on appropriate terms, one can sympathize with the reluctance of SEC staff to weaken board oversight of this linchpin for investor protection. Industry representatives, however, clearly also have a point that even the best intentioned of mutual fund directors must rely to a considerable extent on the efforts of others to handle the implementation of fair valuation processes daily, making it difficult to square practice with the 1940 Act requirement that fund boards "determine" fair value.

iv NEW CHALLENGES TO REGULATORY BOUNDARIES

I now turn from traditional supervisory accommodations within the basic structure of mutual fund regulation to another manner in which industry participants have reduced the costs of mutual fund regulation: instances in which industry innovations have moved a portion, or in some cases all, of a pooled investment vehicle outside of the structure of mutual fund regulation, reducing compliance costs, but also engaging in a form of regulatory arbitrage.[48] As will be seen, some of the cases I discuss have generated litigation or enforcement actions, but a number simply illustrate accepted practices whereby industry participants are understood to have found lawful ways in which to avoid the full application of mutual fund regulation to financial products that are functionally equivalent to pooled investment vehicles, often designed for retail customers. For current purposes, I do not focus on the most familiar path away from mutual fund regulation, the 1940 Act exemptions for private funds, as these exemptions are both well-understood and targeted primarily at institutional investors and extremely wealthy individuals.[49] For the most part, I also do not touch upon the emergence of functionally similar insurance products designed to comply with section 3(a)(8) of the Securities Act of 1933, as the courts, with the acquiescence of Congress, have interpreted this provision to grant these insurance products full exemption from federal securities laws, including mutual fund regulation.[50] What I examine here are innovations in distribution practices that allow for mutual

---

[47] *See* SEC Proposal on Fair Valuation, *supra* note 27. *See* Clifford J. Alexander, Mark P. Goshko, Pamela A. Grossetti, Steven B. Levine & Jacob M. Derr, *SEC Proposes New Fair Value Rule 2a-5*, 10 NAT'L L. REV. (2020).

[48] Some time ago, I wrote an essay exploring the tendency of industry participants (or in some cases, plaintiff counsel) to attempt to relocate financial functions away from their presumptive regulatory regimes. *See* Howell E. Jackson, *Regulation in a Multisectored Financial Services Industry: An Exploratory Essay*, 77 WASH. U.L.Q. 319 (1999). There, I identified mutual fund regulation as the presumptive U.S. regulatory regime for pooled investment vehicles and discussed several examples of functionally similar products located in other legal regimes. *See id.* at 379–97. Some of the practices discussed in the text are analogous to examples discussed in that essay, but many represent subsequent developments.

Within the academic literature, there is extensive literature on the topic of regulatory arbitrage, generally focusing on the costs and consequences of allowing functionally equivalent activities moving outside of a well-defined regulatory perimeter. *See, e.g.*, Victor Fleischer, *Regulatory Arbitrage*, 89 TEX. L. REV. 227, 229 (2010) (defining regulatory arbitrage as "a perfectly legal planning technique used to avoid taxes, accounting rules, securities disclosures, and other regulatory costs"); Annelise Riles, *Managing Regulatory Arbitrage: A Conflicts of Laws Approach*, 47 CORNELL INT'L L.J. 63 (2014).

[49] For an overview of the regulation of private funds, see BARR-JACKSON-TAHYAR, *supra* note 2, ch. 10.5.

[50] The jurisdictional divide between securities and insurance products has been contested since the Supreme Court determined that some insurance products should be subject to federal securities regulation. *See* Sec. & Exch. Comm'n v. Variable Annuity Life Ins. Co. of America, 359 U.S. 65 (1959). *See also* Prudential Ins. Co. of America v. Sec. & Exch. Comm'n, 326 F.2d 383 (3rd Cir. 1964). In the recent past, the SEC reentered the fray and attempted to exert jurisdiction over fixed income annuities by adopting a new regulation narrowing the scope of Securities Act of 1933 § 3(a)(8), 15 U.S.C. § 77c(8) (2018). The D.C. Circuit struck down the regulation on procedural grounds in

funds and similar investment vehicles to bypass, at least in part, the enhanced system of fiduciary protections that mutual fund regulation affords.

A Omnibus Accounts

The first example is fairly prosaic: the use of omnibus accounts by brokerage houses to hold their client's shares of mutual funds.[51] In traditional distribution arrangements for mutual funds, retail customers hold shares directly with a transfer agent hired by the fund and overseen by the associated investment fund complex. For a fee known as a transfer agent fee, the transfer agent would handle communications with the investor, keep track of account balances, and administer financial transactions and distribute disclosure materials. With an omnibus account, the retail investor does not engage directly with a fund's transfer agent but rather interacts with the brokerage firm as a sub-transfer agent. The sub-transfer agent holds shares in an omnibus account with the fund's transfer agent, and that account aggregates the holdings of all the brokerage firm's clients. So, the real work of shareholder administration is handled by the brokerage firms as a sub-transfer agent, and for that, these firms receive a negotiated fee from the fund, with the transfer agent presumably receiving a lower fee than would have been earned had the fund shares all been held directly.

In recent years, sub-transfer agent fees have been the subject of SEC enforcement actions and considerable examination scrutiny.[52] The problem here is sometimes referred to as "distribution in guise." The SEC's concern is that these sub-transfer agency fees are being used to pay for distribution efforts rather than fund administration and thus constitute a violation of Rule 12b-1, which (as discussed earlier) establishes specific procedures that must be followed if fund assets are to be used to finance distribution costs. These enforcement actions are symptomatic of the phenomenon I describe in this chapter. By relying on outside brokerage firms to distribute fund shares and then also moving out of the fund complex an administrative function like sub-transfer agency services, the risk arises that fees nominally designated for one purpose (shareholder administration) are actually being used for another (distribution), but without the safeguards

---

American Equity Life Ins. Co. v. Sec. & Exch. Comm'n, 613 F.3d 166 (D.C. Cir. 2010), and shortly thereafter Congress adopted the Harkin Amendment, effectively barring the Commission from revisiting the matter. *See* section 989J of the Dodd-Frank Wall Street Reform and Consumer Protection Act, Pub. L. No. 111–203 (2010) (instructing the SEC how to treat certain insurance products under section 3(a)(8) of the Securities Act of 1933). While beyond the scope of this chapter, the jurisprudence in this area depends on the so-called supererogation theory, which presumes that insurance products exempt under section 3(a)(8) are fully outside the scope of federal securities laws as opposed to exempt only under the limited terms provided by section 3(a)(8). *See* Tcherepnin v. Knight, 389 U.S. 332, 342, n.30 (1967) (discussing, in dicta, the supererogation theory as applied to insurance products). This interpretive approach, however, is inconsistent with modern practice, especially when extended to the Securities Exchange Act of 1934, which has a quite narrowly exemption for insurance products. *See* Securities Exchange Act of 1934 § 12(g)(2)(G), 15 U.S.C. § 78*l*(2)(G) (2018). Accordingly, while the matter is not free from doubt, the SEC, or a disgruntled purchaser of certain insurance products, could plausibly seek redress under the 1934 Act for fraudulent sales practices in connection with such products. Even without such a revisiting of federal securities jurisdiction, state insurance commissioners could model disclosure and reporting standards in line with suggestions made below.

[51] For an introduction to the evolution toward omnibus accounts, see Gwendolyn A. Williamson, *Tackling Mutual Fund Risks in the Omnibus Channel*, 19 INV. LAW. 1, 1–2 (2012) ("two-thirds of mutual fund shareholders invested outside of an employer-sponsored retirement plan, approximately 80 percent own fund shares through financial intermediaries.").

[52] For an overview of the SEC's work in this area, see U.S. SEC. & EXCH. COMM'N DIVISION OF INVESTMENT MANAGEMENT GUIDANCE UPDATE NO. 2016–01 (Jan. 2016).

that SEC Rule 12b-1 demands.[53] In other words, enforcement efforts in this area are intended to prevent the evasion of one element of the system of mutual fund fiduciary protections by moving one service — sub-transfer agency — beyond direct oversight of the mutual fund and its board.[54]

B *Distribution of Funds through Individual Accounts*

Another industry development in this area has also produced enforcement actions,[55] and is almost certainly of greater significance. Increasingly, brokerage firms and investment advisors are in the business of allocating retail investor accounts into mutual funds of various sorts instead of positions in individual securities, into which securities firms traditionally steered their customers.[56] Thus, these firms represent both important distribution channels for a mutual fund complex and are, effectively, asset allocators for retail investors. In many cases, securities firms follow common investment strategies for many customers, based on a limited number of considerations, such as risk-return preferences, the projected length of investment holdings, and tax considerations. The automation of this process is even more pronounced with robo-advisors that rely heavily on algorithmic models and very little on personal discretion. As a functional matter, what these securities firms are offering their clients is a financial product similar to a fund-of-funds mutual fund.[57] While the underlying mutual funds may be held in the account of an individual customer, these investments are aggregated at the omnibus account level and generate very similar, if not identical, returns for a large number of retail investors with similar risk-return preferences and other characteristics.

Of course, the regulation of these mutual fund allocation accounts is quite different from the regulation of a fund-of-funds mutual fund. Among other things, there is no independent board overseeing the operation of allocation accounts or ensuring that the total fees charged by the account managers are reasonable. Perhaps even more importantly, the regulatory requirements of brokerage firms do not demand clear and consistent disclosures of aggregate fees (including both securities firm level fees and underlying fund fees) nor are these brokerage accounts subject to standardized disclosures of past performance as measured against benchmark indices. Indeed,

---

[53] *See, e.g.*, In the matter of First Eagle Inv. Mgmt. et al., Investment Company Act Release No. 31,382 (Sept. 21, 2015) (a widely publicized SEC action against an investment advisor found to have caused a fund to pay a sub-transfer agent for distribution-related activities outside of Rule 12b-1).

[54] More recently, SEC staff has focused its attention on the use of revenue sharing by investment advisors used to support distribution efforts through intermediaries. As these payments do not constitute the direct application of fund assets for distribution expenses, Rule 12b-1 does not come into play. The staff's enforcement efforts here focus rather on the adequacy of disclosures made to investors about these practices and the possibility that such payments might induce intermediaries to steer investors towards mutual fund share classes with higher costs, a concern at the heart of Regulation BI. *See* Carmen Germaine, *SEC Case Takes Revenue-Sharing Rules in a Completely New Direction*, IGNITES (Aug. 9, 2019).

[55] *See* Press Release, U.S. Sec. & Exch. Comm'n, SEC Share Class Initiative Returning More than $125 Million to Investors (Mar. 11, 2019) (on file with author).

[56] For an overview of these developments, see *The Evolution of Advice: Digital Investment Advisers as Fiduciaries*, MORGAN LEWIS (Oct. 2016), https://www.morganlewis.com/-/media/files/publication/report/im-the-evolution-of-advice-digital-investment-advisers-as-fiduciaries-october-2016.ashx?la=en&hash=7A28D9586FD8ACADC9731733 BFE4281F4E6FEB49. Even before the rise of robo-advisors, there was empirical evidence that investment advisors tended to structure their clients' portfolios in a similar and not especially efficient manner. *See, e.g.*, Stephen Foerster, Juhani T. Linnainmaa, Brian T. Melzer & Alessandro Previtero, *Retail Financial Advice: Does One Size Fit All?*, 72 J. FIN. 1441 (2017) (offering evidence that an advisor's own asset allocation strongly predicts the allocations of its clients).

[57] Notwithstanding these functional similarities, investment advisory programs enjoy a broad safe harbor exemption under Investment Company Act of 1940 Rule 3a-4, 17 C.F.R. § 270.31–4 (2020). Wrap accounts are also subject to special disclosure requirements under Investment Advisers Act of 1940 Rule 204(c)(3)(d), 17 C.F.R. § 275.204(c)(3)(d) (2020).

FINRA and SEC disclosure rules discourage past performance reporting on individual accounts in marketing literature.[58]

Though not often framed in this way, the Department of Labor's now defunct fiduciary rule and SEC's recent adoption of Regulation BI and associated guidance can be seen as attempts to impose a more rigorous regulatory structure primarily around the distribution of mutual fund shares of various classes to retail investors. The DOL rule attempted to resolve the problem by elevating the fiduciary obligations of broker-dealers to preclude certain sales practices and force firms to distribute "clean" share classes with lower fees and also lower-priced index funds. The SEC's Regulation BI and associated guidance rely more heavily on disclosure rules for potential conflicts but address essentially the same problem. Neither approach attempts to bring allocated accounts up to the same level of disclosure of funds-of-funds, and neither approach imposes the kind of gatekeeper protections that mutual fund boards provide. To be sure—and as is explored below—replicating mutual fund regulation at the broker-dealer or investment advisor level would face non-trivial challenges.[59] But with the likely growth of robo-advisors, functionally similar pooled investment vehicles consisting largely, if not exclusively, of allocations to mutual fund investments are destined to become a serious competitor to funds-of-funds, but a competitor operating under a quite different regulatory regime.[60]

C *Managed Accounts*

Another common substitute for mutual funds as a pooled investment vehicle is the managed or separate account. Frequently, investment advisors offer clients with large balances the opportunity to invest through these accounts rather than through mutual funds.[61] In many instances, the managed accounts will have precisely the same investment strategy and portfolio of securities as existing mutual funds. Indeed, asset managers often use their mutual fund performance as a marketing vehicle to attract institutional investors, and in some instances wealthy clients, to managed accounts. This practice, which is widespread in the financial services industry, demonstrates how relatively simple it is for asset managers to replicate the performance of mutual funds in other pooled vehicles. To the extent that managed accounts have traditionally been distributed in the institutional market and to wealthy individuals, issues of investor

---

[58] For an overview of SEC regulation of performance advertising by registered investment advisors and broker-dealers, see U.S. Sec. & Exch. Comm'n, Study on Investment Advisers and Broker-Dealers, As Required by Section 913 of the Dodd-Frank Wall Street Reform and Consumer Protection Act, 30, 71 (Jan. 2011). *See also* Investment Adviser Advertisements; Compensation for Solicitations, 84 Fed. Reg. 67,518 (proposed Dec. 10, 2019) (adopted in final form 86 Fed. Reg. 13,026 (Mar. 5, 2021)); U.S. Sec. & Exch. Comm'n Office of Compliance and Examinations, *The Most Frequent Advertising Rule Compliance Issues Identified in OCIE Examinations of Investment Advisers*, 11 Nat'l Exam Program Risk Alert (Sept. 14, 2017).

[59] Interestingly, however, some analysts have suggested that robo-advisors should, in some instances, be regulated as mutual funds. *See, e.g.,* Melanie L. Fein, *Robo-Advisors: A Closer Look* 16 (Federated Investors, Inc., Jun. 30, 2015), https://papers.ssrn.com/sol3/papers.cfm?abstract_id=2658701. (stating that "[r]obo-advisors may be acting as unregistered investment companies in violation of the Investment Company Act of 1940 and SEC regulations thereunder" and questioning whether they meet the requirements of Rule 3a-4 "to the extent they do not manage client accounts on the basis of each client's financial situation and clients do not have reasonable access to personnel who are available to consult with the client").

[60] For a flavor of the competitive pressures from these new automated distributions channels, see Carmen Germaine, *Direct Platforms Steadily Encroach on Advisors' Turf*, Ignites (Jan. 18, 2019). For a recent article exploring ways to enhance the disclosure obligations of robo-advisors, see Nicole G. Iannarone, *Rethinking Automated Investment Adviser Disclosure*, 50 U. Tol. L. Rev. 433 (2019).

[61] *See, e.g.,* Legg Mason, A Guide to Separately Managed Accounts, at 4 (2019), https://www.leggmason.com/content/dam/legg-mason/documents/en/insights-and-education/brochure/investor-education-sma.pdf (comparing separately managed accounts to mutual funds and noting, among other things, the lower administrative costs of SMAs).

protection may not have been especially acute in this context.[62] Sophisticated parties can insist on performance reports, possibly demand GIPS compliance,[63] and seek detailed information on fees and other expenses. The choice of asset managers to place these larger customers into managed accounts is often justified as reducing compliance costs for the managed accounts as opposed to those costs associated with mutual fund regulation (presumably with savings shared at least in part with managed account customers).[64] The allure of such savings in regulatory costs encourages asset managers to avoid, if possible, the burdens of mutual fund regulation in other contexts as well, including distribution channels where the ultimate investor is an unsophisticated individual.[65] It is to those other contexts that I now turn.

D *Placement of Mutual Fund Shares in Other Pooled Vehicles for Retail Investors*

There are a host of contexts in which mutual fund shares are distributed to retail investors through pooled vehicles not directly subject to mutual fund regulation. These "outer wrappers" are often trusts or other legal entities with different and less onerous regulatory requirements. Investment advisors—either directly or more commonly through affiliated entities—often charge additional fees for these outer wrappers. Those fees are not, as currently structured, subject to mutual fund board oversight or the kinds of enhanced fiduciary protections that mutual fund regulation affords.

---

[62] Of course, to the extent that financial services firms lower the minimum balances required for separately managed accounts, there is the possibility that more individuals without a high net worth or investing sophistication will be drawn into those investment vehicles. *See* Legg Mason, *supra* note 61at 5 (reporting $50,000 minimum balance requirements for separately managed accounts). In that case, separately managed accounts begin to resemble some of the other pooled investment vehicles discussed below.

[63] For an overview of GIPS performance standards, *see* ACA Compliance Group & BNY Mellon, Practical Guidance: the GIPS Standards for Asset Owners, at 3 (2018), https://www.bnymellon.com/_global-assets/pdf/our-thinking/practical-guidance-the-gips-standards-for-asset-owners.pdf ("The popularity and worldwide adoption of the Global Investment Performance Standards (GIPS) by investment management firms is largely due to demand by asset owners. In order to trust investment performance when hiring an outsourced manager, asset owners increasingly require investment managers to comply with the GIPS standards."). *See also* CFA Institute, Global Investment Performance Standards (2020), https://www.gipsstandards.org/standards/2020/Pages/asset_owners.aspx.

[64] One context in which managed account programs interact with mutual fund regulation is in the annual section 15(c) procedures where mutual fund boards assess the reasonableness of fund fees and may consider, among other things, the fees charged by investment advisors to other customers. Often times, lower prices charged on managed accounts are a subject of discussion, and the issue of differences in regulatory costs is a factor advanced as a justification for the differentials. *See* Jones v. Harris Assoc. L.P., 559 U.S. 335, 349–51, n.8 (2010) (recognizing pricing differentials between mutual funds and institutional accounts). As one astute reader of an earlier draft of this chapter notes, the point I make here turns the *Jones v. Harris* litigation on its head, in that managed accounts are not here introduced as evidence that mutual fund fees are too high, but rather to raise the possibility that the relatively lax supervisory safeguards underlying managed accounts may raise issues of regulatory concern.

[65] Indeed, one can see this process at work in a recent trend of employer-sponsored 401(k) plans to "transition" participants from target-date funds into customized managed accounts at a certain age. *See* Carmen Germaine, *Schwab Planning Hybrid Target-Date Fund, Managed Account Service*, Ignites (Nov. 15, 2019) ("Managed accounts were available in 59% of defined contribution plans in 2018, up from just 36% in 2016 … [a]nd DC plan assets in managed accounts grew by more than 80% in the five years ended with 2018 … "). In this hybrid model, the underlying investments in the managed accounts can remain the same mutual fund products, but with customized rebalancing to reflect investor characteristics and with additional fees charged at the managed account level. *See* Anne Tergesen, *How Your 401(k) Could Imitate Netflix*, Wall St. J. (Feb. 14, 2019) (reporting fees at the managed account level of 8 to 23 basis points, in addition to the underlying investment fees). These hybrid products function in a manner quite similar to robo-advised accounts (discussed earlier) with automated allocations to mutual funds. This form of managed account is conceptually similar to the retail products analyzed in the next sub-section, although the design components—limiting access to retirement accounts of older workers—suggests that many investors in these accounts will have substantial balances and, in many instances, qualify as accredited investors and thus arguably constitute wealthy households traditionally targeted for separately managed accounts.

1 Collective Investment Trusts

One economically significant example of this phenomenon is the collective investment trust, which many 401(k) plans now feature on their retirement platforms, often for their default investment option.[66] Unlike traditional target-date funds (organized as funds-of-funds), these collective investment trusts are not regulated as 1940 Act investment companies, even though their underlying holdings may consist entirely, or almost entirely, of mutual funds and are often designed to replicate comparable target-date funds offered by the sponsoring asset manager.[67] In other instances, the collective investment trusts may be customized based on employer specification, but remain functionally similar to target-date funds operated as funds-of-funds. The collective investment trusts are governed by ordinary trust principles and, if the trustee is a regulated entity, such as a bank, may also be subject to additional regulatory obligations.[68] But legal protections at the collective investment trust level are not fully comparable to mutual fund regulation, and, again, one of the justifications for moving to this structure is a lowering of regulatory costs. Even proponents of CITs recognize the need to improve product transparency, including more comprehensive disclosure of all-in costs.[69]

2 ERISA Pension Plans

Even without collective investment trusts, investment advisors and their affiliates often provide services to retirement plans at the plan level—such as recordkeeping and other administrative services—and charge the plan sponsor fees for those services. In some cases, and increasingly, the plan sponsors will deduct those fees (or a portion thereof) from employee retirement accounts. As a matter of legal design, these affiliated services and fee arrangements all occur outside of mutual fund regulation and are primarily regulated by the Department of Labor under ERISA.[70] Over the past decade, the Department has examined the economic relationship between asset managers and ERISA retirement plans, primarily focusing on accurate and complete disclosures, including fee disclosures and revenue-sharing practices.[71] But the relationship of this practice in terms of mutual fund regulation has not, as best I can tell, been carefully examined.

[66]   *See* Press Release, Cerulli Assoc., CITs Offer Major Cost Advantages, but Transparency Will Be Essential (Aug. 2019), https://www.cerulli.com/about-us/press/2019-august-ccit-pr/ ("CIT assets stood at $3 trillion as of year-end 2018. The vehicle exhibited a compound annual growth rate (CAGR) of 7.25% over the five-year period ended 2018.").

[67]   *See* Robert Powell, *Retirement: Everything You Need to Know About Collective Investment Trusts*, THE STREET (July 30, 2018) ("The trustee of the CIT is on the hook for everything to do with the CIT, including deciding who is going to make the day-to-day investment decisions. Sometimes it is the trustee of the CIT themselves, but often they will hire a sub-advisor to pick the stocks or bonds to be held in the CIT. When the trustee decides to own one or more mutual funds in a CIT, they are by default outsourcing the day-to-day investment decisions to the portfolio manager of the mutual fund(s). The trustee of the CIT would then only be responsible for deciding which mutual funds (and the allocation to each if more than one), although the trustee would hire yet another investment professional to do that also.").

[68]   For an overview of the operations and regulation of CITs, see COALITION OF COLLECTIVE INVESTMENT TRUSTS, WHITE PAPER ON COLLECTIVE INVESTMENT TRUSTS (Mar. 31, 2015) (describing legal structure including OCC regulations, 12 C.F.R. 9 (2020) (Fiduciary Activities of National Banks). On some dimensions, such as ERISA coverage, CITs may actually be more heavily regulated than mutual funds.

[69]   *See* Press Release, *supra* note 66. ("Another challenge that CIT providers face is addressing investors' expectations for transparency."). *See also* Cerulli Associates, CIT Provider Survey 7 (2019) (reporting that less than a quarter of CIT providers report to the public on all-in costs).

[70]   For a discussion of the relationship between ERISA's regulation of investment vehicles and the broader landscape of fiduciary duties, see Arthur B. Laby, *Trust, Discretion, and ERISA Fiduciary Status*, ch. 4 (this volume).

[71]   These DOL disclosure requirements relate both to service-provider disclosures to plan fiduciaries and fiduciary disclosures to plan participates. *See* U.S. DEP'T OF LABOR, EMPLOYEE BENEFITS SECURITY ADMINISTRATION, RETIREMENT PLAN FEE DISCLOSURES. For current purposes, it is the latter category of disclosure that is relevant. According to

Adding a layer of fees (paid to investment advisors or their affiliates) at the plan level is in certain respects analogous to the sub-transfer agency fee problem discussed earlier. If those charges were imposed at the mutual fund level, they would be subject to a high degree of board scrutiny and regulation under mutual fund disclosure and performance rules. However, when those charges are moved out to the ERISA retirement plan level, their regulation changes and weakens on many critical dimensions. This differential encourages asset managers to lower mutual fund fees distributed through ERISA retirement plans and bulk up plan level charges. And, of course, the retail investor faces the challenge of combining fee disclosures at two different levels in order to get a clear picture of fund costs.

3 Other Examples

Once one is attuned to this phenomenon, one can find illustrations of mutual funds being distributed in less regulated outer layers with separate fees in a variety of contexts. Two prominent examples are two-tier variable annuity products, where the investment level is regulated as a mutual fund, but the outer layer is an insurance product not subject to mutual fund regulation and subject to separate and, often, quite substantial, additional fees.[72] Tax-favored 529 plans for education savings also have this structure. In many cases, these plans are limited to investing in underlying mutual funds but are wrapped at the plan level by another legal entity with separate pricing arrangements, often offsetting fee changes at the underlying fund level, but with additional charges imposed outside the purview of mutual fund regulation.[73]

V POLICY CONSIDERATIONS GOING FORWARD

What are the policy implications of these developments? To be sure, the evolution of industry practices described could be viewed simply as a nice example of regulatory arbitrage. Quite naturally, asset managers have an incentive to organize their operations to minimize regulatory costs and maximize operational flexibility. In many contexts—especially where the client at issue is truly a sophisticated institutional investor with its own money at risk—the regulatory arbitrage may be socially desirable with few adverse consequences.[74] Conceivably, as industry acquires more experience with less regulated pooled investment vehicles, the SEC might want

---

Fidelity, participant fee disclosures extend to "two broad types of information: (1) plan information, including administrative and individual expenses that may be charged against an individual's account; and (2) investment-related information for the plan's designated investment alternatives." *See* Fidelity Participant Summary of Disclosure Regulations, https://www.fidelity.com/retirement-ira/small-business/participant-disclosure-regulations-summary. For an insightful overview of revenue sharing practices under ERISA, see Dana M. Muir, *Revenue Sharing in 401(k) Plans: Employers as Monitors*, 20 CONN. INSUR. L.J. 485 (2013).

[72] For a recent overview of the regulation of two-tier variable annuities, see Gary O. Cohen, *SEC Proposes Summary Prospectus for Variable Insurance Products*, 52 R. SEC. & COMMODITIES REG. 143 (2019).

[73] The Municipal Securities Rulemaking Board (MSRB) has jurisdiction over 529 Plans. For an overview of the Board's requirements and fee disclosures, *see* Municipal Securities Rulemaking Board, Investor's Guide to 429 Savings Plans, http://www.msrb.org/msrb1/pdfs/MSRB-529-Investor-Guide.pdf. ("There are certain fees and charges assessed under a 529 savings plan that you may pay directly and indirectly. The fees and charges that you may pay directly are charged at the account or investment option level.").

[74] The caveat that the institutional investor must put itself at risk is an important one. While this may typically be true of managed accounts for some institutional investors, like defined benefit plans and insurance companies, it may not be true for defined contribution retirement plan arrangements, such as 401(k) plans or 529 plans. In those contexts, investment risk is borne by an employee, and the employer/sponsor of the plans may well have an incentive to shift fees to plan participants. *See* Howell E. Jackson, *The Trilateral Dilemma in Financial Regulation, in* IMPROVING THE EFFECTIVENESS OF FINANCIAL EDUCATION AND SAVINGS PROGRAMS (Anna Maria Lusardi ed., 2008).

to consider relaxing some of the required obligations of funds-of-funds and other investment companies under mutual fund regulation in light of industry innovations in analogous contexts if only to maintain a level playing field. On the other hand—and especially where the ultimate ownership of investments is at the retail level—policy-makers might have legitimate concerns that the movement of pooled investment accounts outside of mutual fund regulation has deleterious consequences for individual investors. Moreover, the creation of a multi-tiered system of federal regulation for these vehicles could create pressures for more assets to move out into these hybrid arrangements and away from full compliance with mutual fund regulation. Without attempting to offer a definitive answer to these complex issues of regulatory design, I conclude this chapter with a few thoughts on what I think are some of the key issues.

A *Integrated Disclosure for Mutual Funds Distributed to Retail Investors through Other Pooled Vehicles*

A significant concern about the propagation of outer wraps outside the reach of mutual fund regulations is that individual investors in ERISA pension plans or some other pooled collective vehicles will be misled about the costs of investing in these funds because they will focus on the fee information in underlying fund prospectuses and not consider the additional costs imposed at the wrapper level. Omitting these outer wrapper fees will also tend to overstate reported performance. This is a disclosure problem that the SEC has addressed with considerable care in the context of fund-of-funds disclosures. A comparable approach could be developed for other pooled vehicles, perhaps drawing on industry standards for GIPS reporting. In many cases, however, the requirements would need to be imposed by other regulatory authorities, such as the Department of Labor for ERISA retirement plans and bank regulators for trusts with bank trustees. State law would presumably be required to address 529 plans disclosures and two-tier insurance annuity products.[75]

Differences in fiduciary oversight of mutual fund charges, as opposed to fees leveled on non-mutual fund pooled vehicles is a slightly more challenging problem. As noted, the 1940 Act's approach to mutual fund fees is highly stylized and relies on boards of directors with independent members and a supporting system of enhanced fiduciary obligations. Conceivably, some attention could be given to expanded fiduciary obligations on other parties, but precise or even approximate alignment with the mutual fund regime would be difficult to achieve. One modest accommodation could be addressed through traditional mutual fund regulation in the context of annual section 15(c) reviews of investment advisor fees. Among the criteria that board members must consider in assessing the reasonableness of advisory fees under the *Gartenberg* test are the profitability of the fund to the advisor as well as any "fall out" benefits the advisor obtains as a result of advising the fund. Fees and other revenue sources associated with the management of an outer wrapper used to distribute mutual funds could (and arguably should) be factored expressly into the consideration of these *Gartenberg* criteria.[76] Such an approach would put at least a modest constraint on fees and other charges imposed in the outer wrapper, at least when

---

[75] The SEC does have specialized disclosure rules for variable insurance products, and the 1940 Act itself does impose some soft obligations with respect to the reasonableness of overall fees on variable insurance products, but these standards do not replicate the kind of oversight or disclosure requirements for funds of funds. *See* Investment Company Act of 1940 § 26(f)(2)(A), 15 U.S.C. § 80a-26(f)(2)(A) (2018); Updated Disclosures Requirements and Summary Prospectus for Variable Insurance Products and Variable Life Insurance Contracts, 85 Fed. Reg. 25,964 (May 1, 2020).

[76] *See* Krinsk v. Fund Asset Mgmt., Inc., 715 F. Supp. 472, 494–95 (S.D.N.Y. 1988) (discussing primary and secondary fall-out benefits).

the underlying investments are made through registered funds and the outer wrapper is managed by, or contractually connected to, affiliated entities.[77]

B *Aligning Regulation of Allocated Accounts for Individual Retail Investors*

The challenges of aligning regulation of discretionary accounts managed for retail investors are thornier but perhaps even more pressing. As technological developments and consumer preferences promote robo-advising, one can easily imagine steady growth of discretionary accounts — primarily invested in mutual funds through automated allocation software — replacing an ever larger share of retail investment. This process could even extend to a large fraction of the retirement savings space through brokerage platforms available on many ERISA retirement plans. As a legal matter, the regulation governing these accounts has traditionally been rules designed for broker-dealers and registered investment advisors making recommendations with respect to specific securities. In certain respects, the SEC's recent efforts to clarify the duties of broker-dealers and investment advisors can be understood as stiffening the legal obligations of those firms to act in the best interest of clients invested in pooled vehicles.[78] But, as argued above, the financial products increasingly offered through these distribution channels are functionally similar to personalized funds-of-funds, fully subject to mutual fund regulation. How might the rules for broker-dealers and investment advisors be aligned in this context?

As mentioned earlier, performance data and comprehensive fees data (that is fee data including not just wrapper fees but underlying mutual fund fees and commissions) is not something that broker-dealers and registered investment advisors are typically required to report to the public. While a limited body of academic research suggests that returns on retail brokerage accounts are not good and perhaps should be better publicized,[79] there are practical difficulties in requiring brokerage firms to produce these disclosures. Assembling the data could be complicated on an individual level, and it is not entirely clear how a brokerage house or registered investment advisor would report results for their entire client base. Would they report on the median or average customer or the distribution of all customers? The administrative difficulties have been daunting, which perhaps explains why reforms such as the SEC's Regulation BI and associated guidance have gravitated toward softer standards of conduct and disclosure obligations. On the other hand, one might legitimately worry whether these softer protections will create the same degree of protection (and marketplace discipline) that

---

[77] An alternative and more heavy-handed approach would be to bring all of these outer-wrapper charges into approval procedures of the sort required for Rule 12b-1 fees.

[78] See *supra* notes 58–59 (discussing Regulation BI). To be sure, these enhancements may have a positive impact on investors and may focus examination personnel on the selection of mutual fund share classes and best execution practices in discretionary connects. But the question remains whether the articulation of open-ended duties in this context — which are apt to be diluted over time by disclosures and safe-harbor relief — will offer as effective protections for investors and consistent performance and total fee reported of the sort I advocate here.

[79] The evidence that individual investment portfolios underperform the stock market averages is fairly substantial. *See* Brad M. Barber & Terrance Odean, *Trading Is Hazardous to Your Wealth: The Common Stock Investment Performance of Individual Investors*, 55 J. Fin. 773 (2000). *See also* Brad M. Barber & Terrance Odean, *The Behavior of Individual Investors*, in 2 Handbook of Economics of Finance, (George Constantinides, Hilton Harris & Rene M. Stulz eds., 2013). The extent to which this underperformance derives from poor investment advice is less well established, but certainly, a number of recent empirical studies point in that direction. *See, e.g.*, Juhani Linnainmaa, Brian Melzer & Alessandro Previtero, *The Misguided Beliefs of Financial Advisors*, (Kelley School of Business Research, Working Paper No. 18–9) (poor performance in personal accounts of advisors replicated in accounts recommended for their clients); Mark Egan, Gregor Matvos & Amit Seru, *The Market for Financial Adviser Misconduct*, 127 J. Pol. Econ. 233 (2019) (empirical study of advisor misconduct suggest that some financial firms specialize in misconduct and catering to unsophisticated customers).

standardized disclosures and more rigorous fiduciary protections have afforded mutual fund investors in recent decades.

The rise of robo-advisors and algorithmic allocation models, while exacerbating the problem, also allows for new solutions.[80] For one thing, the automation inherent in robo-advising almost certainly diminishes the administrative challenges of producing standardized reports of all-in performance and total fees at the individual account level. More importantly, the standardization of investment advice from robo-advisors makes it possible to imagine the SEC developing a handful of model client profiles with stylized risk-return preferences, investment time horizons, and tax positions. Firms offering allocated accounts to individual investors could be required to report on the historical performance that their accounts would have earned for each model for standardized periods (e.g., one-, three-, five-, and ten- year horizons) along with information on total fees for comparable periods and prospectively.[81] This would replicate the fund-of-funds approach to disclosure and also generate the information that outside vendors, like Morningstar and Broadridge, could use to rank quality and promote effective competition. While this approach would not replicate the fiduciary oversight afforded under mutual fund regulation, it would substantially align market oversight.

VI CONCLUSION

Some degree of regulatory arbitrage is inherent in our fragmented system of financial regulation. Arbitrage can — and perhaps often does — facilitate beneficial innovation. Many of the boundary crossings documented in this chapter are likely of this character. However, regulatory arbitrage can evade important regulatory protections. That almost certainly was the case with money market mutual funds, an exercise of regulatory arbitrage with considerable consumer benefits in the 1990s and substantial negative externalities in the Financial Crisis of 2008. How much government officials should allow pooled investment vehicles for retail investors to escape mutual fund regulation requirements is an important and unresolved question in today's financial markets. At a minimum, it calls out for informed public debate and thoughtful regulatory consideration.

---

[80] For a recent paper exploring new approaches to the regulation of robo-advisors, *see* Nicole G. Iannarone, *Rethinking Automated Investment Adviser Disclosure*, 50 U. Tol. L. Rev. 433 (2019). *See also* Braiden Colman, Kenneth J. Merkley & Joseph Pacelli, *Man Versus Machine: A Comparison of Robo-Analyst and Traditional Research Analyst Investment Recommendations* (Feb. 2020), https://papers.ssrn.com/sol3/papers.cfm?abstract_id=3514879 (offering evidence that robo-advisors outperform traditional analysts).

[81] Recently, the SEC signaled its openness to revisit performance advertising in the context of investment advisors. *See* Investment Adviser Advertisements; Compensation for Solicitations, 84 Fed. Reg. 67,518 (proposed Dec. 10, 2019).

8

Equitable Duty: Regulating Corporate Transactions in the Vicinity of Insolvency from a Comparative Perspective

Edward J. Janger

I INTRODUCTION

Last year, the U.K. Government conducted a consultation on insolvency law and corporate governance.[1] The consultation was triggered by two high-profile cases, *Carillion* and *BHS* ("British Home Stores"): in *Carillion*, it was believed that earlier action by the board of directors to place the company into administration might have preserved the enterprise's viability;[2] in *BHS*, the firm's principal sold the company, leaving a shortfall in the pension fund, after having paid significant dividends over time.[3] Both cases involved allegations of breach of fiduciary duty by officers and directors, but in one case, the focus was on an action against the directors themselves for the decision they had made. In the other, the focus was on the recovery of the dividends from the investors/shareholders through avoidance of the transactions. The consultation proposed, among other things, (1) to extend the fiduciary duties of the officers and directors of holding companies to include the creditors of subsidiaries, and (2) to increase the administrator's clawback and investigative powers in relation to such so-called "value extraction schemes."[4]

Somewhat similar concerns have been raised in the United States. The U.S. courts, particularly Delaware, take a relaxed approach to fiduciary duties in the vicinity of insolvency[5]. This has led to academic commentary[6] and a reform proposal by Senator and former candidate for President, Elizabeth Warren, with her proposed "Accountability in Capitalism Act" (though her views are not limited to the vicinity of insolvency).[7] These proposals offer an opportunity to think, from first principles, about the role of fiduciary duties and clawbacks in governing the behavior of officers, directors and investors when firms enter financial distress.

---

[1] U.K. Dep't of Bus., Energy & Indus. Strategy, Consultation on Insolvency and Corporate Governance: Government Response (Aug. 26, 2018), https://www.gov.uk/government/consultations/insolvency-and-corporate-governance ("Government Response").

[2] For a collection of news stories about Carillion, *see* FT Collections: Carillion's collapse: risk and failure, Fin. Times, https://www.ft.com/content/2cab2ac2-fb83-11e7-9b32-d7d59aace167. A discussion of the Board's role can be found here: https://www.ft.com/content/2095beca-fb8b-11e7-a492-2c9be7f3120a.

[3] Ian Clark, *The British Home Stores Pension Scheme: Privatised Looting?*, 50 Indus. Rel. J. 331, 331–32 (2019).

[4] Government Response at 5–7.

[5] N. Am. Catholic Educ. Programming Foundation, Inc. v. Gheewalla, 930 A.2d 92 (Del. 2007); Trenwick Am. Litig. Trust v. Ernest & Young, L.L.P., 906 A.2d 168 (Del. Ch. 2006) (the "Chancery Opinion" or "Trenwick"), aff'd, No. 495, 2006, 2007 WL 2317768 (Del. Aug. 14, 2007).

[6] Jared A. Ellias & Robert J. Stark, *Bankruptcy Hardball*, 108 Calif. L. Rev. 745 (2020).

[7] Alexis Arumbul, *Elizabeth Warren's Accountable Capitalism Act, Explained*, Medium (Oct. 16, 2018), https://medium.com/question-consumption/elizabeth-warrens-accountable-capitalism-act-explained-85215ccifa6.

When a business is in difficulty, the officers and directors face consequential choices. They must consider whether to continue the business or liquidate it. If they wish to continue the business, they must consider whether to open a formal proceeding or seek to deal with their creditors outside of bankruptcy. The creditors and owners also face consequential decisions: whether to cooperate with a collective strategy to return the business to financial health, or try to protect their own position at the expense of others—to hold, coerce, or extract value from the firm as it fails. Fiduciary duties address the decisions of the officers and directors. Clawbacks address the behavior of the investors.

This chapter compares the U.K. and U.S. approaches to fiduciary duty and clawback as they relate to transactions when the firm is in the vicinity of insolvency. Historically the United States and the United Kingdom have balanced directors' duties and trustees' avoidance powers in opposite ways.[8] In the United Kingdom, officers and directors have a duty of fairness to creditors in the vicinity of insolvency; in Delaware, no such duty arises. The United States takes a strict approach to avoidance of preferential and fraudulent transfers; the United Kingdom requires culpability. Both regimes are under tension.

This chapter suggests that the stress on the duty and clawback regimes on both sides of the pond stems from the difficulties in adapting the law of fiduciary duty and clawback to the exigencies of an insolvency regime oriented toward "rescue." In particular, the chapter concludes, that both jurisdictions fail to appreciate that duty and clawback serve complementary functions in the vicinity of insolvency—equitable treatment of creditors; and that a more balanced approach would be better than either of the lopsided approaches taken by the United States and the United Kingdom.

In formulating this common approach, I draw on previous work done with Melissa Jacoby, where we developed a principle we called "equitable realization." We first developed this concept in the context of managing entitlements over time in a formal Chapter 11 proceeding—a rescue proceeding. We derived it from positive law, finding that, in a Chapter 11 proceeding, value is realized for creditors in two steps: (1) equitable realization; and (2) value realization. At the beginning of the case, the relative position of unsecured creditors is fixed, as is the pool of collateral encumbered by secured creditors. The value of the firm, in contrast, is realized when assets are liquidated, or the firm is recapitalized pursuant to a plan of reorganization. In our view, this vision of rescue is justified on normative grounds. By fixing the priority claims when the proceeding is opened, governance decisions remain with the residual claimants, who share the upside and downside of the continuation decisions ratably.

This chapter extends this principle of equitable realization backward in time to the vicinity of insolvency, applying it to both fiduciary duty and clawback. While "equitable realization" is triggered, as a legal matter, by the opening of a Chapter 11 proceeding, conceptually, the same equitable principles come into play as soon as there is concern that debt claims may not be paid in full. That is the moment when the question of shifting or expanding duties for officers and directors, and possible avoidance liability for investors come into play; decisions of the officers and directors must be made with reference to the imperative that the priority of debt over equity be maintained, and debt claims must be treated ratably.

---

[8] With regard to directors' duties, *compare* N. Am. Catholic Educ. Programming Found., Inc. v. Gheewalla, 930 A.2d 92 (Del. 2007) and Trenwick Am. Litig. Trust v. Ernest & Young, L.L.P., 906 A.2d 168 (Del. Ch. 2006), aff'd, No. 495, 2006, 2007 WL 2317768 (Del. Aug. 14, 2007) *with* Nicholson and another v. Fielding and others [2017] All ER (D) 156 (Oct). *See also* Ryan Beckwith, Dan Butler, & Samuel Naylor, *Nicholson: Decision to Keep Trading Not Always Wrongful*, 15 Int'l Corp. Rescue 157, 157 (2018), https://www.freshfields.com/49ed41/globalassets/services-page/restructuring-and-insolvency/publication-pdfs/icr_nicholson_decision_to_keep_trading_not_always_wrongful.pdf. For a discussion of clawbacks, *compare* 11 U.S.C. § 548 (2018) *with* Insolvency Act of 1986, § 423.

Therefore, I suggest a corollary approach to "equitable realization"—"equitable duty"—that merges concepts of duty and equity. It is implemented through fiduciary duty (focused on officers and directors) and clawback (focused on investors). I argue that fiduciary principles (duty) and avoidance (equity) can (and should) work together to instantiate the following two-pronged principle: When a firm is insolvent, or in its vicinity,

1) the fiduciary should not enter into any transaction that alters the priority of distribution as a legal or economic matter, even if the course of action would increase the value of the estate as a whole. Where there is doubt about whether a course of action will benefit all stakeholders, the fiduciary should obtain consent or seek judicial blessing by opening a proceeding.

2) Shareholder dividends and creditors repayments should be subject to avoidance where forbearance or further investment (choose one: has been conditioned on; results in) an alteration of the distributional scheme.

In other words, when a firm is in the vicinity of insolvency, a duty to either the shareholders or the corporation to maximize value is insufficient. In the absence of consent or judicial approval, a fiduciary must be able to justify its acts with reference to a "best interests" test or "no worse than" treatment. "Equitable duty," thus, imposes a practical constraint of Pareto superiority or "best interests"—no constituency should be made worse off.[9] With this principle in mind, both fiduciary duty and clawback can work together to effectuate both efficient rescue and equitable treatment.

The analysis proceeds in five steps. First, I assert a normative baseline, asking, what "should" officers and directors do under fiduciary principles? I will argue that they should seek to do two things that seem obvious: (1) maximize the value of the firm; (2) distribute that value according to legal entitlements. To put it another way, the fiduciary should maximize the estate's value to the extent it can do so legally and equitably— without distorting ex ante legally enforceable priorities and discriminating among similarly situated creditors. This is what I will call the fiduciary's "equitable duty."

Second, I will consider the decisional environment in the vicinity of insolvency and show that unless the principle of equitable duty is followed, conflicting (or absent) duties of loyalty will leave officers and directors rudderless when the imperative to maximize the value of the estate conflicts with the duty to respect the priority of debt over equity. This is true whether one views the duty of the officers as being owed "to the company" or to particular "stakeholders."

Third, I will consider avoidance powers or to "clawbacks." Clawbacks implement the same equitable principle, but after the fact—unwinding transactions that altered distributional entitlements. Fraudulent conveyance law unwinds transactions that favor equity over debt, and preference law unwinds transactions that violate the principle of equal treatment among creditors. In broad strokes, I will compare the U.S. and U.K. regimes for fiduciary and investor liability. Notwithstanding the common root in equitable duty, the United States and the United Kingdom calibrate their enforcement regimes very differently. The U.S. regime chooses weak fiduciary duties and relatively robust clawback powers, while the United Kingdom would impose a fiduciary duty with regard to creditors but takes a more relaxed approach to avoidance. This difference has its roots in differing historical approaches to rescue.

---

[9] As is discussed below, a version of "equitable duty" was articulated by the U.S. Supreme Court in regard to reorganization cases. Czyzewski v. Jevic Holding Corp., 137 S. Ct. 973, 985 (2017) ("In doing so, these courts have usually found that the distributions at issue would 'enable a successful reorganization and make even the disfavored creditors better off.'"). Here I argue that the same principle operates in the vicinity of insolvency as well.

Fourth, I will suggest that both regimes get it wrong; in rescue, fiduciary duties and clawback complement each other to implement the principle of "equitable duty." Fifth, I will give a report from the field in the United States, and offer the following takeaways:

- In the vicinity of insolvency (and once insolvent) it is essential (but hard) to separate decisions about value maximization (governance) from decisions about distribution (legal entitlement and priority).
- The fiduciary duty of loyalty, standing alone, *does not* give meaningful guidance to decision-makers about distributional choices in the vicinity of insolvency, unless interpreted to include a duty of "equitable treatment" that prohibits trading off one beneficiary against another, even to maximize value, without consent.[10]
- Clawbacks *can* police transactions that violate the duty of equitable treatment prior to the opening of a formal proceeding and the advent of "supervision." They do so by recovering the funds from the creditor or investor.
- Both the United States, through Chapter 11, and the United Kingdom, through recent reforms, seek to encourage rescue, even once a proceeding has been opened. In this regard, judicial supervision, and mechanisms such as the automatic stay and Chapter 11's plan confirmation process *can* preserve the business, while encouraging consent and facilitating rescue.
- The principle of equitable treatment, implicit before opening a proceeding, becomes explicit once a proceeding has been opened. Limiting the power of creditors to use situational leverage, once a proceeding has opened, helps ensure that bargaining happens in the shadow of entitlement and that the principle of equitable treatment is honored. The same can be said of the power to unwind transactions that violate that principle that arises upon the filing of a bankruptcy petition.
- Fiduciary duty and clawbacks are thus complementary and should be given roughly equal prominence in a regime that seeks to encourage efficient rescue.

II DUTY AND ENTITLEMENT IN, AND NEAR, INSOLVENCY

The fiduciary duty of loyalty contemplates (and works best in) a simple world where the firm is solvent, and an agent with discretion can identify the principal and act in its interest. Officers and directors seek to maximize and realize the value of the firm and allocate that value according to legal entitlements. Creditors get paid, shareholders receive dividends. For a solvent firm, shareholder primacy firmly situates the fiduciary's duty of loyalty with the owners.[11] The business judgment rule protects the officers in the exercise of their discretion.[12] Mostly conscientious officers and directors are free to do their jobs without fear of liability for breach of fiduciary duty.

Financial distress changes all of that. For most officers and directors, the "vicinity of insolvency" is seen as a complex state of limbo, where conflicting duties can cause paralysis.[13] Even

---

[10] As discussed below, this duty should apply only to non-ordinary course transactions, and it is a standard, rather than a rule.

[11] Milton Friedman, *The Social Responsibility of Business Is to Increase Its Profits*, N.Y. Times (Sept. 13, 1970), http://umich.edu/~thecore/doc/Friedman.pdf.

[12] N.Y. Bus. Corp. Law § 717 (McKinney 2020).

[13] As Hu and Westbrook suggest:

> Our prescription is to abolish this century-old doctrine. Regardless of financial condition, a corporation and its directors should never owe a duty to creditors, apart from constraints arising in contract and tort. Only when a corporation has passed on as a legal matter—to the heaven or hell of federal bankruptcy law (and perhaps

worse, insolvency, if it occurs, is a realization event—the end of the road. Most of the time, in most jurisdictions, the firm is wound up, and its value distributed amongst its disappointed investors.

A *Rescue: Delaying Realization to Preserve Going Concern Value*

For those familiar with Chapter 11 in the United States, schemes of arrangement in the United Kingdom, as well as emerging "pre-insolvency" mechanisms envisioned by the E.U. Directive on Preventive Restructuring Frameworks, insolvency (or its vicinity) need not lead to realization. Bankruptcy is no longer necessarily the end of the firm, as an operating entity, but a tool to preserve going concern value through recapitalization or sale.[14] It is not an endpoint but a forum that allows viable businesses to continue while restructuring their debt in the shadow of liquidation and non-bankruptcy entitlements.

However, to preserve a business as a going concern, the realization of value must be delayed. The firm must continue to operate, even after it is apparent that the firm *may* not be able to service its existing debt. Outside of bankruptcy, the desire to continue the business may mean incurring debt that may not be paid in full, or current services may be obtained using cash or other assets that might instead have been paid to existing creditors or the shareholders. Every choice contains uncertainty, and that uncertainty will be borne in different proportions by different corporate constituencies.

B. *Rescue and the Problem of Value Allocation*

When a firm's solvency is uncertain, officers and directors face difficult choices along two axes: value maximization/governance and value realization/distribution. In the vicinity of insolvency, the officers and directors must consider three highly consequential corporate decisions about how to maximize the value of the firm. Should they liquidate the firm's assets piecemeal, sell the firm as a going concern, or seek to recapitalize and restructure the debt?

If the value of the firm is realized by continuing to operate, then the value of the cash flow must be allocated among creditors with asset-based priority, creditors, and equity. This allocation must be made, even though the future value of the firm is uncertain, encumbered assets were not sold, and the option value of equity was not foreclosed. Further, this allocation may not follow a strict "waterfall" priority. There may be multiple, distinct pools of value and claims because of corporate structure, national boundaries, or competing claims over assets. If so, how does one identify the residual claimant? To whom does the fiduciary owe a duty?

The following example illustrates the dilemma faced by corporate fiduciaries (officers and directors). And, fiduciary principles, as currently understood, are insufficient to resolve it.

---

a reincarnation)—would matters change. A formal bankruptcy filing, unlike changes in financial condition, initiates the structural changes in governance systems and ownership rights that are essential to the proper resolution of the interests of creditors.

Henry T. C. Hu & Jay Lawrence Westbrook, *Abolition of the Corporate Duty to Creditors*, 107 Colum. L. Rev. 1321, 1324–25 (2007).

[14] Directive (EU) 2019/1023 of the European Parliament and of the Council of 20 June 2019, on preventive restructuring frameworks, on discharge of debt and disqualifications, and on measures to increase the efficiency of procedures concerning restructuring, insolvency and discharge of debt, and amending Directive (EU) 2017/1132 (Directive on restructuring and insolvency) (Recital 2 provides: "Restructuring should enable debtors in financial difficulties to continue business, in whole or in part, by changing the composition, conditions or structure of their assets and their liabilities or any other part of their capital structure").

1. **OpCo is in the vicinity of insolvency.** It has severe cash flow difficulties.
   - On Friday, it must make a payment to its principal financial creditor and also make payroll. It does not have cash on hand to do both.
   - The CEO of the company is confident of two things: (1) this firm is worth more alive than dead; and (2) it will be a close call whether the firm's long-term value will be sufficient to service its existing debt load.

2. **If OpCo is liquidated piecemeal today, equity will be wiped out, and both secured and unsecured creditors will have a shortfall.**
   - The unsecured creditors (UC) are owed $1,000,000.
   - The secured creditor (SC) is owed $2,000,000, but their collateral is only worth $1,500,000.
   - In liquidation, the firm's assets would yield $2,000,000. The SC would receive $1,500,000 from the sale of its collateral.
   - Liquidation of the remaining unencumbered assets would yield $500,000.
   - This would yield a distribution of 33 percent to UC. ($500 K/$1.5MM). This is calculated by dividing the value of the unencumbered assets by the total unsecured claims, which consist of the original $1,000,000 owed to UC plus the $500,000 unsecured deficiency of SC.
   - The value of the unencumbered assets would be distributed $333,333.33 to UC and $166,666.67 as an additional payment to the SC on account of its deficiency.
   - Nothing will be left over for equity.

3. **There are two investors who are interested in purchasing the firm.**
   - Under the proposal of Investor A, the price would be $2.5MM, and the proceeds would be distributed according to existing priorities: SC gets a secured claim of $1.5MM (the value of its collateral) and UC + SP's deficiency each get 67 percent. Equity would still receive nothing.
   - Under Investor B's proposal, the price would be $2.75MM, but the purchaser insists that the distribution will be $2MM (payment in full) to SP, 250 K to UC (25%) and $500 K to equity.
   - Both proposals contain a "kicker" under which the creditors will be paid in full, if, several years out, the company has achieved specific (very optimistic) performance goals.
   - The fiduciary does not know why Investor B prefers a different value allocation, nor does the fiduciary benefit from one over the other.

Insolvency and the vicinity of insolvency put "distributional" questions before the fiduciary that are not present for a solvent firm. If the two offers were $3.25 and $3.5 million respectively, there would be no concern about allocation. The creditors would be paid in full, and the difference in the value of the two offers, if any, shared by the owners. In contrast, where neither offer is likely to be sufficient to pay the various creditors in full, questions of equitable distribution of value are posed starkly. Value maximization is in tension with value allocation.

In this example, therefore, whether a fiduciary has a duty to creditors, to shareholders, to both, or to the corporation affects which of the two options the fiduciary will or can choose. The option which maximizes the value of the firm does so at the expense of the UC and allows both the senior (SC) investor and junior investor (equity) to extract value at the expense of the middle tier (UC) investor. The scenario that "does no harm" produces less value overall. If the fiduciary has no duty to creditors, but only to the shareholders or the firm, then it is free to, and perhaps must, take the proposal of Investor B. If the fiduciary owes a duty to the creditors, but not equity, then it must take the proposal of Investor A and cannot accept the proposal of Investor B. If the fiduciary has a duty to both debt and equity, this scenario places the fiduciary in an uncertain, and perhaps impossible position. It cannot benefit one group without harming the other.

C Rescue and Equity

Nothing empowers the officers or directors to give the creditors a haircut to preserve value for equity or pay the SC more than the value of its collateral plus its *pari passu* share on the deficiency. The fiduciary is only "safe" if it obtains consent or adopts a principle of "non-discrimination" or "do no harm" to everyone with a claim to the value of the firm. In the vicinity of insolvency, this problem presents as a principal agent problem; it is, however, really a problem of trust accounting. The equitable obligation of the fiduciary is to distribute the funds held in trust according to legal entitlements. This is the principle that I will call the fiduciary's "equitable duty." It is a duty to distribute value in a way that treats similarly situated claimants similarly, in accordance with legal entitlements.

D Officers and Directors in the Vicinity of Insolvency in the United Kingdom and the United States

Officers and directors are, however, charged both with operating the firm and distributing its value. When a debtor continues to operate, these two roles are in tension. Multiple creditors may each have the practical power to block a rescue—shutter the business.[15] Creditors may seek to use this situational leverage over value maximization as leverage to extract extra value from the debtor. This leverage influences practical operational decisions. A single creditor may hold out and insist on a larger share of the reorganization surplus, thereby endangering the rescue. Where equity is involved, the shareholders have the power to vote and bind minority shareholders. When debt is involved, however, there is no formal voting mechanism by which the firm can bind dissenting creditors.[16] Holdouts can pinion the fiduciary, leaving them torn between the duty to maximize value (by postponing the day of reckoning) and the duty to distribute according to entitlement. These practical questions lead to a legal one. Can and should fiduciary principles regulate the behavior of officers and directives as they seek to satisfy imperatives of value maximization and distribution based on entitlement?

   The U.K.'s answer is yes. Officers and directors are held to account by a fiduciary duty to creditors once the firm is in the vicinity of insolvency. Officers and directors are potentially liable for wrongful trading if the company continues to operate while insolvent without seeking to minimize the loss to creditors. In the vicinity of insolvency, officers and directors must have a good faith belief that the company will be able to continue in operation as a solvent entity, and

---

[15]   As we will discuss, avoidance powers police equitable distribution, but from the investor perspective. They unwind the transaction and allow the estate to recover assets from the beneficiaries after it is shown to have been problematic. Instead of recovering against the fiduciary, avoidance law unwinds transactions that benefit corporate insiders or particular creditors at the expense of the corporation or creditors. It allows the trustee in bankruptcy to reverse transactions that allowed one stakeholder to disregard or reallocate the priority of payment for the benefit of one stakeholder at the expense of another. They force the investor to consider whether the proposed transaction will be treated as final.

[16]   Bondholders may be able to bind each other, but that only works with regard to a single series of bonds. Bondholders are not bound by trade creditors, and vice versa.

that its actions will benefit the creditors as a whole.[17] But liability may also arise if the company is put into insolvency proceedings prematurely.

In the United States, or at least in Delaware, the courts have decided that the game is not worth the candle. They have exited the field: the Delaware Supreme Court stated in *North American Catholic Educational Programming* v. *Gheewalla* that, in the vicinity of insolvency, the officers and directors do not owe a duty to creditors;[18] similarly, the theory of "deepening insolvency," which would have imposed wrongful trading-like liability has not gained traction in U.S. courts.[19]

Delaware decisions interpreting *Gheewalla* have suggested that in both the vicinity of insolvency and insolvency itself, the duty runs to the corporation as a whole.[20] This does not help much, however, when an officer must choose between options A and B above. It offers no guidance on what to do when the goal of maximizing value requires the officer to choose among constituencies by distorting distributional priorities.

In his contribution to this book, Amir Licht offers a potentially useful suggestion—a duty of impartiality that would come into play any time that conflicts arose in multiple duty situations. He is concerned about a duty with substantive bite and limits his recommendation to a "lean" "procedural" duty to consider the interests of the affected stakeholders. In other words, the duty would have the limited utility of exposing overt, unjustifiable favoritism.[21] This approach holds

---

[17] Insolvency Act of 1986, § 214. *See, e.g.*, Grant v. Ralls EWHC 243 (Ch)(continued training did not worsen the position of the creditors as a whole); *Re Hawkes Hill Publishing Co Ltd* [2007] BCC 937 ("The question is whether they knew or ought to have concluded that there was no reasonable prospect of avoiding insolvent liquidation").

[18] N. Am. Catholic Educ. Programming Foundation, Inc. v. Gheewalla, 930 A.2d 92 (Del. 2007).

[19] Trenwick Am. Litig. Trust v. Ernest & Young, L.L.P., 906 A.2d 168 (Del. Ch. 2006), aff'd, No. 495, 2006, 2007 WL 2317768 (Del. Aug. 14, 2007).

[20] After *Gheewalla*, the law in Delaware has been summarized as follows:

- "There is no legally recognized 'zone of insolvency' with implications for fiduciary duty claims. The only transition point that affects fiduciary duty analysis is insolvency itself."

- "Regardless of whether a corporation is solvent or insolvent, creditors cannot bring direct claims for breach of fiduciary duty. After a corporation becomes insolvent, creditors gain standing to assert claims derivatively for breach of fiduciary duty."

- "The directors of an insolvent firm do not owe any particular duties to creditors. They continue to owe fiduciary duties to the corporation for the benefit of all of its residual claimants, a category which now includes creditors. They do not have a duty to shut down the insolvent firm and marshal its assets for distribution to creditors, although they may make a business judgment that this is indeed the best route to maximize the firm's value."

- "Directors can, as a matter of business judgment, favor certain non-insider creditors over others of similar priority without breaching their fiduciary duties."

- "Delaware does not recognize the theory of 'deepening insolvency.' Directors cannot be held liable for continuing to operate an insolvent entity in the good faith belief that they may achieve profitability, even if their decisions ultimately lead to greater losses for creditors."

- "When directors of an insolvent corporation make decisions that increase or decrease the value of the firm as a whole and affect providers of capital differently only due to their relative priority in the capital stack, directors do not face a conflict of interest simply because they own common stock or owe duties to large common stockholders. Just as in a solvent corporation, common stock ownership standing alone does not give rise to a conflict of interest. The business judgment rule protects decisions that affect participants in the capital structure in accordance with the priority of their claims."

  Quadrant Structured Prod. Co., Ltd. v. Vertin, 115 A.3d 535 (Del. Ch. 2015). Some states go even further, stating that no duty to creditors arises unless the company is both insolvent and no longer a going concern. Beloit Liquidating Trust v. Grade, 677 N.W.2d 298 (Wis. 2004).

[21] Amir N. Licht, *Stakeholder Impartiality: A New Classic Approach for the Objectives of the Corporation*, ch. 16 (this volume).

promise in situations where solvent companies are involved. However, as discussed below, the vicinity of insolvency pits continuation against priority and equality, even where the fiduciary is impartial. A more rigorous mechanism is required to ensure that equitable principles of distribution are respected.

Both the United States and the United Kingdom do go further than a weak procedural duty to be impartial, at least in the vicinity of insolvency. Both face the issue of equitable distribution in insolvency squarely but in different ways. In the United Kingdom, the officers and directors have a duty to creditors to minimize losses. In the United States, there is no such duty, but avoidance addresses the problem of equitable distribution of value, albeit after the fact; preferences and constructive fraudulent conveyances are avoidable on a strict liability basis. The U.K. law contains similar avoidance principles, but avoidance is only available if the recipient of the transfer had reason to know that the transfer was a preference or fraudulent.

In sum, while U.S. and U.K. law address the same question—how can principles of equitable (entitlement-based) distribution be honored in the vicinity of insolvency—they do not necessarily yield the same answer. For example, under U.S. law, entering into transaction B would probably not violate the fiduciary duty of loyalty, but some of the transfers would be avoidable: the payments to the SP in excess of the value of the collateral could be recovered for the benefit of the estate as a preference; the dividend to equity could be considered a fraudulent conveyance. In the United Kingdom, option B might violate the duty of fairness to creditors, but the transfers would likely not constitute avoidable preferences.

iii DUTY V. RESCUE IN THE VICINITY OF INSOLVENCY: AGENCY AND SITUATIONAL LEVERAGE

Neither the United Kingdom nor the United States approach to fiduciary duty is ideal from the perspective of facilitating efficient rescues. Each is hamstrung because governance questions in the vicinity of insolvency raise distributional questions. In the United States, courts have concluded that officers and directors need not address these questions because they are too hard. The reckoning is preserved for the investors, after the fact, through avoidance. In contrast, in the United Kingdom, the duty of fairness forces the officers and directors to deal with these distributional questions in real time, but largely frees the investors from concern.

From an operational perspective, the U.K. approach may force the officers to abandon attempts to recapitalize in order to avoid liability. Opening a proceeding in the United Kingdom pushes the company toward a sale, even after the move from receiverships to administrations.[22] It is widely reported that a dominant form of insolvency proceeding is the so-called "pre-pack" where the floating charge holder pre-arranges a sale of the firm that is then ratified through a quick administration.[23] While the going concern value of the firm may be preserved through a quick sale, the resulting allocation of value may not be fair to junior creditors. The "upside" of the business is transferred to the purchasers while the firm is still in distress, at a time when the value of the firm is axiomatically low.

The obverse U.S. approach is no better. Under basic principles of corporate finance, the *Gheewalla* view seems perverse. Governance rights and fiduciary duties run to the residual

---

[22] Adrian J. Walters, *Statutory Erosion of Secured Creditors' Rights: Some Insights from the United Kingdom*, 2015 U. Ill. L. Rev. 543, 586 (2015).

[23] *Id. See also In re* T&D Indus. PLC, [1999] 1 W.L.R. 646 at 657 (Eng.); *In re* Transbus Int'l Ltd., [2004] 1 W.L.R. 2654 at 2656 (Eng.); DKLL Solicitors v. Her Majesty's Revenue and Customs, [2007] B.C.C. 908 (Eng.); *In re* Kayley Vending Ltd, [2009] B.C.C. 578 (Eng.); *In re* Hellas Telecomms. (Lux.) II SCA, [2010] B.C.C. 295 (Eng.).

claimant. For solvent firms, able to pay their debts, that is the shareholders. If a firm is insolvent, the firm is investing the creditors' money. If the shareholders are out of the money, the residual claimant is the creditors. Therefore, in the vicinity of insolvency, where the situation is uncertain, the shareholders should take care not to take risks with the creditors' money. *Gheewalla*, by contrast, turns this principle on its head and would seem to validate such risk-taking. Indeed, two commentators have suggested that *Gheewalla* has ushered in an era of "bankruptcy hardball."[24] A more charitable, but still quite problematic reading of *Gheewalla* was suggested by professors Hu and Westbrook. They argue that the need for relaxed fiduciary obligation derives from the very desire to delay realization.[25] Rescue is premised on the fact that financial distress should not require cessation of the business and realization on the value of its assets. However, strong fiduciary duties create a problem for the corporate officer when the company needs to prefer a particular creditor to survive. This situation arises, for example, when a key vendor insists on payment in full of its outstanding receivable, when other creditors stand to receive cents on the dollar, or an under-secured creditor threatens to repossess unless additional collateral is provided. Individually, each of these decisions may help keep the business afloat, but they also shift the burden of insolvency inequitably to powerful creditors, often at the expense of less powerful employees, tort claimants, and so on.

Thus, this type of preference raises two fiduciary concerns: (1) risk alteration and (2) equality of treatment. Equity, which is, at least at the moment, out of the money, chooses to gamble the creditors' money on the hope that the firm will return to solvency. And, to do so, they pay one creditor in full, when, if the gamble turns out badly, the other creditors will receive reduced payments.

As demonstrated by the hypothetical that began this chapter, in the vicinity of insolvency, an officer or director seeking to maximize the value of the firm is inherently conflicted. They owe duties to two distinct constituencies—equity and debt. Or maybe three—equity, debt, and priority debt. To make matters worse, within the categories of priority, they owe duties of equal or *pari passu* treatment. Whenever a value-maximizing decision requires the corporate fiduciary to privilege one class or creditor within a class over others, the officer is conflicted. An inherent problem with fiduciary duties in such situations is that they do not provide a mechanism or a principle for making choices.

Thus, for Hu and Westbrook, the practical difficulties of keeping a firm alive require a relaxation of fiduciary principles to account for the situational leverage of the various people whose cooperation is needed to continue the business. Examples of this situational leverage include a key supplier who could stop delivering; a bank that could freeze a line of credit; a key employee who could quit. Each may condition continued cooperation on being brought current. This ability to hold the business hostage means that continuing the business frequently requires the officers to balance the continuation of the business against equal treatment of similarly situated stakeholders. Officers and directors may need to privilege particular creditors in the present to preserve the possibility of a future. The officers and directors are thus in a difficult position as they seek to avoid sending the firm into a death spiral as customers flee, and creditors start to grab the firm's assets.

This tightrope-walk between preserving the value of the firm and acceding to situational leverage facilitates and indeed occasions, a wide variety of familiar abuses. A short list may suffice. The debtor may prefer certain creditors over others.[26] This act of preferring one creditor

---

[24] Ellias & Stark, *supra* note 6.
[25] Hu & Westbrook, *supra* note 13.
[26] 11 U.S.C. § 547 (2018).

over another can take many forms. For example, extortionate credit terms may be used to reallocate the value of future operations from one incumbent creditor to another.[27] High prices might be charged for current services. Assets may be moved about within the firm to improve the position of particular stakeholders. Beyond simple preferences, parties with leverage may simply extract value. They may engage in transactions at under value (constructive fraudulent conveyances), or intentional fraudulent conveyances, where assets are removed from the failing enterprise before it fails.[28] Or, officers may simply walk off with the assets of the firm.

Hu and Westbrook acknowledge that recognizing a fiduciary duty to creditors may put the officers and directors in an impossible situation. They argue that corporate governance law is only suited to address the rights of shareholders, while bankruptcy, at least in the United States, was better suited to realizing and allocating the value of a distressed firm.[29] Their point is twofold. As a governance matter, the Chapter 11 regime in the United States places the firm under judicial supervision while continuing to operate. The choices of the officers and directors are more participatory supervised by a committee of creditors, as well as the court. Assets are protected against a run by a broad automatic stay and current operating creditors are protected against the firm's insolvency through administrative expense priority.[30] Finally, value is distributed under a court approved plan of reorganization.[31] Hu and Westbrook address the conflict problem with a proceeding.

Thus, Hu and Westbrook envision a binary world: (1) no fiduciary duty to creditors outside of bankruptcy; (2) participatory judicially supervised decisions about governance once the case has been opened. The problem is that the rescue regime blurs the line by saying that operations can continue in either regime. To which side should one allocate cases where the solvency of the debtor is uncertain. By eliminating the duty to creditors, Hu and Westbrook leave the decision up to incumbent management and leave management free to trade the interest of creditors against the continuation of the company.

For a firm operating in the vicinity of insolvency, *prior* to opening a proceeding, relaxed fiduciary duties may facilitate the continuation of the business; however, they provide no protection against the situational leverage created by financial distress. While the firm continues in business, high leverage creditors will seek to capture value at the expense of low leverage creditors with similar legal status. Indeed, they may do so in partnership with equity, thereby subordinating other creditors, not merely diluting them.

The only line of defense in Hu and Westbrook's world is clawback. Hu and Westbrook acknowledge, as they must, that the puzzle lies in working out the appropriate transition regime between the *Gheewalla* (no duty) regime and Chapter 11.[32] The problem remains as to how to prevent opportunistic behavior in the period *before* the debtor enters a formal proceeding, and what legal mechanism will, or should, drive the debtor to open a formal rescue proceeding.

In sum, under the U.K. approach, the threat of wrongful trading liability may force the debtor to open a proceeding that will prematurely force realization on the value of the firm. Meanwhile, the U.S. approach may allow the directors to delay realization while the value of the firm

[27]   Shapiro v. Saybrook Mfg. Co. (In re Saybrook Mfg. Co.), 963 F.2d 1490 (11th Cir. 1992).

[28]   11 U.S.C. § 548 (2018).

[29]   Hu & Westbrook, *supra* note 13.

[30]   But weak fiduciary duties present the opposite problem. They facilitate rescue by allowing the company to continue trading. However, they provide no bulwark against situational leverage. This may allow a firm to continue in business but it can also allow high leverage claimants to capture value at the expense of low leverage claimants with similar legal status.

[31]   11 U.S.C. § 1129 (2018).

[32]   Hu & Westbrook, *supra* note 13, at 1399 ("Future research should focus primarily on the transition between the two governance systems.").

dissipates and/or legal entitlements are disregarded when opening a proceeding would, in fact, facilitate rescue and protect entitlements.

IV CLAWBACKS IN BANKRUPTCY AS AN ALTERNATIVE TO THE DUTY OF LOYALTY

As a practical matter, under U.S. law, *Gheewalla* shifts the legal regulation of pre-insolvency behavior from fiduciary duty, which regulates directors and officers, to avoidance, which acts on investors. Instead of the corporate decisionmaker, U.S. law places risk on the investors—the creditors and shareholders—themselves, that money they receive in the form of payments or dividends may be clawed back. Transactions with debtors who turn out to have been insolvent lack finality. United States law contains a number of avoidance provisions that subject the recipients of transfers from the debtor to the risk that the pre-bankruptcy transaction might later be unwound. Creditors might have to return a pre-petition debt repayment as a preference.[33] Recipients of a dividend might have to refund the payment as a fraudulent conveyance.[34] The bank that lends into a leveraged buyout transaction might have its liens avoided if the subject firm is left insolvent.[35] A brief list of avoidable transactions includes:

- *Fraudulent conveyances* may be unwound by creditors under state law (the UFCA, UFTA, or UVTA), all of which contain provisions that avoid both transactions "intended" to "hinder delay or defraud" creditors, as well as provisions that allow avoidance of transfers made while the debtor is insolvent for which the debtor does not receive "reasonably equivalent value." The Bankruptcy Code vests a similar power in the Bankruptcy Trustee pursuant to section 548 of the Code.
- Payments on the eve of bankruptcy that prefer one creditor over another can be unwound by the bankruptcy trustee as *preferences* (11 U.S.C. § 547 (2018)).
- Bankruptcy courts may *recharacterize* debt claims as equity based on the substance, rather than the label of the transaction.
- Finally, where there is creditor misbehavior prior to the bankruptcy, bankruptcy courts have the power to equitably subordinate the claim pursuant to 11 U.S.C. § 510(a) (2018).

For both constructive fraudulent conveyance and preference law, in the United States, liability is strict. The trustee need not prove that the debtor intended to prefer a particular creditor or hinder creditors generally. Neither is it necessary to prove that the transferee had reason to believe it was receiving a preference or a deal that was too good to be true. It is sufficient that the transaction happened. Under the law of constructive fraudulent conveyances in section 5 of the Uniform Voidable Transfers Act and Section 548 of the Bankruptcy Code, if a transfer of property is made by the debtor that is not for reasonably equivalent value, it can be unwound. These provisions allow a trustee in bankruptcy to police pre-petition leveraged buyouts, and to reexamine dividends, the interest rate and fees on loan transactions, as well as transfers within a corporate group. Under section 547 of the Bankruptcy Code, preference law, allows the trustee to avoid payments to creditors that violate the *pari passu* principle.[36]

---

[33] 11 U.S.C. § 547 (2018).
[34] 11 U.S.C. § 548 (2018); Uniform Voidable Transfers Act.
[35] *In re* Revco D.S., Inc., 118, B.R. 468, 511 (Bankr. N.D. Ohio 1990) (appendix containing the Preliminary Report of Examiner Professor Barry L. Zaretsky, July 16, 1990); *see also* Barry L. Zaretsky, Final Report of Examiner Professor Barry L. Zaretsky 201–30 (Dec. 17, 1990).
[36] 11 U.S.C. § 547(b)(5) (2018).

This is a significant difference from the approach in the United Kingdom, where for both causes of action, the transfer is not avoidable unless it can be shown that the debtor intended to prefer a particular creditor,[37] or secret assets[38] — in effect that there was a breach of fiduciary duty. This results in far fewer transactions being avoided and less discipline on the creditors who might receive the funds.

Thus, the comparative position looks like this:

	US	UK
Fiduciary Duty	Weak	Strong
Clawback	Strong	Weak

The puzzle is, which one, if either, gets it right?

v FIDUCIARY DUTY AND CLAWBACK IN RESCUE: "EQUITABLE DUTY"

As the discussion above shows, the United Kingdom and the United States offer mirror images of how to regulate transactions in the vicinity of insolvency: relatively weak fiduciary duties and strong clawbacks in the United States; relatively strong fiduciary duties and weak clawbacks in the United Kingdom. One possible way of explaining this difference may lie in the historically different approaches in the two countries to rescue as a goal of insolvency law. Chapter 11 focuses on rescue under judicial supervision while in the United Kingdom, until relatively recently, the opening of a proceeding meant the sale of the firm or its assets to realize value on the claims. In most of the world the line is even starker. Opening a formal proceeding led to piecemeal liquidation — the end of the road.[39] Chapter 11, by contrast, contemplates a judicially supervised rescue regime. Until the proceeding is open, there is no stay, and once a proceeding is open, the enterprise is brought within judicial supervision, but the business continues to operate. The Hu and Westbrook account suggests that weak or at least weaker fiduciary duties are a necessary attribute of a rescue regime. Hence the U.K. approach might just be a sign that they have not fully evolved to the rescue model. This may have some merit as a descriptive account, but it is wrong as a normative matter as I will discuss below. That said, there is tension within a rescue regime between the desire to continue the business, and the need for legal and/or judicial supervision. In this section, I seek to untangle the exigencies of rescue from the norms of corporate governance, to argue for a more balanced approach to duty and avoidance — equitable duty — that allows for the continuation of the business, while honoring principles of distributional equity.

A *Priority and Rescue*

By now, it should be clear that corporate rescue carries within it an inherent tension between value maximization by continuing the business and respect of distributional entitlements to

---

[37] Insolvency Act of 1986, § 239.

[38] Insolvency Act of 1986, § 238.

[39] A further note, the European Union has recently promulgated Directive on Preventive Restructuring Frameworks. Member states are directed to promulgate so-called "pre-insolvency" regimes that seek to facilitate rescue and are ostensibly modeled on the United States' Chapter 11. Key aspects of the U.S. regime are that the restructuring process is court supervised and subject to a stay. Creditors are given an express role in governance through a creditors' committee, but their rights are otherwise suspended. Court supervision is a quid pro quo for both the stay and continuation of the business without displacing management.

priority. Delayed reckoning introduces time and leverage as forces that can be used to distort the allocation of firm value.

1 Time

Preserving an insolvent or near insolvent business prior to opening a proceeding can distort priority in ways that implicate the hypothetical that introduced this essay. How can one simultaneously respect the priority of debt over equity, the *pari passu* principle, and asset-based priority, while the business continues to operate, using encumbered assets to continue the business, paying some creditors in full while withholding payment from others, and, all the time, continuing to incur debt to others? As the firm continues to operate, the relative allocation of value may shift within the enterprise from assets to operations, from present to future, and the allocation of risk may shift as well. Choices about the business will affect different investor constituencies differently. Indeed, the puzzle remains, even once a proceeding has been opened.

2 Situational Leverage

As emphasized above, the problem is even worse than that. Where the business is more valuable than the assets, business partners with leverage may seek to use their power to allocate part of that extra value to their pre-petition claim. This problem was discussed above in connection with the vicinity of insolvency, but it persists, even once the debtor files for bankruptcy. There will be times when payments to pre-petition creditors constitute fair compensation for services rendered post-petition, and there are times when the creditor may use situational leverage to distort the priority scheme. Indeed, these reallocations may occur as a result of teamwork. A buyer may join forces with incumbent management and a SC to present a take it or leave it sale of the company. An incumbent lender may join forces with management to credit bid and take control of the firm. A key supplier or lender may use its power to extort payment. In particular, attention must be paid to transactions that utilize insolvency induced crisis leverage to distort distributional entitlements. Melissa Jacoby and I have written about this in much greater detail, elsewhere.[40] Again, the goal of maximizing the value of the estate gives the officers and directors no guidance in choosing among the various constituencies. Simply seeking to maximize the value of the firm is not an answer.

B *"Equitable Realization" in Chapter 11 and the Vicinity of Insolvency*

Once a proceeding is opened, Chapter 11 has a well-developed set of tools to address these problems. First, it provides various mechanisms to allow the continuation of the business once a proceeding has been opened. These include: (1) providing breathing space through the automatic stay; (2) leaving incumbent management in control through the concept of the debtor in possession; (3) allowing the debtor to continue to operate the business and use and sell encumbered assets; (4) allowing the debtor to continue to obtain credit; and (5) providing a participatory system for governing the debtor under creditor and court supervision while allowing the business to continue.

---

[40] Melissa B. Jacoby & Edward J. Janger, *Ice Cube Bonds: Allocating the Price of Process in Chapter 11 Bankruptcy*, 123 YALE L.J. 862 (2014).

Second, it provides a process for allocating the reorganized business's value through the plan process. That process is organized around a negotiation in the shadow of non-bankruptcy entitlements. The debtor continues to negotiate with creditors to restructure pre-petition debt. The power of holdouts is limited through class voting and the power to cramdown a non-consenting class of creditors.

The problem is that fixing the business and confirming a plan take time. The question is, how can the entitlements be defended long enough to negotiate while doing what is necessary to continue the business?

C *"Tracing Equity" in Bankruptcy*

As Melissa Jacoby and I have described elsewhere, the Bankruptcy Code provides a mechanism that manages entitlements over time while the business continues to operate in bankruptcy. We describe the mechanism as "equitable realization."[41] The Bankruptcy Code uses the moment of filing the petition as a temporal reference point and then separates the process of realization into two steps: one which fixes entitlements and the second that realizes value and allocates it pursuant to those entitlements. It works as follows:

- First, the relative positions of creditors are frozen as of the petition date. The pool of collateral available to the SC is frozen, and the pro rata share available to UC is also fixed. This is the moment we call "equitable realization."
- For UC, their pro rata share of the estate is fixed based on the amount of debt owed on the petition date.[42]
- For SC, the pool of liened assets is fixed on the petition date as well.
- The SC are guaranteed that they will receive the value of their collateral plus any appreciation,[43] and UC, including the secured creditors' deficiency claims, receive their aliquot share of the residuum.
- Increases in the value of the firm that result from preservation of the going concern are allocated pro rata to cover the unsecured deficiencies that exist on the petition date.

Once a proceeding has been opened, reallocation of value stops. Liens stop floating,[44] interest stops accruing,[45] and the automatic stay prohibits payments of pre-petition debt post-petition,[46] unless it can be shown that this benefits all of the creditors.[47] Through this mechanism of equitable realization, the relative position of creditors is maintained over time, and an entitlement floor is established.

Allocation can then be accomplished either through negotiation or litigation. Chapter 11 contemplates a negotiation in the shadow of these legal entitlements and creates a voting mechanism for creditors to accept or reject the plan. If no agreement is reached, however, a plan can still be confirmed over the objection of a class of creditors if it complies with the entitlement baselines described above.

---

[41] Melissa B. Jacoby & Edward J. Janger, *Tracing Equity: Realizing and Allocating Value in Chapter 11*, 96 Tex. L. Rev. 673 (2018).

[42] 11 U.S.C. § 502 (2018).

[43] 11 U.S.C. §§ 362(d)(1), 361, 506, 1129(b)(2)(A) (2018).

[44] 11 U.S.C. § 552 (2018).

[45] 11 U.S.C. § 502(b) (2018).

[46] 11 U.S.C. § 362 (2018).

[47] Czyzewski v. Jevic Holding Corp., 137 S. Ct. 973, 985 (2017) ("In doing so, these courts have usually found that the distributions at issue would 'enable a successful reorganization and make even the disfavored creditors better off.'").

Returning to the opening hypothetical, Option A could be confirmed over creditor objection because it complies with pre-bankruptcy entitlements—it is "fair and equitable," to use the statutory term. Option B could be confirmed, but only if all affected classes agreed. The debtor could not accept the proposal of Investor B in the hypothetical above, at least in the context of a sale prior to confirmation of a plan of reorganization.[48] While the price would not be problematic, adjusting the priority scheme would be *ultra vires* outside the context of a consensual plan of reorganization.[49] Equitable realization in bankruptcy thus explains how the Bankruptcy Code allocates value once a case has been opened. The fiduciary can seek to maximize the estate's value because distribution is (or at least should be) off the table until a plan can be confirmed.

D *Equitable Realization, Clawback, and Fiduciary Duty: "Equitable Duty"*

While equitable realization happens as a formal matter only once a Chapter 11 proceeding is opened, conceptually, the conflict between equity and debt, and hence between priority and continuation, arises as soon as the firm enters the vicinity of insolvency. Thus the duty to the corporation carries with it a duty to act equitably with regard to the various investor constituencies regardless of whether a proceeding is opened. Therefore, the concept of equitable realization in Chapter 11 should have a cognate in the vicinity of insolvency—"equitable duty." Once it is recognized, this concept ties together many loose ends and resolves the tension described above. It gives content to the U.K.'s duty of fairness to creditors while highlighting the complementary goal of avoidance.

With regard to fiduciary duty, equitable duty looks a lot like the U.K.'s duty of fairness, but it is also consistent with Delaware's duty to the corporation. While the corporate fiduciary has a duty to act for the benefit of the corporation, it does not have the power to reallocate priorities. Thus even, before opening a proceeding, the fiduciary ought to go beyond impartiality. And here is where the complementarity of duty and clawback manifests. A transaction that prefers equity over debt is a fraudulent conveyance. A transaction that violates equality of treatment is a preference. These transactions reorder the corporate capital structure without attending to corporate formalities. In other words, when seeking to continue the firm, the fiduciary cannot reallocate priorities without consent. Where consent cannot be obtained, resort can be had by opening a Chapter 11 proceeding and confirming a plan of reorganization, either through a "consensual" plan of reorganization or through cramdown.

E *Recalibrating the Relationship between Fiduciary Duty and Clawback in Rescue*

Thus, the fiduciary duty to creditors in the vicinity of insolvency and clawback complement each other. But the question remains, what independent work is fiduciary duty doing in rescue cases? The fiduciary is disempowered—prohibited from choices that would distort allocation unless

---

[48] It is not unheard of for judges to approve going concern sales of a business prior to plan confirmation where the purchaser seeks to dictate the distribution of sale proceeds. *Chrysler* and *GM* are notable examples. However, whether such sales would survive the principles later articulated by the Court in *Jevic* remain open to question.

[49] Such a plan could be confirmed if, after, negotiation, disclosure, and voting, it was approved by the requisite majority of affected creditors. 11 U.S.C. § 1129(a) (2018). It could not, however, be confirmed through cramdown (over the objection of a class of creditors), *see* 11 U.S.C. § 1129(b), because it does not comply with the absolute priority rule, and it could not be confirmed over the objection of a creditor who could show that he or she was made worse off than they would have been in a liquidation. 11 U.S.C. § 1129(a)(7) (2018).

particular processes are followed, and avoidance undoes the fiduciaries' choices where they distort entitlements.

Hu and Westbrook argue that the fiduciary duty to creditors endangers rescue by paralyzing the fiduciary. However, they acknowledge that judicial supervision is crucial to the U.S. model, and the "transition" mechanism is, therefore, also crucial. Once the debtor files, the restructuring is supervised. Post-petition financing, use of cash, and major transactions are all subject to court approval. While the business may continue in the ordinary course, the court, along with processes for notice and objection, operate as a backstop. Unfortunately, the permissive regime of *Gheewalla* leaves directors with no incentive to seek judicial supervision of the rescue by filing for bankruptcy. By contrast, in the United Kingdom, opening the case triggers the end of rescue and the shift to sale, so in U.K. schemes, virtually all of the work must be done without invoking judicial intervention, and without meaningful protection from situational leverage. So, the *Gheewalla* regime may be essential to rescue, but fatal to entitlement. The U.K. system, as well, by delaying opening, may similarly sacrifice entitlement at the altar of rescue.

Two recent U.S. cases, however, may open the door to a complementary solution. First, in *Quadrant Structured Products Co.* v. *Vertin*,[50] the Delaware Court of Chancery clarified *Gheewalla* stating that while there was no distinct duty to creditors in the vicinity of insolvency, the duty remained at all time, to the corporation. The difficulty remains in fleshing this out. The *Quadrant* court clarified that so long as a decision can be made by reference to value maximization, there is no conflict of interest:

> When directors of an insolvent corporation make decisions that increase or decrease the value of the firm as a whole and affect providers of capital differently only due to their relative priority in the capital stack, directors do not face a conflict of interest simply because they own common stock or owe duties to large common stockholders. Just as in a solvent corporation, common stock ownership standing alone does not give rise to a conflict of interest. The business judgment rule protects decisions that affect participants in the capital structure in accordance with the priority of their claims.

The *Quadrant* court makes clear that there is no conflict of interest so long as the priorities built into the capital structure are maintained. The question remains, what does this mean when, in the vicinity of insolvency, the interests of different corporate constituencies do not coincide? The answer lies in the concept of equitable duty. Do not reallocate prebankruptcy entitlements in the service of reorganization. Where this cannot be done, the officers can seek the comfort of judicial approval by opening a bankruptcy proceeding.

In *Czyzewski* v. *Jevic Holdings*,[51] the U.S. Supreme Court came close to endorsing the principle of equitable duty in bankruptcy. In discussing payments made to critical vendors to keep the business alive, the Court imposed a condition not of impartiality, but Pareto Optimality, saying that, in approving distributions to creditors prior to a plan, "[T]hese courts have usually found that the distributions at issue would 'enable a successful reorganization and make even the disfavored creditors better off.'"

This principle that any discrimination must improve on the entitlement baseline, cuts through rescues, whether prior to or after opening a proceeding. Officers and directors can only safely make decisions that raise all boats. Investors who seek preferential treatment face the

---

[50] 115 A.3d 535 (Del. Ch. 2015).
[51] 137 S. Ct. 973, 985 (2017) ("In doing so, these courts have usually found that the distributions at issue would 'enable a successful reorganization and make even the disfavored creditors better off.'").

risk of avoidance. Where there is doubt, there are two alternatives, seek actual consent, or seek judicial blessing in Chapter 11.

VI CONCERNS ABOUT THE U.S. MODEL

Since *Gheewalla*, serious questions have been raised about whether the Delaware regime strikes the proper balance. Jared Ellias and Robert Stark[52] blame *Gheewalla* and its progeny for a decline in the behavioral norms inside and on the threshold of bankruptcy. They note that prior to *Gheewalla*, attorneys advised their clients that in the vicinity of insolvency, the officers and directors potentially owed duties to both creditors and shareholders and should ensure that they were treated fairly. After *Gheewalla* the advice was that no duty was due to creditors. The result has been to usher in an era where the combination of creditor and debtor opportunism, coupled with the advent of sophisticated claims trading and distressed debt investing is akin to the Wild West. They advocate a return to a regime where, in the vicinity of insolvency, creditors are owed a duty. However, they do so without an account of how an officer or director might satisfy that duty. The puzzle posed at the beginning of the article remains, how can a conflicted fiduciary choose among beneficiaries?

The recent bankruptcy docket is replete with practices used by debtors and creditors to short cut the bankruptcy process to gain a distributional advantage. Melissa Jacoby and I have written extensively about concerns raised by "hurry up all asset sales" that distort the distributional scheme, even in bankruptcy.[53] An incumbent lender's stranglehold on the debtor's financing can be used to exercise control.[54] Deals negotiated on the eve of bankruptcy can be rushed through the bankruptcy process through side deals known as restructuring support agreements.[55] Critical vendor orders and employee retention plans, while sometimes essential, have been the subject of criticism.[56]

Again, in *Jevic Holding Corp.*,[57] the U.S. Supreme Court criticized such end runs around bankruptcy procedures. There, post liquidation, a debtor sought to dismiss the case, while distributing funds in a way that deviated from the prescribed statutory priority waterfall. The reason for the deviation was that the estate was settling litigation with a third party—the former owners—who had possible independent liability to the debtor's former employees. The employees also had priority claims in the case. A condition of the settlement was that the employees be excluded from any distribution in the case. The Supreme Court rejected this proposal, saying that it constituted an end run around the statutory plan confirmation process, which would have required either approval by statutory majorities or adherence to the statutory waterfall. This case emphasizes the importance of judicial supervision and procedural safeguards as complements to both fiduciary duty and avoidance.

This is where the principle of equitable duty comes in. At least as a conceptual matter, the duty arises at the same time as the duty to creditors—upon entering the vicinity of insolvency. Similarly, as a conceptual matter, the threat of avoidance arises upon entering the vicinity of insolvency. Viewed together, as a package, equitable duty both guides the fiduciary and threatens the investor with a loss of transaction finality. It may cause a fiduciary to recognize

---

[52]   Ellias & Stark, *supra* note 6.

[53]   Jacoby & Janger, *supra* note 40.

[54]   Jay L. Westbrook, *Secured Creditor Control and Bankruptcy Sales: An Empirical View*, 2015 U. ILL. L. REV. 831 (2015).

[55]   Edward J. Janger & Adam J. Levitin, *Badges of Opportunism: Principles for Policing Restructuring Support Agreements*, 13 BROOK. J. CORP. FIN. & COM. L. 169(2018).

[56]   LYNN LOPUCKI, COURTING FAILURE 137–83 (2005).

[57]   137 S. Ct. 973 (2017).

when it needs help—when rescue cannot be achieved fairly without the assistance of a formal proceeding, and limits the benefits to investors of acting opportunistically to use leverage to reorder the firm's capital structure.

VII PULLING IT TOGETHER

In concluding, I would like to suggest that the U.K. Government Consultation may have suggested a way to reconcile the conceptual tension between Hu and Westbrook's observation that fiduciaries cannot choose, with Ellias and Stark's observation that where there is no duty to creditors, the result is not judicial supervision in bankruptcy, but chaos. The Government Consultation proposed a strengthening of creditor protections at both the front end, by extending the duty to creditors to include the directors of a debtor's corporate parent and at the back end, by enhancing the trustee's powers to recover fraudulent conveyances. Both are consistent with the principle of equitable realization. The continuing lack in the U.K. system is a rescue regime with a greater focus on rescue rather than sale.

Hu and Westbrook and the Delaware court are right that there is no fiduciary duty to creditors. There is, however, the duty of a trustee to behave equitably toward all beneficiaries of a trust. Neither the U.K. nor the U.S. regime adequately implements this principle in the context of the rescue of an operating business. Both the U.K. and U.S. regimes fail to recognize the complementary role that fiduciary duty and avoidance play when a creditor seeks to exercise situational leverage. When a creditor forces the debtor to choose between rescue and the statutory waterfall, the answer must be that the fiduciary is at risk and the transaction is subject to clawback. As Hu and Westbrook noted, the piece missing from the post *Gheewalla* regime is the transition mechanism. If bankruptcy is the way to protect creditors, there needs to be an incentive for the directors to commence a proceeding. The principle of equitable realization as a principle of fiduciary duty and avoidance drives the transition for the trustee and threatens the investor who is behaving opportunistically.

In sum, the above analysis suggests the following takeaways:

- In the vicinity of insolvency (and once insolvent), it is essential (but hard) to separate decisions about value maximization (governance) from decisions about distribution (legal entitlement and priority).
- Where the fiduciary has a duty to the corporation, it must be impartial and cannot trade off debt against equity or violate the principle of equal treatment.
- In the vicinity of insolvency, stakeholders *will*, where they can, use situational leverage to distort legal priorities and value allocations.
  - In the vicinity of insolvency, fiduciary duty and clawback serve the complementary function of implementing the principle of equitable realization both before and after a proceeding is opened.
  - If a proceeding is opened, mechanisms such as the automatic stay *can* facilitate rescue by limiting the power of creditors to use situational leverage, once a proceeding has been opened, while preserving the business as a going concern.
  - Clawbacks *can* police transactions that seek to distort the distributional scheme prior to the opening of a proceeding. They do so by recovering the funds from the creditor or investor.

Thus, in rescue, fiduciary duties and clawbacks police the principle of equitable realization both in the vicinity of insolvency and after a proceeding has been opened.

9

Equity, Majoritarian Governance, and the Oppression Remedy

Paul B. Miller[*]

I INTRODUCTION

Equity has made many important—if now largely forgotten[1]—contributions to the law of organizations. It has articulated, in whole or in part, venerable legal forms that enable coordinated activity and investment, including trusts and partnerships. Also, it contributed indirectly to the legislative development of modern forms of organization, including LLPs, statutory trust entities, and corporations.[2] And equity has added a variety of equitable constraints and remedies to those available at law.

Perhaps the most prominent of equity's contributions to the law of organizations is its provision for fiduciary constraints on the exercise of fiduciary powers. Trustees, partners, directors, officers, and other managers of organizations are deemed fiduciaries, and so are subjected to fiduciary duties, backstopped by equitable remedies.[3]

The fiduciary regulation of managers is important. Fiduciary duties and remedies are the primary legal[4] mechanisms for ensuring managerial accountability relative to an organization's purposes.[5] This, in turn, is an important kind of protection for an organization's members; it vindicates their expectations that the organization's purposes bind those allied to it. Fiduciary regulation also safeguards wider social and economic interests in the law's facilitation of private organization. Barriers to trust requisite to coordination[6]—and, thus, effective organization—are

[*] I am grateful for comments from Deborah DeMott, Christine Hurt, Jennifer Hill, Ted Janger, Lyman Johnson, Christoph Kumpan, Arthur Laby, Amir Licht, Asaf Raz, Andrew Tuch, Kelli Alces Williams, and participants at a workshop at Rutgers Law School.
[1] The contributions live on; it is equity's authorship that is forgotten. On equity's jurisdiction over corporations, see Roscoe Pound, *Visitatorial Jurisdiction over Corporations in Equity*, 49 HARV. L. REV. 369 (1936). Pound explains that since the 17th century, "corporations were subject to visitation in order to maintain their good government and secure their adherence to the purposes of their institution." *Id.* at 371.
[2] Peter G. Turner, *Equitable Doctrines in Business Associations, in* EQUITY AND ADMINISTRATION 149 (Peter G. Turner, ed., 2016).
[3] *See generally* Samuel L. Bray, *Fiduciary Remedies, in* THE OXFORD HANDBOOK OF FIDUCIARY LAW 449 (Evan J. Criddle, Paul B. Miller & Robert H. Sitkoff eds., 2019); Paul B. Miller, *Justifying Fiduciary Duties*, 58 McGILL L. J. 969 (2013); Paul B. Miller, *Justifying Fiduciary Remedies*, 63 U. TORONTO L. J. 570 (2013).
[4] I use words "legal" and "law" here and, occasionally, elsewhere, in a generic sense meant to encompass legal and equitable doctrine.
[5] As discussed in Paul B. Miller, *Corporations, in* THE OXFORD HANDBOOK OF THE NEW PRIVATE LAW (Andrew S. Gold et al. eds., forthcoming).
[6] On trust and coordination in organizations, *see* Piotr Sztompka, Trust: A Sociological Theory (1999); Russell Sage Found., Trust and Reciprocity: Interdisciplinary Lessons for Experimental Research (Elinor Ostrom & James Walker eds., 2003); Rafael La Porta, Florencio Lopez-de-Silanes, Andrei Shleifer & Robert W. Vishny, *Trust in Large*

high enough as it is.[7] Absent a reasonable level of legal security for expectations that managers respect the representative nature of their mandates,[8] those considering whether to contribute to an organization might not risk disappointment of trust. For these reasons and more, it is understandable that several chapters in this volume address the fiduciary duties of managers.

When one thinks of corporate governance, one often thinks immediately of directors and officers. But shareholders contribute significantly to governance, too, and only partly through franchise.[9] As we will see, in a way that is characteristic of its relationship to the law more widely, equity normally leaves it to law—here: contract and corporate law—to supply the terms on which shareholders are to interact and jointly contribute to corporate governance.[10] Equity contributes adjectivally to corporate law to protect minority shareholders from conduct by controlling shareholders that is *inequitable* but perfectly *lawful*. Through these interventions, equity aims to ensure that shareholders treat each other fairly concerning their respective legitimate expectations.

I have said that equity intervenes to ensure fairness in relationships between shareholders. However, "fairness" is not, on its own, an operative construct in equity. Rather, equity has different ways of articulating, doctrinally, what is required by way of fair treatment. And that is significant here because equity has vacillated between two strategies in achieving fairness between shareholders: (1) imposition of fiduciary duties on controlling shareholders, which operate generally and prospectively to force alignment of shareholders' interests; and (2) provision for relief on the grounds of oppression,[11] a doctrine that operates exceptionally and retrospectively to facilitate shareholder exit or rectify the effects of misalignment in the interests of shareholders.

There is a clear preference for the fiduciary approach in American equity, in marked contrast to the preference for the oppression doctrine in Commonwealth jurisdictions. As I will explain, the direction taken by American equity is hard to defend. It is so significantly out of step with the direction taken elsewhere that it might be symptomatic of creeping amnesia about equity.[12] But whatever the explanation, I will argue that American equity has responded to a problem that calls for equitable intervention but has done so inaptly, generating confusion about what shareholders owe each other and why. Convergence on the oppression remedy in

---

Organizations, 87 Am. Econ. Rev. 333 (1997); Janine Nahapiet & Sumantra Ghoshal, *Social Capital, Intellectual Capital, and the Organizational Advantage*, 23 Acad. Mgt. Rev. 242 (1998).

7 Brian Broughman, Elizabeth Pollman & D. Gordon Smith, *Fiduciary Law and the Preservation of Trust in Business Relationships, in* FIDUCIARIES AND TRUST: ETHICS, POLITICS, ECONOMICS AND LAW 302 (Paul B. Miller & Matthew Harding eds., 2020).

8 Paul B. Miller, *Fiduciary Representation, in* FIDUCIARY GOVERNMENT 21 (Evan J. Criddle et al. eds., 2018).

9 Though the literature is focused primarily on franchise; in particular, whether it is effective, and should be enhanced. *See* Lucian A. Bebchuk, *The Case for Increasing Shareholder Power*, 118 HARV. L. REV. 833 (2005); Lucian A. Bebchuk, *The Myth of the Shareholder Franchise*, 93 VA. L. REV. 675 (2007); Stephen M. Bainbridge, *Director Primacy and Shareholder Disempowerment*, 119 HARV. L. REV. 1735 (2006); William W. Bratton & Michael L. Wachter, *The Case Against Shareholder Empowerment*, 158 U. PA. L. REV. 653 (2010); Ronald J. Gilson & Jeffrey N. Gordon, *The Agency Costs of Agency Capitalism: Activist Investors and the Reevaluation of Governance Rights*, 113 COLUM. L. REV. 863 (2013).

10 On civilian alternatives to equitable intervention, see Pierre-Henri Conac, Luca Enriques & Martin Gelter, *Constraining Dominant Shareholders' Self-Dealing: The Legal Framework in France, Germany, and Italy*, 4 EUR. COMPANY & FIN. L. REV. 491 (2007).

11 In U.S. case law and commentary, it is common to refer to "oppression" as a description of *behavior* justifying or giving rise to controlling shareholder's fiduciary duties. I mean here to refer to oppression in the narrower, technical sense as a distinctive *doctrinal basis* of equitable intervention.

12 For discussion, see Samuel L. Bray, *Equity: Notes on the American Reception, in* EQUITY AND LAW: FUSION AND FISSION (John C.P. Goldberg et al. eds., 2019); Henry E. Smith, *Fusing the Equitable Function in Private Law, in* PRIVATE LAW IN THE 21ST CENTURY (Kit Barker et al. eds., 2017).

Commonwealth jurisdictions, by comparison, reveals equity to be a vibrant and essential part of modern private law, even as there remain important questions about the bases and limitations of the remedy.

The analysis will unfold as follows. The second section introduces shareholder participation in corporate governance, explains why and how law provides for it on majoritarian terms and notes how pathologies common to majoritarian governance—including, especially, the tyranny of the majority problem—occur in corporations. The third section positions fiduciary duties and the oppression remedy, implicating two divergent modes of equitable intervention—supplemental and corrective—in response to manifestations of the tyranny of the majority problem in corporations. The fourth section explains why the fiduciary response is inapt and overbroad relative to that afforded by the oppression remedy. In recognition that these variants on the oppression remedy are the product of modern legislative innovation, the fifth section demonstrates that and how they are nonetheless substantively equitable. The sixth section canvasses insights that experience with the oppression remedy supplies to those interested in equity more generally.

II THE PROBLEM: CORPORATE TYRANNY OF THE MAJORITY

In organizations that feature enfranchised members, there inevitably arises a question central to their role in organizational governance: by what principle(s) and process(es) is group decision-making to be achieved? Rules must be settled upon if the group is to act corporately. For these rules to be workable, they must make it possible for actions taken by a group to be (a) deciphered as decisions; and (b) accepted as decisions that reflect—in an authoritative, and thus legally effective, way—the will of the group.

A *Majority Rule*

There are, of course, several options. One is a unanimity rule. Sometimes—especially in closely held organizations—members will contract for such a rule. However, unanimity rules have obvious drawbacks. Apart from the obvious ones of protracted indecision and costly bargaining, they skew the incentives of members toward rent-seeking and hold-up behavior. Thus, it is more customary to see the adoption of a variant on majority rule. By relaxing modestly (via a supermajority rule) or significantly (via a simple majority rule) the extent of the agreement required for group decision-making, majority rule makes group decision-making more feasible and efficient—and, thus, viable—as a mechanism of organizational governance.

Independently of these considerations in favor of majority rule are other contingent, but still significant, factors. Where control rights in economic organizations are tied to investment and granted to members on a votes-per-share rather than votes-per-person basis,[13] and where shares are freely transferrable, members with a controlling stake[14] will usually have a vested economic

---

[13] I recognize that shareholder voting rights are configured differently in different corporations and that these differences raise a variety of important questions. I set these aside here and assume for the sake of argument the conventional "one vote per share" configuration of voting rights for a corporation with a single class of shares. For critical analysis of other configurations, *see* Henry T. C. Hu & Bernard S. Black, *The New Vote Buying: Empty Voting and Hidden (Morphable) Ownership*, 79 S. CAL. L. REV. 811 (2006).

[14] The shareholder with effective control will normally hold a majority of shares, but that is not always the case. Courts are focused on regulating the exercise of control, however realized. *See* Jedwab v. MGM Grand Hotels, Inc., 509 A.2d 584, 593 (Del. Ch. 1986); Smith v. Atlantic Properties, Inc., 12 Mass. App. Ct. 201, 422 N.E.2d 798, (1981). I am grateful to Lyman Johnson for emphasizing this point.

interest in the control premium embedded in the market value of their shares. To the extent that the practical capacity to command such a premium is a function of private ownership of the nature and number of shares requisite to control, our system of private property warehouses a rich set of additional legal and moral reasons for continued recognition of a settled framework of legal rules that enable majority rule.

B *Tyranny*

Contrary to one popular line of thought about corporate organization, the corporate form does not mimic the legal and political structure of the state, nor is corporate governance, in principle or practice, usually democratic.[15] Corporate governance does not assume the formal equality of shareholders, nor does it promote deliberation, debate, and voting for its own sake. However, pathologies of majority rule in democratic government have echoes in corporations. Some of these pathologies coalesce as a tyranny of the majority problem.

In political communities, tyranny of the majority manifests in a number of ways, including popular indifference or outright hostility to the interests of a minority. The effects and under-lying attitudes are problematic for political communities precisely insofar as conventional law and politics (reasonably) assume the moral sensibility of majority rule, and on that basis (unreasonably) excuse or neglect realities of minority oppression. Support for majority rule can lead one to excuse or ignore morally base or egregious conduct simply because it reflects the will of a properly constituted majority.

Corporate tyranny is admittedly not as consequential as political tyranny as it implicates a narrower range of morally salient interests; notably, the vested economic interests (investment) of members and associated expectancies. But that is not to diminish the context-relative significance of the problem, because economic organizations that feature enfranchised members are normally premised (and so invite reliance) on their relative equality of interest, however those interests are defined, and however many defined classes of member there might be in an organization.

C *Manifestations, in General Terms*

Turning to corporate tyranny of the majority, I offer a few observations. The first is that at the highest level of abstraction, corporate tyranny parallels that of politics. It manifests in injury or unfairness suffered by a minority at the behest of a majority or controlling interest, whether motivated by malice, prejudice, indifference, or obliviousness to the interests of the minority.

Second, because the motives of an enfranchised group can be difficult to identify and correct as a matter of law, and because the mechanisms by which groups act are often central to effective governance and not readily adjusted so as to prevent tyranny, legal responses to tyranny of the majority are often, sensibly, focused on remedying its *effects*.

Third, narrowing our focus to corporate tyranny, it should be borne in mind that, people being people, the motivations for behavior that is objectively tyrannical are multifarious and some-times mindboggling. Why would one shareholder (or faction) treat another shareholder (or faction) unfairly through the abusive exercise of control rights? In some cases, it is nothing personal; just sheer opportunism, driven by greed or a desire for other perquisites and privileges

---

[15] As noted in Robert B. Thompson & Paul H. Edelman, *Corporate Voting*, 62 VAND. L. REV. 129 (2009); *see also* Grant M. Hayden & Matthew T. Bodie, *One Share, One Vote and the False Promise of Shareholder Homogeneity*, 30 CARDOZO L. REV. 445 (2008).

of control. But as cases involving close corporations reveal, in other cases it *is* personal; deeply so. A conflict between shareholders that manifests in tyrannical behavior is, in these contexts, but an expression of strife between friends, family members, and associates who have had a falling out and, predictably, cannot cabin their personal conflicts. In such cases, an appreciation of whether and how behavior is tyrannical cannot be arrived at by merely analyzing the relative legal and economic positions of the parties in an organization by virtue of their formal roles and standing. It requires searching examination of motive in the wider context of their personal lives, interactions, and relationships.

Fourth, corporate tyranny is complex in respect of means as well as motive. A controlling shareholder looking to punish, extract value from or otherwise injure a minority shareholder may do so in different ways. Corporate tyranny is thus often polycentric in its manifestation. It could simply implicate the parties in their mutual relationship as shareholders, as where a controlling shareholder agitates successfully for the alteration of rights attached to shares, attempts to dilute the minority's interest, or alters the capital structure of the corporation. But given that the corporate form enables shareholders to relate to corporations and each other in multiple capacities (e.g., as employees, creditors, directors, or officers), tyrannical behavior can be accordingly complex, implicating several relational nexuses through which one party can attempt to gain leverage over, exploit, or injure another. And this behavior will often be directed at pressure points that arise because of the minority's non-shareholding positions (e.g., as employee or director). A controlling shareholder can exploit control over the fate of a minority shareholder in respect of non-shareholding positions for reasons of spite (e.g., to more effectively or pervasively cause injury) or to force concessions or exit from a shareholding position. An effective response to polycentric problems here, as elsewhere, requires a flexible approach to investigation, analysis, and remedies. To restrict one's attention to the relative position of the parties as shareholders is to miss much of the tyranny and its ingenuity and to leave its victims without adequate redress.

D Specific Examples

We may now consider illustrations of corporate tyranny drawn from reported cases. Before we do, though, it bears repeating that decisions made based on principles of majority rule are *lawful in form* but *potentially tyrannical in substance and effect*. The risk of tyranny inheres in the technically valid exercise of decision-making power by a group on the basis of majority rule; it is uniquely problematical, partly because it is likely to be excused or discounted for the reason of its lawfulness and because of the moral and prudential reasons that favor majority rule.

Examples of lawful but tyrannical exercise of power by shareholders cover matters susceptible to the direct or indirect exercise of such power. Consider cases in which controlling shareholders exercise their power to approve the sale of corporate assets or bring about approval or ratification of a contract or other transaction in order to profit personally from it, effectively expropriating value from the corporation and, by extension, minority shareholders.[16] Then there are cases in which a controlling shareholder directs the issuance of new shares, or amendment of rights attached to existing shares, diluting the interest of a minority and/or their representation on the board, or depriving the minority of the benefit of rights attached to their shares.[17] Consider also cases in which a controlling shareholder directs the board to terminate the employment of

---

[16] Donahue v. Rodd Electrotype Co. of New England, 367 Mass. 578, 328 N.E.2d 505 (1975).
[17] eBay Domestic Holdings, Inc. v. Newmark, No. 3705, 16 A.3d 1 (Del. Ch. 2010).

a minority shareholder or forces their removal from the board, notwithstanding settled expectations of a position on the board or continued employment.[18] And reflect on cases in which a controlling shareholder tries to force the minority out of their shareholding position, coercing a sale of the shares at less than fair market value.[19]

III TWO EQUITABLE SOLUTIONS

For a time, the courts took a hard luck approach to cases like these. With a nod to caveat emptor, it was suggested that minority shareholders should be understood to have accepted the risk of harsh treatment in purchasing a minority stake. They should not, having come to regret the burdens of their bargain, be heard to complain about harsh but lawful conduct.[20] In other cases, courts — understandably — expressed worry about eroding majority rule and destabilizing commercial expectations that had coalesced around it.

A *Early Indecision about Intervention*

Courts gradually recognized that a policy of non-intervention was hard to justify.[21] But while it became clear that intervention would be premised on an assertion of equitable jurisdiction, it was unclear what avenue(s) of intervention could and should be taken.

Indecision is reflected in early English cases in which courts offered moral exhortation — in terms that could be taken as implying a number of possible grounds for intervention — without settling on a doctrinal entry point.[22] It appears that judges in these cases were genuinely unclear about how to frame the problem juridically. What, if anything, do patterns in objectively tyrannical behavior suggest about general terms of interaction that are apt for shareholders? How ought such conduct be remedied? These were, and are, genuinely difficult questions. Thus the grasping moral exhortation, with judges variously suggesting: that shareholders are parties to a contract of sorts, and that those with a controlling interest ought not to be permitted to act unconscionably; that all shareholders have an implied obligation to exercise their control rights in good faith and the common interest of all shareholders; and that shareholders, while entitled to act in self-interest, are constrained in equity from exercising control in a manner that is oppressive, burdensome, or harsh in its effects on other shareholders.

Indecision over doctrinal bases of intervention took place against a backdrop of a narrow but important avenue of relief open to members of companies since the nineteenth century in

---

[18] Matter of Kemp & Beatley, Inc., 64 N.Y.2d 63, 70, 473 N.E.2d 1173, 1178 (1984); Balvik v. Sylvester, 411 N.W.2d 383 (N. D. 1987). For discussion, see Douglas K. Moll, *Shareholder Oppression v. Employment at Will in the Close Corporation: The Investment Model Solution*, 1999 U. ILL. L. REV. 517 (1999).

[19] See cases discussed in Mary Siegel, *Fiduciary Duty Myths in Close Corporation Law*, 29 DEL. J. CORP. L. 377, 384 (2004).

[20] Some commentators have suggested that the reticence reflected courts' settled attitudes toward equitable intervention in the affairs of partnerships, reflecting the derivation of equitable mechanisms of intervention in companies and corporations from that developed in the context of general partnerships. See A.J. Boyle, *The Minority Shareholder in the Nineteenth Century: A Study in Anglo-American Legal History*, 28 MOD. L. REV. 317, 318 (1965) (explaining that "[i]n the previous century [i.e., the 18th] it had been established that the Chancellor would not interfere in the internal disputes of a partnership 'except with a view to dissolution'") (alteration in original).

[21] Not least because many shareholders cannot be said to have consented to anything by virtue of acquisition of their shares (e.g., those holding shares by way of inheritance). I am grateful to Deborah DeMott for emphasizing this point.

[22] Brian Cheffins, *The Oppression Remedy in Corporate Law: The Canadian Experience*, 10 U. PA. J. INT'L BUS. L. 305, 308 (1988) ("[E]quitable protection afforded by the courts was at best erratic and uncertain and at worst completely ineffective.") (alteration in original).

England and much of the wider Commonwealth.[23] The avenue was introduced by way of an equitable principle, adapted from partnership law, that enabled shareholders to seek an order that a corporation be wound up on the grounds of "justice and equity."[24] Just and equitable wind-up was an extreme remedy (forced dissolution) and so viewed as reserved for extreme circumstances (e.g., fraud, or conduct akin to fraud).[25] This made it less than attractive to shareholders. While valuable in extreme cases, it was inadequate as a general solution to the problem of corporate tyranny.

Cumulatively, though, these experiences proved generative. As courts sifted through imprecise exhortations that shareholders be "fair," act conscionably, and show good faith, they also experimented with the wind-up remedy. Some read a wider jurisdiction into underlying statutory provisions: one allowing the award of alternative equitable remedies. Unfortunately, access to the alternative remedies was conditioned on the petitioner's ability to meet the high bar of establishing a good claim to a wind-up order. This scuppered the effort to widen the remedy, limiting its effectiveness.

Ultimately, the pressures placed on the wind-up remedy were too much for it to bear without it becoming wholly unfocused. Equity had to find another way forward. But by what doctrinal avenue could it respond aptly without unsettling majority rule? As noted earlier, equity came to take divergent paths in different parts of the world. The first, taken in most American states, including Delaware, engaged equity's jurisdiction over fiduciary relationships. The second, initiated in England and subsequently adopted in much of the Commonwealth, premised intervention on oppression, with analysis of same involving searching, fact-intensive assessment of shareholders' reasonable expectations. Each of these modes of intervention has become part of the settled landscape of corporate law in the jurisdictions in which they operate. I will briefly present each in turn before turning to evaluative reflections in the fourth section.

B *Equity's Modes of Intervention: Supplemental and Corrective*

Equity contributes to the legal systems in which it figures by way of two modes of intervention.[26] Some of equity's best-known contributions are primary rights that it has supplied sporadically or in complex forms of interaction. Where equity intervenes by supplying new rules of general application such as primary rights, it serves as a gap filler in the system of first-order law by *generating supplemental law.*[27]

Equity's other important contributions have a different character. Equity makes them through doctrines that enable and channel ex post judicial review of conduct that is lawful but inequitable. Ex post review enabled by equity involves tailored correction of inequities generated by first-order law through one-off adjustments that usually involve intervention in the enforcement of legal rights or exercise of legal powers. The doctrines through which equity's *remedial or corrective* interventions are engaged are a form of second-order law, directed at judges and designed to ensure integrity in the administration of justice. The products of equity's corrective

[23]   Michael J. Trebilcock, *A New Concern for the Minority Shareholder*, 19 McGill L. J. 106 (1973); *See also* Nigel Furey, *The Statutory Protection of Minority Shareholders in the United Kingdom*, 22 Wake Forest L. Rev. 81, 82 (1987).

[24]   *In re* Yenidje Tobacco Co., [1916] 2 Ch. 426 (AC) (Eng.); Ebrahimi v. Westbourne Galleries, Ltd., [1973] AC 360 (HL) (appeal taken from Eng.).

[25]   Cheffins, *supra* note 22, at 309. For critical discussion, see Carlos L. Israels, *The Sacred Cow of Corporate Existence: Problems of Deadlock and Dissolution*, 19 U. Chi. L. Rev. 778 (1952).

[26]   Paul B. Miller, *Equity as Supplemental Law, in* Philosophical Foundations of the Law of Equity 92 (Dennis Klimchuk, Irit Samet & Henry E. Smith eds., 2020).

[27]   *Id.*

interventions are not new law but rather a vanishing trace of fine adjustments to enforcement practices.[28]

Courts engaging equity ordinarily deem a grievance to merit intervention in *either* supplemental *or* corrective mode. That is, a grievance is either—usually over a run of cases—found to be generic and so amenable to supplemental intervention, *or* idiosyncratic and so to require corrective intervention. Equity will sometimes pivot from corrective to supplemental mode where repeat litigation establishes genericity. But it tends to default to its corrective mode and usually chooses between corrective and supplemental intervention.

C *Equity in Supplemental Mode: Ex Ante Fiduciary Regulation*

Given wide variation in manifestations of corporate tyranny, it might come as a surprise that equity would intervene in supplemental mode. But, as noted, in the United States, the dominant response came to be supplementation of ex ante rules of corporate governance through the extension of fiduciary duties to controlling shareholders.

Of course, equity had already contributed importantly to corporate governance by defining fiduciary duties for directors and eventually extending them to officers.[29] The juridical basis for attributing presumptive fiduciary status to directors and officers—consistent with that of other fiduciaries—lies in their being entrusted with the authority to act representatively for the corporation and its shareholders.[30] In that light, and as I will explain in the fourth section below, it is rather more surprising that American equity extended fiduciary duties to shareholders. But that has been our experience.[31] American equity protects minority shareholders from abuse by deeming controlling shareholders accountable as their fiduciaries, and therefore subject to fiduciary duties that operate as ex ante constraints on the exercise of their rights and powers as shareholders. This engagement of equity's supplemental mode of intervention implies that the problem of abuse of power by controlling shareholders is generic and of a "fiduciary" nature, such that fiduciary duties promise an apt resolution of it. More specifically, it suggests that corporate tyranny is uniformly generated by self-interested behavior, and that self-interested behavior by shareholders in the exercise of their rights and powers is generally inappropriate.

In some respects, the extension of fiduciary duties to shareholders has been doctrinally idiosyncratic. Save in close corporations in which the relationship between shareholders is analogous to that between partners in a general partnership,[32] courts have generally *not* held that shareholders are categorically fiduciary as such—i.e., qua shareholders—based on the actual or presumed factual or legal incidents of shareholding. Thus, shareholders are not—in contrast to partners, for example—fiduciaries of one another in respect of the exercise of rights and powers attached to their stake in an entity. Instead, *controlling* shareholders are fiduciaries of *minority* shareholders only by virtue of the type and/or concentration of shares owned and/or the material influence they have over the corporation and its management. Furthermore,

---

[28] Henry E. Smith, *Equity as Second-Order Law: The Problem of Opportunism*, (Harvard Pub. Law Working Paper No. 15–13, 2015), https://ssrn.com/abstract=2617413.

[29] For critical discussion, see Lyman Johnson, *The Three Fiduciaries of Delaware Corporate Law—and Eisenberg's Error*, ch. 3 (this volume); Kelli Alces Williams, *Self-Interested Fiduciaries and Invulnerable Beneficiaries: When Fiduciary Duties Don't Fit*, ch. 18 (this volume).

[30] Miller, *supra* note 8; Paul B. Miller, *The Fiduciary Relationship*, in Philosophical Foundations of Fiduciary Law 63 (Andrew S. Gold & Paul B. Miller eds., 2014); Paul B. Miller, *The Identification of Fiduciary Relationships*, in The Oxford Handbook of Fiduciary Law 367 (Evan J. Criddle, Paul B. Miller & Robert H. Sitkoff eds., 2019).

[31] Americas Mining Corp. v. Theriault, 51 A.3d 1213 (Del. 2012); Donahue v. Rodd Electrotype Co. of New England, 367 Mass. 578, 328 N.E.2d 505 (1975); Wilkes v. Springside Nursing Home, Inc., 370 Mass. 842, 353 N.E.2d 657 (1976).

[32] *See* Wilkes, 370 Mass. at 842.

controlling shareholders are not subject to conventional standards of fiduciary loyalty. They are not prohibited from acting in self-interest, nor are they forbidden from making profits from their "fiduciary" position. Instead, they are prohibited from profiting *unfairly* by reaping gains at the expense or otherwise to the exclusion of minority shareholders.

D *Equity in Corrective Mode: Ex Post Judicial Review for Oppression*

In England and most Commonwealth jurisdictions, there is a clear preference for corrective rather than supplemental intervention as a modality of response to corporate tyranny, structured by way of statutory provisions that enable judicial review of grievances on the basis of oppression. Where they have considered it, courts in these jurisdictions have rejected the notion that any shareholder is a fiduciary of another simply through ownership of shares and enjoyment or exercise of associated rights, irrespective of the extent of control they have by virtue of the nature and/or concentration of shares owned.[33]

Unlike its precursor, the wind-up remedy, the oppression remedy grants courts wide discretion in determining the merits of grievances *and* in remedying a grievance deemed well-founded. Under the oppression remedy, a petitioner alleges that the conduct of the controlling shareholder (or faction) directly or indirectly (e.g., through action or inaction by the board) violated its reasonable expectations and resulted in oppressive or unfair consequences suffered by the petitioner personally. The petitioner invites the court to exercise its unlimited remedial discretion in vindication of those expectations.

The modern oppression remedy was inaugurated by the 1948 U.K. *Companies Act*.[34] Designed specifically for the protection of minority shareholders, section 210 of the *Act* granted courts broad powers to investigate and remedy claims of oppression.[35] The remedy was limited to shareholders and, at least initially, courts were inclined to construe "oppression" narrowly.[36] Thus, some concluded that conduct is oppressive only where it evinces a "lack of probity" and/or is "burdensome, harsh and wrongful" in its effects.[37] The U.K. legislators responded by relaxing the grounds for relief,[38] adding "unfair prejudice"[39] to "oppression," mindful that effective cabining can be achieved by traditional limiting principles in equity (e.g., the requirement that a petitioner establish that they have no adequate remedy at law).

Other jurisdictions followed the lead of U.K. law. The Australian remedy is framed more broadly than that of the United Kingdom, with stated grounds for intervention including "oppression," "unfair prejudice," and "unfair disregard," but remains limited to shareholders. The Canadian variant[40] is broader still and has been considered the most potent remedy in

---

[33] The position taken in commonwealth jurisdictions is nicely summarized by Turner, *supra* note 2, at 156 ("[M]embers of joint stock companies and, later, companies incorporated under the general Acts of incorporation, did not and generally do not owe fiduciary obligations to one another. The doctrine that developed is that members may vote in their several interests provided they do so in good faith. Members who vote with a desire to oppress a minority of their number are seen by equity to act in bad faith. Otherwise the members . . . are essentially free to act as they wish.").

[34] Companies Act 1948, 11 & 12 Geo. 6 c.38 (U.K.), https://www.legislation.gov.uk/ukpga/1948/38/contents/enacted.

[35] Scottish Co-operative Wholesale Society Ltd. v. Meyer, [1959] AC 324 (HL) (appeal taken from Scot.).

[36] As explained by Hoffmann LJ in *Re Saul D. Harrison & Sons plc*, [1995] 1 BCLC 14, [1994] BCC 475 (AC) (Hoffmann LJ) (Eng.).

[37] *See* discussion in Cheffins, *supra* note 22, at 320.

[38] Furey, *supra* note 23, at 93 ("Unfortunately, section 210 was so beset with prerequisite conditions to court intervention that it proved to be almost totally ineffective . . . . Accordingly, in 1962 the Jenkins Committee recommended various changes to section 210 . . . these changes were realized in sections 459–461 of the Companies Act of 1985 by the repeal of section 210 and the incorporation of section 75 of the Companies Act of 1980.") (citation omitted).

[39] For current provisions, see Companies Act 2006 c. 46, §§ 994–996 (U.K.).

[40] Canada Business Corporations Act, R.S.C. 1985, c. C-44, § 241 (Can.).

Anglo-American corporate law.[41] Like its Australian cousin, the Canadian remedy allows claimants to plead "oppression," "unfair prejudice," or "unfair disregard." Canadian courts have pointedly refused invitations to closely define these grounds for intervention.[42] Furthermore, Canadian law, like Australia and the United Kingdom, grants courts unlimited remedial discretion. Finally, Canadian law does not limit the remedy to shareholders. Directors and officers can petition for relief, and, most controversially, creditors can, too.

A few U.S. states have pivoted from fiduciary regulation to the oppression remedy. Different states have different iterations of the remedy, but generally speaking, like other jurisdictions, they focus on protecting the reasonable expectations of minority shareholders from an inequitable violation.[43] While the remedy is reasonably broad in its responsiveness to the multifarious kinds of inequity that shareholders can suffer, it is usually narrower than the variants in U.K. and Commonwealth law. Some states have grafted the oppression remedy into the wind-up remedy, making oppression an independent equitable basis for wind-up rather than a stand-alone remedy.[44] Others have read a broader remedial discretion into wind-up provisions.[45] In either event, many states limit access to the remedy to shareholders in closely held corporations. And American iterations sometimes provide for intervention on the basis of fraud, illegality and oppression rather than "unfair disregard" and "unfair prejudice," though the upshot of these differences is not clear.[46]

Having briefly canvassed the development of the oppression remedy, I wish to offer some observations about oppression analysis that holds for most iterations of the remedy and explain how oppression litigation is structured.

First, as to modality of analysis: the oppression remedy is engaged by way of petitions for discretionary relief rather than the assertion of an ex ante entitlement or allegation of breach of same. The oppression remedy does not define general terms of interaction for shareholders, nor does it even operate on the basis of fixed assumptions about which ex ante entitlements might be placed in issue in connection with a shareholder's petition for relief. Rather, the remedy signals the availability of judicial review and equitable relief in vindication of expectations reasonably held by shareholders[47] that are not protected—or were not adequately protected—at law.[48]

---

[41]   Cheffins, *supra* note 22, at 305 (1988).

[42]   BCE Inc. v. 1976 Debentureholders [2008] 3 S.C.R. 560 (Can.).

[43]   Robert C. Art, *Shareholder Rights and Remedies in Close Corporations: Oppression, Fiduciary Duties, and Reasonable Expectations*, 28 J. CORP. L. 371, 376–95 (2003).

[44]   The history is related by Robert B. Thompson, *The Shareholder's Cause of Action for Oppression*, 48 BUS. LAW. 699, 709 (1993); *see also* MODEL BUS. CORP. ACT § 14.30(2) (AM. BAR ASS'N 2001).

[45]   Thompson, *supra* note 43, at 699 ("Courts . . . are more likely today than in the past to interpret the statutory grounds for dissolution in a way that provides relief for minority shareholders . . . Judges are more inclined to use buyouts or other alternative remedies, even in the absence of specific statutory authorization.") (citation omitted); *see also* Douglas K. Moll, *Shareholder Oppression in Close Corporations: The Unanswered Question of Perspective*, 53 VAND. L. REV. 749, 760 (2000).

[46]   According to Art, *supra* note 43, courts have emphasized that conduct complained of by a minority shareholder need not be fraudulent or illegal to justify intervention, but oppression has been interpreted in different ways. Some equate it with fiduciary disloyalty, others with conduct that reveals some general moral fault or failing. He also notes an emerging tendency to frame oppression in terms of the unfair violation of reasonable expectations.

[47]   Matter of Kemp & Beatley, Inc., 64 N.Y.2d 63, 70, 473 N.E.2d 1173, 1179 ("[O]ppression should be deemed to arise . . . when the majority conduct substantially defeats expectations that, objectively viewed, were both reasonable under the circumstances and were central to the petitioner's decision to join the venture.") (alteration in original); *See also* Douglas K. Moll, *Reasonable Expectations v. Implied-in-Fact Contracts: Is the Shareholder Oppression Doctrine Needed?* 42 B.C. L. REV. 989, 1001–03 (2001).

[48]   The expansive reading of provisions enabling "just and equitable" wind up of companies was conducted in the same spirit. *Per* reasons given by Lord Wilberforce in *Ebrahimi*: "The words [just and equitable] are a recognition of the fact that a limited company is more than a mere legal entity, with a personality in law of its own: that there is room in

While different jurisdictions express the grounds for intervention in different ways, they are usually treated as open-textured. Finally, the oppression remedy calls for the exercise of broad and discretionary remedial powers under which a court may devise a remedy that responds aptly to the material effects of an inequity suffered by the petitioner.[49] Significantly, aptness is understood to encompass due regard for the legitimate expectations of persons other than the petitioner, including such expectations as defined by law rather than equity.[50]

Second, oppression litigation usually proceeds through five phases. First, a petitioner (aggrieved shareholder) must give notice to the respondent(s) in such a manner as to afford them the opportunity to take corrective action. Second, assuming that there is no obstacle on standing, the petitioner must make filings which plead facts suggestive of unfair violation of a reasonable expectation, held personally, that is not protected at law.[51] Third, in some jurisdictions, the petitioner's filings will be expected to engage with stipulated grounds for intervention through pleadings showing that and how conduct complained of was fraudulent, oppressive, or unfair. Fourth, the petitioner may petition for a particular remedy, understanding that remedies are left to the discretion of the court. And fifth, the court will, based on its investigations and review of the pleadings and evidence, determine whether the claimant suffered oppression and, if so, whether and how it should be remedied.

IV EVALUATING THE SOLUTIONS

Recognizing that fiduciary regulation of shareholder relationships is settled law in much of the United States, I nevertheless believe that it stands as a serious misstep. The forces that generate shareholder conflicts, and the material inequities that result from same, are not amenable to effective resolution through general law. Equity ought to have intervened, but not in supplemental mode. Furthermore, fiduciary regulation is a particularly inapt form of supplemental law in this context. Fiduciary duties are not an all-purpose salve for sharp or opportunistic behavior. They have a narrower remit.

By contrast, the oppression remedy is a more effective and appropriate avenue for intervention. It does not involve reordering the ex ante entitlements of shareholders, diminishing the rights of one through the allocation of new rights to another. Instead, it enables petitions for discretionary relief on the conventional basis of inequity in the exercise or enforcement of rights. As I will explain, this form of intervention is valuable and apt where, as here, the problem is not with the law's initial allocation of rights but with varieties of inequity in their exercise. It is also valuable

---

company law for recognition of the fact that behind it, or amongst it, there are individuals, with rights, expectations and obligations inter se which are not necessarily submerged by the company structure ... *The 'just and equitable' provision ... does, as equity always does, enable the court to subject the exercise of legal rights to equitable considerations; considerations, that is, of a personal character arising between one individual and another, which may make it unjust, or inequitable, to insist on legal rights, or to exercise them in a particular way.*" Ebrahimi v. Westbourne Galleries, Ltd., [1973] AC 360 (HL) (appeal taken from Eng.) (emphasis added) (citation omitted).

49 In commonwealth jurisdictions, it is customary that remedial discretion is granted in sweeping terms. *See, e.g.*, Canada Business Corporations Act, R.S.C. 1985, c. C-44, § 241(3) (Can.) ("In connection with an application under this section, the court may make any interim or final order it thinks fit including, without limiting the generality of the foregoing [a lengthy schedule of possible remedies].") (alteration in original). Some American jurisdictions have recognized in courts a similarly broad remedial discretion. *See* Baker v. Commercial Body Builders, Inc., 507 P.2d 387, 395–96 (Or. 1973).

50 Naneff v. Con-Crete Holdings Ltd., 23 O.R. 3d 481, [1995] O.J. No. 1377 (Can. Ont. C.A.).

51 A now-dated study of Australian cases indicated that the most commonly pleaded factual basis of a petition under the Australian oppression remedy is exclusion from participation in management. *See* Ian M. Ramsay, *An Empirical Study of the Use of the Oppression Remedy*, 27 AUSTL. BUS. L. REV. 23, 28 (1999).

insofar as it enables exceptional responses to exceptional circumstances, leaving first-order law intact to benefit the vast majority of shareholders who act equitably in the exercise of control rights.

A *The Case Against Fiduciary Regulation*

The first critical observation that I will venture about the fiduciary regulation of shareholder relationships is to note how odd it is, in general, to alter terms of interaction that obtain between shareholders ex ante in response to problems that arise sporadically ex post from the improper use or leveraging of such terms. In virtue of ownership of an individual share, each shareholder is in a position of formal equality relative to other shareholders in a given class of shares. The entire point of defining rights attached to shares by class is to ensure the formal equality of shareholders and the fungibility of their securities. The mischief at issue in corporate tyranny is not a product of shareholders' rights in their shares, nor even the implications of these rights for corporate governance. It is, rather, a product of the concentration of shares and associated rights, and thus the extent of practical control that might be wielded by a shareholder (or faction) who has amassed sufficient shares in a given corporation. Furthermore, given that corporate tyranny is highly variable in its manifestation, it is surprising that one would look to equity to address the problem by supplying new general terms of interaction (fiduciary duties) that do not apply to all shareholders, and so do not respect their formal equality. This produces an asymmetry in the relative legal position of shareholders, effectively redistributing *post hoc* the legal benefits and burdens of share ownership. Given that equity ordinarily supplements the law in a manner that respects and leaves intact surrounding law,[52] one would have expected that supplementation of the rights and duties of shareholders—if justified—would take the form of a new law that respects their formal equality as well as their property in their shares.

Independently of the misfit between the tyranny of the majority problem and equity's supplemental mode of intervention, there are reasons to think that fiduciary regulation, specifically, is inapt.[53]

One is that shareholder relationships do not bear the hallmarks of a fiduciary relationship. In fiduciary relationships properly so-called, one party—the fiduciary—undertakes a mandate calling for the exercise of discretionary legal powers for other-regarding purposes (those of the grantor of the mandate).[54] Relationships of long-settled fiduciary status conform to this general description, including those between trustees and beneficiaries, agents and principals, and directors and corporations. But relationships between shareholders do not. Shareholders' interest in their shares and any associated control rights is fundamentally proprietary in nature. An individual does not, in purchasing or otherwise acquiring shares, receive or accept a mandate to act for others.[55] The rights and powers incidental to her ownership of shares are personal to her, as is her property in the security itself. There is nothing in the acquisition of a majority or controlling block of issued shares of a corporation that should cause us to think that the acquirer has been authorized or has undertaken to act for others, or that she has willingly relinquished property in her shares and the standing to deal with same in self-interest.[56] Whereas directors and

---

52   Miller, *supra* note 26.

53   For other criticisms, see Benjamin Means, *A Voice-Based Framework for Evaluating Claims of Minority Shareholder Oppression in the Close Corporation*, 97 Geo. L.J. 1207, 1223–26 (2009).

54   See works cited, *supra* note 30.

55   As is sometimes recognized by American courts. For example, the Oregon Supreme Court emphasized that "each shareholder represents himself and his own interests only, and he in no sense acts as a trustee or representative of others." Ostlind v. Ostlind Valve, 165 P.2d 779, 788 (Or. 1946).

56   As has been noted—without recognition of paradox—in Brodie v. Jordan, 857 N.E.2d 1076 (Mass. 2006).

officers assume offices under which they receive fiduciary powers to bind the corporation and its shareholders, shareholders clearly do not undertake to represent anyone and their powers are properly construed as personal.

Further evidence of doctrinal misfit is found in turning one's attention to fiduciary duties and remedies. Consistent with the representative nature of the mandates they have undertaken, fiduciaries are obligated to suppress self-interest and actively pursue the interests or ends of others. The fiduciary duty of loyalty is normally specified by strict prophylactic rules that require fiduciaries to avoid even the appearance of conflict.[57] It is telling that the "fiduciary" duties of controlling shareholders are not framed in this way. Shareholders are not forbidden from considering their own interests in acting on their rights or exercising their powers. Nor are they prohibited from buying shares in corporations that are, or may be, adverse in commercial interest. The standards that have been imposed are decidedly more permissive and amorphous,[58] calling for good faith and solidarity, and are consistent with a shareholder acting in an entirely self-regarding way. These thin constraints are fiduciary only by designation.

Finally, the approach taken to remedying shareholder "disloyalty" is telling that underlying misconduct is not treated as a genuinely fiduciary wrong. The default form of relief for fiduciary disloyalty is a set of profit-stripping equitable remedies.[59] These remedies reallocate gains from disloyal fiduciaries to beneficiaries on the basis that the latter has the rightful claim to them in equity. Other important remedies correct for impropriety in the exercise of power by fiduciaries by treating acts in excess of power as void or voidable at the instance of the beneficiary.[60] Neither of these kinds of remedy, so prominent in fiduciary law, are typically awarded in response to the "fiduciary" misdeeds of a controlling shareholder. The latter might be required to compensate a minority shareholder for losses, sell his shares, or buy out the shares of a minority shareholder at fair market value. However, a controlling shareholder is not required to forfeit his property in his shares or profits realized on his investment. And that is because shareholders are not *really* fiduciaries of one another; the position otherwise in U.S. law is taken half-heartedly, at best.

All of this being said, it is not entirely surprising that courts less versed in equity would turn to fiduciary law in this context. After all, in *some* cases, the pathologies of majority rule are revealed through self-seeking behavior by shareholders. Furthermore, in *all* cases, the pathologies attend majority *power* or *control*. I have insisted that the powers—legal and factual—wielded by shareholders through ownership of shares are acquired and held in a personal rather than fiduciary capacity. But one who cares less for doctrinal analyticity than effective policy might maintain that fiduciary constraints are an effective instrument through which to curb abuse of power between shareholders.

This view betrays a superficial assessment of the pathologies of majoritarian governance in corporations. While sometimes conduct complained of by a minority shareholder will involve opportunistic behavior by a controlling shareholder, in other cases it does not. In Commonwealth jurisdictions, courts have been careful to note that conduct need not be self-interested or suggestive of bad faith to be considered oppressive. In some cases, it might involve intentional or reckless infliction of harm upon a minority shareholder without any corresponding gain for the controlling shareholder. In other cases, there may be neither harm to be redressed, nor gain against which to make attachment; rather, the basis of the complaint will

---

[57] MATTHEW CONAGLEN, FIDUCIARY LOYALTY: PROTECTING THE DUE PERFORMANCE OF NON-FIDUCIARY DUTIES (2010).

[58] One court described them as a "compilation of platitudes." *See* Chiles v. Robertson, 767 P.2d 903, 911 (Or. App.), *opinion modified on reconsideration*, 774 P.2d 500 (Or. App. 1989).

[59] Miller, *Justifying Fiduciary Remedies, supra* note 3; Bray, *supra* note 3.

[60] Bray, *supra* note 3.

be the denial of information or participation or repudiation of an expectancy of employment or some other benefit. Across the cases, one finds a recurrent theme: the pathologies of majoritarian governance manifest as *violations of reasonable expectations that are not, and could not readily have been, protected at law*. Accepting that to be so, one must also accept that fiduciary regulation will be an inadequate (because incomplete) response to the problem it addresses.

B *The Case for the Oppression Remedy*

Despite decades of experience, there continue to be hard questions about how the oppression remedy should be delineated. For example, it is unclear which constituents' interests should be protected and why. Similarly, it is unclear whether there might be value in closer—if still non-exhaustive—stipulation of the meaning of "oppression" and cognate grounds for intervention. Furthermore, the factors that should inform judicial discretion in settling specific remedies for oppression remain opaque.

Therefore, without supposing that the oppression remedy offers a panacea for shareholder conflict, and without endorsing for a particular iteration of it, I wish presently to explain why, in general terms, *some version* of an oppression remedy is the preferable means by which to structure equitable intervention in corporate tyranny cases.[61]

To a considerable extent, the relative advantages of the oppression remedy are attributable to general characteristics of equity's corrective mode of intervention. Recall that, in corrective mode, equity neither supplies first-order law nor displaces or varies it. Rather, it intervenes exceptionally in the enforcement or routine application of the law on the basis of grievances that raise issues of conscience or abuse of right. These grievances do not impugn first-order law *precisely because* corrective equity proceeds on the assumption that the grievances it hears could not be addressed through the development of first-order law.

The first point in favor of the oppression remedy is that it does not presume to rewrite corporate law or fetter contract and property law as they apply to corporations and shareholders. For example, it does not inhibit the concentration of shares among shareholders, require that certain rights or duties be attached to shares, or impose duties, liabilities or other burdens on the exercise of rights or powers by shareholders. Rather, equity here takes notice of existing first-order law and assumes its soundness. It seeks only to ensure that first-order law is not abused or misused to defeat the reasonable expectations of a minority shareholder.

The second point in favor of the oppression remedy lies in its invocation of familiar grounds for equitable intervention, and marshalling of equity's traditional institutional strengths in the inquisitorial evaluation of grievances for which good merits assessment requires fact-intensive investigation and judgment. Because the oppression remedy is not premised on the assertion of a legal entitlement, courts enjoy discretion in determining whether to entertain grievances and in merits assessment is not artificially cabined by ex ante substantive or procedural rules. Merits assessment is not unbounded: courts must be able to articulate reasons for deciding whether there was an inequitable violation of a reasonable expectation that was unprotected or inadequately protected at law. However, courts are afforded wide latitude making a merits assessment on the basis of an encompassing view of material facts, law and policy. Latitude for judge-led, inquisitorial probing of merits is important in this context because the conduct that generates *prima facie* meritorious grievances knows no consistent pattern. If experience teaches

---

[61]   For an economic analysis in support of the remedy on the basis of transactions costs savings, see Brian R. Cheffins, *An Economic Analysis of the Oppression Remedy: Working Towards a More Coherent Picture of Corporate Law*, 40 U. Toronto L. J. 775, 789–811 (1990).

anything, it is that controlling shareholders can misuse or abuse their rights and powers in innumerable ways, through schemes or lapses as varied as the personalities behind them. The oppression remedy proves equal to this variegation by permitting courts to reach fact-driven assessments of the propriety of conduct that is, strictly speaking, entirely lawful, but offensive to justice for reasons that cannot be reduced to a rule.

The third point in favor of the oppression remedy is that it affords courts unparalleled remedial flexibility, again in a way that is consistent with tradition in equity. Because the grievances that sound in oppression admit no general measure, so the remedies that promise an apt response to oppression will be correspondingly varied. A shareholder can petition for a particular remedy, but the petition will not be treated as a "claim" as of "right" precisely because the intervention is not premised on enforcement of a right such as might narrow the scope of apt remedies. A court may consider not just the equity of the petitioner's cause but the equities of anyone with a direct interest that might be affected by a remedial order. Remedial discretion thus enables courts to ensure that no inequity is done in the name of equity. This is a matter of particular importance and delicacy in the context of disputes over the governance of complex organizations.

V THE SENSE IN WHICH THE OPPRESSION REMEDY IS (CORRECTIVELY) EQUITABLE

I have said that the oppression remedy is an instantiation of equity's corrective mode of intervention, contrasting it with equitable supplementation of first-order law. However, this framing might strike some as unusual. It might be thought unusual because the oppression remedy is a modern legislative innovation. It is not a legacy of the centuries-old judge-made equity of chancery courts. So, those who view equity as a thing frozen in time—a body of doctrines encased, as if in resin, in the equity that predates the *Judicature Acts*—might view my framing with skepticism. As I will explain, the skepticism is unfounded because the premises underlying it are wrong. But, if only because it is an acid test that helps clarify the oppression remedy *and* the continuing importance of corrective equity to modern law, it is worth asking: *In what sense is the oppression remedy equitable?*

The reasons for viewing the oppression remedy as an instantiation of corrective equity are neither historical nor institutional. They are substantive. The oppression remedy is substantively equitable in that it bears distinguishing hallmarks of doctrines that channel correctively equitable intervention.[62] I highlight six hallmarks in what follows.

First, the oppression remedy is engaged ex post by way of application for judicial review. Corrective equity is distinguished from law—and supplemental equity—in that it does not contribute to the law's ex ante specification of terms of interaction.[63] Rather, it enables second-order intervention in first-order law for reasons of conscience and justice having to do with the use or enforcement of first-order law.[64] As noted above, the oppression remedy operates in just this way. It does not displace or amend terms of interaction supplied by corporate law. It is invoked and operates ex post upon petition by an aggrieved shareholder. It permits the court to

---

[62] Many of the properties highlighted below have been isolated as distinguishing features of equity by Henry Smith in his work on equity as a system providing for second-order correction of opportunistic misuse of first-order law. *See* Smith, *supra* note 28. It should be emphasized that the properties adverted to below are distinguishing marks of remedial or corrective but *not* supplemental equity, given that supplemental equity fills out first-order law. *See* Miller, *supra* note 26.

[63] Miller, *supra* note 26.

[64] Smith, *supra* note 28.

determine whether, *notwithstanding the law* (which would leave the shareholder's grievance unrecognized), the petition reveals an inequitable violation of the shareholder's reasonable expectations.

Second, the oppression remedy is addressed primarily to judges. Consistent with its ex post operation, corrective equity is also distinguished from first-order law in that it does not articulate norms for the guidance of individuals. Rather, it articulates broad bases for judicial intervention in first-order law. In other contexts, these bases are framed in terms of fraud, breach of confidence or trust, and undue influence. Here, they are put in the similarly open-textured language of oppression and unfairness. These bases for intervention have sometimes been criticized for their failure to provide shareholders with clear guidance. But these criticisms miss the point because the rubrics are addressed to judges, not shareholders. Vague, morally inflected language is intended to indicate to judges the kinds of situation that might call for exceptional equitable intervention.

Third, judges have broad discretion in determining whether to hear a petition and whether it has merit. Generally speaking, consistent with our commitment to the rule of law, judges are required to hear and impartially adjudicate claims brought on the basis of a legal rule and, where (in the case of a duty-imposing rule) they find it abrogated, they must respond in a particular way (e.g., by giving public reasons that announce and explain their findings in light of the rule, and/ or by issuing remedial and enforcement orders that are responsive to the rule and the fact and manner of its violation). Because corrective equity is exceptional and premised on the primacy and soundness of the law in relation to which corrective intervention is sought, judges are widely acknowledged to have broader discretion in deciding whether to hear and how to dispose of petitions in equity. Here, too, the oppression remedy is consonant with corrective equity. Pertinent legislative provisions grant courts wide latitude in determining whether to hear petitions on the basis of oppression and in evaluating their merit.

Fourth, judicial assessment of the merits of petitions brought under the oppression remedy involves often laborious inquisitorial investigation and review of facts material to the relationship between the parties, including those bearing on the personal, institutional, market, and other contexts within which their interactions took place. Courts must consider the relative position of the parties as a matter of law, but the investigation of the factual basis of a petition is focused primarily on identifying the petitioner's material interests and associated expectations that lie beyond protection at law, as well as the fate of those interests and expectations. Doctrinal analysis is focused on determining whether the petitioner's expectations were reasonably held *considering that they were not protected at law*, and if so, whether they were violated through conduct that is objectively inequitable. Here, too, the oppression remedy is of a piece with corrective equity more broadly. Equitable doctrine frames a court's decision whether to intervene but determining the merits of a petition and how a merited grievance should be remedied is highly fact contingent.

Fifth, petitions deemed to present well-founded grievances in oppression typically involve opportunism or polycentric problems. As Henry Smith has explained, corrective equitable intervention is often premised on opportunistic misuse or abuse of law, or polycentric problems that complicate and confound the just application of legal rules.[65] Recognizing that these problems do not exhaust the grounds for corrective equitable intervention, it is nevertheless telling that many successful petitions for relief on the basis of oppression involve facts suggestive of them. Thus, for example, cases in which a controlling shareholder agitates to force a minority

---

[65]   Smith, *supra* note 28.

shareholder to sell its shares at less than fair market value or instigates profit-gouging self-dealing transactions clearly involve opportunism. Equally, cases in which a grievance canvasses the petitioner's treatment in multiple roles (e.g., as shareholder, director, and/or employee) involve polycentric problems of fact and law (i.e., sorting out the reasonable expectations held by the petitioner, recognizing differences in the materiality of considerations of fact and law across roles, and that these differences might have been exploited by the controlling shareholder).

Sixth, courts have unlimited discretion in the choice of remedies for oppression and, in exercising it, generally seek to provide tailored, corrective responses to meritorious grievances. As others have noted, legal remedies are also subject to judicial discretion (e.g., as to kind and quantum) and so cannot be viewed as but an entailment of the violation of a primary right.[66] Nevertheless, discretion is narrower concerning legal remedies than equitable remedies. That is in part because some legal remedies are an apt response to a wrong and others not. Discretion over equitable remedies is wider because they are often not responses to wrongs but are, rather, responses to inequities that resist generalization. Legislative conferral of unlimited remedial discretion upon courts under the oppression remedy has been much commented upon. However, viewed in light of characteristic features of equitable remedies, it is unremarkable. Here, as elsewhere, wide remedial discretion is compelled by the recognition that the circumstances calling for corrective relief in equity are idiosyncratic, and equity's interventions must be tailored to suit them.

VI CONCLUSION: LESSONS ON THE PLACE OF EQUITY IN MODERN LAW

We have established that the oppression remedy is a correctively equitable form of intervention in corporate law. It allows minority shareholders to seek vindication of reasonable expectations inadequately protected at law in exceptional circumstances. We have also established that the oppression remedy promises superior (more apt, and effective) handing of the tyranny of the majority problem in corporations than does the extension of fiduciary duties to controlling shareholders.

I conclude now with some general lessons for current scholarship on equity. We may begin on the negative side of the ledger. Perhaps most notable is further confirmation of the costs of a now-moribund sensibility about equity. It is striking that American equity has charted a path that diverges so sharply from Commonwealth countries. The path taken here might well be counted as doctrinal evidence of the negative consequences of collective amnesia about equity; a condition already lamented by American scholars[67] but is surely not confined to the United States. Wherever it arises, amnesia might mean that lawmakers are less likely to think of legislating for correctively equitable intervention, even where it provides the best means by which to respond to a problem.

Cheeringly, though, there are also positive lessons. And these go to the constructive contributions of equity to modern law. Several jurisdictions have provided for equitable intervention in corporate law through a legislated oppression remedy. The remedy has been developed differently in different jurisdictions and not without controversy, with much criticism echoing the familiar charge that equity threatens to destabilize law. But decades of experience have shown the charge to be overblown. The oppression remedy is now an unexceptional fixture of

---

[66] Nicholas Cornell, *What Do We Remedy?*, in Civil Wrongs and Justice in Private Law 209 (Paul B. Miller & John Oberdiek eds., 2020); Charlie Webb, *Duties and Damages*, in Oxford Studies in Private Law Theory, Vol. 11 (Paul B. Miller & John Oberdiek eds., 2020).

[67] See works cited, *supra* note 12.

Commonwealth corporate law. And this, in itself, is a good news story for equity. It shows that corrective equity is not a redundant appendage or crystalline set of doctrines.

Finally, experience with the oppression remedy suggests that the time has come for rethinking equity's place amongst legal institutions. Some traditionalists will see as genuinely equitable only those doctrines devised by chancery courts before the *Judicature Acts*. However, viewing equity in this way requires one to ignore evidence of its continuing relevance and vitality, and suppresses the impulse lawmakers might otherwise have to innovate through equity. There is no reason to think that innovations achieved through equity need to come from judges, much less judges in specialist courts. Rather, experience with the oppression remedy suggests quite the opposite: legislators can see the need for corrective equity in modern law and provide judges with sensible bases for expanded equitable jurisdiction.

10

Fiduciary Relationships in Employee Benefit Plans

Dana M. Muir

I INTRODUCTION

A complex web of fiduciary, or near-fiduciary, relationships exists in modern day employee benefit plans. For example, financial advisors provide expertise on the investment of plan assets.[1] Plan assets may be invested in mutual funds with the attached fiduciary obligations.[2] A plan's fiduciary functions may be outsourced piecemeal to third parties.[3] The web would not exist, though, without the employers who sponsor plans and the employees who participate in them. This chapter focuses on the relationships between those key actors in plans, the plan sponsors and participants,[4] and how the law addresses tensions in those relationships.

Fiduciary law has long played a role in governing employers' benefit plan promises, particularly in pension plans. The enactment of federal statutory law in 1974 provided the platform for a regulatory regime that imposed extensive minimum requirements on the types of retirement plans that predominated at the time. The statute also included fiduciary provisions that track the obligations of loyalty and care developed in trust law. The relationships between the key actors in benefit plans, however, never mapped neatly onto the trust law structure of settlors, trustees, and beneficiaries.[5]

Trust law relies on subsidiary rules, also known as implementing rules, to adapt the flexible and broad fiduciary obligations of loyalty and care to situations that commonly arise with grantor trusts.[6] Trust law's implementing rules are similar to the rules and regulations developed by agencies such as the Securities and Exchange Commission to provide guidance on statutory provisions. Those rules and regulations also sometimes are referred to as implementing rules.[7]

---

[1] Arthur B. Laby, *Trust, Discretion, and ERISA Fiduciary Status*, ch. 4 (this volume) (arguing that some providers of investment advice on plan assets should be treated as fiduciaries); *see also* Quinn Curtis, *Conflicts of Interest in Investment Advice: An Expanded View*, ch. 6 (this volume) (discussing conflicts of interest of advice providers to retirement savers).

[2] Howell E. Jackson, *A System of Fiduciary Protections for Mutual Funds*, ch. 7 (this volume) (referring to the mutual fund regulatory regime as "likely the world's most elaborate system of fiduciary protections for investors").

[3] Colleen E. Medill, *Regulating ERISA Fiduciary Outsourcing*, 102 IOWA L. REV. 505 (2017).

[4] Participants are employees or former employees covered by benefit plans. Family members of participants may be covered by or have rights in benefit plans in which case they are known as plan beneficiaries. For simplicity, this chapter refers to participants even when the reference includes beneficiaries.

[5] *See infra* section III.A.

[6] Robert H. Sitkoff, *The Economic Structure of Fiduciary Law*, 91 B.U. L. REV. 1039, 1044–45 (2011). Sitkoff further developed the concept in later work, including Robert H. Sitkoff, *An Economic Theory of Fiduciary Law, in* PHILOSOPHICAL FOUNDATIONS OF FIDUCIARY LAW 197, 202–03(Andrew S. Gold & Paul B. Miller eds., 2014).

[7] *See, e.g.*, James J. Park, *Insider Trading and the Integrity of Mandatory Disclosure*, 2018 WIS. L. REV. 1133, 1134 n.1 (2018) (referring to a regulation promulgated by the Securities and Exchange Commission as an implementing rule).

Examples of trust law's implementing rules include the prudent investor rule and the duty of impartiality.[8]

In the setting of employee benefit plans, courts have developed implementing rules to address recurring fiduciary issues that arise due to the nature of the relationships between plan sponsors and participants. As in the trust law context, the implementing rules provide guidance for plan actors, particularly fiduciaries, and should, as a result, decrease decision costs. This chapter interrogates the basis for and the operation of two of those implementing rules.

Beginning in the 1980s, the structure of retirement plans changed, and health care benefits increased in importance. Those plans largely operate outside the minimum requirements the statute had imposed on the previously popular type of retirement plan. The relationships between the key actors in the new retirement and health care plans differed significantly from the relationships in the earlier plans. The general fiduciary obligations of loyalty and prudence govern all of those relationships.

The second section briefly describes the statutory minimum requirements and fiduciary provisions of the Employee Retirement Income Security Act (ERISA),[9] the statute that governs employee benefit plans sponsored by private-sector employers. The third section explains how the relationships between employers as plan sponsors and fiduciaries, and employees as participants in the plans, vary across the three major types of employee benefit plans. The fourth section examines two implementing rules used to address tensions in those relationships.

II OVERVIEW OF BENEFIT PLAN REGULATION AND PLAN TYPOLOGY

This section outlines the basic statutory minimum requirements that govern employee benefit plans. It then describes the increasing importance of defined contribution (DC) and health care plans. It also explains the extent to which the statutory requirements govern DC and health care plans.

A ERISA—Minimum Terms and Fiduciary Obligation

When enacted in 1974, ERISA's goal was to address two types of problems that existed in the retirement plans of the time. First, in what is known as the gratuity theory of pensions, employers had held out potential pension benefits as a gift for long service but had no obligation to pre-fund the benefits. Ultimately, entitlement to those benefits depended on the employer's generosity and financial strength when it came time to pay benefits.[10] Second, even those plans that did pre-fund benefits often neither funded the full amount necessary to guarantee all benefits could be paid nor protected the assets from being diverted to other uses.[11] At times the assets were mismanaged or embezzled. As a result of the gratuity theory and the lack of protected pre-funding, employees often did not receive the benefits they had anticipated.[12]

---

[8] Sitkoff, *An Economic Theory of Fiduciary Law, supra* note 6, at 202–03.
[9] Employee Retirement Income Security Act of 1974 [hereinafter ERISA] §§ 1–4402, 29 U.S.C. §§ 1001–1461 (2018). Although ERISA only applies to benefit plans sponsored by private-sector employers, courts frequently rely on concepts from ERISA when deciding issues that arise in public sector benefit plans. DAVID WEBBER, THE RISE OF THE WORKING-CLASS SHAREHOLDER: LABOR'S LAST BEST WEAPON 2119–21 (2018).
[10] Kathryn L. Moore, *An Overview of the U.S. Retirement Income Security System and the Principles and Values It Reflects*, 33 COMP. LAB. L. & POL'Y J. 5, 26 (2011).
[11] Dana M. Muir, *Plant Closings and ERISA's Noninterference Provision*, 36 B.C. L. REV. 201, 204 (1995).
[12] Moore, *supra* note 10, at 26 (explaining the gratuity theory of pensions); Natalya Shnitser, *Trusts No More: Rethinking the Regulation of Retirement Savings in the United States*, 2016 B.Y.U. L. REV. 629, 640–42 (referring to mismanagement and manipulation of plan assets by union officials or employers).

At the time of ERISA's enactment, retirement plans typically were structured as defined benefit (DB) plans. Those plans calculate benefits according to a formula, often based on years of employment and salary. A DB plan commits to paying lifetime retirement benefits in the form of an annuity.[13] The statutory standards for DB plans require (i) minimum accruals to ensure participants earn benefits incrementally over time, (ii) vesting periods for those accruals, so they are not forfeited even after long periods of work, and (iii) funding of plans, so money is available to pay the vested accrued benefits.[14] These provisions work in concert to prevent employers from treating plan benefits as forms of gratuities.

To address problems of asset mismanagement and theft that had occurred in the pre-ERISA period, Congress incorporated fiduciary principles based on traditional trust law.[15] The statutory provisions require fiduciaries of all plans to act for the exclusive purposes of providing benefits to participants and their beneficiaries and defraying reasonable expenses of administering the plan (a loyalty obligation); to act prudently (a care obligation), to diversify investments to minimize the risk of large losses except to the extent it is clearly prudent not to do so or certain other limited circumstances apply (a prudent investment obligation), and to administer the plan in accordance with its terms to the extent the terms do not violate ERISA.[16] The fiduciary obligations cannot be waived.[17]

B Regulatory Arbitrage — The Rise of Defined Contribution Plans

Beginning in the 1980s, plans shifted from the DB format to a DC format.[18] DC plans may take any of a variety of forms; however, the two primary types are 401(k) plans and Employee Stock Ownership Plans (ESOPs). In the most common type of DC plan, a 401(k) plan,[19] employees may elect whether to contribute to their plan accounts; employers may contribute to the accounts, and ultimately the participant's benefit entitlement is the sum of contributions adjusted for investment gains or losses.[20] ERISA requires ESOPs to invest primarily in employer stock, whereas no such provision exists for standard 401(k) plans.[21] ESOPs typically hold that stock in a suspense account. Over time, as participants earn plan contributions through their employment, the plan transfers stock from the suspense account to participant accounts.[22]

Many of the basic undertakings necessary to operate a DC plan do not differ from those in a DB plan. Both types of plans must be funded, the integrity of plan assets must be protected,

---

[13] Dana M Muir, *Contemporary Social Policy Analysis and Employee Benefit Programs: Boomers, Benefits, and Bargains*, 54 Wash. & Lee L. Rev. 1351, 1361–62 (1997).

[14] Dana Muir & Norman Stein, *Two Hats, One Head, No Heart: The Anatomy of the ERISA Settlor/Fiduciary Distinction*, 93 N. C. L. Rev. 459, 471 (2015).

[15] Shnitser, *supra* note 12, at 632.

[16] ERISA § 404(a)(1), 29 U.S.C. § 1104(a)(1) (2018).

[17] ERISA § 410, 29 U.S.C. § 1110 (2018).

[18] Dana M. Muir, *Counting the Cash: Disclosure and Cash Balance Plans*, 37 J. Marshall L. Rev. 849, 855 (2004).

[19] Because of the popularity of 401(k) plans, this chapter concentrates on them although other types of plans such as 403b and 457 plans sponsored by government entities are similar.

[20] Muir & Stein, *supra* note 14, at 497.

[21] ERISA § 407(d)(6)(A), 29 U.S.C. § 1107(d)(6)(A) (2018).

[22] *See* Michael W. Melton, *Demythologizing ESOPs*, 45 Tax L. Rev. 363, 364–65 (1990). A KSOP is a hybrid of a 401(k) and an ESOP. KSOPs permit participants to make contributions, which are treated as 401(k) contributions, although they may be invested in employer stock. In addition, the employer may contribute employer stock to plan accounts, typically used to "match" participant contributions at a specified rate. See Proceedings, *Employee Stock Ownership After Enron: Proceedings of the 2003 Annual Meeting, Association of American Law Schools Section on Employee Benefits*, 7 Emp. Rts. & Emp. Pol'y J. 213, 236 (2003) (explaining that a "KSOP is an amalgamation of 401(k) and ESOP") (Louis H. Diamond).

assets invested, and benefits paid. However, a number of the statutory minimum requirements outlined above[23] do not apply to DC plans. DC plan benefits are not backloaded at a high cost to employers, so there is no need for accrual rules. Likewise, there is no need for minimum funding standards in DC plans because participants are only entitled to whatever assets are in their accounts.

The mandatory rules that do apply to DC plans tend not to be rules that impose substantial costs on employers. The immediate vesting of contributions voluntarily made by participants simply ensures participants do not forfeit earned compensation that they could have taken in cash. Vesting rules applied to employer contributions permit forfeitures by participants in the plan for a short period and do not require employers to make future contributions. Disclosures may provide useful information to participants; however, doctrinal developments largely mean that only the plan terms are enforceable; other mandatory or voluntary disclosures do not create benefit obligations.[24] Most commentators agree that the lower regulatory burden played an important role in moving from DB to DC plans.[25]

C *Increasing Importance of Welfare Benefit Plans*

In addition to retirement plans, ERISA regulates what in its parlance are welfare benefit plans. Those plans include almost any employee benefit other than those that defer compensation to termination of employment or retirement. The most important welfare benefit plan types are health care and disability insurance plans. By the time of ERISA's enactment in 1974, the costs of health care coverage had begun to increase, but were not yet a significant issue to plan sponsors or participants.[26]

The undertakings necessary to operate health care plans differ from those in retirement plans. For current participants, plans reimburse health care costs as they are incurred.[27] Thus, there is no need to invest plan assets or protect their integrity. The primary undertaking of a health care plan is to pay participants' health care costs according to the plan's terms.

Perhaps it is not surprising then that ERISA only lightly regulates health care plans. The concepts of vesting and accrual do not apply to those plans. Plan sponsors are not required to pre-fund health care benefits for current participants. Health care plans must comply with many of the statute's disclosure requirements, but as noted above, typically those disclosures do not create enforceable promises.[28] In the words of one staff member involved in drafting ERISA, "The answer as to why ERISA didn't do more respecting health and other welfare plans is quite simple: Unlike pension plans, there was no crisis in health plans in 1974."[29] ERISA's fiduciary provisions, however, apply to all benefit plans, including welfare benefit plans.

Since 1974, health care costs have increased, and the United States has struggled to reform its health care system. Problems with the determination of benefit entitlements became acute when in the late 1990s, employers actively began to try to limit their health

---

[23] *Supra* text accompanying notes 13–14.
[24] *See generally* Peter J. Wiedenbeck, Unbelievable: ERISA's Broken Promise (Wash. U. St. Louis Sch. L. Legal Stud. Rsch. Paper Series, No. 19-08-01, 2019), https://papers.ssrn.com/sol3/papers.cfm?abstract_id=3430686.
[25] *For example*, Martin Gelter, *The Pension System and the Rise of Shareholder Primacy*, 43 SETON HALL L. REV. 909, 929–31 (2011).
[26] See Brendan S. Maher, *Regulating Employment-Based Anything*, 100 MINN. L. REV. 1257, 1267–68 (2016).
[27] John Bronsteen et al., *ERISA, Agency Costs, and the Future of Health Care in the United States*, 76 FORDHAM L. REV. 2297, 2308–12 (2008).
[28] *See supra* text accompanying note 24.
[29] Phyllis C. Borzi, *There's "Private" and Then There's "Private": ERISA, Its Impact, and Options for Reform*, 36 J. L. MED. & ETHICS 660, 661 (2008) (quoting Michael S. Gordon) (citation omitted).

care expenditures.[30] Health care costs have continued to rise, although the rate of increase slowed after the 2010 enactment of the Affordable Care Act (ACA).[31]

III FIDUCIARY RELATIONSHIPS AMONG THE KEY PARTIES IN BENEFIT PLANS

Two attributes of employee benefit plans increase the complexity of the fiduciary relationship as compared to the fiduciary relationships in grantor trusts. First, the roles played by the primary actors in employee benefit arrangements, and particularly in DC and health care plans, are not separated, in contrast to the relatively clearly defined roles of the settlor, trustee, and beneficiary in a typical donative trust.[32] Second, differences in the operation of DC and health care plans compared to DB plans affect the relationships among the key parties.[33] This section considers the ways the roles of key plan actors differ across plan types.

A *The Roles of Settlors, Trustees, and Beneficiaries in Benefit Plans*

Both participants and employers act as employee benefit plan settlors. Employers formally establish plans, and, within any relevant regulatory and labor market constraints, they decide on the terms of the plans they sponsor. Employers often pay at least a portion of the costs of the benefits provided by the plans. They bear the costs of creating, amending, and terminating plans. Participants also act as plan settlors. In some plans they explicitly contribute by, for example, allocating a portion of their earnings to a 401(k) plan or paying a portion of the expenses of a health care plan. Participants always contribute their labor in return for plan benefits.[34]

Similarly, both participants and employers are plan beneficiaries. The benefits that plan participants enjoy are obvious; employers' benefits are more subtle. The Supreme Court has made clear that an employer may receive incidental benefits from the plans it sponsors. As examples, employers may benefit from plans through increased competitiveness in the labor market or the use of DB assets to fund early retirement programs during financial downturns.[35] From a practical standpoint, if they did not receive at least indirect benefits from employee benefit plans, employers would have no reason to sponsor them.[36]

Employers become plan fiduciaries through two routes. Every plan must have a named fiduciary. The plan sponsor nearly always serves in that role. ERISA also provides that an actor will become a fiduciary to the extent it is assigned or undertakes particular responsibilities. Employers typically also become fiduciaries through this functional fiduciary route.[37]

An employer's triple status as a settlor, beneficiary, and fiduciary gives rise to the tension that the implementing rules discussed below address—how can an employer control plan terms,

---

[30] Barry R. Furrow, *Health Reform and Ted Kennedy: The Art of Politics ... and Persistence*, 14 N.Y.U. J. Legis. & Pub. Pol'y 445, 451 (2011).

[31] Patient Protection and Affordable Care Act, Pub. L. No. 111-148, 124 Stat. 119 (2010) (codified as amended in scattered sections of 26 and 42 U.S.C.); Abbe R. Gluck & Thomas Scott-Railton, *Affordable Care Act Entrenchment*, 108 Geo. L. J. 495, 508 (2020).

[32] *See infra* section III.A.

[33] *See infra* section III.B.

[34] Shnitser, *supra* note 12, at 634.

[35] Hughes Aircraft Co. v. Jacobson, 525 U.S. 432, 445 (1999) (holding that amending a plan to use DB plan assets to provide early retirement incentives to some participants was not a fiduciary act).

[36] Daniel Fischel & John H. Langbein, *ERISA's Fundamental Contradiction: The Exclusive Benefit Rule*, 55 U. Chi. L. Rev. 1105, 1117–18 (1988).

[37] Dana Muir, *From Schism to Prism: Equitable Relief in Employee Benefit Plans*, 55 Am. Bus. L. J. 599, 617–18 (2018).

benefit from the plan, and fulfill its fiduciary duty of acting for the exclusive purpose of benefiting participants? Professors Daniel Fischel and John Langbein observed that "the simple trust law model of exclusive benefit does not ... comport with the reality of the interests in employee benefit plans."[38] The relationships in DC and health care plans differ in some ways from the DB plans that were the core of Fischel and Langbein's concern, but the reality of those relationships diverge from the trust law model at least as much as did the relationships in DB plans.[39]

B *Fiduciary Relationships in DC Plans Compared to DB Plans*

For many of the operations of a DC plan, the employer's relationship with the participants is similar to the relationship in DB plans. Employers transmit their own or participants' contributions to the plans. Employers establish and maintain a trust to ensure the integrity of the plan assets. Employers ensure participants receive their plan benefits, which typically do not involve controversial calculations, at the appropriate time. Each of these undertakings requires the employer to act on behalf of the participant.

For investment decisions, the relationships vary among types of plans. In DB plans, decisions on the management or control of plan assets are fiduciary decisions.[40] In contrast, in 401(k) plans the plan can, and most do, delegate responsibility for making investment decisions regarding their account assets to participants. In these participant-directed plans, participants choose from an investment menu. If the plan provides a menu that meets regulatory requirements designed to ensure participants can appropriately diversify their investments, then plan fiduciaries do not have any fiduciary responsibility for the participants' specific investment decisions.[41] As discussed in the next section, an exception to the implementing rule that otherwise might apply means that menu selection is a fiduciary function.

In many instances, an ESOP owns a high percentage, sometimes one hundred percent, of the company's issued stock.[42] Three differences in the relationships among the parties flow from the requirement that ESOPs must invest primarily in employer stock. First, in addition to the company whose stock was sold to the ESOP, the creation of an ESOP may benefit a shareholder, such as a company founder, who sells stock to the ESOP or an acquirer of the company who uses an ESOP to fund the acquisition. Challenges to the valuation of the stock purchased by the ESOP are not unusual. Second, because all or most of the value of ESOP accounts is attributable to employer stock, business-related decisions by the employer that affect the price of that stock obviously have a particularly strong effect on the value of participants' ESOP accounts at such companies.[43] Third, an employer or company insider acting as an ESOP fiduciary may

---

[38] Fischel & Langbein, *supra* note 36, at 1117–18. The authors also observe that the participants' preferences in large DB plans vary with respect to their plan interests depending on whether they continue to be employed at the plan sponsor, their status as working or retired, and their age. Although ERISA does not contain an analogue to trust law's duty of impartiality, they argued for that standard to be imported to employee benefits law. *Id.* at 1159–60; *cf.* Amir N. Licht, *Stakeholder Impartiality: A New Classic Approach for the Objectives of the Corporation*, ch. 16 (this volume) (advocating a process-oriented impartiality duty to address the interests of corporate stakeholders).

[39] Shnitser, *supra* note 12, at 632.

[40] Thole v. U.S. Bank, 140 S. Ct. 1615, 1620–21 (2020) (discussing legal actions against a DB plan fiduciary for breaches related to plan investments).

[41] ERISA § 404(c)(1)(A), 29 U.S.C. § 1104(c)(1)(A) (2018).

[42] Norman Stein, *Three and Possibly Four Lessons about ERISA that We Should, But Probably Will Not, Learn from Enron*, 76 St. John's L. Rev. 855, 860 (2002).

[43] Sean M. Anderson, *Risky Retirement Business: How ESOPs Harm the Workers They Are Supposed to Help*, 41 Loy. U. Chi. L. J. 1, 13–21 (2009).

have non-public information about the type of serious financial risk to the stock that could trigger the right or obligation to review the suitability of the stock as a plan asset.[44]

C *Fiduciary Relationships in Health Care Plans*

As explained above, the primary undertaking of a health care plan is to pay participant health care costs according to the plan's terms.[45] That undertaking defines the basic nature of the relationship between the key actors in the plan. Unlike DB and DC plans, where a plan's terms are typically clear on the amount of benefits any given participant is entitled to, some terms of health care plans are ambiguous and give rise to moral hazard for the fiduciaries in determining eligibility for particular treatments.

In many instances, determining eligibility for a particular benefit is clear. By their terms, health care plans often provide coverage for broad categories of benefits such as preventative care or prescription drugs. The plan terms will govern whether a plan covers a routine visit to a physician or a prescription. The plan will also establish any participant cost sharing and whether it takes the form of a share of the premium for the coverage or co-pays for services. These types of plan terms rarely require the exercise of discretion as to eligibility for plan benefits.[46]

Eligibility for benefits based on other plan terms may be more ambiguous. For example, most plans provide an exclusion for treatments that are not "medically necessary." In this way, plans can meet their goal of providing coverage for needed and effective care while avoiding the costs of procedures that are ineffective, experimental, or solely cosmetic. The medically necessary requirement also provides a mechanism for plans to question the validity of procedures that might be in a physician's best interest, but not that of the patient.[47] Professor William Sage has opined that "ambiguity in the interpretation of medical necessity is inevitable."[48]

A second difference between the nature of the relationship between employers and participants in health care plans compared to DB and DC plans is attributable to the nature of the funding of health care benefits. Regardless of the extent to which a plan is insured, decisions on benefits entitlement are zero-sum decisions. For every dollar of health care benefits paid, the insurer or plan sponsor contemporaneously incurs a dollar of cost that has not been pre-funded.[49] The decision maker's need to interpret ambiguous plan terms provides the opportunity for it to engage in opportunistic behavior. The zero-sum nature of the decisions provides the incentive for opportunistic behavior.

Perhaps reputational effects constrain such opportunism. Langbein observed that benefit determinations occur over long periods and involve repeat players. As a result, in his view, plan sponsors and the decision makers they hire typically "have strong incentives not to acquire a reputation for sharp practice in handling benefit claims."[50]

Countervailing factors may offset those reputational costs. The potential for opportunism in zero-sum decision-making may be of most concern in highly individualized decisions where numerous health and treatment factors are relevant. The individualized nature of the decisions

---

[44] *See infra* text accompanying notes 63–66 (discussing the fiduciary analysis applied to decisions about the continued use of employer stock in an ESOP when that stock has become an inappropriate investment).

[45] *See supra* text following note 27.

[46] William M. Sage, *Managed Care's Crimea: Medical Necessity, Therapeutic Benefit, and the Goals of Administrative Process in Health Insurance*, 53 Duke L. J. 597, 605 (2003).

[47] *Id.* at 605–06.

[48] *Id.* at 604.

[49] Bronsteen et al., *supra* note 27, at 2308–12.

[50] John H. Langbein, *The Supreme Court Flunks Trusts*, 1990 Sup. Ct. Rev. 207, 216 (1990).

and confidentiality of health-related information could make it difficult for other plan participants and prospective employees to identify any patterns of opportunistic or imprudent decision-
making.[51] In an article analyzing denials of health care benefits published after he made the
observation above about reputational constraints, Langbein recognized that the potential gain
from benefit denials could more than offset any reputational cost.[52] In such an environment,
short term financial considerations may outweigh longer term benefits from approvals of
preventative or early treatment of conditions that may become more expensive and lead to
higher future costs.

iv IMPLEMENTING RULES

No law requires employers to sponsor DB or DC plans. Federal health care law provides some
employers with flexibility to provide a plan and all employers with considerable latitude on the
generosity of benefits promised by any plan they do sponsor.[53] Plan sponsors benefit from their
sponsorship of employee benefit plans, and bear at least some of the plan costs. And, they are
plan fiduciaries. The confluence of the benefits plan sponsors enjoy, the costs they absorb, and
the fiduciary obligations they must meet is at the heart of the tension between a plan sponsor's
role as an employer and its role as a fiduciary. The resolution of the tension implicates
employers' willingness to sponsor benefit plans. This section considers two implementing
rules that address that tension by adapting ERISA's fiduciary obligations of loyalty and prudence
to the employee benefit plan environment. This section probes the particular salience of those
rules for DC and health care plans, respectively.

A *The Settlor Doctrine*

The settlor doctrine addresses the tension between a plan sponsor's roles by bifurcating those
roles. For any given act, the employer is said to wear one of two hats — a settlor hat for acts taken
as the "settlor" of the plan even if assets are not trusted, and a fiduciary hat for actions as
a fiduciary. The doctrine promotes plan sponsorship by providing employers with flexibility in
amending their plans and reducing costs associated with fiduciary obligations, but at some cost
to participants' benefit expectations.[54] An exception exists for investment-related decisions in
DC plans, which aligns with the nature of the relationship between plan sponsors and participants in those plans.

1 Operation of the Settlor Doctrine

According to the settlor doctrine, plan sponsors do not act as plan fiduciaries when they establish
plans, determine or amend plan terms, or terminate plans; all of these are decisions on plan
design.[55] Plan sponsors do not act in a fiduciary role when they make business decisions that
affect the plan or the benefits a plan provides. The settlor doctrine generally applies across all

---

[51] Dana M. Muir, *Fiduciary Status as an Employer's Shield: The Perversity of ERISA Fiduciary Law*, 2 U. Pa. J. Lab. &
      Emp. L. 391, 408–09 (2000).
[52] John H. Langbein, *Trust Law as Regulatory Law: The UNUM/Provident Scandal and Judicial Review of Benefit
      Denials Under ERISA*, 101 Nw. U. L. Rev. 1315, 1328 (2007).
[53] Nicholas Bagley, *Legal Limits and the Implementation of the Affordable Care Act*, 164 U. Pa. L. Rev. 1715, 1716–21
      (2016) (discussing essential benefits and the employer mandate).
[54] For a critique of the settlor doctrine, see generally Muir & Stein, *supra* note 14.
[55] *Id.* at 463.

types of employee benefit plans.[56] The Supreme Court grounded its development of the settlor doctrine on statutory language. According to the Court, design decisions are not fiduciary acts because the definition of an ERISA functional fiduciary does not refer to discretionary acts that affect plan design.[57]

For example, in *Hughes Aircraft v. Jacobson*, one of the three cases in which the Supreme Court developed the settlor doctrine,[58] the employer had made two amendments to its over-funded DB plan.[59] One of the amendments provided a specified subset of participants with a window of opportunity to retire with enhanced early retirement benefits. This encouraged voluntary separations by older, more expensive employees which, in turn, reduced the employer's payroll expenses.[60] It also enabled the employer to decrease its labor force without having to bear the costs of unemployment benefits associated with a layoff. Because the enhanced retirement benefits were provided through a plan amendment, the Court held that the settlor doctrine applied.[61]

2 The Exception for Investment-Related Decisions in DC Plans

However, the selection of investment options in 401(k) plans does not appear to be a settlor function even if the options are defined in a plan's terms. The DOL was first to designate the selection of investment options as a fiduciary function, stating in 1991 that:

> [T]he act of limiting or designating investment options which are intended to constitute all or part of the investment universe of a [participant-directed 401(k)] plan is a fiduciary function ... whether achieved through fiduciary designation or express plan language ... Thus ... the plan fiduciary has a fiduciary obligation to prudently select such [investment options], as well as a residual fiduciary obligation to periodically evaluate the performance of such [investment options].[62]

The Supreme Court appears to agree with the DOL, although the question the Court addressed, in *Fifth Third Bancorp v. Dudenhoeffer*, was not exactly on point.[63] Former employees of Fifth Third Bancorp alleged that the ESOP's fiduciaries breached their duty of prudence by not decreasing the plan's holdings of company stock when the fiduciaries "should have known—on the basis of both publicly available information and inside information ... that Fifth Third stock was overpriced and excessively risky."[64] Although the approaches differed slightly, most of the circuit courts of appeals had developed a presumption that ESOP investments in employer stock met the prudence requirement. The Supreme Court rejected that presumption. The fiduciaries argued, among other things, that ESOP's have a special purpose in addition to those of an ordinary plan, namely, to "promote employee ownership of employer stock."[65] The Court did not accept

---

[56] Hughes Aircraft Co. v. Jacobson, 525 U.S. 432, 445 (1999) (holding that amending a plan to used DB plan assets to provide early retirement incentives to some participants was not a fiduciary act).

[57] Lockheed Corp. v. Spink, 517 U.S. 882, 890–91 (1996).

[58] Dana M. Muir, *The Plan Amendment Trilogy: Settling the Scope of the Settlor Doctrine*, 15 Lab. Law. 205, 205 (1999).

[59] *Hughes Aircraft Co.*, 525 U.S. at 436.

[60] Muir, *supra* note 58, at 213.

[61] *Hughes Aircraft Co.*, 525 U.S. at 443. Arguably, because the plan assets were used to pay benefits, the decision would have fulfilled the loyalty obligation of acting for the exclusive purpose of providing benefits. *Id.* at 438–39 (rejecting an anti-inurement challenge on this basis).

[62] Final Regulation Regarding Participant Directed Individual Account Plans (ERISA Section 404(c) Plans), 57 Fed. Reg. 46,906, 46,924 n.27 (Oct. 13, 1992) (codified at 29 C.F.R. § 2550.404c-1).

[63] Fifth Third Bancorp v. Dudenhoeffer, 573 U.S. 409 (2014).

[64] *Id.* at 413.

[65] *Id.* at 420.

the notion that the decision makers could take into account nonpecuniary goals even if the plan sponsor memorialized the goals in the plan's terms. According to the Court, "the duty of prudence trumps the instructions of a plan document" because ERISA only requires fiduciaries to follow plan documents to the extent those documents are consistent with the statute.[66]

Professor Peter Wiedenbeck observed that the Court's holding appears inconsistent with its often-stated insistence that decisions memorialized as plan terms never constitute a fiduciary act.[67] In *Fifth Third Bancorp.*, the Court did not explain the implicit distinction it drew between plan terms that govern plan investments and the Court's otherwise uniform application of the settlor doctrine to plan terms. In fact, the *Fifth Third Bancorp* Court never mentioned the settlor doctrine.[68]

3 The Rationale and Implications of the DC Exception from the Settlor Doctrine

Wiedenbeck speculates that the Court may view employer decisions on plan investments as an "inherent fiduciary function."[69] Assuming Wiedenbeck is correct, that begs the question of why investment choice is an inherent fiduciary function and exempt from the application of the settlor doctrine. The rationale may signal whether the Court is beginning to mitigate its insistence that the type of plan at issue does not affect the settlor analysis, perhaps because of the nature of the relationships between the key actors in DC plans with respect to investments.[70]

Traditional trust law offers a starting point in searching for a rationale for the Court's treatment of investment selection as an inherent fiduciary function. Trust law's corollary of the settlor doctrine provides few limits on a settlor's ability to establish the terms of a trust. Nor does it impose fiduciary responsibilities on settlors simply because they establish a trust that contains investment restrictions.

Wiedenbeck suggested that the presumption of prudence the circuit courts developed for ESOP sponsors originally began as a parallel to trust law's frustration doctrine. That doctrine permits trust fiduciaries to act outside a trust's terms if required to avoid the frustration of the trust's purposes.[71] The presumption of prudence operated in a similar fashion by protecting investment decisions made in compliance with the plan terms unless the employer's prospects were so dire they would compel a prudent trustee to act outside the terms. The exception the Fifth Third Bancorp Court established appears, though, to go much further than the trust law concern with frustration. In benefit plans, fiduciary obligation appears to trump any investment provisions included in terms of a benefit plan with the result that all of a decision maker's actions with respect to investments are subject to the fiduciary obligation.

The detailed statutory provisions regarding fiduciary definitions, obligations, and investments, provide an alternative rationale for the investment-related exception to the settlor doctrine. Recall that the *Hughes Aircraft* Court treated the plan sponsor's action in offering the early retirement window as a plan design decision. Because the fiduciary definition does not include

---

66   *Id.* at 421.
67   Peter J. Wiedenbeck, *Untrustworthy: ERISA's Eroded Fiduciary Law*, 59 Wm. & Mary L. Rev. 1007, 1067 (2018).
68   *Id.* at 1068.
69   *Id.*
70   *See* Hughes Aircraft Co. v. Jacobson, 525 U.S. 432, 443–44 (1999) ("Our conclusion [that the settlor doctrine applies to decisions on plan terms] applies with equal force to persons exercising authority over a contributory plan, a noncontributory plan, or any other type of plan.").
71   Wiedenbeck, *supra* note 67, at 1068.

design decisions, the DB plan sponsor did not act as a fiduciary when establishing the early retirement window benefits.[72]

In contrast, the investment-related exception may be explained by the existence of statutory language, rather than the absence of language. The statute requires that ESOPs be invested primarily in employer stock and provides an explicit exemption from the fiduciary duty of diversification. By exempting fiduciaries from the diversification requirement, the implication is that the other fiduciary obligations regarding ESOP investments remain intact.[73] Similarly, participant-directed 401(k) plans must offer a menu of investment options that permits participants to diversify their assets. If the plan fails to meet that requirement, it retains fiduciary responsibility for the participants' investment selection.[74] By exempting fiduciaries from responsibility for participants' investment selection, the implication is that the other fiduciary obligations remain intact, including loyal and prudent selection and monitoring of the plan's investment menu.

Similarly, the statute defines as a fiduciary anyone that "exercises any authority or control respecting management or disposition of [plan] assets."[75] ESOP decision makers responsible for determining whether employer stock is an appropriate plan investment do exercise authority or control over the management of plan assets. The *Fifth Third Bancorp* decision may mean that when the primary effect of a plan-related decision is on management or disposition of assets rather than on the determination of a benefit entitlement the plan sponsor's fiduciary obligations will not be trumped even by memorialization of the decision in the plan terms.

The settlor doctrine and its exception for investment-related decisions appear to preserve fiduciary obligation where the duty of prudence is particularly salient and eliminate it where the existence of a conflict of interest typically is of primary concern. That stands in contrast to fiduciary law, which typically treats prudence as secondary to loyalty. Frankel writes that the fiduciary duty of care is weaker and less strict than the duty of loyalty.[76]

Consider the general application of the settlor doctrine, for example, in cases such as *Hughes*. The doctrine treats conflicts of interest as irrelevant. It allows a plan sponsor to decide on plan terms that redound to its benefit even if the decision provides additional benefits to a subset of participants and decreases the benefit entitlements other participants will earn in the future. In contrast, the exception for investment-related decisions in DC plans preserves the plan sponsors' fiduciary obligation but tends to implicate prudence rather than loyalty. Plan sponsors may benefit directly from decisions on investment menus.[77] More generally, though, the concern with investment menus is that a plan sponsor has not been sufficiently diligent in choosing appropriate investments.[78]

The differences in the relationships between the key actors in DB and DC plans means the allocation of the settlor role also differs. When the settlor role is unbundled, 401(k) plan participants take on a larger portion of the settlor obligations than do participants in a DB

---

[72] *See supra* text accompanying note 57.

[73] Fifth Third Bancorp v. Dudenhoeffer, 573 U.S. 409, 421 (2014).

[74] *See supra* text accompanying note 41.

[75] ERISA § 3(21)(A)(i), 29 U.S.C. § 1002(21)(A)(i) (2018).

[76] Tamar Frankel, Fiduciary Law 169–70 (2011).

[77] This is not to say that loyalty issues never occur when plan sponsors establish 401(k) investment menus. For example, a plan sponsor that as part of its business offers mutual fund investments may select those investments for its plan menu. Or a plan sponsor could agree to include particular investments in its menu in return for discounted nonplan services from the investment provider.

[78] Ian Ayers & Quinn Curtis, *Beyond Diversification: The Pervasive Problem of Excessive Fees and "Dominated Funds" in 401(k) Plans*, 124 Yale L. J. 1476, 1510–11 (2015).

plan. Plan sponsors plan a more limited settlor role in 401(k) plans.[79] Providing less settlor protection for plan sponsors in DC plans plausibly reflects that decreased role.

In sum, the settlor doctrine adapts trust law's distinction between settlors and fiduciaries to the benefit plan ecosystem and thereby addresses the tension between an employer's self-interest and the statute's fiduciary obligation. Although employers perform both settlor and fiduciary roles, the settlor doctrine establishes clear and easily applied rules for when employers act as settlors — when they establish plans, amend them, or terminate them. More recently, the Court has moderated the effect of the settlor doctrine as applied to DC plans. The exception, which treats investment-related decisions as fiduciary decisions even if memorialized in terms of a plan, may reflect the nature of the relationships between plan sponsors and participants in those plans. Although the exception adds nuance to the settlor doctrine, it fulfills the expectation that an implementing rule will provide clear direction on applying fiduciary standards, and thereby will reduce decision costs.

B *Standard of Review for Benefit Claim Denials*

Another implementing rule establishes the standard of review when a participant challenges the denial of a benefits claim. Unlike the settlor doctrine, the standard of review doctrine applies without exception. It is similar to the settlor doctrine in that it addresses the tension between a plan sponsor's self-interest and the statute's fiduciary obligations that apply to discretionary decisions in plan administration. In this context, the tension occurs when a plan administrator makes a discretionary determination on benefits eligibility. The standard of review doctrine has struggled to reflect the realities of the relationships between plan sponsors and beneficiaries in the type of plan for which the tension is most salient — health care plans. As a result, the doctrine fails to provide clear guidance that decreases decision costs.

1 Development and Operation of the Standard of Review Doctrine

In *Firestone Tire & Rubber Co. v. Bruch*, the Supreme Court considered the standard of review to be used when a participant challenges a benefit denial. Firestone had refused to pay benefits under a termination plan to former employees. Firestone did not regard the individuals as terminated because Firestone had sold their division, and the new owner had hired them to work for the division. In violation of ERISA's requirement, no formal written plan document existed.[80]

The Supreme Court held that, in the absence of a grant of discretion to the plan decision maker, a de novo standard of review applied. The Supreme Court also advised that a deferential standard of review ("arbitrary and capricious") is appropriate when a benefit plan grants interpretative discretion to the appropriate plan fiduciary.[81] The Court then cautioned that: "Of course, if a benefit plan gives discretion to an administrator or fiduciary who is operating under a conflict of interest, that conflict must be weighed as a 'facto[r] in determining whether

---

[79] *See supra* text accompanying notes 40–41. A plan sponsor's decision to establish a plan that transfers the risks associated with investment decision-making to participants could be viewed as a decision to divide the fiduciary obligations for investments between itself as a fiduciary and the participants. In an ESOP, the plan participants bear the enhanced risk posed by their plan benefits being particularly sensitive to the business decisions made by the plan sponsor.

[80] *See* Firestone Tire & Rubber Co. v. Bruch, 489 U.S. 101, 104 (1989).

[81] *Id.* at 115.

there is an abuse of discretion.'"[82] As discussed below, the Court has twice returned to the question of how to weigh conflicts of interest.[83]

2 Rationale and General Operation of the Standard of Review Doctrine

The *Firestone* Court pointed to trust law as providing the rationale for its decision. Langbein has explained, however, that the Court misunderstood the basic trust law principles.[84] The demarcation line in trust law is between trusts with explicit provisions denying discretion to the plan trustee and all other trusts. If a trust's terms explicitly deny discretion to the trustee, then the trustee's decisions are not accorded deference and courts apply a de novo standard of review. In trusts that provide discretion or are silent on the matter, the law treats trustees as having the discretion to interpret the terms of the trust subject to review under the arbitrary and capricious standard.[85] Because the plan at issue in *Firestone* lacked a plan document, under trust law, the fiduciary would have had discretion. The Supreme Court adopted the opposite default standard for benefits plans—review is de novo unless the plan states otherwise.

Even if based on a misunderstanding of trust law, the decision to apply de novo review as the default standard in benefit plans aligns with differences between trust and benefits law in the extent to which the regimes accept self-interested fiduciaries. The trust law standard of review doctrine, which defaults to deferential review, assumes trustees are free of conflicts of interest. Trustees are prohibited from acting under a conflict of interest not explicitly permitted by a trust unless fiduciaries disclose the conflict and obtain permission for the transaction from the beneficiaries or a court. A transaction that does not meet those criteria and to which no exception applies is subject to the no further inquiry rule. That deems the transaction to be a fiduciary breach. It is irrelevant that the trustee did not profit or that the transaction's terms were fair. In an interested trustee transaction where an exception applies, or the trustee has met one of the criteria to permit the transaction, the standard of review will be "especially careful scrutiny."[86]

Using a de novo standard as the default in benefits law, which permits self-interested fiduciaries, theoretically parallels trust law's use of enhanced scrutiny for its permitted interested fiduciary transactions. In practice, though, decisions by self-interested benefit plan fiduciaries rarely face a high level of enhanced scrutiny. After the *Firestone* decision, employee benefit plans were quick to adopt discretionary grants of authority.[87] As a result, the starting point for review is the deferential arbitrary and capricious standard. As discussed below, the doctrine lacks clarity in its application when decision makers act under a conflict of interest.

3 Implications and Challenges of the Standard of Review Doctrine

Although the deferential standard of review doctrine applies to decisions in all types of benefit plans, it has particular salience in health care plans. The opioid crisis provides a useful context to consider both the ambiguity in applying plan terms such as the medically necessary standard and

---

[82] *Id.* (quoting Restatement (Second) of Trusts § 187, cmt.d (Am. Law Inst. 1959)).
[83] *See infra* text accompanying notes 93–94.
[84] *See* Langbein, *supra* note 50, at 218.
[85] *See id.* at 217–19.
[86] Robert H. Sitkoff, Fiduciary Principles in Trust Law, in THE OXFORD HANDBOOK OF FIDUCIARY LAW 41, 44–46 (Evan J. Criddle, Paul B. Miller & Robert H. Sitkoff eds., 2019).
[87] Wiedenbeck, *supra* note 67, at 1073–74.

the zero-sum nature of health care coverage decisions.[88] Addiction treatment raises factual complexities and difficulties when deciding whether any given treatment meets the "medically necessary" requirement. Questions that significantly affect the cost of care provided can include, for example, whether it is necessary to provide expensive in-patient treatment and the length of treatment that is required to address the addiction.[89]

The assessment above of the relationships in health plans between plan sponsors and participants explained the opportunity and incentives for opportunistic decision-making that exist in those plans. It also considered the competing arguments on whether reputational concerns sufficiently constrain such opportunism.[90] The nature of these relationships raises both loyalty and prudence concerns, which may be best illustrated by considering how standards of review affect agency costs.

As compared to a de novo standard, a more searching standard of review can be expected to increase a plan sponsor's decision costs in two ways. First, a fiduciary decision maker either will invest more to reach correct outcomes or incur higher costs due to more frequent and successful claims appeals. The scrutiny also may result in the approval of marginal claims in an attempt to avoid review costs. Second, knowing that a claims denial will be scrutinized under a de novo standard may discourage a self-interested decision maker from acting opportunistically. Plan sponsors may respond to the higher decision costs imposed by searching standards of review by terminating benefit plans or decreasing plan generosity.

Alternatively, a deferential standard of review may result instead in increased errors that are either randomly distributed, or if a decision maker acts opportunistically, that disproportionately result in inappropriate denials. Social stigmas associated with some health conditions such as addiction may increase the likelihood of inappropriate denials. Randomness would spread the error costs across plan sponsors and participants. However, participants would not bear those costs equally; instead, randomness would result in inconsistent decisions for participants with similar health situations or who receive similar types of health care treatments. The highest error cost for a participant would be death caused by loss of access to a treatment to which the participant was entitled under the plan's terms.[91]

The decrease in decision costs from a deferential standard of review directly reduce the administrative costs of plan sponsorship. The deferential review also could decrease plan costs associated with the approvals of marginal claims. As with the basic application of the settlor doctrine, the deferential standard of review resolves the tension between a plan sponsor's self-interest and fiduciary obligation in a way that may impose costs on the benefits expectations of participants. At the same time, the decreased costs may encourage plan sponsorship.

The agency cost analysis shows that in health care plans, the duties of care and loyalty are intertwined. In a situation where the application of a plan's terms is ambiguous, it can be costly to determine whether an inappropriate denial is due to self-interest or lack of prudence. To understand the complexity and how the complexity undermines the value of the standard of review doctrine as an implementing rule, recall the Supreme Court's advice for determinations made by a decision maker with a conflict of interest. In *Firestone*, the Court directed that the conflict of interest be weighed as a "facto[r] in determining whether there is an abuse of

---

[88]   Katherine T. Vukadin, *On Opioids and ERISA: The Urgent Case for a Federal Ban on Discretionary Clauses*, 53 U. Rich. L. Rev. 687, 698–703 (2019).

[89]   *Id.* at 704.

[90]   *See supra* text accompanying notes 50–52.

[91]   Muir, *supra* note 37, at 601–02 (observing that ERISA may not provide any remedy for a denial of health care benefits that results in the death of the covered individual).

discretion."[92] How to assess the relevance of a conflict and adjust the standard of review continues to trouble courts and commentators even after the Supreme Court addressed the question in two subsequent cases.

In the first decision, *Metropolitan Life Ins. v. Glenn*, the Court observed that both plan sponsors and the entities they hire to make determinations of benefit eligibility might benefit financially from denying benefits and negating a conflict of interest. In a 6–3 opinion, the Court advised the lower courts to use a facts and circumstances test in a holistic way to determine how much deference to afford to a conflicted decision maker.[93] In the second case, the *Metropolitan Life* dissenters gained enough votes to capture a majority. The lower courts had determined that the benefits denial by a conflicted fiduciary violated the abuse of discretion standard, remanded the claim to the fiduciary, and the fiduciary again denied the claim. The question for the Court, which it answered in the affirmative, was whether the decision maker could be entitled to deference to its second decision. The Court held that a "single honest mistake" should not cause a conflicted fiduciary to forfeit the deferential standard of review.[94] While the Court's first decision appeared to require a serious examination of the decision-making process, the second hewed closer to a presumption of deference even for conflicted decision makers.

The two rules examined in this section take very different approaches to the tension between the plan sponsor's conflicts of interest and their fiduciary obligations. The settlor doctrine declares the conflicts to be irrelevant when plan sponsors make particular decisions. It moderates the doctrine through an equally categorical approach to investment-related decisions in DC plans. The standard of review doctrine uses what in its initial application is a categorical approach based on whether the terms of the plan provide discretion to fiduciary decision makers. That doctrine's value in decreasing decision-making costs drops, however, because of its nuanced and ambiguous adjustment of the standard of review to account for the decision maker's conflict of interest.

V CONCLUSION

The increased use of DC and health care plans means that many plans operate largely outside ERISA's minimum requirements. The relationships between the plan sponsor and the participants differ in each of those plans in important ways as compared to the traditional DB plans that existed at the time of the statute's enactment. The relative absence of other substantive regulation and the nature of the relationships in DC and health care plans increases the tension between the employers' role, as plan sponsors and fiduciaries, and employees as participants.

Although the duties imposed by ERISA track the traditional duties of trust law, the relationships between plan sponsors and beneficiaries do not track the relationships in traditional grantor trusts. To address the tensions specific to the employment benefit plans, courts have developed implementing rules to adapt and provide guidance on the fiduciary standards. In one implementing rule discussed here, the courts have used a categorical approach that declares particular actions either outside fiduciary obligation or fully subject to the fiduciary obligation. The other rule discussed here uses a more nuanced approach that attempts to assess the degree of self-interest and adjust the level of deference to the fiduciary accordingly. This chapter does not make normative judgements about the approaches, but the former rule is more effective in providing clear direction and reducing decision costs.

---

[92]　Firestone Tire & Rubber, 489 U.S. 101, 115 (quoting RESTATEMENT (SECOND) OF TRUSTS § 187, cmt.d (AM. LAW INST. 1959)).
[93]　Metro. Life Ins. v. Glenn, 554 U.S. 105, 112–18 (2008).
[94]　Conkright v. Frommert, 559 U.S. 506, 509–11 (2010).

PART III

Historical and Comparative Perspectives

11

Delaware Corporate Law and the "End of History" in Creditor Protection

Jared A. Ellias & Robert J. Stark[*]

I INTRODUCTION

It is well-understood that shareholders of a corporation occasionally need to ask judges for redress after directors and officers behave in a careless or disloyal way.[1] The primary equitable doctrine that judges use to force careless and disloyal directors and officers to pay damages to shareholders is, of course, fiduciary duty claims that sound in corporate law. Over the past generation, Delaware courts have refined the conditions under which directors and officers will be held liable to shareholders and created rules widely understood by businesspeople that shape the very way solvent American businesses operate.[2] This clarity stands in contrast to the struggle of American judges in deciding how, and whether, corporate law should extend similar protections to creditors, when insolvency sets in and creditors replace shareholders as the primary economic stakeholders. While the "zone of insolvency" doctrine is familiar to business law scholars, we suspect many are unfamiliar with the long history in which it developed.

In this chapter, we chronicle the evolution of Delaware corporate law as judges have struggled to decide what help if any, there should be to creditors of insolvent firms. Corporate law has little to do for the creditors of healthy firms because the downside of a business decision falls first on shareholders who can rely on the familiar protection of fiduciary duty law.[3] However, when a firm becomes financially distressed, the downside of a business decision may fall squarely on the creditors' shoulders. As things now stand, Delaware corporate law largely eschews protecting creditors, holding that creditors should instead look for redress in bankruptcy law, fraudulent transfer law, and contract law. But, as the discussion below reveals, history would suggest that Delaware judges will one day return to the question of what, if anything, corporate law should do to protect creditors when they become the victims of disloyal or negligent managers. The law has waxed and waned on this question throughout American history, and tomorrow is unlikely to be an exception.

This chapter proceeds as follows. The next section summarizes the rise of the so-called "trust fund" doctrine, which provided an initial corporate law framework used by judges to protect

---

[*] The authors thank Uriel Pinel for superb research assistance and Elizabeth Pollman and Vince Buccola for helpful conversations.

[1] Guth v. Loft, Inc., 5 A.2d 503, 510 (Del. 1939).

[2] The famous "business judgment rule" is widely taught at business schools and creates a form of judicial deference to decisions made by boards of directors that are: (a) the products of an analysis of some kind; (b) made without an undisclosed conflict of interest. The business judgment rule thus shapes fiduciary conduct in business law by providing a framework that boards can use to make decisions without fear of liability if the decision looks bad ex post.

[3] *See* Brent Nicholson, *Recent Delaware Case Law Regarding Director's Duties to Bondholders*, 19 DEL. J. CORP. L. 573, 575 (1994) ("In the context of the solvent corporation, it is settled Delaware law that directors do not owe bondholders any duty other than compliance with the terms of the bond indenture").

creditors of insolvent firms. The doctrine held that directors and officers had an obligation, once a firm became insolvent, to use the same care as a trustee in protecting the firm's assets for the benefit of creditors. As we explain, the doctrine was mostly used for asset misappropriation claims but did occasionally venture toward a more modern director liability doctrine that looks more similar to modern fiduciary duty law.[4] This doctrine fell out of favor in modern times. The third section describes the emergence of new Delaware jurisprudence in the 1990s, as Delaware courts crafted an "insolvency exception" to the fiduciary duty law and began finding that management owed creditors fiduciary duties when the firm fell into insolvency.[5] This theory reached its zenith at the turn of the twenty-first century, as Delaware courts tiptoed toward embracing "deepening insolvency" and the notion that creditors might have a tort cause of action against directors and officers who exacerbated a firm's financial distress and reduced the value that would otherwise have been available for distribution to creditors.

In the fourth section, we recount how Delaware's corporate law judges effectively abandoned this theory through a series of decisions immediately prior to and following the financial crisis. In this "third generation" of jurisprudence, Delaware told creditors to look to other areas of law to protect themselves from opportunistic misconduct, such as bankruptcy law, fraudulent transfer law, and their loan contracts. Today, the directors and officers of Delaware corporations face perhaps the least amount of corporate law liability exposure than at any previous point in history.[6] Elsewhere, we have argued that this is problematic and suggested Delaware judges should do more to protect creditors and push back against control opportunism.[7] Here, we trace the path that the law walked to arrive at this point.

II THE RISE AND FALL OF THE "TRUST FUND" DOCTRINE.

The intellectual foundation for corporate law's use of equitable doctrines to protect creditors lies in an obscure corner of nineteenth-century corporate law called "the trust fund doctrine."[8] The idea was famously articulated by Justice Story in 1824 while riding circuit in the recently established state of Maine. In connection with a failed bank corporation, Justice Story ruled, in *Wood* v. *Drummer*, that "[t]he charters of our banks make the capital stock a trust fund for the payment of all the debts of the corporation."[9] Under the doctrine, a higher responsibility is imposed on managers of an insolvent business—similar to that of a trustee.[10] Significantly, the

---

4   *See* Royce de R. Barondes, *Fiduciary Duties of Officers and Directors of Distressed Corporations*, 7 GEO. MASON L. REV. 45, 64 (1998) (describing the "trust fund doctrine" as the "seminal theory" justifying creditor fiduciary duties).

5   Geyer v. Ingersoll Publications Co., 621 A.2d 784, 787 (Del. Ch. 1992) ("[W]hen the insolvency exception [arises], it creates fiduciary duties for directors for the benefit of creditors.").

6   *See generally* Jared A. Ellias & Robert J. Stark, *Bankruptcy Hardball*, 108 CALIF. L. REV. 745 (2020).

7   *See id.*

8   *See, e.g.*, Norwood P. Beveridge, Jr., *Does a Corporation's Board of Directors Owe a Fiduciary Duty to Its Creditors?*, 25 ST. MARY'S L. J. 589, 594 (1994) ("The idea of a director's fiduciary duty which runs directly to corporate creditors, as opposed to a director's fiduciary duty to the corporation which can be enforced indirectly by creditors under certain circumstances, can be traced to the 'trust fund doctrine.'").

9   Wood v. Dummer, 30 F. Cas. 435, 436 (C.C.D. Me. 1824); *see also* Hollins v. Brierfield Coal & Iron Co., 150 U.S. 371, 383 (1893) (insolvency has the effect of placing corporate assets "in a condition of trust, first for the creditors, and then for the stockholders"); MacKenzie Oil Co. v. Omar Oil & Gas Co., 120 A. 852, 857 (Del. Ch. 1923) (upon insolvency, creditors "have the right to regard the corporate assets as being impressed with a new nature, something in the nature of a trust").

10 *See* Bovay v. H.M. Byllesby & Co., 38 A.2d 808, 813 (Del. 1944) ("An insolvent corporation is civilly dead in the sense that its property may be administered in equity as a trust for the benefit of creditors. The fact which creates the trust is the insolvency, and when that fact is established, the trust arises, and the legality of the acts thereafter performed will be decided by very different principles than in the case of solvency.").

nature of a director's duty shifts, from protecting the interests of shareholders to preserving existing asset value for the benefit of creditors.[11] Insolvency, thus, requires management to oversee corporate assets with conservatism (as a trustee might), in a manner that is cognizant (if not deferential) to creditor interests.

The trust fund doctrine originated with a desire to remedy a common mischief: corporate managers or shareholders hiding assets from creditors.[12] Historically, the trust fund doctrine was brought to bear to allow creditors to recover property that had been distributed to the shareholders of either a dissolved corporation or an insolvent corporation.[13] Under the common law, a corporation's dissolution ended its existence as a legal entity, thus abating all pending actions by and against it and terminating its capacity to sue or be sued.[14] Against this harsh rule, the trust fund doctrine arose, in part, to give creditors some protection in the event of a corporate dissolution.[15] Essentially, the trust fund doctrine gave creditors an equitable right to follow corporate assets after dissolution, with the assets held in a trust in which the creditors have a claim superior to that of the shareholders.[16] In the event of dissolution, the trust fund theory imposed a constructive trust or equitable lien upon corporate assets to guarantee the absolute priority of payment to creditors before any distribution to stockholders.[17]

A Nineteenth-Century: Rise of the Trust Fund Doctrine in Equity Jurisprudence.

As a testament to Justice Story's legal stature, the trust fund doctrine quickly rose from a novel equitable theory to adoption by the United States Supreme Court.[18] Ten years after *Wood v. Dummer*, Justice Story, now sitting as a United States Supreme Court Justice, applied the trust fund doctrine in *Mumma v. Potomac Company*.[19] In *Mumma*, the plaintiff was an unsatisfied judgment creditor of the Potomac Company.[20] The charter of the Potomac Company had been annulled by surrender to the Chesapeake and Ohio Canal Company under state legislation.[21] When the old company's assets were transferred to the new company, the plaintiff complained that the legislation impaired the obligation of the contracts of the old company by depriving the

---

[11] Gregory V. Varollo & Jesse A. Finkelstein, *Fiduciary Obligations of Directors of the Financially Troubled Company*, 48 Bus. Law. 239, 244 (1992). One variation of this theme appears to recognize that once a company becomes insolvent, directors continue to owe duties to shareholders, while duties to creditors also arise. *See, e.g.*, Hollins v. Brierfield Coal & Iron Co., 150 U.S. 371 (1893).

[12] Today, these situations are often dealt with through fraudulent transfer law or bankruptcy law.

[13] Edwin S. Hunt, *The Trust Fund Theory and Some Substitutes for It*, 12 Yale L. J. 63, 64 (1902).

[14] In re Citadel Indus., Inc., 423 A.2d 500, 503 (Del. Ch. 1980).

[15] In re RegO Co., 623 A.2d 92, 95 (Del. Ch. 1992).

[16] *Id.* (citations omitted).

[17] Ann E. Conaway Stilson, *Reexamining the Fiduciary Paradigm at Corporate Insolvency and Dissolution: Defining Directors' Duties to Creditors*, 20 Del. J. Corp. L. 1, 77 (1995); *see also* Varollo & Finkelstein, *supra* note 11at 244. Where strictly applied, the trust fund doctrine holds that upon insolvency, directors no longer owe a duty to stockholders, who no longer have a viable economic interest in the entity; instead, directors owe their duty to creditors. *Id.*

[18] Justice Story also legitimized the trust fund theory's place in equity jurisprudence in his celebrated treatise on the subject. *See* 2 Joseph Story, Commentaries on Equity Jurisprudence, As Administered In England and America § 1252 (1877) ("Perhaps, to this same head of Implied Trusts upon presumed intention (although it might equally well be deemed to fall under the head of Constructive Trusts by Operation of law), we may refer that class of cases where the stock and other property of private corporations is deemed a trust fund for the payment of the debts of the corporation; so that the creditors have a lien or right of priority of payment on it, in preference to any of the stockholders in the corporation."); *see also* Fletcher's Cyclopedia of the Law of Private Corporations § 7369 (perm. ed., rev. vol. 1981).

[19] 33 U.S. 281 (1834); Beveridge, Jr., *supra*, note 8.

[20] *Mumma*, 33 U.S. at 284.

[21] *Id.* at 285.

company of assets.[22] In considering the legislation's constitutionality, the Court applied the trust fund doctrine and held that there was no impairment of obligations because creditors could still pursue the assets of the old company in the hands of the new company.[23]

In a period that would come to represent the trust fund doctrine's zenith, a series of subsequent nineteenth-century Supreme Court opinions not only affirmed the doctrine but expanded its application.[24] In *Wood* v. *Drummer*, shareholder liability was limited to the amount of the corporation's capital stock; however, dicta in the 1853 Supreme Court case of *Curran* v. *Arkansas* suggested that all of the corporations' general assets are the subject of a trust fund for the benefit of creditors.[25] The Court's opinion seemingly implies that the fact of insolvency is not the triggering event for the creation of the trust. Rather, the trust fund arises at the corporation's inception and embraces not only paid-in capital but all of the corporation's assets.[26]

In *Sawyer* v. *Hoag*, the Supreme Court again broadened the applicability of the trust fund doctrine to include unpaid subscriptions to capital stock.[27] There, the defendant was an insurance company operating under a special charter and with a required capital stock of $100,000, only $10,000 of which had been paid-in.[28] As soon as the company became insolvent, and this fact became known to the appellant, the right of setoff for an ordinary debt to its full amount terminated.[29] Moreover, it became a fund belonging equally in equity to all the creditors, and could not be appropriated by the debtor to the exclusive payment of his own claim.[30] Just two years after *Sawyer*, the Supreme Court again affirmed the trust fund doctrine's applicability to unpaid stock.[31]

Writing in 1904, Edwin S. Hunt, a lawyer and instructor at Yale Law School, described the trust fund doctrine as most commonly invoked in three situations:

1. Where the property of a corporation has been divided among its stockholders without paying creditors.
2. Where an insolvent corporation has preferred a creditor.
3. Where it is sought to recover unpaid or partially paid subscriptions to capital stock.[32]

Creditors today would mostly seek to address these situations with fraudulent transfer law or bankruptcy law, but the trust fund doctrine was once used by creditor's lawyers to fashion a comparable remedy under corporate law.

In at least one outlying decision, the trust fund doctrine was used in a way that resembles modern fiduciary duty analysis and to force directors and officers of an insolvent firm to pay damages for failing to maximize value.[33] In a 1953 case, *New York Credit Men's Adjustment Bureau* v. *Weiss*, the New York Court of Appeals heard a claim from a bankruptcy trustee representing the

---

22   *Id.* at 284–85.
23   *Id.* at 286 ("[T]he obligation of those contracts survives; and the creditors may enforce their claims against any property belonging to the corporation, which has not passed into the hands of bona fide purchasers; but is still held in trust for the company, or for the stockholders thereof, at the time of its dissolution, in any mode permitted by the local laws.").
24   *See* Sanger v. Upton, 91 U.S. 56, 60 (1875); Sawyer v. Hoag, 84 U.S. 610 (1873); Curran v. Arkansas, 56 U.S. 304 (1853).
25   56 U.S. 304 (1853).
26   *Id.* at 307.
27   Sawyer v. Hoag, 84 U.S. 610 (1873). *See also* Upton v. Tribilcock, 91 U.S. 45, 47–48 (1875) (stating that stockholder's obligation to pay a subscription cannot be released by the corporation).
28   *Id.* at 622.
29   *Id.*
30   *Id.*
31   Sanger v. Upton, 91 U.S. 56, 60 (1875) ("The capital stock of an incorporated company is a fund set apart for the payment of its debts.... The creditors have a lien upon it in equity.").
32   *See* Hunt, *supra* note 13 at 69.
33   *See* New York Credit Men's Adjustment Bureau v. Weiss, 110 N.E.2d 397 (N.Y. 1953).

creditors of a wholesaler of electric supplies.[34] The trustee charged that the creditors had been wronged by decisions that the officers and directors made in deciding how to liquidate the firm's assets.[35] After deciding the firm could not remain in business, the firm's directors and officers conducted a public auction sale properly noticed to the public, which resulted in a disappointing sale price that did not fully cover the debts owed to creditors.[36] The trustee's theory was, essentially, that the officers and directors could have done something different, like sell the assets in bankruptcy or enter into an assignment for the benefit of creditors.[37] Writing for the majority, Judge Conway began by citing the seminal fiduciary duty case of *Meinhard* v. *Salmon* and then describing the directors and officers of an insolvent firm as being, in effect, trustees for creditors who can be forced to pay damages if they failed to maximize the value of the corporate assets.[38] In this case, the majority held, the assets could have been sold for more money through different transactions, and the directors and officers would need to pay damages.[39]

Writing in dissent, Judge Desmond argued that this legal theory—liability for directors and officers to creditors for failing to maximize value, without any allegation of fraud, self-dealing or bad faith—was unheard of in New York law.[40] Judge Desmond reviewed the facts and suggested that, at worst, the directors and officers had made a bad business decision, which should be protected under the business judgment rule.[41] He suggested that the theory most resembled a corporate law waste claim, but waste requires a showing of bad faith, and there was none in this case.[42] He closed by arguing that the trust fund doctrine simply means that creditors have priority over shareholders and therefore that this "much debated theory" has "nothing whatever to do with this case."[43]

B *The Slow Decline of the Trust Fund Doctrine*

While the trust fund doctrine firmly established itself in equity jurisprudence over the nineteenth century,[44] its influence began to recede around the turn of the twentieth century, including in Delaware courts. Furthermore, the enactment of corporate wind-down

---

[34] *See id.* at 398.

[35] *See id.*

[36] *See id.* at 398–99.

[37] *See id.* at 398.

[38] Judge Conway wrote:

We have had occasion to point out the nature of the obligation resting upon fiduciaries which is applicable to those, such as defendants, who are, in effect, trustees. Meinhard v. Salmon, 249 N.Y. 458, 464, 164 N.E. 545, 546, 62 A.L.R. 1. There we said: "Uncompromising rigidity has been the attitude of courts of equity when petitioned to undermine the rule of undivided loyalty by the 'disintegrating erosion' of particular exceptions. Wendt v. Fischer, 243 N.Y. 439, 444, 154 N.E. 303 (304)." We have also pointed out that "questions of bad faith as matters of fact" may be absent from a case and yet "breaches of duty as matters of law" may be present. Matter of Ryan's Will, 291 N.Y. 376, 386, 52 N.E.2d 909, 912. Quasi trustees must be held to accountability for the performance of obligations thrust upon them by circumstances. The safety and protection of the trust res is of primary significance. If the assets the trust fund for the creditors were actually improvidently wasted or depleted as a result of defendants' unilateral action the plaintiff is entitled to recover the amount of the loss thus sustained. If, on the other hand, the assets were not thus wasted or depleted the defendants are not liable. Defendants are not to be cast in judgment solely because they neglected to give creditors notice of the sale.

New York Credit Men's Adjustment Bureau v. Weiss, 110 N.E.2d 397, 399–400 (N.Y. 1953).

[39] *See id.* at 400.

[40] *See id.*

[41] *See id.* at 401 ("At very worst, they were guilty of an error of judgment, but for that the law provides no punishment or remedy").

[42] *See id.*

[43] *See id.* at 401–02.

[44] *See* JOHN POMEROY, EQUITY JURISPRUDENCE: A TREATISE ON EQUITY JURISPRUDENCE, AS ADMINISTERED IN THE UNITED STATES OF AMERICA; ADAPTED FOR ALL THE STATES, AND TO THE UNION OF LEGAL AND EQUITABLE REMEDIES UNDER THE REFORMED PROCEDURE § 1046 (4th ed. 1918).

legislation[45] over the twentieth century provided statutory redress that was nonexistent under the common law abatement regime, thus abrogating much applicability of the trust fund theory.[46] As Judge Learned Hand observed in a 1928 opinion, however, the trust fund doctrine "was a hardy weed and would not die at the first uprooting."[47] Other courts writing in the early 1900s were more direct in their criticism: "The [trust fund doctrine] has been repudiated as a fiction unsound in principle and vexing in business practice."[48] As these statements convey, the trust fund doctrine spurred much controversy in this period.[49]

The reining in of the trust fund doctrine began in earnest when the Supreme Court issued its ruling in *Hollins* v. *Brierfield Coal & Iron Co.*[50] The *Hollins* court posited that the "trust" was one which attached "after possession [of the assets] by a court of equity"; in other words, after the commencement of insolvency proceedings under applicable law.[51] Relying on *Hollins*, in 1923, a Delaware Supreme Court decision considered how the enactment of a statute granting stockholders or creditors the right upon insolvency to seek the appointment of a receiver impacted the trust fund doctrine.[52] In *MacKenzie Oil Co.* v. *Omar Oil & Gas Co.*, the Delaware Supreme Court concluded that insolvency alone "can have no effect as impressing upon corporate assets a trust which creditors may appeal to equity to take cognizance of and administer for their benefit."[53]

---

[45]   See, e.g., DEL. CODE ANN. tit. 8, § 278 (2020) ("All corporations, whether they expire by their own limitation or are otherwise dissolved, shall nevertheless be continued, for the term of 3 years from such expiration or dissolution or for such longer period as the Court of Chancery shall in its discretion direct, bodies corporate for the purpose of prosecuting and defending suits, whether civil, criminal or administrative, by or against them, and of enabling them gradually to settle and close their business, to dispose of and convey their property, to discharge their liabilities and to distribute to their stockholders any remaining assets, but not for the purpose of continuing the business for which the corporation was organized. With respect to any action, suit or proceeding begun by or against the corporation either prior to or within 3 years after the date of its expiration or dissolution, the action shall not abate by reason of the dissolution of the corporation; the corporation shall, solely for the purpose of such action, suit or proceeding, be continued as a body corporate beyond the 3-year period and until any judgments, orders or decrees therein shall be fully executed, without the necessity for any special direction to that effect by the Court of Chancery.").

[46]   See, e.g., Marsh v. Rosenbloom, 499 F.3d 165, 172 (2d Cir. 2007); Reconstruction Fin. Corp. v. Teter, 117 F.2d 716 (7th Cir. 1941) (refusing to apply trust fund theory to tort claim arising after the corporate defendant's dissolution and expiration of the statutory survival period post-dissolution); Green v. Oilwell, 767 P.2d 1348, 1353 (Okla. 1989); Pacific Scene, Inc. v. Penasquitos, Inc., 758 P.2d 1182, 1185 (Cal. 1988); Blankenship v. Demmler Mfg. Co., 411 N.E.2d 1153 (Ill. App. Ct. 1980); Gonzales v. Progressive Tool & Die Co., 463 F.Supp. 117, 119 (E.D.N.Y. 1979) (disallowing action against the corporation when a claim for injury accrued after distribution of corporation's assets was made).

[47]   Wood v. Nat'l City Bank, 24 F.2d 661, 662 (2d Cir. 1928).

[48]   Reif v. Equitable Life Assur. Soc'y of U.S., 197 N.E. 278, 280 (N.Y. 1935). Note that New York Credit Men's Adjustment Bureau, *supra* note 34, was decided in 1953, demonstrating the unevenness of the trust fund doctrine's trajectory. A full chronicle of the trust fund doctrine is outside the scope of this Chapter, which focuses on the doctrine's rise and falls within Delaware law. As discussed *infra* in note 68, the trust fund doctrine remains at least arguably alive and well in some jurisdictions.

[49]   See American Nat'l Bank of Austin v. MortgageAmerica, (In re MortgageAmerica), 714 F.2d 1266, 1268–69 (5th Cir. 1983) ("Although 'corporate trust fund' doctrine is the theory that has been the most thoroughly studied by both courts and commentators, it is nonetheless often poorly understood ... [S]ince [its creation, it] has become such a source of confusion that a leading commentator has introduced his forty-page treatment of the subject with the warning that 'perhaps no concept has created as much confusion in the field of corporate law as has the "trust fund doctrine."'") (*citing* FLETCHER'S CYCLOPEDIA OF THE LAW OF PRIVATE CORPORATIONS § 7369 (perm. ed., rev. vol. 1981)); *see also* Beveridge, Jr., *supra* note 8, at 594.

[50]   150 U.S. 371, 382 (1893).

[51]   Id. at 383, 385 ("The officers of a corporation act in a fiduciary capacity in respect to its property in their hands and may be called to an account for fraud or sometimes even mere mismanagement in respect thereto; but as between itself and its creditors the corporation is simply a debtor, and does not hold its property in trust, or subject to a lien in their favor, in any other sense than does an individual debtor.... Neither the insolvency the corporation, nor the execution of an illegal trust deed, nor the failure to collect in full all stock subscriptions, nor all together, gave to these simple contract creditors any lien upon the property of the corporation, nor charged any direct trust thereon.").

[52]   120 A. 852 (Del. Ch. 1923).

[53]   Id. at 857–59.

A subsequent Delaware Chancery Court ruling limited the trust fund doctrine in a second significant manner.[54] In *Asmussen v. Quaker City Corp*, the court refused to hold corporate directors personally liable under the trust fund theory for preferring some creditors over others, stating that the creditor of an insolvent or dissolved corporation has an adequate statutory remedy in seeking the appointment of a receiver.[55] The court stated that it is the commencement of equitable proceedings that creates the trust fund.[56] Significantly, the court concluded that the "trust fund" was not a rule preventing directors of insolvent corporations from treating some creditors more favorably than other creditors:

> While the trust fund doctrine is supported by the overwhelming weight of authority in cases where the conflict is between creditors on the one hand and stockholders on the other, and also in cases where the corporate assets have been drawn within the administrative power of courts or statutory agencies for liquidation and distribution, yet the weight of authority favors the view that as among creditors, no trust exists which prevents the directors of an insolvent corporation from preferring some over others, notwithstanding the corporation is in failing circumstances and manifestly headed for disaster.[57]

While the court acknowledged that "all courts recognize a trust fund doctrine of some sort," the difficulty was in defining the limits of the concept that corporate assets are a trust fund for the benefit of creditors upon insolvency.[58] The *Asmussen* court departed from other courts that had interpreted the doctrine to hold directors of an insolvent corporation personally responsible for breach of trust, commenting that "some courts have been unable to extricate themselves from the logic of the rule."[59] Finally, in language clearly showing disdain for a liberal application of the doctrine, the court wrote that "the risks of liability on the part of honest directors, which inhere in the contentions of the complainant if they be accepted, are so great and hazardous, that I think the courts should not subject them to it by so carrying to its extreme length the logic of a catchy phrase."[60]

Just three years later, following *Asmussen*, the Delaware Chancery Court again entertained the applicability of the trust fund doctrine in *Pennsylvania Co. for Insurances v. South Broad Street Theatre Co.*[61] There, the court concluded that the directors and others in a position of control over an insolvent corporation could not prefer their own claims as creditors over the claims of outside creditors.[62] The court, declining an opportunity to rest its ruling on the trust fund doctrine, instead reasoned that the prohibition against insiders favoring themselves after insolvency was founded upon "common honesty."[63] The court's remarks in dicta stopped just short of characterizing the doctrine as completely superfluous: "Yet [the trust fund doctrine] if traced to its source appears to be nothing more than a particular expression of the fundamental principle which good morals exact, that men should act in honesty and fairness."[64]

---

[54]   156 A. 180 (Del. Ch. 1931).
[55]   *Id.* at 182.
[56]   *Id.*
[57]   *Id.*
[58]   *Id.* at 181.
[59]   *Id.*
[60]   *Id.* at 182.
[61]   174 A. 112 (Del. Ch. 1934).
[62]   *Id.*
[63]   *Id.* at 116 (*quoting* Stuart v. Larson, 298 F. 223, 227 (8th Cir. 1924)).
[64]   *Id.*

Over time, the trust fund theory continued to wane.[65] By the mid-twentieth century, scholarly critique of the trust fund doctrine ballooned.[66] Courts marginalized the doctrine, dismissing lawsuits that claimed waste arising from decisions of clear business rationality or when business necessity required management to choose among competing creditor interests. Eventually, Delaware courts superseded the doctrine altogether, holding that the "business judgment" rule applies to disinterested management decision-making, even when a company is in distress or insolvent.[67] The final blow to the trust fund doctrine in Delaware was dealt in a 2015 Delaware Chancery Court opinion—*Quadrant Structured Products* (discussed *infra*)—thereby eradicating it from the equitable arsenal once accessible to creditors to hold directors and officers accountable.[68]

iii SHIFTING OF FIDUCIARY DUTIES: ZONE OF INSOLVENCY AND DEEPENING INSOLVENCY

Toward the end of the twentieth century, as the trust fund doctrine's viability was fading fast, a "duty shifting" framework began to emerge in Delaware.[69] A central tenant of corporate law

---

[65] *See, e.g., id.*; Bovay v. H. M. Byllesby & Co., 38 A.2d 808, 813 (Del. 1944).

[66] FLETCHER, *supra* note 18, § 7369; 2 GARRARD GLENN, FRAUDULENT CONVEYANCES AND PREFERENCES § 596 (rev. ed. 1940); ROBERT S. STEVENS, CORPORATIONS § 185 (1936); James R. Ellis & Charles L. Sayre, *Trust-Fund Doctrine Revisited — Part I*, 24 WASH. L. REV. & ST. B. J. 44 (1949) (citing HENRY W. BALLANTINE, BALLANTINE ON CORPORATIONS 348, 349 (rev. ed. 1946)); Hunt, *supra* note 13 at 64 ("There would perhaps be little reason to object to calling the property of a corporation a trust fund for the benefit of its creditors, if all that the phrase meant was, that a corporation must pay its debts before dividing its assets among its stockholders. But the trouble is that the 'trust fund theory' thus originated has not been confined to the case to which Judge Story first applied it"); Pomeroy, *supra* note 44; George W. Wickersham, *The Capital of a Corporation*, 22 HARV. L. REV. 319 (1909); Hyman Zettler, *The Trust Fund Theory: A Study in Psychology*, 1 WASH. L. REV. 81 (1925).

[67] *See, e.g.*, In re Hechinger Inv. Co. of Delaware, 327 B.R. 537, 548–49 (D. Del. 2005) (holding that business judgment rule applies respecting management decisions made when the debtor was "in the vicinity of insolvency"); Prod. Res. Group, L.L.C. v. NCT Group, Inc., 863 A.2d 772, 788 n.53 (Del. Ch. 2004) ("[T]he business judgment rule remains important and provides directors with the ability to make a range of good faith, prudent judgments about the risks they should undertake on behalf of troubled firms.").

[68] Despite Delaware courts' shift away, the trust fund doctrine remains a viable theory in a sizeable number of jurisdictions. *See, e.g.*, Ed Peters Jewelry Co., Inc. v. C & J Jewelry Co., Inc., 124 F.3d 252 (1st Cir. 1997) ("[T]he value of the shareholders' investment in an insolvent company is negligible, and the corporation's directors thereafter become trustees of 'the creditors to whom the [company's] property . . . must go.'") (quoting Olney v. Conanicut Land Co., 16 R.I. 597, 599, 18 A. 181 (1889) (emphasis added)); Askanase v. Fatjo, 130 F.3d 657, 663 (5th Cir. 1997) ("[The trust fund doctrine . . . prohibits an insolvent corporation from paying money or distributing assets to its directors in preference to creditors."); *see also* Alexander v. Hillman, 296 U.S. 222 (1935); Unsecured Creditors' Comm. v. Noyes (In re STN Enters.), 779 F.2d 901, 904–05 (2d Cir. 1985); American Nat'l Bank v. Mortgage Am. Corp. (In re Mortgage Am. Corp.), 714 F.2d 1266 (5th Cir. 1983); Federal Deposit Ins. Corp. v. Sea Pines Co., 692 F.2d 973 (4th Cir. 1982); Clarkson Co. Ltd. v. Shaheen, 660 F.2d 506, 512 (2d Cir. 1981); United States v. F. D. Rich Co., 437 F.2d 549 (9th Cir. 1970); Automatic Canteen Co. of America v. Wharton, 358 F.2d 587 (2d Cir. 1966); Snyder v. Nathan, 353 F.2d 3 (7th Cir. 1965); Stewart v. United States, 327 F.2d 201 (10th Cir. 1964); Davis v. Woolf, 147 F.2d 629, 633 (4th Cir. 1945); King v. Coosa Valley Mineral Prod. Co., 283 Ala. 197 (1968); New York Credit Men's Adjustment Bureau, Inc. v. Weiss, 110 N.E.2d 397 (N.Y. 1953); Tatung Co., Ltd. v. Hsu, Case No. SA CV 13-1743-DOC (ANx), 2016 WL 3475328 (C.D. Ca. 2016) (citing Berg & Berg Enter., LLC v. Boyle, 100 Cal. Rptr. 3d 875, 893 (Cal. Ct. App. 2009)); Ass'n of Mill & Elevator Mut. Ins. Co. v. Barzen Int'l Inc., 553 N.W.2d 446 (Minn. Ct. App. 1996); Whitley v. Carolina Clinic, Inc., 455 S.E.2d 896 (N.C. Ct. App. 1995); Collie v. Becknell, 762 P.2d 727, 731 (Colo. App. 1988); Fagan v. La Gloria Oil & Gas, 494 S.W.2d 624, 628 (Tex. App. 1973); Zinn v. Bright, 87 Cal. Rptr. 736 (Cal. Ct. App. 1970); Plastic Contact Lens Co. v. Frontier of Northeast Inc., 324 F. Supp. 213 (W.D.N.Y. 1969); Wortham v. Lachman-Rose Co., 440 S.W.2d 351 (Tex. Civ. App. 1969); Drew v. United States, 367 F.2d 828 (Ct. Cl. 1968).

[69] *See* Bovay v. H.M. Byllesby & Co., 38 A.2d 808, 813 (Del. 1944) (describing an insolvent firm as property "administered in equity as a trust" for creditors); Production Resources Group LLC v. NCT Group Inc., 863 A.2d 772 (Del. Ch. 2004); Credit Lyonnais Bank Nederland N.V. v. Pathe Comm. Corp., No. Civ. A. No. 12150, 1991 WL 277613

dictates that officers and directors owe a fiduciary duty to the corporation and its shareholders.[70] In addition to serving shareholders, the fiduciary duties of corporate directors and managers are also articulated by reference to the best interests of the corporation.[71] A permutation of this principle instructs that when a corporation is insolvent or nearing insolvency, the duties of care and loyalty that normally run from directors to the corporation to benefit its shareholders shift to the corporation's creditors.[72] This marks a departure from standard operating corporate law: Directors do not generally owe fiduciary duties to creditors.[73]

While some scholars had always felt that fiduciary duty law ought to protect creditors, the leveraged buy-out boom and rise of junk bonds in the 1980s increased the urgency of the call for corporate law to do more to protect creditors.[74] Writing in the *Journal of Corporation Law* in 1988, Morey W. McDaniel, a finance lawyer in Kansas City, wrote:

> Fueled by enormous quantities of debt, the restructuring of corporate America shows no signs of running out of steam. It is a wrenching phenomenon. But we are witnessing far more than a reallocation of resources to their highest valued use. We also are witnessing a massive transfer of wealth from bondholders to stockholders, possibly the largest expropriation of investors in American business history. Leveraged takeovers, buyouts and recapitalizations are having a devastating impact on existing bondholders. Stockholders are getting rich in part at bondholder expense. Some call it the bondholder ripoff. Contractual, legal and market constraints have failed to prevent the exploitation of bondholders, and bondholder losses continue to mount.
>
> Bondholders urgently need a solution; a solution that is both fair and efficient. This Article proposes a two-part solution. First, courts should declare that directors have a fiduciary duty to deal fairly with all the investors in a corporation—bondholders as well as stockholders . . .[75]

Similarly, Professor Lawrence Mitchell argued that leaving bondholders to look solely to their contracts to protection left them with the "lowest common denominator" and urged judges to provide creditors with fiduciary duty protection.[76]

Perhaps in response, the Delaware Chancery Court introduced a modified regime in 1991, known as the "zone of insolvency." The concept was first expressed in *Credit Lyonnais Bank Nederland, N.V.* v. *Pathe Communications, Corp.* as follows: "At least where a corporation is operating in the vicinity of insolvency, a board of directors is not merely the agent of the residue risk bearers [i.e., the shareholders], but owes its duty to the corporate enterprise."[77] Upon

---

(Del. Ch. Dec. 30, 1991); *see also* Marshall S. Huebner & Darren S. Klein, The Fiduciary Duties of Directors of Troubled Companies, AM. BANKR. INST. J. 18, 19 (2015).

[70] *See e.g.*, Arnold v. Soc'y for Sav. Bancorp, Inc., 678 A.2d 533, 539 (Del. 1996) ("Fiduciary duties are owed by the directors and officers to the corporation and its stockholders.").

[71] Rutheford B. Campbell & Christopher W. Frost, *Managers' Fiduciary Duties in Financially Distressed Corporations: Chaos in Delaware (and Elsewhere)*, 32 J. CORP. L. 491 (2007).

[72] Geyer v. Ingersoll Publications Co., 621 A.2d 784, 787-89 (Del. Ch. 1992).

[73] *See, e.g.*, United States v. Jolly, 102 F.3d 46, 48 (2d Cir. 1996); Simons v. Cogan, 549 A.2d 300, 304 (Del. 1988); Katz v. Oak Indus., Inc., 508 A.2d 873, 879 (Del. Ch. 1986).

[74] *See* Lawrence E. Mitchell, *The Fairness Rights of Corporate Bondholders*, 65 N.Y.U. L. REV. 1165, 1168 (1990) ("Recently, attempts have been made, tentatively in the courts and more strongly in the law reviews, to extend fiduciary rights to bondholders"). Important voices in this debate included, among others, Morey McDaniel and William Bratton. Writing in 1928, Adolf A. Berle argued that creditors should have the standing to ask judges for a remedy in the event of "credit manipulation" even if such manipulation was outside the scope of the debt contract. *See* Dalia T. Mitchell, *From Vulnerable to Sophisticated: The Changing Representation of Creditors in Business Reorganizations*, 16 N.Y.U. J.L. & BUS. 123, 140 (2019).

[75] Morey W. McDaniel, *Bondholders and Stockholders*, 13 J. CORP. L. 205, 206 (1988).

[76] *See generally* Mitchell, *supra* note 744. This call was hotly disputed by other scholars. *See, e.g.*, Beveridge, Jr., *supra* note 8.

[77] Credit Lyonnais Bank Nederland N.V. v. Pathe Comm. Corp., No. Civ. A. No. 12150, 1991 WL 277613 (Del. Ch. Dec. 30, 1991) at *34.

entering the zone of insolvency, the court provided, fiduciary duties are owed to the "community of interests" in the corporation rather than solely to shareholders.[78] This shift was necessary, given directors' incentives to put creditors' money at risk while looking out for shareholder interests.[79] In other words, directors must disregard conflicting incentives of various claimants and avoid promoting the interests of one group at the expense of another.[80]

In the year following *Credit Lyonnais*, another Chancery Court decision reaffirmed the duty-shifting framework providing creditors fiduciary duties when a corporation enters insolvency.[81] In *Geyer* v. *Ingersoll*, the Delaware Chancery Court held that fiduciary duties run to creditors during insolvency, but the court did not specify the nature of fiduciary duties owed to creditors nor did it decide whether creditors could sue when the company was in the "zone of insolvency."[82] Notwithstanding these loose ends, a short passage from the court's opinion demonstrates how settled it had then become that fiduciary duties shift to creditors in times of insolvency: "[N]either party seriously disputes that when the insolvency exception does arise, it creates fiduciary duties for directors for the benefit of creditors. Therefore, the issue the parties present to me is when do directors' fiduciary duties to creditors arise via insolvency."[83] The court cogently reasoned why the shift is necessary and self-evident:

> The existence of the fiduciary duties at the moment of insolvency may cause directors to choose a course of action that best serves the entire corporate enterprise rather than any single group interested in the corporation at a point in time when shareholders' wishes should not be the directors only concern. Furthermore, the existence of the duties at the moment of insolvency rather than the institution of statutory proceedings prevents creditors from having to prophesy when directors are entering into transactions that would render the entity insolvent and improperly prejudice creditors' interests.[84]

As articulated in *Credit Lyonnais* and *Geyer*, duty shifting constituted a coherent legal doctrine instituted to protect creditor interests during hazardous financial times.[85]

In addition to the zone of insolvency doctrine, a separate framework began emerging, known as the "deepening insolvency" doctrine. This doctrine created potential liability for corporate managers and third-parties responsible for the artificial extension of distress, resulting in a worsened financial situation for the company.[86] Under this theory, a creditor could bring

---

[78] *Id.* Even prior to Credit Lyonnais, courts generally agreed that the fiduciary duties of directors shifted from the corporation's stockholders to its creditors when the corporation was in fact insolvent. *See, e.g.,* Fed. Deposit Ins. Corp. v. Sea Pines Co., 692 F.2d 973, 976–77 (4th Cir. 1982); Clarkson Co. Ltd. v. Shaheen, 660 F.2d 506, 512 (2d Cir. 1981).

[79] Credit Lyonnais Bank Nederland, N.V. v. Pathe Comm., at *34 n.55.

[80] Myron M. Sheinfeld & Judy Harris Pippitt Sheinfeld & Pippitt, *Fiduciary Duties of Directors of a Corporation in the Vicinity of Insolvency and After Initiation of a Bankruptcy Case,* 60 BUS. LAW. 79, 88 (2004).

[81] Geyer v. Ingersoll Publications Co., 621 A.2d 784 (Del. Ch. 1992).

[82] *Id.* at 787–89, 791.

[83] *Id.* at 787.

[84] *Id.* at 789.

[85] *See, e.g.,* In re Kingston Square Assocs., 214 B.R. 713, 735 (Bankr. S.D.N.Y. 1997); In re Buckhead Am. Corp., 178 B.R. 956, 968 (Bankr. D. Del. 1994). *See generally* Sheinfeld & Pippitt, *supra* note 80 at 89. *See also* Frederick Tung, *Gap Filling in the Zone of Insolvency,* 1 J. BUS. & TECH. L. 607, 613 (2007) (stating that shifting the fiduciary duty to creditors upon insolvency is "fairly settled law in Delaware and other jurisdictions").

[86] Official Comm. of Unsecured Creditors v. R.F. Lafferty & Co., Inc., 267 F.3d 340 (3d Cir. 2001); In re Oakwood Homes Corp., 340 B.R. 510, 531 (Bankr. D. Del. 2006) (holding that Delaware, New York, and North Carolina courts would recognize deepening insolvency as a cause of action); In re LTV Steel Co., Inc., 333 B.R. 397, 422 (Bankr. N.D. Ohio 2005) (determining that deepening insolvency would be a valid cause of action under Delaware and New Jersey law). *See generally* Ronald R. Sussman & Benjamin H. Kleine, *What is Deepening Insolvency?,* 15 J. BANKR. L. & PRAC. 6 Art. 4 (2006) (summarizing the history of deepening insolvency as both a separate cause of action and a theory of damages).

a tort claim against officers and directors, as well as financing sources, for credit extensions that allowed continued operations and facilitated value deterioration and positioning for the new lender to assume ultimate ownership.[87] In 1991, the Delaware Courts first acknowledged that a cause of action for deepening insolvency might exist in the *Credit Lyonnais Bank* decision.[88] The predicate fact pattern for deepening insolvency cases is as follows: a corporation is nearing insolvency, officers and directors overly extend the corporation's life, and in doing so, take on further debt and decrease chances of recovery for creditors.[89] For example, in *In re Exide Technologies, Inc.*, a Delaware bankruptcy court held that deepening insolvency could be a legitimate cause of action where there was "damage to corporate property," as in cases where lenders pushed a corporation towards increased insolvency by issuing more debt.[90] Plaintiffs used the theory of deepening insolvency in a number of cases to show that management wrongfully ran the company into the ground, unnecessarily hurting creditors.[91]

This turn in the law quickly drew criticism from scholars, who viewed creditors as plenty capable of defending their interests through contract law and, thus, in no need of fiduciary duty protections.[92] And even if they were not, a framework based on "duty shifting" required identifying insolvency in real-time, while it was occurring, which seemed manifestly unfair.[93]

---

[87] *See, e.g.*, In re Exide Techs., Inc., 299 B.R. 732 (Bankr. D. Del. 2003).

[88] *See* Credit Lyonnais Bank Nederland N.V. v. Pathe Comm. Corp., No. Civ. A. No. 12150, 1991 WL 277613 (Del. Ch. Dec. 30, 1991). *See also* In re Inv'rs Funding Corp. of N.Y. Sec. Litig., 523 F. Supp. 533, 541–49 (S.D.N.Y. 1980) (an earlier decision in the Southern District of New York where a court first considered a claim that insiders in the failing company wrongfully extended the life of the company, holding that every act that prolongs a company's existence is not necessarily beneficial). *See also* Schacht v. Brown, 711 F.2d 1343, 1350 (7th Cir. 1983) (a bankruptcy case where the Seventh Circuit first used the phrase "deepening insolvency" in cases where management extended the life of a corporation to its detriment).

[89] *See* Sussman & Kleine, *supra* note 86 (summarizing the history of deepening insolvency as both a separate cause of action and a theory of damages).

[90] *See* In re Exide Techs., Inc., 299 B.R. 732, 752 (Bankr. D. Del. 2003) (an opinion that weighed whether Delaware state law supported an action for deepening insolvency). *See also* Ian T. Mahoney, *The CitX Decision: Has the Tort of "Deepening Insolvency" Gone Bankrupt?*, 52 VILL. L. REV. 995 (2007) (outlining the limitations of deepening insolvency cases within Third Circuit jurisprudence).

[91] *See* Official Comm. of Unsecured Creditors v. R.F. Lafferty & Co., Inc., 267 F.3d 340, 344 (3d Cir. 2001) (holding that Pennsylvania law would recognize "deepening insolvency" as a valid cause of action where a third party persuaded the corporation's shareholders to participate in a Ponzi scheme. However, the court held that the specific complaint was properly dismissed because the Committee of Creditors who brought suit was in pari delicto with the third parties it sued, meaning the defendants' wrongdoing imputed on the bankrupt corporation itself). *See also* In re Oakwood Homes Corp., 340 B.R. 510, 531 (Bankr. D. Del. 2006) (denying a motion to dismiss on a deepening insolvency claim, outlining the history of deepening insolvency and finding, as the choice of law was still unclear, that courts in Delaware, New York, and North Carolina would all recognize deepening insolvency as a cause of action); Buckley v. O'Hanlon, No. 04-955GMS, 2007 WL 956947, at *7 (D. Del. Mar. 28, 2007) (following the deepening insolvency standards in Lafferty, and denying a motion to dismiss on a deepening insolvency claim where defendants misrepresented the corporate creditworthiness, increased debt, and prolonged the corporate life); In re Inofin Inc., No. 11-11010-JNF, 2012 WL 5457415, at *29 (Bankr. D. Mass. Nov. 8, 2012) (reviewing different approaches to deepening insolvency since Lafferty and holding that it was too soon to tell whether Massachusetts would allow deepening insolvency, thus finding that granting a motion to dismiss was premature).

[92] *See* Ellias & Stark, *supra* note 6, notes 86–88 and accompanying text. *See also* Henry T. C. Hu & Jay Lawrence Westbrook, *Abolition of the Corporate Duty to Creditors*, 107 COLUM. L. REV. 1321, 1348 (2007)(stating that "duty shifting doctrines are flatly inconsistent with the long-held aspirations of the field of corporate governance and they preclude the use of analytical techniques made possible by modern finance"); Frederick Tung, *Gap Filling in the Zone of Insolvency*, 1 J. BUS. & TECH. L. 607, 608 (2007) (suggest[ing] "that at least for commercial creditors, fiduciary duties that include such creditors are unnecessary.")

[93] *See generally* Anil Hargovan & Timothy M. Todd, *Financial Twilight Re-Appraisal: Ending the Judicially Created Quagmire of Fiduciary Duties to Creditors*, 78 U. PITT. L. REV. 135 (2016). *See also* Alan Schwartz & Robert E. Scott, *Contract Theory and the Limits of Contract Law*, 113 YALE L. J. 541 (2003). The authors argued that commercial parties "want the state to enforce the contracts that they write, not the contracts that a decisionmaker with a concern for fairness would prefer them to have written." *Id.* at 618.

IV ELIMINATION OF DIRECT CLAIMS AGAINST OFFICERS
AND DIRECTORS: *GHEEWALLA*

Perhaps under the weight of this criticism, both the idea of "duty-shifting" in the "zone of insolvency" as well as "deepening insolvency" as a new tort theory were soon sent to join the "trust fund" doctrine in Delaware corporate law's dust bin. In *Trenwick v. Ernst & Young*, the Delaware Supreme Court eliminated deepening insolvency as a cause of action.[94] There, the court held that deepening insolvency was as baseless a complaint as "shallowing profitability," contrasting the doctrine of deepening insolvency with that of the business judgment rule.[95]

Likewise, the duty-shifting framework prescribed in *Credit Lyonnais* was diminished and ultimately extinguished as a legitimate cause of action in a series of subsequent Delaware court opinions. In *Production Resources Group*, although not dispositive to the case, the court noted that the zone of insolvency concept was "an admittedly confusing one, escaping easy definition."[96] Recognizing the "uncontroversial proposition" that a firm's directors are said to owe fiduciary duties to the company's creditors, the court narrowly applied *Credit Lyonnais* to mean that directors' duties did not change in the zone of insolvency but, rather, that directors had expanded discretion to consider creditors' interests in decision-making.[97] While the existence of such duties may have been "uncontroversial," the court qualified how creditors might enforce a breach of those duties. The court recognized that most such claims are likely to be derivative in nature, though it acknowledged there might be some circumstances in which "directors display such a marked degree of animus towards a particular creditor with a proven entitlement to payment that they expose themselves to a direct fiduciary duty claim by that creditor."[98]

In a 2007 opinion, the Delaware Supreme Court eliminated any notion of creditor rights' to bring direct fiduciary claims.[99] In *North American Catholic Educational Programming Found., Inc. v. Gheewalla*, the court held that the breach-of-fiduciary-duty count stated no claim because the defendant directors owed no duty to the plaintiff-creditors.[100] The court concluded, "[t]he creditors of a Delaware corporation that is either insolvent or in the zone of insolvency have no right, as a matter of law, to assert direct claims for breach of fiduciary duty against its directors."[101] The court reasoned that such a right would create uncertainty for directors who have a fiduciary duty to exercise their business judgment in the best interests of an insolvent corporation. As such, a direct right of action would create a conflict between the duty of the directors to "maximize the

---

94 *See* Trenwick Am. Litig. Trust v. Ernst & Young, L.L.P., 906 A.2d 168, 170–74 (Del. Ch. 2006) (echoing the reasoning of the Chancery Court that deepening insolvency was only a "catchy term" and not a legitimate cause of action). *See also* Hugh M. McDonald, Hugh M. Fishman, Todd S. Fisherman & Laura Martin, *Lafferty's Orphan: The Abandonment of Deepening Insolvency*, 26 AM. BANKR. INST. J. 1 (2008) (explaining the origins of deepening insolvency since the Lafferty decision and offering reasons the theory is a redundant cause of action); John Tully, *Plumbing the Depths of Corporate Litigation: Reforming the Deepening Insolvency Theory*, 2013 U. ILL. L. REV. 2087 (2013) (recapping the history of deepening insolvency across state laws and ultimately recommending that Illinois allow it as a valid cause of action).

95 *See* Trenwick, 906 A.2d at 205.

96 Prod. Res. Group, L.L.C. v. NCT Group, Inc., 863 A.2d 772, 787–88 (Del. Ch. 2004).

97 *Id.* at 790–91 (emphasis added) (citations omitted). *See* U.S. Bank Nat'l Ass'n v. U.S. Timberlands Klamath Falls, L. L.C., 864 A.2d 930, 947 (Del. Ch. 2004) (defendant admitted that fiduciary duties extend to creditor interests when a firm is insolvent but contested insolvency).

98 Prod. Res. Group, L.L.C. v. NCT Group, Inc., 863 A.2d 772, 798. *See also* Big Lots Stores v. Bain Capital Funds VII, 922 A.2d 1169 (Del. Ch. 2006); Bryan Anderson, *Gheewalla and Insolvency: Greater Certainty for Directors of Distressed Companies*, 11 U. PA. J. BUS. L. 1031, 1037 (2009).

99 N. Am. Catholic Educ. Programming Found., Inc. v. Gheewalla, 930 A.2d 92, 100 (Del. 2007).

100 *Id.* at 103. *See also* Sabin Willet, *Gheewalla and the Director's Dilemma*, 64 BUS. LAW. 1087, 1089 (2008).

101 Gheewalla, 930 A.2d at 103.

value of the insolvent corporation for the benefit of all of those having an interest in it, and the newly recognized direct fiduciary duty to individual creditors."[102] The court further noted that creditors, unlike shareholders, already have an arsenal of protections available to them, including contractual agreements, security instruments, the implied covenant of good faith and fair dealing, and fraudulent conveyance laws that "render the imposition of an additional, unique layer of protection through direct claims for breach of fiduciary duty unnecessary."[103] Thus, the *Gheewalla* court concluded that creditors might only assert a breach of fiduciary duty claims on a derivative basis.

The most recent iteration of the *Gheewalla* doctrine was articulated by the Delaware Chancery Court in *Quadrant Structured Products Co., Ltd. v. Vertin*:

> In light of *Gheewalla*, I do not believe it is accurate any longer to say that the directors of an insolvent corporation owe fiduciary duties to creditors. It remains true that insolvency "marks a shift in Delaware law," but "that shift does not refer to an actual shift of duties to creditors (duties do not shift to creditors). Instead, the shift refers primarily to standing: upon a corporation's insolvency, its creditors gain standing to bring derivative actions for breach of fiduciary duty, something they may not do if the corporation is solvent, even if it is in the zone of insolvency."[104]

If any uncertainty remained following *Gheewalla*, the *Quadrant* court endeavored to debunk any lasting myths about purported fiduciary duties owed to creditors: "After *Gheewalla* ... the following principles are true:

- There is no legally recognized zone of insolvency with implications for fiduciary duty claims.[105] The only transition point that affects fiduciary duty analysis is insolvency itself.[106]
- Regardless of whether a corporation is solvent or insolvent, creditors cannot bring direct claims for breach of fiduciary duty.[107] After a corporation becomes insolvent, creditors gain standing to assert claims derivatively for breach of fiduciary duty.
- The directors of an insolvent firm do not owe any particular duties to creditors.[108] They continue to owe fiduciary duties to the corporation for the benefit of all of its residual claimants, a category which now includes creditors.[109] They do not have a duty to shut down the insolvent firm and marshal its assets for distribution to creditors,[110] although they

---

[102]   *Id.*

[103]   *Id.* at 100.

[104]   Quadrant Structured Prod. Co. v. Vertin, 102 A.3d 155, 176 (Del. Ch. 2014) (*citing* Robert J. Stearn, Jr. and Cory D. Kandestin, *Delaware's Solvency Test: What Is It and Does It Make Sense? A Comparison of Solvency Tests Under the Bankruptcy Code and Delaware Law*, 36 Del. J. Corp. L. 165, 171 (2011)).

[105]   *Id.* (*citing Gheewalla*, 930 A.2d at 94 ("When a solvent corporation is navigating in the zone of insolvency, the focus for Delaware directors does not change: directors must continue to discharge their fiduciary duties to the corporation and its shareholders by exercising their business judgment in the best interests of the corporation for the benefit of its shareholder owners.")).

[106]   *Id.* (*citing Gheewalla*, 930 A.2d at 101 (rejecting the zone of insolvency because of the need for providing directors with definitive guidance)).

[107]   *Id.* (*citing Gheewalla*, 930 A.2d at 101).

[108]   *Id.* (*citing Gheewalla*, 930 A.2d at 103 (Recognizing that directors of an insolvent corporation owe direct fiduciary duties to creditors, would create uncertainty for directors who have a fiduciary duty to exercise their business judgment in the best interest of the insolvent corporation. To recognize a new right for creditors to bring direct fiduciary claims against those directors would create a conflict between those directors' duty to maximize the value of the insolvent corporation for the benefit of all having an interest in it, and the newly recognized direct fiduciary duty to individual creditors); *Shandler*, 2010 WL 2929654, at *14 (A plaintiff "cannot base his fiduciary duty claim on the premise that the board did not do what was best for a particular class of [the corporation's] creditors.").

[109]   *Id.* (*citing Prod. Res.*, 863 A.2d at 791; *Trenwick*, 906 A.2d at 174–75).

[110]   *Id.* (*citing Trenwick*, 906 A.2d at 195 n.75).

may make a business judgment that this is indeed the best route to maximize the firm's value.[111] ...

- When directors of an insolvent corporation make decisions that increase or decrease the value of the firm as a whole and affect providers of capital differently only due to their relative priority in the capital structure, directors do not face a conflict of interest simply because they own common stock or owe duties to large common stockholders. Just as in a solvent corporation, common stock ownership standing alone does not give rise to a conflict of interest. The business judgment rule protects decisions that affect participants in the capital structure in accordance with the priority of their claims."[112]

As *Quadrant* confirms, *Gheewalla* succeeded in turning on its head what was once an resilient principle of corporate law—that directors owed fiduciary duties to creditors during times of insolvency. While creditors may still bring derivative claims in prescribed scenarios, this remaining right represents scant consolation for the protections previously enjoyed under traditional equity jurisprudence, most notably under the trust fund doctrine.[113]

v CONCLUSION

As the brief survey in this chapter shows, American judges have always struggled over what protections, if any, creditors deserve under corporate law. Presumably, Delaware law will continue to evolve, perhaps returning to greater willingness to punish directors and officers who behave in a way that shocks the conscience. Without a doubt, the spate of court decisions since the Great Recession that scaled backed creditor protections that had existed in the law in one form or another since the 1800s has played an important role in emboldening some managers and shareholders to take aggressive actions that disadvantage creditors, as we have discussed elsewhere.[114] But the pendulum has swung before, and could again, and future judges may be tempted anew to return creditors to the warm embrace of fiduciary duty law, prompting a new round of scholarly and judicial debates that have gone back and forth for nearly all of American history.

---

[111]   *Id.* (*citing Prod. Res.*, 863 A.2d at 788).

[112]   *Id.* (*citing Shandler*, 2010 WL 2929652, at *14 (applying business judgment rule to decision by the board of insolvent entity and explaining that "[e]ven when [the entity] was insolvent, the board was entitled to exercise a good faith business judgment to continue to operate the business if it believed that was what would maximize [the entity's] value").

[113]   *See* Barry E. Adler & Marcel Kahan, *The Technology of Creditor Protection*, 161 U. Pa. L. Rev. 1773, 1786 (2013) ("Delaware law, including the provision of potential liability to creditors, thus imposes little risk of personal liability unless directors personally benefit from wrongdoing").

[114]   *See generally* Ellias & Stark, *supra* note 6.

12

The Independent Director in Delaware and German Corporate Law

Christoph Kumpan[*]

I INTRODUCTION

The Delaware courts have stressed the importance of independent directors in protecting the interests of shareholders by preserving the integrity of the corporate governance process. For example, transactions between the company and a self-interested director which, in principle, give rise to concerns that the director may face a conflict between his fiduciary duties to the company and his own interests will be considered less problematic if independent directors on the company's side approve the transaction.[1] Independent directors have a similarly important role if a shareholder wishes to bring a derivative suit against a director who has breached his or her duties.[2] In that situation, the shareholder has first to ask the board to pursue the claim. However, this demand will be excused if there is reasonable doubt as to whether a majority of the directors at the time when the complaint was filed could have considered the demand impartially (so-called demand futility). In order to avoid such a finding by the court, it is vital to have sufficient independent directors on the board. Hence, although the statutes in Delaware do not require independent directors, case law incentivizes and rewards the use of independent directors in various settings, including the approval of conflicted transactions and the dismissal of derivative suits.[3]

The role of independent directors is also of worldwide concern as institutional investors and proxy advisors, such as ISS[4] and Glass Lewis[5], demand non-U.S. companies to instate independent directors as well, because having independent directors is seen as an important aspect of good corporate governance. Even in Germany, where corporations have a completely different

[*]   The author is grateful to Arthur Laby and Jacob Russell for their helpful comments and kind support. He thanks the participants of the workshop for this volume for their inspiring ideas and thoughts, and Paul Corleis for his research assistance.

[1]   *See* Kahn v. M & F Worldwide Corp. 88 A.3d 635, 642 (Del. 2014).

[2]   *See, e.g.,* Aronson v. Lewis, 473 A.2d 805, 812 (Del. 1984).

[3]   Independent directors are, however, required by stock exchanges. *See, e.g.,* NASDAQ STOCK MARKET RULES § 5605(b)(1) (2020) (regarding a majority independent board).

[4]   Institutional Shareholder Services. Regarding the Voting Policies of ISS with regard to Europe see ISS, Continental Europe, Proxy Voting Guidelines, Benchmark Policy Recommendations (Jan. 21, 2020), https://www .issgovernance.com/file/policy/active/emea/Europe-Voting-Guidelines.pdf. For other guidelines, see ISS, Voting Policies (2020), https://www.issgovernance.com/policy-gateway/voting-policies.

[5]   Regarding the Policy Guidelines of Glass Lewis with regard to Germany, see Glass Lewis, 2020 Proxy Paper, Guidelines, An Overview of the Glass Lewis Approach to Proxy Advice, Germany (2020), https://www .glasslewis.com/wp-content/uploads/2016/12/Guidelines_Germany.pdf. For other guidelines, see Glass Lewis, Policy Guidelines (2020), https://www.glasslewis.com/guidelines/.

corporate structure, independent directors have been installed. In contrast to U.S. corporations with their one-tier board that combines management and control functions, German law separates those two functions and provides for a two-tier board, divided into a management board and a supervisory board. Hence, the demand of institutional investors and proxy advisors for independent directors contributes significantly to the growing convergence of corporate governance structures and the perception of what constitutes good corporate governance.

This paper will focus on the corporate law systems of Delaware and Germany. Delaware is the leading corporate law jurisdiction in the United States where many U.S. corporations have been incorporated. As one of the major European jurisdictions, Germany follows a vastly different structural approach to corporate law compared to Delaware. Both systems, however, converge with regard to the corporate structure. With the incentive to use independent directors, Delaware moves towards a stronger structural distinction between management and control. Germany, on the other hand, has introduced the concept of independent directors in addition to its already existing structural distinction between management and control.

This paper presents an overview of how the independence of directors is determined in Delaware and Germany and compares both approaches. The comparison shows that while the concept of the independent director is the same in both jurisdictions, it is implemented rather differently. From that comparison, the paper develops cautious suggestions regarding how to improve the approach in Delaware to ensure more legal certainty for the affected directors and shareholders, something the current approach is in dire need.

In the following, the paper will illustrate the problem of who can be considered independent in more detail (II). Then follows a short overview of recent case law in Delaware on independent directors with a primary focus on derivative suits where this issue is highly relevant (III). Subsequently, the German approach will be presented in comparison to Delaware (IV) and, finally, a few tentative conclusions will be drawn regarding the determination of independence in Delaware (V).

II THE CHALLENGE OF DEFINING INDEPENDENCE

A *Standardized vs. Case-by-Case Determination of Independence*

Given the significance of independent directors for good corporate governance, it appears particularly important to determine as clearly and unambiguously as possible when directors are independent and when they are not. However, determining when someone is considered to be independent can be done in very different ways. The approach in Delaware determines independence case-by-case (i.e. with regard to the concrete individual case) and is based on factors largely developed through case law, not statute. Such an approach raises significant problems as it undermines legal certainty. Under this approach, the persons concerned are unable to determine whether they meet the requirements for independence as it leaves the courts ample room for unpredictable decisions. A standardized or abstract approach, on the other hand, would ensure legal certainty, but would not show consideration for the individual cases. While, so far, Germany has followed a more standardized approach, recent amendments to the German Corporate Governance Code (GCGC)[6] have changed the legal approach in the direction of a more case-by-case determination as in Delaware. However, the approach has been implemented rather differently leaving, for example, the determination of independence to the

---

[6] For more on the GCGC, see section IV.B.

board itself while in Delaware, the courts decide whether a director is regarded as independent or not.

B *The Concept of Independence*

In general, independence means the absence of dependence,[7] that is the absence of or the freedom from restrictive ties. In the context of decision-making, independence, that is the freedom from restrictive ties, is regularly meant to ensure that the decision maker is impartial in decision-making[8] and can make decisions free from extraneous influences.[9] Accordingly, the requirement of independence serves to protect the decision-making process.[10]

Independence can be subdivided into internal and external independence.[11] Internal independence, "impartiality," or "unbiasedness," is a mental state of the person concerned in which that person considers only aspects relevant to the fulfillment of the task.[12] In contrast, external independence means the absence of legal, personal, and economic influences by third parties.[13] It is a necessary prerequisite for internal independence[14] for decision makers can only be completely unbiased if they are entirely indifferent to the result of their activities because the decision does not affect their present or future economic or personal circumstances.[15] If there is no external independence or the person concerned is not considered independent, this regularly leads to the conclusion that this person is not internally independent either and thus unable to make unbiased decisions.[16] Whoever appears independent does not give rise to concerns of being biased, and whoever is considered biased does not appear to be independent.

---

[7] Jean Nicolas Druey, *Unabhängigkeit als Gebot des allgemeinen Unternehmensrechts [Independence as a requirement of general company law], in* FESTSCHRIFT PETER DORALT ZUM 65. GEBURTSTAG, 151, 153 (Susanne Kalss, Christian Nowotny & Martin Schauer eds., 2004).

[8] Wibke Schramm, *Interessenkonflikte bei Wirtschaftsprüfern, Steuerberatern und Rechtsanwälten unter dem besonderen Aspekt der beruflichen Verschwiegenheit [Conflicts of interest of auditors, tax advisors and lawyers in consideration of professional secrecy] in* DEUTSCHES STEUERRECHT, 1364, 1367 (2003).

[9] *Cf.* Report of the Regierungskommission Corporate Governance, BUNDESTAGS-DRUCKSACHE 14/7515, 46; Professional Statute of Auditors (Berufssatzung für Wirtschaftsprüfer/vereidigte Buchprüfer (BS WP/vBP)) of 12 February 2010, 29 (Independence as freedom from ties that interfere or could interfere with the freedom of professional decision-making). *Cf.* KATHARINA OBERHOFER, DIE UNABHÄNGIGKEIT DES AUFSICHTSRATS [THE INDEPENDENCE OF THE SUPERVISORY BOARD] 79 (2008); Paul Davies, *Die Struktur der Unternehmensführung in Großbritannien und Deutschland: Konvergenz oder bestehende Divergenz? [The structure of corporate governance in Britain and Germany: convergence or existing divergence?], in* ZEITSCHRIFT FÜR UNTERNEHMENS- UND GESELLSCHAFTSRECHT, 268, 275 (2001).

[10] DRUEY, *supra* note 7, at 153.

[11] *Cf.* KATRIN MÜLLER, DIE UNABHÄNGIGKEIT DES ABSCHLUSSPRÜFERS, 23–24 (2006); OBERHOFER, *supra* note 9, at 86–87; Volker Röhricht, *Unabhängigkeit des Abschlussprüfers [Auditor Independence], in* WPG (DIE WIRTSCHAFTSPRÜFUNG) - SONDERHEFT, 80 (2001).

[12] Röhricht, *supra* note 11, at 80. *Cf.* MÜLLER, *supra* note 11, at 24; Holger Fleischer, *Das Doppelmandat des Abschlussprüfers – Grenzen der Vereinbarkeit von Abschlußprüfung und Steuerberatung [The auditor's dual mandate – the limits of the compatibility of audit and tax advice], in* DEUTSCHES STEUERRECHT, 758, 760 (1996); Christian Schwandtner, *Die Unabhängigkeit des Abschlussprüfers [Auditor Independence], in* DEUTSCHES STEUERRECHT, 323, 324 (2002). *See also* Commission Recommendation of 16 May 2002, *Statutory Auditors' Independence in the EU: A Set of Fundamental Principles*, O.J. L 191/22, Annex A, 1, Para 4 (p. 34); OBERHOFER, *supra* note 9, at 86; Röhricht, *supra* note 11, at 80.

[13] NICOLE D. DEMME, DIE UNABHÄNGIGKEIT DES ABSCHLUSSPRÜFERS NACH DEUTSCHEM, US-AMERIKANISCHEM UND INTERNATIONALEM RECHT [AUDITOR INDEPENDENCE UNDER GERMAN, U.S., AND INTERNATIONAL LAW] 37 (2003); ROLAND KITSCHLER, ABSCHLUSSPRÜFUNG, INTERESSENKONFLIKT UND REPUTATION [AUDIT, CONFLICT OF INTEREST AND REPUTATION], 28 (2005).

[14] Fleischer, *supra* note 12, at 760; Schwandtner, *supra* note 12, at 325.

[15] Röhricht, *supra* note 11, at 81.

[16] If external ties cannot be recognized, the person concerned may be externally independent, but can still be internally prejudiced or biased.

However, determining whether someone is internally independent is not easy. For example: Can a director be considered independent if he or she is a friend of the director who has potentially breached his or her fiduciary duties? Can a relative of a director be considered independent if there is no personal, emotional relationship with that director, meaning both are as emotionally distant from each other as they are from other directors to whom they are not related? What about existing business relationships between a director and a fellow director who might have breached his or her duty, or what about the joint pursuit of a charitable purpose?

In general, it is easier to determine whether someone is externally independent than whether someone is internally independent. Therefore, independence requirements are usually based on external independence. Thus, whether someone is independent is usually determined by searching for externally visible influences. In that respect, most legal approaches, such as those in Delaware and Germany, are very similar. At the same time, however, the two mentioned jurisdictions follow vastly different approaches when it comes to the details, not least because of their very different governance structures. Thus, the same idea is implemented very differently. Examining these different approaches is not only enlightening in itself, but it can also provide helpful insights for the other legal system. With regard to Delaware, the comparative perspective may help to make the mystical case-by-case approach in Delaware clearer and more predictable.

III THE LEGAL FRAMEWORK IN DELAWARE

According to the Delaware courts, the inquiry whether a director is independent examines whether "the director's decision is based entirely on the corporate merits of the transaction and is not influenced by personal or extraneous considerations."[17] Thus, "[i]ndependence means that a director's decision is based on the corporate merits of the subject before the board rather than extraneous considerations or influences."[18]

A *Beholdenness*

When determining whether directors are independent the courts in Delaware look into more subjective types of ties that can generate "a sense of 'beholdenness.'"[19] Accordingly, directors are not independent if they are "beholden" to the interested party, or subject to that party's influence in such a way that the director's "discretion would be sterilized."[20] Delaware courts examine the totality of the factual allegations in each situation to assess whether the business or personal relationships of a director "give rise to human motivations compromising the participants' ability to act impartially toward each other on a matter of material importance."[21] In other words, a director is not independent if his or her relationship to the interested party is "so close that one could infer that the non-interested director would be more willing to risk his or her reputation than risk the relationship with the interested director."[22]

---

[17] Cede & Co. v. Technicolor, Inc., 634 A.2d 345, 362 (Del. 1993).
[18] Aronson v. Lewis, 473 A.2d 805, 816 (Del. 1984).
[19] Usha Rodrigues, *The Fetishization of Independence*, 33 J. Corp. L. 447, 466 (2008). *See also* Rales v. Blasband, 634 A.2d 927, 936 (Del. 1993) ("beholden").
[20] *Rales*, 634 A.2d at 936; *see also* Beam ex rel. Martha Stewart Living Omnimedia, Inc. v. Stewart, 845 A.2d 1040, 1050 (Del. 2004); Robotti & Co. v. Liddell, No. 3128-VCN, 2010 WL 157474, at *12 (Del. Ch. Jan. 14, 2010).
[21] Sandys v. Pincus, 152 A.3d 124, 126 (Del. 2016).
[22] Robotti & Co. v. Liddell, No. 3128-VCN, 2010 WL 157474, at *12 (Del. Ch. Jan. 14, 2010).

That leads to a fact-intensive inquiry made on a transaction- or decision-specific basis.[23] Thus, a director may be independent with regard to one transaction or decision but lack independence with regard to another. Much of the case law in this area focuses on business relationships or other economic ties. But the courts have also stressed that noneconomic factors, such as close personal relationships, coinvestment in significant assets, or large philanthropic or charitable contributions, can influence human behavior and therefore must be considered when evaluating director independence.

B *Network of Business Relationships*

While financial ties can raise concerns regarding independence, according to the Delaware Supreme Court "the existence of some financial ties between the interested party and the director, without more, does not disqualify the director … ; the inquiry must be whether, applying a subjective standard, those ties were material, in the sense that the alleged ties could have affected the impartiality of the individual director."[24] Thus, limited financial ties to an interested party—which are not "material" to the director—are not enough to raise concerns about that director's independence.[25]

In *Greater Pennsylvania Carpenters' Fund v. Giancarlo*,[26] the Court of Chancery rejected challenges to the independence of three directors. It held that it was not sufficient that one director was a long-time partner of a venture capital firm that had coinvested in businesses with the interested party and another director had served as CEO of other businesses in which a venture capital firm had invested alongside the interested party. The reason was that the plaintiff did not show how such coinvestments were material to the directors. With regard to the third director, the court came to the same conclusion, despite allegations that the director was a partner in a private equity firm that invested in companies affiliated with the interested party because the affiliated companies did not provide continuous ongoing revenue, nor did they present an opportunity to profit from the transaction at issue for the private equity firm.

In contrast, in *Sandys v. Pincus*, the Delaware Supreme Court held that a network of business relationships between certain directors and the company's controlling stockholder raised reasonable doubts regarding the impartiality of those directors.[27] The court held that two outside directors were not independent, because they were partners of a venture capital firm that owned a 9.2 percent stake in the company of which they were directors and also had invested in a company cofounded by the interested director's wife and another company where an interested director was also a member of the board. The court found these connections were evidence of a "network" of "repeat players who cut each other into beneficial roles in various situations."[28] That created "human motivations" that "might have a material effect on the parties' ability to act adversely to each other."[29]

---

[23] *See, e.g., Beam*, 845 A.2d 1040.

[24] Kahn v. M & F Worldwide Corp., 88 A.3d 635, 636 (Del. 2014).

[25] *See* In re Gaylord Container Corp. S'holder Litig., 753 A.2d 462, 465 n.3 (Del. Ch. 2000) (no issue of fact concerning director's independence where director's law firm "has, over the years, done some work" for the company because plaintiffs did not provide evidence showing that the director "had a material financial interest" in the representation).

[26] Greater Pa. Carpenters' Fund v. Giancarlo, C.A. No. 9833-VCP (Del. Ch. Sept. 2, 2015) (Transcript), aff'd, No. 531, 2015 (Del. Mar. 11, 2016) (Order).

[27] 152 A.3d 124, 126 (Del. 2016).

[28] *Id.* at 134.

[29] *Id.*

C Personal Relationships

With regard to personal relationships, Delaware courts have held that in and of themselves they do not negate the independence of a director, but they do matter when evaluating director independence.[30] On the one side, in *Beam ex rel. Martha Stewart Living Omnimedia, Inc.* v. *Stewart*, the court rejected the view that directors were not independent because they "moved in the same social circles, attended the same weddings, developed business relationships before joining the board, and described each other as 'friends.'"[31] However, in *Delaware County Employees Retirement Fund* v. *Sanchez*, the court found that one director lacked independence because the director had been "close friends" with the interested party for fifty years, and the director and his brother's primary employment was with a company over which the interested party had substantial control.[32] According to the court, this went beyond "the kind of thin social-circle friendship" that the court has found to be insufficient to rebut the presumption of independence.[33] Hence, "[a] couple of rounds of golf a year is one thing, shared family vacations every year for a decade is quite another, because the friendship may be more in the nature of a familial one."[34] Therefore, it should not only be identified whether a personal relationship exists, but also be determined how "thick" the relationship is.

D Co-Ownership of a Significant Asset

Co-ownership of a unique asset with an interested director can be indicative of a close personal relationship. In *Sandys* v. *Pincus*, the court held that one of the outside directors could not be considered to be independent of the CEO because they co-owned a private airplane together.[35] Although the investment could not be regarded as material to either director, the co-ownership did reflect that the two directors enjoyed a significant personal relationship which compromised the independence of the director concerned. The court noted that an airplane "requires close cooperation in use, which is suggestive of detailed planning indicative of a continuing, close personal friendship."[36] That "signaled an extremely close, personal bond" that, "like family ties, one would expect to heavily influence a human's ability to exercise impartial judgment."[37] Hence, the court concluded, the director could not act independently.

In *Cumming* v. *Edens*, the Court of Chancery concluded that joining the ownership group—of which the interested director was a member—for a professional basketball team negated the independence of the director concerned.[38] The court noted that it was "a relatively small group of investors who would own a highly unique and personally rewarding asset" and that the director assisted in an effort to build a new arena for the team they co-owned.[39] Although the joint ownership would not necessarily require the two directors to work together on the management of the team, it was "revealing of a unique, close personal relationship."[40]

---

[30] Park Employees' & Ret. Bd. Employees' Annuity & Benefit Fund of Chicago on behalf of BioScrip, Inc. v. Smith, No. 1100-VCG, 2017 WL 1382597, at *10 (Del. Ch. Apr. 18, 2017) (citing *Sandys v. Pincus*, 152 A.3d 124 (Del. 2016)).
[31] Beam ex rel. Martha Stewart Living Omnimedia, Inc. v. Stewart, 845 A.2d 1040, 1051 (Del. 2004).
[32] Delaware Cty Emp. Ret. Fund v. Sanchez, 124 A.3d 1017, 1021, 1022 (Del. 2015).
[33] *Id.* at 1022.
[34] Leo E. Strine, Jr., *Documenting the Deal: How Quality Control and Candor Can Improve Boardroom Decision-Making and Reduce the Litigation Target Zone*, 70 Bus. Law. 679, 689 n.19 (2015).
[35] Sandys v. Pincus, 152 A.3d 124, 126 (Del. 2016).
[36] *Id.* at 130.
[37] *Id.*
[38] Cumming on behalf of New Senior Inv. Group, Inc. v. Edens, No. 13007-VCS, 2018 WL 992877 (Del. Ch. Feb. 20, 2018).
[39] *Id.* at 17.
[40] *Id.*

E *Philanthropic Contributions*

In *In re Oracle Corp. Derivative Litigation*, the court found that indirect ties, such as philanthropic contributions, could also affect director independence.[41] In *Cumming v. Edens*, the court found that a director was not independent because she received "substantial and clearly material director fees" from service on boards at the behest of the interested director and her primary employment was with a non-profit organization that received substantial support from the interested director's family.[42] On the other hand, in *In re J.P. Morgan*[43] the court found that contributions made by the affected company to a museum where the director in question was the president were not enough to negate the director's independence since it was not alleged that the contributions were important to the director, or whether they had affected the decision-making process.

F *Other Influences*

Moreover, the Delaware courts have had numerous other opportunities to deal with the determination of independence and have pointed to a variety of other relevant factors. For example, it was held that the compensation a director receives for serving as a director does not negate his or her independence, even if it is large compared to the director's other income.[44] The same has been held regarding certain dependencies, for example, when the defendant influenced or controlled the selection and retention of directors[45] or when the director was also a corporate officer and had to decide a matter involving a superior officer.[46] If one person dominates the board, that itself does not negate the independence of the other directors, according to the judges, unless the dominant director is directly interested in the transaction.[47] Past favors of the defendant, such as providing the director with lucrative contracts or compensation, are also regarded as not affecting a director's independence unless the director expects further favors in the future.[48] The same has been held with regard to longstanding business relations.[49] Finally, payments by the corporation to the director's relatives (e.g., monthly lease payments of $7,000) which do not represent a significant departure from fair market value do not affect the director's independence.[50]

---

[41] In re Oracle Corp. Derivative Litig., 824 A.2d 917 (Del. Ch. 2003).

[42] Cumming, 2018 WL 992877 at *14-15.

[43] In re J.P. Morgan Chase & Co. S'holder Litig., 906 A.2d 808 (Del. Ch. 2005).

[44] Cf. In re Walt Disney Co. Derivative Litig., 731 A.2d 342, 359–60 (Del. Ch. 1998), aff'd in part, rev'd in part sub nom., Brehm v. Eisner, 746 A.2d 244 (Del. 2000).

[45] Cf. Aronson v. Lewis, 473 A.2d 805, 816 (Del. 1984).

[46] In re Walt Disney, 731 A.2d at 356.

[47] Heineman v. Datapoint Corp., 611 A.2d 950, 955 (Del. 1992) ("There must be some alleged nexus between the domination and the resulting personal benefit to the controlling party."); In re MAXXAM, Inc., 659 A.2d 760, 773 (Del. Ch. 1995) ("To be considered independent a director must not be 'dominated or otherwise controlled by an individual or entity interested in the transaction.'").

[48] In re Walt Disney, 731 A.2d at 358.

[49] Orman v. Cullman, 794 A.2d 5, 27 (Del. Ch. 2002); see also Crescent/Mach I Partners, L.P. v. Turner, 846 A.2d 963, 980–81 (Del. Ch. 2000).

[50] Litt v. Wycoff, No. Civ. A. 19083-NC, 2003 WL 1794724, at *5 (Del. Ch. Mar. 28, 2003). The court found the evidence insufficient because plaintiffs did not show how close the family relationship was or whether the payments substantially exceeded the market rate or were "material" to the director or his relatives.

III COMPARISON OF THE GERMAN LEGAL ENVIRONMENT TO DELAWARE

A *Structural Differences Compared to Delaware*

With regard to the independence of directors, the situation in Germany is on the one hand, very different and on the other hand, quite similar to the one in Delaware. It is very different with regard to the general structure of the corporations and how independence is established, but similar concerning the relevance attached to the independence of directors as a means of good corporate governance. Moreover, the German approach to independence is more rules-based, while the standards of Delaware appear to be rather vague. In order to understand the relevance of independence of directors in Germany, it is important to understand that the corporate structure in Germany is rather different from the one in Delaware.

1 Two-Tier Board Structure

In contrast to Delaware corporations, which have a single-tier board, German stock corporations are required to have a two-tier board structure.[51] The two-tier board consists of a "management board" and a "supervisory board." This functional division is bolstered by the incompatibility principle that a person cannot be a member of both boards at the same time,[52] and a prohibition exists against the supervisory board assuming management tasks or giving instructions to the management board on how to carry out its duties.[53] While the management board is responsible for running the corporation's business, the supervisory board's main function is to control the management board. Controlling the management board means that the supervisory board examines its past decisions and accounting and bookkeeping, and monitors the corporate policy established by the management board. It thereby ensures that the management board complies with the law and the articles of association and does not engage in mismanagement and does not damage the company. In some instances, the articles of association or supervisory board resolution may stipulate that a measure taken by the management board or a transaction should be subject to the approval of the supervisory board.[54] However, apart from these special cases, the supervisory board may not become involved in managing the company and may not direct the management board on how it should carry out its management tasks.

In addition, the supervisory board assumes an advisory function, meaning it counsels the management board with regard to, for example, the corporate policy and how to avoid mismanagement. Moreover, the supervisory board appoints and dismisses the members of the management board.[55] The appointment is usually for a period of five years; dismissal by the supervisory board is possible only under special circumstances. This differs from the United States, where board members are usually appointed for one year, and election and dismissal are carried out directly by the shareholders. In Germany, shareholders play a relatively minor role in stock

---

[51] For a comparison, see Klaus J. Hopt & Patrick C. Leyens, *Board Models in Europe – Recent Developments of Internal Corporate Governance Structures in Germany, the United Kingdom, France, and Italy*, 1 ECFR 135 (2004). On the two-tier board, see also Klaus J. Hopt, *Law and Corporate Governance: Germany Within Europe*, 27 J. Appl. Corp. Fin. 8, 9–11 (2015). For an overview of the German corporate governance, see Hanno Merkt, *Germany – Internal and external corporate governance, in* Comparative Corporate Governance 521 (Andreas M. Fleckner & Klaus J. Hopt eds., 2013).

[52] § 105 AktG.

[53] § 111 (4) sent 1 AktG.

[54] § 111 (4) sent 2 AktG.

[55] Members of the management board are not elected by the shareholders. However, the shareholders elect the members of the supervisory board.

corporations, although that is slowly changing due to the growing influence of institutional shareholders and proxy advisors.

2 Independent Directors

Even though the functional division between the two boards in Germany solves a number of problems that independent directors in Delaware seek to resolve, Germany has followed the international trend towards independent directors. The concept of director independence has remained controversial in Germany, especially with regard to the relationship between board members and controlling shareholders. Since Germany has many family enterprises and groups of companies, strict independence requirements specified in terms of minimum percentages of independent board members are much more problematic than in countries with dispersed ownership such as the United States.[56]

Moreover, in a two-tier board system such as the one in Germany, independent directors are of less importance than in a one-tier system such as in the United States. In cases such as *Weinberger*[57] or *Unocal*,[58] independent directors were regarded as guardians of the interests of shareholders by preserving the integrity of the corporate governance process.[59] In the German two-tier board system, this task is carried out by the supervisory board. In order to ensure that supervisory board members fulfill their duty to protect the company's interests, the German Federal Court of Justice made it clear in its *ARAG/Garmenbeck*[60] decision that supervisory board members must enforce claims for damages to which the company is entitled against members of the management board who breached their duties and damaged the company.[61] Otherwise, the supervisory board members may be sued themselves for breaching their duty to monitor the management board and protect the interests of the company.

B *2019 GCGC Recommendations on Independence*

While the structure of corporations is regulated in the German Stock Corporation Act (Aktiengesetz or AktG), the recommendations on independence are found in the GCGC.[62] The GCGC plays a rather special role in German corporate law.[63] It complements the AktG, a federal statute and contains recommendations on the governance of listed corporations that reflect standards of good and responsible governance accepted in Germany and internationally.[64] Due to the statutory obligation to report annually on the compliance with or

---

[56] *See* Hopt, *Law and Corporate Governance, supra* note 51, at 8, 10.

[57] Weinberger v. UOP, Inc., 457 A.2d 701 (Del. 1983).

[58] Unocal Corp. v. Mesa Petroleum Co., 493 A.2d 946 (Del. 1985).

[59] Randy J. Holland, *Delaware Directors' Fiduciary Duties: The Focus on Loyalty*, 11 U. OF PA. J. BUS. L. 675, 685 (2009).

[60] Bundesgerichtshof [BGH] [Federal Court of Justice] April 21, 1997, NEUE JURISTISCHE WOCHENSCHRIFT [NJW] 1926 (1997).

[61] § 93 AktG. Only in exceptional cases may the supervisory board abstain from such a procedure, namely if it is required to protect the interests of the company.

[62] Only for a brief period did § 100 (5) AktG contain a provision requiring that one member of the supervisory board be independent and financially competent.

[63] The GCGC was drafted and is regularly reviewed by the Regierungskommission Deutscher Corporate Governance Kodex. The commission is a self-regulatory body of the industry financed by the industry and completely independent in its decisions. The government cannot instruct it as to what should or should not be included in the Code, and there are no government or political representatives in the commission.

[64] These standards are formulated as recommendations—from which listed companies may only depart when they disclose and explain their departure—and suggestions—from which corporations may depart without disclosure.

deviation from the recommendations (so-called comply-or-explain approach[65]), the recommendations have a considerable (practically) binding effect.

In 2019, the GCGC was substantially amended. Changes and additions include the formulation of general principles and the general explanatory notes preceding the preamble.[66] Significant changes have also been made with regard to the recommendations on the independence of supervisory board members.[67]

1 Objective of the Independence Requirement

In line with the monitoring function of the supervisory board, the independence requirement under the GCGC aims to ensure that members of the supervisory board effectively perform their monitoring duties in the interest of all stakeholders and without improper consideration of the persons to be monitored.[68] With regard to the supervisory board as a whole, this is done by limiting the number of supervisory board members who could be subject to a potential conflict of interest due to a loyalty or role conflict,[69] and by reserving certain positions—the chair of the supervisory board, the chair of the audit committee and the chair of the remuneration committee—for persons who are independent or lack independence only in a certain respect (meaning they are independent of the management board but not of the controlling shareholder).[70] This is intended to prevent potential conflicts of interest on an individual level and the board level. The independence requirement thus has a preventive effect, well before an actual conflict of interest arises.

2 Point of Reference for Independence: Company, Management Board, Controlling Shareholder

According to the GCGC, members of the supervisory board should be considered independent if they are independent of the company and its management board as well as of any controlling

---

[65] *See* § 161 AktG.

[66] For more changes see Klaus J. Hopt & Patrick C. Leyens, *Der Deutsche Corporate Governance Kodex 2020* [*The German Corporate Governance Code 2020*], ZEITSCHRIFT FÜR UNTERNEHMENS- UND GESELLSCHAFTSRECHT [ZGR] 929, 933 (2019).

[67] These recommendations can be found in C.6-C.12 GCGC and complemented by recommendation C.1 sentence 4 of the Code, according to which the corporate governance statement "shall also provide information about what the shareholder representatives on the Supervisory Board regard as the appropriate number of independent Supervisory Board members representing shareholders, and the names of these members." The recommendations on independent directors are restricted to the shareholder representatives; the Code thus avoids the dispute over the independence of employee representatives on the supervisory board which is a highly contested topic due to the German codetermination rules which require large firms (with 2,000 and more employees) to have half of the members of the supervisory board be employee representatives.

[68] Regierungskommission Deutscher Corporate Governance Kodex, Second Draft, 3 (22 May 2019). *See also* Michael Hoffmann-Becking, *Unabhängigkeit im Aufsichtsrat* [*Independence in the supervisory board*], in NEUE ZEITSCHRIFT FÜR GESELLSCHAFTSRECHT 801, 802 (2014); Kai Hasselbach & Janis Jakobs, *Die Unabhängigkeit von Aufsichtsratsmitgliedern* [*The independence of supervisory board members*], in BETRIEBS-BERATER 643 (2013); Thomas Kremer & Axel von Werder, *Unabhängigkeit von Aufsichtsratsmitgliedern: Konzept, Kriterien und Kandidateninformationen* [*Independence of Supervisory Board members: Concept, criteria and candidate information*], in DIE AKTIENGESELLSCHAFT 340, 341 (2013).

[69] Regierungskommission Deutscher Corporate Governance Kodex, Second Draft, 3 (22 May 2019); *cf.* Kremer & von Werder, *supra* note 68, at 340.

[70] Recommendation C.10 GCGC: "The Chair of the Supervisory Board, the Chair of the Audit Committee, as well as the Chair of the committee that addresses Management Board remuneration, shall be independent from the company and the Management Board. The Chair of the Audit Committee shall also be independent from the controlling shareholder."

shareholder.[71] The management board, its members and the "controlling shareholders" are the key players who are in a position to negatively influence the monitoring and advisory activities of the supervisory board. From the mention of the controlling shareholder, it also follows that an essential aspect of the independence requirement is the protection of minority shareholders.[72]

A COMPANY AND MANAGEMENT. A member of the supervisory board must be independent of the management board in order to be able to control it properly. In this context, independence means more than the separation of personnel between the two bodies.[73] It also excludes certain relationships between members of the supervisory board and the management board, if these relationships may endanger the independence of a supervisory board member. In view of this, the term "management board" as used in this context must be understood broadly in a sense that also includes the relationship to individual members of the management board. Hence, independence is required from the management board as a whole as well as from members of the management board individually.

The reference to the company must be seen in light of the fact that the management board manages the company and therefore, could influence the supervisory board member via the company, for example, by entering into transactions with supervisory board members on behalf of the company.

B CONTROLLING SHAREHOLDER. With regard to the controlling shareholder,[74] the explanatory memorandum to the GCGC makes it clear that although the controlling shareholder should be adequately represented on the supervisory board, minority protection should not be neglected and the number of representatives delegated by the controlling shareholder should therefore be limited.[75] Thus, independent supervisory board members also have the duty to protect the interests of outsiders, such as minority shareholders and creditors, against powerful controlling shareholders.[76] Controlling shareholders can exercise their influence in the general meeting and on the supervisory board to enforce their own entrepreneurial interests against the interests of the company if necessary.[77] Even if their interests often coincide with the interests of minority shareholders, this does not always have to be the case.[78] In particular, controlling

---

[71] Recommendation C.6 (2) of the GCGC.

[72] *See also* Hopt & Leyens, *supra* note 666, at 959.

[73] As provided for in § 105 AktG. See the Government Draft, Bilanzrechtsmodernisierungsgesetz, BUNDESTAGS-DRUCKSACHE 16/10067, 101.

[74] According to the explanatory memorandum to the GCGC, a controlling shareholder is a shareholder with whom the Company has concluded a control agreement or who holds an "absolute majority of votes" or at least a "sustainable voting majority" at the general meeting. *See* Regierungskommission Deutscher Corporate Governance Kodex, *Rationale German Corporate Governance Code*, 9 (16 Dec. 2019).

[75] Regierungskommission Deutscher Corporate Governance Kodex, *Rationale German Corporate Governance Code*, 9 (16 Dec. 2019).

[76] Matthias Habersack, *Kirch/Deutsche Bank und die Folgen* ["*Kirch vs. Deutsche Bank*" *and the Consequences*], in FESTSCHRIFT FUER WULF GOETTE ZUM 65 GEBURTSTAG 121, 128 (Matthias Habersack & Peter Hommelhoff eds., 2011); Peter Hommelhoff, *Aufsichtsrats-Unabhängigkeit in der faktisch konzernierten Börsengesellschaft* [*Independence of the supervisory board in the listed stock corporation of a de facto group of companies*], in ZEITSCHRIFT FÜR WIRTSCHAFTSRECHT 1645, 1647 (2013); Uwe Hüffer, *Die Unabhänbgigkeit von Aufsichtsratsmitgliedern nach Ziffer 5.4.2 DCGK* [*The independence of supervisory board members in accordance with no. 5.4.2 GCGC*], ZEITSCHRIFT FÜR WIRTSCHAFTSRECHT 637, 642 (2006); *see also* Walter Bayer, Grundsatzfragen der Regulierung der aktienrechtlichen Corporate Governance [*Fundamental issues of the regulation of corporate governance of stock corporations*], NEUE ZEITSCHRIFT FUER GESELLSCHAFTSRECHT, 1, 11 (2013); Hasselbach & Jakobs, *supra* note 68, at 645.

[77] Kremer & von Werder, *supra* note 68, at 342.

[78] *See* Final Report by the High-Level Group of Company Law Experts on a Modern Regulatory Framework for Company Law in Europe, 63-64.

shareholders can easily have a conflict of interest if they do business with the dependent company.[79] Since controlling shareholders have both legally and factually significant opportunities to influence the composition of the supervisory board, they can influence its (control) activities.[80] This means that the controlling shareholders or their representatives have the opportunity to safeguard their special interests, which in individual cases may conflict with the interests of the minority shareholders and also with those of the (subsidiary) company.

3 Absence of a Permanent and Material Conflict of Interest

According to the GCGC, a supervisory board member will only be deemed independent from the company or management board if that member has no personal or business relationship with the company or its management board that may cause a substantial and not merely temporary conflict of interest.[81]

The recommendation thus centers around the absence of conflicts of interest. Conflicts of interest arise when a person has diverging interests due to different positions or relationships.[82] This is regularly the case if someone has to safeguard the interests of another person,[83] as in the case of the supervisory board member who must safeguard the interests of the company, that is the shareholders and—depending on the jurisdiction—(other) the stakeholders. At the same time, the person concerned has his or her own interests or is in another relationship with a third party which requires safeguarding other (conflicting) interests of that third party.[84] With regard to the recommendations on independence in the GCGC, both types of conflicts of interest are conceivable.

Furthermore, the conflict of interest must be "substantial," that is material, and not merely temporary.[85] This provides both a time- and content-related characterization of the conflict setting a de minimis requirement in order to exclude minor conflicts of interest that do not generally impair the monitoring activities of a supervisory board member.[86]

A PERMANENT CONFLICT OF INTEREST. A conflict of interest that is not merely temporary is permanent. Conflicts of interest can be divided into permanent and occasional conflicts:[87]

---

[79]   Habersack, *supra* note 76, at 128.
[80]   Oberhofer, *supra* note 9, at 85.
[81]   Recommendation C.7 (1) sent. 2 GCGC.
[82]   About conflicts of interest in German law, see Christoph Kumpan, Der Interessenkonflikt im deutschen Privatrecht [*Conflicts of Interest under German Private Law*] (2014); *see also* Ulrich L. Göres, Die Interessenkonflikte von Wertpapierdienstleistern und -analysten bei der Wertpapieranalyse [*Conflicts of Interest of Financial Services Providers and Analysts*] 33 (2004); Heinz-Dieter Assmann, *Interessenkonflikte und „Inducements" im Lichte der Richtlinie über Märkte für Finanzinstrumente (MiFID) und der MiFID-Durchführungsrichtlinie* [*Conflicts of interest and "inducements" in the light of the Markets in Financial Instruments Directive (MiFID) and the MiFID implementing Directive*], *in* Österreichisches Bank-Archiv (ÖBA) 40, 43 (2007); Kay Rothenhöfer, § 63 WpHG Allgemeine Verhaltensregeln, Verordnungsermächtigung [*General rules of conduct, authorisation of ordinances*], *in* KAPITALMARKTRECHTKOMMENTAR § 63 mn 42 (Eberhard Schwark & Daniel Zimmer eds., 5th ed. 2020); Christoph Kumpan & Patrick C. Leyens, *Conflicts of Interest of Financial Intermediaries*, 5 ECFR 72, 84 (2008); *cf.* Kay Rothenhöfer, *Verhaltens- Organisations- und Aufzeichnungspflichten nach dem WpHG* [*Duties of conduct, organisation and recording according to the WpHG*], *in* BANK- UND KAPITALMARKTRECHT, mn 13.9–13.14 (Siegfried Kümpel/Peter O. Mülbert/Andreas Früh/Thomas Seyfried, eds., 5th ed. 2019).
[83]   Raschid Bahar & Luc Thévenoz, *Conflicts of Interest: Disclosure, Incentives, and the Market, in* CONFLICTS OF INTEREST, 1, 2–3 (Luc Thévenoz & Raschid Bahar eds., 2007).
[84]   On the different kinds of conflicts of interest, see KUMPAN, *supra* note 82, at 37–44.
[85]   *See* recommendation C.7 GCGC.
[86]   Hasselbach & Jakobs, *supra* note 68, at 646.
[87]   KUMPAN, *supra* note 82, at 41.

Permanent conflicts are continuous from when they occur, such as in the case of a supervisory board member for the entire or at least a longer part[88] of the appointment period and play a recurring role in decisions made by the supervisory board member concerned. In contrast, occasional conflicts only occur in individual cases or for a limited period. A conflict with the interests of other parties involved that is not merely temporary, that is permanent, can arise, for example, if the supervisory board member is related to a member of the management board because kinship is not a temporary condition. On the other hand, an occasional conflict of interest can arise if the supervisory board member negotiates a one-time purchase agreement with the company for a single item.[89] Occasional conflicts do not permanently impair the activities of the supervisory board, but only occur during individual supervisory board votes. Accordingly, in such cases, it is sufficient that the supervisory board member concerned abstains from the respective voting and, if necessary, even from the discussions on the concerned issue affected by the conflict.[90]

B SUBSTANTIAL CONFLICT OF INTEREST. Whether a conflict is "substantial," that is material, depends on whether it poses a serious risk of impairing the supervisory board member's ability to judge, so that the member no longer decides solely in the interest of the company, but is guided by the influence that gives rise to the conflict of interest.[91] This can be assumed if the conflict-laden relationship or decision has significant effects on the supervisory board member concerned or related persons.[92] In particular, this can be assumed if the relationship or decision has a significant impact on the income and financial situation of the supervisory board member or a related person.[93] However, this can only provide an indication of the conflict's significance, because a purely quantitative approach to assessing the significance of a conflict—that is taking only into account the turnover or income that a supervisory board member achieves within the scope of the relationship—would be too narrow.[94] A conflict can also be "substantial" if the supervisory board member is emotionally or personally affected.[95] Moreover, consideration must be given to whether there is a cluster risk for the supervisory board member,[96] meaning that various insignificant influences taken together lead to a substantial conflict.

C POTENTIAL CONFLICT OF INTEREST. According to the GCGC supervisory board members should "be considered independent from the company and its management board if they have no personal or business relationship with the company or its management board that may cause a substantial—and not merely temporary—conflict of interest."[97] From the words "may cause" it

---

[88] Jens Koch, *§ 100 Persönliche Voraussetzungen fuer Aufsichtsratsmitglieder* [*Personal requirements for supervisory board members*], in AKTIENGESETZ § 100 mn. 40 (Uwe Hüffer & Jens Koch eds., 14th ed. 2020).

[89] For more examples, *see* Martin Klein, *Die Änderungen des Deutschen Corporate Governance Kodex 2012 aus Sicht der Unternehmenspraxis* [*The amendments to the German Corporate Governance Code 2012 from the perspective of corporate practice*], in DIE AKTIENGESELLSCHAFT 805, 806 (2012).

[90] Hasselbach & Jakobs, *supra* note 68, at 646; Henrik-Michael Ringleb, Thomas Kremer, Marcus Lutter & Axel von Werder, *Die Kodex-Änderungen vom Mai 2012* [*The amendments to the Code as of May 2012*], in NEUE ZEITSCHRIFT FÜR GESELLSCHAFTSRECHT 1081, 1087 (2012); *see also* Koch, *supra* note 88, at mn 40, Jens Koch, *§ 108 Beschlussfassung des Aufsichtsrats* [*Resolutions of the Supervisory Board*], in AKTIENGESETZ § 108 mn. 10 (Uwe Hüffer & Jens Koch eds., 14th ed. 2020); in more detail KUMPAN, *supra* note 82, at 508-557.

[91] *Cf.* Klein, *supra* note 89, at 807. *See also* Koch, *supra* note 88, at mn 40.

[92] Klein, *supra* note 89, at 807; *see also* Kremer & von Werder, *supra* note 68, at 345.

[93] Hasselbach & Jakobs, *supra* note 68, at 646.

[94] Kremer & von Werder, *supra* note 68, at 345. *See also* Koch, *supra* note 88, at mn 40.

[95] Hasselbach & Jakobs, *supra* note 68, at 646.

[96] Kremer & von Werder, *supra* note 68, at 345.

[97] Recommendation C.6 GCGC.

can be inferred that the mere possibility of a conflict of interest, that is a potential conflict of interest, is sufficient to preclude independence.[98] In other words, the abstract or typical risk of a conflict of interest suffices; the conflict does not need to become an actual or concrete conflict.[99] Accordingly, there is no need to set too high a standard for the assumption of a conflict of interest.

4 Indicators for a Lack of Independence

The GCGC also provides examples or "indicators" for assuming when a board member is not independent of the company and the management board.[100] These exemplary[101] indicators should be taken into account when assessing independence and, according to the explanatory memorandum to the GCGC, are suitable for ruling out that a supervisory board member is independent, but do not inevitably do so.[102]

The GCGC mentions four cases or indicators when it should be assumed that a board member is not independent: (1) if the supervisory board member was a member of the management board of the company during the two years prior to the appointment;[103] (2) if the supervisory board member has a significant business relationship (e.g., as a customer, supplier, lender or consultant) with the company or one of its dependent companies or had one in the year prior to his or her appointment, either directly or indirectly as a shareholder or in a responsible function of another company outside the group; (3) if he or she is a close family member of a member of the management board; or (4) if he or she has been a member of the supervisory board for more than twelve years.[104]

A FORMER MEMBERS OF THE MANAGEMENT BOARD. The first case concerns the transition from the management board to the supervisory board. It focuses on the risk that the previous member of the management board does not have a neutral, independent view of the company's business activities.[105] The reason is that in the case of an immediate transition to the supervisory board, the former member of the management board has usually played an active role in shaping the company during his or her time on the management board, or he or she is still loyal to their former colleagues on the management board, which may cloud his or her judgment. On the other hand, the company and industry knowledge of former members of the management board is also valuable for the supervisory board's monitoring activities.[106] In order to bridge the gap between the

---

[98] *See* Hasselbach & Jakobs, *supra* note 68, at 645; Klein, *supra* note 89, at 806; Kremer & von Werder, *supra* note 68, at 345.

[99] An actual conflict of interest would often be difficult to prove in practice and subject to very subjective assessments. *See* Hasselbach & Jakobs, *supra* note 68, at 645.

[100] *See* recommendation C.7 (2) GCGC.

[101] Due to the words "in particular" used in the recommendation.

[102] Regierungskommission Deutscher Corporate Governance Kodex, *Rationale German Corporate Governance Code,* 9 (Dec. 16, 2019).

[103] Internationally, longer periods are common. In the United States, e.g., a period of three years after retirement is usually required; the European Commission even provides for five years after retirement (see Annex II No 1 lit. a of the Recommendation of the Commission of 15 February 2005, O.J. L 52/51).

[104] Internationally, twelve years is considered long in terms of independence. *See, e.g.,* CalPERS, Governance & Sustainability Principles, 17 (Sept. 2019); Glass Lewis, 2019 Guidelines Germany, 6 (2019). The UK Corporate Governance Code recommends nine years, *see* Financial Reporting Council, The UK Corporate Governance Code, Provision 10 (p. 7) (July 2018).

[105] Kremer & von Werder, *supra* note 68, at 343.

[106] A similar argument is used in the United States with respect to why nonindependent directors are important for any board, as they have the necessary knowledge about the company and the industry to help ensure that the business will thrive.

necessary independence and valuable expertise, the GCGC provides for a two-year cooling-off period between leaving the management board and taking up a supervisory board mandate.[107]

B BUSINESS RELATIONSHIPS: CUSTOMER, SUPPLIER, LENDER, ADVISOR. The second case concerns business relationships. In particular, these include business relationships with the company as a customer, supplier, lender, or advisor. As the GCGC makes it clear that this list is not exhaustive, this second case could be understood more broadly to encompass all types of relationships aiming at an economic exchange.[108] Whether such a (usually contractual) relationship is legally effective does not matter if the parties actually "live" the relationship.[109] Since the relationship is intended to be a "business relationship," "pro bono" activities are generally not covered unless they are of particular importance for the reputation of a supervisory board member or the preparation of future orders and are therefore of economic significance.[110] The interests of customers, suppliers, lenders, and advisors will often, but not always, coincide with those of the company. Hence, there is a risk that in borderline situations, they could be guided by their own interests rather than the interests of the company.[111]

C FAMILY MEMBERS. The third case concerns family membership, a special "personal relationship."[112] In family relationships, there is usually a certain loyalty between the parties involved[113] that usually has a strong influence on the ability to judge.[114] According to the explanatory memorandum to the GCGC, the term "close family member" should be understood as defined in IAS 24.9.[115] Accordingly, "close family members" of a person are family members who can be assumed to influence or be influenced by that person; they include the children and the spouse or partner of that person, the children of that person's spouse or partner, and dependent relatives of that person or of that person's spouse or partner.[116]

D OTHER PERSONAL RELATIONSHIPS. In principle, the recommendations on independence in the GCGC also cover other personal relationships than family relationships, because the term "personal relationship" which is used in the GCGC[117] is broader than the term "family membership." Moreover, the list of indicators for ruling out independence contains only examples and is not exhaustive. Thus, "other personal relationships" could also encompass, for example, friendships as special, self-chosen, emotional relationships. However, friendships are not suitable as a starting point for a legal provision. Since friendship is an internal state of mind that can only be determined by each person individually, third parties cannot be sure of the existence or non-existence of a friendship without a corresponding statement by the person

---

[107] That is in line with the cooling-off period in § 100 (2) sentence 1 no. 4 AktG.
[108] Koch, *supra* note 88, at mn 42; Kremer & von Werder, *supra* note 68, at 344.
[109] Hasselbach & Jakobs, *supra* note 68, at 646.
[110] *Id.*
[111] Kremer & von Werder, *supra* note 68, at 342.
[112] Personal relationships can naturally only exist between natural persons. *See* Kremer & von Werder, *supra* note 68, at 343.
[113] Kremer & von Werder, *supra* note 68, at 341.
[114] Jan Lieder, *Das unabhängige Aufsichtsratsmitglied* [*The independent member of the supervisory board*], in NEUE ZEITSCHRIFT FÜR GESELLSCHAFTSRECHT 569, 572 (2005). *Cf.* Kremer & von Werder, *supra* note 68, at 341. Accordingly, no 13.1 of the Commission Recommendation regards family relationships as negating independence.
[115] Regierungskommission Deutscher Corporate Governance Kodex, *Rationale German Corporate Governance Code*, 9 (16 Dec. 2019).
[116] *Id.*
[117] *See* recommendation C.7 (1) sent. 2 GCGC.

concerned. In addition, the concept of friendship is indefinite and different people have different opinions on what characterizes a friendship. Since a legally viable approach needs an externally recognizable and objectively determinable connection, friendships cannot be regarded as covered by the concept of personal relationships in the GCGC.[118]

E TWELVE YEARS ON THE SUPERVISORY BOARD. The fourth case concerns supervisory board activity of more than twelve years as an indicator of a lack of independence. While a long term in office does not necessarily mean that the respective member is conflicted, such a long term in office at a company may lead to a certain degree of habituation, which makes it difficult for the supervisory board member to react to changes and critically question a practice that has been in place for a long period of time.[119] Even if there is no conflict of interest at issue, this indicator appears appropriate to regard the supervisory board member concerned as no longer independent.[120]

5 Independence in Spite of the Indicators

If one (or more) of these criteria or indicators is met, it must be assumed that the person concerned is not independent within the meaning of the GCGC. However, the GCGC does not automatically rule out independence—in contrast to international practice.[121] On the contrary, the supervisory board member in question can still be considered independent.

The determination of independence is to be made at the "dutiful discretion"[122] of the supervisory board.[123] If the directors take into account the indicators mentioned above[124] and conclude that the supervisory board member in question is nevertheless to be classified as independent, this does not constitute a deviation from the Code, so that no comply-or-explain-declaration[125] is required (only the required justification in the corporate governance statement).[126]

This decision-making structure enables the directors to assume independence in a specific case even though the requirements of a potential or "abstract" conflict of interest are fulfilled. While generally, independence as a preventive legal instrument builds on the absence of a potential or abstract conflict of interest, the directors may decide on the specific, concrete situation at hand. This is particularly useful in a "borderline situation," for example when the cooling-off period has not yet fully expired.[127] In certain cases, it may well be that the company's situation has changed or that the former member of the management board has already been cut

---

[118] These problems of the vague concept of "personal relationships" are avoided by the more concrete concept of "family membership." *Cf.* Lieder, *supra* note 114, at 572.

[119] Hasselbach & Jakobs, *supra* note 68, at 646; Koch, *supra* note 88, at mn 42 (operational blindness).

[120] Hasselbach & Jakobs, *supra* note 68, at 646.

[121] Hopt & Leyens, *supra* note 66, at 962.

[122] Koch, *supra* note 88, at mn 43; *see also* Theodor Baums, *Unabhängige Aufsichtsratsmitglieder* [*Independent members of the Supervisory Board*], *in* ZEITSCHRIFT FÜR DAS GESAMTE HANDELS- UND WIRTSCHAFTSRECHT 697, 699 (2016).

[123] Regierungskommission Deutscher Corporate Governance Kodex, *Rationale German Corporate Governance Code*, 10 (16 Dec. 2019).

[124] *See* recommendation C.7 (2) GCGC.

[125] Pursuant to § 161 AktG.

[126] For a critique, see Hopt & Leyens, *supra* note 66, at 962.

[127] That, however, does not release from the requirement of a cooling-off period according to § 100 (2) sent. 1 no. 4 AktG. See Daniel Rubner & Jan-Benedikt Fischer, *Unabhängigkeit des Aufsichtsrats – Die Empfehlungen des DCGK 2019* [*Independence of the supervisory board – The recommendations of the GCGC 2019*], *in* NEUE ZEITSCHRIFT FÜR GESELLSCHAFTSRECHT 961, 965 (2019).

off from the company or management board in such a way that the concerns regarding independence are no longer warranted.

However, it must be taken into account that such an approach, which allows the directors to focus on the specific, concrete conflict of interest in the individual case, is associated with greater uncertainty for the external observer than an approach which focuses solely on potential or abstract conflicts of interest. In case of an abstract conflict of interest, the decision determining independence would always be the same, regardless of the individual case. For example, a family relationship leads to an abstract conflict, even if, for example, a sibling has no emotional relationship with the other. In contrast, if the determination of independence focuses on whether there is an individual, concrete conflict of interest, that decision would be based on the individual situation and therefore not as predictable for third parties like it would be for a decision based on an abstract conflict of interest. However, this uncertainty is countered by the obligation to provide reasons in the corporate governance statement.[128] This ensures that outsiders get informed why no conflict of interest is to be assumed in that specific case.

6 Independence Requirement with Regard to the Controlling Shareholder

The GCGC also focuses on independence from a controlling shareholder.[129] This concept of independence is defined slightly differently from the independence of the company and the management board: A supervisory board member is considered to be independent of a controlling shareholder if the board member or a close family member is neither a controlling shareholder nor a member of the executive body of the controlling shareholder, and does not have a personal or business relationship with the controlling shareholder that may cause a "substantial," that is material—and not merely temporary—conflict of interest.

The reference point of independence, in this case, is different from that of independence from the company and management board. Moreover, the GCGC does not contain a list of indicators with regard to the independence from the controlling shareholder. There is also no possibility of a different assessment of independence in a specific individual case. Accordingly, it is only relevant if there is a relationship to the controlling shareholder, meaning a potential or abstract conflict of interest. The abstract conflict, however, must also be "substantial" and not just temporary, giving the board some leeway in determining whether a director is independent.

C *Same Concept, Different Implementation*

As the foregoing explanations show, the concept of independent directors is handled quite differently in Delaware and Germany. This begins with the question of who assesses whether a director is independent or not. While in Delaware the courts decide that question, in Germany, it lies essentially with the supervisory board itself. Thus, in Delaware outsiders decide, while in Germany insiders decide. However, in Germany, the supervisory board has to communicate its decision to the public, so that in the end, the decision is monitored by the market.

Determination by the courts or the supervisory board also means a different approach with regard to when the decision is made. Courts decide ex post, while the decision by the supervisory board is made ex ante. With an ex ante perspective, the susceptibility to errors is higher because later events are not known in advance. In contrast, an ex post perspective is prone to hindsight

---

[128] *See* recommendation C.8 GCGC. *See also* Regierungskommission Deutscher Corporate Governance Kodex, *Rationale German Corporate Governance Code*, 9 (16 Dec. 2019).
[129] Recommendation C.9 GCGC.

bias. At the same time, the lack of independence or "beholdenness" in Delaware has larger consequences than in Germany: In the case of a derivative suit in Delaware, for example, it decides on whether or not a shareholder is entitled to sue. In contrast, in Germany, there are mainly indirect sanctions via the market or during voting at general meetings. In view of this, one could have assumed that there is a greater need in Delaware for a legally secure determination of independence or "beholdenness" and that an ex ante approach would be more appropriate.

There are also differences with regard to the way independence is determined. Both legal systems use typified cases, such as "business relationships." In both legal systems, however, the concrete individual case is considered as well. But then both legal systems proceed differently. Whereas in Delaware considering the individual case at hand serves to refute an initially assumed independence, the approach in Germany aims at the opposite outcome by enabling the supervisory board to still assume individual independence despite the fact that one or more of the indicators that hint at a lack of independence are fulfilled.

Both legal approaches reach their limits when it comes to emotionally subjective relationships, such as friendship. Although the non-exhaustive enumeration of case groups lacking independence in the German Code allows for considering friendship as negating independence, the primary focus on abstract, typifying and objectively verifiable cases rather excludes such an approach. In Delaware, too, a friendship will not immediately lead to the exclusion of independence. The question of the "thickness" of a personal relationship as raised by the courts, however, shows a generally greater openness to consider such subjectively shaped states of mind.

V CLARIFYING THE MYSTICAL APPROACH IN DELAWARE

The focus on the individual specific situation at hand has led the Delaware courts to follow a facts and circumstances test, which not only creates challenges for practitioners but also appears difficult when dealing with independence requirements. The determination of director independence under Delaware law involves a fact-intensive inquiry made on a transaction- or decision-specific basis. Thus, under Delaware law, a director may be independent for one transaction or decision but lack independence with respect to another.

The downright mystical approach in Delaware becomes obvious in the requirement of "beholdenness." Instead of this intangible concept, shaped by the courts on a case-by-case basis, the courts should clearly identify the actual problem in these cases: the conflict of interest, which in the respective situation prevents or can prevent an uninfluenced, proper decision. Focusing on the conflict of interest will make it clearer that it is always only a matter of one's own- or third-party interests which have to be weighed or suppressed.

However, a mere renaming to "conflict of interest" does not suffice. Since internal independence cannot be measured objectively,[130] but is felt subjectively and is therefore difficult to prove, the concept of internal independence cannot be used for a viable legal approach to determining independence. Hence, a legal definition of independence must be based on external independence, because, in contrast to internal independence, standardized (typifying) criteria for the absence of external independence can be specified by law.[131] This standardization of the criteria

---

[130] Wolfgang Ballwieser, *Die Unabhängigkeit des Wirtschaftsprüfers – eine Analyse von Beratungsverbot und externer Rotation [The independence of the auditor – an analysis of the ban on consulting and of external rotation]*, in DER WIRTSCHAFTSPRÜFER ALS ELEMENT DER CORPORATE GOVERNANCE, 99, 101 (Marcus Lutter, ed., 2001); Baums, *supra* note 122, at 702; Müller, *supra* note 11, at 24. *See also* BJÖRN LAUKEMANN, DIE UNABHÄNGIGKEIT DES INSOLVENZVERWALTERS [THE INDEPENDENCE OF THE INSOVENCY PRACTITIONER], 84 (2010).

[131] On the necessity of a typification and objective consideration, see Laukemann, *supra* note 130, at 84; Joachim Schindler & Udo Rosin, *Die Unabhängigkeit des Wirtschaftsprüfers nach Deutschem und Amerikanischem Recht – insbesondere*

means that independence requirements are regularly formulated in an abstract way. As shown in the comments above, they are usually based on situations where there is typically a conflict of interest.

Hence, a distinction must be made between a typical, abstract conflict of interest, when a conflict could generally be assumed, for example, due to a family relationship, and a conflict of interest in the individual situation under consideration, which could deviate from the general assessment, for example, because a sibling is emotionally detached from the other and treats him or her like any other third party. The abstract and the concrete conflict of interest represent two different levels of threat to the interests of the company:[132] The first level implies an abstract threat to the interests of the company. Such a threat can be assumed if certain typical or abstract criteria are met that usually hint at a conflict of interest. While that endangers the interests of the company, the danger is more remote than in case of a concrete conflict. However, in this case (i.e., abstract danger), independence will already be excluded. At the second level are concrete conflicts of interest of a person, leading to an actual concrete threat to the company's interests. The concrete conflict is more severe than an abstract conflict as it is a real conflict of a real person, not merely a situation in which a conflict might occur. At the third level, there is a breach of duty, which, however, only occurs if the director actually gives preference to interests other than the interests of the company and thus actually violates the interests of the company.

Hence, the status-related requirement of independence provides protection against conflicts of interest—and, thus, ultimately against an actual breach of duty—at a very early stage.[133] The preventive protection of the independence requirement will take effect long before a concrete conflict of interest occurs and already counteracts concerns of dependency.[134] In individual cases, a concrete conflict of interest may go undetected if no abstractly typifying case would be fulfilled, but a conflict of interest in the specific situation nevertheless exists, as can be the case in a "friend" relationship. As a rule, however, an abstractly typifying approach tends to be over-inclusive and therefore restricts the persons concerned more than an individualized approach, for not every typified bond will restrict everyone in the same way. However, in view of the intended preventive effect of the independence requirement, a more restrictive approach is preferable to the opposite case, that is, being under-inclusive.

Although much of Delaware corporate law is about improving the governance process for which a robust decision-making process is important, Delaware does not preclude a conflict of interest approach. On the contrary, since independence serves to protect the decision-making process, it is necessary to be as transparent as possible about when independence can be assumed. Robust decision-making needs legal certainty, which is advanced by a clear conflict-of-interest approach. Without legal certainty, decision-making will always be under the sword of Damocles of insecurity and, hence, actually not robust.

If one argues that the amorphousness of "beholdenness" could be designed precisely to capture something wider than conflicts of interest, this argument will also not be valid. "Something wider" implies that "beholdenness" goes beyond (abstract) conflicts of interest.

Beratungsverbot und Rotation [*The independence of the auditor under German and American law – in particular the prohibition of consulting and rotation*], *in* DER WIRTSCHAFTSPRÜFER ALS ELEMENT DER CORPORATE GOVERNANCE, 117, 119 (Marcus Lutter, ed., 2001); Marco Staake, *Der unabhängige Finanzexperte im Aufsichtsrat* [*The independent financial expert on the supervisory board*], *in* ZEITSCHRIFT FÜR WIRTSCHAFTSRECHT 1013, 1015 (2010).

[132] Regarding the following, see Frank Scholderer, *Unabhängigkeit und Interessenkonflikte der Aufsichtsratsmitglieder* [*Independence and conflicts of interest of supervisory board members*], *in* NEUE ZEITSCHRIFT FÜR GESELLSCHAFTSRECHT 168, 171 (2012).

[133] Hoffmann-Becking, *supra* note 68, at 802.

[134] *Id.*

However, it has already been mentioned that it is not easy to make specific (concrete) conflicts of interest legally accessible in a predictable way. It is even more difficult to legally grasp phenomena that go beyond concrete conflict of interest. But this is precisely the focus of the present criticism, as it is exactly this that leads to great legal uncertainty and leaves those subject to the law ultimately to the arbitrariness of the courts.

VI CONCLUSION

The ongoing convergence of global corporate governance systems is reflected by the increasingly important legal institution of the independent director. Even legal systems, like Germany, which require a dualistic board structure and thus have less need for independent directors, have introduced independent directors. However, a legal comparison shows that the regulatory framework has been implemented quite differently compared to the United States or more specifically, Delaware. The German approach explicitly focuses on conflicts of interest as obstacles to independence and uses typified cases of conflicts of interest to facilitate the application and ensure legal certainty. Although the individual situation of a director can be considered as well, that does not endanger legal certainty, since it is the directors who decide on that matter. Thus, the recommendations of the GCGC can provide useful information for dealing with independence requirements, because its recommendations are aligned with the preventive objective of the independence requirement and entail greater legal certainty than the mystical "beholdenness" formula of the Delaware courts.

13

For Whom Are Nonprofit Managers Trustees? The Contractual Revolution in Charity Governance

Jacob Hale Russell[*]

I INTRODUCTION

Strapped for both cash and visitors, a museum's board decides on radical change. It votes to sell off artwork to finance a shift towards a new mission, one it believes will bring in more visitors and reestablish the museum's role in the community. Aggrieved parties protest the shift. Donors, artists represented in the collection, and the visiting public all assert particular harms to their interests. Do these parties' claims implicate a breach of fiduciary duty? And if so, do they have standing to sue?

Battles like these have become common in recent years. They are the most visible sign of an equally hard-fought, if more obscure, war over the paradigm that defines the nature of the charitable sector[1] in general. That battle, waged in scholarly journals, court decisions, and American Law Institute conferences, has been nearly as messy as the high-profile public clashes at specific institutions. It involves the blurry overlap between two converging bodies of doctrine, trust law and corporate law, both of which have influenced the development of charitable law. And it implicates foundational questions about "what sort of charity we as a society want to have."[2]

This chapter sketches the intellectual history of the transformation of charitable law, which is a microcosm of a broader intellectual current: the adoption of the contract paradigm across business law. The paradigm's rise in corporate law is well known and widely debated. My focus here is on its less-known cousin, nonprofit law, which has also been transformed by ideas of

---

[*] I use words like "charity," "nonprofit," and "independent sector" interchangeably in this chapter. To be sure, these terms mask important distinctions between specific structures and legal regimes employed in the sector (operating not-for-profit corporations, charitable trusts, family foundations, and so on). Because my narrative is about an overall trend in thought, those details are not usually important here. Also, using them interchangeably is consistent with the growing convergence in the law of charitable organizations. (The ongoing restatement project by the American Law Institute on charitable nonprofits adopts an approach based on the convergence of the various bodies of law that used to be considered separate.).

[1] I use words like "charity," "nonprofit," and "independent sector" interchangeably in this chapter. To be sure, these terms mask important distinctions between specific structures and legal regimes employed in the sector (operating not-for-profit corporations, charitable trusts, family foundations, and so on). Because my narrative is about an overall trend in thought, those details are not usually important here. Also, using them interchangeably is consistent with the growing convergence in the law of charitable organizations. (The ongoing restatement project by the American Law Institute on charitable nonprofits adopts an approach based on the convergence of the various bodies of law that used to be considered separate.).

[2] Rob Atkinson, *Unsettled Standing: Who (Else) Should Enforce the Duties of Charitable Fiduciaries?*, 23 J. CORP. L. 655, 658 (1998).

contract, in ways that have not been noticed nor even likely intended. A fear once expressed by Deborah DeMott—that corporate scholars would "resort[] unreflectively to contract rhetoric"[3]—has become the norm, even in an unlikely corner of the law.

Consider the debate, which reached peak fever roughly a decade ago, over whether donors to charitable nonprofits should have the standing to sue organizations over misuse of gift funds. Common law had long avoided providing a private right of action for donors, limiting enforcement in the charitable context primarily to the attorney general. Donors had no standing to sue charities except in unusual cases, such as when they maintained a formal reversionary right in a trust. These longstanding rules came under fire, as a number of reform efforts contemplated expanding donor standing, and fights broke out over particular gifts at well-known institutions, including Princeton, the University of Southern California, and Lincoln Center.[4] The debates have subsided somewhat in the last few years, and donor power has expanded slightly, if not dramatically.

I argue that the rise of the contract paradigm explains much about this debate—why it took place, and why it resulted in expanded donor rights. The debate was, in fact, a necessary outcome of the logic of contract. Contract's implications led naturally to a search for specific principals to whom fiduciary loyalty might be owed; that focus unearthed new concerns about charitable responsiveness to various constituencies—both as a doctrinal and normative matter. Even arguments by those who oppose donor standing, but still adopt contract-based arguments, reveal the sweeping success of the contract paradigm's takeover.

Prior to the early 1980s, a perspective on charitable entities that might be called "institutionalist" reigned, doctrinally grounded more in concepts from property and trust law. By institutionalist, I mean that the primary focus was on the organization's relationship to society, rather than on the interaction between specific individuals— director's obligation to shareholders, for instance—familiar from the contractarian view. The institutionalist perspective emphasized developed and widely understood, if also messy and indeterminate, ideas of the "public," embodied in concepts like the "public trust" or public ownership. This is not to say that people did not question the selflessness of particular philanthropists, but a broad consensus still existed about the public purposes of the independent sector. Boards had broad autonomy. Fiduciary duties and other aspects of governance were seen primarily as constraints to avoid outright fraud or self-dealing, not to limit the permissible scope of an organization's mission.

The contractual turn, developed as part of the rise of law and economics theory within the field of business organizations, displaced that view, in ways both intended and unexpected. By contract paradigm, I particularly mean its positive sense: reconceptualizing the corporation or in this case, the charitable nonprofit, as a nexus of contracts. (Its closely linked normative aspect—the idea that most of corporate law should be non-mandatory rules—has had an impact as well.) The resulting idea—charity-as-contract—stressed fixed ex ante promises made to specific constituencies, most notably donors. It is embodied in various legal theories—such as the donor standing cases, or cases that invoke nonprofit directors' "duty of obedience" in novel ways—as well as in practice—by organizations themselves, their donors, and state attorneys general who enforce nonprofit law.

Of course, debates in legal theory did not by themselves cause a wholesale change in the charitable sector.[5] Instead, legal ideas could do their work in part because they intersected with

---

3   Deborah A. DeMott, *Beyond Metaphor: An Analysis of Fiduciary Obligation*, 37 DUKE L. J. 879 (1988).

4   Reid Kress Weisbord, *Reservations about Donor Standing: Should the Law Allow Charitable Donors to Reserve the Right to Enforce a Gift Restriction?*, 42 REAL PROP., PROB., & TR. J. 245 (2007).

5   That said, there is good reason to believe that theoretical debates will be more important in charity law than for-profit corporate law. The charitable sector is governed less by formal litigation and published decisions, simply because

a series of other social, cultural, and intellectual changes in the nonprofit world — each of these trends resonated with the more bargain-driven conception of charities. Meanwhile, the focus of charitable governance moved further from its trust law origins and more towards the law of business organizations, which further aided and abetted the shift in paradigm.

My approach here is one of intellectual history, and my goal is not to argue whether charitable law actually "is" or should be contract law. Paradigms are not right or wrong, so much as helpful or unhelpful — or more accurately, helpful at some things, unhelpful at others. Debates about contractarianism are usually cast as an argument between those who support mandatory and non-mandatory regimes. Few scholars have noticed the contract paradigm's descriptive move also has implications: it redirects scholarly focus, reframes doctrinal beliefs, and swallows and recasts old ideas.

This chapter proceeds in two sections. First, I tell the story of how the contract paradigm entered discussions of charitable law. It represents a remarkable conversion in the rhetoric used to discuss charity, from a few tentative forays in the 1980s within law and economics to the fairly wholesale adoption of contract vocabulary by scholars today. Second, I show that the idea has had far more influence over the nonprofit sector than is widely assumed, and I give examples in doctrine, in transactional practice, and reigning sector norms. These include debates over donor rights and the role of the attorney general in enforcement.

II FROM PUBLIC TRUST TO CONTRACT

Ideas of contract are today so dominant across business law that it can be hard to resurrect what came before. This is partly the nature of reigning paradigms, and partly the explicit work of legal scholars: for instance, John Langbein's famous article applying contract principles to a trust argues that the nature of trust law has *always* been contract, not just that trust law *should* be contractual.[6] Prior to the 1980s, however, the language of charitable nonprofit law was generally quite different from today's rhetoric. In the earlier period, commentators emphasized widely recognized, if sometimes ambiguous notions of the "public trust." Today, commentators on nonprofits — even those with normative positions strikingly different from Langbein's — stress contract over trust.

This section first briefly sketches the public trust language. It then traces the intellectual assault on that earlier paradigm, focusing particularly on Henry Hansmann and Langbein. My final sub-section describes the contract paradigm's ultimate widespread adoption.

A *Public Trust and Public Ownership*

Ideas of the public trust are, like all broad standards, amorphous, but have long legal roots. Today public trust is little discussed except in certain pockets of law, notably environmental law, where it remains an active strategy for litigation over access to and protection of public resources. However, for centuries, public trust dominated how scholars and jurists thought about charitable organizations.

---

various incentives align to make litigation substantially less likely than in for-profits, so perceptions of the law have an outsized role in actual nonprofit practice.

[6] John Langbein, *The Contractarian Basis of the Law of Trusts*, 105 YALE L. J. 625 (1995). For one exposition of the argument that Langbein misreads the history of trust law, see M. W. LAU, THE ECONOMIC STRUCTURE OF TRUSTS: TOWARDS A PROPERTY-BASED APPROACH (2011).

The language employed under the trust paradigm could often be quite lofty. For Justice Coleridge, writing in the nineteenth century, a museum did not own paintings as an end in itself but as "a means to give the people an ennobling enjoyment." He rejected a request that a museum take steps to relocate art which would, according to proponents, keep the paintings safer, but at the expense of access by a wider audience. If displaying a painting for more viewers meant that "a great picture perished in the using," he wrote, it would still have "fulfilled the best purpose of its purchase . . . in its results to the nation." In the blitz of World War II, trustees of the National Gallery considered, and accepted, the suggestion of a letter writer who proclaimed that it would be "wise and well to risk one picture for exhibition each week."[7] These examples show that the public trust concept stressed public purpose; these cases were decided neither based on narrow views of ownership and control by the charitable organization nor based on promises or contracts between the organization and the donor or any other identifiable constituent.

This notion paralleled earlier conceptions of philanthropy, which were also less bargain-driven than their modern counterpart. It is important to remember that America's views on charitable giving have morphed over time. There is a current tendency to tell the story of American philanthropy as a continual tradition. A familiar trope of such accounts, present in scores of scholarly articles on charity, invokes Alexis de Tocqueville's 1835 observation that Americans are "forever forming associations." In fact, the comparison to Tocqueville—usually used by contemporary commentators to buttress their pluralist, democratic conception of the philanthropic sector—is historically problematic. For one, he was referring not so much to philanthropic or charitable causes as political associations; moreover, the economic structure of society was very different at the time.[8] Moreover, as legal historians have noted, the early nineteenth century was a time of legal hostility to the charitable trust and "prejudice against vested charitable institutions."[9] At the same time, it was also a moment where many would-be donors shared a "widespread acceptance of a common set of moral values and economic principles," a commitment to a shared set of "middle-class standards of thrift, sobriety, and responsibility." What appears today as a patchwork of unrelated, pluralistic organizations were linked by a fairly unified set of views about public purposes, embodied, for instance, in the so-called "Benevolent Empire" of Protestant reform groups that promoted an interlinked set of causes including temperance, abolition, and educational reform.[10]

Philanthropy today is often regarded in transactional terms—the donor's decision to give comes first, whether motivated by altruistic or selfish (tax or ego) reasons, and the agreement is less a pure gift than a bargain.[11] Contrast that to the description of philanthropy given in 1924 by Carl Zollmann, author of the leading treatise on charities of the first half of the twentieth century, and a serious doctrinal scholar of diverse fields from air law to religious law, whose views were hardly radical or socialist. "Modern thought," Zollmann writes, "tends more and more to the conclusion that the ownership of great wealth is not merely for the transmission of it to one's own family but is largely a public trust." Although Zollmann makes clear he was certainly not unaware of how donor vanity might influence a decision, his overall conception is one of

---

7   All three quotes in this paragraph, and the accompanying stories, are to be found in the text of a lecture by the former British Museum director. *See* Neil MacGregor, *A Pentecost in Trafalgar Square, in* WHOSE MUSE? ART MUSEUMS AND THE PUBLIC TRUST (Cuno ed., 2004). The edited volume in which it appears overall represents a contemporary (and therefore increasingly rare) endorsement of what I call the public trust conception of not-for-profits.

8   Emma Saunders-Hastings, "Is American Philanthropy Really Democratic in the Tocquevillian Sense?" (2015), https://histphil.org/2015/07/15/is-american-philanthropy-really-democratic-in-the-tocquevillian-sense.

9   Lawrence Friedman, *The Dynastic Trust*, 73 YALE L. J. 547, 590 (1964).

10 ROBERT H. BREMNER, AMERICAN PHILANTHROPY 40–45 (2d ed. 1988).

11 On the turn from gift to transaction, see Weisbord, *supra* note 4.

charitable giving not as a voluntary transaction, but as a moral obligation to "appropriate a part of [this wealth] to serve the public welfare or the general benefit of his community."[12] Giving is not so much a decision as an inherent feature of the acquisition of great wealth.

Zollmann's words echo those of Andrew Carnegie, whose famous 1889 "Gospel of Wealth" saw philanthropy as solving a problem that would be inevitably faced by successful capitalists like him: they had "more revenue than can be judiciously expended upon themselves" because of their "peculiar talent for affairs." That "surplus wealth" traditionally could be left upon death to one's children, which was "most injudicious," or others. Better, said Carnegie, was to put it while alive into structures to administer money to improve the "general condition of the people . . . for the common good." To be sure, Carnegie's motives can easily be questioned, as can his assertion that his fortune was amassed through pure skill "under the free play of economic forces."[13] Contemporaries questioned the consequences of his scheme; one worried that Carnegie's philanthropy was creating a "vast system of patronage," but he nonetheless shared a concern about finding the right framework for dealing with the "moral significance of great fortunes" in society.[14] This emphasis on the social obligations of wealth, whether in the rhetoric of Carnegie or his critics, put more emphasis on public obligation than on voluntary bargain.

Even the most aggressive donors imagined that the results of their gifts would evolve with the needs of the public. Particularly telling is the story of the Rockefeller Foundation. Retired in 1987 and with wealth far surpassing what he could easily give away through piecemeal gifts, Rockefeller, like Carnegie and others, hit upon the idea of setting up a "foundation, a trust, and engage directors who will make it a life work to manage . . . this business of benevolence properly and effectively."[15] How did Rockefeller intend to do this? Not with a private trust, but rather with a large gift to the federal government modeled after the earlier grant that produced the Smithsonian museums.[16] The governing structure would be picked through a political process, not by Carnegie. For years he tried to do this, getting a bill introduced in Congress in 1910 and finally accepting Congress's "no"—driven by politics that had turned increasingly on Rockefeller in the wake of the Standard Oil antitrust prosecutions—in 1913.[17] Even then, Rockefeller and his foundation maintained the rhetoric of "public trust," even establishing a governance structure that required a degree of public (if elitist) representation.

Depicting the decline of the notion of the public trust is not meant to caricature the elite patrons of either generation: in other words, this is not the story of entirely altruistic, public-spirited civil servants of old giving way to greedy, private minded, egotistical barons of today. The early philanthropists were motivated, among other things, by their personal views about the benefits of industry and capitalism for society, and a strong and often unpleasant sense of paternalism. Structural factors played a role, too, in their conception of philanthropy. As two scholars of philanthropy have argued, the strength and nature of the early twentieth century foundations owed in part to the weakness of the federal government in that era, alongside a widely shared view that the federal government should not make unified social policy—a

---

[12] CARL ZOLLMANN, AMERICAN LAW OF CHARITIES 120–1 (1924).

[13] ANDREW CARNEGIE, THE GOSPEL OF WEALTH AND OTHER TIMELY ESSAYS 1-46 (1901).

[14] William Jewett Tucker, *The Gospel of Wealth*, 15 ANDOVER REV. 644–45 (1891).

[15] Bremner, *supra* note 10, at 111.

[16] James Smithson's estate was given to the United States in 1836, and the Smithsonian Institution was established by Congress in 1846. For an extensive discussion of the influence of the Smithsonian trust on Rockefeller, see Elizabeth A. Harmon, The Transformation of American Philanthropy: From Public Trust to Private Foundation, 1785-1917 (2017) (unpublished Ph.D. dissertation) (University of Michigan) (on file with author).

[17] Bremner, *supra* note 10, at 112–13.

view that has since eroded.[18] But that simply underscores the broader point: although private foundations were indeed private, "private" had a different connotation, one that still emphasized a shared set of views about the public purposes and consequences of charity.[19]

B *Hansmann and the Missing Principal of Charitable Law*

Henry Hansmann was among the first legal scholars to devote sustained attention to the organizational structure of not-for-profits. His early work, as in the other papers subsequently collected together as *The Ownership of Enterprise*, sought to understand why particular organizational forms were selected by different types of enterprise.[20] His guiding concept was that a firm's choice of form must be driven by a desire to minimize misalignments and conflicts particular to that sector. For each type of entity, Hansmann works by identifying a principal (or beneficiary) whose agency costs needed minimization—a method which seems innocuous enough, but which in the charitable context resulted in a remarkable new characterization of charitable purpose.

Hansmann starts by identifying the key feature of charitable organizations as the "nondistribution constraint"—the prohibition from "distributing any profits it earns to persons who exercise control over the firm."[21] The lack of distribution meant there were also no owners with either control or residual claimant rights. What problem was solved by this unique configuration? It obviously could not, as the traditional corporate form did, minimize agency issues between managers and owners—as there were no owners. So Hansmann decided a nonprofit's principals must be its "customers," much like in a consumer-owned cooperative. If "customers are in a peculiarly poor position to determine ... the quality or quantity of the services they receive from a firm," it makes sense to construct a nonprofit, which "abandons any benefits of full ownership in favor of stricter fiduciary constraints on management."[22]

But who were the customers? This was perhaps the greatest conceptual leap: for Hansmann, the donor came first. Relief and aid groups' "customers"—its principals—are its donors, who worry about whether the organizations will serve as effective intermediaries in channeling their contributions to those in need. In Hansmann's depiction of the structure, relief organizations only indirectly serve those who receive aid; the donor is their principal, using the organizational structure to ensure the organization does a good job on their behalf in supplying relief. Similarly, in nonprofit broadcasting organizations, the nondistribution constraint is a form of patron ownership; it helps donors be sure that their contributions will help on the margins but without the collective action problems of actual patron ownership.

Hansmann claimed not to be revolutionary. On the contrary, he noted that while his jargon might sound foreign, his view was no different from characterizing nonprofits "in much the same way that we have always viewed charitable trusts—that is, as fiduciaries."[23] But it was a revolution, not just in the way his depiction gave donors primacy. Even the attempt to identify

---

[18]   Barry D. Karl & Stanley N. Katz, *The American Private Philanthropic Foundation and the Public Sphere 1890–1930*, 19 MINERVA no. 2, 236 (1981).

[19]   *Id.* at 238–40. For a useful discussion of how the contract theories of business law were tied to a move away from a public conception of the corporation towards a private one, *see* Jennifer G. Hill, Corporations, Directors' Duties and the Public/Private Divide, ch. 15 (this volume).

[20]   Henry Hansmann, *The Role of Nonprofit Enterprise*, 89 YALE L. J. 835 (1980). Hansmann is situated within the broader history of contractarianism in Jacob Hale Russell and Arthur B. Laby, *The Decline and Rise of Fiduciary Obligations in Business*, introduction (this volume).

[21]   *Id.* at 838–9.

[22]   HENRY HANSMANN , THE OWNERSHIP OF ENTERPRISE 228 (2000).

[23]   Hansmann, *supra* note 20, at 845.

the primary beneficiary of a nonprofit marked a break from prior nonprofit theory. For Hansmann, given his systematic approach, identifying a beneficiary no doubt seemed logical; if the fiduciary relationship is a principal-agent relationship, identifying the principal is essential. In turn, that led him to another bigger, and more novel, leap, one that fundamentally recasts the purpose of the nonprofit form as existing *"primarily to protect the interests of the organization's patrons* from those who control the corporation" (emphasis added).[24]

This analysis violated a longstanding view among scholars in the nonprofit community that one should avoid identifying or naming principals. There was a modest doctrinal reason for that and a bigger philosophical reason. The modest reason, almost tautological, was that charitable trusts always had indefinite beneficiaries, which made them by nature unidentifiable. Under black-letter law, naming definite identifiable beneficiaries, like family members, made it all too likely that a trust did not truly serve charitable purposes. As both *Restatements of Trusts* published before Hansmann's article had put it: "In the case of a charitable trust there need not be and ordinarily is not a definite beneficiary, and the trustee is ordinarily not in a fiduciary relation to any specific person."[25] Rather than a beneficiary, the "property is devoted to the accomplishment of purposes beneficial to the community."[26]

Hansmann's decision to identify a beneficiary—and then decide the donor held that role—was thus a significant philosophical leap, but one made with no acknowledgment of the break. Previous case law and the leading treatises on trust law explicitly argued that any attempt to identify a beneficiary in a nonprofit organization—even an indefinite one—was not just doctrinal error but based on a "fundamental misconception of the nature of the charitable trust." As one leading commentator put it, that misconception was "the failure to distinguish between the public or the community which is the real beneficiary of every charitable trust and the particular human beings who are mere conduits of its social benefits to the public."[27]

That point had been made time and again by earlier scholars and judges: If a charitable trust is created to serve a particular group, members of that group are still not its beneficiaries but "are merely the means through which the public receives benefits." An art museum could never have beneficiaries, "even in the broadest sense," because its advantages flow to visitors and the community more broadly.[28] For commentators across much of the twentieth century, this explained many distinctive features of charitable law, including the limitation of standing to the attorney general. "While the human beings who are to obtain advantages from charitable trusts may be referred to as beneficiaries, the real beneficiary is the public and the human beings involved are merely the instrumentalities from whom the benefits flow," one court observed in language rather typical of the public trust conception.[29]

What is most notable about Hansmann's break with this idea is that it appears not to be a result of a particular normative agenda around donors or the role of nonprofits, so much as the inexorable result of his approach. Indeed, he is at pains to stress that his idea represents only new labels and while he may or may not believe that there is no reason to believe this represented part of a particular normative agenda with respect to charitable purposes. Instead, Hansmann follows a paradigm, one which requires the identification of a principal whose contracting

---

[24]   *Id.*
[25]   Restatement (Second) of Trusts § 348 (Am. Law Inst. 1959) (same as the prior Restatement of Trusts (Am. Law Inst. 1935)). This language does not appear in the closet corresponding section of the third restatement adopted in 2003. *See* Restatement (Third) of Trusts § 28 (Am. Law Inst. 2003).
[26]   *Id.* at § 364.
[27]   George Gleason Bogert, The Law of Trusts and Trustees § 363 (1935).
[28]   *Id.*
[29]   *In re* Freshour's Estate, 345 P.2d 689 (Kan. 1959).

problems need help from organizational law. Once that leap is made, it is easy to start seeing donors as continuous owners in a contract relationship, rather than one-off givers.[30]

Hansmann's leap was no doubt buttressed by the trend in nonprofit law towards convergence with corporate law. The first Model Nonprofit Corporation Act, drafted in the 1960s, sought to mimic many aspects of the Model Business Corporation Act. That begged the question of whether nonprofits had any equivalent to shareholders. The public trust model had not needed to answer that question; it was either irrelevant or in fact, dangerous, to identify constituents.

Perhaps the most compelling evidence of the early intellectual foothold of these ideas is that even the early critics of Hansmann adopted his essential logic and vocabulary. One critique challenged Hansmann's narrow focus on particular types of nonprofits but then extended his logic, by identifying other forms of contract (besides donor-patron contracts) that might be the centerpiece in other types of organizations.[31] The title of another work in this vein, "Agents Without Principals," might first seem to be drawing a contrast or distinction between for-profit and not-for-profit law, or critiquing the idea that one can find fiduciary duties in the absence of a meaningful principal-agent relationship.[32] Instead, its author, Evelyn Brody, responds to Hansmann's argument and employs agency theory more broadly to consider ways of aligning incentives with multiple constituents of the nonprofit sector. She identifies three particular constituencies—donors, clients, and the government—rather than the older, messier, but nonetheless longstanding concept of the "public" at large. The argument suggests that the problems of nonprofits are not that unique, and powerful explanations from the agency model of corporations still work well in the shareholderless world of nonprofits. Even Hansmann's critics, then, were using the same new contractarian scaffolding to build their visions of the charitable sector.

C Charity as Contract

John Langbein's "Contractarian Basis of the Law of Trust," published in 1995, represents perhaps the most visible moment of contract law breaching trust law's barricades. Langbein claims that fiduciary duties under trust law are actually "contractarian" in nature because they are meant "to capture the likely understanding of the parties to the trust deal."[33] Default duties are merely standardized contract terms, but when they exist, "express terms dominate default rules in fiduciary law." One of the key implications of his account is an increased role for settlors; for settlors, as much or more than beneficiaries, are part of the bargain struck in the creation of

---

[30] That method explains some of the empirical quirks of Hansmann's chapter, such as telling just-so stories about organizations that gloss over much of their real-world texture—and render his descriptions less availing. (His hospital chapter, by contrast, draws far more on solid empirical data than the primary nonprofit chapter.) For instance, even if it is right that some donor-sponsored organizations produce a public good and solicit donations based on the marginal valuation placed on the public good by each donor, it is harder to extend that to large organizations where a small number of patrons provide very large gifts (museums and performing arts organizations, for which he applies a similarly dubious price discrimination model); additional explanations, both altruistic and non-altruistic, are more compelling than simply donor-as-consumer, in particular, because many such donors are not really consumers. (A donor of works to an art museum was able to consume those works better before their donation; performing arts donors regularly do not attend events they fund.)

[31] Ira Mark Ellman, *Another Theory of Nonprofit Corporations*, 80 MICH L. REV. 999 (1982).

[32] Evelyn Brody, *Agents without Principals: The Economic Convergence of the Nonprofit and For-Profit Organizational Forms*, 40 N. Y. L. SCH. L. REV. 457 (1996). The critique one might expect from the title parallels Kelli Alces Williams's critique of the meaningfulness of the principal-agent terminology in the public corporate context. Kelli Alces Williams, *Self-Interested Fiduciaries and Invulnerable Beneficiaries*, ch. 18 (this volume).

[33] Langbein, *supra* note 5.

a trust. Thus, for Langbein and others who believe trusts are simply species of contract, settlor standing ought to be the default.

Still, a charity might have been a hard test for the success of the contract model. Despite the breadth of his claims, Langbein himself explicitly excluded charity from his 1995 account. He characterized charity as a "quasi-public institution" that must satisfy "standards of public benefit" whose genesis is regulatory law and common law, not contract.

Yet others, and eventually Langbein himself, drew an explicit connection between charitable trusts and contract. The most common early example involved discussions over the role of donor intent, such as in legal doctrines like *cy près* and deviation that deal with the administration of a gift when circumstances change.[34] Once the contract model was adopted by scholars of charitable law, cy près found a seemingly obvious, if novel, purpose: solving the problem of incomplete contracts. "The charitable trust is in some respects the prototypical relational contract," proclaimed two scholars in 1989,[35] using language that would have been unrecognizable a decade or two previously. Fiduciary standards were, in their contract-laden view, "a bonding mechanism to monitor the activities of one of the parties to the agreement" by the other party—donors—to this "long-term, inherently flexible arrangement."[36] As with any paradigm, contract tended to politely and unreflectively marginalize any disconfirming evidence. For instance, as to why donors did not, in fact, write contracts if they intended their gifts to be contracts, the predominant explanation became a technical one: they must have hoped to avoid potential challenges based on the consideration requirements of contract law.

Despite his early statement that his contractarian approach to trust law should not apply to charitable law, Langbein himself ultimately adopted contractarian ideas in his own future considerations of the cy près and deviation doctrines. A later article categorized the mandatory rules of trust law along two dimensions: "intent-defeating rules" and "intent-serving rules whose purpose is to discern and implement the settlor's true intent." The change-of-circumstance doctrines were, in his mind, clearly "intent-serving ... imputed-intent doctrines,"[37] there to help ensure that future generations followed the intentions of the writer of the contract—the donor.

This new characterization of cy près marked a break from historical perspectives on the doctrine, which did not originate to serve donor intent. In fact, quite the contrary: it originated for entirely collective reasons—to save charitable gifts from escheating back into private hands by repurposing them without violating the trust instrument, and as late as the twentieth century was primarily used to further the public interest in charitable gifts. Zollmann, writing in the 1920s, is characteristic in his description of the doctrine's shifts. In its earliest use, in Roman times, the purpose of the doctrine was to save a gift that became illegal—that is, to prevent it from being forfeited by the city, not to protect the donor. In the Medieval era, the doctrine's goal revolved around the saving of souls, which required the saving of gifts that allowed the souls an afterlife. The American colonists put their own spin on it; their principal fear was that the sovereign would use cy près to abrogate a citizen's goal in favor of their own.[38] In the early twentieth century, commentators widely agreed the doctrine was about preserving gifts in the

---

34 Roughly speaking, cy près is used to rewrite a charitable gift's purpose to be as "near as possible" to the original intent; the related doctrine of equitable deviation is used to rewrite specific restrictions on a gift to better serve its purpose.

35 Alex M. Johnson & Ross D. Taylor, *Revolutionizing Judicial Interpretation of Charitable Trusts*, 74 IOWA L. REV. 545, 571 (1989). *See also* Allison Anna Tait, *Keeping Promises and Meeting Needs: Public Charities at a Crossroads*, 102 MINN. L. REV. 1789 (2018) (adopting the relational contracting logic).

36 Johnson & Taylor, *supra* note 35, at 571.

37 John Langbein, *Mandatory Rules in the Law of Trusts*, 98 NW. U. L . REV. 1105 (2004).

38 CARL ZOLLMANN, AMERICAN LAW OF CHARITIES (1924).

realm of charity.[39] To be sure, these uses are not inherently *in*consistent with donor intent—a donor might well want their gift saved (although then why would they not say so, and why would they specify that the gift should fail)—but donor intent was never the central justification for the doctrine.

The modern leap—seeing cy près as predominantly about helping donor intent—was, once again, dictated by the logic of contract. Once contract became the central metaphor, a mandatory rule could only be justified if it filled in the intent of the parties. Most significantly for my claim about the power of reigning paradigms, even those who disputed the idea that cy près should be broadened to enhance relational contracting used contract-based arguments. For instance, other scholars argued against expanded cy près not based on the social grounds of old (fears of the dead hand controlling too many assets), but rather on an argument drawn from central law and economics theorizing about contracts: the idea that "penalty defaults" can force contracting parties, in this case, donors, to be more complete in their contracting.[40]

Other aspects of contractarian approaches to the corporation were also ported to the nonprofit realm, including the broader corporate agency costs literature. Geoffrey Manne, son of Henry Manne and like his father, an advocate for widening the use of law and economics approaches, made an early foray with his "Agency Costs and the Oversight of Charitable Organizations,"[41] but many others, on the left and right, followed. Authors soon began to assume, without noting the novelty of this assumption, that the central governance problem facing nonprofits was the lack of plaintiffs—that is, because it was hard or impractical to sue nonprofits, boards were likely to shirk or self-deal. "The market forces that constrain the scope of authority of corporate officials do not appear to constrain similarly the trustees and employees of foundations," wrote Jonathan Macey, in a theoretical leap subsequently adopted by others.[42]

Could this scholarly move towards seeing charitable organizations as predominantly contractual entities, with problems parallel to their for-profit corporate counterparts, simply be academic efficiency at work? Perhaps contract, in other words, was the best way to solve the existing problems of the nonprofit sector. It is not impossible, but what is most significant about the paradigm shift is that these moves did not actually answer the questions swirling at the time. Instead, the new theory announced its own questions—ones that had never been asked before but for which it already had answers—and then real-world events seemed to confirm that the paradigm's questions were the right ones.

In other words, charity-as-contract needed a nonprofit governance crisis: after all, this was what agency cost theories were designed to solve. The collapse of Enron in 2000, and the ensuing literature on the failures of corporate governance, resulted in concerns being extended to the not-for-profit sector, although nobody really explained why or whether there was a comparable crisis. A handful of anecdotes—some bad, but none necessarily systematic—seemed to suffice. As if to confirm the crisis, various rumblings in the mid-2000s about a crackdown against nonprofits by state attorney general offices, the IRS, and Senate Committees provided a few scattered anecdotes. Notably, most of the anecdotes were about self-dealing, excessive

---

[39]   As *American Jurisprudence*, one of the leading synopses of American common l put it in the early twentieth century:
    "Gifts or trusts for charitable purposes are favorites of the law and the courts. It is the fixed policy of the law to uphold charitable gifts and trusts whenever possible. The courts will construe charitable trusts to give them effect, if possible, and to carry out the general intention of the donor. . . . [Courts] will go to the length of their judicial power to sustain such gifts. . . . [A] gift must be interpreted in favor of a charity."
    15 AM. JUR. 2D CHARITIES § 114 (1962).

[40]   Jonathan R. Macey, *Private Trusts for the Provision of Private Goods*, 37 EMORY L. J. 295 (1988).

[41]   Geoffrey Manne, *Agency Costs and the Oversight of Charitable Organizations*, 199 WISC. L. REV. 227 (1999).

[42]   Macey, *supra* note 24, at 298.

compensation, and other breaches easily categorized as breaches either of the duty of loyalty or regulatory law. However, the literature quickly morphed into concerns over the governance problem of "mission drift," perhaps because that focus was a better fit with its donor-as-principal, nonprofit-as-relational-contract model.

Once agency costs had been spotted as a central problem, many of those articles further adopted the claim—never studied empirically—that donations depended on reducing agency costs. In Macey's model, for instance, the donor decision to "allocate his money will depend on the probability that the fund ultimately will in fact" do what the donor wants.[43] The assumption— that donors give in exchange for a kind of control right—has become widespread.[44]

These two trends in combination—the governance "crisis" made central in business law research by Enron's collapse, and the rise of donor centrality—morphed the nature of the governance threat that fiduciary duties and nonprofit governance were meant to solve. Where before the primary fear had been self-dealing and embezzlement, now the primary fear was lack of fealty to mission and especially donors. Even scholars who did not share the donor-centric assumptions began to worry that the attorney general's traditional enforcement focus—"simply protecting nonprofit assets from theft and charitable contributions from misdirection"—was insufficient, and oversight was needed over "mission creep and organizational integrity."[45] A series of high-profile national disputes—fights over the Buck Trust in Marin County in the 1980s, the Barnes Foundation collection's move to Philadelphia from the suburbs in the 1990s, or the current fight at the Berkshire Museum over its conversion from art museum to science museum—were recast as fiduciary disloyalty cases: that is, the boards were allegedly disloyal to donors.

What is perhaps most surprising about all of this is how quickly and extensively the contract thinking became adopted outside of its most obvious quarters, including by not-for-profits themselves and by scholars outside the law and economics framework. Civil society theorists who stress the role of philanthropy in revitalizing the public sphere have made arguments for increased donor standing and explicitly picked up Langbein's contract model.[46] Advocates against strict enforcement of donor intent often lean on relational contracting and the idea of a "bargain" with donors,[47] and not merely as an effective strategy to counter opponents' claims— they explicitly endorse the aptness of the paradigm.

III THE REVERBERATIONS OF THE CONTRACT PARADIGM

Once the contract paradigm had been introduced into scholarly and theoretical discussions of charitable law, it slowly spread to affect real-world charitable practices. Again, the claim is not that legal theory did all the work; rather, the contract paradigm interacted with a set of issues internal to the nonprofit sphere, with a broader turn towards contract language in related

---

[43] *Id.* at 299.

[44] In one rare exception, Reid Weisbord and Peter DeScioli suggest that, in fact, the best available psychological evidence implies that allowing donors to sue in order to alleviate agency costs might have opposite, deleterious consequences on charitable giving. Reid Kress Weisbord & Peter DeScioli, *The Effects of Donor Standing on Philanthropy: Insights from the Psychology of Gift-Giving*, 45 Gonz. L. Rev. 225 (2009).

[45] Dana Brakman Reiser, *Enron.org: Why Sarbanes-Oxley Will Not Ensure Comprehensive Nonprofit Accountability*, 38 U. C. Davis L. Rev. 205 (2004).

[46] Iris Goodwin, *Donor Standing to Enforce Charitable Gifts: Civil Society vs. Donor Empowerment*, 58 Vand. L. Rev. 1093 (2005).

[47] Allison Anna Tait, *The Secret Economy of Charitable Giving*, 95 B. U. L. Rev. 1663 (2015); Tait, *supra* note 35.

dimensions of law, and with a set of restatement and uniform act projects that opened up policy windows for rethinking aspects of charitable doctrine.

This section sketches a handful of examples of how the contract paradigm has put its fingerprint in discussions of fiduciary duties in not-for-profits. The first example is donor rights — the increased sense that organizations are responsible to, and donors should be permitted to sue, charitable organizations. The second involves attorney general offices, the traditional focus for the enforcement of fiduciary duties, and the changing conception of their role as being about enforcing bargains rather than interpreting public interest. The third example is found in discussions of the duty of obedience. Finally, I review a few smaller debates more internal to the not-for-profit world, engaged by both scholars and the independent sector itself, and suggest that many of these, too, implicitly draw on ideas of contract.

Although doctrine is a part of the story, simply looking at published fiduciary duty suits — for instance to see if more donors have been awarded standing, or if courts talk about fiduciary duties in contract terms — is not a particularly useful method on its own. There are only a handful of such cases, and although there are certainly cases suggestive of this move, it is hard to draw an unambiguous trend line. This difficulty points to something fundamental about studying the not-for-profit sector versus the for-profit sector: litigation will *always* be rare in the nonprofit sector, and the "shadow of the law" will be more important than actual law. Of course, even in the corporate context, fiduciary duties are often said to have minimal teeth — worn thin by the business judgment rule, exculpation for duty of care breaches, the paucity of out-of-pocket payments, the expansive discretion of special litigation committees, and other widely documented features of derivative litigation. All those limitations will be even more salient in nonprofits. Incentives to sue are even rarer in the not-for-profit context, because of ambiguity in standing, conventional collective action problems, financial incentives, various statutory forms of indemnification, and social norms.

Moreover, the "shadow of the law" in the nonprofit sector is even more informal. Volunteer boards, not always advised by lawyers, but trying to "do the right thing," are likely to turn to whatever resources they have — colloquial restatements of the law and training materials put out by nonprofit oversight groups. In a sector driven by informality and little litigation, what board members are told about their fiduciary duties arguably matters more than what the few published cases say.

Consider the fundamental change cases discussed in opening the chapter. These usually involve tough decisions, with good faith arguments on both sides. In a traditional business law sense, good faith ought to be enough to take fiduciary duties out of the picture — the business judgment rule would insulate almost any good faith board decision in the courtroom. But in the nonprofit world, there is a heightened sense that these boards may be violating their fiduciary duties; fiduciary language is used as a rhetorical device, as much or more than as a legal tactic, by aggrieved parties.

A *Donor Standing and Donor Rights*

The "donor rights" movement is largely a modern phenomenon, buttressed by organizations like the Philanthropy Roundtable that have focused heavily on attempting to increase fidelity to donor intent. The view that fidelity to donors' wishes is sacrosanct appears to have popular psychological resonance, with near-unanimous support for the notion that ignoring donor intent is a "serious" matter.[48] It is therefore unsurprising that many believe donors should obviously be

---

[48]   Harvy Lipman, "Donors Say Intentions Are Key," Chronicle of Philanthropy (Jan. 12, 2006) (reporting on a Zogby poll on the issue of donor intent). (Given the phrasing of the question, the poll may or may not accurately capture

entitled to the right to vindicate their intent in court. From a doctrinal standpoint, however, it is hard to overstate how dramatic a shift donor rights, especially standing to sue, marks from traditional rules.[49] The old, highly limited rules about standing to bring fiduciary or trust enforcement cases essentially meant donor intent merged with public intent. Donor intent could never be enforced unless the attorney general (or, in very limited contexts, certain beneficiaries) wanted it to be—and would typically only do so because of public interest in it.[50] With no remedy, there was simply no clear sense of a right to donor intent.

But the pressure to expand donor standing—either formally through doctrine, or informally through campaigns about donor rights—was a logical result of the contract paradigm. It is probably the area that has obtained the greatest influence on formal written doctrine. To take one example, the Uniform Trust Code has departed from the Restatement of Trusts and longstanding common law to give settlors standing to enforce a charitable trust.[51] Since the majority of gifts to charity are not made through trusts, this has not led to a flood of litigation, but it is significant. Moreover, it is perhaps surprising given the early intellectual history of these debates—recall that Langbein, who advocated for increased settlor standing, excluded charities in his early work—and yet the UTC provides it *only* for charitable trusts.

The uniform acts governing charity funds show a similar trend if we compare the 1970s Uniform Management of Institutional Funds Act (UMIFA) to the 2006 Uniform Prudent Management of Institutional Funds Act (UPMIFA).[52] In a way, the acts also reflect the preoccupations of their eras: UMIFA was largely about protecting organizations facing economic troubles from a stagnant economy, by expanding their investment rights. By contrast, written in better economic times and a new charitable economy, UPMIFA explicitly acknowledges the role of donors throughout, cites the "overarching duty to comply with donor intent," and "improves the protection of donor intent" with respect to endowment spending.[53] The comments to the full draft explicitly critique UMIFA for inadequately protecting donor intent in its treatment of rules around deviation. Although it does not take a hard line against modifications by charities, attorney general notification is required as is a court order or donor consent for many changes to donor restrictions.

Outside of formal law, not-for-profits appear to have accepted much of the rhetoric. The issue of enhanced donor standing was similarly the subject of a major debate over several years in the Restatement project on charity law. Fundraising professionals have widely endorsed a "Donor Bill of Rights."[54] Donor intent is increasingly characterized as an "ethical" obligation; in the most widely used summary of not-for-profit governance principles, the board has the "primary responsibility" to live up to the organization's "legal and ethical obligations to its donors, consumers, and the public."[55]

Arguments in favor of donor standing are not new, but the rhetoric behind them has changed in ways that illustrate the paradigmatic shift. In 1950, in an article still widely cited in these

nuanced views but combined with the high degree of media scrutiny that typically surrounds donor intent cases, it is clear that something about the importance of donor wishes captures the public imagination.)

[49] This shift is well documented by Weisbord, *supra* note 4.

[50] Weisbord & DeScioli, *supra* note 44, at 237.

[51] Unif. Trust Code §405(c) (Unif. Law Comm'n 2000) ("The settlor of a charitable trust, among others, may maintain a proceeding to enforce the trust.").

[52] Unif. Mgmt. of Inst. Funds Act (Unif. Law Comm'n 1972); Unif. Prudent Mgmt. of Inst. Funds Act (Unif. Law Comm'n 2006).

[53] Unif. Prudent Mgmt. of Inst. Funds Act §§ 3, 15.

[54] "Donor Bill of Rights" (Assoc. of Fundraising Prof'l. 2015), https://afpglobal.org/donor-bill-rights.

[55] "Principles for Good Governance and Ethical Practice" (Indep. Sector 2015), https://independentsector.org/programs/principles-for-good-governance-and-ethical-practice/.

debates today, Kenneth Karst pointed to the limitations of attorney general enforcement and raised, among other ideas, the possibility of expanded donor standing. But, coming from a different paradigm, his actual concern is quite different from modern scholars who worry about breaches of trust with the donors. Karst is not interested in the problem of enforcing the donor's bargain, as the phrasing used in the title of his article—the "efficiency of the charitable dollar"—makes clear. For Karst, donors might be allowed to sue only because of their knowledge—their incentives to watch the organization on behalf of the public—not because of their actual interest. His fears are self-dealing, not mission drift. Moreover, donor standing is not his preferred solution, which instead is an administrative agency. The article is framed around the idea of "public funds." Nothing in the article contemplates a contract view. He specifically notes the decline in granting visitatorial powers to donors, because "we now recognize that property given by a donor to charity is no longer 'his own' in any sense which allows him to dispose of it as he pleases."[56]

When Hansmann turned to the absence of donor standing, he assumed very different reasons underlay the attorney general's sole role in fiduciary enforcement: he explained it entirely through the lens of donors' interest in enforcing their contractual rights in the enterprise, and assumed the limited standing was the preferred approach donors would take to solving their collective action problems. He argued for expanded patron standing (for both donors and customers) because he could see no difference between the patron's interest in enforcing an organization's charter than that which a commercial customer "has in having an ordinary profit-seeking merchant adhere to the terms of a contract of sale." Calling their donations gifts instead of contracts "define[s] away these important elements of the transaction." In taking a gift, "management pledges to devote all of those funds, beyond reasonable compensation, to the organization's general purposes, or to the particular services requested by the patron."[57]

The donor-intent movement has blurred the history of many doctrines that implicate donor intent, such as discussions about whether or not to liberalize cy près. Commentators often make the assumption that "traditional" courts were "hesitant to employ cy près for fear of sacrificing individual property rights by exalting the use of property for the 'community' over its use and control by the donor."[58] This "traditional" concern is, in fact, a very modern concern. As noted before, cy près had long been a gift-saving doctrine—one that prevented the failure of a trust and its loss to the community—not a donor-intent doctrine. Its focus on intent was largely an American colonial need to limit sovereign power, versus a British version that permitted prerogative sovereign rights.[59] The fear was not wronging donors; it was granting too much power to the state. And in most of the twentieth century, the underlying purpose continued to be saving gifts, not helping donors. The courts would nearly always find that the donor had manifested "general charitable intent"—meaning the desire to have their gift rewritten to serve other charitable purposes, a requirement before invoking cy près—even in cases where little textual evidence supported their claim.[60]

---

56   Kenneth L. Karst, *The Efficiency of the Charitable Dollar: An Unfulfilled State Responsibility*, 73 HARV. L. REV. 433, 433, 446 (1960).

57   Henry Hansmann, *Reforming Nonprofit Corporation Law*, 129 U. PA. L. REV. 497, 608 (1981).

58   Johnson & Taylor, *supra* note 21, at 567.

59   Zollmann, *supra* note 23; *see also* 10 AM. JUR. CHARITIES 124 (1937).

60   The explicit breadth of courts' willingness to do so was made clear in a 1974 case summarizing the doctrine. Wesley United Methodist Church v. Harvard Coll., 366 Mass. 247, 252–53 (1974). The court was quite frank that general charitable intent could—should—be found even when the donor's stated intents seem quite specific. After all, the court reasoned, one would never bother describing a general charitable intent because, by definition, one gave a gift "fully expecting his scheme to be effective, [he] never contemplates alternative dispositions, or at least fails to include

B *Attorneys General and the Turn to Donor Protection*

The attorney general has long played an outsized role in enforcing fiduciary obligations in the charitable sector, but the contract paradigm has subtly morphed the nature of that role. The attorney general's role had long been explicit as the representative of the public trust. As noted previously, commentators stressed that the reason for giving the attorney general power was not to solve the lack of donor standing but to provide the appropriate party to represent the sole beneficiary of any charity, the public at large.[61] Even the classical term used to justify the attorney general's powers, *parens patriae* (parent of the nation), draws attention to the attorney general's role as representative of the *nation*, not the individual.

Since the rise of the contract metaphor, an increasing number of scholars have suggested a different role for the attorney general, one of ensuring smooth donor enforcement of their interests. For these commentators, donors have incentive issues that lead them either to over-enforce (the possibility of seeking personal gain on a gift) or to underenforce (collective action problems if the issue is widespread rather than specific to their gift, and the paucity of financial rewards in the nonprofit sector). In the contract model, the attorney general's job has been recast to "represent the intended beneficiaries and enforce their collective rights against the trustee."[62] The power of the paradigm is suggested in one footnote where an author notes that this theory poorly matches the facts on the ground: even if the attorney general has a useful role, why make it entirely impermissible to have private enforcement? Rather than questioning the paradigm, the author dismisses the evidence that does not fit the paradigm.[63]

Attorneys general have begun to adopt donor primacy language in their own guiding documents. Oregon's attorney general, for instance, tells nonprofit directors that it is "important to keep faith with donor intentions."[64] In its briefs on the recent court battles about the Berkshire Museum, the Massachusetts attorney general took several positions that were explained as protective of the donor, rather than grounded in the public interest. A major portion of its brief is devoted to the claim that Norman Rockwell "appears to have intended" that his two paintings never be sold, an "implied trust" based on his long-term friendship with the then-director of the museum, and social norms against deaccessioning that it argued existed at the time of Rockwell's gifts. Even in its broader arguments, the attorney general focused narrowly on interpreting the museum's old legislative charter, characterizing it in quasi-originalist terms—ensuring its "charitable and legislative mandate to be a museum of art, science, and history," which it claimed did not allow the board to substantially reduce the artistic component. The language used in many of these discussions is not one focused on the public trust or public

---

them in his testamentary design." Thus the court ruled that even though the donor's gift was quite specific—even providing that if funds grew beyond expectations, they could be used for additional scholarships only "subject to the qualifications and limitations as above provided"—the donor's intent was general. Put differently, general charitable intent always existed unless a donor goes out of his way to waive it, and it is not even clear how one would do that (possibly a "gift over" clause, which specified the gift would be returned to a different purpose if the charitable purpose failed in a particular way, or language demonstrating "purposeful and permanent exclusion of all others").

61   *See, e.g.*, Bogert, *supra* note 27. Masayuki Tamaruya discusses how the Japanese model of nonprofit governance has moved away from a sole emphasis on external, state-based enforcement and towards internal, fiduciary-based systems for ensuring public trust and limiting corruption. *See* Masayuki Tamaruya, *Fiduciary Law and Japanese Nonprofits: A Historical and Comparative Synthesis*, ch. 14 (this volume).

62   Johnson & Taylor, *supra* note 21, at 572.

63   *Id.* at 573, n. 199 (stating "I find it extremely odd, even counterintuitive, that the settlor of the trust is not allowed to sue to enforce the trust."). (To be clear, this is at least partly a feature, not a bug, of paradigms: a model is meant to simplify reality and make it tractable, and in doing so will focus attention on some aspects while blurring others.)

64   Oregon Office of the Attorney General, "A Guide to Nonprofit Board Service in Oregon" (2020), https://www .doj.state.or.us/wp-content/uploads/2017/03/guide-nonprofit-board-service.pdf.

interest, merely of following the charter and donor will—ideas entirely grounded in contractual relationships.[65]

Increasingly it has begun to be assumed this had *always* been the attorney general's primary role. When, in a dispute over the Hershey Trust, the Pennsylvania attorney general asserted its ability to represent the "public welfare" beyond the strict terms of the trust, commentators suggested this had broadened the narrower definitions of the attorney general's power, as being limited to enforcing the trust on behalf of its named beneficiaries. But the attorney general's historical role had been very much as the representative of the public interest; ensuring fidelity to charitable intent was subservient, at best a means to, serving public goals which an accountable public officer such as the attorney general could best assess.[66]

C *The Recasting of the Duty of Obedience*

A third change has been a rise in references to the "duty of obedience" in the nonprofit sector, which is increasingly taken to mean a duty to the contract with one's donors. In part, this rise appears to stem from doctrinal confusion, the result of the collapse of a clear distinction between trust and corporate law within the nonprofit sector. Many scholars today regularly assert that directors of nonprofit organizations owe a "duty of obedience," separate from their duties of care and loyalty, although others (consistent with for-profit corporate law) reject the notion that there is a third, separate duty.

On a practical level, most guides that explain the law to not-for-profit directors appear to recognize a duty of obedience and break it out as a separate, third category. These colloquial restatements often create more confusion than clarity. They often refer to the duty of "obedi-ence" as being a duty owed to original "mission" or to "donor intent"—rather than more accurately framing it as a duty to the organization itself. Further confusion occurs because these explanations do not distinguish between corporate fiduciary obligations, versus fiduciary obligations that might be owed under trust law if and when the nonprofit organization itself is the trustee of a formal trust. (Any particular gift may or may not be given as a trust.)

Historically, in the business law context, directors' duty of obedience existed as a requirement that fiduciaries must not commit ultra vires acts. Once that doctrine faded from relevance, the term has rarely been used, although it is occasionally used by scholars to refer to *Caremark*-style duties, owed as a result of the duty of loyalty, to ensure that a company complies with governing law.[67] The duty appears much more prevalent in not-for-profit discussions, which has led some to say that the duty of obedience "survived" as a peculiar residual in not-for-profit organizational law. However, a more accurate statement would be that it was resurrected or rediscovered in the last few decades—and made consistent with the new paradigm of contract.

Indeed, there were scarce mentions of the phrase in law reviews or case law until a 1999 New York state case. In a statement that is now regularly quoted, that court ruled that the board's "duty of obedience ... mandates that a board, in the first instance, seek to preserve its *original* mission" (emphasis added). "Original" appears to have come from nowhere, and tellingly, the court cites no cases, as this was a novel use of the duty of obedience. Its justification was simply that such a duty was "axiomatic." A decision by the board to reprioritize its mission was not, in

---

[65] Attorney General's Response to Plaintiff's Motion for Temporary Restraining Order, filed in Rockwell et al. v. Trustees of the Berkshire Museum, No. 1776CV00253 (Berkshire County Superior Court), Oct. 30, 2017.

[66] *See, e.g.*, 10 AM. JUR. CHARITIES 115.5 (1937).

[67] Alan R. Palmiter, *Duty of Obedience: The Forgotten Duty*, 55 N.Y. L. SCH. L. REV. 457, 459–65 (2010).

this court's view, a viable option, even though it obviously would be in a for-profit context; instead, "all reasonable effort[s] to preserve the mission" was required.[68]

The justification drew on an old chestnut: now that the contract paradigm had arrived, the nonprofit needed a principal. The court quoted a New York treatise co-authored by Kurtz to find that the equivalent of the shareholder-profit motive here was the "perpetuation of particular activities." The *perpetuation*, tellingly, has become the "raison d'etre of the organization." In turn, this language has crept in elsewhere, without acknowledgment of its controversial role.[69] Even if it does not constitute formal law in most places, the heightened rhetoric around the original mission will likely influence the practice of not-for-profit boards.

The contractual paradigm plays a clear role in morphing the doctrine, without those using the phrase seemingly being aware of the change. In earlier common law, the duty of obedience referred to obeying governing law; now it is about obedience to private contract. It is regularly characterized as a duty to the "charter," to "original mission," or even more specifically to the wishes of a donor. One influential guide to director liability describes the duty of obedience as "akin to that of a trustee in a manner faithful to the expressed wishes of the creator."[70] This recent rhetoric essentially revives the doctrine of ultra vires, arguably in an even more aggressive form, in the not-for-profit sector. The ABA's guide for directors refers to the duty of obedience "adhering to the mission for which it was established."[71] Other scholars speak of the duty of obedience as "honoring a donor's intent."[72]

A similar trend, towards a more "originalist," charter-bound view of an organization's purpose, also emerged in debates over the ALI project on charities. An early 2005 draft made it clear that a board could change its purpose at will, drawing more from corporate law principles.[73] More recent iterations specified that the fiduciary duty of loyalty includes an affirmative obligation on directors to seek cy près or deviation to change a gift, rather than simply assuming that the threat of impermissible deviations would be protected sufficiently by existing state laws restricting deviations. Even the ALI's basic statement of the fiduciary duty of loyalty encompasses the concept of an organization's "purposes," and its text would restrict the use of assets to "that charity's purpose at the time the assets were acquired." The ALI authors emphasize the general applicability of cy près to corporate assets for "reflect[ing] the expectations of donors,"[74] which again was not the original goal of cy près.

The prior public trust paradigm did not have anything analogous to such a duty to the original purpose or a donor. Loyalty was owed to the organization itself, whose ultimate purposes had to be public-serving. By contrast, the contract model required that one spell out what and to whom agents were loyal. These moves, which suggest a view of boards far narrower than their for-profit counterparts, have been further buttressed by new state laws that provide state oversight for changes of purpose. An example is a Massachusetts law passed in the late 1980s requiring

---

68 Manhattan Eye, Ear & Throat Hosp. v. Spitzer, 186 Misc. 2d 126 (Sup. Ct. N.Y. 1999).

69 Commonwealth v. New Foundations, Inc., 182 A.3d 1059, 1067 (Pa. Commw. Ct. 2018) (stating, without citation to authority, that a "director of a nonprofit also has the duty of loyalty and obedience.").

70 DANIEL KURTZ, BOARD LIABILITY: GUIDE FOR NONPROFIT DIRECTORS (1988). The mention of "trustee" in many of these discussions has led some to suggest that the duty of obedience comes from trust law, but the term is not mentioned in any Restatement of Trust. Of course, loyalty duties in trust law do require faithful execution of trust instruments — but the instruments involved in the contemporary not-for-profit duty of obedience cases are not trusts.

71 AMERICAN BAR ASSOCIATION COORDINATING COMMITTEE ON NONPROFIT GOVERNANCE, GUIDE TO NONPROFIT CORPORATE GOVERNANCE IN THE WAKE OF SARBANES-OXLEY (2005).

72 Thomas Lee Hazen & Lisa Love Hazen, *Punctilios and Nonprofit Corporate Governance: A Comprehensive Look at Nonprofit Directors' Fiduciary Duties*, 14 U.PA.BUS.L. 347 (2012).

73 Principles of the Law of Nonprofit Orgs. § 240 (Am. Law. Inst. Council Draft No. 5, 2007).

74 Restatement of the Law of Charitable Nonprofit Org. § 3.01 (Am Law. Inst. Tentative Draft No. 1, 2016).

notification of the attorney general for changes in a nonprofit's mission. That trend towards an originalist contract also appears in revisions to the model nonprofit acts. The drafting committee of the 1988 Revised Model Nonprofit Act was "virtually unanimous" in its decision to reject such an idea.[75] But in revisions in 2008, expanded language gestures towards the idea of making it difficult to shift mission.[76]

How do we know the contract paradigm played a role in this shift? Again, the most compelling evidence is the fact that even critics of these moves have adopted the language of contracts and agency costs.[77] One critic who supports more leniency for boards—that is, drawing more from corporate law than trust law—nonetheless views nonprofit law as addressing an agency costs problem of balancing the trustee-beneficiary and trustee-settlor relationships. The argument is based on a comparative assessment of different types of contractual default rules. Other skeptics of donor standing, including one who argues for establishing new nonprofit organizations to monitor other nonprofits, still use the contractarian language of agency costs and monitoring incentives.[78] Others have drawn on other aspects of the contractarian literature, such as using the market for corporate control as a way of improving nonprofit governance.[79]

D Contract Theory in Other Key Debates

Other live debates in the not-for-profit sector—largely outside of formal law, but more about not-for-profit-practice—also appear rooted in, and influenced by, the contract paradigm. This is not surprising, in part because the contract paradigm resonated with other trends in the nonprofit sector. These include the professionalization of the nonprofit sector in the 1970s and 1980s; the uncertainty and vulnerability wrought on many nonprofit institutions by the culture wars of the 1980s; responses to a sequence of scandals in the nonprofit sector in the 1990s; the "new" philanthropy of the 1990s and 2000s, with its more muscular, results-oriented donors; and efforts to "democratize" the independent sector in the 2000s through today.

One challenge has been to the concept of "public ownership." As noted earlier, the prevailing conception of charities as being grounded in the public trust, prior to contract's rise, regularly invoked sweeping language about public ownership of wealth. Charitable property was, for American Jurisprudence, "public property . . . consecrated to the public use, and becomes part of the public resources for promoting the happiness and well-being of the people of the state"—a reference not found anywhere in today's edition of American Jurisprudence.[80] The contract paradigm has no room for "public ownership." Contemporary scholars routinely reject arguments about the idea of public ownership. In a paper commissioned by the Philanthropy Roundtable, the most prominent lobbyist for donor rights, Evelyn Brody and John Tyler argue that public pressure on nonprofits (for compliance or anything else) cannot be justified on the basis of their assets being "public money," for "philanthropic assets cannot fairly be characterized as public money."[81]

---

[75] Lizabeth Moody, *The Who, What, and How of the Revised Model Nonprofit Corporation Act*, 16 N. Ky. L. Rev. 251 (1988).

[76] Model Nonprofit Corporation Act § 10.09 (3d ed.) (Am. Bar Ass'n 2008).

[77] Robert Katz, *Let Charitable Directors Direct: Why Trust Law Should Not Curb Board Discretion Over a Charitable Corporation's Mission and Unrestricted Assets*, 80 Chi.-Kent L. Rev. 689 (2005).

[78] Atkinson, *supra* note 2.

[79] Dana Brakman Reiser, *Nonprofit Takeovers: Regulating the Market for Mission Control*, 2006 B.Y.U. L. Rev. 1181.

[80] 10 Am.Jur. Charities § 121 (1937).

[81] Evelyn Brody & John Tyler, "How Public is Private Philanthropy? Separating Reality from Myth" (Philanthropy Roundtable 2009).

A broad trend towards professionalization in the nonprofit sector has gone alongside this. This trend often stresses commitments to constituencies, such as a "donor bill of rights," or the idea of "accountability" to particular groups. Funders, too, are more likely to require particular rules, to specify governance constraints, or to receive audits, to protect their contractual rights. Even arguments against "undemocratic" and self-perpetuating boards draw on ideas of contract, as their focus is the importance of "accountability" and "representativeness" to those party to the not-for-profit's "bargain."

The growth of transactional sophistication in the not-for-profit context has also tended to make charitable gifts more contract-like. The traditional means of giving was either a family foundation or a direct gift to charity. Today, the number of options for giving has exploded—from charitable LLCs to directed trusts to venture philanthropy forms that employ a mix of for-profit and nonprofit structures. Many of these options exist in large part to give donors more control over their investments—to be able to more efficiently direct and enforce their bargain.

Donor-advised funds, a prevalent modern vehicle for giving, are a remarkable example of the success of charity-as-contract. The idea of a donor-advised fund is to provide a large umbrella fund that allows donors to pool funds and take an immediate tax write-off while maintaining some autonomy over how the funds will ultimately be used but saving on transaction costs. In practice, donor-advised funds nearly always do what their donors want; but in their formal language, they *must* insist on maintaining absolute discretion over the final disposition of funds and being able to overrule their donors' wishes, because of IRS requirements. A recent case has called that discretion into question and essentially adopted the donor-as-contract model. Fidelity Charitable Fund, which maintains a large pool of donor-advised funds, was sued by a client who had placed funds in that pool. The court rejected Fidelity's argument that the plaintiff could not possibly have standing, despite the typical bar on beneficiary standing. The court noted that charitable trust governance was not solely about public interest but also about "the interest of the donors who have directed that their contributions be used for certain charitable purposes."[82]

IV CONCLUSION

Charitable law should have been a hard field for the contract paradigm to rewrite. Not only did early contributors to the contractarian school exclude charities, but charities raise particular challenges that are not present elsewhere in business law. It is hard to apply principal-agent models to charitable organizations, largely because it remains hard to identify a clear principal. And charities implicate the "public" in a way that traditional corporations do not, given the tax code's requirement that a charity provide a public benefit.

Yet the contract paradigm now pervades charity—and largely without it having been noticed. Reigning paradigms often swallow the history that came before, decontextualizing old arguments that rested on a very different set of assumptions. Consider one final example, based on one of the oldest and most famous cases of not-for-profit law in the United States, the 1819 case of *Dartmouth College* vs. *Woodward*.[83] It is today invoked as an "early and influential theory of charitable giving ... grounded in the importance of donor intent."[84] Now that the contract

---

[82] Fairbairn v. Fidelity Investments Charitable Gift Fund, 2018 WL 6199684 (N.D. Cal., Nov. 28, 2018).

[83] 17 U.S. 481 (1819).

[84] Tait, *supra* note 35, at 1673. Others have done the same: In the ALI project, *Dartmouth* is said to be about the "implied contract between the state and every benefactor who should give money to the corporation" and a case about the "importance of honoring restrictions on charitable assets to encourage donations," because of a quote saying gifts would "flow forever in the channel which the givers have marked out for it." RESTATEMENT OF THE LAW OF CHARITABLE NONPROFIT ORG. §§ 1.02; 4.01 (AM. LAW. INST. 2019).

paradigm is here, commentators have recast it as a case about implied contracts with donors. But this is not true, and not just because this is not the focus of the case (it was primarily a case about a constitutional issue, was an outlier at its time, and was quickly relegated by a quick technical fit). It is not true because *Dartmouth* quite explicitly *rejects* many of the ideas of donation-as-contract, such as the possibility of third-party standing. In fact, a better reading sees it as standing directly in the stream of public trust theory: courts there, and in related cases, were limiting doctrines that would block change and evolution and thus "prevent the state from preserving and protecting the public interest."[85]

Paradigms are powerful at recasting history, and at refocusing scholarly inquiry. This does not mean they are wrong, or that the normative results of the contract paradigm have led to worse outcomes in the not-for-profit world. However, it does point to contract theory's influence in shaping scholarship that otherwise claims to be neutral. And it is a reminder of how hard it can be to observe or recognize the prevailing paradigm when one is standing in the middle of it.

---

[85]   R. N. Denham, *An Historical Development of the Contract Theory in the Dartmouth College Case*, 7 MICH. L. REV. 201 (1909).

14

Fiduciary Law and Japanese Nonprofits: A Historical and Comparative Synthesis

Masayuki Tamaruya[*]

I INTRODUCTION

Ensuring the proper governance of nonprofit organizations while simultaneously encouraging robust voluntary works has posed a perennial challenge for policy makers around the globe. In recent years, Japanese law regarding nonprofits has undergone extensive changes. In 2006, legislation was introduced to replace the then-110-year-old Civil Code provisions for public-interest corporations. In fact, the 2006 legislative changes represent the culmination of a nonprofit law reform that has spanned nearly a quarter of a century. The process is not yet complete. The Legislative Council within the Japanese Ministry of Justice has recently published the General Outline for the reform of public-interest trust legislation.

This chapter will present the evolution of Japanese law regarding nonprofits from a comparative historical perspective and assess its achievements. Section II will provide a historical overview of Japanese law regarding nonprofits, beginning with the introduction of the Civil Code in 1896 and continuing until the 1980s. The evolution of Japanese nonprofit law is characterized by complex interactions among the indigenous nonprofit tradition and influences from both civil law and common law jurisdictions. The post-World War II expansion of the administrative state amplified the role of the government in the governance of nonprofits. Beginning in the 1970s, however, growing criticism of mismanagement and corruption involving public-interest corporations and supervising government authorities created momentum for reform.

The major theme of this chapter is the shift in the governance approach brought by the reform movement since the 1990s. As outlined in Section III, the overhaul of nonprofit legislation in 2006 represented a shift of emphasis from external governance through government regulation to internal governance that relies on fiduciary principles and transparency. The shift has not been without challenges. The fiduciary governance introduced in public-interest corporations through statute does not automatically apply to many other entity forms used by the nonprofit sector. Even with regard to public-interest corporations, only a few cases have been decided to indicate how the new approach applies in practice. Section IV will use the available statistics and empirical studies to critically examine the reform's achievements and consider any remaining issues.

[*] I am grateful for valuable comments from Deborah DeMott, Daniel Foote, Arthur Laby, Mark Levin, Mark Ramseyer, Jacob Russell, Yoshiharu Shiraishi, and other participants in the following workshops: Fiduciary Obligations in Business (Rutgers Law School, October 2018), New Perspectives in Japanese Law (Harvard Law School, September 2018), Sixth Annual Fiduciary Law Workshop (Washington University School of Law, June 2018). I am also grateful for the generous research funding provided by Japan Society for the Promotion of Science, KAKENHI Grant Numbers JP15KK0100 and JP26380017.

A note on the terms "public interest (*koeki*)" and "charitable (*jizen*)" is warranted here. The term "public interest" has a broad meaning that includes "charitable" purposes. According to the version of the Civil Code introduced in 1896, a "public-interest corporation" was to serve the open-ended purposes of "worship, religion, *charity*, scholarship, art, or other public interests," subject to governmental permission and oversight.[1] By the end of the twentieth century, the broad concept of public interest in the nonprofit context had attracted criticism in connection with concerns about the degree of government influence that could be exerted through its supervisory capacity. Following the 2006 reform, "public interest" has been understood more narrowly. Under the current statute, public-interest corporations must still serve "scholarship, art, charity, or other public interests" and benefit members of the general public, but a table appended to the statute specifies twenty-three categories of services to which public-interest corporations can direct their effort.[2] These statutory categories parallel the charitable purposes commonly listed in charity legislation in common law jurisdictions.[3] Today, many Japanese lawyers use the term "public-interest corporation" or "public-interest trust" in a way that is equivalent to the common law terms "charitable organization" and "charitable trust."

II THE JAPANESE LAW OF NONPROFITS IN COMPARATIVE PERSPECTIVE

The Civil Code of 1896 introduced the modern law of nonprofits to Japan.[4] It was, however, not the only source, as common law trust was introduced in 1922, and both of these Western influences had to interact with local conditions, most notably the charitable enterprises indigenous to Japan, and the growing administrative state after World War II.

A *The Civil Law Tradition*

The Civil Code provided for two forms of public-interest corporations. One was an association, a membership-based corporation that could not distribute profits to its members but allowed them flexibility in designing their activities according to the collective will. The other was a foundation, an endowment-based entity without membership, typically established for enduring functions, such as educational or medical institutions. The Civil Code provided that "an association or foundation that concerns worship, religion, charity, scholarship, art, or other public interests, and whose purpose is not profit-making, may be incorporated by receiving permission (*kyoka*) from the competent governmental authority."[5] This contrasted with a for-profit corporation under the Commercial Code, which could be created automatically if certain statutory requirements were satisfied. According to Kenjiro Ume, a drafter of the Japanese Civil Code, the corporations involving public interests required special governmental regulation.[6]

---

[1] MINPŌ (CIVIL CODE), Law No. 89 of 1896 [hereinafter Civil Code], § 34 (repealed by the Law No. 50 of 2006) (emphasis added).

[2] Kōeki Shadan Hōjin oyobi Kōeki Zaidan Hōjin no Nintei tō ni kansuru Hōritsu [Public Interest Association Corporation and Public Interest Foundation Corporation Authorization Act] [hereinafter Public Interest Corporation Authorization Act], Law No. 49 of 2006 [hereinafter Public Interest Corporation Authorization Act], § 2(iv), Beppyō [Appended Table].

[3] *Compare* Appended Table to the Public Interest Corporation Authorization Act § 2 *with* Charities Act 2011 c 25, s 3(1) (U.K.); RESTATEMENT (THIRD) OF TRUSTS § 28 (AM. LAW INST. 2001); UNIF. TRUST CODE § 405 (UNIF. LAW COMM'N 2010).

[4] Civil Code §§ 33–83.

[5] *Id.* § 34.

[6] KENJIRŌ UME, MINPŌ YŌGI I [LECTURE ON CIVIL CODE I], 68 (1896).

In the nineteenth century, the law of nonprofit organizations was still evolving in Continental Europe. The Napoleonic Code of 1804 contained no provision for legal personality.[7] Anti-association attitudes prevailed in the subsequent French Republic, where the public interest was considered the exclusive prerogative of state bodies. The Japanese Government entrusted a French lawyer, Gustave Boissonade, with the task of drafting the Japanese Civil Code. As introduced in parliament, the Boissonade Code only provided that "[a] legal person, whether public or private in nature, can only be created by virtue of statutory authorization; it can enjoy private right only in accordance with the statutory provisions."[8] Although it was passed by the Parliament in 1890, it never came into force for political reasons. The Japanese drafters of the Civil Code then looked to Germany, which was in the process of drafting its own Civil Code.[9] This second Civil Code, which came into effect in Japan in 1896, mirrors many aspects of the German Civil Code, which came into effect in 1900.[10]

Significant parallels between the German and Japanese Civil Codes can be observed in their distinction between membership-based associations and endowment-based foundations,[11] as well as their organizational structure. Both associations and foundations acted through directors, who represented the entity in all transactions relating to the corporation.[12] Although neither Code prescribed a director's specific duties, limitations were imposed on transactions that may represent a conflict of interest,[13] and directors were subject to rules applicable to agents acting under the contract of mandate.[14] In Japanese contexts, directors were regarded as owing "the duty of care of faithful managers,"[15] a term of art found in the Japanese Civil Code that encompasses duties of care and loyalty in common law formulations.[16] For associations, the general assembly of the members had the power to appoint directors[17] and make decisions on corporate matters,[18] while foundations were not member-based and had no general assembly to convene. In Japan, an auditor could be appointed and tasked with auditing the corporate books and assets, as well as supervising directors' role in running

---

7   The French Civil Code did contain provisions on partnership (*société*), which has no legal personality. Voluntary association (*association*) was only made legal by statute in 1901. Edith Archambault, *France, in* Defining the Nonprofit Sector: A Cross-National Analysis 103, 104–05 (Lester M. Salamon & Helmut K. Anheier eds., 1997).

8   Minpō Jinji-hen [Civil Code Book of Person], Law No. 98 of 1880, § 5 (repealed by Minpō [Civil Code], Law No. 89 of 1896).

9   Masaaki Tomii, Minpō Genri Dai-Ikkan: Sōron [The Principles of Civil Code I: General Principles] 184–85 (1905).

10   Bürgerliches Gesetzbuch (Civil Code) [hereinafter German Civil Code]. Following discussion relies on the English translation of the 1900 German Civil Code in Chung Hui Wang, The German Civil Code: Translated and Annotated with an Historical Introduction and Appendices (1907). For Japanese studies comparing Japanese and German Civil Codes provisions on associations and foundations, *see* Minoru Tanaka, Kōeki Hōjin to Kōeki Shintaku [Public Interest Corporations and Public Interest Trusts] 7–8 (1980); Toshiji Hayashi, [Zaidan, Zaidan Hōjin no Kenkyū [Studies on Foundation and Incorporated Foundations] 377–402 (1983).

11   Japanese Civil Code § 34. The German Civil Code has separate sets of provisions for associations (§§ 21–79) and foundations (§§ 80–88).

12   Japanese Civil Code §§ 52, 53; German Civil Code §§ 26, 86.

13   Japanese Civil Code § 57 (a conflicted director cannot represent the corporation); German Civil Code §§ 27(3), 86, 668 (the director as an agent must pay interest).

14   German Civil Code §§ 27(3), 668 (application *mutatis mutandis* of the Code §§ 664–670 on the contract of mandate). Japanese law reached the same conclusion through statutory interpretation. Sakae Wagatsuma, et al., [Wagatsuma, Ariizumi Konmentāru Minpō, Sōsoku, Bukken, Saiken [Wagatsuma and Ariizumi's Commentary on Civil Code: General Principles, Property, and Obligation] 131 (4th ed. 2016). Mandates, understood as a species of contracts in civil law jurisdictions are modern descendants of Roman law analogous to the agency relationship in common law. Martin Gelter & Geneviève Helleringer, *Fiduciary Principles in European Civil Law Systems, in* Oxford Handbook of Fiduciary Law 581, 588–90 (Evan J. Criddle, Paul B. Miller & Robert H. Sitkoff eds., 2019).

15   Japanese Civil Code § 644 (the duty of care of a faithful manager).

16   J. Mark Ramseyer & Masayuki Tamaruya, *Fiduciary Principles in Japanese Law, in* Oxford Handbook of Fiduciary Law 643, 643 (Evan J. Criddle, Paul B. Miller & Robert H. Sitkoff eds., 2019).

17   Japanese Civil Code § 6; German Civil Code § 27.

18   Japanese Civil Code § 63; German Civil Code § 32.

a given entity.[19] Nevertheless, it was still possible for the auditor to fail to provide sufficient oversight or even collude with the directors in their pursuit of illicit objectives. Thus, as stated by a drafter of the Civil Code, Masaaki Tomii, the government was expected to provide "supreme supervision" over public-interest corporations.[20]

In broad terms, the Japanese Code provisions echoed the stable pattern of cooperation between the state and the nonprofit sector, which paralleled that of nineteenth-century Germany.[21] At the same time, the Japanese approach to the supervision of the nonprofits tended to be more centralized. Under the German federal system, the supervision of nonprofit entities was delegated to each state, which seemingly exercised broad discretion.[22] In comparison, Japanese public-interest corporations were subject to discretionary supervision that applied nationally.[23] Eiichi Hoshino, an eminent scholar on the Civil Code in Japan, remarked that the idea that the determination of the public interest belongs exclusively to the government held sway well into the latter half of the twentieth century.[24] Until the 2006 reform, the governance of public interest corporations, beginning from their creation and continuing through the ongoing management to dissolution, was largely entrusted to discretionary oversight by the government.

Another departure from the German Civil Code was the Japanese Code's focus on "the public interest." As already discussed,[25] the scope of operation the Japanese Civil Code allowed for public-interest corporations—service to "worship, religion, charity, academic activities, art, or other public interests"[26]—was open-ended compared to that of common law charity regulation.[27] Nevertheless, compared to the German Code, which distinguished between for-profit and non-profit entities but did not create a category for charitable or public-interest purposes,[28] the Japanese focus was narrow. Because the 1896 Civil Code disallowed the incorporation of an organization unless sanctioned by the Code or other specific legislation, those organizations that pursued mutual benefit or undefined nonprofit purposes had to either operate as unincorporated organizations or seek specialized legislation to incorporate themselves.[29]

The Civil Code provisions for public-interest corporations remained unchanged for over a century. However, World War II had a profound impact on the operation of Japanese public-interest corporations. During the war, practically all public-interest corporations were required to align themselves with the government's war efforts. After World War II, constitutional constraints were imposed on the government to prohibit the use of public funds for religion and education.[30] In response, special legislation was introduced to create different types of legal personalities for religious[31] and school corporations.[32] The destruction and subsequent hyperinflation caused by the war also posed a challenge for many public-interest organizations. One

---

19 Japanese Civil Code §§ 58, 59.
20 TOMII, *supra* note 9, at 234.
21 Helmut K. Anheier & Wolfgang Seibel, *Germany, in* DEFINING THE NONPROFIT SECTOR: A CROSS-NATIONAL ANALYSIS 128 (Lester M. Salamon & Helmut K. Anheier eds., 1997).
22 German Civil Code §§ 43, 44. *See* TANAKA, *supra* note 10, at 7; HAYASHI, *supra* note 10, at 381-82.
23 Japanese Civil Code § 67.
24 EIICHI HOSHINO, MINPŌ NO SUSUME [LEARNING THE CIVIL CODE] 96 (1998).
25 *See supra* notes 1–3, and accompanying text.
26 Japanese Civil Code § 34.
27 *See* Charitable Uses Act 1601; *Income Tax Special Purposes Commissioners v Pemsel* [1891] All ER Rep 28 (Lord McNaughten); Charities Act 1960 (U.K.).
28 German Civil Code § 21.
29 Japanese Civil Code § 6.
30 NIHONKOKU KENPŌ [KENPŌ] [CONSTITUTION] § 20 (freedom of religion and separation of religion and state), § 89 (restriction on public spending on any religious or educational institutions).
31 Shūkyō Hōjin Hō [Religious Corporations Act], Law No. 125 of 1951.
32 Shiritsu Gakkō Hō [Private Schools Act], Law 270 of 1949, §§ 25–58.

major avenue for survival was an organization's option to convert itself into a newly created entity as a social welfare[33] or medical corporation,[34] which was then placed under the auspices of the Ministry of Health and played an integral role in providing national social and medical services. These major nonprofit sectors were thus carved out of the public-interest corporation sector, and an idiosyncratic management and governance regime developed within each sector.[35]

This brief overview of the comparative and historical context reveals the notable features of Japanese nonprofit legislation. While the oversight of nonprofit management was delegated to separate governmental departments with discretionary authority, the rules of internal fiduciary governance remained unarticulated for an extended period. While numerous forms of government-sponsored entities were introduced to partition the Japanese nonprofit sector, no legal mechanism existed through which a grassroots nonprofit organization could be incorporated. These features would become the major foci of reform in the late twentieth century.

B Indigenous Nonprofits

Before the introduction of the modern Civil Code, Japan had its own tradition for nonprofit or charitable enterprises. Since the seventh and eighth centuries, large Buddhist temples established hospitals and charities to provide food for the poor.[36] Buddhist temples were not necessarily independent institutions but established to further the interests of the state or powerful clans. More recently, in the eighteenth or nineteenth century, thousands of village institutions known as *Terakoya* (temple schools) were in operation, thus contributing to a high rate of literacy that resulted in the country's modernization, which began in the late nineteenth century.[37]

Nevertheless, the transition from indigenous charities to modern public-interest corporations was not easy. This is illustrated by the history of a secular nonprofit called *Kan'on-kō* (Society of Gratitude) founded in 1829 in Akita, a northeastern region of Japan.[38] A wealthy merchant named Sukenari Naba and his followers donated 2,000 *ryō* (equivalent to 260 million yen or $2.5 million today) to the domain government (*han*), which purchased farmland so feudal revenue could alleviate the region's poverty and prepare for possible famines.[39] Although Naba intended to donate the funds to the domain government, the government delegated its practical management to him and his fellow managers. They later agreed, with the approval of the authority, that the fund belonged to neither the authority nor its subjects.[40]

In 1871, *Kan'on-kō* faced a major challenge soon after the Meiji restoration, when the newly established government confiscated the endowment as part of the centralization of the government structure and the modernization of the property system. Following repeated petitions, the government returned 6,000 yen in 1874 and 53,350 yen in 1881 (the total amount is equivalent to 1.18 billion

[33] Shakai Fukushi Jigyō Hō [Social Welfare Services Act], Law No. 45 of 1951, renamed as Shakai Fukushi Hō [Social Welfare Act] by Law No. 111 of 2000.

[34] Iryō Hō [Medical Care Act], Law No. 205 of 1948.

[35] Masayuki Deguchi, *Globalization, Glocalization, and Galapagos Syndrome: Public Interest Corporations in Japan*, 18 INT'L J. NOT-FOR-PROFIT L. 5, 6 (2016).

[36] Takayoshi Amenomori, *Japan*, in DEFINING THE NONPROFIT SECTOR: A CROSS-NATIONAL ANALYSIS 188, 190–91 (Lester M. Salamon & Helmut K. Anheier eds., 1997).

[37] *Id.* See also Wataru Fujiwara, *Nihon no Minkan Hieiri Soshiki no Genryū [The Sources of Private Nonprofit Organizations in Japan]*, in NIHON NO NPO-SHI: NPO NO REKISHI WO YOMU, GENZAI, KAKO, MIRAI [THE HISTORY OF JAPANESE NPO: READING THE HISTORY OF NPO, PRESENT, PAST AND FUTURE] 1, 13–14 (Makoto Imada ed., 2006).

[38] KAN'ON-KŌ, KAN'ON-KŌ SHI [KAN'ON-KŌ JOURNAL] (1921); TANAKA, *supra* note 10, at 27–56.

[39] The legal history of *Kan'on-kō* is narrated in Zennosuke Nakagawa, *Kan'on-kō Hōritsushi: Nihon Hōjinshi no Ichi Shiryō [The Legal History of Kan'on-kō: A Material for the History of Organizational Law in Japan]*, 49 HŌGAKU-KYŌKAI ZASSHI [J. JURIS. ASS'N] 80 (1931).

[40] KAN'ON-KŌ, *supra* note 38, at 5.

yen and \$10.8 million today).[41] Another crisis struck *Kan'on-kō* shortly thereafter when donors sued its managers (*nenban*) based on their assertion of partial ownership of the fund and the right to be informed of its management.[42] The case was eventually brought to the Supreme Court (*Taishin'in*), which ruled in favor of *Kan'on-kō*'s managers in 1890.[43] The Court held that *Kan'on-kō* could be understood as a foundation without an owner, and upheld the lower court judgment, which characterized *Kan'on-kō* as a moral person for charitable purposes. The Supreme Court held that the donor relinquished ownership to the property in the form of a gift to the *Kan'on-kō* and had no entitlement to its funds.

These legal challenges prompted *Kan'on-kō* to codify its governing rules. After excavating old documents and practices and seeking legal advice, a constitutional document (*kanrei*) was drawn up in 1892.[44] The drafting process attracted the attention of Boissonade, who was finishing the draft of the initial Civil Code. Boissonade provided several rounds of editing support, and personally contributed fifty yen (1 million yen or \$9,100 today) to the fund. When the new Civil Code was introduced to replace the Boissonade Code, *Kan'on-kō* was duly registered as a foundation in 1898.

During World War II, the organization suffered a more serious blow. After the war, the Supreme Commander for the Allied Powers issued a series of orders intended to democratize Japan. As part of the farmland reform, large landholdings were repossessed by the government and redistributed to numerous tenant farmers. *Kan'on-kō*'s land was also subject to repossession, thereby depriving it of the property basis for its poverty relief works.[45] Work could only be continued via reliance on a government subsidy provided by the Social Welfare Services Act of 1948. In 1951, *Kan'on-kō* converted itself to a social welfare corporation and has since served the community by running an orphanage.

In Akita alone, at least 18 *Kan'on-kō*s followed Naba's example, and numerous *ko*s were scattered throughout pre-modern Japan. Their purposes and structures varied.[46] The introduction of uniform rules applicable to charitable institutions did not occur until the Meiji restoration. Yet the same government was hostile to such local charitable initiatives, and the modernization of the landholding system through the abolition of feudal incidents was irreconcilable with the basic structure of such indigenous endeavors.[47] The same may be said of the democratization of landholdings after World War II, and the subsequent growth of the welfare state. Very few *ko*s and other indigenous charitable arrangements survive today as legally recognized entities.[48]

C *Governance in the Nonprofit Sector*

By the end of World War II, each public-interest corporation was subject to supervision by either one of the national government departments possessing jurisdiction over its activities or the governor of the prefecture within which it operated. The supervision was highly discretionary, as the Japanese

---

[41] *Id.* at 15, 21.

[42] Nakagawa, *supra* note 39, at 109–10.

[43] Taishin'in Judgment of July 9, 1890, as quoted by Nakagawa, *supra* note 39, at 110–11.

[44] KAN'ON-KŌ, KAN'ON-KŌ KANREI GIKAI [KAN'ON-KŌ CUSTOMARY RULES EXPLAINED] (1893).

[45] MICHIO AOKI & SHOJI TAKUYA, KINSEI SHAKAI FUKUSHI SHIRYŌ: AKITA KAN'ON KŌ BUNSHO [HISTORICAL MATERIAL ON MODERN SOCIAL WELFARE: AKITA KAN'ON-KŌ DOCUMENTS] 14 (2000).

[46] Masayuki Deguchi, *Nihon ni okeru Minpō Sekō Mae no Kō to Gendai Hieiri Soshiki to no Tokusei no Kyōtsuusei* [*Similarities between the "Kō" of the Pre-Civil Code era and present-day Nonprofit Organizations (NPOs) in Japan*], 38 KOKURITSU MINZOKUGAKU HAKUBUTSUKAN KENKYŪ HŌKOKU [NATIONAL MUSEUM OF ETHNOLOGY STUDIES REPORT] 299, 305–08 (2014).

[47] Takuya Shoji, *Meiji Zenkin ni okeru Chiiki teki Kyūsai Soshiki no Sonzoku Katei: Kan'on-kō no Hōjinka wo Megutte* [*The Survival of Local Poverty Relief Arrangements in Early Meiji: Kan'on-kō's Transition to a Legal Entity*], 33 SENSHŪ SHIGAKU [SENSHŪ HISTORY REVIEW] 67, 82 (2002).

[48] Deguchi, *supra* note 46, at 310.

Civil Code did not contain specific standards to be applied by the government in reviewing application to the creation of a public-interest corporation or by way of ongoing supervision.[49] By the early 1970s, it was standard practice for those who wished to create a public-interest corporation to consult with government officials in advance of application and adhere to any administrative guidance that was given.[50]

The Japanese court shied away from scrutinizing the government's determination of public-interest corporation status. In *Adachi River-North Medical Association* v. *Governor of Tokyo* (1988),[51] the Tokyo Metropolitan Government denied a petition submitted by a group of physicians to form a new local medical association as a public-interest foundation following their separation from the local Adachi Medical Association due to internal conflict. The lower court sided with the petitioners, asserting that the denial constituted an unlawful abuse of discretion because no factual basis existed for the government's assumption that the establishment of rival medical associations could confuse and disrupt the provision of public health services. However, the Supreme Court reversed this judgment. Citing past instances in which the local government struggled to reconcile the feuding members of the Adachi Medical Association, the Court held that when a governmental decision has a certain factual foundation and is *prima facie* rational, absent exceptional circumstances, the decision does not constitute illegal excess or abuse of administrative discretion.

The supervising departments occasionally made genuine efforts toward enhancing internal governance when issuing permission for a new public-interest corporation. One such method was requiring the bifurcation of the board of directors to create a supervisory council called *hyogi-kai*.[52] The creation of this council was useful for foundations because they had no separate general meeting to which the final authority to monitor directors could be assigned. Such a separate board was created by the founding document and typically given the power to nominate directors and approve fundamental changes to the foundation. The membership-based association did have a general meeting for members, which had the power to determine matters not exempted by the constitutional document and dissolve the association by a three-quarters majority.[53] Nonetheless, members had diverse and sometimes contradictory interests that were not always consistent with those of the general public. The disjunction between members' interest and that of the public remained unarticulated well into the 1990s, even in academic writings.[54]

In the 1960s and 1970s, a series of publicized scandals questioned the effectiveness of governmental supervision over public-interest corporations. One such instance involved the Postal and Transportation Association, a foundation created in 1955 with the Ministry of Posts and Telecommunication's permission.[55] Although its board was filled with prominent figures in politics and industry, including then Prime Minister Eisaku Sato, the foundation had long remained dormant. In 1967, Tokuji Kojima, its newly appointed director, proceeded to collect 450 million yen ($1.3 million) from small business owners as an advance payment for using the welfare facilities center he promised would be built by the Central Tourism Corporation, a for-

[49] Japanese Civil Code § 34 (repealed).

[50] Nihon Kōeki Hōjin Kyōkai [Japan Association of Charitable Organizations] (JACO), Kōeki Hōjin no Setsuritsu, Un'ei, Kantoku no Tebiki [A Handbook for the Establishment, Management, and Supervision of Public Interest Corporations] 12–13 (editorial support by Sōmushō Daijin Kanbō Kanri Shitsu [Internal Affairs Minister's Secretarial Management Office], 6th ed. 2003).

[51] 1297 Hanji 29 (Supreme Court, July 14, 1988).

[52] Tanaka, *supra* note 10, at 16–18. This is similar to the German style of corporate governance. James J. Fishman, *The Development of Nonprofit Corporation Law and an Agenda for Reform*, 34 Emory L. J. 617, 679–83 (1985).

[53] Civil Code §§ 63, 69 (repealed).

[54] Nobuko Kawashima, *Governance of Nonprofit Organizations: Missing Chain of Accountability in Nonprofit Corporation Law in Japan and Arguments for Reform in the U.S.*, 24 UCLA Pac. Basin L. J. 81, 103–105 (2006).

[55] *Chūō Kankō Aratana Kuroi Kiri [Central Tourism and New Dark Fog]*, Yomiuri Shimbun (Aug. 10, 1967).

profit corporation led by him.[56] While Kojima took advantage of the trust that the name of the public foundation generated, his fellow directors and the regulator, the Ministry of Posts and Telecommunication, were apparently unaware of his general operations.[57] After Central Tourism went bankrupt in 1967, the Postal and Transportation Association's permission to operate was revoked, and Kojima and a fellow director investigated for the criminal forgery of private and public documents.[58]

Kojima was then involved in another publicized scandal implicating the National Association for the Traffic Safety of Children. This foundation was established in 1966 with the permission of the Prime Minister's Office and presided by the then ruling Liberal Democratic Party (LDP)'s vice secretary-general, Yuzo Matsuzawa. After becoming the foundation's Vice President, Kojima embezzled five million yen ($13,900) using various tactics, including charging a donor for the cost of printing 100,000 copies of "Safety Booklet for Good Children" while only printing 30,000.[59] Kojima concealed this and other misconduct through off-book transactions.[60]

These revelations were just the tip of the iceberg. In 1971, the Government conducted an inquiry into public-interest corporations and found evidence of inappropriate management in 40 percent of the 106 entities randomly selected from 4,407 public-interest corporations.[61] Issues included the absence of operational records, excessive profit-making, the use of accumulated assets for staff and related persons' benefit and offering directorships to supervising department officials.

Faced with criticism, governmental departments with jurisdiction over public-interest corporations created a standing committee in 1971 to coordinate their guidance and supervisory work.[62] The Civil Code was amended in 1979 to explicitly provide the supervising department with the power to issue supervisory orders and revoke permission upon a public-interest corporation's failure to comply.[63] In July 1986, the standing committee published a standard for the guidance and supervision of the administration of public-interest corporations.[64] These informal standards were updated in the 1980s and 1990s and formalized through the Cabinet Resolution in September 1996.[65] This guidance required organizations to adopt a more rigid organizational structure and accounting procedures. All public-interest corporations were asked to disclose their constitutional and financial documents via the internet, and those entities that provided services under government contract were required to disclose more extensive information on the government department's website.[66] The Cabinet Resolution exhorted public-interest corporations to

[56] *Id.*
[57] *Kōeki Hōjin wo Arai Naose: Ninka Torikeshi Shobun mo [Thorough Investigation Needed for Public Interest Corporation: Possible Revocation of Permissions]*, YOMIURI SHIMBUN (Aug. 10, 1967).
[58] *Shushōin nado Gizō Mitomeru: Teishin Un'yu Kyōkai no Moto Riji [Forgery of Prime Minister's Seal Admitted: Former Director of Postal and Transportation Association]*, YOMIURI SHIMBUN (Sept. 27, 1967).
[59] *Jidō Kōtsū Kyōryoku Kai: Kojima Fukukaichō wo Taiho [Children Traffic Safety Association: Vice President Kojima Arrested]*, YOMIURI SHIMBUN (Jun. 2, 1971).
[60] *Id.*
[61] Administrative Management Agency's report submitted to the Cabinet Meeting on December 21, 1971, as reported in *Daidassen no Kōeki Hōjin: Datsu Mokuteki, Kane Mōke, Zentai no 40 percent mo to Gyōkan Happyō [Public Interest Corporation in Disarray: Lost Purposes and Money Making in over 40 percent of the PICs, Administrative Management Agency Says]*, YOMIURI SHIMBUN (Dec. 21, 1971).
[62] Standing Committee the Supervision of Public Interest Corporations, *Agreement on Standards of Permission for Creation of Public Interest Corporations* (Mar. 1972); *see* JACO, *supra* note 50, at 8.
[63] Civil Code §§ 67(2), 71 (as amended by the Law No. 68 of 1979).
[64] Standing Committee for the Guidance and Supervision of Public Interest Corporations, *Standards of Guidance and Supervision for Public Interest Corporations* (1979).
[65] Cabinet Resolution, *Standards of Permission for Creation and Guidance and Supervision of Public Interest Corporations* (Sept. 1996).
[66] Agreement among Cabinet Ministers Responsible for Guidance and Supervision of Public Interest Corporations, *Disclosure of Public Interest Corporation through the Internet* (Aug. 2001).

actively pursue the benefit of numerous unascertained individuals and demonstrated the intention of eliminating entities that only pursue mutual benefit or provide welfare services for members of a certain group, such as industry associations.[67] Public-interest corporations whose services overlapped and competed with those of for-profit corporations were required to broaden their scope of services or add new ones in the public interest; otherwise, their permission to operate was revoked.[68] However, these tightened regulations ironically made it more difficult for newly formed nonprofits to receive permission for incorporation.

Despite these measures, issues persisted. A government inquiry in 1992 found that nearly 20 percent of a sample comprising 923 public-interest corporations showed evidence of improper administration of charity affairs or weakness in their governance structure.[69] For instance, one unnamed foundation made a profit of 583 million yen ($3.9 million) in 1989 and accumulated almost 2 billion yen ($13.3 million), but showed minimal expenditure toward any public interest.[70] Another foundation, whose ten directors and three auditors were also the officials of a for-profit corporation, invested 43 percent of the foundation's endowment into the for-profit and its affiliates.[71] The report meticulously described and categorized the instances of abuse and mismanagement, while avoiding the identification of any entity or person by anonymizing their names. Nevertheless, these instances of underperformance and corruption fueled the momentum for reform.[72]

D The Evolution of Public-Interest Trusts

The controversy over public-interest corporations led the philanthropists to seek an alternative model of charitable giving: public-interest trusts. Although the Trust Act of 1922 contained eight sections on public-interest trusts, trusts were used exclusively in commercial contexts, and no public-interest trusts had been created for over half a century.[73] In 1976, the government commissioned a comprehensive study of public-interest trusts. The Japan Association of Charitable Organization (JACO) submitted a report, which supported the Japan Business Federation (*Keidanren*) in advocating the use of trusts for philanthropic activities.[74] The first two public-interest trusts in modern Japanese history were created in 1977.

As the 1922 Trust Act was silent on regulatory matters, public-interest trusts were assigned to individual governmental departments for oversight. Of the first two public-interest trusts created in 1977, one was assigned to the Ministry of Foreign Affairs and the other to the Ministry of Infrastructure (now the Ministry of Land, Infrastructure, Transport, and Tourism). Guidance similar to that provided for public-interest corporations was published in 1994, which in practice limited the scope of public-interest trusts to grant-making and providing scholarships.[75] Trusteeship for virtually all public-interest trusts was undertaken by trust banks.

---

[67] Cabinet Resolution, *supra* note 65, at para.1.

[68] *Id.* at para. 2(2).

[69] Ministry of Internal Affairs Administrative Inspection Bureau, *The Present Status and Issues of Public Interest Corporations: Observation from Ministry of Internal Affairs' Audit Result*, 13 (1992).

[70] *Id.* at 15.

[71] *Id.* at 35.

[72] Hiroyasu Nakata, *Kōeki Hōjin, Chōkan Hōjin, NGO [Public Interest Corporations, Intermediate Corporations, and NGOs]*, 1126 JURIST 53, 56 (1998).

[73] Shintaku Hō [Trust Act], Law No. 62 of 1922, §§ 66–73.

[74] Tatsuo Ohta, *Charitable Trust in Japan: An Article submitted to "Charitable Trust Session" at China Charity Fair in Shenzhen, China*, 3–4 (Sept. 19, 2015).

[75] Standing Committee on Guidance and Supervision of Public Interest Corporations, *Standard for Permission to Undertake Public Interest Trusts* (Sept. 1994).

Since 1977, the number of public-interest trusts has steadily increased. By 1990, 304 public-interest trusts had been created to hold 20.9 billion yen ($140 million), and total assets peaked in 2001 at 73.7 billion yen ($615 million), held by 566 public-interest trusts.[76] While the scale of trust assets pales when compared with the 13.6 trillion yen ($124 billion) held by 9,371 public-interest corporations, it is noteworthy that no alleged or proven case of misused public-interest trust had emerged even in the 1980s and 1990s, when public-interest corporations were under incessant criticism and scrutiny. Unlike managers of public interest corporations, trust banks are under the regulatory oversight of the financial authorities. The limited purposes served by the public-interest trusts also made it relatively easy to maintain transparency in operation and management of the funds.

III REFORM MOVEMENTS IN THE 2000S AND 2010S

Toward the end of the twentieth century, criticism of both public-interest corporation misman-agement, and overbearing government oversight, led to a series of reforms in nonprofit law. Legislation was introduced in 1998 to allow a new form of nonprofit organization; the Civil Code provisions governing public-interest corporation were replaced by a new set of legislation in 2006; and as of 2020, a new public interest trust legislation has been proposed. These changes represent a significant shift of emphasis from external governance through government regula-tion to internal governance that relies on fiduciary principles and transparency.

A *Background Shifts*

In 1990, the Japanese economic bubble burst. Political instability came alongside the economic downturn as the LDP lost its almost forty-year-long parliamentary majority in 1993. In 1994, Tomiichi Murayama became the first Socialist Prime Minister in forty-seven years, but this was just the first of several short-lived coalition governments that jostled for control for the remainder of the century. However, the 1990s were a springboard for the comprehensive reform of the Japanese charity sector.[77] In 1995, a disastrous earthquake hit the Hanshin-Awaji area. The earthquake triggered broad civic participation in volunteer works and charitable activities. Various grass-root organizations emerged and demanded recognition of their status as legal entities to facilitate volunteer works. The non-LDP administration was more receptive to the public demand for the reform of public-interest corporations.

In 2000, a scandal erupted at a public-interest corporation called KSD, founded by a former Labor Ministry bureaucrat, Tadao Koseki, with the permission of the Tokyo Metropolitan Government to provide mutual insurance and welfare services for small businesses. In actuality, he hired other retired bureaucrats from the Labor Ministry, paid politicians lavishly for political and bureaucratic advantage, and embezzled massive amounts of money for himself. The courts eventually convicted him and other involved parties on criminal charges.[78] By the 2000s, the administrative reform had attracted national attention calling for a reorganization of the manner in which government works were

---

[76] Shintaku Kyōkai [Trust Companies Association of Japan], *Kōeki Shintaku no Jutaku Jōkyō 2019 Nen 3 Gatsu Genzai [The Status of Charitable Trust Business as of March, 2019]*, 279 SHINTAKU [TRUSTS] 88, 89 (2019).

[77] Masayuki Deguchi, *The Distinction between Institutionalized and Noninstitutionalized NPOs: New Policy Initiatives and Nonprofit Organizations in Japan*, in THIRD SECTOR POLICY AT THE CROSSROADS: AN INTERNATIONAL NON-PROFIT ANALYSIS 153, 158–63 (Helmut K. Anheier & Jeremy Kendall eds., 2001).

[78] 1832 HANREI JIHŌ 39 (Tokyo D.Ct. May 20, 2003), *aff'd*, 62 SAIHAN KEISHŪ 507 (Tokyo High Ct. Dec. 19, 2005), *aff'd*, 1457 HANREI JIHŌ 6 (S. Ct. Mar. 27, 2008).

delegated and subsidies distributed through non-governmental organizations. Thus, the revision of Civil Code provisions on public-interest corporations became a major reform agenda.[79]

The criticism of the governmental supervision of public-interest corporations was complex. On the one hand, regulators were criticized for being too lax. Once public-interest corporations were recognized as such via government permission, many perpetuated abuse and mismanagement beneath the supervisory radar. Government officials operated under conflicts of interest because they were often offered director seats from the public-interest corporations they regulated and received hefty compensation in return upon retirement. On the other hand, regulators were criticized for being overly restrictive. Faced with mounting criticism, regulators allowed incorporation only when a proposed entity possessed sufficient funds and had a managerial structure in place. Meanwhile, the Civil Code granted no entity status for organizations that operated as nonprofits but were non-charitable in nature. This prevented start-up or grassroots voluntary organizations from incorporating themselves.[80]

In 1996, the Civic Activities Promotion Bill was introduced in the legislature as a parliamentary member's bill (*giin rippo*), a rare deviation from the standard practice where the government introduces a bill.[81] In 1998, it ultimately became law as the Specified Nonprofit Activities Promotion Act.[82] The law is intended to enable citizens' groups to obtain a legal personality without discretionary intervention from the government. Thus, a specified nonprofit corporation, commonly known as an *NPO Hōjin* (NPO [nonprofit organization] corporation), can be established by filing the requisite papers with the relevant government office,[83] and the government must approve the application if the papers satisfy the prescribed requirements.[84] Although the 1998 Act contained very limited provisions on directors' fiduciary duties, tax legislation was introduced in 2001 that allowed tax-deductible donations to an NPO corporation that maintains proper governance and contributes to the public interest.[85] Mirroring the American test of public support, such corporations must have a geographically broad funding base or service area, cannot provide more than half of their services to members or other specified groups, and must receive at least one-third of their revenue through donations.[86]

B *The Nonprofit Reform in 2006*

In 2006, the reform momentum of the 1990s culminated in a comprehensive overhaul of public-interest corporation law when three sets of legislation were passed to replace the

---

[79] Cabinet Resolution, *The Comprehensive Reform of Public Interest Corporation Legislation* (Mar. 2002); Cabinet Resolution, *The Principles of Administrative Reform* (Dec. 2004).

[80] Hiroyasu Nakata, *Outline of the General Association and Foundation Corporation Legislation*, 1328 JURIST 2 (2007); AKIRA MORIIZUMI, STUDIES IN PUBLIC INTEREST CORPORATION 6–8 (1977).

[81] Deguchi, *supra* note 77, at 162–63.

[82] Tokutei Hieiri Katsudō Sokushin Hō [Specified Nonprofit Activities Promotion Act], Law No. 7 of 1998 [hereinafter NPO Corporation Act].

[83] NPO Corporation Act § 10.

[84] *Id.* § 12.

[85] NPO Corporation Act § 44; Sozei Tokubetsu Sochi Hō [Tax Special Measures Act], Law No. 26 of 1957, § 41-18-2 (as inserted by Law No. 7 of 2001). The requirement for tax privileges was relaxed through successive amendment to tax legislation in 2003, 2005, 2006, 2008, and 2011.

[86] NPO Corporation Act § 45(i).

previous Civil Code provisions.[87] The statute divides nonprofit corporations into two categories: general and public-interest corporations. General corporations can be created simply by filing with the local registration office without government permission.[88] If the general corporation pursues one or more of the statutorily enumerated public interests and receives authorization from the newly created Public-Interest Commission (*Koueki Nintei-tō Iinkai*), it becomes a public-interest corporation and enjoys certain tax benefits.[89] Modeled after the Charity Commission in England and Wales,[90] the Commission comprises seven commissioners from outside of the government with the mandate to act independently from the administrative body. The Commission administers the standard for permission and operational requirements reformulated and incorporated in the 2006 Public Interest Corporation Authorization Act.[91]

A general corporation can take the form of either an association or a foundation. Although general corporations cannot distribute profits, the range of activities in which they may engage is unlimited. This created the possibility for the incorporation of business interest organizations and mutual benefit groups. A set of governance mechanisms parallel to those used by for-profit corporations was introduced for both general and public-interest corporations. For associations, the general meeting of the members ultimately has the power to determine all matters relating to the corporation,[92] and appoints directors and auditors whom it can remove through a resolution.[93] Foundations must have at least three councilors, who collectively have the power to select and dismiss directors and auditors, approve accounting documents, and determine other organizational matters.[94] This board of councilors is now required by statute and is no longer an informal practice encouraged by administrative guidance. The directors' duties entailing loyalty and non-competition are now also prescribed in the statute.[95] The statute further clarifies that directors, auditors, and foundation councilors are agents of the corporation, which means that they each owe the corporation the duty of care of faithful managers.[96]

A general corporation can apply to become a public-interest corporation if it engages in activities relating to scholarship, art, charity, or other public interests for the benefit of unascertainable beneficiaries.[97] The corporation must also demonstrate that it possesses the requisite accounting base and technical capability; does not provide special interests to its members, officials, or

---

[87] Ippan Shadan Hōjin oyobi Ippan Zaidan Hōjin ni Kansuru Hōritsu [General Association and General Foundation Act], Law No. 48 of 2006 [hereinafter, General Corporation Act; Public Interest Corporation Authorization Act; Ippan Shadan Hōjin oyobi Ippan Zaidan Hōjin ni Kansuru Hōritsu oyobi Kōekishadan Hōjin oyobi Kōeki Zaidan Hōjin no Nintei tō ni Kansuru Hōritsuno Sekō ni Tomonau Kankei Hōritsu no Seibini Kansuru Hōritsu [General Corporation Act and Authorization Act Implementation Act], Law No. 50 of 2006 (hereinafter Implementation Act).

[88] General Corporation Act § 22.

[89] Public Interest Corporation Authorization Act §§ 4–10.

[90] In England, the Charity Commission was established in 1853. Charitable Trust Act 1853, 16 & 17 Vict. c. 137.

[91] Public Interest Corporation Authorization Act §§ 4–26. The Public Interest Commission has also published detailed guidance and associated Q&As. Koueki Nintei-tō Iinkai [Public Interest Commission], *Koueki Nintei-tō ni Kansuru Un'yō ni Tsuite (Koueki Nintei-tō Gaidorain) [On the Application of Public Interest Standard etc. (Public Interest Standard etc. Guideline)]* (April 2008, last updated March 2019); Koueki Nintei-tō Iinkai [Public Interest Commission], *Koueki Nintei Hōjin Seido-tō ni Kansuru Yoku Aru Shitsumon (FAQ) [Frequently Asked Questions (FAQ) on the Public Interest Corporation System]* (Mar. 2020).

[92] General Corporation Act § 35.

[93] *Id.* §§ 63, 70.

[94] *Id.* §§ 173, 176, 177.

[95] General Corporation Act §§ 83, 84, 197.

[96] *Id.* §§ 64, 172, applying *mutatis mutandis* the Civil Code provisions on mandate contracts. For discussion of civil law mandates and their implication on Japanese law, *see supra* notes 14–16 and accompanying text, as well as references cited therein.

[97] Public Interest Corporation Authorization Act §§ 2(iv), 5(i). The appendix to the Act lists 23 activities deemed to contribute to the public interests.

employees and their related persons; and no single director and spouse or relatives comprise more than a third of the board.[98] Three financial constraints are imposed. First, if a corporation raises revenue from public-interest activities, the revenue cannot exceed the expenses covering the proper costs for such services.[99] Second, the expenditure for public-interest services must comprise at least 50 percent of the total.[100] Third, the value of unused assets cannot exceed the projected expenditure for the public-interest activities for the following year.[101] These statutory requirements are intended as a departure from the discretionary supervision of governmental departments, although the Authorization Act delegated the definition of many key concepts and procedural requirements to the administrative regulation issued by the Cabinet Office.[102]

C *The Reform of Public-Interest Trusts*

As of 2020, the reform of the public-interest trust was underway.[103] In 2018, the Legislative Council published a General Outline for the proposed reform, laying the groundwork for the bill's presentation to parliament.[104]

The General Outline proposes the broadening of trustee bases by enabling ordinary individuals or corporations to serve as trustees.[105] This was controversial, as it signaled a shift from the previous practice where the trusteeship was almost invariably undertaken by trust banks. The debate also reflected a lingering concern regarding the abuse of public-interest entities. This concern has been further augmented because the General Outline proposes using public-interest trusts for more extensive works compared to the prior parameters for use, which were limited to the distribution of grants or scholarships.[106]

The General Outline makes various proposals toward enhancing accountability in trust management.[107] One such proposal consists of the introduction of a trust supervisor (*shintaku-kanrinin*) as a mandatory oversight mechanism.[108] The supervisor cannot be related to the trustees, the settlors, or their family or employees to ensure independence.[109]

IV ASSESSING NONPROFIT REFORM IN JAPAN

The reform of nonprofit law put greater emphasis on internal governance through fiduciary principles and transparency. The reform was not without challenges, and this section will use available empirical evidence to assess the reform's achievements and consider any remaining issues that pose ongoing challenges.

---

[98] These requirements are listed in Public Interest Corporation Authorization Act § 5 (ii)-(xviii).

[99] *Id.* § 14.

[100] *Id.* § 15.

[101] *Id.* § 16.

[102] *Kōeki Shadan Hōjin oyobi Kōeki Zaidan Hōjin no Nintei-tō ni Kansuru Hōritsu Sekou Kisoku [Order Implementing the Public Interest Corporation Authorization Act]*, Cabinet Office Order No. 68 of 2007.

[103] Yuichiro Nakatsuji, *Kōeki Shintaku Hō no Minaoshi ni Kansuru Chūkan Shian no Gaiyō [Outline of the Interim Proposal on the Revision of the Charitable Trust Act]*, 273 SHINTAKU [TRUST] 152 (2018).

[104] HŌMUSHŌ HOUSEI SHINSAKAI [MINISTRY OF JUSTICE LEGISLATIVE COUNCIL], KŌEKI SHINTAKU HŌ NO MINAOSHI NI KANSURU CHŪKAN SHIAN [GENERAL OUTLINE FOR THE REVISION OF PUBLIC INTEREST TRUST ACT] (Dec. 18, 2018) [hereinafter GENERAL OUTLINE].

[105] GENERAL OUTLINE § 4, at 3–4.

[106] *Id.* at § 9.

[107] *Id.* at § 5 (trust supervisor), §§ 7, 8 (administrative authorization), § 11 (disclosure).

[108] GENERAL OUTLINE § 5, at 5–6. The enforcer had been introduced for private trusts in 2006. Trust Act §§ 258(4); 123–30.

[109] *Id.* § 5–2(2).

A *Transition to the New Public-Interest Regime*

After the 2006 reform was implemented in 2008, public-interest corporations formed under the former Civil Code provisions were given five years to either register as general corporations or apply for reauthorization as public-interest corporations. Of the 24,317 public-interest corporations at the beginning of the transition period, nearly half (11,679) opted for status as a general corporation, and little more than a third (9,050) completed the transition to new public-interest corporations.[110] Of the remaining entities, 3,588 dissolved themselves or merged with other entities, and 426 simply disappeared, along with assets worth at least 9.92 billion yen ($90 million).[111]

As of December 2018, 9,561 public-interest corporations existed in Japan, with assets totaling 14.9 trillion yen ($135 billion).[112] During 2018, they received 281 billion yen ($2.6 billion) in donations, raised 3.3 trillion yen ($30.0 billion) from service provision, and spent 4.7 trillion yen ($42.7 billion) for public-interest services.[113]

According to an international survey published in 2016, the total amount of individual charitable giving in Japan was estimated at 7.0 billion dollars, compared to 258.5 billion dollars in the United States, 17.4 billion dollars in the United Kingdom, and 6.9 billion dollars in South Korea.[114] When compared to the GDP, the Japanese figure is 0.12 percent, which is much lower than those of the United States (1.44 percent), the United Kingdom (0.54 percent), and South Korea (0.50 percent). However, it should be noted that the Continental European jurisdictions tend to have lower figures, as demonstrated by Germany (0.17 percent) and France (0.11 percent).[115] Against these figures, the reform of nonprofit legislation can be assessed.

B *The Public-Interest Commission*

The Public-Interest Commission has been positively received by the general public as the overseer of public-interest corporations. The Commission administers the statutory standard for authorizing public-interest corporations, thereby replacing the prior administrative guidance. The publication of their decisions and underlying reasoning contributes to the regulatory process's transparency.[116] This English Charity Commission model of supervision will likely be extended to public-interest trusts.[117]

While the Commission reports to the Cabinet Office, the seven commissioners are selected from outside of the government ministries and appointed by the Prime Minister with the approval of both Houses of Parliament.[118] Each commissioner is guaranteed a three-year term

---

[110] Takako Amamiya, *Kōeki Hōjin Seido Kaikaku no Genjō to Kongo no Kadai [The Present State and Future Prospects of the Public Interest Corporation Reform]*, in Shimin Shakai Sekutā no Kanōsei: 110 Nenburi no Daikaikaku no Seika to Kadai [The Potentials of the Civil Society Sector: Achievements and Remaining Issues of the Major Reform in 110 Years] 17, 22 (Masahiro Okamoto ed., 2015).

[111] NHK Kurōzu Appu Gendai Shuzai Han [NHK Close-up Modern Times Investigative Team], Kōeki Hōjin Kaikaku no Fukai Yami [The Deep Darkness of the Public Interest Corporation Reform] 38 (2014).

[112] Naikakufu [Cabinet Office], *Heisei 30 Nen Kōeki Hōjin no Gaikyō oyobi Kōeki Nintei tō Iinkai no Katsudō Hōkoku [The Overview of Public Interest Corporations and the Annual Report of the Public Interest Commission for the Fiscal Year 2018]*, 3, 24 (Dec. 2019).

[113] *Id.* at 27, 29.

[114] Charities Aid Foundation, Gross Domestic Philanthropy 12 (Jan. 2016).

[115] *Id.*

[116] Masahiro Okamoto, *Kōeki Hōjin Seido Kaikaku no Bunmyaku to Igi [The Context and Implication of Public Interest Corporation Legislation Reform]*, in Shimin Shakai Sekutā no Kanōsei: 110 Nenburi no Daikaikaku no Seika to Kadai [The Potentials of the Civil Society Sector: Achievements and Remaining Issues of the Major Reform in 110 Years] 13, 16 (Masahiro Okamoto ed., 2015).

[117] General Outline §§ 7, 8.

[118] Public Interest Corporation Authorization Act §§ 32, 34, 35.

and is under the statutory obligation to exercise his or her duty independently.[119] Nevertheless, some critics have voiced concern.[120] The administrative staff serving the Commission are officials of the Cabinet Office, who came from various governmental departments that formerly exercised broad discretion in supervising public-interest corporations. Tsutomu Hotta, a prominent advocate for nonprofit reform, charged that the officials of the Cabinet Office

> failed to understand the Authorization Act's purposes or appreciate the significance of the new public-interest corporation regime. They continued to follow their past experience characterized by absolute discretion, posing questions to applicants that do more harm than good. They wasted a significant amount of applicants' energy by requesting useless documentation, and disincentivized their application by providing an incorrect interpretation of the law.[121]

To the credit of the officials, Hotta notes that the situation improved beginning in the second year when new personnel arrived, and full-time staff began handling the applications in earlier stages of the authorization process.[122]

Given the scarcity of cases, it is premature to identify a shift in the Court's deferential attitude to the administrative authorization of public-interest company status. Nonetheless, in the *Japan Society for Dying with Dignity* v. *Japan*,[123] the Tokyo District Court reversed the Public-Interest Commission's denial of authorization. One of the main functions of the Japan Society for Dying with Dignity was to run an unofficial registration service for living wills, and the Commission denied the application because such service cannot be regarded as a public-interest activity. It ruled that conferring the status of a public-interest corporation would give the public the undue impression that the government gave official approval to the registration of living wills, which could exert undue pressure upon the physicians who provide necessary medical services in terminal care. The Court, however, held that such findings were based on incorrect premises, given that various guidelines published by public bodies, including the Ministry of Health and Labor and the Japan Medical Association, recognize the primacy of patient autonomy, and physicians could continue following these guidelines to provide proper care.

C *Fiduciary Governance and Internal Checks and Balances*

As discussed earlier, the 2006 legislation introduced an elaborate set of rules on fiduciary governance, including the codified duty of loyalty owed by the directors of general and public-interest corporations.[124] However, the significance of the formal changes should not be overstated. Even before the reform, these officials were considered as acting under the Civil Code provisions applicable to agency relationships,[125] and the Civil Code provided that self-dealing transactions were void.[126]

The Japanese courts' approach can be illustrated by *Japan Kanji Aptitude Testing Foundation* v. *Okubo*,[127] involving extensive self-dealing and asset diversion within a public-interest corporation before the transition to the new statutory regime. The Court ordered a remedy without

---

[119] *Id.* §§ 36, 37, 38.

[120] Okamoto, *supra* note 116, at 15–16.

[121] Tsutomu Hotta, *Seido Sekkei no Yugami ga Okosu Mondaiten [Problems that Have Arisen from the Skewed System Design]*, 1421 JURIST 32, 36–37 (2011).

[122] *Id.* at 37.

[123] 2019 WLJPCA 01186004 (Tokyo Dist. Ct., Jan. 18, 2019).

[124] General Corporation Act §§ 83, 84, 197.

[125] Ramseyer & Tamaruya, *supra* note 16, at 663.

[126] Civil Code § 57 (repealed).

[127] Kyoto District Court Judgment of Jan. 12, 2015, LLI/DB and LEX/DB.

relying on the duty of loyalty provision. The Japan Kanji Aptitude Testing Foundation (*Nihon Kanji Noryoku Kentei Kyokai*) was approved in 1992 and offered ten different levels of Chinese character writing tests, attracting 2.7 million examinees in 2007. The chairman and his son, who was also the vice-chairman of the foundation, authorized a series of unnecessary transactions between the foundation and their four family companies that constituted conflicts of interest.[128] The Kyoto District Court ordered them to pay 2.4 billion yen ($21.8 million) for failure to exercise the due care of faithful managers, and four of their family companies were required to divulge their unjust enrichment. In separate criminal proceedings, the two directors were convicted for criminal breach of trust and sentenced to two and a half years in prison.[129] The foundation's public-interest corporation status was revoked, and it received reauthorization in 2013 only after the board reorganized and implemented a series of reforms.

Public-interest corporations are subject to additional governance requirements. Public-interest authorization is not available if over one-third of the applying general corporation's board comprises the spouse or other relatives within three degrees of any single director.[130] The directors and employees of an outside corporation cannot comprise more than one-third of the corporation's board.[131] The public-interest corporation cannot provide special benefits to any member, official, or employee,[132] and when paying remuneration to officers, it must follow a disclosed standard from within the range specified by the Cabinet Order.[133]

For foundations, a board of councilors that oversees the board of directors is now mandatory.[134] The board of councilors is expected to serve as an autonomous body to monitor the board of directors.[135] In practice, it is unclear whether the board of councilors constitutes a truly informed and independent body that can provide checks. At present, the checks and balances between the separate boards are expected to be self-executing, and no case regarding councilors' responsibility and liability has been reported. The same applies to the trust supervisor, who must provide a similar check and balance mechanism for the proposed public-interest trusts.[136]

D *Preventing Abuse*

The abuse in the Kanji Aptitude Testing Foundation was revealed before the 2006 reform through an inspection by the Ministry of Education, which had supervisory authority over the education-related public-interest corporation at the time. Nevertheless, the Ministry of Education was also criticized for its failure to ensure compliance and detect more serious violations.[137] Prior to the revelation of the large-scale asset diversion, the Ministry had merely

---

[128] *Monka-shō Kanken ni Torihiki Kaishō Shidō: Rijichō Kanren Ni-sha to [Guidance by the Ministry of Education: The Kanji Testing Foundation to dissolve transaction with two Chairman-related companies]*, YOMIURI SHIMBUN (Mar. 11, 2009).

[129] Kyoto District Court Judgment of February 29, 2012, LLI/DB and LEX/DB, *affirmed by* Osaka High Court Judgment of March 26, 2013, and Supreme Court Judgment of December 9, 2014.

[130] Public Interest Corporation Authorization Act § 5(x).

[131] *Id.* § 5(xi).

[132] *Id.* § 5(iv).

[133] *Id.* §§ 5(xiii), 20; Cabinet Order § 3.

[134] General Corporation Act §§ 170, 172–96.

[135] Fishman, *supra* note 52, at 679–80.

[136] GENERAL OUTLINE § 5, at 5–6.

[137] *Kyōkai to Monkashō no Mitsugetsu: Shōeki Yūsen Kumotta Shidōryoku [Honeymoon of the Foundation and the Ministry of Education: Ministry Interest Advanced and Ability to Guide Reduced]*, YOMIURI SHIMBUN (May 22, 2009).

faulted the foundation for making an excessive profit. It had issued guidance to reduce the testing fee, but the foundation failed to comply.

Some commentators feared the emergence of another organization like the Kanji Testing Foundation. However, since its establishment in 2007, the Public-Interest Commission has observed no case similar in scale. The Commission has the power to require reports from a public-interest corporation, enter its office, and inspect the organizational operation, the books, and other documents.[138] During the fiscal year 2017, the Commission entered the offices of 2,915 public-interest corporations. This is intended to subject each corporation to entry by the Commission once every three years.[139]

Until 2018, only three public-interest corporations had been deauthorized by the Commission.[140] In one such case, the Japan Life Foundation (*Nihon Raifu Kyokai*) had guaranteed the payment of medical and service fees to hospitals and care houses on behalf of elderly people who had no relatives or friends to sign a guarantee contract for them. The foundation diverted 270 million yen ($2.5 million) from funds deposited by service recipients and underwent voluntary reorganization. In 2016, the Commission moved to revoke its authorization because it had failed to secure sufficient financial resources for the provision of public-interest services.[141] Three directors were later arrested for violation of money lending regulations, and the foundation was declared bankrupt.

Given the reduced transparency of general corporations, they are more susceptible to abuse than public-interest corporations. For instance, a tax evasion scheme was quickly devised to exploit the general corporation.[142] One must merely create a general corporation and fund it with family assets, so that family members continue to run the corporation as their own upon his or her death, without paying inheritance tax. This loophole was plugged by the 2018 tax reform.[143] Further, the name of an association or foundation generates a sense of trustworthiness among the general public, which is also problematic. Some general corporations have reportedly taken advantage of such trust and collected money that was ultimately exhausted for illegitimate purposes.

Other nonprofits have also made headlines for abusive practices. In 2014, it was reported that a social welfare corporation was being sold at a high price.[144] Although the social welfare corporation had no share to trade as a nonprofit foundation, the steady flow of government subsidy for social welfare services and the sense of entitlement from endowing the foundation made the chairmanship a lucrative commodity. According to a newspaper article in *The Asahi Shimbun*, the chairman of the board of directors for the Sakuragaoka Welfare Association received 125 million yen ($1.1 million) for ceding his position. In a related article, the same paper asserted that some social welfare corporations were run by the chief director for his own interest and the boards of directors and councilors often failed to provide effective checks. Among the various social welfare corporations mentioned, the chief director of the Sunflower Society (*Himawari-no-kai*) was named as having sold donated property, thereby increasing his

138 Public Interest Corporation Authorization Act §§ 27, 59.
139 Cabinet Office, *supra* note 112, at 70.
140 *Id.* at 78.
141 Naikakufu [Cabinet Office], *Heisei 28 Nen Kōeki Hōjin no Gaikyō oyobi Kōeki Nintei tō Iinkai no Katsudō Hōkoku* [*The Overview of Public Interest Corporations and the Annual Report of the Public Interest Commission for the Fiscal Year 2016*], 73–74 (Sept. 2017).
142 Shin'ya Oshino, *Ippan Shadan: Sōzoku ni Kazei* [*General Corporation: Taxation on Inheritance*], NIKKEI SHIMBUN (Mar. 26, 2018).
143 Inheritance Tax Act, Law No. 73 of 1950, § 66-2, as inserted by Law No. 7, 2018.
144 *Shafuku Riken, Tobikau Kane: Enchō no Za Kōnyū* [*Concessions over Social Welfare, Money Flying Around: Chairman's Seat on Sale*], ASAHI SHIMBUN (May 19, 2014).

salary without the board's authorization.[145] However, the corporation successfully sued the newspaper, which agreed to publish an article apologizing for the inadequate verification of facts and inaccurate statements.[146]

E Encouraging Voluntary Works

While the prevention of abuse is an important policy objective, it should not defeat the original purpose of facilitating works for the public interest. Gift giving is increasing. The Japan Fundraising Association estimates that 45.7 million individuals donated 775.6 billion yen ($7.1 billion) in 2016 after a steady increase from 545.5 billion yen ($5.0 billion) in 2009.[147] The year 2011 was an exceptional year when the Great Tohoku earthquake and tsunami disaster generated donations of over 1 trillion yen ($9.3 billion). Corporate donations increased from 477 billion yen ($4.3 billion) in 1994 to 790.9 billion yen ($7.2 billion) in 2015.[148]

Generally, tax incentives for donations increase people's willingness to donate to charities. In Japan, however, that is not necessarily the case. Of all nonprofit donors in 1994, only 14.3 percent claimed their donations on their tax returns (although over 40 percent of those donating over ten thousand yen did claim the donation).[149] A further shift in the volunteer and donation culture in Japan may be required before tax benefits create significant incentives to donate.

More relevant to fiduciary governance, a recent study suggests that people tend to donate to entities with stronger governance and derive more revenue from the government and other independent sources. Entities that publish their accounting documents on their websites receive 370 thousand more yen ($3,360) than those that do not, on average.[150] Research also shows that donors are interested in financial information regarding efficiency in the management of expenses, the extent of revenue-raising activities, and the donation balance.[151]

However, critics argue that public-interest corporations are overburdened by a rigid set of financial requirements.[152] The provision mentioned most frequently in this context is the requirement that the income from revenue-generating activities must not exceed the expenditures required to provide services for public benefit.[153] The restriction made sense in the 1990s when the government endeavored to stop inactive or old public-interest corporations from accumulating unnecessary cash or assets. Nonetheless, the requirement that corporate books be kept in the red contradicts sensible directors' notions of healthy fiscal management.[154] It also prevents a corporation from preparing for contingencies and deploying its assets strategically.

More generally, many regulations and restrictions apply to all public-interest and general corporations of all types. Smaller start-up organizations have found it too cumbersome to engage

---

[145] *Shafuku Hōjin no Shibutsu-ka: Wanman Rijichō "Bōsō" [Social Welfare Corporation Made Personal Possession: One-man Chief Director Running out of Control]*, ASAHI SHIMBUN (May 26, 2014).

[146] *Shakai Fukushi Hōjin "Himawari-no Kai" no Kiji wo Teisei-shi, Owabi Shimasu: Asahi Shimbunsha [Asahi Shimbun Correct the Errors in an Article on Social Welfare Corporation Himawari-no-kai and Make an Apology]*, ASAHI SHIMBUN (Apr. 17, 2015).

[147] Nihon Fando Reijing Kyōkai [JAPAN FUNDRAISING ASS'N], KIFU HAKUSHO 2017 [GIVING JAPAN 2017] (2017) at 26–27.

[148] *Id.* at 48–49.

[149] *Id.* at 80.

[150] *Id.* at 76–77.

[151] *Id.* at 78.

[152] Hotta, *supra* note 121, at 32–34.

[153] Authorization Act § 14.

[154] KŌEKI HŌJIN KYŌKAI [JACO], KŌEKI HŌJIN NO UN'EI OYOBI KIFU TŌ NI KANSURU ANKĒTO CHŌSA KEKKA [QUESTIONNAIRE RESEARCH ON THE ADMINISTRATION OF AND GIFT GIVING TO PUBLIC INTEREST CORPORATION AND GENERAL CORPORATION] 46–66 (Aug. 2019).

a certified accountant and, in the case of foundations, a separate board of councilors. Although JACO has proposed the need for a more simplified organizational structure for small nonprofits, no legislative response has been delivered thus far.[155] The ongoing reform of public-interest trusts is premised on the assumption that they are "lightweight and lightly equipped" compared to public-interest corporations.[156] Even so, some commentators call for governance mechanisms more stringent than proposed to allay the fear of abuse.[157]

F *Transparency*

The 2006 legislation expanded the disclosure obligations of public-interest corporations. Public corporations must now prepare a yearly project plan, budget, list of assets, list of officials, and compensation payment standards, which must be submitted to the Public-Interest Commission and made accessible to the general public.[158] Public corporations and large-scale general corporations with debt that exceeds 20 billion yen ($182 million) are generally required to undergo a third-party audit by professional accountants.[159]

The volume of information available to the public has increased.[160] Although disclosure via the internet is not required, 86 percent of public-interest corporations publish information through their websites.[161] The Cabinet Office publishes information and statistics on public-interest corporations online on behalf of the Public-Interest Commission, as required by statute.[162] Many nongovernmental organizations were established to provide logistical and other support for individual nonprofits. For instance, the Japan NPO Center was established in 1995 to serve as an information center for NPO corporations and other volunteer organizations.[163] The Japan Fundraising Association, created in 2009, began publishing statistical analyses and reports in 2010.[164]

However, it is noteworthy that most former public-interest corporations opted to continue as general corporations. They can be readily created and have no duty to disclose beyond publishing their balance sheet and retaining their financial statements for inspection by members and creditors.[165] Online disclosure is voluntary, and only 62.2 percent of general corporations publish information online.[166] The reduced transparency of these organizations means that the public (and the media) can no longer access their lists of directors (possibly former bureaucrats), cash flow statements (possibly government subsidies) or project plans (how the money is spent).[167]

---

[155] Kōeki Hōjin Kyōkai [JACO], Kōeki Hōjin Seido Kaikaku Yōbō ni Kansuru Hōkokusho [The Report on Public Interest Corporation Reform Proposal] 18–19 (June 2012).

[156] Hōmushō [Ministry of Justice], Kōeki Shintaku Hō no Minaoshi ni Kansuru Chūkan Shian no Hosoku Setumei [Supplementary Explanation for the Interim Proposal for the Revision of Public Interest Trust Legislation] 79 (2017); Nakatsuji, *supra* note 107, at 153 n.6.

[157] Takeshi Sakuma, *Kōeki Shintaku Hō Kaisei no Ronten [Issues Relating to the Revisions of Public Interest Trust Legislation]*, 271 Shintaku [Trust] 4, 8–10 (2017).

[158] Authorization Act §§ 21, 22.

[159] General Corporation Act §§ 62, 171; Authorization Act § 5(xii).

[160] Tadashi Sato, *Kōzō Kaikaku-ki to Hanshin Awaji Dai-Shinsai [The Structural Reform Period and Hanshin-Awaji Earthquake]*, in Nihon no NPO-shi: NPO no Rekishi wo Yomu, Genzai, Kako, Mirai [The History of Japanese NPO: Reading the History of NPO, Present, Past and Future] 217 (Makoto Imada ed., 2006).

[161] Kōeki Hōjin Kyōkai & Nihon NPO Sentā [JACO & NPO Center], Hi-Eiri Hōjinkaku Sentaku ni Kansuru Jittai Chōsa [Survey Report on the Selection of Nonprofit Entity Form] 36 (February 2017).

[162] Public Interest Corporation Authorization Act, § 57.

[163] Sato, *supra* note 160, at 236.

[164] Japan Fundraising Association, *supra* note 147.

[165] General Corporation Act §§ 128, 129, 199.

[166] JACO, *supra* note 154, at 34.

[167] NHK Close-up Modern Times Investigative Team, *supra* note 111, at 144–48.

G *Integration of the Nonprofit Sector*

The Japanese nonprofit sector remains fragmented. Although the authorization and oversight procedure for public-interest corporations was consolidated under the Public-Interest Commission, school, religious, social welfare, and medical corporations remain outside its jurisdiction.[168] Furthermore, the NPO corporations were introduced by a 1998 statute, and before the 2006 reform, they formed a nonprofit sector distinct from public-interest corporations.[169] In fact, when the government declared its intention to undertake the comprehensive reform of nonprofit legislation in 2002, the representatives of NPO corporations lobbied extensively to remove them from the reform's scope.[170]

Nonetheless, there are signs that policy makers are beginning to view the nonprofit sector from a more comprehensive perspective.[171] When the governance mechanism for medical corporations was reformed in 2006, and that of social welfare corporations in 2016, a number of provisions were introduced that parallel the general corporation legislation. The directors of these corporations now owe statutory fiduciary duties,[172] and they and their board are accountable to the general meeting (if acting as an association) or separate board of councilors (if acting as a foundation).[173] Although school corporations have not undergone such thorough reform, as of 2014, their directors were assigned the statutory duty of loyalty to their corporation;[174] meanwhile, the same reform gave the Ministry of Education additional powers to monitor and intervene in schools found to be in breach of legal or government orders or improperly managed.[175] Furthermore, accounting standards, which were previously idiosyncratic in each corporate category, are now gradually harmonizing.[176]

v CONCLUSION

A nation's charity sector cannot be reformed in one day. The twisted history of Japanese public-interest corporation legislation has meant that its nonprofit sector has long been divided into complex subsectors and governed by a kaleidoscope of legal norms derived from various civil and common law jurisdictions. Such an amalgam of legislation, which has been in conflict with indigenous charitable works from its inception, has undergone significant transformation over the years. The government's supervisory role has shifted from direct control to a more detached approach toward ensuring sound fiduciary governance.

This chapter has looked at Japan's continuous attempt toward a conceptual and comparative synthesis of fiduciary principles and the integration of the nonprofit sector. The assessment has revealed reasons to be both optimistic and cautious. While the greater emphasis on internal governance has generally been accepted, the limited number of court cases has made it difficult

---

[168] For historical background, see nn. 31–35, and accompanying text.

[169] Nobuko Matsumoto, *Recent Changes in Laws Regarding Nonprofit Corporations and Charitable Trusts in Japan*, 45 ZEITSCHRIFT FÜR JAPANISCHES RECHT /J. OF JAPANESE L. 129, 135 (2018).

[170] Masayuki Deguchi, *Seido Tōgō no Kanōsei to Mondai: Garapagosuka to Gurobaruka [The Potential and Concerns with Systemic Integration: Galapagos and Globalization]*, in SHIMIN SHAKAI SEKUTĀ NO KANŌSEI: 110 NENBURI NO DAIKAIKAKU NO SEIKA TO KADAI [THE POTENTIALS OF THE CIVIL SOCIETY SECTOR: ACHIEVEMENTS AND REMAINING ISSUES OF THE MAJOR REFORM IN 110 YEARS] 157, 160–63 (Masahiro Okamoto ed., 2015).

[171] Aya Okada, Yu Ishida, Takako Nakajima, & Yasuhiko Kotagiri, *The State of Nonprofit Sector Research in Japan: A Literature Review*, 2 VOLUNTARISTICS REVIEW 1, 7–8 (2017).

[172] Social Welfare Act §§ 45-13, 45-16, 45-20, 64, 172; Medical Care Act §§ 46-6 through 46-6-4, 46-4(2), 46-5(3), 47-49-3.

[173] Social Welfare Act §§ 45-8 through 45-15, and Medical Care Act §§ 46-7, 46-8, 46-3 through 46-3-6; 45-8; 46-4-46-4-7.

[174] Private Schools Act § 40-2.

[175] *Id.* §§ 60, 63.

[176] Deguchi, *supra* note 35, at 9–10.

to assess how fiduciary principles are to be implemented on the ground. The greater emphasis on transparency and the newly created Public Interest Commission has been received positively. While no new case of blatant abuse or corruption has surfaced under the new regime created by the 2006 legislation, and the Commission's periodic entries may have prevented potential abuse, the limited number of enforcement actions makes it difficult to see the hidden abuse. While one can observe a steady effort to integrate the nonprofit sector and encourage healthy public-interest works, the sector has yet to overcome its excessive fetishism of entity forms.

PART IV

Stakeholders and Society

15

Corporations, Directors' Duties, and the Public/Private Divide

*Jennifer G. Hill**

I INTRODUCTION

In their classic 1932 text, *The Modern Corporation and Private Property*,[1] Berle and Means viewed the public corporation as a profoundly ambiguous entity, straddling the divide between public and private law. This public-private divide created ongoing tension in corporate law history and practice.[2]

A decidedly private conception emerged in the 1980s, in the form of the law and economics "nexus of contracts" theory of the corporation.[3] Under this theory, which subsequently became the dominant corporate law paradigm in the United States and a number of other jurisdictions,[4] shareholder interests and corporate performance took center stage. However, recently, the pendulum has swung in the opposite direction, and there is far greater attention to stakeholder interests and the social responsibilities of corporations and their directors and officers.

According to the Greek poet, Archilochus, "[t]he fox knows many things, but the hedgehog knows one big thing."[5] The law and economics theory of the corporation embodies the latter

* I would like to thank participants at Rutgers Law School's workshop for this volume. Particular thanks go to Marc Gross, Arthur Laby, Vice Chancellor Joseph Slights and Jacob Russell for helpful suggestions and references, and Mitheran Selvendran for excellent research assistance. I am grateful to Monash University for providing funding for this project under a Networks of Excellence (NoE) Research Grant on the topic, "Enhancing Corporate Accountability."

[1] ADOLF BERLE & GARDINER MEANS, THE MODERN CORPORATION AND PRIVATE PROPERTY (2d ed. 2017).

[2] *See generally* William T. Allen, *Our Schizophrenic Conception of the Business Corporation*, 14 CARDOZO L. REV. 261 (1992).

[3] The "nexus of contracts" economic theory represents a private aggregational concept of the corporation, which is viewed merely as a "complex set of explicit and implicit contracts." Frank H. Easterbrook & Daniel R. Fischel, *The Corporate Contract*, 89 COLUM. L. REV. 1416, 1418 (1989). *See also* William W. Bratton Jr., *The "Nexus of Contracts" Corporation: A Critical Appraisal*, 74 CORNELL L. REV. 407, 417–20 (1989). Given that non-shareholder stakeholder contracts are included in the contractual nexus, there is nothing *per se* about this theory that compels a shareholder-centered view of the corporation. Nonetheless, under the classical economic "nexus of contracts" theory of the corporation, shareholder interests are treated as preeminent. *See, e.g.,* Jonathan R. Macey, *An Economic Analysis of the Various Rationales for Making Shareholders the Exclusive Beneficiaries of Corporate Fiduciary Duties*, 21 STETSON L. REV. 23 (1991); David Millon, *Theories of the Corporation*, 1990 DUKE L. J. 201, 229–31. This theory also treats shareholders as principals and corporate managers as their agents. *See* Michael C. Jensen & William H. Meckling, *Theory of the Firm: Managerial Behavior, Agency Costs, and Ownership Structure*, 3 J. FIN. ECON. 305, 308–09 (1976). However, similar aggregational theories have been used by some scholars to subvert any presumption of shareholder primacy. *See, e.g.,* Margaret M. Blair & Lynn A. Stout, *A Team Production Theory of Corporate Law*, 85 VA. L. REV. 247, 253–54 (1999) (arguing that boards of directors exist to protect the interests of all members of the corporate "team," not merely the interests of shareholders, and claiming this approach is consistent with the "nexus of contracts" approach to corporate law).

[4] *See* William W. Bratton, Jr., *The "Nexus of Contracts" Corporation: A Critical Appraisal*, 74 CORNELL L. REV. 407, 439–40 (1989); David Millon, *Theories of the Corporation*, 1990 DUKE L. J. 201, 229–31.

[5] As retold by Isaiah Berlin. *See* ISAIAH BERLIN, THE HEDGEHOG AND THE FOX: AN ESSAY ON TOLSTOY'S VIEW OF HISTORY (1953).

approach, representing "a single, universal, organising principle,"[6] whereby the key agency problem of corporate law is the misalignment of the interests of company directors and officers with the interests of shareholders.[7]

However, recent financial scandals, such as the Wells Fargo fraudulent accounts scandal in the United States and scandals at some of Australia's leading banks,[8] have emphasized the fact that there is not one, but rather multiple, problems in corporate law. These scandals highlighted two distinct problems in corporate law. The first is a legitimate concern about corporate financial performance.[9] This is a critical issue, given that we now live in an age of "forced capitalism"[10] where, in a number of jurisdictions, members of the public have become involuntary investors in the stock market via mandatory retirement saving schemes.[11] The second problem is the danger that corporate conduct may result in negative externalities and harm to society.[12] These scandals demonstrated in an acute way that enhanced financial performance can have a dark side in terms of harm to stakeholders or society as a whole. They also showed that corporate governance techniques designed to address the first problem might exacerbate the second by creating perverse incentives for corporate misconduct.[13] One of the consequences of an increasing focus on this second problem of corporate law is greater regulatory attention to the issue of corporate culture.[14] This is closely tied to a more public conception of the corporation,[15] and renewed attention to the need to ensure responsibility and accountability for corporate actions.[16]

---

6   *Id.*

7   Some scholars in the field of financial economics view corporate governance more broadly as applying to "suppliers of finance" to the corporation, which includes creditors as well as shareholders. *See* Andrei Shleifer & Robert W. Vishny, *A Survey of Corporate Governance*, 52 J. Fin. 737, 737 (1997). Nonetheless, Shleifer and Vishny acknowledge that "[o]ur perspective on corporate governance is a straightforward agency perspective, sometimes referred to as separation of ownership and control. We want to know how investors get managers to give them back their money." *Id.*, at 738.

8   *See infra*, text accompanying notes 57–72.

9   *See, e.g.*, Donald C. Langevoort, *The Effects of Shareholder Primacy, Publicness, and 'Privateness' on Corporate Cultures*, 43 Seattle U. L. Rev. 377, 377–78 (2020) (interpreting the norm of wealth-maximization for shareholders as an antidote to agency costs in the form of managerial selfishness).

10   Leo E. Strine, Jr., *Toward Common Sense and Common Ground? Reflections on the Shared Interests of Management and Labor in a More Rational System of Corporate Governance*, 33 J. Corp. L. 1, 4–5 (2007).

11   According to Chancellor Strine, most U.S. employees in the private sector with 401(k) retirement plans "have little choice but to invest in the market." *Id.*, at 4. The position in Australia is similar, given its distinctive system of retirement ("superannuation") funding. *See, e.g.*, Super System Review Final Report, Part One, Overview and Recommendations, app. B at 69 (2010) ("Cooper Review"). *Cf.* Lynn A. Stout, *The Mythical Benefits of Shareholder Control*, 93 Va. L. Rev. 789, 801 (2007) (adopting a traditional "voluntary investment" paradigm, stating "investors are not forced to purchase shares in public corporations at gunpoint").

12   *See, e.g.*, Richard M. Buxbaum, *Corporate Legitimacy, Economic Theory, and Legal Doctrine*, 45 Ohio St. L. J. 515, 517–18 (1984) (supporting the view that the external effects of corporate action in the public domain cannot be ignored). *See also* Langevoort, *supra* note 9 (discussing the concept of "publicness" as a form of legitimacy and "social licence").

13   *See* Jennifer G. Hill, *Deconstructing Sunbeam – Contemporary Issues in Corporate Governance*, 67 U. Cin. L. Rev. 1099, 1120–25 (1999) (discussing the Sunbeam scandal, arguably an early example of the risk posed by perverse incentives).

14   *See, e.g.*, Langevoort, *supra* note 9; Vicky Comino, *"Corporate Culture" is the 'New Black' – Its Possibilities and Limits as a Regulatory Mechanism for Corporations and Financial Institutions* (2019) (forthcoming, 44 U.N.S.W.L.J. ___ (2021)). Definitions of corporate culture abound. The definition adopted by the Australian Banking Royal Commission, e.g., was: "shared values and norms that shape behaviours and mindsets." *See* Commonwealth of Austl., Final Report Royal Commission into Misconduct in the Banking, Superannuation and Financial Services Industry Vol. 1 334 (2019) (Austl.) ("Banking Royal Commission").

15   *See, e.g.*, Hillary A. Sale, *Fiduciary Law, Good Faith and Publicness, in* The Oxford Handbook of Fiduciary Law 763 (Evan J. Criddle, Paul B. Miller & Robert H. Sitkoff eds., 2019) (discussing the concept of "publicness" in relation to the corporation).

16   *See, e.g.*, Phillip I. Blumberg, *The Corporate Entity in an Era of Multinational Corporations*, 15 Del. J. Corp. L. 283, 285 (1990); Christopher D. Stone, *The Place of Enterprise Liability in the Control of Corporate Conduct*, 90 Yale L. J. 1 (1980).

This chapter argues that there are multiple problems in corporate law, and different problems may come to the forefront at different times, creating a tension between public and private conceptions of the corporation. The chapter also explores the implications of this tension for the duties and accountability of company directors and officers. The chapter proceeds as follows. Part II provides a snapshot of the history and theory of corporations from a public-private perspective. Part III discusses the implications of the public-private tension for directors' fiduciary duties and examines the divergent approaches taken in the famous Berle-Dodd debate. Part IV considers some recent developments concerning corporate culture and societal harm against the backdrop of the recent U.S. and Australian banking scandals. Part V explores, from a comparative law perspective, the issue of directors' liability for flawed corporate cultures that result in negative externalities or breach of the law, and Part VI concludes.

II CORPORATE LAW HISTORY, LEGAL THEORY, AND THE PUBLIC/ PRIVATE DIVIDE

The tension between public and private conceptions of corporate law has a long history.[17] As a result of its group characteristics, the corporation traditionally occupied an ambiguous and intermediate position within liberal theory's dichotomy between state and individual.[18] From one perspective, corporations could appear to be creations of the state, justifying clear limitations on their powers as a result of their public status. Through a different lens, however, they could be viewed as private organizations, protecting the rights of individuals from state incursion.

U.S. corporations had strong quasi-public roots and derived from early U.K. royal chartered corporations,[19] which were effectively viewed as arms of the state.[20] Most U.S. chartered corporations prior to the American Revolution were in fact "bodies politic," such as towns, districts, and religious and educational institutions,[21] and it was not until the late eighteenth century that chartered "for-profit" business corporations became ascendant.[22] Yet, American corporate law did not distinguish between business corporations and bodies politic during this period .[23] All

---

[17] This chapter focuses on historical developments in this regard in common law jurisdictions only. For discussion of historical developments regarding public interest corporations in a civil law jurisdiction, Japan, *see* Masayuki Tamaruya, *Fiduciary Law and Japanese Nonprofits: A Historical and Comparative Synthesis*, ch. 14 (this volume).

[18] *See generally* PHILIP SELZNICK, LAW, SOCIETY AND INDUSTRIAL JUSTICE 37–38 (1969); Gerald E. Frug, *The City as a Legal Concept*, 93 HARV. L. REV. 1057 (1980); Gregory A. Mark, *The Personification of the Business Corporation in American Law*, 54 U. CHI. L. REV. 1441, 1445 (1987).

[19] *See* L. C. B. Gower, *Some Contrasts Between British and American Corporate Law*, 69 HARV. L. REV. 1369, 1370–72 (1956).

[20] As such, royal chartered corporations were required to fulfil societal purposes. *See generally* LAWRENCE M. FRIEDMAN, A HISTORY OF AMERICAN LAW 159–71 (4th ed. 2019); Gower, *supra* note 19, 1370–72; Jennifer G. Hill, *The Trajectory of American Corporate Governance: Shareholder Empowerment and Private Ordering Combat*, 2019 U. ILL. L. REV. 507, 541–44 (2019). *See also* Joel Seligman, *A Brief History of Delaware's General Corporation Law of 1899*, 1 DEL. J. CORP. L. 249, 255 (1976).

[21] *See* Pauline Maier, *The Revolutionary Origins of the American Corporation*, 50 WM. & MARY Q. 51, 53 (1993); Samuel Williston, *History of the Law of Business Corporations Before 1800: Part II*, 2 HARV. L. REV. 149, 165 (1888).

[22] *See generally* ROBERT E. WRIGHT, CORPORATION NATION 62–63 (2013); Harwell Wells, *Shareholder Power in America 1800–2000: A Short History, in* RESEARCH HANDBOOK ON SHAREHOLDER POWER 13, 14 (Jennifer G. Hill & Randall S. Thomas eds., 2015). Early U.S. chartered business organizations had both public and private facets since most charter grants effectively involved private ownership of public utilities. These public utilities included, e.g., mills, banks, bridges, toll roads and later, railroads. William J. Carney, *Fundamental Corporate Changes, Minority Shareholders, and Business Purposes*, 1980 AM. B. FOUND. RES. J. 69, 82 (1980). *See also* Gregory A. Mark, *Some Observations on Writing the Legal History of the Corporation in the Age of Theory, in* PROGRESSIVE CORPORATE LAW 67, 68–69 (Lawrence E. Mitchell ed., 1995).

[23] *See* Seligman, *supra* note 20, at 254; Samuel Williston, *History of the Law of Business Corporations Before 1800: Part I*, 2 HARV. L. REV. 105, 105–06 (1888).

chartered corporations were regarded as "public agencies," and, as such, heavily restricted in their activities[24] and required to serve a societal purpose.[25]

During the nineteenth century, however, the corporation attempted to dissociate itself from the state and fought to secure rights and freedom of association.[26] This led to the emergence of a private contractual conception of the corporation (a forerunner to the law and economics theory) by the close of the century,[27] swiftly followed by the rise of state competition for incorporation charters.[28] These developments supported a new image of U.S. state corporate law as "enabling."[29] They also created the modern U.S. bifurcation between private and public law—whereby business corporations came to be classified as private organizations, attracting legal protection under modern "enabling" legislation while municipal corporations continued to be treated as public entities, requiring strong public law constraint.[30]

This tension and conceptual ambiguity lay close to the surface of *The Modern Corporation and Private Property*,[31] in which Berle and Means portrayed the modern public corporation as straddling the public/private divide. The authors described the public corporation as a kind of "economic empire"[32] while at the same time, highlighting its "quasi-public" characteristics.[33] In view of these chameleon-like qualities, Berle and Means considered that corporate law of the future could develop into either a species of private or public law.

III THE PUBLIC/PRIVATE DIVIDE, DIRECTORS' DUTIES, AND THE BERLE-DODD DEBATE

This public-private tension has implications for directors' fiduciary duties,[34] as shown in the famous Berle-Dodd debate. In 1932, Professors Berle and Dodd engaged in an intense debate

---

[24] *See* Seligman, *supra* note 20, at 254; Leo E. Strine, Jr. & Nicholas Walter, *Originalist or Original: The Difficulties of Reconciling Citizens United with Corporate Law History*, 91 NOTRE DAME L. REV. 877, 897–99 (2016). Even after the charter system had been replaced by general incorporation statutes, these statutes continued to impose substantial restrictions on corporations and their boards of directors. *See generally* Naomi R. Lamoreaux, *Revisiting American Exceptionalism: Democracy and the Regulation of Corporate Governance: The Case of Nineteenth-Century Pennsylvania in Comparative Context*, in ENTERPRISING AMERICA: BUSINESSES, BANKS, AND CREDIT MARKETS IN HISTORICAL PERSPECTIVE 32, tbl. 1.1 (William J. Collins & Robert A. Margo eds., 2015); Maier, *supra* note 21, 55–57; John Morley, *The Common Law Corporation: The Power of the Trust in Anglo-American Business History*, 116 COLUM. L. REV. 2145, 2163 (2016); Elizabeth Pollman, *Constitutionalizing Corporate Law*, 69 VAND. L. REV. 639, 649 (2016); Williston, *supra* note 23, 110–11.

[25] *See* Oscar Handlin & Mary F. Handlin, *Origins of the American Business Corporation*, 5 J. ECON. HIST. 1, 22 (1945); Maier, *supra* note 21, 55–57; Williston, *supra* note 23, 110–11. *See also* David Ciepley, *Can Corporations be Held to the Public Interest, or Even to the Law?*, 154 J. BUS. ETHICS 1003 (2018).

[26] *See* Mark, *supra* note 18; Gunther Teubner, *Enterprise Corporatism: New Industrial Policy and the "Essence" of the Legal Person*, 36 AM. J. COMP. L. 130 (1988).

[27] *See* William W. Bratton, Jr., *The New Economic Theory of the Firm: Critical Perspectives from History*, 41 STAN. L. REV. 1471, 1472–73; Katsuhito Iwai, *Persons, Things and Corporations: The Corporate Personality Controversy and Comparative Corporate Governance*, 47 AM. J. COMP. L. 583, 587–92 (1999).

[28] *See generally* Charles M. Yablon, *The Historical Race Competition for Corporate Charters and the Rise and Decline of New Jersey: 1880–1910*, 32 J. CORP. L. 323 (2007).

[29] *See* Pollman, *supra* note 24, at 651. *See also* Michal Barzuza, *Inefficient Tailoring: The Private Ordering Paradox in Corporate Law*, 8 HARV. BUS. L. REV. 131 (2018) (discussing the link between the largely enabling structure of US corporate law and contemporary private ordering).

[30] *See generally* Frug, *supra* note 18.

[31] Seligman, *supra* note 20, at 254.

[32] *See* BERLE & MEANS, *supra* note 1, at 5.

[33] *Id.* at 4.

[34] The classification of directors as fiduciaries developed by analogy to agents and trustees was fundamental to early British corporate law. *See generally* Jennifer G. Hill & Matthew Conaglen, *Directors' Duties and Legal Safe Harbours: A Comparative Analysis*, in RESEARCH HANDBOOK ON FIDUCIARY LAW 305 (D. Gordon Smith & Andrew S. Gold eds., 2018). *See also* Cassimatis v. ASIC [2020] FCAFC 52, [126]-[157] (Austl.); ASIC v. Cassimatis (No 8)

concerning the nature of directors' responsibilities.[35] Although both men agreed that directors were "trustees,"[36] and as such, owed fiduciary duties, they vehemently disagreed as to whom those duties were owed.[37] Berle adopted a private aggregate theory of the corporation, which supported his claim that directors held their powers in trust for shareholders as beneficiaries.[38] Dodd, on the other hand, regarded the corporation as a public institution and argued that directors owed their duties to a diverse group of stakeholders, including employees, creditors, and consumers.[39] Berle, a pragmatist, considered that Dodd's model failed to represent any effective constraint on managerial power.[40]

The Berle-Dodd debate is said to represent a "clash between the different visions of corporatism."[41] Furthermore, those visions are regarded as binary and irreconcilable. For example, the Berle-Dodd debate laid the groundwork for the ongoing dispute concerning shareholder primacy versus stakeholder primacy.[42] Yet, the divide between Berle and Dodd was perhaps less clear-cut than often thought, because both men later appeared to swap positions, acknowledging that the other had won the debate.[43]

By the 1980s, however, Professor Berle's original idea of corporatism appeared to prevail in the form of the law and economics "nexus of contracts" theory.[44] However, even Milton Friedman, the quintessential proponent of a private model of the corporation, acknowledged that corporate law operates within a public matrix of laws and norms. Friedman famously declared that "[t]here is one and only one social responsibility of business – to use its resources and engage in activities designed to increase its profits."[45] Nonetheless, he followed that edict with the less familiar coda — "so long as it [*i.e.* business] stays within the rules of the game, which is to say, engages in open and free competition without deception or fraud."[46]

A number of recent international business law scandals and corporate governance developments have highlighted the importance of recognizing the external effects of corporate conduct in the public domain and the need to ensure accountability when corporations deviate from the "rules of the game." They have also revived issues concerning the role and duties of directors, with which Berle and Dodd grappled almost a century ago.

[2016] FCA 1023, [417]-[428] (Austl.); Joseph W. Bishop, Jr., *Sitting Ducks and Decoy Ducks: New Trends in the Indemnification of Corporate Directors and Officers*, 77 YALE L. J. 1078, 1096–97 (1968). This constraint on directors' power was subsequently transmitted to the United States, and in 1926, the Delaware Court of Chancery explicitly acknowledged company directors as fiduciaries in Bodell v. General Gas and Electric Corp., 132 A. 442 (Del. Ch. 1926), *aff'd*, 140 A.2d. 264 (Del. 1927). *See generally* Randy J. Holland, *Delaware Directors' Fiduciary Duties: The Focus on Loyalty*, 11 U. PA. J. BUS. L. 675, 680–81 (2009).

35   *See* Adolf A. Berle, Jr., *Corporate Powers as Powers in Trust*, 44 HARV. L. REV. 1049 (1931); Adolf A. Berle, Jr., *For Whom Corporate Managers Are Trustees: A Note*, 45 HARV. L. REV. 1365 (1932); E. Merrick Dodd, Jr., *For Whom Are Corporate Managers Trustees?*, 45 HARV. L. REV. 1145 (1932).

36   Although company directors are no longer regarded as trustees, trust law continues to play an important role in other areas of fiduciary law. *See, e.g.*, Arthur B. Laby, *Trust, Discretion and ERISA Fiduciary Status*, ch. 4 (this volume).

37   *See generally* Jennifer G. Hill, *Then and Now: Professor Berle and the Unpredictable Shareholder*, 33 SEATTLE U. L. REV. 1005, 1009–10 (2010).

38   *See* Berle, *supra* note 35(1931); Berle, *supra* note 35(1932).

39   *See* Dodd, *supra* note 35.

40   *See* Berle, *supra* note 35(1932).

41   William W. Bratton & Michael L. Wachter, *Shareholder Primacy's Corporatist Origins: Adolf Berle and the Modern Corporation*, 34 J. CORP. L. 99, 124 (2008). Berle's "private" conception of the corporation and directors' duties would later become the dominant paradigm under the law and economics model of the corporation.

42   *See, e.g.*, Lynn A. Stout, *The Toxic Side Effects of Shareholder Primacy*, 161 U. PA. L. REV. 2003 (2013).

43   *See* Bratton & Wachter, *supra* note 41, at 103–04, 132–34; Joseph L. Weiner, *The Berle–Dodd Dialogue on the Concept of the Corporation*, 64 COLUM. L. REV. 1458, 1462–64 (1964).

44   *See* Bratton, *supra* note 27, at 1472–73; Iwai, *supra* note 27, at 585.

45   Milton Friedman, *The Social Responsibility of Business is to Increase its Profits*, N.Y. TIMES, Sept. 13, 1970, at 126.

46   *Id.*

IV DEVELOPMENTS CONCERNING STAKEHOLDERS, CORPORATE CULTURE AND SOME RECENT SCANDALS

The pendulum, which swung so clearly in favor of a private conception of the corporation from the 1980s onward, is arguably in the process of changing direction. There is a growing focus on stakeholder interests and the public corporation's responsibilities to society as a whole. In 2018, for example, Larry Fink, CEO of BlackRock, one of the world's largest institutional investors, declared that companies "must benefit all of their stakeholders, including shareholders, employees, customers, and the communities in which they operate."[47] The U.S. Business Roundtable recently declared a similar goal.[48] The British Academy's *Future of the Corporation* research project also reflects a return to the idea that corporate purpose needs to be aligned with a social purpose.[49]

"Corporate culture" is closely connected with these developments. Although the concept has been described as "inherently slippery,"[50] international regulators[51] are now promoting the need for a positive corporate culture. This use of corporate culture in this way is closely tied to the risk of negative externalities and harm to stakeholders and the public. The New York Federal Reserve, for example, recently introduced the idea of "cultural capital" as a way of mitigating misconduct risk in financial institutions.[52]

Culture has also become an increasingly important feature of many corporate governance codes.[53] Although these codes, which originated in the United Kingdom, are generally non-binding, they may interact with, and complement, legal duties, including directors' fiduciary duties.[54] Many codes now explicitly focus on the social role and responsibilities of public corporations. The 2018 U.K. Corporate Governance Code, for example, notes that the role of a successful company is not only to create value for shareholders but also to contribute to "wider

---

[47]   *See* BLACKROCK, LARRY FINK'S 2018 LETTER TO CEOS A SENSE OF PURPOSE (2018); Peter Horst, *BlackRock CEO Tells Companies to Contribute to Society. Here's Where to Start*, FORBES (Jan. 16, 2018), https://www.forbes.com/sites/peterhorst/2018/01/16/blackrock-ceo-tells-companies-to-contribute-to-society-heres-where-to-start/.

[48]   *See, e.g.*, Press Release, Business Roundtable, Business Roundtable Redefines the Purpose of a Corporation to Promote "An Economy that Serves All Americans" (Aug. 19, 2019), https://www.businessroundtable.org/business-roundtable-redefines-the-purpose-of-a-corporation-to-promote-an-economy-that-serves-all-americans; David Gelles & David Yaffe-Bellany, *Feeling Heat, C.E.O.s Pledge New Priorities*, N.Y. TIMES, Aug. 20, 2019, at A1.

[49]   *See* THE BRITISH ACAD., FUTURE OF THE CORPORATION: RESEARCH SUMMARIES, 4–5 (2018) (U.K.); THE BRITISH ACAD., FUTURE OF THE CORPORATION: PRINCIPLES FOR PURPOSEFUL BUSINESS (2019) (U.K.). According to The British Academy's *Future of the Corporation* project, "the purpose of business is to solve the problems of people and planet profitably, and not profit from causing problems." *Id.* at 8.

[50]   *See* Dan Awrey, William Blair & David Kershaw, *Between Law and Markets: Is There a Role for Culture and Ethics in Financial Regulation*, 38 DEL. J. CORP. L. 191, 205 (2013); Justin W. Schulz, *Tapping the Best That is Within: Why Corporate Culture Matters*, 42 MGMT. Q. 29, 32 (2001). *See also* John M. Conley & William M. O'Barr, *The Culture of Capital: An Anthropological Investigation of Institutional Investment*, 70 N.C. L. REV. 823 (1992).

[51]   These include, for example, the Australian Securities and Investments Commission; Basel Committee on Banking Supervision; the U.K. Financial Reporting Council; and the Central Bank of Ireland. *See generally* Michael Roddan, *Culture at Top of Watch List: ASIC Boss*, THE AUSTL., Feb. 17, 2018, at 29; BASEL COMMITTEE ON BANKING SUPERVISION, CORPORATE GOVERNANCE PRINCIPLES FOR BANKS, Principle 1, [29]-[32] (Jul. 2015); FIN. REPORTING COUNCIL, CORPORATE CULTURE AND THE ROLE OF BOARDS: REPORT OF OBSERVATIONS (2016) (U.K.); CENTRAL BANK OF IR., BEHAVIOUR AND CULTURE OF THE IRISH RETAIL BANKS (2018).

[52]   *See* Kevin J. Stiroh, Executive Vice President, Federal Reserve Bank of New York, Remarks at the GARP Risk Convention, Reform of Culture in Finance from Multiple Perspectives (Feb. 26, 2019), https://www.newyorkfed.org/newsevents/speeches/2019/sti190226.

[53]   *See, e.g.*, ASX CORP. GOVERNANCE COUNCIL, CORPORATE GOVERNANCE PRINCIPLES AND RECOMMENDATIONS, Recommendation 3.1 and Principle 3 (4th ed. 2019) (Austl.); FIN. REPORTING COUNCIL, THE UK CORPORATE GOVERNANCE CODE, 1, 4, Principle B (Jul. 2018) (U.K.).

[54]   *See generally* Ronald J. Gilson, *From Corporate Law to Corporate Governance*, in THE OXFORD HANDBOOK OF CORPORATE LAW AND GOVERNANCE 3 (Jeffrey N. Gordon and Wolf-Georg Ringe eds., 2018).

society."[55] Furthermore, corporate culture features prominently in The British Academy's current *Future of the Corporation* research project, as a means of promoting societal trust in corporations.[56]

Several recent banking scandals demonstrate that poor financial performance, which was regarded as the key agency problem under the law and economics theory of the corporation, is not the only challenge in modern company law. These scandals include the U.S. Wells Fargo fraudulent accounts scandal[57] and several high profile scandals at some of Australia's leading financial institutions.[58] The Australian scandals resulted in two important reports, which suggested that the misconduct identified was directly tied to defective corporate cultures. The first of these reports, by the Australian Prudential Regulation Authority ("APRA Prudential Report")[59] in 2018, assessed the governance, culture and accountability structures of the Commonwealth Bank of Australia, after numerous incidents at the bank, including breaches of anti-money laundering and counter-terrorism laws.[60] The second report by the Australian Banking Royal Commission[61] examined misconduct in the financial services industry generally.[62] The Commission published its Interim Report in 2018[63] and its Final Report in February 2019.[64]

Although wrongdoing at Wells Fargo and the Australian banks was originally attributed to a "few bad apples,"[65] it later became apparent that there were problems, involving perverse financial incentives, that caused the misconduct.[66] At Wells Fargo, for example, unrealistic sales targets and bonus arrangements induced employees to engage in fraud.[67] More senior bank

---

[55] FIN. REPORTING COUNCIL, *supra* note 53, at 4, Principle A (Jul. 2018) (U.K.).

[56] *See* THE BRITISH ACAD., *supra* note 49, 11, 32–33 (2018) (U.K.).

[57] *See* Jackie Wattles, Ben Geier, Matt Egan & Danielle Wiener-Bronner, *Wells Fargo's 20 Month Nightmare*, CNN MONEY (Apr. 24, 2018), https://money.cnn.com/2018/04/24/news/companies/wells-fargo-timeline-shareholders/index.html.

[58] These financial services scandals led to the introduction of the 2019 amendments to the ASX Corporate Governance Principles and Recommendations. *See* ASX CORPORATE GOVERNANCE COUNCIL, *supra* note 53; Elizabeth Johnstone, Chairman, ASX Corporate Governance Council, Address at Launch of the 4th Edition of the Corporate Governance Principles & Recommendations, 2–3 (Feb. 27, 2019), https://www.asx.com.au/documents/asx-compliance/ej-speech-press-version.pdf (Austl.).

[59] *See* AUSTL. PRUDENTIAL REGULATORY AUTH., PRUDENTIAL INQUIRY INTO THE COMMONWEALTH BANK OF AUSTRALIA (Apr. 30, 2018) (Austl.).

[60] *Id.* at 6, 15–16.

[61] COMMONWEALTH OF AUSTRALIA, ROYAL COMMISSION INTO MISCONDUCT IN THE BANKING, SUPERANNUATION AND FINANCIAL SERVICES INDUSTRY TERMS OF REFERENCE (2017) (Austl.).

[62] For background on the establishment of the Australian Banking Royal Commission, see Kevin McCann AM, Conference Presentation, The Supreme Court of New South Wales Annual Corporate and Commercial Law Conference 2018, Corporate Governance: Lessons from the Interim Report of the Financial Services Royal Commission, 3–7 (Nov. 20, 2018), http://www.supremecourt.justice.nsw.gov.au/Documents/Publications/Corporate%20and%20Commercial%20Law%20Conference/2018/KMcCann%20_Lessonsfromthereportofthe financialservroyalcom_Supreme_Court_of_NSW_Corporate_and_Commercial_Conference_2018_11_20.pdf (Austl.).

[63] The Banking Royal Commission published its interim findings in September 2018. *See* COMMONWEALTH OF AUSTL., INTERIM REPORT ROYAL COMMISSION INTO MISCONDUCT IN THE BANKING, SUPERANNUATION AND FINANCIAL SERVICES INDUSTRY VOL. 1 (2018) (Austl.).

[64] *See* COMMONWEALTH OF AUSTL., *supra* note 14. The Australian Banking Royal Commission's Final Report contained 76 Recommendations. *See id.* at 20–42.

[65] *See* Lucinda Shen , *Former Wells Fargo Employees to CEO John Stumpf: It's Not Our Fault*, FORTUNE, Sept. 19, 2016.

[66] *See* Renae Merle, *Wells Fargo Fired 5,300 Workers for Improper Sales Push. The Executive in Charge is Retiring with $125 Million*, WASH. POST, (Sept. 13, 2016), https://www.washingtonpost.com/news/wonk/wp/2016/09/13/wells-fargo-fired-5300-workers-for-illegal-sales-push-executive-in-charge-retiring-with-125-million/.

[67] *Id. See generally* Jennifer G. Hill, *What Do Colonialism and Pizza Delivery Policies Have to Do with the Wells Fargo Scandal?*, OXFORD BUS. L. BLOG (Nov. 2, 2016), https://www.law.ox.ac.uk/business-law-blog/blog/2016/11/what-do-colonialism-and-pizza-delivery-policies-have-do-wells-fargo.

employees also benefited from the misconduct due to the prevalence of performance-based pay. It seems that compensation incentives may not only encourage wrongdoing, but also undermine its detection. It has recently been argued, for example, that stock-based executive compensation can create systematic perverse incentives to underinvest in compliance programs that could identify misconduct.[68]

The Australian Banking Royal Commission considered that remuneration practices and policies were the main drivers of culture at the relevant financial institutions it examined.[69] Commissioner Hayne, in his interim findings, made the "simple, but telling observation"[70] that all the impugned conduct delivered financial benefits for the individuals and entities concerned.[71] The Final Report devoted an entire chapter to "Culture, Governance and Remuneration."[72]

These banking scandals highlighted the importance of non-financial risks.[73] The relevant misconduct and compliance failure benefited shareholders (at least until the discovery of the misconduct), while simultaneously harming customers. Indeed, one of the key findings of the APRA Prudential Report was that the exceptional financial success of the Commonwealth Bank of Australia had "dulled the senses" of the institution and senior management to the dangers posed by non-financial risks.[74] The Australian Banking Royal Commission inquiry also highlighted the danger of reputational loss due to non-financial risks.[75]

The banking scandals demonstrated that flawed corporate cultures could result in serious harm to stakeholders, such as customers. In the Australian Banking Royal Commission's Final Report, Commissioner Hayne rejected a binary shareholder versus stakeholder approach to corporate law, stating:

> It is not right to treat the interests of shareholders and customers as opposed. Some shareholders may have interests that are opposed to the interests of other shareholders or the interests of customers. But that opposition will almost always be founded in differences between a short-term and longer-term view of prospects and events.[76]

Commissioner Hayne also placed blame for the misconduct squarely at the feet of the financial institutions, and their directors and officers. He stated:

> [T]here can be no doubt that the primary responsibility for misconduct in the financial services industry lies with the entities concerned and those who managed and controlled those entities: their boards and senior management. Nothing that is said in this Report should be understood as diminishing that responsibility.[77]

---

[68] *See* John Armour, Jeffrey Gordon & Geeyoung Min, *Taking Compliance Seriously*, 37 YALE J. ON REG. 1 (2020). Failure to invest in adequate risk management and compliance systems has been raised as a potential problem in a recent scandal, involving serious allegations of compliance failure at Westpac, one of Australia's four largest banks. *See* Karen Maley, *What the Hell Went Wrong: Bob Joss*, AUSTL. FIN. REV., Nov. 30, 2019 at 15.

[69] COMMONWEALTH OF AUSTL., *supra* note 63, at 301.

[70] *Id.*

[71] *Id.*

[72] *See* COMMONWEALTH OF AUSTL., *supra* note 14, at Ch. 3.5.

[73] *See* AUSTL. SEC. & INV. COMM'N, REPORT 631 CORPORATE GOVERNANCE TASKFORCE – DIRECTOR AND OFFICER OVERSIGHT OF NON-FINANCIAL RISK REPORT (2019) (Austl.).

[74] *See* AUSTL. PRUDENTIAL REGULATORY AUTH., *supra* note 59, at 3.

[75] *See* COMMONWEALTH OF AUSTL., *supra* note 14; AUSTL. SEC. & INV. COMM'N, *supra* note 73.

[76] *See* COMMONWEALTH OF AUSTL., *supra* note 14, at 403.

[77] *Id.*, at 4.

v DIRECTOR AND OFFICER LIABILITY FOR BREACH OF THE DUTY OF OVERSIGHT: A COMPARATIVE ANALYSIS

These financial scandals raise interesting questions about community expectations regarding a "public accountability"[78] role for company directors and officers. Moreover, a key issue is the extent to which those expectations are matched by legal liability.[79]

Since the 1960s, in response to the work of Professor Melvin Eisenberg,[80] independent directors have been viewed as corporate monitors, with a fundamental duty of oversight.[81] This image of directors has been a central aspect of the modern shift around the world toward majority independent boards.[82] However, as another doyen of U.S. corporate law, Professor Victor Brudney, once noted, to describe directors as monitors is not the end of the story—we need to know precisely what it is they are supposed to be monitoring.[83]

Brudney suggested at least three possibilities in this regard, which intersect with the division between Berle and Dodd in their famous debate. According to Brudney, independent directors could be described as monitoring: (i) integrity;[84] (ii) efficiency/performance;[85] or (iii) corporate social responsibility.[86]

During the 1990s, the dominance of the law and economics theory of the corporation, coupled with increased interest in corporate governance by financial economists,[87] led to an almost exclusive focus on monitoring corporate efficiency/performance.[88] To what extent, however, are directors and corporate officers today expected to monitor corporate culture failures that result in negative externalities involving integrity or social responsibility issues? And to what extent can they be liable for breach of their duty of oversight in failing to recognize and address non-financial and ethical risks associated with flawed corporate culture? There are

---

[78] Professor Langevoort has, e.g., argued in favor of such an interpretation of the U.S. Sarbanes-Oxley Act 2002. *See* Donald C. Langevoort, *The Social Construction of Sarbanes-Oxley*, 105 Mich. L. Rev. 1817, 1829 (2007).

[79] In a 2017 speech, U.S. Federal Reserve Governor Jerome H. Powell stated "we simply expect much more of boards of directors than ever before. There is no reason to expect that to change." Jerome H. Powell, Speech at the Large Bank Directors Conference, The Role of Boards at Large Financial Firms (Aug. 30, 2017), https://www.federalreserve.gov /newsevents/speech/powell20170830a.htm. The same point was made more than 50 years ago by an Australian High Court judge, who warned that where community expectations lead, the law will usually follow. *See* Douglas Menzies, *Company Directors*, 33 Austl. L. J. 156 (1959) (Austl.).

[80] *See generally* Melvin A. Eisenberg, The Structure of the Corporation: A Legal Analysis (1976).

[81] *See, e.g.,* Jeffrey N. Gordon, *The Rise of Independent Directors in the United States, 1950–2005: Of Shareholder Value and Stock Market Prices*, 59 Stan. L. Rev. 1465 (2007).

[82] *See, e.g.,* Independent Directors in Asia: A Historical, Contextual, and Comparative Approach (Dan W. Puchniak, Harald Baum & Luke Nottage eds., 2017).

[83] Victor Brudney, *The Independent Director—Heavenly City or Potemkin Village?*, 95 Harv. L. Rev. 597 (1982).

[84] Professor Brudney focuses on "managerial" integrity (e.g., precluding self-dealing by management), though similar arguments can be made in relation to "organizational" integrity. *Id.* at 607–31, 653.

[85] *Id.* at 632–39.

[86] *See id.* at 602–03, 658. Professor Brudney considered that there are practical difficulties involved in all three types of monitoring, on the basis that the independent director's leverage is "modest." *Id.* at 658–59. In relation to monitoring efficiency, for example, he stated that the generally accepted view is that independent directors "cannot and do not diligently police management's wealth-maximizing function." *Id.* at 638. *Cf.* Gordon, *supra* note 81 (arguing that a shift in the role of independent directors from advisors to monitors of shareholder wealth maximization was facilitated by technological and informational improvements regarding stock prices).

[87] *See, e.g.,* Gilson, *supra* note 54 at 5 (noting that, between 1995 and 2013, 25% of all articles in the prestigious *Journal of Financial Economics* related to corporate governance).

[88] For example, Professor Gordon, writing in 2007, stated that the "now-conventional understanding" of directors in public companies is that they are "supposed to 'monitor' the managers in view of shareholder interests." Gordon, *supra* note 81, at 1468. According to Gordon, the 1990s and 2000s were characterized by a principle of "unalloyed shareholder wealth maximization." *Id.* at 1469. *See, e.g.,* Julian Velasco, *Shareholder Primacy in Benefit Corporations*, ch. 17 (this volume) (distinguishing between the wealth maximization norm and shareholder primacy).

significant differences between the traditional approaches of U.S., U.K. and Australian law in this regard.[89]

Under U.S. state law, the most important of which is Delaware law, directors have traditionally faced "miniscule likelihood"[90] of liability with respect to their duty of oversight, unless it can be demonstrated that they had actual knowledge of the wrongdoing. The leading modern U.S. case on the duty of oversight is the landmark 1996 decision, *In re Caremark International Inc. Derivative Litigation ("Caremark")*.[91] This case, bolstered by later important decisions, such as *Stone v. Ritter*[92] and *In re Citigroup Shareholder Derivative Litigation*,[93] demonstrated that directors will generally be protected from liability in all but extreme circumstances. Mere negligence is insufficient, given the capacious protection of the business judgment rule.[94] Even gross negligence[95] does not suffice, due to the ubiquitous presence of exculpation clauses in U.S. corporate charters.[96]

According to the *Caremark* case, directors will only be liable for "bad faith" breaches of oversight responsibility, falling within the more stringent duty of loyalty.[97] The court stated that to establish lack of good faith, the plaintiff must show "a sustained or systematic failure of the board to exercise oversight—such as an utter failure to attempt to assure a reasonable information and reporting system exists."[98] Dicta in the *Disney* litigation and *Stone v. Ritter* went even further, requiring, as a precondition to liability, egregious conduct, in the form of *intentional* infliction of harm or *conscious* dereliction of duty by a director.[99]

Although some scholars have perceived this duty of good faith under U.S. corporate law as implicating a public accountability role for directors,[100] the practical effect of the judicial definition of "bad faith" in these decisions was such as to render the U.S. duty of oversight aspirational only.[101] In many of the banking scandals, for example, directors and officers were completely ignorant of the misconduct and compliance failures within the organization.[102] The

---

[89] *See generally* Hill & Conaglen, *supra* note 34. For an excellent historical analysis of how U.S. and U.K. fiduciary law, which had the same roots, came to diverge radically, see DAVID KERSHAW, THE FOUNDATIONS OF ANGLO-AMERICAN CORPORATE FIDUCIARY LAW (2018). *See also* Edward J. Janger, *Equitable Duty: Regulating Corporate Transactions in the Vicinity of Insolvency from a Comparative Perspective*, ch. 8 (this volume) (discussing differences between the approach of U.S. and U.K. law relating to fiduciary duties in the context of corporate insolvency).

[90] *See* Brudney, *supra* note 83, at 614.

[91] 698 A.2d 959 (Del. Ch. 1996). For detailed background to the *Caremark* case, see Jennifer Arlen, *The Story of* Allis-Chalmers, Caremark, *and* Stone: *Directors' Evolving Duty to Monitor, in* CORPORATE LAW STORIES 323 (J. Mark Ramseyer ed., 2009).

[92] Stone v. Ritter, 911 A.2d 362 (Del. 2006).

[93] In re Citigroup Inc. S'holder Derivative Litig., 964 A.2d 106 (Del. Ch. 2009).

[94] *See* E. Norman Veasey, *An Economic Rationale for Judicial Decisionmaking in Corporate Law*, 53 BUS. LAW. 681, 689–92 (1998).

[95] Gross neglect (or "crassa negligentia") was the standard of diligence required under eighteenth-century U.K. law in the famous case of Charitable Corporation v. Sutton, (1742) 2 Atk 400, 406; 26 ER 642.

[96] *See* Malpiede v. Townson, 780 A.2d 1075 (Del. 2001).

[97] *See* Louis J. Bevilacqua, *Monitoring the Duty to Monitor*, N.Y.L.J., Nov. 28, 2011, at 2. *See also* Hill & Conaglen, *supra* note 34; Hillary A. Sale, *Monitoring Caremark's Good Faith*, 32 DEL. J. CORP. L. 719 (2007); Veasey, *supra* note 94, at 691–92.

[98] In re Caremark Int'l Inc. Derivative Litig., 698 A.2d 959 at 971 (Del. Ch. 1996).

[99] *See In re* Walt Disney Co. Derivative Litig., 906 A.2d 27, 66–67 (Del. 2006). *See also* Stone v. Ritter, 911 A.2d 362, 370 (Del. 2006).

[100] *See, e.g.,* Sale, *supra* note 15.

[101] *See* Julian Velasco, *The Role of Aspiration in Corporate Fiduciary Duties*, 54 WM & MARY L. REV. 519 (2012) (criticizing the increasing use of the term "aspiration" in relation to binding legal duties).

[102] *See, e.g.,* AUSTL. PRUDENTIAL REGULATORY AUTH., *supra* note 59, at 3 (referring to the fact that financial success had "dulled the senses" of senior managers to the dangers posed by non-financial risk). Similar issues seem to have arisen in relation to the recent Westpac scandal. See Elizabeth Knight, "Westpac vs AUSTRAC – The Stakes Just Got

narrow contours of the *Caremark* doctrine led some commentators to question whether investors are, in fact, provided with any "meaningful oversight protection."[103] Although this legal regime is often justified on policy grounds,[104] it has recently been claimed that the standard policy arguments do not necessarily justify the complete exclusion of liability.[105]

Two recent Delaware Supreme Court decisions, however, suggest a judicial shift may be occurring regarding the interpretation of the "good faith"/"bad faith" dichotomy in the *Caremark* doctrine and that this shift could potentially offer broader scope for liability of directors for public harm caused by corporations.[106] The first of these decisions, a 2017 demand futility case, *City of Birmingham Retirement and Relief System v. Good*,[107] highlights the traditionally narrow scope of *Caremark*-style claims, yet at the same time demonstrates the potential for change. The case involved a claim that the directors of Duke Energy Corp. breached their duty of oversight when the company discharged highly toxic coal ash and wastewater into a North Carolina river.[108] The majority judgment affirmed the Court of Chancery's decision that the plaintiffs had failed to show that the directors acted in "bad faith," the standard for *Caremark*-style oversight liability.[109] However, Chief Justice Strine disagreed, and the grounds for his dissenting judgment are noteworthy. He stated that:

> It was the business strategy of Duke Energy, accepted and supported by its board of directors, to run the company in a manner that purposely skirted, and in many ways consciously violated, important environmental laws ... Duke's executives, advisors, and directors used all the tools in their large box to cause Duke to flout its environmental responsibilities, thereby reduce its costs of operations, and by that means, increase its profitability. This, fiduciaries of a Delaware corporation, may not do.[110]

The second case, the 2019 Delaware Supreme Court decision in *Marchand v. Barnhill*,[111] involved a suit against the directors of a dairy company, Blue Bell Creameries USA, Inc., which had distributed contaminated ice cream, resulting in the deaths of several customers. The

Bigger," *The Sydney Morning Herald*, Jun. 13, 2020; Karen Maley, "Westpac Veteran Asks What Went Wrong," *Australian Financial Review*, Nov. 30, 2019.

[103] Bevilacqua, *supra* note 97. *See also* Ronald Barusch, *CBS and the Need to Hold Directors Accountable*, WALL ST. J., Sept. 16, 2018.

[104] The high level of protection provided to U.S. directors under the duty of care has sometimes been justified on the basis of the "stupefying disjunction between risk and reward," which could apply if directors were to be held liable for negligence. *See* Gagliardi v. Trifoods Int'l, Inc., 683 A.2d 1049, 1052 (Del. Ch. 1996).

[105] Holger Spamann, *Monetary Liability for Breach of the Duty of Care?*, 8 J. LEGAL ANALYSIS 337 (2016). *See also* Lyman Johnson, *The Three Fiduciaries of Delaware Corporate Law — and Eisenberg's Error*, ch. 3 (this volume) (noting that "a robust duty of care for officers — the law on which is surprisingly undeveloped in Delaware — might revive the prospect of remedies for a care breach by senior executives, who cannot be exculpated").

[106] It should also be noted that directors can potentially be liable under U.S. securities law for oversight failures relating to public responsibilities, where they have made corporate misstatements, even if those misstatements were made in good faith. *See* Hillary A. Sale & Donald C. Langevoort, *"We Believe": Omnicare, Legal Risk Disclosure and Corporate Governance*, 66 DUKE L. J . 763 (2016) (discussing the decision in Omnicare Inc. v. Laborers Dist. Council Constr. Indus. Pension Fund, 575 U.S. 175 (2015)).

[107] 177 A.3d 47 (Del. 2017).

[108] *See, e.g.*, Brudney, *supra* note 83, at 603 (discussing the potential role of directors in addressing "the social costs of externalities, such as pollution of the environment").

[109] *See* City of Birmingham Retirement & Relief Sys. v. Good, 177 A.3d 47, 51, 64 (Del. 2017) (per Seitz J.).

[110] *Id.* at 65. *See also* In re Massey Energy Co. Derivative & Class Action Litig., 160 A.3d 484 (Del. Ch. 2017); In re Massey Energy Co., C.A. No. 5430-VCS, 2011 WL 2176479, at *6, *20 (Del. Ch. May 31, 2011) (where similar issues arose in the context of worker safety).

[111] Marchand v. Barnhill, 212 A.3d 805 (Del. 2019). The parties in Marchand v. Barnhill entered into a $60 million settlement on April 24, 2020, shortly before the trial was due to commence. *See* Meredith Kotler, Pamela Marcogliese & Marques Tracey, *Recent Delaware Court of Chancery Decision Sustains Another Caremark Claim at the Pleading Stage*, HARV. L. SCHOOL F. ON CORP. GOVERNANCE (May 25, 2020), https://corpgov.law.harvard.edu/2020/05/25/

plaintiffs successfully pleaded that the company's directors were not protected under the *Caremark* doctrine. Although the company had U.S. Food and Drug Administration ("FDA") compliance systems in place, the court held that the directors had not implemented any "system to monitor food safety *at the board level*,"[112] and that the absence of such board level monitoring amounted to "bad faith indifference"[113] for the purposes of the *Caremark* doctrine. *Marchand v. Barnhill* signals a significant deviation from the previously accepted contours of the *Caremark* doctrine. It has already been relied upon to support potential *Caremark* liability in a recent Delaware Court of Chancery decision, *In re Clovis Oncology, Inc. Derivative Litigation*,[114] and could have major personal liability ramifications for directors and officers in the future.[115]

At first sight, the position in the United Kingdom appears to be quite different from the traditionally narrow contours of U.S. *Caremark*-style liability. Directors in the United Kingdom have been subject to a clear oversight responsibility for financial mismanagement as part of their duty of care and diligence ("duty of care") since the landmark 1925 decision in *In re City Equitable Fire Insurance Co.*[116] The standard for this duty, originally one of gross negligence, rose significantly during the 1990s.[117] The U.K. case law also suggests that directors have a responsibility to monitor, from both a competence and an integrity perspective, any functions that they have delegated to other persons in the organization.[118] The 2018 U.K. *Corporate Governance Code* states that directors "must act with integrity, lead by example and promote the desired culture."[119]

Although this might suggest that U.K. directors face a high risk of liability for oversight failure, that is not, in fact, the case.[120] There is a dearth of litigation under the U.K.'s private enforcement model for breach of directors' duties. The directors of U.K. public companies have faced virtually no risk of being sued for damages for breach of their duty of care,[121] even following the global financial crisis, where blame could often be traced to board policies.[122] The reasons for

---

recent-delaware-court-of-chancery-decision-sustains-another-caremark-claim-at-the-pleading-stage/. The former chief executive officer of Blue Bell Creameries USA, Inc. was also charged with conspiracy in relation to the listeria outbreak. *See* Christopher Mele, *Blue Bell's Ex-C.E.O. Charged in Conspiracy to Cover Up Listeria Outbreak*, N.Y. TIMES, May 1, 2020, at A23.

[112]   Marchand v. Barnhill, 212 A.3d 805, 823 (Del. 2019).

[113]   *Id.* at 823.

[114]   In re Clovis Oncology, Inc. Derivative Litig., C.A. No. 2017–0222–JRS, 2019 WL 4850188 (Del. Ch. Oct. 1, 2019) (where the plaintiffs alleged that the board directors of Clovis, a pharmaceutical company, had ignored red flags regarding failure by the company to comply with clinical testing protocols for a particular drug, and then allowed Clovis to issue misleading public statements about the relevant drug trials). For discussion of some judicial developments since In re Clovis Oncology, Inc., see Kotler, Marcogliese & Tracey, *supra* note 111.

[115]   *See* Martin Lipton & Wachtell Lipton, *Spotlight on Boards*, HARV. L. SCHOOL F. ON CORP. GOVERNANCE (Jun. 28, 2019), https://corpgov.law.harvard.edu/2019/06/28/spotlight-on-boards-4/. *See also* Kotler, Marcogliese & Tracey, *supra* note 111, arguing that cases, such as Marchand v. Barnhill, represent "unique or extreme examples of certain corporate behavior," rather than signaling a change in the law.

[116]   [1925] Ch 407 (U.K.).

[117]   *See, e.g.*, Re D'Jan of London Ltd [1993] BCC 646 (U.K.); Norman v. Theodore Goddard [1992] BCC 14 (U.K.).

[118]   *See* Re Barings Plc (No 5); Secretary of State for Trade and Industry v. Baker (No. 5) [2000] 1 BCLC 523 (U.K.). *See generally* PAUL L. DAVIES & SARAH WORTHINGTON, GOWER & DAVIES PRINCIPLES OF MODERN COMPANY LAW [10–10], 247 (10th ed., 2016); Joan Loughrey, *The Director's Duty of Care and Skill and the Financial Crisis*, in DIRECTORS' DUTIES AND SHAREHOLDER LITIGATION IN THE WAKE OF THE FINANCIAL CRISIS 12, 17 (Joan Loughrey ed., 2013).

[119]   FIN. REPORTING COUNCIL, *supra* note 53, at 4.

[120]   Note, however, that director disqualification orders, including for recklessness and incompetence are relatively common in the United Kingdom. *See generally* DAVIES & WORTHINGTON, *supra* note 118, at [10–2], [10–10], 237–38, 246–47.

[121]   John Armour, Bernard Black, Brian Cheffins & Richard Nolan, *Private Enforcement of Corporate Law: An Empirical Comparison of the United Kingdom and the United States*, 6 J. EMPIRICAL LEGAL STUD. 687, 687, 690, 699–700, 710 (2009).

[122]   *See generally* Loughrey, *supra* note 118, at 12–13.

this lack of litigation are mainly procedural,[123] yet they create what has been described as "an accountability firewall"[124] in the United Kingdom.

In spite of some superficial similarities, Australian law relating to directors' oversight duties differs significantly from the traditional U.S. *Caremark* standard and U.K. company law.[125] Australian directors and officers are subject, not only to general law (i.e. common law and equitable) duties but also to statutory duties under the *Corporations Act*,[126] including the duty of care,[127] which form part of a broader civil penalty enforcement regime.[128]

In contrast to the strongly private, contractual interpretation of corporate law under contemporary Delaware case law,[129] the Australian courts have increasingly viewed directors' statutory duties as public obligations, which have an important social function.[130] According to the 2011 decision, *ASIC v. Healey*,[131] "[t]he role of a director is significant as their actions may have a profound effect on the community, and not just shareholders, employees and creditors."[132]

Australian case law also accepts that directors have an obligation to oversee and monitor the activities of their company,[133] and that failure to ensure that the company has proper control systems in place, to enable directors to fulfil their monitoring responsibilities, can constitute a breach of the duty of care.[134] These oversight responsibilities may, in certain circumstances, implicate matters traditionally associated with corporate social responsibility, when those matters expose the company to significant risk, including, for example, risks associated with climate change.[135] In the wake of the Banking Royal Commission's findings,[136] the Australian Securities and Investments Commission ("ASIC") released a report, which confirms that boards of

---

[123] Procedural reasons for the negligible U.K. case law on breach of the duty of care include the absence, until recently, of class actions and the loser-pays litigation system. *See generally* Armour et al., *supra* note 121; Hill & Conaglen, *supra* note 34; Marc T. Moore, *Redressing Risk Oversight Failure in UK and US Listed Companies: Lessons from the RBS and Citigroup Litigation*, 18 Eur. Bus. Org. L. Rev. 733 (2017).

[124] *See* Joan Loughrey, *Breaching the Accountability Firewall: Market Norms and the Reasonable Director*, 37 Seattle U. L. Rev. 989, 989 (2014) (citing UK Parliamentary Commission on Banking Standards, *Changing Banking for Good*, Vol. 1. 2013–14, H.L. 27–1, H.C. 175–1, at 10 (U.K.)).

[125] *See generally* Hill & Conaglen, *supra* note 34.

[126] *See Corporations Act* 2001 (Cth), ss 180–84 (Austl.).

[127] *Corporations Act* 2001 (Cth), s 180(1) (Austl.).

[128] *See Corporations Act* 2001 (Cth), Part 9.4B; s 1317E(1) (Austl.). *See generally* Hill & Conaglen, *supra* note 34.

[129] *See, e.g.,* ATP Tour, Inc. v. Deutscher Tennis Bund, 91 A.3d 554 (Del. 2014); Boilermakers Local 154 Retirement Fund v. Chevron, 73 A.3d 934 (Del. Ch. 2013); James D. Cox, *Whose Law Is It? Battling over Turf in Shareholder Litigation*, in Research Handbook on Shareholder Power 333 (Jennifer G. Hill & Randall S. Thomas eds., 2015). *See also* Jacob Hale Russell, *For Whom Are Non-Profit Managers Trustees?: The Contractual Revolution in Charity Governance*, ch. 13 (this volume) (stating that "[i]deas of contract are today so dominant across business law that it makes it hard to resurrect what came before").

[130] *See* Jason Harris, Anil Hargovan & Janet Austin, *Shareholder Primacy Revisited: Does the Public Interest Have Any Role in Statutory Duties?*, 26 Co. & Sec. L. J. 355 (2008); Michelle Welsh, *Realising the Public Potential of Corporate Law: Twenty Years of Civil Penalty Enforcement in Australia*, 42 Fed. L. Rev. 217, 223–28 (2014).

[131] (2011) 196 FCR 291 (Austl.). *See generally* Jennifer G. Hill, *Centro and the Monitoring Board – Legal Duties Versus Aspirational Ideals in Corporate Governance*, 35 U.N.S.W.L.J. 341 (2012); John Lowry, *The Irreducible Core of the Duty of Care, Skill and Diligence of Company Directors: Australian Securities and Investments Commission v. Healey*, 75 Mod. L. Rev. 249 (2012).

[132] ASIC v. Healey, (2011) 196 FCR 291, 297 (Austl.).

[133] *See* ASIC v. Adler (2002) 168 FLR 253, 347 (Austl.); Daniels v. Anderson (1995) 37 NSWLR 438, 503–04 (Austl.).

[134] ASIC v. Adler (2002) 168 FLR 253, 347 (Austl.).

[135] A Memorandum of Opinion, co-authored by a senior corporate law barrister, has argued that Australian directors who disregard the risks to their business associated with climate change could potentially face liability for breach of the statutory duty of care. *See* The Centre for Policy Development and the Future Business Council, Climate Change and Directors' Duties, Supplementary Memorandum of Opinion (Mr Noel Hutley SC and Mr Sebastian Hartford Davis) (Mar. 26, 2019).

[136] *See* Commonwealth of Austl., *supra* note 14.

Australian public companies are responsible for both financial and non-financial risks.[137] The report also emphasizes that these two forms of risk are closely connected, because "non-financial risks have very real *financial* implications for companies, their investors and their customers."[138]

Finally, in contrast to both the United States and the United Kingdom,[139] Australia relies on a predominantly public, rather than private, enforcement model,[140] as a result of its civil penalty regime.[141] The 2016 decision, *ASIC v. Cassimatis (No 8)*,[142] accepted that breach of the statutory duty of care is not only a private, but also a public wrong, and there is a public interest in the enforcement of directors' duties in Australia.[143] Under this public enforcement regime, actions for breach of directors' duties are usually brought by the business conduct regulator, ASIC. The regulator has a very high success rate in such actions to date,[144] and recently benefited from a major expansion of the sanctions available to it under this regime.[145]

An increasing number of ASIC's civil penalty applications in recent times have involved so-called "stepping stone" liability.[146] This developing form of liability comprises a two-step process, whereby directors and officers may be personally liable for failure to prevent contraventions of the law by their corporation.[147] In recent stepping stone liability cases, ASIC has argued that directors breached their statutory duty of care by allowing the corporation to contravene another provision of the *Corporations Act*, thereby jeopardizing the corporation's interests by exposing it to a penalty.[148] Stepping stone liability is particularly well-suited to the kind of

---

[137] AUSTL. SEC. & INV. COMM'N, *supra* note 73.

[138] *Id.* at 2.

[139] *See* Armour et al., *supra* note 121. There are, however, some aspects of public enforcement in the United Kingdom. *Id.* at 716–17.

[140] For a comparison of the U.S. and Australian enforcement models relating to directors' duties, see Renee M. Jones & Michelle Welsh, *Toward a Public Enforcement Model for Directors' Duty of Oversight*, 45 VAND. J. TRANSNAT'L L. 343 (2012).

[141] *Corporations Act* 2001 (Cth), Part 9.4B; s 1317E(1) (Austl.).

[142] ASIC v. Cassimatis (No 8) [2016] FCA 1023 (Austl.). An appeal against this decision was dismissed in March 2020 by the Federal Court of Australia in Cassimatis v. ASIC [2020] FCAFC 52 (Austl.).

[143] *See* ASIC v. Cassimatis (No 8) [2016] FCA 1023, [455], [461], [503] (Austl.). *See also* Cassimatis v. ASIC [2020] FCAFC 52, [27], [240] (Austl.).

[144] *See* Greg Golding, *Tightening the Screws on Directors: Care, Delegation and Reliance*, 35 U.N.S.W.L.J. 266, 273–74 (2012); Ian M. Ramsay & Benjamin B. Saunders, *An Analysis of the Enforcement of the Statutory Duty of Care by ASIC*, 36 CO. & SEC. L. J. 497, 510–11 (2019). *See also* Belinda Gibson & Diane Brown, *ASIC's Expectations of Directors*, 35 U.N.S.W.L.J. 254 (2012); Jasper Hedges & Ian M. Ramsay, *Has the Introduction of Civil Penalties Increased the Speed and Success Rate of Directors' Duties Cases?*, 34 CO. & SEC. L. J. 549, 552–53 (2016); Welsh, *supra* note 130, at 233–39.

[145] *See Treasury Law Amendment (Strengthening Corporate and Financial Sector Penalties) Act* 2019 (Cth) (Austl.); AUSTL. SEC. & INV. COMM'N, *Media Release 19–032 ASIC to pursue harsher penalties after laws passed by Senate* (Feb. 15, 2019), https://asic.gov.au/about-asic/news-centre/find-a-media-release/2019-releases/19-032mr-asic-to-pursue-harsher-penalties-after-laws-passed-by-senate/.

[146] On the evolution of "stepping stone" liability, *see* Tim Bednall & Pamela Hanrahan, *Officers' Liability for Mandatory Disclosure: Two Paths, Two Destinations?*, 31 CO. & SEC. L.J. 474 (2013); Abe Herzberg & Helen Anderson, *Stepping Stones – From Corporate Fault to Directors' Personal Civil Liability*, 40 FED. L. REV. 181 (2012).

[147] *See* Alice Zhou, *A Step Too Far? Rethinking the Stepping Stone Approach to Officers' Liability*, 47 FED. L. REV. 151 (2019).

[148] *See, e.g.*, ASIC v. Maxwell [2006] NSWSC 1052, [104]–[106] (Austl.). *See generally* Harris et al., *supra* note 130. Although some judges have expressed concern about stepping stone liability being used as a back-door means of imposing accessorial liability on directors, this type of liability has been successful in a number of recent Australian cases. *See, e.g.*, ASIC, in the matter of Sino Australia Oil and Gas Ltd (in liq) v. Sino Australia Oil and Gas Ltd (in liq) [2016] FCA 934, [85]–[86] (Austl.); ASIC v. Cassimatis (No 8) [2016] FCA 1023 (Austl.). *See* Ramsay & Saunders, *supra* note 144, at 519. However, in Cassimatis v. ASIC [2020] FCAFC 52 (Austl.), the judges expressed doubt as to the value of the term, if not the concept, of "stepping stone liability," as an analytical tool for assessing breach of s 180(1) of the *Corporations Act* 2001 (Cth) (Austl.). *See id.* at [79], [221], [465].

misconduct that results in stakeholder or social harm. The Banking Royal Commission[149] criticized ASIC for its frequent use of enforceable undertakings[150] (a form of negotiated settlement, not dissimilar from deferred or non-prosecution agreements), rather than pursuing litigation against regulated entities and their directors and officers.[151] ASIC has responded by indicating that it intends to use its enforcement powers more aggressively in the future.[152]

VI CONCLUSION

Underlying business history and theory, there is tension between the public and private conceptions of the corporation. This tension is embodied in the famous Berle-Dodd debate, in which the two sides to the debate are often viewed as binary and irreconcilable. The Berle-Dodd debate provides the basis for contemporary clashes between "different visions of corporatism,"[153] such as the conflict between shareholder primacy and stakeholder-centered versions of the corporation.[154]

This chapter provides two central insights. The first is that there is not one problem, but multiple problems in corporate law and different problems may come to the forefront at different times. Although financial performance is a legitimate concern in corporate law, it is also essential to recognize, and address, the danger that corporate conduct may result in negative externalities and harm to society. It is, therefore, a mistake to view the two sides of the Berle-Dodd debate as binary and irreconcilable. The second insight is that corporate governance

---

[149] COMMONWEALTH OF AUSTL., *supra* note 14.

[150] *See* AUSTL. SEC. & INV. COMM'N, REGULATORY GUIDE (RG) 100, ENFORCEABLE UNDERTAKINGS (Feb. 2015) (Austl.). *See also* AUSTL. SEC. & INV. COMM'N, *Media Release 18–325: Research study on Enforceable Undertakings Released*, Oct. 25, 2018 (discussing the findings in Nehme et al., *The General Deterrence Effects of Enforceable Undertakings on Financial Services and Credit Providers*, 2018, https://download.asic.gov.au/media/4916053/18-325mr-deterrence-effects-of-enforceable-undertakings-on-financial-services-and-credit-providers.pdf).

[151] *See* COMMONWEALTH OF AUSTL., *supra* note 14, at 440–42. Note, however, that a recent interim discussion paper on corporate criminal liability by the Australian Law Reform Commission ("ALRC") has suggested that current Australian law may inappropriately target directors for corporate misconduct while providing too many opportunities for senior officers to evade personal liability. AUSTL. L. REFORM COMM'N, DISCUSSION PAPER 87, CORPORATE CRIMINAL RESPONSIBILITY, Nov. 2019, [7.30]- [7.33]. *See generally id.*, [7.19]-[7.66]. *See also* Johnson, *supra* note 105 (distinguishing between the fiduciary duties owed by executive officers and directors under Delaware Law). On the issue of individual liability of directors and officers for corporate misconduct, *see also* AUSTL. L. REFORM COMM'N, CORPORATE CRIMINAL RESPONSIBILITY: INDIVIDUAL LIABILITY FOR CORPORATE MISCONDUCT: AN UPDATE, Mar. 2020, in which the ALRC confirms its view that there is an "accountability gap" under Australian law in terms of holding senior officers of large corporations liable for corporate misconduct. *Id.* 4. *See also* DEPARTMENT OF THE TREASURY (CTH), IMPLEMENTING ROYAL COMMISSION RECOMMENDATIONS 3.9, 4.12, 6.6, 6.7 AND 6.8 FINANCIAL ACCOUNTABILITY REGIME: PROPOSAL PAPER, Jan. 2020.

[152] In the Banking Royal Commission's Final Report, Commissioner Hayne stated that the regulator's first question, upon becoming aware of any entity's breach of the law, should be "Why not litigate?" COMMONWEALTH OF AUSTL., *supra* note 14, at 427. It is anticipated that this will result in a far greater volume of litigation, including for breach of statutory directors' duties, in the future. *See, e.g.*, Michael Pelly, *ASIC Set for Hayne Court Blitz*, AUSTL. FIN. REV., Aug. 19, 2019 (Austl.). *See also* AUSTL. SEC. & INV. COMM'N, *Report 625: ASIC Enforcement Update: January to June 2019*, 3 (Aug. 2019) (Austl.); AUSTL. SEC. & INV. COMM'N, *ASIC Enforcement Update: September 2019 to February 2020*, 3–4 (Feb. 2020) (Austl.).

[153] Bratton & Wachter, *supra* note 41, at 124.

[154] For discussion of the enduring "stockholder/stakeholder dilemma," *see* Amir N. Licht, "Stakeholder Impartiality: A New Classic Approach for the Objectives of the Corporation," ch. 16 (this volume). *See also* Julian Velasco, supra note 88. *Cf.* Lucian A. Bebchuk & Roberto Tallarita, *The Illusory Promise of Stakeholder Governance* (forthcoming, CORNELL L. REV., Dec. 2020); Colin Mayer, *Shareholderism versus Stakeholderism – A Misconceived Contradiction. A Comment on 'The Illusory Promise of Stakeholder Governance' by Lucian Bebchuk and Roberto Tallarita*, (European Corporate Governance Institute, Working Paper No. 522/2020, Jun. 2020).

techniques (such as performance-based pay), which are designed to ameliorate one problem in corporate law,[155] can, at the same time, exacerbate other problems.

A number of recent developments in corporate law have highlighted the negative externalities and social harm that corporate actions can cause. These developments suggest the emergence of a more cohesive vision of the corporation that encompasses both private and public aspects. They also potentially affect the role and duties of company directors, who are no longer seen merely as monitors of corporate performance but also as monitors of corporate integrity and the risk of social harm.

---

[155]	For example, performance-based pay, which is designed to address agency problems related to financial perform-ance, can provide perverse incentives for misconduct affecting stakeholders and society. *See, e.g.,* COMMONWEALTH OF AUSTL., *supra* note 14, at 347–74.

16

Stakeholder Impartiality: A New Classic Approach for the Objectives of the Corporation

Amir N. Licht[*]

I INTRODUCTION

Former Delaware Chief Justice Leo Strine, Jr. recently argued extrajudicially that "[d]espite attempts to muddy the doctrinal waters, a clear-eyed look at the law of corporations in Delaware reveals that, within the limits of their discretion, directors must make stockholder welfare their sole end, and that other interests may be taken into consideration only as a means of promoting stockholder welfare."[1] For many years, the semi-official position of the U.S. business community, reflected in the Business Roundtable's Statement on Corporate Governance, has espoused a similar principle—that "the paramount duty of management and of boards of directors is to the corporation's stockholders."[2]

In direct response to this position, U.S. Senator Elizabeth Warren (D-Mass.) in 2018 introduced her Accountable Capitalism Act. Inspired by "the thriving benefit corporation model," the Act would require very large American corporations to consider the interests of all corporate stakeholders—including employees, customers, shareholders, and communities—with a view to balancing their interests.[3] In a turnaround from its prior position, the Business Roundtable in 2019 promulgated a new statement on the purpose of a corporation, in which prominent corporate leaders announced that they "share a fundamental commitment to all of our stakeholders."[4] As reporters noted, however, the Business Roundtable did not provide specifics on *how* it would carry out its newly stated ideals.[5]

[*] For helpful comments I am grateful to Richard Brooks, Matthew Conaglen, Lior Frank, Jennifer Hill, Lyman Johnson, Amnon Lehavi, Paul Miller, Asaf Raz, Steven Schwarcz, Andrew Tuch, and Julian Velasco, and especially to the editors, Arthur Laby and Jacob Russell. Special thanks to Former Chief Justice Leo E. Strine, Jr. for his comments on an earlier draft. Accountability for all errors remains with me.

[1] Leo E. Strine, Jr., *The Dangers of Denial: The Need for a Clear-Eyed Understanding of the Power and Accountability Structure Established by the Delaware General Corporation Law*, 50 Wake Forest L. Rev. 761, 768 (2015). In tandem, Strine recently advanced a reform proposal that, inter alia, would ensure that large companies consider worker concerns through dedicated board committees. Leo Strine, *Toward Fair and Sustainable Capitalism* (U. of Penn. Inst. for L. & Econ. Research Working Paper No. 19–39, 2019).

[2] Bus. Roundtable, *Statement on Corporate Governance*, at 3 (1997).

[3] Press Release, Office of Senator Elizabeth Warren, Warren Introduces Accountable Capitalism Act (Aug. 15, 2018), https://www.warren.senate.gov/newsroom/press-releases/warren-introduces-accountable-capitalism-act.

[4] Bus. Roundtable, *Statement on the Purpose of a Corporation*, at 1 (2019), https://opportunity.businessroundtable.org/ourcommitment/.

[5] David Gelles & David Yaffe-Bellany, *Shareholder Value Is No Longer Everything, Top C.E.O.s Say*, N.Y. Times (Aug. 19, 2019), https://www.nytimes.com/2019/08/19/business/business-roundtable-ceos-corporations.html.; *see also* Joseph Stiglitz, *Can we Trust CEOs' Shock Conversion to Corporate Benevolence?*, Guardian (Aug. 29, 2019), https://www.theguardian.com/business/2019/aug/29/can-we-trust-ceos-shock-conversion-to-corporate-benevolence (echoing decades-old concerns about such position, Joseph Stiglitz questioned the statement's ingenuity).

A duty to consider stakeholder interests is already a pressing reality for large companies in the United Kingdom. Section 172 of the Companies Act 2006 requires directors to act in a way they consider, in good faith, would be most likely to promote the success of the company for the benefit of its members[6] as a whole. In doing so, directors are *required* to have regard, among other things, to the interests of the company's employees, business partners, the community, and the environment. Government regulations promulgated in 2018 require large companies, whether listed or non-listed, to include in their strategic reports a new statement on *how* the directors have considered stakeholders' interests in discharging their duty under section 172.[7]

The new U.K. provision brings a significant twist to a plot that has been unfolding—in circles, it must be said—at least since Lord Justice Bowen in 1883 famously stated in *Hutton* v. *West Cork Ry.*:

> A railway company, or the directors of the company, might send down all the porters at a railway station to have tea in the country at the expense of the company. Why should they not? It is for the directors to judge . . . The law does not say that there are to be no cakes and ale, but there are to be no cakes and ale except such as are required for the benefit of the company.[8]

From Lord Justice Bowen to Chief Justice Strine (and/or Senator Warren and/or Mr. Jeff Bezos & co.), the debate over the objectives of the corporation has been oscillating between two polar positions, dubbed "monistic" and "pluralistic" in business management parlance. The monistic position endorses a single maximand (that which is to be maximized)—invariably, shareholder interest—while the pluralistic position supports a multiple-objective duty that would balance the interests of several stakeholder constituencies, shareholders included. With few exceptions, this debate has been limited to the substantive question of whether non-shareholder stakeholders *deserve* consideration in their own right. The practical question of *how* to perform this balancing has been largely neglected. As we shall see below, when the Supreme Court of Canada discussed this practical point in an *obiter dictum* in *BCE Inc.* v. *1976 Debentureholders*, the Court explicitly eschewed giving it an answer.[9] Lawyers are similarly at sea with regard to a multiple-stakeholder-objective provision in India's Companies Act, 2013.

This paper advances a new, yet classical, approach for the task of considering the interests of various stakeholders by directors and other corporate fiduciaries who are required by law, or opt, to adopt a stakeholderist approach—that is, to consider such different interests together with shareholders' interest in a pluralistic mode. I argue that for lawfully accomplishing this task, while also complying with their standard duties of loyalty and care, directors should exercise their discretion impartially. Judicial review of directors' conduct in terms of treating different stakeholders accordingly should implement the concomitant doctrine of impartiality. This approach is new, as it has not yet been implemented in this context.[10] At the same time, this approach is also classical, even orthodox. The duty of impartiality (or even-handedness, or fairness; courts use these terms interchangeably) has evolved in traditional trust law mostly during the nineteenth century. In recent years, it has been applied in trust cases in several

---

[6]   That is, shareholders, in the U.K. statute's terminology.

[7]   The Companies (Miscellaneous Reporting) Regulations 2018, SI 860, art. 2, ¶ 4 (UK).

[8]   Hutton v. West Cork Railway Co. (1883) 23 Ch.D. 654, 672 (U.K.). *Hutton* was followed, with extensive quotes, in Parke v. Daily News Ltd [1962] Ch. 927 (U.K.).

[9]   BCE Inc. v. 1976 Debentureholders, [2008] S.C.C. 69 (Can.). *See infra*, text accompanying note 36.

[10] For an early version of some of the present ideas, see AMIR LICHT, FIDUCIARY LAW—THE DUTY OF LOYALTY IN THE CORPORATION AND IN THE GENERAL LAW 203–10 (2013) (in Hebrew).

common law jurisdictions. More importantly, this duty has been applied during the latter part of the twentieth century in modern, complex settings of pension funds, where fund trustees face inescapable conflicts among subgroups of members. These conflicts resemble the tensions among different stakeholders in business corporations—a feature that renders this doctrine a suitable source of inspiration for the task at hand.

In a nutshell, the duty of impartiality accepts that there could be irreconcilable tensions and conflicts among several trust beneficiaries who, in all other respects, stand on equal footing vis-à-vis the trustee. Applying the rule against duty-duty conflict (dual fiduciary) in this setting would be ineffective, as it would disable the trustee—and consequently, the trust—without providing a solution to the conundrum. The duty of impartiality calls on the trustee to consider the different interests of the beneficiaries impartially, even-handedly, fairly, etc.; it does not impose any heavier burden on the good-faith exercise of the trustee's discretion. Crucially, the duty of impartiality does not imply equality. All that it requires is that the different interests be considered within extensive margins.

The upshot is a light though not hollow regime, whose main advantage is that it is workable. This is precisely where impartiality holds promise for advancing the discourse and actual legal regulation of shareholder-stakeholder relations through fiduciary duties. A normatively appealing legal regime is unlikely to satisfy even its proponents if it does not lend itself to practical implementation, *a fortiori* for its opponents. For legal systems and individual lawyers that champion a pluralistic stakeholder-oriented approach for the objective of the corporation, having a workable doctrine for implementing that approach is crucial—an absolute necessity.

While this chapter does not purport to advance a (yet another) normative argument for stakeholderism, those who endorse this approach would find the present proposal a useful tool for ensuring its workability. In tandem, this proposal might make stakeholderism more palatable to its opponents, as the impartiality duty is mostly compatible with applying the business judgment rule to directors' discretion. Stakeholder impartiality is thus particularly suitable for legal systems that endorse a pluralistic stance on the objectives of the corporation, such as Canada's and India's open-ended stakeholderist approaches. Such a doctrinal framework might also prove useful for systems and individuals who endorse a monistic, shareholder-focused approach. That could be the case in the United Kingdom and Australia, for instance, where directors could face liability if they do not consider creditors' interest in a timely fashion even before the company reaches insolvency. Moreover, this approach could be helpful where the strictest versions of doctrinal shareholderism arguably rein, such as Delaware law post-*NACEPF v. Gheewalla*[11]—in particular, with regard to tensions between common and preferred stockholders post-*Trados*.[12]

II *E PLURIBUS UNUM?* MONISM AND PLURALISM IN THE CORPORATE OBJECTIVE

This section lays the ground for introducing impartiality as a workable legal framework for considering multiple stakeholders in strategic decisions aimed at promoting the best interest of the corporation. My goal is neither to justify nor debunk a pluralistic approach to strategic management. In fact, there is reason to believe that this debate cannot be resolved, as it is values-laden and political in essence. This section, therefore, begins with a comparative overview of the

---

[11] N. Am. Catholic Educ. Programming Found., Inc. v. Gheewalla, 930 A.2d 92 (Del. 2007).
[12] In re Trados Inc. S'holder Litig., 73 A.3d 17 (Del. Ch. 2013).

positive legal regimes that govern this subject, primarily in common law jurisdictions. Next, it deals briefly with the normative aspect of the subject and points out the implementation challenge that bedevils it.

A *A Positive Comparative Overview*

1 The World

A superficial observation might lead one to think that corporate laws around the world have converged to shareholder value as the single maximand of corporate governance. When Henry Hansmann and Reinier Kraakman announced "the end of history for corporate law," they argued that "there is convergence on a consensus that the best means to ... the pursuit of aggregate social welfare is to make corporate managers strongly accountable to shareholder interests and, at least in direct terms, only to those interests."[13] Some ten years later, they insisted that their ideological or normative claim (which was stated quite positively) "is holding up extremely well."[14]

The OECD's Principles of Corporate Governance convey a similar impression.[15] In their third edition since 1999, now published together with the G20 forum of the world's largest economies and after consultation with business and labor representatives, the Principles purport to reflect a universal consensus. Moreover, they guide international financial institutions and countries in assessing corporate governance reforms. Principle VI on the responsibilities of the board states that "[t]he corporate governance framework should ensure ... the board's account-ability to the company and the shareholders."[16] On the role of stakeholders, the Principles state that "[t]he corporate governance framework should recognise the rights of stakeholders estab-lished by law or through mutual agreements ... "[17] Despite their claim for universality, the Principles adopt a very American approach. By declaring the board accountable to the company and the shareholders, the Principles closely follow the ruling in *Guth* v. *Loft*, that "[c]orporate officers and directors ... stand in a fiduciary relation to the corporation and its stockholders."[18] Other stakeholders only have the protection of other laws or contracts but not of directors' fiduciary accountability.

This appearance of uniformity is misleading, however. Legal systems vary considerably on the objectives of the corporation and the board's mission. The following sections present glimpses into a number of common law systems in this regard. Fiduciary law constitutes an important segment of private law in all of these systems, exhibiting the same basic principles of fiduciary loyalty, yet they differ significantly in how they address this issue.[19]

---

[13] Henry Hansmann & Reinier Kraakman, *The End of History for Corporate Law*, 89 Geo. L. J. 439, 441 (2001).
[14] Henry Hansmann & Reinier Kraakman, *Reflections on the End of History for Corporate Law, in* The Convergence of Corporate Governance: Promise and Prospects 32 (Abdul A. Rasheed & Toru Yoshikawa eds., 2012).
[15] Org. for Econ. Co-operation & Dev., G20/OECD Principles of Corporate Governance 51 (2015), https://www .oecd.org/daf/ca/Corporate-Governance-Principles-ENG.pdf.
[16] *Id.* at 45.
[17] *Id.* at 34 (Principle IV).
[18] Guth v. Loft, Inc., 5 A.2d 503, 510 (Del. 1939).
[19] Some scholars argue that common law systems are shareholder-oriented while civil law systems are stakeholder-oriented. *See* Michael Bradley, Cindy A. Schipani, Anant K. Sundaram & James P. Walsh, *The Purposes and Accountability of the Corporation in Contemporary Society: Corporate Governance at a Crossroads*, 62 L. & Contemp. Probs. 9 (1999); Hao Liang & Luc Renneboog, *On the Foundations of Corporate Social Responsibility*, 72 J. Fin. 853 (2017). A full discussion of this hypothesis, which still awaits a rigorous empirical confirmation, exceeds the present scope.

2 The United States

U.S. law—in particular, Delaware law—represents the strongest doctrinal version of shareholder primacy. To begin, only shareholders have the power to appoint directors, such that in one way or another, directors are bound to serve their interest both practically and, one could argue, also deontologically. As just noted, *Guth* directs the directors' fiduciary obligations to the company and shareholders, implicitly implying that the interests of the two overlap. This doctrine has been solidified in a number of recent cases. In *eBay Domestic Holdings, Inc. v. Newmark*, the Delaware Chancery Court stated that "[d]irectors of a for-profit Delaware corporation cannot deploy a rights plan to defend a business strategy that openly eschews stockholder wealth maximization—at least not consistently with the directors' fiduciary duties under Delaware law."[20] In a more broadly applicable and prominent context, that of a near-insolvent company, the Delaware Supreme Court in *Gheewalla* ruled as follows:

> When a solvent corporation is navigating in the zone of insolvency, the focus for Delaware directors does not change: directors must continue to discharge their fiduciary duties to the corporation and its shareholders by exercising their business judgment in the best interests of the corporation for the benefit of its shareholder owners.[21]

Gheewalla is particularly noteworthy because the Court goes to great lengths "to provide the directors with clear signal beacons and brightly lined channel markers as they navigate with due care, good faith, and loyalty on behalf of a Delaware corporation and its shareholders."[22] So much so, that by drawing a sharp distinction between solvency and insolvency, it effectively denies, as a matter of law, the existence of a murky zone of insolvency. In reality, however, vagueness and uncertainty characterize this setting, as the Court itself notes.

In *Trados*, the Delaware Chancery took shareholder primacy to its logical extreme, in distinguishing between common stockholders as residual claimants and thus ultimate beneficiaries of the firm's value, who are protected by fiduciary duties, and preferred stockholders with contractual rights, who are not owed fiduciary duties based on such rights.[23] By holding the contractual element to be the appropriate basis for a preferred shareholder to bring suit, *Trados* relegates the preferred to the stakeholder category in the OECD Principles framework. While doctrinally and economically sound, this distinction, too, has a certain air of denial to it, since preferred stocks are actually a hybrid of debt and residual-claim-type equity.

The legal landscape in the United States is broader and more varied than Delaware law. For one, scholars still debate shareholder primacy in fiduciary duties in U.S. corporations.[24] In addition to case law, there is a substantial body of statutory law in numerous states, including, in particular, "constituency statutes" and benefit corporation statues. The effect of these statutes on the content and exercise of fiduciary duties in regular business corporations is, at best unclear.[25]

---

[20] eBay Domestic Holdings, Inc. v. Newmark, 16 A.3d 1, 35 (Del. Ch. 2010).

[21] Gheewalla, 930 A.2d 92, 100 (Del. 2007); *see also* Quadrant Structured Prods. Co. v. Vertin, 102 A.3d 155 (Del. Ch. 2014).

[22] Gheewalla, 930 A.2d at 101.

[23] In re Trados Inc. S'holder Litig., 73 A.3d 17, 63 (Del. Ch. 2013); *see also* Frederick Hsu Living Trust v. ODN Holding Corp., 2017 Del. Ch. LEXIS 67 (Del. Ch. 2017) (same).

[24] See Robert J. Rhee, *A Legal Theory of Shareholder Primacy*, 102 MINN. L. REV. 1951 (2018) for a recent survey.

[25] *See, e.g.*, Brett H. McDonnell, *Corporate Constituency Statutes and Employee Governance*, 30 WM. MITCHELL L. REV. 1227 (2004); Brett McDonnell, *Benefit Corporations and Strategic Action Fields or (The Existential Failing of Delaware)*, 39 SEATTLE U. L. REV. 263 (2016); Jonathan D. Springer, *Corporate Constituency Statutes: Hollow Hopes and False Fears*, 1999 ANN. SURV. AM. L. 85 (1999); Julian Velasco, *Shareholder Primacy in Benefit Corporations*, ch. 17 (this volume); David G. Yosifon, *Opting out of Shareholder Primacy: Is the Public Benefit Corporation Trivial*, 41 DEL. J. CORP. L. 461 (2017). One may note that the Model Benefit Corporation Legislation only requires that directors

3 The United Kingdom

U.K. law is more loyal to the classical formula of fiduciary loyalty by making the company alone the beneficiary of directors' fiduciary duties. Moreover, it has traditionally taken a comprehensive approach to the best interests of the company by referring to "the company as a whole."[26] The Companies Act 2006 preserves this approach.[27] Section 172 of the Act is explicit in designating shareholders as the ultimate beneficiaries of the company. Crucially, this section requires directors to consider other stakeholders, yet stakeholders' interests are subordinated to the interests of shareholders.[28] In tandem, the manner in which this consideration is to be carried out—for example, as between shareholder value and combating climate change and promoting human rights—is left to the discretion of the directors.[29]

The relations between shareholders' and creditors' interests as the subject of directors' good-faith judgment as to the best interest of the company are more nuanced in U.K. law than in Delaware law. Section 172 preserves prior statutory and case law "requiring directors, in certain circumstances, to consider or act in the interests of creditors of the company"—namely, in the vicinity of insolvency.[30] In those circumstances, the contours of which are decidedly fuzzy,[31] the director must "have proper regard for the interest of [the company's] creditors and prospective creditors."[32] In *BTI 2014* v. *Sequana*, the Court of Appeals acknowledged that "the interests of creditors are identified as interests different from, and potentially in conflict with, the promotion of the success of the company for the benefit of its members as a whole."[33] The Court further indicated that these interests are mutually exclusive, suggesting that they should dominate directors' discretion sequentially.[34]

4 Canada

At first glance, Canadian law closely resembles U.K. law on the present subject, as section 122 of the Canada Business Corporations Act renders the corporation the nominal beneficiary of directors' and officers' fiduciary duties. A seemingly small difference in the provision on oppression, which refers to creditors,[35] has led to a radical departure of the Canadian approach

---

consider the interests of other stakeholders, not unlike the present proposal. *See* William H. Clark, Jr. & Larry Vraka, *White Paper: The Need and Rationale for the Benefit Corporation: Why It Is the Legal Norm That Best Addresses the Needs of Social Entrepreneurs, Investors, and Ultimately, the Public*, Benefitcorp.net 17 (2013), https://benefitcorp .net/sites/default/files/Benefit_Corporation_White_Paper.pdf.

[26] *See* Greenhalgh v. Arderne Cinemas Ltd. [1951] Ch. 286, 291 (C.A.); Allen v. Gold Reefs of West Africa Ltd. [1900] 1 Ch. 656, 671 (C.A. 1897).

[27] Companies Act 2006, c. 46, § 170(1) (U.K.) ("Companies Act 2006").

[28] For discussions, see, e.g., Andrew Keay, *Tackling the Issue of the Corporate Objective: An Analysis of the United Kingdom's Enlightened Shareholder Value Approach*, 29 Sydney L. Rev. 577 (2007); Georgina Tsagas, *Section 172 of the Companies Act 2006: Desperate Times Call for Soft Law Measures*, in Shaping the Corporate Landscape: Towards Corporate Reform and Enterprise Diversity 131 (Nina Boeger & Charlotte Villiers eds., 2018).

[29] *See* R on the application of People & Planet v. HM Treasury [2009] EWHC 3020 (Admin), [35] (U.K.).

[30] *See* Liquidator of West Mercia Safetywear Ltd v. Dodd (1988) 4 BCC 30; Kristin van Zwieten, *Director Liability in Insolvency and Its Vicinity*, 38 Oxford J. Legal Stud. 382 (2018).

[31] *See* BTI 2014 LLC v. Sequana S.A. [2019] EWCA Civ 112 (U.K.).

[32] Jetivia SA v. Bilta (UK) Ltd. [2015] UKSC 23, [123] (U.K.).

[33] BTI 2014, at [198].

[34] *Id.* at [199].

[35] Canada Business Corporations Act, R.S.C. 1985, C-44, § 241(2). *Compare* the parallel provision on unfair prejudice in § 994 of the U.K. Companies Act 2006.

to the treatment of stakeholders from the traditional rule. In considering a petition by institutional bondholders in 2008, the Supreme Court of Canada in *BCE* said:

> [T]he duty of the directors to act in the best interests of the corporation comprehends a duty to treat individual stakeholders affected by corporate actions equitably and fairly. There are no absolute rules. In each case, the question is whether, in all the circumstances, the directors acted in the best interests of the corporation, having regard to all relevant considerations, including, but not confined to, the need to treat affected stakeholders in a fair manner, commensurate with the corporation's duties as a responsible corporate citizen.
>
> Directors may find themselves in a situation where it is impossible to please all stakeholders ... There is no principle that one set of interests—for example, the interests of shareholders—should prevail over another set of interests.[36]

The Court thus put on the table what many have swept under the carpet. By using fairness rather than loyalty as the framework of analysis, *BCE* allows for conflicting interests to be weighed against one another. However, as the Court candidly acknowledges, it gives directors no guidance as to how they should resolve this dilemma, and notes that "the court looks beyond legality to what is fair, given all of the interests at play."[37] A 2019 amendment to section 122 (re-) locates the issue within fiduciary duties, as it authorizes directors and officers to consider the interests of shareholders, employees, retirees and pensioners, creditors, consumers, and governments; the environment; and the long-term interests of the corporation. Consistent with *BCE*, this new provision does not prioritize any of these interests.[38]

5 Israel

In line with other modern corporate law statutes, the Israeli Companies Law, 1999 includes a specific provision on the objective of the corporation, stating that "[t]he purpose of a company is to operate in accordance with business considerations for maximizing its profits, and within the scope of such considerations, the interests of its creditors, its employees and the public may *inter alia* be taken into account."[39] While the Law does not specifically mention shareholder welfare as the objective of the corporation, it expresses this objective by calling for profit maximization, since only shareholders are entitled to profits when dividends are paid out, this section thus reads like a stronger version of its U.K. counterpart. Both provisions implement a shareholder primacy approach, but while in the U.K. statute considering the interests of other stakeholders is mandatory, the Israeli provision renders it discretionary.

Despite the relatively clear language of the statute, the Israeli Supreme Court in *Mishmar HaEmek v. Manor*—a case dealing with equitable subordination of shareholder loans—interpreted it as requiring the company at all times to balance the interests of all stakeholders, especially creditors.[40] The Court reasoned that such balancing is called for in light of the duty of good faith that governs the company's relations with all of its commercial counterparts.[41] It stands to reason that in discharging their fiduciary duty to act in the

---

[36] BCE Inc. v. 1976 Debentureholders, 2008 SCC 69, para. 82–84 (Can.).

[37] *Id.* at para. 71.

[38] The new section 122(1.1) resembles Peoples Department Stores Inc. (Trustee of) v. Wise, 2004 SCC 68, para. 42 (Can.) ("[I]n determining whether they are acting with a view to the best interests of the corporation it may be legitimate, given all the circumstances of a given case, for the board of directors to consider, *inter alia*, the interests of shareholders, employees, suppliers, creditors, consumers, governments and the environment.").

[39] Companies Law, 5759-1999, § 11(a), 44 (1999) (Isr.).

[40] CA 4263/04 Mishmar HaEmek v. Manor, Adv., as Liquidator of Efrochei HaZafon Ltd., 63(1) PD 458 (2009) (Isr.).

[41] *Id.* at [18] (Procaccia J).

interest of the company,[42] directors, and officers should implement such balancing, although the manner for doing so remains elusive, much like in Canada.

6 India

India's Companies Act of 2013 presents the most dedicated attempt to date to implement a formal pluralistic, stakeholder-oriented duty. Section 166 of the Indian Act provides that "[a] director of a company shall act in good faith in order to promote the objects of the company for the benefit of its members as a whole, and in the best interests of the company, its employees, the shareholders, the community and for the protection of environment." The language and the legislative history of this provision make it clear that the intention was to put the interests of all stakeholder constituencies on the same level.[43]

On the one hand, the Indian provision echoes the parallel Israeli and U.K. provisions in terminology and style. On the other hand, its content bears substantial resemblance to the Canadian ruling in *BCE* and section 122(1.1). Specifically, there is no hint in it (or in related materials) as to *how* directors should balance the potentially conflicting interests of different stakeholders. Moreover, as Mihir Naniwadekar and Umakanth Varottil powerfully argue, this provision suffers from additional implementation problems, as stakeholders lack any means for enforcing whatever rights they may have.[44] "Arguably," they aver, "the magnanimity of its verbiage and rhetoric in favour of stakeholders merely pays lip service to them and obscures any real teeth or legal ammunition available to non-shareholder constituencies to assert those rights as a matter of law."[45]

B *Some Normative Aspects*

Let us now move from the positive to the normative. In the seminal dialogue between Adolf Berle and E. Merrick Dodd in the 1930s, Berle actually sided with Dodd on the principled normative desirability of a pluralistic approach.[46] He nonetheless rejected it for being unworkable:

> Now I submit that you can not [sic] abandon emphasis on "the view that business corporations exist for the sole purpose of making profits for their shareholders" until such time as you are to be prepared to offer a clear and reasonably enforceable scheme of responsibilities to someone else.[47]

Arguments for the monistic, shareholder-centered approach are diverse. One strand invokes shareholder sovereignty and ownership of the corporation, manifested in shareholder voting, for

---

[42] *See* § 254(a) of the Companies Law. This section codifies the traditional duty of loyalty formerly recognized in case law. *See* Mo. 100/52 Hevra Yerushalmit LeTaasiya Ltd v. Aghion, 6 PD 887, 889 (1952) (Isr.), citing *Cook v. Deeks*, [1916] UKPC 10 (P.C.).

[43] *See, e.g.*, Afra Afsharipour, *Redefining Corporate Purpose: An International Perspective*, 40 Seattle U. L. Rev. 465 (2017); Umakanth Varottil, *The Evolution of Corporate Law in Post-Colonial India: From Transplant to Autochthony*, 31 Am. U. Int'l L. Rev. 253 (2016). On a related obligation of corporate philanthropy under section 135 of the Act, see, e.g., Arjya B. Majumdar, *India's Journey with Corporate Social Responsibility – What Next*, 33 J. L. & Com. 165 (2015).

[44] *See* Mihir Chandrashekhar Naniwadekar & Umakanth Varottil, *The Stakeholder Approach Towards Directors' Duties under Indian Company Law: A Comparative Analysis*, in The Indian Yearbook of Comparative Law 2016 95 (Mahendra Pal Singh ed., 2017).

[45] *Id.* at 97.

[46] For a detailed analysis see Amir N. Licht, *The Maximands of Corporate Governance: A Theory of Values and Cognitive Style*, 29 Del. J. Corp. L. 649, 690–98 (2004).

[47] A. A. Berle Jr., *For Whom Corporate Managers are Trustees: A Note*, 45 Harv. L. Rev. 1365, 1367 (1932); *see also* Victor Brudney, *Contract and Fiduciary Duty in Corporate Law*, 38 B.C. L. Rev 595, 645–46 (1997).

example, to support this view.[48] Another invokes the agency problem and economic efficiency more generally. The former argument, from agency, holds that allowing corporate insiders to shift among several maximands of different stakeholders will dilute the accountability of those insiders. Pointing to shareholders as the residual financial claimants in the corporation, the argument from efficiency holds that maximizing profits in the interest of shareholders promotes the interest of all other (financial) claimants, whose interests are largely fixed.[49]

Some proponents of the pluralistic approach marshal ethical and political arguments in support of that view.[50] Another strand of the literature draws on insights about prosocial motivations from psychology and behavioral economics in support of entrusting insiders with discretion to consider all the stakeholders who participate in the firm's team production.[51]

Economists who have entered into this debate tend to uphold the shareholderist approach.[52] Vikas Mehrotra and Randall Morck underscore the danger that "[e]xpanding the corporate objective function to include non-equity stakeholders has the side effect of magnifying top managers' scope for opportunism;" they therefore wryly conclude that "shareholder value maximization might be the worst option save all the others."[53] Acknowledging this risk, Roland Bénabou and Jean Tirole nonetheless aver that investors and other stakeholders could have some demand for corporate managers to adopt socially responsible strategies on their behalf, notwithstanding profit sacrifice.[54] Oliver Hart and Luigi Zingales argue that given that in reality, many investors are prosocial, managers should be tasked with adopting socially responsible strategies.[55] This approach seems to suffer from an implementation problem, too, however. Entrusting corporations with promoting prosocial preferences could run into the impossibility of forming a consensus among investors and/or stakeholders.[56]

Empirical evidence on the desirability of these approaches is equivocal. A number of meta-analyses find a weak but significantly positive correlation between firms' social performance and

---

[48]   *See, e.g.,* Lawrence A. Hamermesh & Leo E. Strine Jr., *Fiduciary Principles and Delaware Corporation Law: Searching for the Optimal Balance by Understanding that the World is Not, in* OXFORD HANDBOOK OF FIDUCIARY LAW (Evan J. Criddle, Paul B. Miller & Robert H. Sitkoff eds., 2019); Julian Velasco, *Shareholder Ownership and Primacy,* 2010 U. ILL. L. REV. 897.

[49]   FRANK H. EASTERBROOK AND DANIEL R. FISCHEL , THE ECONOMIC STRUCTURE OF CORPORATE LAW 38 (1991).

[50]   *See, e.g.,* Ronald M. Green, *Shareholders as Stakeholders: Changing Metaphors of Corporate Governance,* 50 Wash. & Lee L. Rev. 1409 (1993); Symposium, *Corporate Irresponsibility: America's Newest Export?,* 70 GEO. WASH. L. REV. 867, 890 (2002); Lyman Johnson, *Delaware Judiciary and the Meaning of Corporate Life and Corporate Law,* 68 TEX. L. REV. 865 (1990); David Millon, *Radical Shareholder Primacy,* 10 U. ST. THOMAS L. J. 1013 (2013); Robert J. Rhee, *Fiduciary Exemption for Public Necessity: Shareholder Profit, Public Good, and the Hobson's Choice during a National Crisis,* 17 GEO. MASON L. REV. 661 (2010).

[51]   *See, e.g.,* Margaret M. Blair & Lynn A. Stout, *A Team Production Theory of Corporate Law,* 85 VA. L. REV. 247 (1999); LYNN STOUT, THE SHAREHOLDER VALUE MYTH: HOW PUTTING SHAREHOLDERS FIRST HARMS INVESTORS, CORPORATIONS, AND THE PUBLIC (2012). Bainbridge, however, supports shareholder-centered "director primacy." *See, e.g.,* Stephen M. Bainbridge, *Director Primacy: The Means and Ends of Corporate Governance,* 97 NW. U. L. REV. 547 (2003).

[52]   See, most famously, Milton Friedman, *A Friedman Doctrine —The Social Responsibility of Business Is to Increase Its Profits,* N.Y. TIMES, Sept. 13, 1970, at A31; *see also* MILTON FRIEDMAN, CAPITALISM AND FREEDOM 133 (1962) (same).

[53]   Vikas Mehrotra & Randall Morck, *Governance and Stakeholders, in* THE HANDBOOK OF THE ECONOMICS OF CORPORATE GOVERNANCE 637, 673, 638 (Benjamin Hermalin & Michael Weisbach eds., 2017). *See also* Richard M. Frankel, S.P. Kothari, & Luo Zuo, Why Shareholder Wealth Maximization Despite Other Objectives (unpublished manuscript) (Aug. 7, 2019) (on file with author).

[54]   Roland Bénabou & Jean Tirole, *Individual and Corporate Social Responsibility,* 77 ECONOMICA 1 (2010).

[55]   Oliver Hart & Luigi Zingales, *Companies Should Maximize Shareholder Welfare Not Market Value,* 2 J. L. FIN. & ACCT. 247 (2017).

[56]   *See* Mehrotra & Morck, *supra* note 53, citing Kenneth J. Arrow, *A Difficulty in the Concept of Social Welfare,* 58 J. POL. ECON. 328 (1950); Frankel *et al., supra* note 53 (same).

financial performance.[57] Even if these results are valid, the mechanism behind them is unclear: Does maximizing shareholder value incidentally help other stakeholders, or can better managers handle several stakeholder constituencies simultaneously to the benefit of all?[58]

Whether or not one is persuaded by the empirical evidence, the normative debate probably cannot be resolved because of another, more fundamental difficulty. I have argued that the two polar positions in this debate express different values, where values are defined according to social psychological theories as conceptions of the desirable.[59] In a joint study with Renée Adams and Lilach Sagiv, we have shown that when board members and CEOs of Swedish public corporations address stylized shareholder-stakeholder conflicts, they systematically contrast between shareholders' and other stakeholders' interests and exhibit a principled stance about favoring one over the other—a stance that in turn is linked to their personal value preferences.[60] In a subsequent study with Adams, we confirm this relationship in a multinational sample of directors and observe robust relations between shareholderism and cultural orientations.[61] These findings indicate that directors address the issue with an intention to "do the right thing," the law notwithstanding. Thus, direct legal regulation of directors' conduct in shareholder-stakeholder dilemmas could face formidable difficulties.

III STAKEHOLDER IMPARTIALITY

A *The Classical Doctrine*

Consider a simple scenario: In preparation for meeting his maker, one settles a trust, instructing the trustee to care for the financial needs of his loved ones at the trustee's absolute discretion. The survivors

---

[57] *See* Mahfuja Malik, *Value-Enhancing Capabilities of CSR: A Brief Review of Contemporary Literature*, 127 J. Bus. Ethics 419 (2015); Gunnar Friede, Timo Busch & Alexander Bassen, *ESG and Financial Performance: Aggregated Evidence from More than 2000 Empirical Studies*, 5 J. Sustainable Fin. & Inv. 210 (2015); Joshua D. Margolis, Hillary Anger Elfenbein & James P. Walsh, Does It Pay to Be Good ... and Does It Matter? A Meta-Analysis of the Relationship between Corporate Social and Financial Performance (Mar. 1, 2009) (unpublished manuscript) (on file with author); Joshua D. Margolis & Hillary Anger Elfenbein, *Do Well by Doing Good? Don't Count on It*, 86 Harv. Bus. Rev. 19 (2008); Marc Orlitzky, Frank L. Schmidt & Sara L. Rynes, *Corporate Social and Financial Performance: A Meta-analysis*, 24 Org. Stud. 403 (2003). While the methodology for assessing financial performance is well-established, that for assessing social performance is still developing. *See generally* Amir Amel-Zadeh, *Social Responsibility in Capital Markets: A Review and Framework of Theory and Empirical Evidence* (Newton Centre for Endowment Asset Management, Working Paper 2018).

[58] *See* Larry Fauver, Michael B. McDonald & Alvaro G. Taboada, *Does It Pay to Treat Employees Well? International Evidence on the Value of Employee-Friendly Culture*, 50 J. Corp. Fin. 84 (2018). *Compare* Lea Cassar & Stephan Meier, *Intentions for Doing Good Matter for Doing Well: The Negative Effects of Prosocial Incentives* (Columbia University, Working Paper 2018); Agne Kajackaite & Dirk Sliwka, *Prosocial Managers, Employee Motivation, and the Creation of Shareholder Value* (IZA Institute of Labor Economics, Discussion Paper No. 11789). *See generally* Wolfgang Breuer, Torbjörn Müller, David Rosenbach & Astrid Salzmann, *Corporate Social Responsibility, Investor Protection, and Cost of Equity: A Cross-Country Comparison*, 96 J. Banking & Fin. 34 (2018); Allen Ferrell, Hao Liang & Luc Renneboog, *Socially Responsible Firms*, 122 J. Fin. Econ. 585 (2016); Philipp Krüger, *Corporate Goodness and Shareholder Wealth*, 115 J. Fin. Econ. 304 (2015); Jan Schmitz & Jan Schrader, *Corporate Social Responsibility: A Microeconomic Review of the Literature*, 29 J. Econ. Surv. 27 (2015); Patricia Crifo & Vanina D. Forget, *The Economics of Corporate Social Responsibility: A Firm-Level Perspective Survey*, 29 J. Econ. Surv. 112 (2015); Ronald W. Masulis & Syed Walid Reza, *Private Benefits and Corporate Investment and Financing Decisions: The Case of Corporate Philanthropy* (European Corporate Governance Institute, Working Paper No. 603/2019).

[59] *See* Licht, *supra* note 46, at 657–58, citing, in particular, Shalom H. Schwartz, *Universals in the Content and Structure of Values: Theoretical Advances and Empirical Tests in 20 Countries*, in 25 Advances in Experimental Social Psychology 1 (Mark P. Zanna ed. 1992).

[60] Renée B. Adams, Amir N. Licht & Lilach Sagiv, *Shareholders and Stakeholders: How Do Directors Decide?*, 32 Strategic Mgmt. J. 1331 (2011).

[61] Amir N. Licht & Renée B. Adams, *Shareholders and Stakeholders Around the World: The Role of Values, Culture, and Law in Directors' Decisions* (European Corporate Governance Institute, Working Paper No. 459/2019).

include a widow and a number of orphans of different ages. The widow is aging and looking at existing and foreseeable medical expenses, whereas the orphans are quite healthy now and will likely enjoy a longer life than the trustee can imagine. Assume for simplicity that the estate consists only of cash and that only securities are to be purchased (thus excluding real property, etc.). In addition, it is undisputed that the trustee operates with the punctilio of an honor the most sensitive and is entirely prudent and fully skilled for the task. What should be the makeup of the trust's investment portfolio in terms of the ratio between stocks and bonds? With regard to equities, should the trustee invest in high-tech start-up companies? Should government bonds be preferred over corporate bonds?

The trustee in this setting faces an irreconcilable conflict between the interests of the two classes of beneficiaries that stem from their different life expectancies. This, in turn, calls for different invest-ment strategies for fulfilling the financial needs of each generation. The widow's needs militate for liquid, low-risk, fixed-income securities. The children can better tolerate market fluctuations, so would rather have high-volatility, high-yield investments. *Any* decision by the trustee could adversely affect one or both of the beneficiary classes. It could thus be challenged under standard fiduciary law analysis—and the trustee called to account—on the basis of breaching the no-conflict rule by way of dual fiduciary or duty-duty conflict, or for failing to act in subjective good faith, or acting in light of an ulterior motive.[62] Fiduciary law's standard response—to disable the trustee—is no answer, as the problem does not lie with the trustee but rather with the beneficiaries. Splitting the estate in two is no cure either: similar tensions will immediately emerge between the commerce-oriented child who would benefit most from a capital infusion and the artsy, dreamy one who needs a stable source of income for living expenses.

This generic dilemma became prominent in late eighteenth-century England.[63] A typical settle-ment would authorize the trustee to manage the estate for the benefit of a life-tenant (the widow) and the remainderman or the residuary (the orphans). Oftentimes, the distinction between the life beneficiary and the remainderman overlapped with different financial (equitable) interests in the estate—to income and to capital, respectively. But this seemingly clear distinction caused as many problems as it purported to solve. For example, what should be the rule if capital assets require current expenses for maintenance? Should dividends from shares be treated as income or as capital? Early nineteenth-century cases established technical rules of apportionment in light of the financial circumstances of the era.[64] Those rules have since been revised or abolished, in line with develop-ments in finance.[65]

Of greater importance here is the substantive conceptual framework for the comparative treatment of beneficiary classes. Originally, the trustee's obligation to treat beneficiaries impartially and fairly as part of their duty of loyalty was understood to imply equal treatment. According to Chantal Stebbings, this was "in accordance with the maxim 'Equality is Equity' and with the very foundation of Equitable jurisprudence in concepts of fairness and even-handedness."[66] This is feasible when the beneficiaries are on equal footing.[67] This laudable principle is incompatible, however, with handling

---

[62] Note that formally, the trustee in this setting is not in breach, because the trust instrument authorizes him to operate while facing this dilemma. The problem is substantive, namely, how should the trustee operate while facing this tension. The duty of impartiality provides the formal doctrine for the latter problem. I am grateful to Matthew Conaglen for this point.

[63] The following draws on the compelling account in CHANTAL STEBBINGS, THE PRIVATE TRUSTEE IN VICTORIAN ENGLAND 65–97 (2002).

[64] *See, e.g.,* Howe v. Earl of Dartmouth (1802) 7 Ves. Jr. 137 (U.K.); Earl of Chesterfield's Trusts (1883) 24 Ch. D. 643 (U. K.); Allhusen v. Whittell [1867] LR 4 Eq 295 (U.K.).

[65] In the United Kingdom, for instance, the rules in *Earl of Dartmouth, Earl of Chesterfield's Trusts,* and *Allhusen* were abolished by the Trusts (Capital and Income) Act 2013, c. 1 (U.K.).

[66] STEBBINGS, *supra* note 63, at 67.

[67] *See, e.g.,* Hutchinson v. Morritt (1839) 160 ER 818, 3 Y & C Ex. 547 (U.K.) ("[I]t is the duty of trustees . . . to divide the profit so made rateably amongst the cestui que trusts.")

differential interests of differently-situated beneficiaries. Moreover, in the social circumstances of Victorian England, in which many trustees were relatives or close friends of the settlor or beneficiaries, it proved difficult to resist pressures to adjust trust administration to the needs of particular beneficiaries—sometimes, with solid justification. The technical rules of apportionment further triggered litigation over equality issues and motivated settlors to opt out of these rules.[68] Due to a confluence of these and additional factors, by the early twentieth century, equality was abandoned as the substantive meaning of the trustee's duty of impartiality.[69]

Today, the duty of impartiality (or even-handedness, or fairness) "regulates trustee/beneficiary conflicts when the trust terms create a conflict that abridges the sole interest rule."[70] It is recognized and implemented largely similarly in all the major common law jurisdictions. Its application has spread during the late twentieth century beyond private trusts—most notably, to the administration of pension funds. This obligation is further implemented with respect to executors in corporate insolvency. The following provides a brief survey of its contemporary meaning.

Succinctly, the duty of impartiality imposes on the fiduciary an obligation to consider the interests of the beneficiaries. Not more than that, but not less either. "[U]nder a discretionary trust," noted the court in *Kain* v. *Hutton*, "there is no right to distributions but only a right to be considered."[71] In *Cowan* v. *Scargill*, probably the most famous case in the modern era dealing with the duty of impartiality, Vice-Chancellor Megarry stated that it is "the duty of trustees to exercise their powers in the best interests of the present and future beneficiaries of the trust, holding the scales impartially between different classes of beneficiaries."[72] In *Nestle* v. *National Westminster Bank*, Hoffmann J clarified:

> [T]he trustee must act fairly in making investment decisions which may have different consequences for different classes of beneficiaries. There are two reasons why I prefer this formulation to the traditional image of holding the scales equally between tenant for life and remainderman. The first is that the image of the scales suggests a weighing of known quantities whereas investment decisions are concerned with predictions of the future . . . . The second reason is that the image of the scales suggests a more mechanistic process than I believe the law requires. The trustees have in my judgment a wide discretion . . . . It would be an inhuman law which required trustees to adhere to some mechanical rule for preserving the real value of the capital when the tenant for life was the testator's widow who had fallen upon hard times and the remainderman was young and well off.[73]

Nestle was approved on appeal, where Staughton LJ and Leggatt LJ said, respectively:

> At times it will not be easy to decide what is an equitable balance. If the life-tenant is living in penury and the remainderman already has ample wealth, common sense suggests that a trustee should be able to take that into account, not necessarily by seeking the highest possible income at the expense of capital but by inclining in that direction. . . .
>
> The very process of attempting to achieve a balance, or (if that be old-fashioned) fairness, as between the interests of life-tenants and those of a remainderman inevitably means that each can complain of being less well served than he or she ought to have been.[74]

---

68 STEBBINGS, *supra* note 63, at 70–71.

69 *Id.* at 79.

70 John H. Langbein, *Questioning the Trust Law Duty of Loyalty: Sole Interest or Best Interest?*, 114 YALE L. J. 929, 939 (2005).

71 Kain v. Hutton [2007] NZCA 199 at [243] (N.Z.).

72 Cowan v. Scargill [1985] Ch. 270, at [286], [287] (U.K.).

73 Nestle v. National Westminster Bank plc [2000] WTLR 795 (Ch), (1988) 10 Tru LI 112 (U.K.). This decision has been cited with agreement several times. *See, e.g.,* X v. A, B, C [2000] EWHC Ch 121 (U.K.); Labrouche v. Frey [2016] EWHC 268 (Ch) (U.K.).

74 Nestle v. National Westminster Bank [1992] EWCA Civ 12 (U.K.).

The courts have emphasized that impartial administration of the trust does not entail equal treatment. In *Edge v. Pension Ombudsman*, the Court of Appeal rejected an attempt to find fault in pension fund trustees who failed to give equal weight to the interests of all groups of savers.[75] In *Forbes Trustee Services Ltd* v. *Jackson*, the court noted that "[s]ome inequalities in treatment are inevitable, but [trustees] must not pursue a course of action which clearly favours one class of members over another."[76] The law in Australia, New Zealand, and Canada is virtually similar;[77] so is trust law and federal ERISA law in the United States, where the trustee is required to have "due regard" to the interests of the different beneficiary classes.[78] For example, *Siskind* v. *Sperry Retirement Program* held that "[i]t was reasonable for the plan fiduciary to approve an amendment that would provide increased benefits to those employees whose jobs were at greater risk of elimination, [because] employees at overstaffed plants and employees at 'lean' plants are not similarly situated."[79] As noted, company liquidators and administrators are subject to a similar duty as well.[80]

Cases holding fiduciaries to account for breaching the duty of impartiality are rare. Still, the trustee's exceptionally ample discretion in discharging their duty to act in the best interests of the body of beneficiaries as a whole does not mean unbridled discretion, let alone immunity from liability. For example, in *Mulligan*, the trustees were held liable for indulging the wishes of the widow by investing solely in high-interest fixed-income assets that did not provide any capital appreciation.[81] Before its judgment was reversed on appeal, the primary court in *Wendt* v. *Orr* held an executor accountable for monies paid out in breach of the duty of impartially to potential claimants and for related costs and ordered his removal.[82] In *Re Smith*, the trustee was removed from office for heeding the objections of the remainderman to purchasing higher-yielding investments that would have benefitted the life-tenant.[83] In *Boe v. Alexander*, a pension fund trustee was found to have breached his duty to balance the interests of all the beneficiaries.[84]

B *The Proposed Approach*

It is the thesis of this paper that the duty of impartiality holds substantial promise as a doctrinal framework for addressing the interests of stakeholder constituencies in business firms. In this view, directors and other corporate fiduciaries with strategic responsibilities will be obliged to treat the company's stakeholders impartially when they make business judgments in the best interest of the company as a whole—an obligation that will be discharged by considering the

---

[75] Edge v. Pension Ombudsman [1999] EWCA Civ 2013 (U.K.).

[76] Forbes Trustee Services Ltd v. Jackson [2004] EWHC 2448 (Ch) (U.K.).

[77] *See, e.g.*, respectively, for Australia: Commonwealth Bank Officers Superannuation Corporation Pty Ltd v. Beck [2016] NSWCA 218 (Aust.); Manglicmot v. Commonwealth Bank Officers Superannuation Corporation [2010] NSWSC 363 (Aust.); for New Zealand: Enright v. Enright [2019] NZHC 1124 (N.Z.); Re Mulligan (Deceased) [1998] 1 NZLR 481 (HC) (N.Z.); for Canada: Neville v. Wynne, [2006] BCCA 460 (Can.); Anova Inc. Employee Retirement Pension Plan (Administrator of) v. Manufacturers Life Insurance Co. [1994] 121 DLR (4th) 162 (ON SC) (Can.).

[78] See, with regard to private trusts, RESTATEMENT (THIRD) OF TRUSTS, § 78–79 (AM. LAW INST. 2007); Uniform Trust Code § 803 (2005); Uniform Principal and Income Act § 103 (2000); Varity Corp. v. Howe, 516 U.S. 489 (1996). With regard to ERISA, see, e.g., Siskind v. Sperry Retirement Program, 47 F.3d 498 (2d Cir. 1995); Morse v. Stanley, 732 F.2d 1139 (2d Cir. 1984). With regard to trust indentures of debt facilities, see Steven L. Schwarcz, *Fiduciaries with Conflicting Obligations*, 94 MINN. L. REV. 1867 (2010).

[79] *Siskind*, 47 F.3d at 506.

[80] *See* In re Contract Corporation (Gooch's Case) (1871) LR 7 Ch App 207 (U.K.); IND Energy Inc v. Langdon [2014] WASC 364 (Aust.); ASIC v. Edge [2007] VSC 170 (Aust.); Bovis Lend Lease v. Wily [2003] NSWSC 467 (Aust.).

[81] Re Mulligan (Deceased) [1998] 1 NZLR 481 (HC) (N.Z.).

[82] *See* Wendt v. Orr [2004] WASC 28 (Can.); reversed in Orr v. Wendt [2005] WASCA 199 (Can.).

[83] *See* Re Smith (1971) 16 DLR (3d) 130 (ON SC) (Can.), affirmed (1971) 18 DLR (3d) 405 (ON CA) (Can.).

[84] Boe v. Alexander [1987] 15 BCLR (2d) 106 (CA) (Can.).

interests of the company's various stakeholders. This obligation of stakeholder impartiality will form part of the directors' duty of loyalty and be discharged with the skill and care reasonably required in the circumstances.

The proposed duty draws on the traditional duty of trustees only as a source of inspiration for its conceptual framework. This is because trustees' duty of impartiality in discretionary trusts cannot be applied directly in a corporate setting. While trust beneficiaries are direct objects of trustee duties, it is the company (as a whole) that is the object and beneficiary of directors' duties in legal systems that derive from English company law.[85] In this conception, shareholders are only secondary notional beneficiaries, whose interest as a general constituency proxies for the company's interest in legal systems that endorse shareholder primacy. Delaware and other U.S. laws are unique in their dual corporation-and-shareholders-oriented duty of loyalty under *Guth*.[86]

The duty of impartiality of liquidators may be perceived as a version of regular directors' duty. It is closer to the proposed duty of regular directors than the trustee's duty, because the liquidator's duty of loyalty, including impartiality, is formally oriented to both creditors and shareholders without ignoring the company's legal personality.[87] On this notional continuum, between regular trustees and liquidators, one could locate trustees of pension funds. The latter owe direct loyalty to the beneficiaries, but different beneficiary classes comprise large and changing numbers of individual beneficiaries akin to shareholders, bondholder, and employees. Common to all three types of fiduciary duties — of trustees, liquidators, and directors (as proposed) — is the discretion that these fiduciaries are required to exercise in good faith in the interest of a body of ultimate beneficiaries as a whole. At the same time, only directors exercise *business* judgment — with a view to taking up risky projects with uncertain payoffs — while trustees' and liquidators' mission and judgment are custodial in nature — with a predominant task of preserving the estate to reasonably ensure payout distribution.

Substantively, stakeholder impartiality would require directors to give proper consideration ("due regard" in U.S. usage) to stakeholders' interests. The duty's contribution to extant obligations — for example, under section 172 of the U.K. Companies Act — lies in providing content and structure. First, this model explicates the obligation as requiring deliberation only, and thus, by construction, not requiring directors to take other kinds of action — for example, to ameliorate certain adverse effects (while not forbidding it either). Second, this model clarifies that the duty is process-oriented rather than outcome-oriented. Specifically, it rejects an obligation to strive for, let alone achieve, any kind of equality among the different stakeholder constituencies. Put otherwise, it does not call for balancing stakeholders' interests. Together, these features ensure that the proposed model is workable — that directors and courts can implement it "with clarity and force," as Berle and Means have insisted.[88]

By eschewing regulation of substantive equality of outcome, the proposed stakeholder impartiality does not encroach on directors' business judgment, thus preserving a sphere that is free of post hoc legal intervention. At the same time, while the proposed duty admittedly has lean content, it is anything but hollow. As a primarily process-oriented duty, it calls on directors to discharge it by conducting a structured and well-documented deliberation that is reasonable in

---

[85] *Compare* JJ Harrison (Properties) Ltd v. Harrison [2001] EWCA Civ 146, [25] (U.K.).

[86] *See supra* text accompanying note 19.

[87] It is also directed to the court. *See Gooch's Case, supra* note 80; *see generally* In re Pantmaenog Timber Co Ltd [2003] UKHL 49 (U.K.).

[88] *See* ADOLF A. BERLE & GARDINER C. MEANS, THE MODERN CORPORATION AND PRIVATE PROPERTY 312 (HARCOURT, BRACE & WORLD rev. ed. 1968) ("It remains only for the claims of the community to be put forward with clarity and force."); *see also supra* note 46 and accompanying text.

the circumstances, in line with jurisprudence on the business judgment rule[89] and with a similar duty of trustees to exercise an informed discretion in a proper procedure.[90]

Procedures that focus on giving due regard to participants are nonetheless not devoid of content and should not be regarded as mere "box-checking." They can yield desirable outcomes despite—and perhaps thanks to—their lean substantive content. Several mechanisms may engender such effects. From the decision makers' perspective, a formal requirement to consider someone in a discussion ensures that his or her issue is indeed discussed at any level of detail rather than neglected, either knowingly or subconsciously. Such a requirement also helps in raising awkward issues for discussion by team members who might otherwise prefer to avoid friction with their fellows. More basically, conducting discussions in an orderly and transparent fashion likely changes the very mode of analysis from intuitive to high-level deliberation.[91] From the stakeholders' perspective, a duty to consider ensures that they would be given "their day in the boardroom." Ample research on procedural justice by Tom Tyler and others has shown that such procedural features could engender positive outcomes, including acceptance of and collaboration with adverse decisions.[92]

Stakeholder impartiality, as a legal doctrine, need not overlap with stakeholder-oriented strategic management. According to Edward Freeman's capacious definition, a stakeholder could be "any group or individual who can affect or is affected by the achievement of the organization's objectives."[93] This is a positive axiomatic definition; it entails neither particular normative implications (which stakeholders deserve what) nor any instrumental implications (what would happen if certain stakeholders got something).[94] The latter aspects would be determined separately, using different methodologies.

Recent jurisprudence in Australia and New Zealand demonstrates this point with regard to executors' duty of impartiality. In light of legislation that gives certain persons not mentioned in a will a right to nonetheless claim benefits from the estate within a limited period, the question arose whether the executor owes a duty of impartiality to such potential claimants. The courts have split on this question, and a full discussion, albeit instructive, is beyond the present scope.[95] The key point is that such potential claimants clearly fall within Freeman's definition of stakeholders, as they affect the administration of the estate. Nevertheless, a court may decline to recognize them as a matter of law and deny them the coverage of the duty of impartiality. A fully analogous analysis would be in place with regard to corporate stakeholder impartiality.

Non-shareholder stakeholders must be able to enforce their right to impartial treatment to ensure that stakeholder impartiality is not merely whitewash for hard-nosed shareholder primacy

---

[89] *See, e.g.,* In re Walt Disney Co. Derivative Litigation, 907 A.2d 693, 750 (Del. Ch. 2005).

[90] *See* Abacus Trust Company (Isle of Man) v. Barr [2003] EWHC 114, [16] (Ch) (U.K.) and references therein.

[91] For overviews of the psychological mechanisms involved in intuitive and analytical thought processes, see, e.g., Gerard P. Hodgkinson & Eugene Sadler-Smith, *The Dynamics of Intuition and Analysis in Managerial and Organizational Decision Making,* 32 ACAD. MGMT. PERSP. 473 (2018); Jonathan St. B. T. Evans, *Dual-Processing Accounts of Reasoning, Judgment, and Social Cognition,* 59 ANN. REV. PSYCH. 255 (2008).

[92] *See* E. ALLAN LIND & TOM R. TYLER, THE SOCIAL PSYCHOLOGY OF PROCEDURAL JUSTICE (1988); *see also* Harris Sondak & Tom R. Tyler, *How Does Procedural Justice Shape the Desirability of Markets?,* 28 J. ECON. PSYCH. 79 (2007); Rebecca Hollander-Blumoff & Tom R. Tyler, *Procedural Justice in Negotiation: Procedural Fairness, Outcome Acceptance, and Integrative Potential,* 33 LAW & SOC. INQUIRY 473 (2008).

[93] R. EDWARD FREEMAN, STRATEGIC MANAGEMENT: A STAKEHOLDER APPROACH 46 (1984).

[94] A large literature elaborates on these issues. For introductions, see, e.g., Thomas Donaldson & Lee E. Preston, *The Stakeholder Theory of the Corporation: Concepts, Evidence, and Implications,* 20 ACAD. MGMT. REV. 65 (1995); Eric W. Orts & Alan Strudler, *Putting a Stake in Stakeholder Theory,* 88 J. BUS. ETHICS 605 (2009).

[95] For comprehensive analyses reaching opposite conclusions, see Wendt v. Orr [2004] WASC 28 (Can.); reversed in Orr v. Wendt [2005] WASCA 199 (Can.) and references therein.

(for those who are concerned about this possibility).[96] While beneficiaries of trusts and estates can bring a personal claim against the trustee, in companies, only shareholders can bring a derivative claim—a point that *Gheewalla* has forcefully underscored.[97] Past experience indeed has shown that this is not a fanciful concern. In *Parke* v. *Daily News*, the court applied *Hutton* to condemn paying employees beyond their legal entitlement.[98] Section 309 of the U.K. Companies Act 1985 was then amended to require the directors to have regard to the interests of the company's employees in general, as well as the interests of its shareholders. That section (now repealed) further provided that "the duty imposed by this section on the directors is owed by them to the company (and the company alone) and is enforceable in the same way as any other fiduciary duty owed to a company by its directors"—that is, excepting the company or a liquidator, by shareholders in a derivative action. Len Sealy famously quipped that "[Section 309] is either one of the most incompetent or one of the most cynical pieces of drafting on record."[99]

In order to prevent a repetition of such a farce, members of stakeholder constituencies should have standing, preferably derivatively or in a direct cause of action, against the directors with regard to the latter's compliance with the duty of impartiality. Granted, such an arrangement would exceed the conventional array of rights and duties among and between the company, its directors and officers, and the shareholders. In tandem, relatively little will suffice to show proper discharge of this obligation—basically, evidence that the directors have indeed given their mind to the relevant stakeholders. There will be no need to mention any actual or potential substantive effect, as this is not called for by the duty, although it would be allowed to do so. One must not dismiss such evidence—typically, records of board meetings and related documents—as useless bureaucratic hassle, since the duty is process-oriented by design.

Stakeholder impartiality could prove particularly useful in legal systems that endorse a pluralistic approach to the objectives of the corporation, Canada being a prime example. Recall how the *BCE* court openly acknowledged that "there is no principle ... ."[100] *BCE* was decided in a legal framework of oppression/unfair prejudice, that in Canada includes the creditors. This outcome-oriented doctrine aims to protect some minimum legitimate expectations; it connotes substantive fairness, not procedural fairness. It is not surprising, therefore that the Court found itself in want of means for providing consistent guidance on the doctrine's content. To clarify: the rule in *BCE* is not meaningless or hollow; it is just not particularly workable, if at all. In contrast, if *BCE* were to be read as implying stakeholder impartiality, it is submitted that both market participants and the courts would be better able to comply with its ruling and promote the legal policy it reflects. A similar analysis would apply to section 166 of India's Companies Act, which formally designates the interest of all stakeholder constituencies as objectives of Indian companies.

Stakeholder impartiality could prove useful also in shareholderistic systems. For example, implementing this approach in the United Kingdom would provide boards of companies subject to the new reporting regulations mentioned in the Introduction, a clear framework for establishing compliance with their duties under section 172. Perhaps surprisingly, this approach might be applied in Delaware, too. Recall that in *Trados* and *ODN*, the courts denied preferred

---

[96] Recall the critique by Naniwadekar and Varottil, *supra* text accompanying note 44.

[97] *See* N. Am. Catholic Educ. Programming Found., Inc. v. Gheewalla, 930 A.2d 92, and text accompanying notes 21.

[98] Parke v. Daily News Ltd [1962] Ch 927 (U.K.).

[99] L. S. Sealy, *Directors' "Wider" Responsibilities – Problems Conceptual, Practical and Procedural* 13 MONASH U. L. REV. 164, 177 (1987).

[100] *See supra* text accompanying note 36.

stockholders the protection of directors' duty of loyalty because common stockholders were deemed more deserving of this protection as residual claimants.[101] These decisions marginalized the residual equity feature of preferred stock. If stakeholder impartiality had been implemented in those cases, the result might have remained the same, but the legal analysis would have been more loyal to the reality of the financial interests involved.[102]

IV CONCLUSION

About twenty years ago, Henry Butler and Fred McChesney complained that "[f]or centuries legal, political, social, and economic commentators have debated corporate social responsibility *ad nauseam*."[103] Nauseating as it may be to some, the debate over shareholders and stakeholders as the focal objective of the corporation appears as lively as ever, even though the positions voiced in it now have a long lineage indeed. This essay does not attempt to resolve this debate, among other things, because the present author believes it cannot be resolved and is bound to go on.[104] The goal of this essay is more modest yet still ambitious—to push the discourse forward by advancing a doctrinal framework for considering the interests of various stakeholders in those legal systems that already do or may in the future require directors to do so—such as in the United Kingdom and, in a very different modus, in Canada—but also in legal systems that currently focus on shareholder interests—for example, in Delaware. As proposed in this essay, stakeholder impartiality is at the same time novel in corporate law yet classical in fiduciary law. Courts who wanted to experiment with it thus would be able to draw on a solid body of jurisprudence that would facilitate its implementation. It is hoped that some indeed will do so.

---

[101] *See supra* note 23.

[102] For proposals to implement impartiality analysis with regard to preferred stock, *see* LICHT, *supra* note 10; Shachar Nir, *One Duty to All: The Fiduciary Duty of Impartiality and Stockholders' Conflict of Interest*, 16 HASTINGS BUS. L. J. 1 (2020).

[103] Henry N. Butler & Fred S. McChesney, *Why They Give at the Office: Shareholder Welfare and Corporate Philanthropy in the Contractual Theory of the Corporation*, 84 CORNELL L. REV. 1195, 1195 (1999).

[104] *See supra* text accompanying notes 59.

17

Shareholder Primacy in Benefit Corporations

*Julian Velasco**

I INTRODUCTION

The goal of the traditional business corporation ("business corporation") has been understood to be the creation of wealth for the benefit of its owners, the shareholders.[1] However, this view has not been universally held. There have always been those who argue that wealth creation must be tempered by socially responsible behavior so that business can benefit all of society and not simply its owners.[2] In each generation, the call for social responsibility is revived;[3] but each time the traditional view of business seems to prevail in the end.[4] Recently, there has been a growing demand on the part of investors and consumers for what has come to be known as "social enterprise." Although the term is difficult to define with precision, it is generally understood to mean businesses that pursue socially beneficial goals in addition to investor profit.[5] This demand for social enterprise has led to the creation of new forms of business organization to support it. The most popular such form is the public benefit corporation ("benefit corporation"), and this chapter will focus on the benefit corporation. Due to space constraints, the focus will be almost exclusively on the benefit corporation as proposed in the Model Benefit Corporation Act.[6] This is reasonable because "[t]he Model Legislation

* I would like to thank the participants of the workshop for this volume at Rutgers Law School and the participants at a colloquium for this essay at Notre Dame Law School for their helpful comments. I would also like to thank Nicole Paige, Mara Case, and Emily Dufner for their excellent research assistance.
1 Dodge v. Ford Motor Co., 170 N.W. 668, 684 (Mich. 1919). *See also* eBay Domestic Holdings, Inc. v. Newmark, 16 A.3d 1, 34 (Del. Ch. 2010).
2 *See generally* CAMBRIDGE HANDBOOK OF SOCIAL ENTERPRISE LAW (Benjamin Means & Joseph Yockey eds., 2017) [hereinafter CHSEL]; PROGRESSIVE CORPORATE LAW (Lawrence E. Mitchell ed., 1995); *see, e.g.,* E. Merrick Dodd, Jr., *For Whom Are Corporate Managers Trustees?*, 45 HARV. L. REV. 1145, 1148 (1932).
3 For historical accounts, see Daniel J. Morrissey, *The Riddle of Shareholder Rights and Corporate Social Responsibility*, *in* CHSEL, *supra* note 2, at 353; C.A. Harwell Wells, *Cycles of Corporate Social Responsibility: An Historical Retrospective for the Twenty-First Century*, 51 U. KAN. L. REV. 77 (2002).
4 In 2001, Professors Hansmann and Kraakman famously declared, albeit not without controversy, that "[t]here is no longer any serious competitor to the view that corporate law should principally strive to increase long-term shareholder value." Henry Hansmann & Reinier Kraakman, *The End of History for Corporate Law*, 89 GEO. L. J. 439 (2001).
5 *Cf.* Lloyd H. Mayer, *Creating a Tax Space for Social Enterprise*, *in* CHSEL, *supra* note 2, at 157, 159 ("The more general definition is: a social enterprise is a business that sells goods or services (or both) and has both the goal of generating a profit and a social benefit goal.").
6 *See generally* Model Benefit Corp. Legis. (2017), *available at* https://benefitcorp.net/sites/default/files/Model%20bene fit%20corp%20legislation%20_4_17_17.pdf (hereinafter, Model Legislation).

promulgated by B Lab has been extremely influential, forming the basis of the vast majority of state benefit corporation laws."[7]

It is commonly believed that the benefit corporation was created to overcome the bias toward shareholder primacy implicit in traditional corporate law.[8] At the very least, it was unclear whether courts would accept business goals that conflicted with wealth creation. In order to assure the viability of social enterprise, new forms of business organization designed for that very purpose were deemed necessary. The purpose of benefit corporations, then, would seem to be to overcome notions of shareholder primacy in traditional corporate law and ensure that certain businesses can be operated not solely in the interests of shareholders, but also for the benefit of society generally.

It is my thesis that this account is incorrect in some critical respects. In particular, I will argue that those benefit corporations are or at least should be considered to be, perfectly consistent with shareholder primacy. Rather, it is only the shareholder wealth maximization norm with which the benefit corporation is at odds.

It is essential to distinguish between these two concepts; they are often considered to be interchangeable, but they are not. The shareholder wealth maximization norm insists that a business must be operated with the primary goal—perhaps even the exclusive goal—of creating wealth for its owners, the shareholders. In my use of the term, shareholder primacy is something different; it insists that the corporation is to be operated primarily—perhaps even exclusively—in the interests of the shareholders. Although the two concepts are highly compatible, they are not identical. Shareholder wealth maximization is a particular implementation of shareholder primacy that assumes that shareholders are interested primarily or exclusively in wealth creation. But that assumption is not necessarily accurate.[9] Shareholders are not necessarily driven solely by profits; they may be altruistic to varying degrees.[10] It is entirely possible for shareholders to consider it to be in their own interests, broadly defined, to create wealth in a responsible, sustainable, and moral way. Such shareholders may find the business corporation to be an inadequate investment vehicle because of its ties to shareholder wealth maximization. Thus, they may seek a legal form that allows them to unite with other

---

[7] Ronald J. Colombo, *Taking Stock of the Benefit Corporation*, 7 Tex. A&M L. Rev. 73, 77 (2019).

[8] *See generally* William H. Clark, Jr. & Larry Vranka, et al., *White Paper: The Need and Rationale for the Benefit Corporation: Why it is the Legal Form That Best Addresses the Needs of Social Entrepreneurs, Investors, and, Ultimately, the Public* 7–14 (2013), available at https://benefitcorp.net/sites/default/files/Benefit_Corporation_White_Paper.pdf [hereinafter White Paper]; *see also* Kevin V. Tu, *Socially Conscious Corporations and Shareholder Profit*, 84 Geo. Wash. L. Rev. 121, 154 (2016) ("The most commonly stated reason for supporting Benefit Corporation statutes is that the traditional for-profit corporation and non-profit corporation models available under existing law do not effectively allow for the pursuit of both profit and non-financial objectives.").

[9] Milton Friedman acknowledges this point. *See* Milton Friedman, *A Friedman Doctrine — The Social Responsibility of Business Is to Increase Its Profits*, N.Y. Times, Sept. 13, 1970, at A17. Friedman insists that the corporate management's responsibility is "to conduct the business in accordance with [the shareholders'] desires." *Id.* According to him, this "generally will be to make as much money as possible," but "in some cases his employers may have a different objective." *Id.* For example, "[a] group of persons might establish a corporation for an eleemosynary purpose—for example, a hospital or a school. The manager of such a corporation will not have money profit as his objectives but the rendering of certain services." *Id.* Thus, Friedman's position is best understood as embodying shareholder primacy with a rebuttable presumption of wealth maximization.

[10] *See id. Cf.* In re *Oracle Corp. Derivative Litig.*, 824 A.2d 917, 938 (Del. Ch. 2003) ("Homo sapiens is not merely homo economicus. We may be thankful that an array of other motivations exist that influence human behavior; not all are any better than greed or avarice, think of envy, to name just one. But also think of motives like love, friendship, and collegiality, think of those among us who direct their behavior as best they can on a guiding creed or set of moral values."); *see also* Oliver Hart & Luigi Zingales, *Companies Should Maximize Shareholder Welfare Not Market Value*, 2 J. L. Fin. & Acct. 247 (2017). It should be noted that wealth maximizing shareholders may be altruistic as well. Such shareholders may simply prefer to engage in altruism at the personal level rather than at the corporate level.

like-minded investors and pre-commit to a purpose that is not limited to wealth creation but allows for altruism. The benefit corporation is such an entity.[11]

In this chapter, I will argue that the benefit corporation, like the business corporation, should be understood through the lens of shareholder primacy. The critical difference between the business corporation and the benefit corporation is that, by adopting the benefit corporation form, the shareholders have signaled their personal interest in pursuing other socially desirable goals in addition to wealth creation. Thus, unlike the business corporation, the benefit corporation rejects the shareholder wealth maximization norm. However, this is itself an alternate implementation of shareholder primacy—one that is not limited to the goal of wealth maximization but allows for altruism in the form of social enterprise.

My thesis rejects the claim that benefit corporations were created for the purpose of benefiting stakeholders or society directly. In other words, the conduct of the benefit corporation should be understood entirely in terms of shareholder altruism rather than in terms of stakeholder rights. Although public benefits will inevitably result from benefit corporation legislation ("BCL"), they are not the primary goal. Rather, the goal of BCL is to empower shareholders who are inclined to be altruistic.[12] Importantly, the goal is not to force shareholders to be altruistic. Properly understood, BCL is as enabling as traditional corporate law and should not be understood as a form of mandatory regulation. As a result, the law should not be interpreted as protecting the interests of other stakeholders over those of the shareholders. Instead, it should be interpreted as protecting the interests of altruistic shareholders over those of profit-maximizing shareholders. This will redound to the benefit of other stakeholders, of course; but only indirectly. Stakeholders should not be understood to have vested rights in the benefit corporation.

My thesis will, no doubt, strike many as counter-intuitive; but it should not. The history of BCL is largely consistent with this view. Moreover, its structure is highly compatible with my thesis and largely incompatible with the contrary view. I will review the evidence, as well as present normative policy arguments, and then consider the implications of this model for the interpretation and future development of the law of benefit corporations.

ii TRADITIONAL BUSINESS CORPORATIONS

The traditional view of the business corporation is that it is owned by its shareholders, and its purpose is to make money for its shareholders.[13] Everybody knows this, but not everyone accepts it.[14] Academics, in particular, have difficulty with the traditional view. Many corporate law scholars insist that the law is not so clear and offer various arguments to demonstrate that shareholders are not truly owners.[15] For some scholars, but by no means all, it follows that the corporation should not be run solely in the interests of shareholders, but instead be run in the

---

[11] See White Paper, *supra* note 8, at 28 ("Benefit corporations best meet the needs of entrepreneurs, investors, consumers and policy makers interested in using the power of business to solve social and environmental problems.").

[12] Cf. Michael B. Dorff, *Why Public Benefit Corporations*, 42 DEL. J. CORP. L. 77, 95 (2017) ("Delaware's primary goal in passing its [BCL] was to provide flexibility to those social entrepreneurs and investors who wanted a legal form that would permit them to pursue social goals alongside profits.").

[13] See *supra* note 1.

[14] See Julian Velasco, *Shareholder Ownership and Primacy*, 2010 U. ILL. L. REV. 897, 899–900 ("[T]hat shareholders do not own corporations . . . enjoys general acceptance in scholarly circles . . . . And yet, outside of the academy, views on the corporation remain quite traditional.").

[15] See, e.g., Stephen M. Bainbridge, *Director Primacy: The Means and Ends of Corporate Governance*, 97 NW. U. L. REV. 547, 564–65 (2003); Lynn A. Stout, *Bad and Not-so-Bad Arguments for Shareholder Primacy*, 75 S. CAL. L. REV. 1189, 1190–95 (2002).

interests of all its stakeholders or for the benefit of society generally.[16] These arguments, however, tend to amount to a claim that shareholders *ought* not to be considered owners rather than that they *are* not owners, and that directors can *get away with* pursuing the interests of non-shareholders rather than that they *have the right* to do so. I have considered such arguments in other work,[17] and will not address them at length here.

For purposes of this chapter, I assume the legitimacy of the traditional view of business corporations—that the shareholders are the owners. I maintain that this is true across the board in the United States. At the very least, however, it is clearly true under Delaware law.[18]

However, many people want to deny shareholder ownership in large public corporations, but few would deny the concept of ownership in closely held corporations.[19] At least for now, most benefit corporations are closely held rather than publicly held.[20] Thus, the typical arguments against shareholder ownership of public corporations simply do not apply.

Because shareholders are owners, the corporation is run in their interests. Such shareholder primacy is not necessarily synonymous with wealth maximization. However, it is reasonable to assume, at least in the absence of evidence to the contrary, that most shareholders in a for-profit business corporation are interested in maximizing the wealth created by their business. Thus, the wealth maximization norm makes sense as a default rule.

Arguments against wealth maximization tend to fall into two categories. On the one hand, they may insist that the law nowhere explicitly requires wealth maximization.[21] Although this may be true, the argument loses its strength once it is acknowledged that the shareholders are the owners. This is because there is no reason that the corporation should be run in the interests of anyone else. If the corporation is truly treated as a separate entity—like a sole proprietorship—then it should seek to maximize its profits. If it does this, it will redound to the benefit of the shareholder owners.[22]

The other argument against wealth maximization is that the law does not enforce it. The business judgment rule provides directors with the discretion to pursue other goals[23]—and, it is argued, must do so necessarily.[24] This argument is correct insofar as it goes, but it does not go very far at all. The argument does not establish that directors are permitted to avoid wealth

---

[16] *See, e.g.*, Margaret M. Blair & Lynn A. Stout, *A Team Production Theory of Corporate Law*, 85 VA. L. REV. 247 (1999); Kent Greenfield, *New Principles for Corporate Law*, 1 HASTINGS BUS. L. J. 87, 89 (2005).

[17] *See* Velasco, *supra* note 14.

[18] *See, e.g.*, North American Catholic Educational Programming Foundation, Inc. v. Gheewalla, 930 A.2d 92, 101 (Del. 2007) ("The directors of Delaware corporations have 'the legal responsibility to manage the business of a corporation for the benefit of its shareholders [sic] owners.'") (*quoting* Malone v. Brincat, 722 A.3d 5, 9 (Del. 1998)). *See also* Leo E. Strine, Jr., *The Dangers of Denial: The Need for a Clear-Eyed Understanding of the Power and Accountability Structure Established by the Delaware General Corporation Law*, 50 WAKE FOREST L. REV. 761, 768 (2015) ("Despite attempts to muddy the doctrinal waters, a clear-eyed look at the law of corporations in Delaware reveals that, within the limits of their discretion, directors must make stockholder welfare their sole end, and that other interests may be taken into consideration only as a means of promoting stockholder welfare.").

[19] *See* Velasco, *supra* note 14, at 934–38.

[20] *See* Brett H. McDonnell, *Three Legislative Paths to Social Enterprise: L3Cs, Benefit Corporations, and Second-Generation Cooperatives, in* CHSEL, *supra* note 2, at 67, 75 ("[T]he vast majority of benefit corporations are small, closely held businesses.").

[21] *See, e.g.*, LYNN STOUT, THE SHAREHOLDER VALUE MYTH: HOW PUTTING SHAREHOLDERS FIRST HARMS INVESTORS, CORPORATIONS, AND THE PUBLIC 25 (2012) ("There is no solid legal support for the claim that directors and executives in U.S. public corporations have an enforceable legal duty to maximize shareholder wealth.").

[22] Velasco, *supra* note 14, at 926–27.

[23] *See, e.g.*, Tu, *supra* note 8, at 140 ("[T]he discretion granted under the business judgment rule effectively eviscerates the claim that corporation managers must be driven by the sole goal of shareholder profit maximization.").

[24] *See, e.g.*, Einer Elhauge, *Sacrificing Corporate Profits in the Public Interest*, 80 N.Y.U. L. REV. 733, 868 (2005) ("Managerial discretion to sacrifice corporate profits [to further the public interest] . . . is inevitable because it cannot be disentangled from the discretion managers need to make profit-enhancing corporate decisions.").

maximization. Rather, it establishes only that directors may be able to get away with doing so. Directors' fiduciary duties require them to act in the interests of shareholders.[25] Directors are given discretion so that they can exercise their expertise to that end.[26] That discretion comes with the ability to abuse shareholders, but not permission or license to do so. For example, if the directors were to admit that they were not acting in the interests of shareholders—something they are generally unwilling to do—they would almost certainly be held liable for breach of fiduciary duty.[27] Thus, the argument is not that the law does not require shareholder wealth maximization, but only that directors have the ability to break the law with some degree of impunity.

A related version of the argument is that directors can skirt wealth maximization by shifting their attention to the long-term interests of the shareholders.[28] This shift in focus allows them to pursue societal interests that sacrifice shareholder wealth in the short run ostensibly to maximize shareholder wealth in the long run. Such an argument is formally valid, but whether it is plausible in any particular case is a question of fact. Wealth maximization need not have a definite horizon, and one very well might sacrifice a small profit today for a larger one tomorrow.[29] Thus, director decisions to do so are perfectly legitimate, provided that they are sincere. However, if such decisions are not sincere and merely ruses for pursuing the interests of others, then they amount to a breach of fiduciary duty.[30] Again, directors may avoid liability for misconduct, but they are not actually authorized to breach their duties.

Even those who would like to reject the traditional view of the corporation generally acknowledge that it is widely and stubbornly held.[31] Thus, the social enterprise movement has largely shifted its focus from the business corporation to new forms of business enterprise.

Before we turn to benefit corporations, it is worth noting that the social enterprise movement need not have given up on the business corporation. Traditional corporate law consists of flexible enabling statutes that allow investors to change the default rules.[32] Thus, it should be possible to amend a corporation's charter to provide that its purpose shall not be limited to shareholder wealth maximization and instead should extend to pursuing the interests of society.[33] Such an amendment would seem to be perfectly legitimate, at least for a new corporation. However, it

---

[25] See Velasco, *supra* note 14.

[26] See Dodge v. Ford Motor Co., 170 N.W. 668, 684 (Mich. 1919) ("The discretion of directors is to be exercised in the choice of means to attain that end, and does not extend to a change in the end itself, to the reduction of profits, or to the nondistribution of profits among stockholders in order to devote them to other purposes.").

[27] See In re Walt Disney Co. Derivative Litig., 906 A.2d 27, 66–67 (Del. 2006) (upholding "intentional dereliction of duty, a conscious disregard for one's responsibilities" as "a legally appropriate, although not the exclusive, definition of fiduciary bad faith"), *aff'd*, 907 A.2d 693 (Del. Ch. 2005).

[28] See, e.g., Elhauge, *supra* note 24, at 746 ("[M]anagers can almost always make a plausible argument that they somehow might increase profits in the long run.").

[29] See Paramount Communications, Inc. v. Time, Inc., 571 A.2d 1140, 1150 (Del. 1989) ("[T]he question of 'long-term' versus 'short-term' values is largely irrelevant because directors, generally, are obliged to chart a course for a corporation which is in its best interests without regard to a fixed investment horizon.").

[30] See *supra* note 27 and accompanying text. *Cf. infra* note 38.

[31] See, e.g., Carol Liao, *Early Lessons in Social Enterprise Law*, in CHSEL, *supra* note 2, at 101, 119 ("The steadfast assumption that shareholder primacy should guide corporate behavior is deeply embedded in Anglo-American ideological beliefs. The fact that the legal basis for shareholder primacy has been debunked by legal scholars time and again as not lessened its intransigence.").

[32] Williams v. Geier, 671 A.2d 1368, 1381 (Del. 1996) ("At its core, the Delaware General Corporation Law is a broad enabling act which leaves latitude for substantial private ordering . . . ."); *see also* Leo E. Strine, Jr., *Delaware's Corporate Law System: Is Corporate America Buying an Exquisite Jewel or a Diamond in the Rough—A Response to Kahan & Kamar's Price Discrimination in the Market for Corporate Law*, 86 CORNELL L. REV. 1257, 1260 (2001) (describing the DGCL as "largely enabling" and as creating "a wide realm for private ordering").

[33] See *also* Elhauge, *supra* note 24, at 859–60 ("Suppose a corporation's initial charter includes a charter provision opting out of the standard legal limits on managers' profit-sacrificing discretion . . . . It seems clear that such an opt

might be problematic for an existing corporation. Minority shareholders would have at least an arguable claim that such an amendment would be unfairly harm them. It is not clear whether such an argument would work, but the *eBay* opinion provides at least some basis for suspecting that it might.[34] Thus, a general corporation law strategy would be risky for social enterprise and is surrounded by uncertainty. It is largely because of this uncertainty that the social enterprise has turned its attention to new forms of business enterprise.

III BENEFIT CORPORATIONS

It is easy to assume that the benefit corporation form was created in order to protect society from shareholders, but this is simply not accurate. This section provides four specific arguments for why BCL should be interpreted consistently with shareholder primacy. These are based on structural considerations that are baked into the law itself. Together, they demonstrate that BCL supports rather than undermines shareholder primacy.

First, BCL was adopted to allow for social enterprise.[35] The legal viability of social enterprise under general corporation law was in question, and BCL was adopted to overcome the legal uncertainty.[36] As the official comment to § 101 of the Model Benefit Corporation Legislation put it, "[t]his chapter authorizes the organization of a form of business corporation that offers entrepreneurs and investors the option to build, and invest in, businesses that operate with a corporate purpose broader than maximizing shareholder value and a responsibility to consider the impact of its decisions on all stakeholders, not just shareholders."[37]

While BCL intentionally rejects the shareholder wealth maximization norm, it is not opposed to shareholder primacy. BCL generally does not take the form of mandatory law that makes demands of or puts limits on shareholders. Instead, it is essentially an enabling law that allows shareholders who are so inclined to pursue a new goal—that is, social enterprise rather than wealth maximization. Such legislation is, in fact, shareholder-friendly—even shareholder-centric. Far from restraining shareholders, it empowers them to pursue their interests beyond the narrow confines of wealth maximization.

It is important to note that, under this view, other stakeholders are not directly relevant. They come into the picture only indirectly, insofar as they are valued by the shareholders.[38] In other words, BCL empowers shareholders to benefit other stakeholders but does not require them to do so.

Second, BCL is not entirely new, but builds on the foundation of corporate law. BCL is merely an extension of corporate law and explicitly provides that traditional corporate law governs except where it is changed by BCL.[39] Rather than start from whole cloth, the drafters

out should be legally permissible."). *See generally* David G. Yosifon, *Opting Out of Shareholder Primacy: Is the Public Benefit Corporation Trivial?*, 41 DEL. J. CORP. L. 461 (2017).

[34] In *eBay Domestic Holdings, Inc. v. Newmark*, 16 A.3d 1 (Del. Ch. 2010), the court struck down the adoption of a shareholder rights plan (poison pill) intended to prevent Craigslist from pursuing shareholder wealth maximization. The court emphasized that there were shareholders who invested in Craigslist as a for-profit corporation who deserved the protection of fiduciary duties. However, the court also suggested that the result might have been different if the founders were the only ones affected by such a decision. *Id.* at 34.

[35] *See* White Paper, *supra* note 8, at 1–4.

[36] *See* White Paper, *supra* note 8, at 7–14.

[37] Model Legislation § 101, cmt.

[38] The same is true in business corporations. *See* Revlon, Inc. v. MacAndrews & Forbes Holdings, Inc., 506 A.2d 173, 182 (Del. 1986) ("A board may have regard for various constituencies in discharging its responsibilities, provided there are rationally related benefits accruing to the stockholders.").

[39] *See* Model Legislation § 101(c).

of BCL chose to build upon the solid foundation of traditional corporate law. As a result, the burden of persuasion falls on those who argue that benefit corporations are different from business corporations.

Nowhere does BCL purport to modify the concept of shareholder ownership or shareholder primacy. Nor does it do away with the goal of wealth creation for the shareholders' benefit. What BCL does is temper business corporation goals with additional other-regarding duties. In doing so, it clearly eliminates the shareholder wealth maximization norm. But the principle of shareholder ownership and the corollary that the business should be run in the shareholder's interests are not thereby affected.

Third, BCL reflects many of the same principles of shareholder primacy evident in traditional corporate law. Not only does it carry over all the standard elements, like shareholder election of directors, but it also introduces new benefit corporation-specific shareholder rights. For example, shareholders are empowered to enforce the directors' fiduciary duties to consider third-party interests by means of derivative litigation.[40] Thus, BCL rules vindicate the shareholders' interests in altruism.

Fourth, stakeholders are essentially powerless under BCL. They have no right to any level of benefits.[41] They have no right to enforce BCL by derivative litigation.[42] And they have no structural rights, such as voting rights, that would enable them to protect any interest they might be thought to have. Structurally, this arrangement would make little or no sense if the goal were to protect the stakeholders: it gives stakeholders no means of protecting themselves and leaves their protection to the whim of the same parties against whom they supposedly need protection. Thus, many advocate for changes to voting rights or the enforcement mechanism.[43] However, stakeholder powerlessness makes perfect sense if the goal of BCL is to enable shareholders to engage in social enterprise—to empower, rather than require, them to be altruistic.

In short, the purpose of BCL seems to be to overcome the shareholder wealth maximization norm but not to benefit other stakeholders at the shareholders' expense. This purpose is shareholder-centric: it empowers shareholders to be altruistic if they so desire and enables them to make credible commitments to that effect.

IV COUNTER-ARGUMENTS

It might be argued that other structural provisions cut against shareholder primacy. In this section, I will consider three structural counter-arguments. I will demonstrate that, although benefit corporations may benefit other stakeholders, they do not do so at the expense of shareholders, but rather promote shareholder primacy by assisting shareholders to effectuate their altruistic purposes.

The first such argument emphasizes that BCL not only authorizes businesses to consider stakeholder interests but actually *requires* them to do so.[44] Arguably, if the law were truly shareholder-centric, it should have been embodied in an enabling law rather than a mandatory law.

---

[40]   *See* Model Legislation § 305(b).
[41]   *See* Model Legislation § 301(d).
[42]   *See* Model Legislation § 305(a)-(b).
[43]   *See, e.g.,* Dana Brakman Reiser, *Theorizing Forms for Social Enterprise*, 62 EMORY L. J. 681, 719 (2013).
[44]   *See* Model Legislation § 301(a)(1).

Although this evidence seems incompatible with shareholder primacy, further consideration exposes the argument's weakness. In the first place, these provisions are not truly mandatory because they are entirely optional. They are binding only if shareholders opt into BCL.[45] Shareholders do so voluntarily because they want to consider other stakeholders. Traditional corporate law does not seem to allow them to do it,[46] so they opt into BCL which requires—and thus clearly allows—them to do so.[47] However, shareholders are free to run their business as ordinary business corporations under traditional corporate law. Thus, the mandatory nature of the provision is illusory.

Moreover, the law does not require very much: it only requires that directors *consider* the interests of other stakeholders.[48] It does not require that they be given any particular weight, nor that stakeholders are entitled to any particular outcome.[49] It certainly does not grant other stakeholders any vested interest in the benefit corporation's conduct.

As much as proponents of BCL might wish for an even split between the interests of shareholders and other stakeholders,[50] the law requires no such thing. The legislative history makes it clear that directors are free to balance competing interests as they see fit.[51] Moreover, under BCL, the business judgment rule expressly applies to directors' decisions.[52] It is clear that, after giving them due consideration, directors are free to reject outright any particular stakeholder interests. Thus, BCL remains shareholder-centric despite the apparent requirement to consider the interests of others.

Finally, as previously discussed, BCL does not empower other stakeholders to enforce its provisions.[53] In addition, directors are exculpated from personal liability for public benefit decisions.[54] This strongly suggests that the interest protected is not the stakeholders' right to benefits, but the shareholders' altruistic interest in providing such benefits.

A second argument that BCL is not shareholder-centric can be based on the public disclosure requirements.[55] After all, public disclosure enables the shaming of benefit corporations that do not live up to public expectations.[56] On the surface, this seems incompatible with shareholder primacy. This argument, however, is not any stronger than the last.

It is possible that, in some cases, BCL disclosure requirements could work against the interest of the shareholders, but that is not its intent. BCL was designed to empower shareholders who

---

[45] *See* Model Legislation § 104.

[46] Many states have constituency statutes that explicitly allow directors to consider the interests of stakeholders in making business decisions. *See* White Paper, *supra* note 7, at 8-11. However, I have argued elsewhere that, "with the benefit of hindsight, it seems clear that constituency statutes are not very significant." Julian Velasco, *The Fundamental Rights of the Shareholder*, 40 U.C. Davis L. Rev. 407, 463 (2006). *See also* White Paper, *supra* note 8, at 10 (concluding that "courts seem reluctant to wade into these issues and often fall back on shareholder primacy").

[47] *See, e.g.*, Tu, *supra* note 8, at 155 ("[T]he creation of a new class of corporation that not only authorizes but also mandates the balancing of various stakeholder incentives is necessary to eliminate the risk of legal uncertainty.").

[48] *See* Model Legislation § 301(a)(1). *See generally* Amir N. Licht, *Stakeholder Impartiality: A New Classic Approach for the Objectives of the Corporation*, ch. 16 (this volume).

[49] *See* White Paper, *supra* note 8, at 24 ("[T]he consideration standard does not require a particular outcome of the directors' decision-making . . . .").

[50] *See* J. Haskell Murray, *Social Enterprise Innovation: Delaware's Public Benefit Corporation Law*, 4 Harv. Bus. L. Rev. 345, 355 n.64 (2014).

[51] *See* White Paper, *supra* note 8, at 22–24 (discussing flexibility of BCL).

[52] *See, e.g.*, Model Legislation § 301(e).

[53] *See supra* note 42 and accompanying text.

[54] *See, e.g.*, Model Legislation § 301(c)(2).

[55] *See* Model Legislation § 402.

[56] *Cf.* Joseph W. Yockey, *The Compliance Case for Social Enterprise*, 4 Mich. Bus. & Entrepreneurial L. Rev. 1, 39 (2014) (raising the possibility of "non-legal sanctions (e.g., public shaming and harm to reputation)").

are interested in social enterprise. Disclosure requirements are a means of this empowerment: without it, shareholders might have no way of knowing whether or to what extent directors are pursuing the public benefits they want them to pursue.[57] Without this information, shareholders would have no choice but to trust the directors. With this information, however, they can take action to ensure that their stated interest in altruism is being pursued adequately—including by replacing directors or by initiating derivative actions. It also protects shareholders who are interested in social enterprise from shareholders who are not: public disclosure and resulting shaming may help ensure that the benefit corporation does not suffer from mission drift—a situation in which "the pursuit of profits starts to overshadow the pursuit of public benefits."[58]

A third requirement that would suggest that BCL is not shareholder-centric is the requirement to prepare the annual benefit report using an independent third-party standard ("third-party standard").[59] It might seem that shareholders are not permitted to do as they please in a benefit corporation but must comply with third-party standards. If so, this could have the effect of forcing the shareholders to act against their own financial interests.

As an initial matter, it is worth noting that this requirement is not as onerous as it may appear. There is no requirement for an audit or certification, only a self-assessment.[60] Moreover, "[t]he Model Legislation does not require a benefit corporation to use any particular third-party standard to prepare its benefit report."[61] Thus, benefit corporations are allowed to select among third-party standards. BCL contemplates the availability of many options.[62] It is entirely foreseeable, and almost unavoidable that different bodies will develop very different standards. This would allow shareholders to select an agreeable standard.[63] Thus, one should not overstate the imposition of the third-party standard requirement.

Disclosure generally and third-party standards specifically could be said to have another beneficiary: the consumer. Such requirements eliminate, or at least minimize, the possibility of greenwashing—"the phenomenon of businesses seeking the cachet of being more environmentally and socially responsible than they actually are."[64] Any corporation can claim to be altruistic, and if consumers are socially conscious, every corporation has an interest in appearing to be. Unfortunately, it is difficult for consumers to discern which corporations are sincere and which are not. Public disclosure requirements and third-party standards can help consumers discriminate more effectively.[65] To the extent that consumers are armed with knowledge, they can support altruistic over traditional businesses if interested in doing so.

However, this benefit for consumers should be understood as little more than a side effect of a provision intended to protect shareholders. Through its disclosure requirements, BCL limits the ability of a benefit corporation to feign social responsibility and therefore allows the company

---

[57] *See generally* Reiser, *supra* note 43, at 707–08 (discussing importance of informational rights for investor enforcement).

[58] Yockey, *supra* note 566, at 6.

[59] *See, e.g.*, Model Legislation §§ 102, 401; *see also id.* at § 102 (defining "independent" and "third-party standard").

[60] White Paper, *supra* note 8, at 25.

[61] *Id.* at 24.

[62] *Id.* at 24–25 (pointing to "more than 100 'raters'").

[63] *Cf.* Anthony Page, *Preserving Social Enterprise's Mission, in* CHSEL, *supra* note 2, at 417, 425 ("Even if third-party organizations are not captured, benefit corporations have the ability to shop around among the many standard-setting organizations . . . .").

[64] Model Legislation § 102 (in definition of "third-party standard").

[65] White Paper, *supra* note 8, at 19 ("By assessing and disclosing the benefit corporation's overall social and environmental performance against an independent third-party standard, shareholders and the public are provided an easy way to evaluate the company . . . .").

to make a more credible claim about its commitment to social enterprise.[66] Although credible commitments may also benefit the like-minded consumer, their primary beneficiary remains the socially-conscious shareholder. BCL benefits investors by helping them distinguish between sincere and insincere social enterprises. The corresponding benefit to consumers is incidental.

Finally, one might argue that the existence of the benefit directors and benefit officers argues against shareholder primacy. These are directors and officers who are "specifically designated to oversee benefit issues."[67] Among other things, the benefit officer has "the duty to prepare the benefit report,"[68] and the benefit director is responsible for "preparing a statement for inclusion in the annual report of whether, in the opinion of the director, the benefit corporation acted in accordance with its . . . benefit purposes."[69] However, it should be noted that benefit officers are entirely optional, and benefit directors are required only for public corporations.[70] Most benefit corporations are not public.[71] Moreover, benefit directors and officers have no power to change corporate policy unilaterally. Finally, they are elected and appointed in the ordinary way,[72] ensuring that they are as subject to the shareholders as any other officers and directors. In short, the benefit directors and benefit officers are better understood as advancing the interests of the shareholders rather than those of the stakeholders.

Thus, the structure of BCL is entirely consistent with shareholder primacy, properly understood. It is opposed to the shareholder wealth maximization norm, but not designed to force shareholders' hands or to privilege stakeholder interests over shareholder interests. It is designed to empower shareholders whose interests extend beyond wealth maximization. It allows them to pursue altruism to an extent that traditional corporate law might not.

v IMPLICATIONS OF SHAREHOLDER PRIMACY

Thus far, I have argued that BCL is shareholder-centric: that although it does away with the shareholder wealth maximization norm, it does not do away with shareholder primacy. In other words, the purpose of the benefit corporation is to pursue the interests of the shareholders, broadly understood to include wealth creation and social consciousness. In this section I will discuss the implications of these principles for BCL.

The simplest way to summarize the implications is to say that BCL should seek to empower altruistic shareholders to enact their vision of social enterprise, rather than to mandate them to be more generous than they wish to be. In other words, BCL generally should be enabling rather than mandatory, and it should be mandatory only to the extent that it enables shareholders to pursue social enterprise more effectively.

Why enabling law? First, because this is the general trend in the law of business organization,[73] and BCL is only an offshoot.[74] Second and more importantly, because the primary purpose of BCL is to enable shareholders to do something that was questionable under traditional corporation law.[75] Thus, BCL should stay true to its enabling roots. Third,

---

[66] Dorff, *supra* note 12, at 102–05 (discussing the signaling or "[b]rand motive" for BCL); *see, e.g.*, Tu, *supra* note 8, at 160–65 (evaluating the market justification for BCL).

[67] White Paper, *supra* note 8, at 21.

[68] Model Legislation § 304(b)(2).

[69] White Paper, *supra* note 8, at 21 (citing Model Legislation § 302(c)).

[70] Model Legislation §§ 302(a), 304(a).

[71] *See supra* note 20 and accompanying text.

[72] Model Legislation §§ 302(b), 304(a).

[73] *See supra* note 32 and accompanying text.

[74] *See supra* note 39 and accompanying text.

[75] *See supra* notes 35–37 and accompanying text.

because BCL is inherently voluntary. No business has to become a benefit corporation. It will do so only if it finds BCL agreeable. The more mandatory the requirements of BCL, the more likely it will be to dissuade shareholders from pursuing the benefit corporation form. If we wish to encourage the formation of benefit corporations, we should use mandatory law sparingly.

In what particulars should BCL be enabling rather than mandatory? In many ways. At the most basic level, BCL should not seek to mandate any particular level of shareholder altruism; it is enough to allow for it. Some companies' shareholders may want to engage in more altruism than others, which should be permitted. One company may want to dedicate half of its potential profitability to the public benefit, while another may only wish to dedicate 10 percent. A rule that would require an even split, as has been suggested,[76] would exclude many potential investors. In fact, it could easily exclude the vast majority of investors, for it seems unlikely (to the author at least) that many benefit corporations would come anywhere near a 50/50 split. Rather than allow only the hardcore to assume the benefit corporation form, we should allow larger numbers of investors to be altruistic on whatever level they are willing to accept.

Also, BCL should not mandate any particular types of altruism. Thus, for example, it should not mandate that the company pursue a general public benefit.[77] Instead, the company should be able to choose freely the types of benefits that it desires to pursue.[78] Some, no doubt, will choose to include general public benefits. Others, however, may not. Some benefit corporations may prefer to focus entirely on a specific type of public benefit. There is no reason why shareholders who want to focus on one cause should be forbidden to do so.[79]

Of course, BCL is flexible enough that it almost certainly allows corporations to focus on a single cause as well.[80] However, a broad mandate gives the directors discretion to pursue public benefits that go beyond the shareholder's interests. BCL should allow shareholders to restrict the freedom of directors to drift from the intended mission. This would also limit the directors' ability to escape accountability by pointing to whatever benefits arise from their decisions.[81] Because the purpose of BCL is to enable shareholders to engage in social enterprise, the law should enable shareholders to decide upon the type of social enterprise in which they wish to engage.

Along similar lines, BCL should not require the directors, in making their decisions, to consider the interests of a specified list of stakeholders.[82] Shareholders may want to sacrifice

---

[76] *See supra* note 50.

[77] Model Legislation § 201(a).

[78] *See* Lyman Johnson, *Managerial Duties in Social Enterprise: The Public Benefit Corporation, in* CHSEL, *supra* note 2, at 341, 352 ("[O]ther states should follow the model of Minnesota which permits the formation of 'specific benefit corporations' designed to advance only those benefits specifically described; they need not advance more amorphous 'general public benefits'.").

[79] The authors of the benefit corporation White Paper insist that proponents of BCL "are interested in creating a new corporate form that gives entrepreneurs and investors the flexibility and protection to pursue all … public benefit purposes," and that allowing only specific public benefits "would undermine one of the main purposes of the legislation." White Paper, *supra* note 8, at 21-22. However, it does not provide much in the way of normative argument other than asserting a preference.

[80] *See* White Paper, *supra* note 8, at 22 ("[T]he general public benefit provision … recognizes that different companies will pursue the creation of a material positive impact on society and the environment in different ways. [It] encourages flexibility and enables innovation by simply setting a 'directional' performance requirement … without creating unnecessarily prescriptive performance requirements … .").

[81] *Cf.* McDonnell, *supra* note 20, at 79 ("The two-masters problem … may make duty especially slippery in social enterprises, as the duty to pursue either profits or social purpose can generally justify any action.").

[82] *Cf.* Johnson, *supra* note 78, at 349 (arguing against mandatory consideration of stakeholders as creating "an odd theoretical amalgam of stakeholderism, stockholderism, and public purposefulness").

their wealth for one specific set of stakeholders only—its employees, for example.[83] Such mandatory consideration provisions empower directors to ignore the shareholders' interests in altruism and substitute their own. Of course, many benefit corporations may choose to include all constituencies within the ambit of their altruism, but they would be able to voluntarily add such a provision to their charter. Those who wish to focus should be permitted to do so. If an opt-in provision seems unnecessary, then there should at least be an opt-out. Most current BCL does not have any way to escape such provisions.

The implications of shareholder primacy extend beyond these considerations. It may be appropriate to eliminate third-party standards and possibly even mandatory public disclosure. Such proposals are not as radical as they may seem. In fact, Delaware law does not require either.[84] It might be argued that this undermines consumers' interests: without disclosure, they would be unable to assess the credibility of the companies' claims of altruism.[85] However, the purpose of BCL is to empower shareholders, not consumers. In any event, it is unlikely to have such an effect. Because consumers tend to favor altruistic companies, public disclosure serves as a form of advertisement. Thus, benefit corporations could be expected to make public disclosures voluntarily.[86] What would be more necessary is a prohibition against fraud or deception. Nevertheless, it is possible that some shareholders would prefer not to have such publicity.[87] A mandatory public disclosure requirement, for example, might discourage "shy altruists"—those who would prefer to keep their altruism secret. There is no need to alienate such actors. Thus, eliminating third-party standards and even disclosure requirements would be consistent with the enabling nature of BCL and, because of the ability to adopt such provisions or undertake such behavior voluntarily, would not be expected to undermine its purposes.

It is often suggested that new mandatory provisions be adopted.[88] One of the more popular suggestions is that the ability to enforce the directors' fiduciary duties be extended beyond the shareholders and given to stakeholders or some stakeholder representatives.[89] The idea is that this would help ensure that the benefit corporation does not suffer from mission drift. If too much attention is given to shareholder wealth creation, shareholders may not be willing to complain. Allowing other stakeholders to sue would ensure that the company pursues its dual purpose: wealth creation and public benefit.

Such a proposal should be rejected for various reasons. First, it is incompatible with the true purpose of BCL, which is empowering shareholders. Stakeholder enforcement would seek to force shareholders to be self-sacrificing rather than empower them to do so voluntarily. Second, it ignores the fact that shareholders may have different levels of public interest in mind. A stakeholder may seek to enforce a 50/50 split, while the shareholders may desire to donate only 10 percent. If the company gives only 10 percent, how can a court conclude that the company has failed to live up to a higher standard as opposed to having lived up to a desired

---

[83] Cf. Sarah Dadush, *A New Blueprint for Regulating Social Enterprise*, in CHSEL, *supra* note 2, at 432, 433 (distinguishing "beneficiaries ... who transact with social enterprises (Customer-Beneficiaries)" from "those who are employed by social enterprises (Worker-Beneficiaries)").

[84] *See* DEL. CODE ANN. tit. 8, § 366(b) (2020).

[85] *See* White Paper, *supra* note 8, at 3 ("The lack of comprehensive and transparent standards is making it difficult for a consumer to tell the difference between a 'good company' and just good marketing.").

[86] Surprisingly, many benefit corporations are not complying with the disclosure requirements. *See generally* J. Haskell Murray, *An Early Report on Benefit Reports*, 118 W. VA. L. REV. 25 (2015). Although this may cut against my argument, it also undermines the argument that disclosure requirements helpful and appropriate.

[87] This may explain the lack of compliance with the disclosure requirements. *See id.*

[88] *See, e.g.*, Page, *supra* note 633, at 428 (listing various proposals).

[89] *See, e.g.*, Page, *supra* note 633, at 428 ("benefit enforcement proceedings could be opened up to non-shareholder stakeholders"); Reiser, *supra* note 433, at 719 ("stakeholders might be granted ... standing to sue for redress").

lower standard? Even if the company once sought to live up to a 20 percent standard, it may change its mind. Enabling legislation should not seek to lock in a choice, lest shareholders cautiously adopt overly-conservative goals.

Another popular proposal is that benefit corporations be required to have stakeholder representation on the board of directors.[90] These stakeholder directors would be motivated to ensure that the company does not shirk its purpose of seeking public benefits. Under the shareholder primacy view of benefit corporations, such a proposal would be wholly inappropriate. As a theoretical matter, it would be inappropriate to interfere with the shareholders' control over the company. Stakeholders should not require shareholders to be more altruistic than they wish to be. As a practical matter, it would be difficult to implement in an appropriate way. Unless there is a clear standard, there would be no objective way for stakeholder directors to determine that the company is shirking. Even if the company adopts a clear standard, stakeholder directors will interfere with the shareholders' ability to modify that optional standard. They may even be able to modify the standard on their own against the wishes of a majority of the shareholder owners.[91] This ends up looking more like a mandatory regime than an enabling one.

Finally, it may be argued that, even if shareholders should not be saddled with mandatory altruism, it may be appropriate to demand a certain level of public benefit in order for a business to be able to claim the title of benefit corporation.[92] After all, it could be misleading, both to investors and to consumers, to allow a traditional profit-maximizing business to masquerade as a benefit corporation. Accordingly, it might be appropriate to expel from the BCL those corporations that do not meet certain minimal standards.[93]

Such minimal standards may be substantive or procedural. Substantive standards might, for example, require a certain level of altruism. We have already discussed how this would be inappropriate.[94] If there were to be a minimum, it should be set fairly low in order to encourage rather than discourage adoption of the benefit corporation form. But some would argue that it would be unwise to signal to companies that they can "get away with" so little altruism.

Thus, it might be better to focus on minimal procedural requirements. These might include compliance with disclosure requirements or even a requirement that the company live up to its announced level of altruism, whatever it may be. This would be much less of an impingement upon shareholder primacy and might seem to be unobjectionable.

However, if mission drift is the concern, it may not be a good idea to revoke benefit corporation status for procedural reasons. The fear is that, over time, a benefit corporation may accumulate shareholders who wish to minimize altruism or even exit benefit corporation status altogether.[95] Under BCL, it would take a two-thirds vote to exit.[96] This makes it difficult for

---

[90] *See, e.g.*, J. Haskell Murray, *Shareholder Representatives for Social Enterprise, in* CHSEL, *supra* note 2, at 373; *see also* J. Haskell Murray, *Adopting Stakeholder Advisory Boards*, 54 AM. BUS. L. J. 61 (2017).

[91] For example, if stakeholder representatives in the aggregate make up half of the board, they would need the vote of only one of the other directors to be able to impose their desired policies on the shareholders.

[92] *Cf.* John E. Tyler III, *Essential Policy and Practice Considerations for Facilitating Social Enterprise: Commitment, Connections, Harm, and Accountability, in* CHSEL, *supra* note 2, at 43, 47–48 (discussing the "requisite level of intent that an investor must have to social impact ... for a business to qualify as a social enterprise" in terms of percentages "towards social good" versus "dedication to financial returns").

[93] *See, e.g.*, MINN. STAT. § 304A.301(5) (2020) ("If a public benefit corporation fails to file ... the annual benefit report required by this section, the secretary of state shall revoke the corporation's status as a benefit corporation.").

[94] *See supra* note 76 and accompanying text.

[95] *See, e.g.*, Dana Brakman Reiser, *Benefit Corporations—A Sustainable Form of Organization?*, 46 WAKE FOREST L. REV. 591, 617 (2011) ("[S]hareholders themselves may become biased toward profit goals or be bought out by others seeking financial over social gains.").

[96] *See* Model Legislation §§ 102, 105 (minimum status vote).

profit-maximizing shareholders to prevail, even if they have achieved majority status. However, if lack of compliance with technical procedural requirements could lead to revocation, this would open up a new avenue for wealth-maximizing shareholders to take over benefit corporations. Such shareholders could obtain control and purposefully fail to live up to the procedural requirements, thereby causing the revocation and reversion to business corporation status.[97] It is unlikely that this would be a desirable result. Thus, although the state may have an interest in compliance with minimal requirements, revocation for lack of compliance is probably not the best way for the state to vindicate its interest.[98]

VI REMAINING PROBLEMS

For many, the shareholder primacy view of benefit corporations will be disappointing. This is especially true for those whose primary concern is not empowering shareholders to be altruistic, but rather protecting other stakeholders from the harm that may be caused by businesses. For those who prefer a mandatory regime, a shareholder primacy view is necessarily unsatisfactory. However, even those who embrace the shareholder primacy view might have some legitimate concerns.

A non-mandatory approach does make it more difficult for benefit corporations to make credible commitments to social enterprise. A strong mandatory regime would make it easy for investors to identify sincere altruists: any business that incorporates under BCL would either be sincere or at least would be required to act as if it were sincere. The form of the benefit corporation would be all that interested parties, including both investors and consumers, would need to know in order to have assurance about the sincerity of the company's commitment.

With a non-mandatory enabling approach, the form is not sufficient to assure anyone of the company's altruistic bona fides. With no legal minimum standards for the level of altruism and an uncertain disclosure system, assessing a benefit corporation's sincerity will require a closer examination of individual companies. Because the investigation is not costless, the public will not be entirely informed. This will make it easier for traditional businesses to masquerade as legitimate social enterprises. Greenwashing will become easier, and therefore likely more prevalent. Moreover, as a direct result, it will be more difficult for legitimate social enterprises to make credible commitments to altruism. Even with perfect disclosure on their part, such businesses will face an audience that will not necessarily bother to digest the disclosure, and not necessarily trust the disclosure if they do read it. Although the exact magnitude of the issue is difficult to gauge, this is an unfortunate side effect of shareholder primacy.

Moreover, there may be less overall public benefit from an enabling model than a mandatory model. This would be because companies would be free to choose smaller commitments. In fact, it could be argued that allowing companies to give less might cause those that would otherwise give more also to give less.[99] By contrast, a mandatory model would force companies to do more than they otherwise might. This could increase the aggregate social benefit.

---

[97] See Murray, *supra* note 86, at 47–48 ("Using the loss of benefit corporation status ... may be unwise, as benefit corporations unsatisfied with the form may try to use not filing a report to convert to a traditional corporation without having to obtain the super-majority shareholder approval generally required.").

[98] Some other penalty, such as a fine or tax, may be more appropriate. However, a draconian penalty likely would scare away potential investors, while a moderate penalty may be ineffective.

[99] See, *e.g.*, Page, *supra* note 633, at 430 (discussing consequences of India's 2013 Companies Act contribution requirement: "Companies that previously contributed a higher percentage to corporate social responsibility projects have reduced their level of contributions to no more than the mandated 2% baseline.").

However, this is by no means certain. It is also quite possible that the enabling model would lead to a greater aggregate benefit than the mandatory model. This would be because it would not exclude companies unwilling to make the minimum mandatory commitment. A greater number of smaller donors could very well lead to a greater aggregate good than a smaller number of larger donors. Ultimately, which model would lead to the greater aggregate benefit is an empirical question for which there are, as yet, no clear answers.

In all likelihood, it would depend on the level of the minimum commitment. To the extent that it is too high, a mandatory requirement would exclude many participants. To the extent that it is too low, it might encourage those who would be willing to do more not to bother. The benefit-maximizing strategy would be to set the minimum level at a level that is high enough to ensure real benefits, but not so high as to exceed companies' willingness to contribute. This would not be an easy figure to calculate in advance.

Moreover, even if the mandatory model would lead to a greater aggregate social benefit, it would almost certainly also lead to less overall engagement in social enterprise. Only those companies that are willing to make the minimum investment would become benefit corporations. All others would remain business corporations and thus have less incentive, and perhaps less ability, to engage in altruism. Presumably, it would be good, both in itself and for long-term benefit maximization, to encourage widespread engagement in social enterprise rather than keep it cabined among the most serious altruists. If so, an enabling approach has a lot to offer that a mandatory approach does not.

Also, the mandatory approach would be unfair on two levels. First, it would be unfair to existing benefit corporations to change the rules of the game in mid-stream.[100] Companies elected benefit corporation status with the understanding that this would enable them to be altruistic. It would be unfair to require them now to do more than they anticipated. The unfairness is exacerbated because it would take a supermajority vote to exit benefit corporation status. This would allow a minority of shareholders to hold the others captive.

Secondly, it might be problematic on a broader level. Corporations are owned by shareholders. They are permitted to pursue their own interests, and arguably required to maximize their wealth creation. Benefit corporations are also owned by shareholders. The shareholders voluntarily choose the form to escape the structures of wealth maximization and pursue their holistic interests, including altruism. Such choices are admirable and ought to be encouraged. But forcing such shareholders to do more than they would like is anything but encouraging. To force shareholders to choose between greater-than-desired sacrifice or nothing seems a heavy-handed way of maximizing societal benefit. Moreover, to the extent that minimum requirements can be characterized as a way to mulct altruistic shareholders, it seems positively objectionable. As a normative matter, benefit corporation status, which is inherently voluntary, should remain essentially and not merely technically voluntary.

VII CONCLUSION

As I have sought to demonstrate, BCL is shareholder-centric. It seeks to eliminate the shareholder wealth maximization norm but does not seek to eliminate shareholder primacy. On the contrary, the elimination of the shareholder wealth maximization norm is in service of

---

[100] *Cf.* Elhauge, *supra* note 244, at 860 ("Such a midstream amendment would presumably be in the interests of the majority of shareholders who approved it, but it would expropriate the investment of other shareholders, who invested based on the default rule that allows only a limited degree of profit-sacrificing.").

shareholder primacy: it intends to empower altruistic shareholders to engage in social enterprise, which might be difficult under traditional corporate law.

As a result, I also have argued that an enabling view of BCL is more appropriate than a mandatory view. Given that BCL is itself entirely voluntary, it would seem incongruous for its provisions to have a mandatory flavor. To be sure, it may be appropriate to have some mandatory provisions; but if BCL is to be successful, even mandatory provisions ought to be designed to appeal to the shareholders. Thus, for example, mandatory disclosure intended to allow altruistic shareholders and entrepreneurs to signal credible commitments to social enterprise would be on much sounder footing than would be mandatory commitment levels or mandatory consideration provisions that have the effect of benefiting other stakeholders at the expense of shareholders. BCL is much more likely to be successful if considered empowering than if it is considered confiscatory.

The enabling view may be considered disappointing for some, especially for progressive corporate law scholars hoping for a more society-centric form of business association. However, it should be seen as a modest success. Although BCL may not achieve all that they desire, it does significantly advance their policy goals. It enables greater altruism than seems to be permitted under traditional corporate law. Thus, current law can be seen as a first step: if an enabling version of BCL is successful, it may be possible to experiment with a more mandatory version in the future. If it has only modest success, then a mandatory version would be unsustainable. By contrast, starting with a heavy-handed mandatory approach would risk strangling the idea of BCL in its infancy.

Whether or not progressive scholars agree, legislatures and courts should resist the temptation to go too far too fast. They should acknowledge the shareholder-centric roots of BCL, stick with the enabling view, and empower shareholders to use the benefit corporation form to engage in social enterprise to the extent they are interested in doing so. If consumers are truly interested, they will reward this sort of behavior and we can expect the benefit corporation form to flourish. If consumers are not as enthusiastic as expected, we can still allow altruistic shareholders to pursue their interests holistically, and not force them into the mold of shareholder economicus.

18

Self-Interested Fiduciaries and Invulnerable Beneficiaries: When Fiduciary Duties Do Not Fit

Kelli Alces Williams[*]

I INTRODUCTION

It is easy to see why the corporate governance bargain, one in which directors and managers operate a business on behalf of its owners, was a fiduciary one *ab initio*. The governance mechanism anticipated knowledgeable managers making business decisions on behalf of passive owners. When there were fewer businesses to invest in, shareholders might risk a substantial portion of their individual capital in investments in corporations managed by others. Even as corporations were first publicly traded, the small numbers meant limited opportunities for diversification and mechanisms for disclosure and consumption of information were slower and less reliable than they are now. In the unruly days before securities regulation, corporate shareholders were fending for themselves, truly entrusting their wealth to the loyalty and good faith of others.

The modern public corporation is a different beast than the corporations envisioned by the drafters of Delaware corporate law, and the governance paradigm has shifted significantly. Investor reliance on fiduciary obligation and selfless corporate decision-making has become fiction. While the expressive function of that legal fiction may provide some benefits, such as encouraging a culture of integrity among corporate directors, believing that the legal fiction is a reality around which all corporate governance law is built is quite harmful. The governance of public corporations simply does not fit within the fiduciary paradigm any longer.

Theoretical definitions of fiduciary relationships abound, but there are a few points of agreement among the differing camps. A fiduciary is responsible for acting on behalf of or for the benefit of another, the beneficiary. The fiduciary is expected to pursue the beneficiary's best interests and not prioritize self-interests or third-party interests above the beneficiary's interest. There is a consensus among scholars that a fiduciary relationship exists when the beneficiary is vulnerable to the fiduciary or the fiduciary's discretion, when one party has placed trust or confidence in another to work on their behalf, for their benefit, and never to their detriment.[1] I'll refer to the doctrine defined by these points of agreement as the "fiduciary model."

[*] I am grateful to the participants in the workshop for this volume at Rutgers Law School for helpful comments on this chapter. Arthur Laby and Jacob Hale Russell did a wonderful job organizing the workshop and gave tremendously valuable feedback on the draft. Particular thanks are also due to Richard Brooks, Jennifer Hill, Christine Hurt, Lyman Johnson, Christoph Kumpman, Arthur Laby, Amir Licht, Masayuki Tamaruya, Paul Miller, Asaf Raz, Steven Schwarcz, Andrew Tuch, and Julian Velasco. Sara Finnigan and Alexander Purpuro provided excellent research assistance.
[1] *See, e.g., In re* Walt Disney Co. Derivative Litig., 907 A.2d 693, 697–98 (Del. Ch. 2005), *aff'd*, 906 A.2d 27 (Del. 2006) ("Fiduciaries who act faithfully and honestly on behalf of those whose interests they represent are indeed granted wide latitude in their efforts to maximize shareholders' investment."); Meinhard v. Salmon, 249 N.Y. 458, 164 N.E. 545, 546

Operating a modern public corporation is not a fiduciary enterprise. In monitoring senior officers, directors are relatively inattentive and protected by the business judgment rule and, in many cases, by contractually-elected exculpation from breach of the duty of care from an obligation to be more attentive. Senior officers make important decisions about corporate strategy and priorities, and directors are rarely called upon to second guess those decisions or change the firm's course. Senior officers are employees, and so are fiduciaries of the corporation within the scope of their employment, but in their decision-making for the firm, they are not bound to consider or represent any particular interest.

The conventional answer to that problem is that officers and directors represent and pursue the interests of the corporate entity. Because a corporation is an inanimate entity, pursuing the corporation's interest is only meaningfully termed a fiduciary obligation if officers and directors are limited in how they can define that interest. In order to act in a fiduciary capacity, officers and directors must act as fiduciaries when deciding what the corporate interest is, meaning, they must be selfless in defining that interest. In this chapter, I explain how and why they do not and cannot act as fiduciaries in choosing the corporate path and, therefore, why fiduciary doctrine does not describe decision-making in large, public corporations. To be sure, there are limited instances where directors act as fiduciaries when performing discrete tasks, such as negotiating a corporate takeover.[2] But when it comes to the bulk of corporate decision-making and defining corporate business, they do not act as fiduciaries because they are not acting on behalf of a well-defined beneficiary and are not selfless in defining what the corporate interest is or how it will be pursued. There is no fiduciary duty that binds directors in the discretion they exercise on behalf of the owners of the assets they control, save for minimal, specific exceptions that are narrowly defined and limited in duration.

One might say that corporate fiduciary duties simply mandate that managers not be conflicted without permission. This proscription absolves them from choosing any one corporate interest to represent.[3] Directors may make whatever decisions they like as long as they are not helping themselves at the expense of the corporation.[4] This might seem like a limited, but important, role for fiduciary duties, but it so distills fiduciary obligation that it

---

(1928) (describing the fiduciary duties that owners of closely held businesses owe each other); Stephen M. Bainbridge, *Must Salmon Love Meinhard? Agape and Partnership Fiduciary Duties*, 17 GREEN BAG 2d 257 (2014) (analyzing trust in the context of partnership fiduciary duties); Deborah A. DeMott, *Beyond Metaphor: An Analysis of Fiduciary Obligation*, 1988 DUKE L. J. 879, 882–83 (describing the general principles of fiduciary obligation as obliging the fiduciary to further the beneficiary's best interests); Tamar Frankel, *Fiduciary Law*, 71 CAL. L. REV. 795, 800 (1983) (describing the fiduciary relation as one where the entrustor is dependent upon the fiduciary); Andrew S. Gold, *On the Elimination of Fiduciary Duties: A Theory of Good Faith for Unincorporated Firms*, 41 WAKE FOREST L. REV. 123, 134–35 (2006) ("Fiduciary duties … preclud[e] managers from acting in their own interest in place of the interests of the business entity.") (alteration in original) (citation omitted); Arthur B. Laby, *The Fiduciary Obligation as the Adoption of Ends*, 56 BUFF. L. REV. 99, 131–33 (2008) (noting the fiduciary has power over the principal yet must act for the principal's benefit); Larry E. Ribstein, *Are Partners Fiduciaries?*, 2005 U. ILL. L. REV. 209, 215 (describing the relationship where an "owner" derives benefit from property and delegates management power to a "manager" as the "paradigm"); D. Gordon Smith, *The Critical Resource Theory of Fiduciary Duty*, 55 VAND. L. REV. 1399, 1400 (2002) (noting that courts impose fiduciary obligations where one person trusts the other and becomes vulnerable as a result).

2 *See infra* notes 43–45 and accompanying text.

3 Amir Licht proposes that directors adhere to a duty of impartiality, which would require them to give "due regard" to the interests of all stakeholders in making corporate decisions. Amir N. Licht, *Shareholder Impartiality: A New Classic Approach for the Objectives of the Corporation*, ch. 16 (this volume). Under a duty of impartiality, directors would be prohibited from preferring the interests of any one stakeholder above others.

4 Edward B. Rock reports that Samuel Arsht "is said to have proposed that the law be simplified to the following principle: Directors of Delaware corporations can do anything they want, as long as it is not illegal and as long as they act in good faith." Edward B. Rock, *Saints and Sinners: How Does Delaware Corporate Law Work?*, 44 UCLA L. REV. 1009, 1015 (1997).

discards the most valuable aspects of the equitable remedy: the ability to respond flexibly to unanticipated betrayals and complex conflicts. Instead, corporate managers are pulled and guided in many directions by regulation, their incentives, and market forces and left to navigate a best personal career path rather than a course that honors particular corporate, shareholder, or stakeholder interests or preferences. Blame the anemic state of corporate fiduciary duties on the business judgment rule, the decline of the duty of care, the complexity of the businesses of large, public corporations, market demands, and political culture, among others; whatever the principle that guides corporate managers and their accountability to a firm, it is not fiduciary.

Continuing to identify the governance relationships as fiduciary when they are not is a problem because the legal fiction has become so mythologized that it appears to be the central, defining piece of corporate governance law. As such, investors are encouraged to take great solace in the managerial integrity fiduciary duties are supposed to inspire. Indeed, I suspect scholars, shareholders, legislators, judges, and even directors are loathe to admit corporate governance has moved beyond fiduciary obligation because to do so would imply that directors could use the corporation as a personal bank account or use their power to pursue personal wealth maximization. Stealing is prohibited by mechanisms other than fiduciary duty. Even non-fiduciaries may not steal. Far from clearing a path for corporate corruption, acknowledging the truth of corporate governance will simply allow those exposed to the externalities of poor or improvident management to better protect themselves and hold managers to account. Rather than basking in a false sense of security promised by high fiduciary rhetoric, the law and those it seeks to protect will be able to respond pragmatically to how corporate officers and directors actually make decisions and prevent the ways they are most likely to cause harm.[5]

In this chapter, I argue that corporate governance relationships are not properly characterized as fiduciary in nature. Continuing to try to paint these relationships as fiduciary has resulted in a mangled understanding of corporate governance and fiduciary doctrine itself. The second section describes the fiduciary model and explains how its general principles have been applied to corporate governance. The third section reveals that corporate fiduciary law omits too many crucial elements of the fiduciary model to accurately describe a fiduciary relationship between a corporation and its managers. The fourth section explains the role of the prohibition against managerial self-dealing and how that prohibition may constitute a fiduciary duty of loyalty in some, but not all, governance situations.

II THE FIDUCIARY MODEL

The competing conceptions of fiduciary obligation have been described in various ways. As in many debates about legal doctrine and theory, one side presents a deontological view and the other, a utilitarian one. These camps are known as "anti-contractarian" and "contractarian," respectively, or "moralist" and "amoralist." On the contractarian side, Larry Ribstein and Gordon Smith have argued that a fiduciary duty exists when one party exercises open-ended discretion over the business or affairs of another.[6] Frank Easterbrook and Daniel Fischel believe that fiduciary relationships are contractual relationships with many important instructions and

---

[5]   *See* Paul B. Miller, *Equity, Majoritarian Governance, and the Oppression Remedy*, ch. 9 (this volume) ("Fiduciary duties are not an all-purpose salve for any sharp or opportunistic behavior. Fiduciary law has a narrower remit.").

[6]   Easterbrook and Fischel describe a continuum with non-fiduciary contracts on one end and fiduciary relationships on another, with the "size" of the gaps in the contract growing larger. Frank H. Easterbrook & Daniel R. Fischel,

terms left undefined.[7] These large "gaps" must be filled with an understanding that the fiduciary will complete the required tasks by pursuing the beneficiary's best interests instead of her own.[8] The contractarians agree that a fiduciary is obliged to pursue the best interests of the beneficiary and eschew conflicts of interest in circumstances defined by the beneficiary's relative vulnerability to the fiduciary's discretion.[9]

Anti-contractarians agree that fiduciary relationships arise when one party is vulnerable to the judgment or discretion of another and that the fiduciary is required to pursue the best interests of the beneficiary.[10] Differing in the business context, however, anti-contractarians believe that fiduciary obligation is fundamentally different from other obligations and fiduciary relationships are not merely contractual. Fiduciaries are supposed to zealously pursue the best interests of a beneficiary with a faithfulness that goes beyond merely avoiding conflicted financial interests. Anti-contractarians hold that we could not specifically define what loyalty would mean in each individual circumstance, rather, courts must be left with the equitable discretion to call a breach of loyalty when they see it, based on the facts before them.[11] This flexibility rightfully defines fiduciary relationships and doctrine. Anti-contractarians also believe that fiduciary loyalty is akin to interpersonal loyalty, a devotion to the health, happiness, and welfare of the beneficiary.[12]

On the contrary, contractarians are more likely to subscribe to the view that corporate directors can do anything legal as long as they act in good faith.[13] That is, as long as they are not actively trying to harm the corporation or take advantage or profit from it for personal benefit, they fulfill their fiduciary obligation.[14] Contractarians are skeptical of expanding the definition of the duty of loyalty beyond a prohibition of explicit self-dealing.[15] Both sides agree that corporate directors are fiduciaries.

In this chapter, I will challenge that conclusion. As a descriptive matter, I will argue that the officers and directors of large, public corporations do not act as fiduciaries of the corporation or its shareholders, with limited exceptions. As a normative matter, I argue that the developments away from fiduciary status are appropriate and do not leave corporate managers unaccountable to investors.

Contract and Fiduciary Duty, 36 J. L. & ECON. 425 (1993); Ribstein, *supra* note 1, at 217; Smith, *supra* note 1, at 1402–03.

[7] Easterbrook & Fischel, *supra* note 6, at 425.

[8] *Id.* at 439–40.

[9] *See, e.g.*, Ribstein, *supra* note 1, at 232 (noting that "fiduciaries consent to forego self-interest"); Smith, *supra* note 1, at 1410 (distinguishing between contracting parties and fiduciaries; noting that the fiduciary must refrain from self-interested behavior that wrongs the beneficiary, whereas contracting parties may engage in self-interested behavior if contemplated by the contract).

[10] *See, e.g.*, DeMott, *supra* note 1, at 902–03; Frankel, *supra* note 1, at 800–01.

[11] Andrew S. Gold, *The New Concept of Loyalty in Corporate Law*, 43 U. C. DAVIS L. REV. 457, 498–503 (2009) (describing different standards of review courts could apply to the duty of loyalty); Arthur B. Laby, *Resolving Conflicts of Duty in Fiduciary Relationships*, 54 AM. U. L. REV. 75 (2004) (noting courts' discretion in applying the duty of loyalty).

[12] *See* Gold, *supra* note 11, at 489 (citing Lyman Johnson, *After Enron: Remembering Loyalty Discourse in Corporate Law*, 28 DEL. J. CORP. L. 27 (2003)); *see also* Stephen R. Galoob & Ethan J. Leib, *Fiduciary Loyalty, Inside and Out*, 92 S. CAL. L. REV. 70, 73–77 (2018) (discussing the moralist position on fiduciary loyalty).

[13] Rock, *supra* note 4, at 1015.

[14] Ribstein, *supra* note 1, at 225; Stephen M. Bainbridge, *Director Primacy: The Means and Ends of Corporate Governance*, 97 NW. U. L. REV. 547 (2003); Smith, *supra* note 1.; Kelli A. Alces, *The Fiduciary Gap*, 40 IOWA J. CORP. L. 351, 393 (2015).

[15] *See generally* D. Gordon Smith, *Contractually Adopted Fiduciary Duty*, 2014 U. ILL. L. REV. 1783.

III WHY THE GOVERNANCE OF A LARGE CORPORATION IS NOT FIDUCIARY

As currently constituted, there are three reasons the officers and directors of large corporations[16] are not fiduciaries of shareholders or the corporation itself. First, managers[17] do not have a sense of the best interests of a beneficiary. Pursuing profit or a corporate strategy is not the same as studying, internalizing, or adopting the ends or interests of another, even if that interest is as broad as "long-term wealth maximization." The shareholder interests served by corporate officers and directors are varied and complex. Even attentive shareholders who actively participate in management might have differing views about how a given corporation should be managed. Officers and directors are responsible for considering the interests of various constituencies and deciding what is "best" for the corporation. That directive is meaningless, though, unless there is some indication of how they are supposed to make those decisions.

Second, corporate managers are expected to carefully consider and follow their own interests in exactly the sorts of situations where fiduciary theory would dictate that they eschew self-interest. Incentive compensation and personal professional reputation guide managers when making important business decisions for the corporation. A manager's personal interest is easier to identify and guide than a monolithic "shareholder interest" or a sense of corporate best interest, particularly when calibrating corporate decisions to a risk preference. Indeed, most executive compensation is designed to change a managers' corporate decision-making, assuming that the manager will make decisions favoring their personal financial interests. Modern executive compensation does not reflect an attempt to align the interests of a fiduciary with a single, identifiable beneficiary, as fiduciary doctrine would ordinarily allow and encourage.[18]

Third, shareholders of large, public corporations are not *vulnerable* to the decisions of corporate managers, at least not uniquely so. Such shareholders should be and usually are, well-diversified. The fact that shareholders do not directly make corporate business decisions does not, by itself, make them the beneficiaries of fiduciary duties. Consumers of corporate products also do not make decisions about how those products function, how well or poorly they are made, what they cost, or how widely available they are. They stand to be injured by mistakes in corporate management and from managers' decisions that favor personal advantage over consumer welfare, but that vulnerability does not make them beneficiaries of a fiduciary relationship in the eyes of the law. Powerlessness over the decision-making of others and standing to lose some amount financially as a consequence are necessary, but not sufficient, components of the kind of vulnerability fiduciary duty protects.

---

[16] This argument does not necessarily apply to limited liability companies or limited partnerships, particularly where passive investors invest large sums of money for long periods. As the vulnerability of investors increases, so does the need for fiduciary obligations. Managers of such firms are unlikely to attract investors if they do not agree to hold the interests of those investors paramount.

[17] In this chapter, I consider officers and directors together as "managers." While their roles differ, as do the extent to which they are held responsible for breaches of fiduciary duty by the law, my focus is on corporate decision-making. To that end, corporate officers and directors both decide what is in the corporate best interest and make vital business decisions for the firm. Because it is that exercise of discretion on behalf of the corporation that I am interested in, I can consider the two groups together for the purposes of my theory. *But see* Lyman Johnson, *The Three Fiduciaries of Delaware Corporate Law — and Eisenberg's Error*, ch. 3 (this volume) (explaining potential pitfalls and inaccuracies of lumping officers and directors together when discussing fiduciary duties).

[18] John H. Langbein has advocated allowing conflicted interests that benefit the beneficiary or align the fiduciary's interests with those of the beneficiary in trust law. John H. Langbein, *Questioning the Trust Law Duty of Loyalty: Sole Interest or Best Interest?*, 114 Yale L. J. 929, 933–34 (2005). Indeed, only *conflicted* self-interest is prohibited by corporate fiduciary doctrine.

A *The Interests of the Beneficiary*

Fiduciary theorists generally agree that a fiduciary must exercise discretion in pursuit of the beneficiary's best interests. To do so, the fiduciary must understand the beneficiary's best interests, and, to the extent best interests and preferences diverge, understand that tension and how to resolve it. While means may be left to a fiduciary's discretion, the ends are not. In business organizations, managers are bound to pursue the wealth maximization of the firm, but the means by which they do so are left to their sole discretion under the business judgment rule.[19] In reality, those ends and means can be blurred—outcomes are uncertain and complicated, and a variety of corporate leaders can make individual decisions that affect those outcomes. A number of paths may lead to wealth maximization but operate on different timeframes and entail different degrees of risk.

The task of balancing risk preferences offers a prime example of how corporate officers and directors are not necessarily bound to pursue a beneficiary's favored interest in their management of a corporation. The riskiness of a business strategy has a direct bearing on its expected return and the potential variance of the outcome of the strategy from that return. Different strategies carry different degrees of risk, and the ultimate decision is a choice about the appropriate degree of risk to take. The riskiness of choice made by a fiduciary must align with the beneficiary's risk preference.[20]

A variety of risk preferences influence corporate decision-making. Well-diversified shareholders would rather individual corporations take more risk than the senior executives of that corporation would prefer.[21] Long-term shareholders would rather the firm take less risk than short-term investors would. Short-term investors often include hedge funds and other private equity firms that might actively lobby and monitor management. Creditors would prefer that the firm avoid risk altogether. While creditors of a solvent firm are not the beneficiaries of fiduciary duties, they can exert pressure on companies through rights reserved in loan agreements and their power over the availability of capital allows them to influence corporate decision-making.[22]

These decisions about risk are often described as falling within the business judgment rule. However, that characterization is further evidence that corporate managers are not fiduciaries: after all, calibrating risk is fundamental to a beneficiary's interests and preferences, not a matter that should be subject to such wide discretion. They represent the very end a fiduciary is required to pursue. A choice among several different strategies that represent the same approximate risk profile would fall within the business judgment rule, but attempts at wealth maximization that significantly depart from a given risk preference cannot honor the preferences of a given set of investors or the imagined preferences of a given "corporation." The differences in expected return and variance are too great.

---

[19] *See, e.g.*, Stephen M. Bainbridge, *The Business Judgment Rule as Abstention Doctrine*, 57 VAND. L. REV. 83, 87 (2004) ("[T]he [business judgment] rule is ... a doctrine of abstention pursuant to which courts in fact refrain from reviewing board decisions unless exacting preconditions for review are satisfied.") (alteration in original).

[20] John H. Langbein, *The Contractarian Basis of the Law of Trusts*, 105 YALE L. J. 625 (1995); Robert H. Sitkoff, *An Agency Costs Theory of Trust Law*, 89 CORNELL L. REV. 621, 654–56 (2004) (discussing the disparities in risk tolerance between beneficiaries and fiduciaries in the context of trusts).

[21] The shareholders have diversified firm-specific risk while a company's executives have invested their time, livelihood, and reputation in the one firm. For a description of the connection between incentive pay and shareholder interests, *see* Michael C. Jensen & William H. Meckling, *Theory of the Firm: Managerial Behavior, Agency Costs and Ownership Structure*, 3 J. FIN. ECON. 305, 353 (1976); Michael C. Jensen & Kevin Murphy, *Performance Pay and Top Manager Incentives*, 98 J. POL. ECON. 225, 242–53 (1990).

[22] *See* Kelli A. Alces, *Strategic Governance*, 50 ARIZ. L. REV. 1053, 1054–59 (2008) (describing the power of creditors in the context of insolvent corporations).

In addition to the varying interests of different shareholders and creditors, corporate managers are also expected to consider the interests of other constituents in making corporate decisions. Employees, consumers, and the communities in which corporations operate make demands on corporate resources and managers' decision-making priorities. Recently, the Business Roundtable has acknowledged the demands of these other constituents and restated the purpose of corporate governance. In the past, the Business Roundtable said that the purpose of corporations is to "serve shareholders." Now, it has announced that the managers of corporations must deliver value to customers, invest in employees, deal fairly with suppliers, "support the communities in which we work," *and* "generat[e] long-term value to shareholders."[23] Almost no one takes the Business Roundtable at its word here. The consensus seems to be that the group is engaged in reputation management in light of the current popularity of populism and the persistent image of corporations and corporate executives as the evil boogeymen of our society. Still, the strategy is interesting. It is quite bold for supposed fiduciaries to tell their beneficiaries what the purpose of their engagement is and even bolder for the fiduciaries to tell their beneficiary that they are no longer solely pursuing the beneficiary's interest when it conflicts with other priorities. If different risk preferences among shareholders pull a corporate manager in too many directions for the manager to be properly considered a fiduciary, adding societal interests to the mix would certainly undermine any claim that corporate managers serve any one beneficiary, particularly as these interests can directly conflict with a goal of shareholder wealth maximization.

In addressing similar concerns about their argument that governments are fiduciary, Evan Criddle and Evan Fox-Decent argue that fiduciaries whose decisions can have significant societal impacts owe "'first-order duties' to the beneficiary" and "'second-order duties' to the broader public or public purposes."[24] Indeed, they argue, "some fiduciary relationships *always* entail multiple commitments."[25] To be sure, corporate managers have always been bound to follow the law when pursuing the goal of shareholder wealth maximization and regulations have confined corporations in dealing with employees and consumers and limit their impacts on the environment. In the examples of second-order duties that Criddle and Fox-Decent offer, fiduciaries are bound not to harm society directly, lawyers must protect the integrity of the judicial system or doctors must protect the public health.[26] They must obey positive law, that is, and part of doing so is having the judgment to know when society-protecting positive law applies.

A command to avoid that which is illegal and do what the law requires is hardly exercising fiduciary judgment in society's favor. It is simply observing the limits the law has placed on the beneficiary's objectives. I would argue that the "second-order duties" Criddle and Fox-Decent recognize are not fiduciary in nature. For that reason, second-order duties do not explain what a putative fiduciary is doing when they balance directly conflicting interests, and the law does not tell them what to do. If the Business Roundtable leaders are serious about investing in employees at the expense of the bottom line, then they are not fiduciaries to a single beneficiary interest. They are noble, and to the extent they succeed in promoting the survival and well-being of their businesses and the world, they deserve high praise, but they are not *fiduciaries*. A *fiduciary* cannot be *loyal* to conflicting interests simultaneously. If the Business Roundtable

23 Bus. Roundtable, Statement on the Purpose of a Corporation (2019), https://opportunity.businessroundtable.org/wp-content/uploads/2019/08/BRT-Statement-on-the-Purpose-of-a-Corporation-with-Signatures.pdf.
24 Evan J. Criddle & Evan Fox-Decent, *Guardians of Legal Order, in* Fiduciary Government 67 (Evan J. Criddle et al., eds., 2018).
25 *Id.* at 82.
26 *Id.*

is disingenuous, as many suspect, then it is revealing a conflict between corporate managers who aim only to maximize the firm's profit and managers who are willing to moderate their pursuit of profits with considerations of societal interests. The fact that both kinds of managers prosper is evidence that whatever fiduciary obligations managers have do not constrain how they make decisions for the firm, at least beyond a command that they refrain from stealing from the company or otherwise acting in bad faith.

The most corporate fiduciary law can do in monitoring strategic decisions about a corporation's business operations is to tell the managers not to be conflicted without permission. I have argued in prior work that a weak duty of care and generous business judgment rule prevent corporate fiduciary duties from requiring very much of a corporate manager's loyalties and zealotry in pursuit of a beneficiary's best interests.[27] But more than that, even if a court were willing to demand that corporate managers pursue a beneficiary's best interest, that interest would be so difficult to discover and follow that the very essence of the fiduciary command would be rendered meaningless. If corporate managers are expected, allowed, and encouraged to pursue a corporate mission, supported by strategies of their own choosing and designed for their own personal risk preferences, then it is not a beneficiary's interest they are pursuing. It is their own. And they are not fiduciaries.

B *The Dominant Self-Interest of the Corporate Manager*

Corporate managers cannot pursue the interests of each shareholder faction at once and cannot simultaneously balance shareholder interests with the contractual demands of creditors, employees, and the consumer markets. Attempts to push managers to do so have not come from fiduciary litigation, and answers to such questions are not found in fiduciary rhetoric or expectations, thanks to the business judgment rule. Rather, corporate decision-making is driven, in large part, by executive compensation, market influences, and expectations, and the importance to officers and directors of their careers and the professional reputations that will help them secure their next job.

Executive incentive compensation seeks to align managerial self-interest with the interests of shareholders. Corporate managers have sunk their entire livelihood and professional reputation into the fortunes of the company they are managing. Managers, then, will prefer to take less risk to avoid betting and losing the house.[28] In order to align managers' interests with relatively risk-preferring, well-diversified shareholders, corporations gave officers stock options and incentive pay that rewarded large increases in stock price.

When executive compensation was perceived as having gone too far in making managers risk-takers, the scholarly response was to suggest aligning executive's personal risk preferences with creditors'.[29] Creditors with fixed claims against the corporation, and no right to participate in corporate profits above the amount of their claim, have no interest in maximizing profits and would rather the company be run as conservatively as possible. The hope was that executive compensation packages containing elements of each level of risk preference might align

---

[27] Kelli A. Alces, *Debunking the Corporate Fiduciary Myth*, 35 J. Corp. L. 239, 250–52 (2009).

[28] David I. Walker, *The Law and Economics of Executive Compensation: Theory and Evidence, in* Research Handbook on the Economics of Corporate Law 232 (Claire Hill & Brett McDonell eds., 2011); Lucian Arye Bebchuk et al., *Managerial Power and Rent Extraction in the Design of Executive Compensation*, 69 U. Chi. L. Rev. 751, 762 (2002).

[29] Frederick Tung & Xue Wang, *Bank CEOs, Inside Debt Compensation, and the Global Financial Crisis* 2, 4 (Bos. Univ. Sch. of Law, Working Paper No. 11–49, 2011), http://papers.ssrn.com/sol3/papers.cfm?abstract_id=1570161.

managerial self-interest with the interest of the corporation. Whether such compensation techniques would be effective in aligning those interests is beyond the scope of this paper.[30]

The important point here is that the governance focus is on manipulating the manager's self-interest rather than expecting managers to put personal financial interest aside in order to pursue the interests of a beneficiary. Aligning a fiduciary's interest with a beneficiary to inspire trust is a common and effective strategy in traditional fiduciary relationships. Using the fiduciary's incentives to define the beneficiary's interest and guide the fiduciary's behavior moves the fiduciary's self-interest to the center of the relationship. A corporate manager does not learn the beneficiary's interest through communication with or detailed knowledge of the beneficiary. Rather, the manager's objectives are communicated to him through his personal motivations and incentives, as enforced by executive compensation, the interpersonal dynamics of a board, or his professional reputation. To be sure, corporate officers and directors may not steal corporate funds or direct corporate funds or business to themselves, friends, or family (without permission), but it is hard to think of an instance in which a corporate manager makes a decision that is deemed to be in the best interest of the corporation that does not also confer a personal benefit upon that manager. The dominance of self-interest here is not malicious or even disloyal. Rather, the interest of the relevant beneficiary is simply too difficult to identify beyond the clues left by executive compensation.

I have argued here that executive compensation has gone too far, that it moved from supplementing fiduciary duty and aligning interests to dominating managers' motives and decision-making. One might ask if that error indicates a willingness to change the fiduciary nature of the relationship or if it is simply an overcorrection that fiduciary concerns might motivate us to walk back. My position in this chapter is that the conventional wisdom is that officers and directors are fiduciaries, and the received wisdom is misguided. That would mean that, while directors and those designing executive compensation did not mean to negate fiduciary duties, they nevertheless have. The ground has shifted over time, and each element I am raising here contributes to a change in the corporate governance relationships, rendering them no longer fiduciary.

Another problem that has troubled corporate law scholars, particularly in the last twenty years, is that corporate decision-making may be influenced more by the squeakiest wheel than by any discerned judgment that something is in the corporate best interest.[31] Activist shareholders, hedge funds, traders with short-term timeframes, securities analysts, and those who follow their expectations and recommendations closely may exert more direct influence on managerial decision-making than a manager's own understanding of how best to guide the corporate ship.[32] Managers note their vulnerability to the demands, trades, and expectations of those investors and analysts and include it in calculating how they will fare by choosing a particular business strategy.

---

[30] Brian Galle and I expressed skepticism on this point in *The False Promise of Risk-Reducing Incentive Pay: Evidence from Executive Pensions and Deferred Compensation*, 38 J. CORP. L. 53 (2012).

[31] *See, e.g.*, Lucian A. Bebchuk, Alon Brav & Wei Jiang, *The Long-Term Effects of Hedge Fund Activism*, 115 COLUM. L. REV. 1085, 1085 (2015) (discussing whether activist hedge funds have detrimental effects on long-term interests of companies and their shareholders); Assaf Hamdani & Sharon Hannes, *The Future of Shareholder Activism*, 99 B.U. L. REV. 971, 974–75 (2019) (arguing the success of activist hedge funds cannot be reconciled with claim that institutional investors have pervasive conflicts of interest that have a substantial market-wide effect); Marcel Kahan & Edward B. Rock, *Hedge Funds in Corporate Governance and Corporate Control*, 155 U. PA. L. REV. 1021, 1022 (2007) (arguing that the value of hedge fund activism outweighs the concerns about conflicts of interests, and additional regulatory intervention is unnecessary).

[32] *See generally* Frederick Tung, *Leverage in the Board Room: The Unsung Influence of Private Lenders in Corporate Governance*, 57 UCLA L. REV. 115 (2009).

There is no way to know for sure what inputs combine, and in which priority when managers make corporate business decisions.[33] It is clear, though, from the ways executive compensation is designed and implemented that we expect and encourage managers to consider their self-interest in making decisions for the firm. We know that they will try to maximize their income, their professional reputation, and minimize the extent to which certain parties can harm them. Commands that a fiduciary advance the beneficiary's best interests and eschew her own simply do not describe corporate governance in large, public corporations.

C *Vulnerability to the Fiduciary's Decision-Making*

A shift away from fiduciary obligation is only a problem if those who invest in corporations are vulnerable to the corporate managers' decision-making. The "beneficiary" in question, the corporation (and its shareholders), must be vulnerable to the fiduciary's discretion. The vulnerability is what necessitates the trust that a fiduciary must only act for the beneficiary's best interest. Vulnerability often exists in relationships that are not fiduciary. There cannot be, however, fiduciary duty without a vulnerable beneficiary.

A central premise of fiduciary doctrine, from either the contractarian or the anti-contractarian position, is that the beneficiary has handed over control of something important to her because she lacks either the time or expertise, or both, to exercise that control herself.[34] The large gaps in the fiduciary contract that Easterbrook and Fischel focus on are there because the beneficiary does not care to monitor the fiduciary carefully and cannot specifically spell out what a fiduciary must do in each instance in which they have to exercise discretion. The beneficiary gives up that discretion only upon receipt of a promise or other assurance that the fiduciary will make the decision that he believes honors the beneficiary's best interests.

But there are a number of common situations in which one party gives someone else the power to make a decision for them that do not implicate fiduciary duties. Consumers delegate control over the safety and quality of the products they purchase to the companies that make them. A consumer may spend far more money for a car than they ever invest in stock, and beyond certain minimum thresholds enforced by the government, they cannot hold anyone liable for a car that is expensive to maintain or generally unreliable. Land Rover is not a fiduciary of its customers, despite the small fortunes it takes for its products. Land Rover's consumers pay thousands to repair the cars above and beyond the tens (or hundreds) of thousands they pay to purchase the vehicles in the first place, putting more money into the performance of the car than an average shareholder has in the performance of the stock of any corporation. Certainly, car companies have figured out how to make cars that operate more reliably than Land Rovers, and I am sure someone could teach Land Rover if it wanted to learn. Its consumers, who bear the substantial cost of that decision, do not have the power to force Land Rover to be more like Toyota; nor do they want to, apparently.[35] No one expects Land Rover to pursue its consumers' best interests because a seller is not a fiduciary of its buyer. Land Rover does not make more reliable cars because it does not have to in order to sell the number of cars it needs to sell.

---

[33] Claire Hill & Richard Painter, *Compromised Fiduciaries: Conflicts of Interest in Government and Business*, 95 MINN. L. REV. 1637, 1647 (2011) ("[B]ecause of the multitude of interests involved, sorting out the legitimate from the illegitimate can be close to impossible.").

[34] *See* Frankel, *supra* note 1, at 808 (noting that a beneficiary may seek a fiduciary because the fiduciary is more of an expert, the beneficiary does not want to perform the duties personally or give up the time to perform the duties).

[35] *See* Steven Symes, *Why People Keep Buying Land Rovers*, WHEELSCENE (Jan. 27, 2016), https://wheelscene.com /buying-land-rovers/.

Vulnerability to decisions beyond their control does not make buyers of Land Rovers beneficiaries of fiduciary duties. And that vulnerability continues after the car is purchased. For the life of a car, the manufacturer can make decisions about upgrades or recalls or the availability of new parts that will affect the experience of a purchaser of that car.

Corporations were originally considered beneficiaries of directors' fiduciary duties because of a structural vulnerability—directors were controlling assets that were not theirs, so of course, they must do so in the interests of another. Because a corporation is inanimate, and it is the directors themselves who are empowered to speak for the corporation, it made doctrinal and practical sense to designate the shareholders the human beneficiaries of directors' duties. It was the shareholders who invested their money in the business that allowed the corporation to buy the assets the directors would manage, and those shareholders would rely on directors' decisions for any hopes they had of realizing a return on those investments. Shareholders simply would not part with their money without knowing that the business would be operating in the interests of realizing the best possible financial return on the money.

But investment in public corporations has changed substantially. The vast majority of corporate equity investors are not vulnerable to the decisions of the managers of any one firm. Many are well-diversified and invest through managed retirement or mutual funds, or indexed funds that track the market generally. Such investors do not know in which corporations they are shareholders and do not find out because they have diversified away firm-specific risk and rely upon securities laws and the market to mitigate systemic risk. More focused shareholders such as activist investors, holding companies, private equity funds, and hedge funds do pressure management to make the decisions they prefer. But because of their sophistication and significant capital, they are hardly vulnerable parties. In some ways, corporate managers and other stakeholders may be more vulnerable to the preferences and power of sophisticated investors than most retail investors are to the decisions of corporate managers.[36] That today's investors are willing to part with their capital in the absence of fiduciary duties is evident in a large and sophisticated derivatives market. Investors holding options on the stock of public corporations are not owed fiduciary duties by the managers of those corporations, but still risk their capital in hopes of a return that relies on the decisions those managers make.

The conventional wisdom holds that fiduciary duties tie managers to the mast, making sure that they do not extract rents from the firms they are supposed to operate for the profit of a group larger than themselves. However, to the extent fiduciary duties achieve that end, it is through the social pressure and signaling they create, rather than by their enforcement through liability.[37] The Delaware courts signal standards for ideal governance through fiduciary rhetoric in their opinions even if those opinions do not impose liability.[38] The signal is sent and received, though,

---

[36] Shlomit Azgad-Tromer, *Corporations and the 99%: Team Production Revisited*, 21 FORDHAM J. CORP. & FIN. L. 163, 176 (2016) (noting the increased role of institutional investors in public companies and that "[m]anagers of public companies start to look at their company through the lens of an activist.") (alternation in original) (citation omitted); David R. Beatty, *How Activist Investors Are Transforming the Role of Public-Company Boards*, MCKINSEY & CO. (Jan. 3, 2017), https://www.mckinsey.com/business-functions/strategy-and-corporate-finance/our-insights/how-activist-investors-are-transforming-the-role-of-public-company-boards [https://perma.cc/U9GG-MB4U].

[37] Rock, *supra* note 4, at 1104 (noting that "public shame" in the corporate context may be sufficient to deter certain behaviors).

[38] *See In re* Walt Disney Co. Derivative Litig., 907 A.2d 693, 697 (Del. Ch. 2005), *aff'd*, 906 A.2d 27 (Del. 2006) ("This Court strongly encourages directors and officers to employ best practices, as those practices are understood at the time a corporate decision is taken. But Delaware law does not ... hold fiduciaries liable for a failure to comply with the aspirational ideal of best practices") (alternation in original) (citation omitted); Brehm v. Eisner, 746 A.2d 244, 256 (Del. 2000) ("[I]deals of good corporate governance practices for boards of directors that go beyond the minimal

and for a variety of reasons, directors, and officers behave themselves most of the time.[39] Culture, incentive compensation, and securities regulation prevent unauthorized self-dealing from becoming a systemic threat.

IV WHAT THE PROHIBITION OF CONFLICTED INTEREST MEANS IN CORPORATE LAW

My argument thus far addresses a minimalist view of corporate fiduciary obligation. Even if we consider the corporate fiduciary duty to be a narrow one, I argue it is still inapt. The anti-contractarian perspective paints a broad picture of the duty of loyalty, arguing that officers and directors owe a devotion to shareholder and corporate interests that is akin to the interpersonal loyalty observed in friendships. Such a notion of loyalty is incompatible with the complex nature of the modern corporation's business. If an officer or director cannot identify one particular interest to advance or one risk preference to adopt, it is impossible to devote themselves to a particular interest above all others. Loyalty is singular. That is the defining characteristic of the fiduciary duty of loyalty and its impracticability in the governance of the modern, public corporation, is why the fiduciary paradigm no longer accurately describes corporate governance.

The contractarian position presents a more difficult challenge to this argument. Contractarians argue that the corporate duty of loyalty simply prohibits officers and directors from engaging in conflicted transactions without the permission of the corporation.[40] Corporate fiduciary duties are narrow because that is how fiduciary principles are most useful in the corporate setting.[41] Indeed, according to the contractarian account, parties are in a fiduciary relationship if they agree to be. Following this argument, I could be correct about my observations in this chapter and wrong that the relationships are not fiduciary in nature.

The first problem with the prohibition of conflicts of interest is that it is disingenuous. The contractual term does not mean that corporate managers can never be conflicted without permission. They are regularly influenced by a variety of factors, including pressure from capital markets, analysts, and particular shareholders. Personal interest in cultivating a career and preparing oneself for the next job can strongly motivate corporate managers and may conflict with whatever corporate interest a court would define as the beneficiary interest in a particular situation. These conflicts can be significant, yet are rarely, if ever, addressed in fiduciary law. Even if we only prohibited financial conflicts, personal financial interests could color a managers' judgment and still not violate the prohibition. The closest the law comes to considering managers' interest in their own employment and employment prospects is in

---

legal requirements of the corporation law are highly desirable ... [b]ut they are not required by the corporation law and do not define standards of liability.") (alternation in original) (citation omitted).

39 Rock, *supra* note 4 (analyzing cases).

40 Guth v. Loft, Inc., 23 Del. Ch. 255, 269, 5 A.2d 503, 510 (1939) ("Corporate officers and directors are not permitted to use their position of trust and confidence to further their private interests."); *In re* Walt Disney Co., No. CIV.A. 15452, 2004 WL 2050138, at *5 n.49 (Del. Ch. Sept. 10, 2004) ("[T]he duty of loyalty ... imposes an affirmative obligation to protect and advance the interests of the corporation and mandates that [a director] absolutely refrain from any conduct that would harm the corporation .... [a] director may not allow his self-interest to jeopardize his unyielding obligations to the corporation and its shareholders."); R. Franklin Balotti & Jesse A. Finkelstein, Delaware Law of Corporations and Business Organizations Statutory Deskbook § 4.16 (2008).

41 I do not mean to ignore the anti-contractarian position that corporate fiduciary duties are much broader here. Again, I am addressing the argument that is most challenging to my position. The claim that the duty of loyalty in corporate law is much broader than I describe has been addressed in the third section of this chapter. But I could be right that corporate managers are largely driven in their decision making by self-interest and that shareholders are not vulnerable and still be wrong that corporate governance is not built on fiduciary obligation if the fiduciary obligation is narrow by design.

regulating defensive responses to hostile takeovers. But even then, the concern is with managers trying to preserve their current job or trying to secure personal side payments (golden parachutes), not that they have more subtle conflicts involving their professional futures. Subtle conflicts can be significant but are impossible to police, so the law does not try.[42] It is more accurate to say that corporate managers cannot be conflicted without permission in a few clearly defined circumstances. That command lacks the trust-building, flexible, capacious nature of fiduciary obligation that can respond to unanticipated problems and allow for the definition of fiduciary obligation as a particular relationship or task unfolds.

Second, when we identify the situations in which we really mean that corporate directors cannot be conflicted without permission (or cannot be conflicted at all), courts issue relatively precise edicts, creating simple, narrow rules. Much of corporate fiduciary jurisprudence in recent years has grown in the mergers and acquisitions context[43] and much of it is the application of the *Revlon* duty.[44] Once it is clear that a corporation will be sold, directors must pursue the highest possible price for their shareholders. They are no longer "guardians of the corporate bastion," and they will not keep their current jobs.[45] They now must turn the reins over to the highest bidder, and their sole obligation is to identify and complete a deal with the highest bidder. This edict does not second guess discretion after the fact; it limits discretion entirely. It defines a precise outcome, leaving managers to evaluate the facts to choose the qualified acquirer, the one offering the most money to shareholders. There is, of course, flexibility in how directors achieve that end. They are expected to use their best efforts and judgment to obtain the best possible outcome for shareholders in the midst of a complicated, dynamic process with a number of potential acquirers with different offerings, whose consequences for shareholders must be well-understood and whose value must be appropriately appraised. Conducting an auction under such circumstances does sound like a fiduciary task.

It is most accurate to say that officers and directors *become* fiduciaries of shareholders when the *Revlon* duty arises. It is at that point at which they are expected to exercise their best judgment and discretion in pursuit of a single beneficiary's interest. Then, managers are to set aside their personal preferences for continued employment or their personal plans for the corporation's business and future in order to pursue the highest price possible for shareholders. At some point, the management team must decide the auction is over and award the corporation to the highest bidder. Finding the moment to end the auction can be difficult and controversial.

---

[42] Hill & Painter, *supra* note 33.

[43] *See, e.g.*, Reith v. Lichtenstein, No. CV 2018–0277-MTZ, 2019 WL 2714065 (Del. Ch. June 28, 2019) (acquiring corporation's stockholder sufficiently alleged that preferred stockholder and directors breached fiduciary duties by causing the acquiring corporation to issue stock cheaply); Ryan v. Armstrong, No. CV 12717-VCG, 2017 WL 2062902 (Del. Ch. May 15, 2017), *aff'd*, 176 A.3d 1274 (Del. 2017) (stockholder pleaded facts supporting a breach of duty of loyalty action against the majority of the board of directors in connection with the cancellation of an acquisition); Chen v. Howard-Anderson, 87 A.3d 648, 693 (Del. Ch. 2014) (analyzing breach of fiduciary duty claims arising out of proposed merger agreement); In re Crimson Expl. Inc. Stockholder Litig., No. CIV.A. 8541-VCP, 2014 WL 5449419 (Del. Ch. Oct. 24, 2014) (class action challenging a stock-for-stock merger alleging breach of fiduciary duties in approving the merger).

[44] RBC Capital Markets, LLC v. Jervis, 129 A.3d 816, 854 (Del. 2015) (finding the board of directors conduct fails *Revlon* enhanced scrutiny); C & J Energy Servs., Inc. v. City of Miami Gen. Employees', 107 A.3d 1049, 1071 (Del. 2014) (finding the court below misapplied *Revlon*); In re Zale Corp. Stockholders Litig., No. CV 9388-VCP, 2015 WL 5853693, at *10 (Del. Ch. Oct. 1, 2015), *opinion amended on reargument*, No. CV 9388-VCP, 2015 WL 6551418 (Del. Ch. Oct. 29, 2015) (applying *Revlon* enhanced scrutiny to a merger consideration of cash paid to the target company's stockholders).

[45] Revlon, Inc. v. MacAndrews & Forbes Holdings, Inc., 506 A.2d 173, 182 (Del. 1986) ("The directors' role changed from defenders of the corporate bastion to auctioneers charged with getting the best price for the stockholders at a sale of the company.").

Though they have one clear interest to pursue, managers must still exercise judgment. And as long as the managers are not indulging interests that conflict with the shareholder interest, they will not be held liable for making business judgments that later turn out to have been suboptimal.

The fiduciary relationship that corporate governance law claims to impose continuously actually only applies in limited situations. In arguing that governments are not fiduciaries, Timothy Endicott argued that "public agencies and officials have many fiduciary duties."[46] The same could be said of corporate officers and directors. They may occasionally have fiduciary duties, but their work to make business decisions on behalf of the corporation cannot be described as fiduciary. Corporate interests are too complex and diverse to overtake the personal managerial interests that the corporate contracts and securities markets make paramount.

V THE EXPRESSIVE FUNCTION OF CORPORATE FIDUCIARY DOCTRINE

Edward Rock has argued that corporate fiduciary duty functions in a way to create a culture of good behavior on the part of corporate managers. The expressive function of fiduciary law alerts corporate managers to what best practices would be, what their priorities should be, and how the corporate community believes they should be running public corporations. In effect, it fulfills the role of a professional association. The National Association of Corporate Directors (NACD) is a friendly, voluntary version of professional associations like the American Medical Association, the American Bar Association, and state attorneys' bars. It provides certification through testing and offers consulting services that evaluate boards' skills and offers recommendations about how they can improve.[47] It also devises statements of best practices and has offered recommendations to regulators about appropriate governance reforms.[48] But membership in the NACD is not compulsory, and neither are its certifications. It does not have the power to punish directors or prevent them from serving on boards. It does the continuing education work of some professional associations but does not perform a disciplinary function. By contrast, a professional association with disciplinary powers could apply reputational penalties for violations of its ethical code and would provide a means to prevent those who are incompetent or unethical from serving on boards or as leaders of public companies. Because the NACD is a voluntary organization, it must sell its vision of good corporate governance to directors. It may not compel or discipline them.

The securities regulations serve a punitive gatekeeping function for those who would serve at the helm of public companies. Those regulations include censure and orders to stop violations and fines for relatively minor violations.[49] Managers guilty of more serious offenses can be suspended or permanently barred from leading public companies.[50] Still more serious offenses can lead to criminal liability.[51] But securities regulations do not reach all corporations and tend to stay out of the day-to-day operation of even the public companies to which they apply.

---

[46] Timothy Endicott, *The Public Trust*, *in* Fiduciary Government 306 (Evan J. Criddle et al. eds., 2018).

[47] NACD Directorship Certification, Nat'l Ass'n of Corp. Dirs., https://certification.nacdonline.org/?_ga=2 .162856251.623507937.1590610094–466197067.1590247523.

[48] *Recommendations from the National Association of Corporate Directors Concerning Reforms in the Aftermath of the Enron Bankruptcy*, Nat'l Ass'n of Corp. Dirs. (May 3, 2002), https://web.archive.org/web/20071025181012/http://www.nacdonline.org/nacd/enron_recommendations.asp.

[49] *See* Securities Exchange Act of 1934 §§ 21, 21B, and 21C, 15 U.S.C. §§ 78u, 78u-2, and 78u-3 (2018).

[50] Securities Exchange Act of 1934 § 21C, 15 U.S.C. § 78u-3 (2018).

[51] Securities Exchange Act of 1934 § 21(d), 15 U.S.C. § 78u(d) (2018).

A compulsory professional association might be useful, but it is not surprising that corporate managers do not have one. Such associations are usually instruments of protectionism, limiting the competition to which the professionals in a given jurisdiction are exposed. No such protectionism is necessary or desirable in corporate governance. Corporations tend to have a variety of people who serve on their boards. One reason is that a corporation's board can help the firm connect to different parts of the communities in which it operates. Making those connections may mean adding board members who are not otherwise businesspeople and who may be in a variety of places.[52] Running professional associations is also expensive. Even if one national association could carry out licensing and discipline for all officers and directors in the country, someone, probably those officers and directors, would have to decide that it is worth the expense. With the SEC and multiple plaintiffs' bars paying attention, officers and directors may not see why they should do more to monitor and punish themselves.

The standards of behavior announced in the dicta of fiduciary cases do much of what a professional association would do. To that end, the rhetoric used by courts and embraced by the corporate bar, scholars, and plaintiffs' attorneys is quite effective, and the role of that ethical voice in governance is, indeed, important and valuable. So, what is the harm? If fiduciary standards keep officers and directors from self-dealing and create useful norms, why does it matter what we call them? Why disabuse ourselves of the illusion of fiduciary loyalty?

Continuing to believe that corporate governance relationships are fiduciary when they are not is a fundamental misunderstanding of the foundation of corporate governance itself. In order to truly protect all of the parties involved effectively, we must understand their rights and powers in relation to one another. To say the relationships are not fiduciary is not to say that managers are free to embezzle from the firm or use its assets for personal benefit to the exclusion of the firm and its investors. It is not to say that they are free to harm the corporation and its shareholders or to otherwise act in bad faith. It is to openly acknowledge what managers are doing when they make decisions. The complex realities of enormous modern corporations make a true fiduciary relation inapt. Honesty and transparency about the realities of governance will give managers the freedom to act and be transparent in how they are making decisions for the firm. That freedom should make managers more effective, and increased transparency in corporate governance will help shareholders understand their investments and calibrate them appropriately. It also allows shareholders to actually protect themselves from potential harms they face. If we acknowledge that managers are selling a governance product, the law can impose more appropriate rules to respond to reality. If it is not selflessness that shareholders require, what limits should the market place on managerial decision-making? What information do investors need? What are the allowable governance products? We will discover the correct answers to these questions once we free the relevant actors from the confines of a fiduciary paradigm. Then, rather than relying on a patently false sense of security, shareholders can be secure in an honest understanding of what they are buying and what their investment represents.

vi CONCLUSION

Path dependence has led us to believe that corporate officers and directors are fiduciaries of the corporation and its shareholders. Because corporate managers are using their discretion to make decisions about how to use property that does not belong to them, we assume fiduciary law must

---

[52] Stephen M. Bainbridge & M. Todd Henderson, Outsourcing the Board: How Board Service Providers Can Improve Corporate Governance 98 (2018).

apply to their decisions. But the realities of modern corporate governance directly conflict with the imposition of fiduciary doctrine. Corporate managers are frequently guided by self-interest in making business decisions for the firm, and modern investors are anything but vulnerable. Further, corporate managers consider a variety of interests, sometimes making decisions for a non-shareholder constituency that directly conflict with a goal of maximizing shareholder returns. Though we certainly want corporate managers to behave with integrity and limit the externalities their decisions visit upon societal well-being, we cannot properly describe them as *fiduciaries* of equity holders or even fiduciaries *to* particular corporate goals. The time has come to understand corporate governance under a new paradigm.

Index

For EU product safety concerns, contact us at Calle de José Abascal, 56–1°,
28003 Madrid, Spain or eugpsr@cambridge.org.

www.ingramcontent.com/pod-product-compliance
Ingram Content Group UK Ltd.
Pitfield, Milton Keynes, MK11 3LW, UK
UKHW030903150625
459647UK00022B/2839